SAMUEL BUTLER

HUDIBRAS

SAMUEL BUTLER

From the gouache and pastel portrait by Edward Lutterel
in the National Portrait Gallery

SAMUEL BUTLER

HUDIBRAS

EDITED
WITH AN INTRODUCTION
AND COMMENTARY
BY

JOHN WILDERS

OXFORD
AT THE CLARENDON PRESS

Oxford University Press, Ely House, London W. 1

GLASGOW NEW YORK TORONTO MELBOURNE WELLINGTON
CAPE TOWN IBADAN NAIROBI DAR ES SALAAM LUSAKA ADDIS ABABA
DELHI BOMBAY CALCUTTA MADRAS KARACHI LAHORE DACCA
KUALA LUMPUR SINGAPORE HONG KONG TOKYO

ISBN 0 19 811844 9

First published 1967
Reprinted 1975

Printed in Great Britain
at the University Press, Oxford
by Vivian Ridler
Printer to the University

PREFACE

THIS edition was undertaken primarily with the object of providing a commentary on *Hudibras* which would make it intelligible to the modern literary student. Before embarking on the commentary, however, I found it necessary to edit the text of the poem on modern bibliographical principles. The only available edition with any claim to textual accuracy was A. R. Waller's, published in the Cambridge English Classics (1905), but there were apparently no good reasons for Waller's choice of copy-texts and his description of the early editions was very far from complete. I therefore decided to make a thorough examination of the early editions and to edit the text afresh before embarking on the commentary which it was my ultimate purpose to compile. The textual introduction to the present edition includes a full description of all the editions of *Hudibras* published during the poet's lifetime, and a statement of the principles upon which I have edited the text. I was, unfortunately, unable to make use of Mr. James L. Thorson's article on the early editions (Papers of the Bibliographical Society of America, lx (1966), 418–38) which did not appear until this book was in proof.

While writing the commentary I have been deeply indebted to the thoroughness and erudition of my eighteenth-century predecessor Zachary Grey, without whose edition my own work would have been almost impossible. As well as attempting to explain obscure allusions, I have provided brief definitions of words which I imagine to be unfamiliar to the average literary student, using my own ignorance as a guide. When in doubt, I have glossed those words which are described in the *OED* as 'obsolete'. Examples of usage have been omitted where they are provided by the *OED*. Dates quoted from documents using Old Style have been converted to New Style throughout this edition.

The introductory matter includes a biography of the poet, an account of his moral and philosophical views, largely illustrated from the commonplace books, and an interpretative essay on the poem itself. I have not attempted to trace Butler's literary influence, since such a study would have involved a survey of the direct imitations of *Hudibras*, of which there are a great many; they have, moreover, already been examined in detail by E. A. Richards in his *Hudibras in the Burlesque Tradition* (1937).

A number of generous financial awards have given me the leisure to write this book. I must thank the Master and Fellows of St. John's College, Cambridge, for the award of a Strathcona Research Studentship, the trustees of the Procter Fund for a Jane Eliza Procter Visiting Fellowship at Princeton, and the committee of the Colston Research Society of Bristol for a grant which helped me to check the typescript. I also wish to express my gratitude to Professor Basil Willey, Mr. Hugh Sykes Davies, the late Hugh Macdonald, and Professor Louis Landa for their supervision of my work in its early stages. Invaluable assistance has been given by the librarians at Cambridge, the Bodleian Library, the British Museum, Princeton, Harvard, Yale, the Huntington Library, and Bristol University. I must particularly thank the Rosenbach Foundation and the curator of its library in Philadelphia for putting Butler's unpublished notebook at my disposal. For permission to reproduce Samuel Cooper's miniature and Edward Lutterel's portrait of Butler, I am indebted to the Duke of Buccleuch and the Trustees of the National Portrait Gallery. Mr. Michael Wilding freely allowed me to make use of his researches into Butler's life in Worcestershire, and Mr. Esmond de Beer generously lent me his own copies of some of the early editions of *Hudibras*. Dr. H. F. Brooks read through the edition in typescript and suggested a number of additions and revisions that I was happy to adopt. Specific information was kindly supplied by Dr. John Cannon, Professor Bruce Dickins, Dr. Alastair Fowler, Mr. R. C. Latham, Fr. Simon Mein, Mr. M. J. Prichard, Miss S. I. Tucker, and others. Finally, I must express my thanks to Dr. A. B. Cottle for assisting in the correction of the proofs, to Mr. and Mrs. John Farrell for compiling the index, and to Mr. Dan Davin of the Clarendon Press for his patience, encouragement, and hospitality.

J. S. W.

University of Bristol

CONTENTS

ILLUSTRATIONS

SIGLA AND ABBREVIATIONS

SIGLA

THE sigla used in the apparatus to the text correspond to those under which the early editions are itemized in the textual introduction (pp. xlviii–liv). A1, B1, and D1, for example, refer to the first editions of each of the three parts, and C1 refers to the first edition of the First and Second Parts. Siglum A (without a number following) is used when a substantively similar reading is to be found in all Marriot's editions of the First Part. In the same way, sigla B and D indicate a substantively similar reading in all the relevant editions of the Second and Third Parts.

ABBREVIATIONS

Adagia	Desiderius Erasmus, *Adagia, Opera Omnia*, 10 vols., Leyden, 1703–6, vol. ii.
Agrippa	*Three Books of Occult Philosophy Written by Henry Cornelius Agrippa of Nettesheim*, Translated ... by J. F., 1651.
Bacon, *Works*	*The Works of Francis Bacon*, edited by J. Spedding, R. L. Ellis, and D. D. Heath, 14 vols. 1857–74.
Birch	Thomas Birch, *History of the Royal Society*, 4 vols. 1756–7.
Blackstone	Sir William Blackstone, *Commentaries on the Laws of England*, 4 vols. 1809.
Characters	Samuel Butler, *Characters and Passages from Note-books*, edited by A. R. Waller, Cambridge, 1908 (also referred to as *Notebooks*).
Clarendon	Edward, Earl of Clarendon, *History of the Rebellion and Civil Wars in England*, edited by W. D. Macray, 6 vols. Oxford, 1888.
Const. Docs.	*Constitutional Documents of the Puritan Revolution, 1625–1660*, selected and edited by S. R. Gardiner, Oxford, 1899.
Davies	Godfrey Davies, *The Restoration of Charles II*, San Marino, 1955.
Don Quixote	*The History of Don Quixote of the Mancha*, translated ... by Thomas Shelton, 4 vols. 1896 (Tudor Translations, vols. xiii–xvi).
ELH	*A Journal of English Literary History*

Firth and Rait	*Acts and Ordinances of the Interregnum, 1642–1660*, collected and edited by C. H. Firth and R. S. Rait, 3 vols. 1911.
Gardiner	S. R. Gardiner, *History of the Great Civil War, 1642–1649*, 4 vols. 1893.
Grey	*Hudibras in Three Parts . . . with Large Annotations and a Preface* by Zachary Grey, 2 vols. 1744.
H.M.C.	Historical Manuscripts Commission.
Jonson, *Works*	*The Works of Ben Jonson*, edited by C. H. Herford and Percy Simpson, 11 vols. Oxford, 1925–52.
Kittredge	G. L. Kittredge, *Witchcraft in Old and New England*, New York, 1956.
Milnes	*Hudibras*, edited by Alfred Milnes, 2 vols. 1881–3.
Minor Caroline Poets	*Minor Poets of the Caroline Period*, edited by George Saintsbury, 3 vols. Oxford, 1905–21.
MLN	*Modern Language Notes.*
MP	*Modern Philology.*
Nash	*Hudibras*, edited by Treadway Russel Nash, 2 vols. 1835.
Neal	Daniel Neal, *History of the Puritans*, 5 vols. 1822.
Notebooks	Samuel Butler, *Characters and Passages from Note-books*, edited by A. R. Waller, Cambridge, 1908 (also referred to as *Characters*).
NQ	*Notes and Queries.*
ODEP	*The Oxford Dictionary of English Proverbs*, Oxford, 1948.
OED	*The Oxford English Dictionary.*
Posth. Works	*Posthumous Works in Prose and Verse . . . by Mr. Samuel Butler . . . with a Key to Hudibras by Sir Roger L'Estrange*, 1715; *The Second Volume of the Posthumous Works of Mr. Samuel Butler . . . with a Key to the II and III Parts of Hudibras by Sir Roger L'Estrange*, 1715.
Purchas, *Pilgrimage*	Samuel Purchas, *Purchas his Pilgrimage*, 1626.
Purchas, *Pilgrimes*	Samuel Purchas, *Purchas his Pilgrimes*, 4 vols. 1625.
RES	*The Review of English Studies.*
Rump	*Rump: or an Exact Collection of the Choycest Poems and Songs relating to the Late Times*, 2 vols. 1662.
Rushworth	John Rushworth, *Historical Collections*, 8 vols. 1659–1701.
Satires	Samuel Butler, *Satires and Miscellaneous Poetry and Prose*, edited by René Lamar, Cambridge, 1928.
Scot	Reginald Scot, *The discoverie of witchcraft*, 1584.
SP	*Studies in Philology.*

Tilley	Morris Palmer Tilley, *Dictionary of the Proverbs in England in the Sixteenth and Seventeenth Centuries*, Ann Arbor, 1950.
TLS	*The Times Literary Supplement*.
Topsell	Edward Topsell, *History of Four-footed Beasts and Serpents*, 1658.
Vaughan, *Works*	Thomas Vaughan, *Works*, edited by A. E. Waite, 1919.
Walker	Clement Walker, *Compleat History of Independency*, 1661.
W.R.O.	Worcestershire Record Office.
Yates	Frances A. Yates, *Giordano Bruno and the Hermetic Tradition*, 1964.

INTRODUCTION

1. The Life and Ideas of Samuel Butler

WHEN the First Part of *Hudibras* was published, Samuel Butler was nearly fifty years old. Until then he had lived in obscurity, earning a living as a clerk or secretary to a succession of noble families. He enjoyed a brief period of fame with the success of his poem, but failed to obtain the preferment for which he had hoped and relapsed again into comparative obscurity, continuing to work as a secretary, or passing the time among the literary men of London who were his friends, until his death. The records relating to his life are therefore few. His childhood and family background can be reconstructed from the wills and parish registers of Worcestershire, where he was born,[1] but from the point where he left home to earn a living, documentation becomes scanty, and almost the only sources of information are the two short biographies written after his death, one by his friend John Aubrey,[2] the other by Anthony à Wood,[3] who took most of his material from Aubrey. A very brief biography of Butler was published with the 1704 edition of *Hudibras*,[4] and has frequently been reprinted, but it is largely based on Wood's and the additional material is unreliable. These three sources were used by John Lockman for the biography he wrote for the *General Dictionary*,[5] to which additional notes were contributed by Charles Longueville, the son of William Longueville, the lawyer who befriended Butler in his last years. More recently, evidence has been found to substantiate some of the statements made by these early biographers,[6] but in general the picture of Butler's life remains

---

[1] See René Lamar, 'Du Nouveau sur l'Auteur d'*Hudibras*', *Revue Anglo-Américaine*, i (1924), 213–27; Michael Wilding, 'Samuel Butler at Barbourne', *NQ*, N.S. XIII, i. 15–19.

[2] *Brief Lives*, ed. Clark, 2 vols. Oxford, 1898, i. 135–8.

[3] *Athenae Oxonienses*, ed. Bliss, 1813–20, iii. 874–6.

[4] William Oldys, in a manuscript note in his copy of the 1726 edition of *Hudibras* (B.M. 11626.aaa.3), attributes the biography to Sir James Astry. For Astry, see R. E. C. Waters, *Genealogical Memoirs of the Families of Chester of Bristol . . . and the Families of Astry*, 1881, pp. 80–81.

[5] 10 vols., 1734–41, vi. 289–99.

[6] See E. S. de Beer, 'The Later Life of Samuel Butler', *RES* iv (1928), 159–66.

sketchy and must be pieced together from material which is not always trustworthy.

Although our knowledge of his life is far from complete, we have a very full record of the poet's opinions.[1] During the latter part of his life he kept at least two commonplace books in which he entered occasional remarks on the books he was reading, a number of verse sketches, and a great many observations of a philosophical kind arranged under appropriate headings. These observations do not amount to a formal system of philosophy, for a commonplace book is essentially made up of random reflections, but they cover a wide range of topics and show a consistent point of view. After his death Butler's manuscripts became the property of William Longueville and, after passing through several hands, reached Robert Thyer, the Keeper of the Public Library in Manchester, who in 1759 published Butler's *Genuine Remains in Verse and Prose*. These two volumes include most of the prose *Characters* and miscellaneous poems and a selection of entries from the commonplace books. The manuscripts used by Thyer are now in the British Museum.[2] Another notebook, not apparently known to Thyer, was for a time the property of T. R. Nash, the eighteenth-century historian of Worcestershire and editor of *Hudibras*, and after disappearing from sight for well over a century was purchased by the American bibliophile A. S. W. Rosenbach. It is now in the library of the Rosenbach Foundation in Philadelphia. Although the text of the other Butler manuscripts has appeared in full, the contents of this book have not been published.[3]

ii

The earliest documents relating to the Butler family show that in the sixteenth century they were living in Claines, a large parish on the northern outskirts of Worcester, where Robert

---

[1] For discussions of Butler's opinions see D. Gibson, 'Samuel Butler', *Seventeenth-Century Studies*, ed. Shafer, Princeton, 1933; R. Quintana, 'Samuel Butler: A Restoration Figure in a Modern Light', *ELH* xviii (1951), 7–31.

[2] B.M. Add. MSS. 32625 and 32626. The former is written in Butler's own hand, the latter is a transcript probably made by Thyer.

[3] The notebook is described and extracts quoted by Norma E. Bentley in 'Another Butler Manuscript', *MP* xlvi (1948), 132–5, and '*Hudibras* Butler Abroad', *MLN* lx (1945), 254–9.

Butler, a yeoman farmer, made a will and an inventory of his goods in 1546.[1] Robert and his wife Joan had five children, of whom the youngest, Richard, was the great-grandfather of the poet. The poet's grandfather, also Richard, lived about eight miles south of Worcester in the tiny village of Strensham, on a farm which he leased from the Russell family, the local lords of the manor. He was buried there in 1599.[2] It was at Strensham that the poet's father, Samuel Butler, spent most of his life. Like his ancestors he was a farmer, having inherited from his father the lease on the farm at Strensham, but he was also employed, presumably as a clerk, by Sir John Russell, with whom he appears to have been on friendly terms.[3] He lived with his family in a long, low, timbered house of one storey, later known as 'Butler's Cot', which was still standing in 1870 but fell into disrepair soon afterwards and was demolished.[4] Samuel and Mary Butler had four sons and four daughters, all except one of whom were baptized at Strensham. The poet, their fifth child, was baptized there on 14 February 1613.

The youngest child, Margaret, was christened in July 1621 at Claines, where the family may have lived for a time, for they owned a house and land at Barbourne in the parish of Claines. But by 1626, when the father died, they were living at Defford, a parish close to Strensham, where they again leased a farm from the Russells.[5] With the death of Samuel Butler senior, the lease at Defford came to an end and his property at Barbourne passed to his children, who presumably returned to live there. By 1626 the poet was attending King's School, Worcester, together with a certain Richard Hill, a boy about four years his junior, who later became an acquaintance of Aubrey's.[6] Hill told Aubrey many years later that the poet was born 'in Worcestershire, hard by Barbon-bridge', but he probably received this impression from the fact that Butler, as a schoolboy, was living in Barbourne.

[1] Worcestershire Record Office 008.7.1546/233, 1546/150.
[2] W.R.O. 008.7.1598/175; Strensham Parish Register.
[3] He witnessed a codicil to Sir John Russell's will, proved in 1598 and now in Somerset House. It contains the item 'I give unto Samuell Butler my servant my black gelding'.
[4] *NQ*, 6th Ser. iv. 387; *Transactions of Worcestershire Naturalists' Club*, 1897, pp. 19–21, 151–2.
[5] Will of Samuel Butler senior, W.R.O. 008.7.1627/29.
[6] See Alec Macdonald, *History of King's School Worcester*, 1936, p. 108; *The Vigornian*, November 1921.

The successive wills and inventories of the Butler family show that, in the course of four generations, they had increasingly prospered. The poet's father owned a house and land in addition to the one he occupied, and he employed two servants and a housemaid. His possessions, listed in the inventory of his goods,[1] include the usual things to be found on a small farm—livestock, implements, and produce—but also a considerable quantity of furniture, brass, pewter, a silver bowl and spoons, and some musical instruments. He was twice churchwarden of Strensham, in 1602 and 1611, and the preamble to his will, an impressive piece of prose, suggests that he was a devout Christian. He was also a man of some education and learning. He wrote his will in a strong, clear hand, dividing between his children a small library of books. Of these, he left to his daughter Susanna his music books, to his son Thomas his English books, but to Samuel, obviously the scholar of the family, 'all my Lawe and Latine bookes of Logicke, Rhethoricke, Philosophy, Poesy, phisicke, my great Dodaneus Herball,[2] and all other my lattine and greeke bookes whatsoever'.

Butler's father made provision in his will for his sons to be bound apprentices, but had apparently neither the intention nor the means to send them to the university. Wood was told by one of Butler's brothers that the poet had been to Cambridge; others in the neighbourhood said that he had been to Oxford, but no records exist of his matriculation at either university. He had, however, inherited some of his father's property at Barbourne and may at first have decided to follow the occupation of his ancestors and become a farmer, for he still held the land and a house in 1628.[3] But if the early biographers are correct, this intention was soon abandoned and shortly afterwards he became a clerk, first with a respected family near his birthplace and later with more eminent employers far from Worcester. He thus severed the connexion with the land that his family had maintained for several generations, moving from the rural environment of

---

[1] W.R.O. 008.7.1627/29.

[2] Rembert Dodoens, *A Niewe Herball or historie of plantes . . . First set foorth in the Doutche or Almaigne tongue . . . nowe first translated out of French into English by H. Lyte*, 1578. Samuel Butler senior had inherited it from his father.

[3] See the account-book of the Bishop of Worcester relating to the Manor of Whistons and Claines (W.R.O. 009.1.BA 2636/4, ii/23399, fol. 54); *NQ*, n.s. xiii. i. 17.

SAMUEL BUTLER

From the miniature by Samuel Cooper in the collection
of the Duke of Buccleuch and Queensberry, K.T.

his childhood into a very different kind of society, one in which he was never wholly at ease.

His first employment is said to have been as a clerk to 'one Mr. *Jefferys* of *Earls-Croom*, an Eminent Justice of the Peace for that County, with whom he liv'd some years in an easie and no contemptible Service'.[1] Leonard Jefferey, one of the most active magistrates in the county, may have been a friend of the Butlers from the time when they lived at Strensham, for his house, Earl's Croome Court, was in the next parish. The poet's cousin, Richard Butler, who also lived at Earl's Croome, helped to compile the inventory of his goods.[2] Since Leonard Jefferey died in 1629, within a year of the time when Butler held the Barbourne property, it is possible that his son Thomas Jefferey, and not Leonard, was the poet's employer.[3] It was while he was working at Earl's Croome that Butler is said to have taken up painting, and some portraits attributed to him were found in the house by T. R. Nash in 1774.[4] Two of them, crudely painted, are still in existence. They are preserved in the vestry of Earl's Croome Church and are said locally to be of Leonard Jefferey and his wife.

'He came when a young man', writes Aubrey, 'to be a servant to the countesse of Kent, whom he served severall yeares. Here, besides his study, he employed his time much in painting and drawing, and also in musique. . . . His love to and skill in painting made a great friendship between him and Mr. Samuel Cowper.' The Dowager Countess of Kent, whose husband, the Earl, died in 1639, lived at Wrest Park in Bedfordshire, and was a friend and patroness of Selden the antiquary, who had been the Earl's steward. Her house has long since vanished and her papers have been destroyed, but a number of circumstances tend to confirm that Butler worked for her. He was certainly acquainted with the miniaturist Samuel Cooper in later years, for Cooper painted his portrait, and in 1668 took him to dine with Pepys.[5] Moreover, one of the pallbearers at his funeral, a Mr. Saunders, described by Aubrey as 'the countesse of Kent's kinsman', said that the poet had been employed as a translator by Selden.

[1] 1704 Biography.
[2] W.R.O. 008.7.1629/104.
[3] See *Worcestershire County Records, Calendar of Quarter Sessions Papers*, ed. J. W. Willis Bund, 2 vols. 1900, i. xlix.
[4] *Collections for the History of Worcestershire*, 2 vols. 1781-2, ii. 391.
[5] *Diary*, 19 July 1668.

Butler's later biographers, following the anonymous *Life* of 1704, tell of his employment by Sir Samuel Luke, of Cople in Bedfordshire, a strict Presbyterian who represented Bedford in the Long Parliament, commanded a troop of dragoons, and was scoutmaster-general to the Earl of Essex. It was while living with Luke, we are told, and having the opportunity to observe Puritanism at close quarters, that Butler was prompted to start the composition of *Hudibras*. Butler's residence with Luke is, however, not mentioned by Aubrey or Wood, nor has any other evidence of it been found. Moreover, the poet himself declared that he began to write *Hudibras* while lodging with a west country knight in Holborn.[1] The idea that he was in some way associated with Luke may perhaps have grown out of the implied allusion to him in the first canto of *Hudibras*,[2] but it is probable that the poet was, in fact, never in his employment.

When he started the composition of *Hudibras*—and the evidence suggests that this was in about 1658[3]—Butler was lodging in Holborn, had already became a familiar figure in Gray's Inn Walk, and had formed an acquaintance with the lawyers.[4] His connexion with Gray's Inn is supported by his frequent use of legal terms in *Hudibras*, and by a manuscript, formerly in the possession of Nash but now lost, in which he made an abridgement of Coke's *Commentary on Littleton*.[5] It is even possible that he lived for a time in Gray's Inn itself and 'studied the Common Lawes of England'.[6]

He next appears in 1661 at Ludlow, where he was steward to Richard Vaughan, Earl of Carbery. Ludlow Castle had been captured during the Civil War by the Roundheads and its contents had been seized and sold. The Court of the Marches was revived there after the Restoration with Carbery as its President, and one of his first tasks was to make the castle habitable again. His account-books record payments made by Butler to craftsmen employed in the repairs.[7] The poet is also said to have been married about this time, but no record of the marriage has been found, and his bride has been variously described as a widow named Morgan[8] and a spinster named Herbert.[9] It is certain that

---

[1] Letter to Sir George Oxenden. See Appendix A.
[2] See Appendix B. [3] See p. xlvi.
[4] Letter from Richard Oxenden to Sir George Oxenden. See Appendix A.
[5] Nash, i. xviii. [6] Aubrey.
[7] *NQ*, 1st Ser. v. 5. The account-books appear to be now lost. Aubrey mentions the stewardship. [8] Aubrey. [9] 1704 Biography.

he was married at some time, however, for he refers to his wife, without mentioning her name, in an undated letter which he wrote to his sister.[1]

Butler gave up his stewardship at Ludlow in January 1662. By December the First Part of *Hudibras* was in the bookshops[2] and his obscurity was temporarily at an end. It became at once the most popular poem in London and was 'not only taken into his majesty's hands, and read by him with great delight, but also by all courtiers, loyal scholars and gentlemen, to the great profit of the author and bookseller'.[3] 'Whether I have performed it well or noe I cannot tell', the poet modestly confessed, 'Onely I have had yᵉ good fortune to have it Genˡˡy esteemᵈ Soe especially by yᵉ King & yᵉ best of his Subjects.'[4] Nine editions were published within a year, four of them by a piratical printer eager to profit from its success, and a spurious Second Part, the work of an anonymous imitator, went into at least three editions. Not surprisingly, Butler expected some kind of preferment, but he was not rewarded until fifteen years later, when he was granted a pension by Charles II. By then the popular legend had probably developed that Butler, the loyal satirist, was wasting his life in poverty and neglect, and since the poet himself did nothing to dispel this impression, even apparently after his pension had been awarded, he acquired a reputation as a patriotic man of letters whom society, to its shame, had left to starve.[5] Dryden was probably not the only author to remind a prospective patron of Butler's alleged fate.[6]

Although Butler gave up his post at Ludlow in 1662, he may have continued to work for Carbery in some other capacity. According to one report,[7] it was Carbery who presented him to Charles II, and the Earl also issued Butler with a protection from arrest in September 1667.[8] In July 1668 he was in London, dining with Pepys and Samuel Cooper, but by July 1670 he had found

---

[1] The letter is printed by Lamar, *Satires*, 399.

[2] Pepys, *Diary*, 26 December 1662.   [3] Wood.

[4] Letter to Sir George Oxenden. See Appendix A.

[5] Butler's poverty is referred to by Dryden ('Hind and the Panther', iii. 247–50), Oldham ('Satire Against Poetry'), Otway (Prologue to Lee's *Constantine*), and others. The legend appears in its fullest detail in Richardson Pack's memoir of Wycherley, attached to Wycherley's *Posthumous Works*, 1728, i. 7.

[6] Dryden, letter to Rochester, ?August 1683, *Letters*, ed. C. E. Ward, 1942, p. 21.

[7] See J. R. Magrath, *The Flemings in Oxford*, Oxford Historical Society, 1904, i. 418.

[8] The protection is now in the possession of Mr. Hugh Hale Bellot, a descendant of Thyer's stepdaughter.

a new post in the service of the Duke of Buckingham. In that summer he and Thomas Sprat, the historian of the Royal Society, went as members of Buckingham's entourage to Versailles, where the Duke had been sent to negotiate a treaty with Louis XIV.[1] The poet took with him a notebook[2] in which he had carefully compiled an English–French dictionary, and in which he recorded his impressions of the French people. He may also have accompanied the Duke to the Hague two years later, when Buckingham was sent to arrange a peace with the Dutch, for he composed a brief 'Description of Holland', and, in another commonplace book, remarked on the cleanliness of the Dutch houses and the unwholesomeness of the air.[3] He was still working for Buckingham in June 1673, now as a secretary for his affairs as Chancellor of the University of Cambridge,[4] a post which he may have held until July 1674, when the Duke ceased to be Chancellor. According to Wood, he helped Buckingham in the composition of *The Rehearsal*.

The Second Part of *Hudibras* had appeared in print almost exactly a year after the First. The rest of Butler's extant work can be ascribed to the years between 1667 and his death,[5] including the prose *Characters*, written, according to Thyer, mainly between 1667 and 1669, the revised version of the First and Second Parts of *Hudibras*, published in 1674, and the Third Part, which was on sale at the end of 1677.[6] This last part was not as successful as the two earlier ones—it went into three editions in three years—and at least one reader noticed in it evidence of the poet's declining powers.[7] In November 1677 he was awarded his pension, an annual grant of £100 together with an immediate gift of the same amount.[8] The pension appears not to have been paid, however, before September 1678, when the King gave instructions for the money to be issued quarterly and for arrears to be made up.[9]

In spite of his past success and ultimate recognition, Butler was, it seems, bitterly disappointed. 'He might have had preferments at first', says Aubrey, 'but he would not accept any but very good ones, so at last he had none at all, and dyed in want.'

---

[1] See Norma E. Bentley, '*Hudibras* Butler Abroad', *MLN* lx (1945), 254–9.
[2] The unpublished notebook in the library of the Rosenbach Foundation.
[3] *Satires*, p. 149; *Characters*, p. 450.
[4] *Cal. State Papers, Domestic, 1673*, p. 395.
[5] E. S. de Beer, 'The Later Life of Samuel Butler', *RES* iv (1928), 162.
[6] H. M. C., *Marquis of Bath at Longleat*, ii. 159.
[7] Ibid.   [8] *Cal. Treasury Books, 1676–9*, p. 479.   [9] Ibid, p. 1116.

He is said to have spent his last years in a room in Rose Alley, Covent Garden, to which he was confined with gout from October 1679 until Easter 1680.[1] In this latter year, possibly as a result of his continued complaints of poverty, he was given £20 by the King 'as of free guift and royal bounty'.[2] He died on 25 September and was buried in the churchyard of St. Paul's, Covent Garden,[3] at the expense of William Longueville, an eminent lawyer who had befriended him towards the end of his life. His pallbearers included Shadwell the dramatist, a Dr. Davenant (presumably Charles, the son of Sir William), a Dr. Cole, who probably came from Worcester, Mr. Saunders, 'the countesse of Kent's kinsman', and Aubrey, his biographer.[4]

Aubrey describes him as 'of a middle stature, strong sett, high coloured, a head of sorrell haire'. Temperamentally he was gloomy, even morose; 'all the Business of this World', he once wrote, 'is but *Diversion,* and all the *Happiness* in it that Mankind is capable of—anything that will keep it from reflecting upon the Misery, Vanity and Nonsence of it.'[5] Yet he was roused to high spirits by wine and company, and is said to have had 'a clubb every night' with John Cleveland.[6] His character was caught vividly by James Yonge, a physician from Plymouth, who saw him at the Wits' Coffee House in Covent Garden two years before his death. 'I saw the famous old Mr. Butler,' wrote Yonge, 'an old paralytick claret drinker, a morose surly man, except elevated with claret, when he becomes very brisk and incomparable company.'[7]

iii

The events of Butler's life, apart from this sudden rise to fame, are unexciting and have little intrinsic interest. His ideas are, however, unusually interesting, for in them we can glimpse the characteristic values of the Augustans in the process of formation. He judges human behaviour from the standpoint of empirical common sense. He values the reasonable, the practical, and the

[1] Aubrey.
[2] H. F. Brooks, 'Gift to Samuel Butler', *TLS*, 1940, 327; Norma E. Bentley, 'A Grant to *Hudibras* Butler', *MLN* lix (1944), 281.
[3] *Registers of St. Paul's Covent Garden*, iv. 89; *Harleian Society Registers*, xxxvi (1908).
[4] Aubrey; de Beer, op. cit.   [5] *Notebooks*, p. 271.
[6] Aubrey, 'Life of Cleveland', *Brief Lives*, i. 175.
[7] *Journal of James Yonge*, ed. F. N. L. Poynter, 1963, p. 157.

useful and sees truth only in statements which can be verified by immediate experience. In these respects he is a Baconian. The Baconians of the mid-century, however, adopted from their master not only an empirical view of knowledge but also a sceptical attitude towards other philosophical endeavours. Bacon himself, as well as foreseeing great intellectual and material progress from scientific empiricism, also denounced the many impediments to knowledge which had to be eradicated before such progress could be made—the 'idols and false notions which . . . so beset men's minds that truth can hardly find entrance'.[1] Baconians like Browne and Glanvill—whose outlook was in some ways similar to Butler's—were therefore as much concerned to eradicate error and superstition as they were to promote 'truth' and scientific endeavour. With Butler the emphasis is markedly different. He was so deeply conscious of the folly, hypocrisy, and gullibility of men that he had little faith in human progress. He regarded the intellectualism of the old philosophy and the experimentation of the new science as equally unprofitable. Moreover, he allied himself to no religious party, since he believed all sects to be misguided and intolerant. He was repelled alike by the self-righteousness of the Puritan régime and by the licentiousness of the age which followed it. His outlook on human endeavour was therefore that of a sceptic and his scepticism found its natural expression in satire.

Butler inherited from the Middle Ages a conception of the universe as an intricate, complex, but beautifully ordered structure, 'every Part of which ha's so rationall a Relation to every other in particular, and the whole in generall; That though it consist of innumerable Pieces and Joynts, there is not the least Flaw imaginable in the whole.'[2] This great artifice, being the handiwork of God, expresses the nature of its creator; it is 'a Copie which the Divine wisdome has drawn of itself'.[3] To apprehend this material universe through the senses and by the exercise of reason is to become aware of the only kind of truth accessible to man, who has 'no meanes of Knowledg but by Sense, and Reason collection, Consequence and Demonstration'.[4] Hence, according to Butler, 'all Knowledge is nothing but a right observation of Nature';[5] 'Truth . . . is but the Putting of those Notions of things

---

[1] *Novum Organum* xxxviii, *Works*, iv. 53.   [2] *Notebooks*, p. 337.
[3] Ibid.   [4] Ibid., p. 281.   [5] Ibid., p. 288.

(in the understanding of Man) into the same order that their Originals are in Nature'.[1]

Unlike more thoroughgoing sceptics, Butler did not doubt the validity of sense-impressions, but he repeatedly questioned man's ability to learn from them or to act upon them. What impressed him, as it was to impress Swift, was man's proneness to delusion. 'There are but few Truths in the world', he said, 'but Millions of Errors and falsities, which prevayle with the Opinion of the world.'[2] The ultimate source of error lay in man's natural tendency to be affected by irrational forces within himself. A man might have a great deal of reason, 'but nothing renders it so utterly unusefull as Passion, to which it has a Naturall Antipathy'.[3] Imagination, too, is deceptive. It is like a sail which carries away the mind with every wind of vanity, when it should be governed by the helm of reason.[4] These irrational forces in the individual create superstition and error in society, which perpetuates them by education. 'So are men broken and bred up to those il-favourd opinions in their infancys by use and Custome, which otherwise Nature had never inclin'd them to.'[2]

The irrational element in man prevails most strongly, however, when he turns his mind to religion, for theology is an area of inquiry in which he has almost no empirical evidence to guide him. It is true that we can infer something of the nature of God from his creation, which is an image of Himself, and from the testimony of the Gospels, but we cannot be sure that our knowledge of nature is correct or that the testimony of Scripture is to be trusted. Our notions of God cannot, therefore, be arrived at rationally and must necessarily be a matter of faith. Theology is 'a Speculative Science of Finding out Reasons for things that are not within the Reach of Reason'.[5] The intellectualism of scholars like Hudibras and the mystical insights professed by Ralpho are equally unprofitable : we can no more define matters of faith than we can 'draw a true Map of Terra Incognita by mere Imagination'.[6] Butler's sceptical attitude towards theology—a natural sequel to his empiricism— was the source of his repeated attacks on the scholastic philosophers. The schoolmen, he believed, made categorical statements about matters in which there could be no certainty.

---

[1] Ibid., p. 290.
[3] Ibid., p. 448.
[5] Ibid., p. 466.

[2] Ibid., p. 349.
[4] Ibid., p. 336.
[6] Ibid., p. 300.

They were 'curious in Subtilties, and ignorant in things of solid Knowledg', 'penny-wise, and Pound-foolish'.[1] The very terms they used, having no reference to observable fact, were meaningless abstractions, and the manipulation of them in accordance with the rules of logic was an ingenious but vain exercise. 'Logitians', Butler declared, 'cannot teach men solid, and substantiall Reason, but only little Tricks and evasions, that are worse then nothing.'[2] Moreover, the schoolmen are by no means the only philosophers to fall under Butler's criticism. Elsewhere he attacks Pythagoras and Hermetic mysticism,[3] Lucretius and Descartes,[4] and ridicules the precepts of the Stoics by making his hero recite them while imprisoned in the stocks.[5] He remarked frequently in his commonplace books on the 'contradictions' and 'inconsistent opinions' of philosophers and, in the *Satire on the Abuse of Human Learning*,[6] exposed the foolishness of all the major classical philosophers in turn.

The comments which Butler entered in his notebooks show that he was continually disturbed by man's natural proneness to error, but he was also aware of the ways in which error is perpetuated. He was on the alert against charlatanism, hypocrisy, and deception, of which he chiefly accuses the clergy. His hostility to the Church was derived in part from his view of theology, which led him to believe that the knowledge professed by the clergy—and by virtue of which they exercised authority—was mere pretence, and that they maintained their position by keeping other men in ignorance. 'The more false any Religion is', he noted, 'the more Industrious the Priests of it are, to keepe the People from prying into the Mysteries of it, and by that Artifice render them the more zealous, and Confident in their Ignorance.'[7] The churches, therefore, were the chief guardians of error: there is no folly so vain and ridiculous 'but if it put it self into the Protection of Piety and Religion, is by the easy credulous reputed Sacred and not to be touchd'.[8] Religion was used not only to perpetuate ignorance but also by unscrupulous men to justify crime—and here Butler's intellectual convictions appeared to be amply confirmed by his experience of the hypocrisy of the

---

[1] *Notebooks*, p. 283. [2] Ibid., p. 293.
[3] Ibid., p. 442; *Hudibras*, I. i. 523–62.
[4] *Notebooks*, p. 398; *Hudibras*, I. ii. 57. [5] Ibid., I. iii. 1013–56.
[6] *Satires*, pp. 73–75. [7] *Notebooks*, p. 304. [8] Ibid., p. 294.

Puritans. 'The modern Saint', he said, 'that believe's himself Priviledg'd, and above Nature, ingage's himself in the most horrid of all Wickedneses . . . and is so far from Repentance, that he puts them upon the Accompt of Pious Duties, and good workes.'[1] Butler's reputation as the author of *Hudibras* has created the impression that he was primarily an anti-Puritan writer, but in the notebooks he is just as critical of the Catholic church, which, he believed, 'Deboshes the Reason and understandings of Men' more than any other in the world.[2] The truth is that he was not narrowly anti-clerical, but saw the clergy as guilty to a high degree of failings common to man in general. His own age had its share of human folly, but was no more corrupt than any other. 'The greatest extravagancys in the world are things that ever have been and ever wilbe, and to reforme them is but to put them into another way, and perhaps a worse, and not to alter their Nature.'[3]

His attitude to religion was not, however, completely sceptical. References in the notebooks show that he was attracted by the views of rational theologians such as Hales, Chillingworth, and Tillotson,[4] and, like them, he seems to have seen a remedy for the intolerance of his age in the establishment of a broad, comprehensive Church and a reasonable Christianity. For 'all men agree in the end of Religion that God is to be worshipd'.[5] The 'differences and distractions' of mankind arise not from their unwillingness to serve God but from uncertainty as to how they should do so. They should have the honesty and humility to confess their ignorance of spiritual matters, and should come to an agreement on those fundamental tenets of religion which are open to rational demonstration and on which all men are agreed. 'If there were but so much generall Certainty in the Doctrines of Religion as there is in some other Knowledges, in which Mankinde may seeme to bee less Concernd, all the world would be of one Church.'[6]

Holding as he did an essentially empirical view of knowledge, Butler might be expected to have sympathized with the growing interest in science and with the deliberations of the Royal Society. In fact, he had little or no respect for the scientists, exposing them to ridicule both in *Hudibras* and in his best minor poem, *The Elephant in the Moon*. It is true that he shared something of their

---

[1] Ibid, p. 307. [2] Ibid, p. 453. [3] Ibid, p. 345.
[4] See Norma E. Bentley, 'In Defense of Butler', *MLN* lxi (1946), 359–60.
[5] *Notebooks*, p. 299. [6] Ibid.

practical, empirical attitude, but he could see little of value in their activities. They were, he believed, as prone to error and misapprehension as other men, and, in their over-exclusive concern for experiment and discovery, were apt to be absorbed by the trivial rather than the useful, or to seek for wonders at the expense of truth. So eager are the astronomers in Butler's poem to discover life on the moon that they mistake a mouse in their telescope for a lunar elephant.[1] The experiments performed by the Royal Society—blood-transfusions, research into the diseases of trees, the invention of new kinds of transport—Butler attributes to Sidrophel, the quack astrologer, with the implication that they are all meretricious and futile. From the modern standpoint, of course, his opinion of the scientists seems prejudiced and reactionary, as does Swift's portrayal of them in the Academy of Lagado, but his criticism was not thoughtless: to him, the virtuosi were debasing their talents in trivialities instead of applying themselves to 'solid and useful knowledge'.

Butler's awareness of intellectual error, and his fear of its consequences, also affected his view of literature, towards which he held a no less rational attitude. For him the imagination was not a source of illumination or insight. It was a 'certaine slight of the Minde' which 'deliver's things otherwise then they are in Nature'.[2] At best, it was a means of creating pleasing fictions; at worst, it deluded the Puritan Saints into imagining they were inspired by God. The poets, Butler believed, should apply themselves to 'the Imitation of *Nature*'; they should not misrepresent it by 'turning the Inside of the Earth outward' or 'making *Nature* shew Tricks like an Ape'.[3] Butler's literary theories are similar to those of Davenant and Hobbes, who also regarded poetry from an empirical point of view. For Hobbes imagination, or fancy, is a product only of experience and memory. The idea that a poet may be inspired is 'a foolish custome, by which a man, enabled to speak wisely from the principles of nature and his own meditation, loves rather to be thought to speak by inspiration, like a Bagpipe'.[4] Davenant, similarly, describes inspiration as 'a spiritual Fitt' simulated by pagan priests in order to arouse reverence among super-

---

[1] 'Elephant in the Moon', *Satires*, pp. 3–16.
[2] *Notebooks*, p. 336.
[3] 'A Small Poet', *Characters*, pp. 53–54.
[4] 'The Answer of Mr. Hobbes to Sr. Will. D'Avenant's *Preface* before *Gondibert*', *Critical Essays of the Seventeenth Century*, ed. Spingarn, 2 vols. Oxford, 1908, ii. 59.

stitious people. Both Hobbes and Davenant turned their attention to the problems of writing heroic poetry in a rationalistic age. Davenant, addressing his own poem *Gondibert* to Hobbes, criticized Homer, Statius, and Tasso for setting their scenes in heaven and hell, thus depriving their narratives of probability, and prided himself on having stayed within the bounds of nature.[1] He thereby earned the approval of Hobbes, who, in reply, criticized the 'impenetrable Armors, Inchanted Castles, invulnerable bodies, Iron Men, flying Horses, and a thousand other such things' to be found in romantic epic, which thereby exceeds not only 'the *work*, but also the *possibility* of nature'.[2]

Butler was familiar with this discussion and alludes to it in *Hudibras*.[3] His contribution to it was not, like Davenant's, to write a heroic poem on 'enlightened' principles, but to write a comic poem revealing the conventions of such poetry as ridiculous when looked at in a rational light. His invocation is not to a 'heavenly muse' but to the 'Ale, or viler Liquors' that inflamed the Puritan controversialists. His heroes, though presented in the elevated terms of epic and romance, are obviously no more than common tradesmen. The magic castle in which Hudibras and Ralpho are imprisoned is simply the village stocks. His satire is directed, moreover, not merely against the literary conventions of the epic, which he sees as an outmoded survival from the superstitious past, but also against the ideals of conduct which the epic, by tradition, holds up for our approval. These ideals, he believed, would be absurd if submitted to the test of actual conduct: 'if any man should but imitate what these Heroical Authors write in the Practice of his life and Conversation, he would become the most Ridiculous Person in the world.'[4] Hence military honour, far from being glorious, is no more than 'Slaughter, and knocking on the head',[5] or, as Davenant had described it, 'onely an impudent courage or dexterity in destroying'.[6]

Butler's poem is, however, not merely an attack on outmoded literary ideals and conventions: it is also a satire on outmoded superstitions and philosophical assumptions. Satire, for Butler, unlike heroic poetry, serves a useful purpose because it exposes

---

[1] 'Preface to *Gondibert, an Heroick Poem*', Spingarn, ii. 2–5.
[2] 'Answer', Spingarn, ii. 61.
[3] See I. i. 515–18, I. ii. 397–402, and notes.   [4] *Notebooks*, p. 278.
[5] I. ii. 323.   [6] 'Preface to *Gondibert*', Spingarn, ii. 10.

error and vice and thereby encourages people to think more rationally and live better. His definition of satire gives some indication of his moral purposes in writing *Hudibras*: it is 'a kinde of Knight Errant that goe's upon Adventures, to Relieve the Distressed Damsel Virtue, and Redeeme Honor out of Inchanted Castles, And opprest Truth, and Reason out of the Captivity of Gyants and Magitians'.[1] His own satire is an attempt to release truth and reason from the captivity of error and hypocrisy. At the same time, much of it is cast in the form of a mock-heroic poem, which itself provides a criticism of heroic poetry.

11. Hudibras: *Content and Form*

For personal reasons on which it would be fruitless to speculate from the slight evidence available, Butler's outlook was unsettled, sceptical, and pessimistic. He found it impossible to sympathize with any of the religious or political factions of his time. One cause was no doubt the nature of the age itself, which was a period of violent political unrest and one in which men's ways of thinking underwent a fundamental change. Long-established beliefs, many of them inherited from classical times, were being shown to be false, and truths derived from theological premises were being replaced by truths based upon empirical observation. This intellectual revolution, of which Bacon was the major prophet, was effected by Hobbes, Locke, and others, and, by the end of the century, its foundations were complete. *Hudibras* is a product of the transitional period. This is clear from the fact that, while Butler's outlook is in some ways very modern, his knowledge was derived from the Middle Ages and beyond. Its sources can be found in such writers as Aristotle, Pliny, and the Roman historians. The period was, moreover, peculiarly favourable to the writing of satire, since the ideas of former ages were being criticized by the standards of the new. Whatever may have been the psychological causes of Butler's scepticism, the age itself induced in him the distinctive tensions of the satirist: a sense of the opposition between the ideal and the actual, between what ought to be and what is. Hence he was impelled, like most satirists, to reveal the reality which he believed to lie behind traditional opinion and popular superstition. In *Hudibras* he attempted to show that

[1] *Notebooks*, p. 469.

scholarship was often no more than futile pedantry, that religion was commonly a pretext for the acquisition of power or wealth, that romantic love was generally a cover for self-interest, and that military honour was the reward for barbarism. The range of his satire is extremely wide, but his point of view is generally consistent both within the poem and with his other writings, particularly the commonplace books. He applies to the objects of his satire the same sceptical attitude which pervades the notebooks, and tests them by the same principles of practical, empirical common sense.

The first of the three parts is undoubtedly the most successful. The action is more complete than that of the other two parts, the wit is more concentrated, and the whole piece is animated by an energy and inventiveness which Butler failed to sustain into the later cantos. It also tackles delusion in a more fundamental way, by examining the basic principles by which men judge the truth, and attacking false kinds of knowledge at their roots. Although the two protagonists, Hudibras and Ralpho, belong to different churches, and although the cause of their frequent arguments is theological, their essential difference lies in the ways in which they believe truth to be ascertainable. The interest of this part, like that of much of Butler's work, is philosophical as well as moral.

The knight is an Aristotelian, 'profoundly skill'd in Analytick', who can examine and dispute any proposition according to the rules of logic. He is well versed in Latin, Greek, and Hebrew, knows all the rules of rhetoric, and is learned in the scholastic philosophy. Yet for practical purposes his intellectual achievements are useless. They either enable him clumsily to discover the obvious or prevent him from seeing things which are apparent to common sense. His logic teaches him what everyone knows—for example, that committee-men are 'rooks'—his mathematical skill induces him to calculate the time by algebra, and his philosophical training has filled his mind with false and useless information. When, in the Second Part, he meets a village procession, he thinks it is a Roman triumph. Whereas Hudibras is encumbered by excessive scholarship, Ralpho prides himself upon his ignorance, his freedom from that carnal knowledge which he sees as an impediment to divine inspiration,

A Liberal Art, that costs no pains
Of Study, Industry, or Brains.[1]

[1] I. i. 477–8.

He is also a neo-Platonist, a follower of the Hermetic philosophers, and a disciple of Thomas Vaughan. He claims to be divinely inspired and to know things beyond the scope of empirical experience. He is, however, shrewder than his master, for he does not take his own prophetic claims seriously. He keeps up the pretence of inspiration for his own ends: the light that inspires him is a light 'for Spiritual Trades to cousen by'.[1] The fundamental differences between the two men are revealed in the great disputation at the end of the First Part.[2] The immediate cause of their quarrel is theological: Ralpho asserts that Presbyterian synods are nothing more than bear-gardens, while Hudibras is roused to defend his own church against the Squire's attack. But, when called upon to defend his accusation, Ralpho follows his inclination to mysticism and describes a synod as a 'type' or emblem of a bear-garden, ingeniously accumulating parallels between the two. Hudibras, a '*Presbyterian* true blew', is anxious to refute Ralpho's arguments, but cannot do so by simple common sense. Instead, he grapples with them by the cumbersome methods of formal logic:

> That both are *Animalia*,
> I grant, but not *Rationalia*:
> For though they do agree in kind,
> Specifick difference we find.[3]

The knight's reply prompts Ralpho to criticize his master, not for his Presbyterian convictions, but for his use of Aristotelian logic, which, to him, is

> An Art t'incumber *Gifts* and wit,
> And render both for nothing fit.[4]

The two now confront each other not as representatives of two opposing religious sects but as a logician and a mystic; and, as Hudibras realizes, the ground for their disagreement is no longer a question of church government but of something more fundamental:

> But to the former opposite,
> And *contrary as black to white;*

---

[1] I. i. 502.   [2] I. iii. 1095 ff.
[3] I. iii. 1277–80.   [4] I. iii. 1343–4.

Mere *Disparata*, that concerning
Presbyterie, this, *Humane Learning*.[1]

At this point the discussion stops, both parties having exhausted themselves without convincing their opponents, but having demonstrated to the reader the futility both of formal logic and of mystical delusion. Both men are blinded by sectarian prejudice, and, while the squire is led by his imagination into making ridiculous statements, the knight is prevented by his scholarship from exposing their absurdity.

With the appearance of Sidrophel, in the Second Part, Butler returns to the theme of intellectual delusion, this time with reference to astrology, astronomy, and experimental science. Sidrophel, like Hudibras, is a learned man who has 'been long t'wards *Mathematicks*, *Opticks*, *Philosophy*, and *Staticks*'.[2] But his learning is, like all theoretical knowledge, useless and deceptive. Seeing a boy's kite through his telescope, he mistakes it for a comet and is struck with terror at the prospect of some universal disaster. Burdened with excessive scholarship, he has failed to make any progress towards the discovery of truth. Butler compares him to a dog turning a spit, who exerts all his energy in the hope of moving forward but is kept by his own weight in the same place.[3]

So in the *Circle* of the *Arts*,
Did he advance his nat'rall Parts;
Till falling back still, for retreat,
He fell to *Juggle*, *Cant*, and *Cheat*.[4]

He has therefore resorted to charlatanism, and has become an astrologer in order to earn a living, selling amulets and charms or drawing up horoscopes for his credulous clients. Butler's criticism of astrology is that, like Ralpho's mysticism, it has no foundation in experience and admits of no empirical proof. The knight demonstrates at length how the astrologers have disagreed amongst themselves over such fundamental questions as the exact location of the stars and the extent of their influence on the affairs of the world.[5] Moreover, besides encouraging delusion, astrology is of no practical value:

So when your Speculations tend
Above their just and useful end,

---

[1] I. iii. 1371-4.   [2] II. iii. 205-6.   [3] II. iii. 209-14.
[4] II. iii. 215-18.   [5] II. iii. 865-928.

> Although they promise strange and great
> *Discoveries* of things far fet,
> They are but idle *Dreams* and *Fancies*.[1]

Sidrophel attempts to answer the knight's criticisms and to
convince him that the art he practises is intellectually sound, but,
failing to do so and finally exposed as a charlatan, he resorts to
violence in order to defend his reputation. This is not the only
occasion in the poem when a character turns to violence in order
to protect his beliefs or pretensions. Talgol, accused of betraying
the Puritan cause, comes to blows with Hudibras, while the
Saints themselves are accused of deciding all controversies by
'Infallible *Artillery*'. Butler believed that one of the logical effects
of error and delusion was often bloodshed—a result which he had
no doubt observed in the controversies of his own age—and
that 'when [a man] is possest with an opinion, the less he understand's of it, the more confident and obstinate he is in asserting it'.[2]

Closely related to his attacks on self-deception is Butler's satire
on hypocrisy, the art of deceiving others. He is especially critical
of religious and political hypocrisy, believing that men in power
can justify practically any crime by appealing to the will of God
or the welfare of the nation. As he remarked in his commonplace
book, 'When Absolom had resolvd to Rebel against the King his
Father, he had no way so proper to put his Designe in execution,
as that of pretending to pay a vow which he had made to the
Lord.'[3] In his discussion of the sanctity of oaths, in the Second
Part,[4] Ralpho looks back on the events of recent history and finds
in them a series of vows all broken on some moral or political
pretext. The King had been attacked on the pretext of his own
safety, the House of Lords, which the Commons had sworn to
preserve, had been abolished as 'dangerous and unuseful', and
Cromwell, pledged to protect the Commons, had used his own
army to destroy it. The real motive behind political and religious
idealism is, according to Butler, self-interest:

> To domineer and to controul
> Both o're the body and the soul,
> Is the most perfect *discipline*
> Of Church-rule, and by *right divine*.[5]

---

[1] II. iii. 777–81.   [2] *Notebooks*, p. 333.   [3] Ibid., p. 301.
[4] II. ii. 102 ff.   [5] I. iii. 1177–80.

Cornered in the dark and terrified of what he believes to be a devil, Hudibras is forced to confess that his pretensions of sanctity are a cover for avarice, and that 'what makes all Doctrines Plain and Clear' is 'about two Hundred Pounds a Year'.[1]

ii

The mode of Butler's attack is extremely varied, ranging from irony to simple invective, and including caricature, mock-disputation, and farce. Parts of *Hudibras* are set loosely in the form of a mock-heroic poem, which, like all works of that kind, depends for its effect on the violent contrast between subject and treatment. In adopting this form Butler was influenced by Cervantes, to whom he alludes several times, and who had created a comic discrepancy between the outmoded ideals of his hero and the reality of the world in which he found himself. Scarron, Butler's near-contemporary, created a more crudely comic antithesis between the stature of his epic heroes and the 'Billingsgate' language in which he described them. In England the wits Sir John Mennis and James Smith had used octosyllabic couplets for comic purposes, and had written short travesties of the epic in their miscellanies *Musarum Deliciae* (1655) and *Wit Restor'd* (1658). Butler may have been influenced by them and certainly adapted several features from *Don Quixote*[2] and the *Virgile Travesti*,[3] but none of these influences was radical: he created a new form, in which several sources may be recognized but which was essentially original. His originality lies partly in the fact that he composed a satire that was simultaneously a criticism of contemporary public morality and outmoded ways of thinking and a parody of what, in common with Hobbes and Davenant, he regarded as an outmoded literary form. For him both the knight's attempts to discover truth by Aristotelian logic and the conventional trappings of heroic poetry, with its chivalric heroes and magic castles, were relics of a superstitious past. Both kinds of satire, the philosophical and the literary, were effected simultaneously by the ingenious device of presenting figures like Hudibras, Ralpho, and Sidrophel

---

[1] III. i. 1277-8.
[2] See E. M. Wilson, 'Cervantes and English Literature of the Seventeenth Century', *Bulletin Hispanique*, l (1948), 45-52.
[3] See S. E. Leavitt, 'Paul Scarron and English Travesty', *SP* xvi (1919), 108-20.

within the framework of a mock-heroic poem. Whereas earlier parodies of the epic, like Scarron's *Virgile Travesti* or James Smith's *Innovation of Ulysses and Penelope*,[1] had been no more than literary *jeux d'esprit*, Butler adapts their mode, the literary travesty, for more serious critical purposes. His was thus the first poem in a new tradition that was later to include *MacFlecknoe* and *The Dunciad*, where the conventions of epic are used for purposes of satire which is both literary and moral.

Hudibras has none of the sustained and detailed ingenuity of *The Dunciad*, where Pope consistently parodies both the general structure and the very phrases of the epic. In *Hudibras* both epic and romance are parodied indiscriminately, and the literary device itself is frequently abandoned in favour of other comic modes, such as the mock-disputation or farce. The poem itself is divided into books and cantos, each canto headed by its appropriate 'argument', in the manner of *The Faerie Queene*. The sudden turns of fortune which occur in the narrative, such as the arrival of the Skimmington in the Second Part, or the burning of the rumps in the Third, are a feature adapted from Italian romance like the *Orlando Furioso*, which Spenser had also used. Mock-heroic elements occur most frequently in the First Part, which, in accordance with convention, plunges *in medias res* with the description of the two chief characters before setting the scene 'in Western Clime' half-way through the first canto. The hero, whose name is taken from *The Faerie Queene*, is presented as a knight-errant setting out on horseback to remedy wrongs. He addresses the rabble in words taken from Lucan[2] and later courts his mistress in phrases adapted from Lucretius.[3] Athene and Mars intervene in the brawl, as they had intervened in the Trojan War (the former assuming the more earthy form of 'rust'),[4] and Orsin laments the loss of his bear, as Hercules had lamented the loss of Hylas in the *Argonautica*.[5] The village stocks are described like an enchanted fortress of romance, and Sidrophel is the comic equivalent of Archimago or Merlin. The most sustained mock-heroic passage is, however, the description of the rabble in the second canto, which parallels the list of epic combatants. Each member is given a suitably high-sounding name appropriate to his trade: the fiddler

[1] Included in Smith and Mennis's *Wit Restor'd*, 1658.
[2] I. ii. 493 ff.
[3] 'Epistle to his Lady', ll. 99 ff.
[4] I. ii. 781.
[5] I. iii. 183–6 and note.

is called Crowdero, the bearwarden Orsin, the butcher Talgol, and the farmer Colon.[1] They are also ironically compared to classical heroes—Crowdero is compared to Chiron, Talgol to Ajax, Colon to Hercules, and Trulla to Camilla. The effect of these literary allusions is by no means simple. At times they emphasize the meanness of the characters in comparison with their epic trappings—and Butler may well have seen himself as living in a mock-heroic age, when tailors claimed divine inspiration and the sons of brewers commanded regiments. But the antithesis between form and subject also acts in the opposite direction, the presence of coarse characters and 'low' actions within a heroic framework reflecting critically upon the literary conventions themselves.

From the notebooks it appears that Butler objected to heroic poetry on the grounds that it 'handle's the slightest, and most Impertinent Follys in the world in a formall Serious and unnaturall way'.[2] In other words, he disliked the style and conventions of such poetry because they were artificial, but also rejected its ideals as trivial and foolish. In *Hudibras* he satirizes both the conventions of heroic poetry and its ideals. He shows up the artificiality of its style by applying its conventions to a crowd of unruly tradesmen. But his criticism is more than literary: one of the themes of *Hudibras* is the foolishness of the ideals of epic and romance when judged by practical, realistic standards.

The two virtues primarily upheld by heroic poetry are those of military valour and chivalric love. That this was Butler's view is shown in the opening to the second canto:

> There was an ancient sage *Philosopher*,
> That had read *Alexander Ross* over,
> And swore the world, as he could prove,
> Was made of *Fighting* and of *Love*:
> Just so *Romances* are, for what else
> Is in them all, but *Love* and *Battels*?

Far from being virtues, however, Butler believed them to be illusory and, in performance, absurd, 'for if any man should but imitate what these Heroical Authors write in the Practice of his life and Conversation, he would become the most Ridiculous

[1] Butler probably coined these epic-sounding names following the example of *The Knight of the Burning Pestle*. See note to 1. ii. 106.
[2] *Notebooks*, p. 278.

Person in the world'.[1] This criticism is implicit throughout much of the First Part, where the high exploits of the Greeks and Trojans are reduced to—and identified with—a common brawl, where the knight's protestations of love are shown to be a cover for the appropriation of his lady's dowry, and the 'noble trade' of the demi-gods and heroes is dismissed as 'slaughter and knocking on the head'. In the Second Part the criticism becomes more explicit, for the conversation between Hudibras and the widow centres chiefly on the subjects of military prowess and romantic love, in which the knight's apparent idealism is rebuked by the widow's realistic common sense. Hudibras, soundly beaten by Trulla and thrown into the stocks, attempts to convince himself that defeat is actually victory, partly by citing the Stoic view of pain and also by claiming that, by chivalric standards, suffering is a virtue:

> For what's more honorable then *scarrs*,
> Or skin to tatters rent in *Warrs*?[2]

—an opinion which is contradicted by his own ridiculous situation in the stocks and by the colloquial realism with which he expresses it. The widow, however, pretends to take the statement literally, and suggests that he should accumulate even greater honours by suffering a whipping:

> But if a *beating* seem so brave,
> What *Glories* must a *Whipping* have?[3]

Hence the knight's heroic ideals are put to the test and he finds himself pledged to thrash his own backside for the sake of honour.

The conversation proceeds to a lengthy debate on the subject of love, in which Hudibras voices the conventionally romantic view, whereas the widow, seeing through his schemes to lay hands on her fortune, attacks the whole notion of love as it is expressed in romantic literature. The knight woos her in the exaggerated manner of contemporary lyric poets:

> The *Sun* and *Day* shall sooner part,
> Then *love*, or you, shake off my heart.
> The *Sun* that shall no more dispence
> His own, but *your* bright influence;

[1] *Notebooks*, p. 278.   [2] II. i. 219-20.   [3] II. i. 275-6.

> I'l carve your name on *Barks* of *Trees*,
> With *true-loves knots*, and *flourishes*;
> That shall infuse eternal *spring*,
> And ever-lasting flourishing.[1]

The widow, however, realizes that these words have no relation to the knight's real feelings:

> For you will find it a hard *Chapter*,
> To catch me with *Poetique Rapture*,
> In which your *Mastery* of *Art*
> Doth shew it self, and not your *Heart*.[2]

Finally, the conversation passes to other matters, and the knight leaves his lady, still protesting love and vowing to keep his pledge of whipping, while actually scheming to lay hands on her money and determined to evade his promise. The conventional attitudes of heroic poetry have been shown to be false; the conventional values have been put to the test and found ridiculous.

iii

It appears from Butler's letter to Sir George Oxenden[3] that, on its first appearance, the characters in the First Part were identified by its readers with certain prominent personalities living at the time. Butler's own comment on this interpretation is that, although the characters of Hudibras and his squire were inspired by an actual knight and his clerk (whom many people recognized in the poem), the rest were not modelled on specific people and were not designed to be identified as such: 'the other Psons as Orsin a Beareward, Talgol a Butcher, Magnano a Tinker, Cerdon a Cobler, Colon a Clowne &c: are such as Commonly make up Bearebaitings', and 'though some curious witts heere pretend to discover ceartaine Psons of Quallity wth whome they say those Characters agree', no such resemblance was intended.

Hardin Craig has also suggested that the characters in the First Part stand for 'ceartaine persons of quallity', and that the action is an allegorical representation of certain political events.[4] His

---

[1] II. i. 561–8.   [2] II. i. 585–8.
[3] See Appendix A.
[4] '*Hudibras*, Part I, and the Politics of 1647', *Manly Anniversary Studies*, Chicago, 1923, 145–55.

theory—put forward before the discovery of the letter to Oxenden
—is that 'the brave resistance of the bear, his flight and establishment in a place of at least temporary comfort' may 'represent the
flight of King Charles from Hampton Court to Carisbrook', and
that the knight's defeat by the rabble 'may represent the defeat
of the Presbyterians and their overthrow by the leaders of the
army'. If this is so, then the bear stands for Charles I, Hudibras for
the Presbyterians, and the mob for the Independent party. The
ruthless Colon may be Cromwell,[1] Talgol the butcher may be
Fairfax, Magnano may be the 'magnanimous' Skippon, and
Cerdon may be Ireton 'the scholar of the rebellion'.

It is true that the First Part, like the rest of *Hudibras*, is full of
political allusion, and that the action appears to take place during
a particular phase of the Civil War.[2] The inclusion of political
allegory would also be in keeping with Butler's intention to write
a parody of heroic poetry, since other poems in that tradition,
notably *The Faerie Queene*, invite such an interpretation. Whether
or not he intended specific political implications to be seen in the
poem can, perhaps, never be known for certain, but the question
depends upon the external evidence and upon the extent to which
the poem itself is intelligible without recourse to allegorical
interpretation. The external evidence of Butler's letter suggests
that there is no such allegory: the figures in the second canto are
consistent only with his purpose in writing a mock-heroic poem.
They are not public figures, but 'a Beareward, a Butcher, a Tinker,
a Cobler, a Clowne', placed ironically in the context of an epic.
It is, of course, possible that Butler's explanation is itself ironical,
but the poem itself makes consistent good sense simply as a parody
of heroic poetry in which no sustained allegorical significance need
be recognized. The bear-baiting and the subsequent brawl are the
comic equivalent of an epic battle, and the knight's duel with
Trulla is a parody of encounters with such warlike women as
Ariosto's Bradamante and Spenser's Radigund. The description
of the rabble in the second canto is the equivalent of the epic roll-
call in which, according to convention, the appearance, character,
and skill of each warrior is described in turn, and, though the
manner is heroic, the meaning relates to the distinctive attributes

[1] Craig points out that Colon's name reversed suggests Cromwell's nickname
'Nol'.
[2] See pp. xliv–xlv.

of the different tradesmen. Talgol, for example, is a butcher (his name means, literally, 'cut-throat'[1]) and he wears the 'Gantlet blew and Bases white'[2]—the blue sleeves and white apron—of his profession. He has, we are told, slaughtered many beasts with his 'keen blade'[3] and, like Don Quixote, has killed many a flock of sheep. Colon is 'right expert in Command of horse', not necessarily because he is a soldier or represents Cromwell, but because he is a farmer (Latin *colonus*) and can both plough a field[4] and 'clense a Stable'. The other characters are likewise presented in heroic terms ironically adapted to their trades.

This does not prevent Butler from making incidental thrusts against contemporary figures from time to time, for it was a fact of seventeenth-century public life that several political and military leaders came from humble origins, as the authors of popular ballads and lampoons were quick to point out. The figure of Cerdon, the cobbler, for example, is used as part of Butler's attempt to deflate the reputation of the epic heroes, but may at the same time have given him the opportunity for a casual allusion to one of Cromwell's officers, Hewson, who had once been a cobbler in Westminster. Colon may have been intended to remind the reader of Desborough who, as the anti-Puritan lampoonists eagerly insisted, was originally a farmer.[5] Such incidental allusions are, however, very different from the full-scale political allegory envisaged by Craig, in which each character is an allegorical figure and in which the narrative parallels actual political events. Both the poem itself and Butler's other writings show that his interests were not primarily political, but that he was much more concerned with the moral and philosophical principles that lie beyond politics. Like most satirists, he attacked human weaknesses in the forms in which his own age presented them to him. Politicians did not interest him, nor did political parties, except in so far as they were guilty of human ambition or self-deception, to which he was always sensitive.

iv

The mock-heroic is only one, and one of the least frequent, of the modes through which Butler reveals the pretensions and

---

[1] See note to I. ii. 288. [2] I. ii. 768. [3] I. ii. 303.
[4] I. ii. 461. [5] See notes to I. ii. 409, 441.

triviality of man. His greatest satirical weapon is his style, with
its earthy, colloquial language, intentionally clumsy rhythms,
and comic rhymes, which debase everything they describe. His
language ranges from the coarse to the elevated and the pedantic.
He can ridicule the idea of divine inspiration, for example, by
describing it in homely images and coarsely realistic terms:

> This Light inspires, and playes upon
> The nose of Saint, like Bag-pipe-drone,
> And speaks through hollow empty soul,
> As through a Trunk, or whisp'ring hole,
> Such language as no mortall ear
> But spiritual Eaves-droppers can hear.[1]

The plain colloquialism of Butler's language is a vehicle for his
practical, realistic outlook. It is one way by which he tests human
behaviour and shows it to be foolish or hypocritical. At other
times he attacks pretension by using the very language by which
it is perpetuated. Butler is well versed in the cant and professional
terms employed by the kind of people he attacks—the Puritans,
the politicians, and the scientists. The use of 'hard words' was,
he says, one of the incitements which led to the outbreak of war.
The poem contains plenty of examples of the political jargon of
the day, including such terms as 'Malignants', 'Delinquents', 'the
well-affected', and Butler can make his characters speak the
characteristic language of the Puritans. Hudibras is said to know
more than forty philosophers 'as far as words and termes could
go', and he sprinkles his conversation with Latin tags, philosophical terms, and the language of the law. Sidrophel, too, and
the lawyer use their own professional jargon, the speciousness
of which Butler reveals by exposing it as a cover for ignorance
and self-interest.

The imagery of *Hudibras*, like its language, is generally of two
kinds. It is either so homely and commonplace that it deflates its
subject or so fantastically learned and pedantic that it mocks
itself by its own excess. It has been pointed out[2] that the 'lowering'
metaphors are often grotesque images of animals:

> Mighty he was at both of these,
> And styl'd of *War* as well as *Peace*.

[1] I. i. 509–14.
[2] Ian Jack, *Augustan Satire*, Oxford, 1952, 31–32.

> (So some Rats of amphibious nature,
> Are either for the Land or Water).[1]

> Beside 'tis known he could speak *Greek*,
> As naturally as Pigs squeek:
> That *Latin* was no more difficile,
> Then to a Blackbird 'tis to whistle.[2]

The rural, animal imagery of *Hudibras* is one of the few evidences of Butler's early experiences as a boy in Worcestershire, but it is also a means of expressing the unpretentious, realistic outlook he may have acquired there, from which he judged the public world that he encountered later.

The peculiarly learned imagery of the poem was no doubt derived from Butler's reading in the libraries of his aristocratic employers. The copiousness and obscurity of its allusions is, in fact, one of the most distinctive and celebrated features of *Hudibras*. There are references to philosophy, theology, science, astrology, witchcraft, alchemy, medicine, the classics, history, and foreign travel. Indeed Butler has acquired a reputation not unlike Burton's as a purveyor of recondite information. He generally alludes to such things, however, in order to discredit them. The poem abounds with references to 'authors', 'histories', and 'antiquaries', both real and imaginary, who are credited with patently absurd opinions—that a Saxon duke, for example, was unwittingly consumed by mice, that the Prince of Cambay feeds on basilisks and kisses his wives to death, or that the Median emperor

> dreamt, his Daughter
> Had pist all *Asia* under water,
> And that a *Vine*, sprung from her *hanches*,
> O'erspread his *Empire*, with its branches;
> And did not *Southsayers* expound it,
> As after by th'event he found it?[3]

'There is no certaine Knowledg', wrote Butler, 'without Demonstration',[4] and his repeated gibes against learned authorities are yet another way in which he shows the difference between practical reality and popular delusion.

---

[1] I. i. 25–28. [2] I. i. 51–54.
[3] II. iii. 691–6. [4] *Notebooks*, p. 282.

Irony, exaggeration, innuendo, the mock-heroic, the use of incongruous language and imagery are among the many indirect means by which Butler carries out his satirical purposes. Some of the most impressive passages in *Hudibras*, however, consist of simple, violent invective. The knight's first speech, in which he inquires the cause why '*Dog* and *Bear* are to dispute', starts as a parody of pedantic and political argument, but moves imperceptibly into an attack on the predatory nature of man, in which the poet seems to be expressing his own convictions:

> But no Beast ever was so slight,
> For man, as for his God, to fight.
> They have more wit, alas! and know
> Themselves and us better then so.
> But we, we onely do infuse
> The Rage in them like *Boute-feus*.
> 'Tis our example that instills
> In them th'infection of our ills.
> For, as some late Philosophers
> Have well observ'd, Beasts that converse
> With Man, take after him, as Hogs
> Get Pigs all th'year, and Bitches Dogs.
> Just so by our example Cattel
> Learn to give one another Battel.[1]

Hudibras is in many ways an unsatisfactory poem. Butler's use of rhythm for comic effect precludes much metrical subtlety or variety. As Ian Jack has pointed out, the metre is scarcely recognizable as that of 'Il Penseroso' or Marvell's 'The Garden'. The comic invention which enlivens the first two parts appears only intermittently in the third, which is also verbose and has little of the terseness of expression of the earlier parts. Moreover, the poem has no coherent form and reaches no satisfactory conclusion. Its greatest qualities are the vigour of Butler's expression and the fertility of his wit. These appear at their best not so much in single, unexpected strokes of ingenuity as in extended speeches and character-sketches where the images are copious and the poet's power of invention rises vigorously to its height. Like Swift, Butler engaged in a kind of desperate intellectual ingenuity as an antidote for his prevailing pessimism. If the total effect of

[1] i. i. 775–88.

his satire is largely destructive, it is probably because he could see little in his age but partisan violence and delusion. Hence he was incapable of sympathizing even with the constructive movements of his time and was compelled to remain an uncommitted but troubled spectator.

TEXTUAL INTRODUCTION

1. *Date of Composition*

BUTLER's natural talent lay in the elaborate development of single themes, such as is possible within the framework of the 'character' or formal disputation, and which he unfolds either through a series of images (as in the prose *Characters*) or through one extended image (as in Ralpho's diatribe against the synods in *Hudibras*). His commonplace books are full of such passages, many in octosyllabic couplets, which he appears to have kept in readiness to incorporate at some stage in a longer work. The fact that *Hudibras* itself consists largely of character-sketches and debates, linked by passages of narrative, suggests that Butler worked into it material he had composed at different times; hence the date of its composition cannot be ascribed to a brief period of years, and portions of the second and third parts may well have been written before the completion of the first. The statement on the title-pages of the First and the First and Second Parts that they were 'written in the time of the late wars' is unhelpful, since, as Quintana has pointed out,[1] this could signify any time between 1640 and 1660. Nor does Butler's remark that he wrote the First Part shortly before meeting Sir George Oxenden[2] enable a more precise date to be fixed, since Oxenden was in England for three separate periods between 1639 and 1662.[3] The most rewarding evidence is to be found within the poem itself, in Butler's allusions to political events and to published works, the dates of which are beyond dispute.

All three parts of *Hudibras* contain references to three successive but distinct phases of history: the early years of the Civil War, on which the characters look back in retrospect, the period in which Butler visualized the action of his poem as taking place, and the period during which he actually wrote the poem. During the course of his first, long address to the bear-baiting mob in the First Part (I. ii. 493–680) the knight reminds his audience of

---

[1] 'The Butler–Oxenden Correspondence', *MLN* xlviii (1933), 7.
[2] See Appendix A.
[3] Quintana, op. cit., p. 6; Appendix A.

a series of political events which have preceded their encounter.
These events range chronologically from the '*Et caetera* Oath' of
1640 to the army petitions of 1647, and include the accusation of
the five members (1642), the defeat of the Royalists at Roundway
Down, and the taking of the Solemn League and Covenant (1643).
They are spoken of as having taken place before the action of the
poem itself and are, in fact, regarded by the knight as leading up
to the immediate event of the bear-baiting. Butler therefore
appears to have imagined the bear-baiting as occurring shortly
after these historical events. The period visualized for the narrative
itself is suggested by the contrast in outlook and allegiance
between Hudibras and his Squire. The knight is a 'Presbyterian
true blew' of the old school, whereas Ralpho is an Independent,
whose disparaging comments on the Presbyterians are the immediate cause of argument with his master. Butler therefore appears
to have set the action of his poem at a time when the conflict
between Presbyterians and Independents was at its height. Such
was the situation between the closing months of 1647, when the
army had forced the withdrawal of eleven Presbyterian members
of parliament, and the end of 1648, when parliament was finally
purged of Presbyterians by Colonel Pride.[1] This was also the
time when, according to Gardiner, the Puritans were most active
in suppressing popular sports.[2]

If the year 1648 is the date visualized by Butler for the action
of the First Part of *Hudibras*, it is not the time during which he
wrote it, for he is himself considering the conflict between
Presbyterian and Independent retrospectively. The knight set
out, he tells us,

> When *civil* Fury first grew high,
> And men fell out they knew not why.

The period from which Butler looked back on recent history is
less easy to deduce from the text of the First Part, but the concluding lines of the first canto seem to refer to a recent situation:

> So have I seen with armed heel,
> A Wight bestride a *Common-weal*;
> While still the more he kick'd and spurr'd,
> The less the sullen Jade has stirr'd.

[1] This is also the date suggested by Hardin Craig in '*Hudibras* and the Politics of
1647', *Manly Anniversary Studies*, Chicago, 1923, p. 150.
[2] Gardiner, iv. 45–46.

The allusion here is almost certainly to Oliver Cromwell, who rose to power and ruled the country with the 'armed heel' of the army. If this is correct, then Butler was engaged in writing this passage towards the end of the period between December 1653, when Cromwell was made Protector, and September 1658, when Cromwell died. Further evidence is provided by allusions in the First Part to printed books, of which the latest is Digby's *Late Discourse*,[1] published both in France and England in 1658. Butler was, however, still at work on the First Part after the Restoration, for in the last canto he describes the influence in England of the French fashions which Charles II brought back from the Continent:

> the *French* we conquer'd once,
> Now give us Laws for Pantaloons,
> The length of Breeches, and the gathers,
> Port-canons, Perriwigs, and Feathers.[2]

There is also a reference to Le Blanc's *Famous Voyages*,[3] which was published in Paris in 1648 but did not appear in an English translation until 1660. Both the literary and political references therefore point to the conclusion that Butler was engaged in the composition of the First Part between 1658 and 1660. This conclusion is supported by the poet's own statement that he wrote it shortly before meeting Sir George Oxenden, for Oxenden was in England between 1659 and 1662.

In the Second Part Butler is less concerned with political and theological divisions in the country than with political conduct generally and with non-political matters like astrology. The historical setting is therefore less precise, and the text does not offer sufficient evidence to determine the date visualized for the action. There is, however, a survey of recent history, as in the First Part, in which the Squire points out the frequency with which parliamentary oaths have been broken.[4] Ralpho alludes again to the early years of the war, mentioning the Protestation (1641) and the Solemn League and Covenant (1643), but also touching upon episodes which happened later than those mentioned in the First Part, including Pride's Purge (1648) and the abolition of the House of Lords in 1649. At one point[5] the squire

---

[1] I. ii. 223-40.   [2] I. iii. 923-6.   [3] I. ii. 282-6.
[4] II. ii. 143-200.   [5] II. iii. 139-42.

mentions that a '*Ledger* to the Devil' has been sent by 'this present
Parliament' to investigate cases of witchcraft, but since the parliament referred to is the Long Parliament, the allusion does not
help to place the time of the action any more exactly.

The fact that the first instalment of *Hudibras* was described on
its title-page as 'The First Part' indicates that Butler had already
begun, or at any rate was planning, to write a sequel. The appearance of the widow in the Second Part is, moreover, prepared for
in the last canto of the First.[1] It is therefore likely that the Second
Part was in existence in an unfinished state by the end of 1662,[2]
and that Butler or the bookseller waited to observe the success of
the First Part before venturing on the publication of a second.
Several of the literary references are to books published shortly
before 1662, such as Peter du Moulin's *Devill of Mascon* (1658)[3]
and Casaubon's account of the exploits of John Dee (1659).[4]
There is also a reference to the ghostly drummer who was said
to have haunted a house near Tedworth in 1662.[5] Some of the
third canto must, however, have been written in 1663, since
Butler makes comic use of the spurious 'Second Part' which
appeared in that year.[6] The 'Epistle to Sidrophel' was composed
much later. It appeared for the first time in 1674, when it was
added to the revised version of the First and Second Parts. The
Epistle contains references to the discourses and experiments of
the Royal Society, including a paper concerning eggs, read in
1672.[7] It must therefore have been written between 1672 and 1674.

Although sections of the Third Part may well have been in
Butler's notebooks at an earlier date, there is no doubt that the
greater part of it was composed after the Restoration, since the
action of the second canto is depicted as taking place in February
1660, concluding as it does with the public burning of the rumps
as Monk and his soldiers put an end to the Rump Parliament.
This same canto also contains a survey of recent history, which is
continued far beyond the events mentioned in the earlier parts to
include the death of Oliver Cromwell, the fall of Richard Cromwell, and the placing of Oliver's head on the top of Westminster
Hall in 1661.[8] Some of the third canto must, however, have been

---

[1] I. iii. 309 ff.
[2] The First Part was on sale by 26 December 1662. See p. xix.
[3] II. iii. 161.   [4] II. iii. 163, 237–8.   [5] II. i. 132.
[6] II. iii. 991–1012.   [7] Epistle 46.   [8] III. ii. 224–6.

D

composed much later than this, for Butler alludes to Herbert Croft's *The Naked Truth*,[1] which was published in 1675. Most of the Third Part was presumably written between 1663, when the Second Part came out, and 1677, when the Third Part was published. The literary allusions are, however, much more scanty than in the rest of the poem, and it is therefore impossible to assign a more specific date.

11. *Early Editions*

THE FIRST PART

A1 *Title-page*: HUDIBRAS. | [rule] | THE FIRST PART. [rule] | *Written in the time of the late Wars.* | [rule] | [device: a wreath] | [rule] | *LONDON,* | Printed by *J.G.* for *Richard Marriot*, under Saint | *Dunstan*'s Church in *Fleetstreet.* 1663.

Collation: 8°. A–R⁸, 136 leaves, pp. [4] 1–70 [71] 72–161 [162] 163–268 [misnumbering p. 171 as 17, 250 as 251, 251 as 250; misprinting p. 23 as ᴈ3 and 227 as ᴈ27 in some copies; numbering p. 38 in inner margin].

Contents: blank A1ʳ; imprimatur A1ᵛ: [line of 34 fleurs-de-lis] | Imprimatur. | *JO: BERKENHEAD.* | Novemb. 11. | 1662. | [line of 33 fleurs-de-lis, inverted, and the ligature 'æ']; title-page A2ʳ; blank A2ᵛ; Canto I pp. 1–70; Canto II pp. 71–161; blank p. 162; Canto III pp. 163–268; errata at foot of p. 268.

Catchword p. 106 misprinted 'One' instead of 'Yet'.

Copies collated: British Museum; Bodleian; Cambridge; Bristol University; Harvard (two copies); Yale (two copies).

A2 *Title-page*: Hudibras. | [rule] | THE FIRST PART. | [rule] | *Written in the time of the late Wars.* | [rule] | [device: a wreath as in A1] | [rule] | *LONDON:* | Printed by *J.G.* for *Richard Marriot*, under | St. *Dunstans* Church in *Fleet-street*, 1663.

Collation: 12°. A–E¹²F⁶, 66 leaves, pp. [4] 1–128 [misnumbering p. 25 as 2, pp. 94–95 as 92–93, 98–99 as 96–97, 102–3 as 100–1, 106–7 as 104–5, 110–11 as 108–9, 114–15 as 112–13 in some copies].

Contents: blank A1ʳ; imprimatur A1ᵛ: [line of ornaments beginning with half-ornament] | IMPRIMATUR. | *Jo: Berkenhead.* | Nov. 11. 1662: | [line of ornaments ending with half-ornament]; title-page A2ʳ; blank A2ᵛ; Canto I pp. 1–34; Canto II pp. 35–77; Canto III pp. 78–128.

Catchword p. 40 printed 'VVith', first word p. 41 'With'; catchword p. 73 'VVhere', first word p. 74 'Where'. Errata noted on p. 268 of A1 have been corrected.

Copies collated: Bodleian; Harvard; Yale.

[1] III. iii. 145.

A3 *Title-page*: identical with A2.

Collation: 12°. A–E¹²F⁶, 66 leaves, pp. [4] 1–128.

Contents: blank A1ʳ; imprimatur A1ᵛ: [line of ornaments ending with half-ornament] | IMPRIMATUR. | *Jo: Berkenhead.* | Nov. 11. 1662. | [line of ornaments beginning with half-ornament]; title-page A2ʳ; blank A2ᵛ; arrangement of text similar to A2.

Catchword p. 1 printed 'When', first word p. 2 'VVhen'; catchword p. 10 'VVhose', first word p. 11 'Whose'; catchword p. 11 'With', first word p. 12 'VVith'; catchword p. 36 'With', first word p. 37 'VVith'; catchword p. 40 'With', first word p. 41 'VVith'; catchword p. 61 'Was', first word p. 62 'VVas'.

Copies collated: British Museum; Bodleian.

A4 *Title-page*: identical with A2 and A3.

Collation: 12°. A–E¹²F⁶, [C5 unsigned in some copies], 66 leaves, pp. [4] 1–128 [misnumbering p. 25 as 1, pp. 28–29 as 4–5, 32–33 as 8–9, 36–37 as 12–13, 40–41 as 16–17, 44 as 20 in some copies].

Contents: arrangement and imprimatur similar to A3.

Running-title on pp. 36, 37, 40, 41, 44 (misnumbered 12, 13, 16, 17, 20) misprinted *Canto* I instead of *Canto* II. Catchword p. 1 printed 'When', first word p. 2 printed 'VVhen'; catchword p. 10 'VVhose', first word p. 11 'Whose'; catchword p. 11 'With', first word p. 12 'VVith'; no catchword p. 31 in some copies; catchword p. 36 'With', first word p. 37 'VVith'; catchword p. 40 'With', first word p. 41 'VVith'; catchword p. 59 'VVhich', first word p. 60 'Which'; catchword p. 79 'Gave', first word p. 80 'Give'; catchword p. 88 'Where', first word p. 89 'VVhere'; catchword p. 96 'VVhen', first word p. 97 'When'; no catchword p. 104.

Copies collated: Bodleian; Princeton; Yale.

A5 *Title-page*: identical with A2, A3, and A4.

Collation: 8°. A–H⁸, 64 leaves, pp. [2] 1–75 [76] 77–125 [126].

Contents: title-page A1ʳ; imprimatur A1ᵛ: [line of ornaments enclosed in brackets] | IMPRIMATUR. | *Jo: Berkenhead.* | Nov. 11. 1662. | [line of ornaments enclosed in brackets]; Canto I pp. 1–34; Canto II pp. 35–75; blank p. 76; Canto III pp. 77–125; blank p. 126.

Catchword p. 106 printed 'VVhy', first word p. 107 printed 'Why'.

Copies collated: Bodleian; Harvard.

A6 *Title-page*: HUDIBRAS. | [rule] | THE FIRST PART. | [rule] | *Written in the time of the late Wars* | [rule] | [device: a crowned rose and thistle] | [rule] | *LONDON,* | Printed in the Year, 1663.

Collation: 8°. A–H⁸, 64 leaves, pp. [2] 1–75 [76] 77–125 [126].

Contents: title-page A1ʳ; imprimatur A1ᵛ: [line of ornaments] | Imprimatur. | *JO: BERKENHEAD.* | Novemb. 11 | 1662. | [line of ornaments]; Canto I pp. 1–34; Canto II pp. 35–75; blank p. 76; Canto III pp. 77–125; errata at foot of p. 125; blank p. 126.

First word on p. 4 printed 'Vnd' for 'And'; catchword p. 70 misprinted 'fO' for 'Of' in some copies; no catchword p. 123. Running-title p. 79 misprints '*CANTO II.*' for '*CANTO III.*'; p. 86 misprints '*CANTO.*' for '*CANTO III.*'.
Copies collated: British Museum (two copies); Bristol University.

A7 *Title-page*: identical with A6.

Collation: identical with A6, but mis-signing sig. E3 as F3 and misnumbering p. 91 as 61.
Contents: arrangement similar to A6. The name in the imprimatur is spelled '*BIRKENHEAD*'; errata noted at foot of p. 125 in A6 have been corrected; running-title p. 90 misprinted '*Canto II*' instead of '*Canto III*'; catchword p. 15 misprinted 'But' instead of 'But'.
Copy collated: Bodleian.

A8 *Title-page*: HUDIBRAS. | [rule] | THE | FIRST PART. | [rule] | Written in the time of the late WARS. | [rule] | [design: 7 lines of ornaments in an inverted pyramid, 14 in top line] | [rule] | *LONDON*, | Printed in the Year, 1663.

Collation: 8°. A–H⁸, 64 leaves, pp. [2] 1–75 [76] 77–125 [126] [misnumbering pp. 106–7 as 108–9, 110 as 112].
Contents: title-page A1ʳ; imprimatur A1ᵛ: [line of 17 ornaments of which 1st, 9th, and 17th are fleurs-de-lis; a colon follows 9th ornament] | Imprimatur. | *JO: BIRKENHEAD*. | Novemb. 11. | 1662. | [line of 17 ornaments of which 1st, 9th, and 17th are fleurs-de-lis; all ornaments inverted except final fleur-de-lis]; arrangement of text similar to A6.
Catchwords misprinted: p. 12 'For' for 'For', p. 26 'But' for 'But', p. 52 'Shal' for 'Shall'. Change to larger (italic) type in running-title at p. 79. Running-title p. 87 misprinted '*CHNTO III.*'; running-titles pp. 88, 90, 104, 106, 120, 122 misprinted '*CANTO II.*' for '*CANTO III.*'.
Copies collated: Bodleian; Harvard (two copies).

A9 *Title-page*: HUDIBRAS | [rule] | THE | FIRST PART. | [rule] | Written in the time of the late WARS. | [rule] | [design: seven lines of fleurs-de-lis in an inverted pyramid, 13 in top line] | [rule] | *LONDON*, | Printed in the Year, 1663.

Collation: 8°. A–H⁸ [sig. G4 misprinted as C4], 64 leaves, pp. [2] 1–75 [76] 77–125 [126] [misnumbering pp. 2–3 as 4–5, 6–7 as 8–9, 10–11 as 12–13, 14 as 16, and 88 as 89].
Contents: title-page A1ʳ; imprimatur A1ᵛ: [line of 15 fleurs-de-lis with a comma after 7th fleur-de-lis] | Imprimatur. | *JO. BIRKENHEAD.* | Novemb. 11. | 1662. | [line of 15 inverted fleurs-de-lis with inverted comma after 7th fleur-de-lis]; arrangement of text similar to A6.
Catchwords misprinted: p. 21 'But' for 'But', p. 34 'THE' for 'THE', p. 62 'The' for 'The', p. 87 'To' for 'To', p. 94 'A' for 'As', p. 101 'Through'

for 'Though'. Running-titles pp. 78, 120, and 122 misprint '*CANTO. II.*'
for '*CANTO. III.*'.
  Copies collated: British Museum; Cambridge.

THE SECOND PART

B1 *Title-page*: HUDIBRAS. | [rule] | *The Second Part.* | [rule] | By
the Authour of the First. | [rule] | [device: a bell, an angel, and the
booksellers' initials, 'M' and 'A'] | *LONDON,* | Printed by *T.R.*
for *John Martyn,* and *James Allestry* | at the Bell in S^t· *Pauls*
Church Yard, 1664.

  Collation: 8°. *A*⁴B–O⁸P⁴ [F3 mis-signed F4], 112 leaves, pp. [*8*] 1–216.
  Contents: blank *A*1ʳ–*A*2ᵛ; title-page *A*3ʳ; blank *A*3ᵛ–*A*4ʳ; imprimatur
*A*4ᵛ: [line of 17 roses] | *Imprimatur,* | ROGER L'ESTRANGE. | *Novemb.*
5th. | 1663. | [line of 17 roses]; Canto I pp. 1–66; Canto II pp. 67–130;
Canto III pp. 131–216; errata at foot of p. 216.
  Copies collated: British Museum; Bodleian; Cambridge; Bristol University;
Harvard; Yale (two copies).

B2 *Title-page*: HUDIBRAS. | [rule] | *The Second Part.* | [rule] | By
the Author of the First. | [rule] | [device as in B1] | *LONDON,*
| Printed by *T.R.* for *John Martyn,* and *James* | *Allestry,* at the Bell
in S^t· *Pauls* Church- | Yard. 1664.

  Collation: 8°. A–H⁸, 64 leaves, pp. [*6*] 7–77 [*78*] 79–125 [*126–8*] [mis-
numbering p. 25 as 21 in some copies].
  Contents: blank *A*1ʳ–*A*2ʳ; imprimatur *A*2ᵛ: [line of 14 roses] | *Imprimatur,* |
ROGER L'ESTRANGE. | *Novemb.* 5th. | 1663. | [line of 14 roses]; title-page
*A*3ʳ; blank *A*3ᵛ; Canto I pp. 7–42; Canto II pp. 43–77; blank p. 78; Canto III
pp. 79–125; blank pp. 126–8.
  Some of the errata noted on p. 216 of B1 have been corrected.
  Copies collated: British Museum (two copies); Bodleian (three copies);
Cambridge (two copies); Harvard (three copies); Yale (three copies);
Princeton.

THE FIRST AND SECOND PARTS

C1 *Title-page Part I*: HUDIBRAS. | [rule] | *The First and Second
Parts.* | [rule] | Written in the time of the | Late Wars. | [rule] |
CORRECTED & AMENDED, | WITH | Several Additions and
Annotations. | [rule] | *LONDON,* | Printed by *T.N.* for *John
Martyn* and *Henry* | *Herringman,* at the *Bell* in *St. Pauls Churchyard,* |
and the *Anchor* in the Lower Walk of | the *New Exchange,* 1674.
  Title-page Part II: HUDIBRAS. | [rule] | *The Second Part.* | [rule]
| By the Author of the First. | [rule] | CORRECTED &
AMENDED, | WITH | Several Additions and Annotations. |

[rule] | *LONDON,* | Printed by *T.N.* for *John Martyn* and *Henry* | *Herringman,* at the *Bell* in *St. Pauls Churchyard,* | and the *Anchor* in the Lower Walk of | the *New Exchange,* 1674.

Collation: 8°. A–2C⁸ [sigs. I4, K3, T3, Y3, Y4, and 2C4 unsigned], 208 leaves, pp. [*2*] 1–220 [*2*] 221–412 [misprinting p. 45 as 54, 65 as 6, and 74 as *ᵗL* in some copies; misnumbering 207–220 as 189–202].

Contents: title-page Part I A1ʳ; blank A1ᵛ; Part I Canto I pp. 1–55; Canto II pp. 56–124; Canto III pp. 125–206; Annotations pp. [207–20]; blank two pages; title-page Part II p. 221; blank p. 222; Part II Canto I pp. 223–74; Canto II pp. 275–324; Canto III pp. 325–91; Heroical Epistle pp. 392–9; Annotations pp. 400–12.

Catchwords misprinted: p. 171 'Tha' for 'That', p. 195 'Wher' for 'Where', p. 293 'Canno' for 'Cannot', p. 323 'Than' for 'Then'; no catchword pp. 206 and 391. Running-title p. 65 and pp. 76–77 misprinted as '*CANTO* I' for '*CANTO* II' in some copies; pp. 326–7, 330–31 misprinted as '*CANTO* II' for '*CANTO* III' in some copies.

Copies collated: British Museum; Bodleian; Harvard (two copies); Yale (two copies).

C2 *Title-page Part I*: HUDIBRAS. | [rule] | *The First and Second Parts.* | [rule] | Written in the Time of the | Late Wars. | [rule] | CORRECTED & AMENDED, | With | Several Additions and Annotations. | [rule] | *LONDON:* | Printed by *T.N.* for *John Martyn* and *Henry* | *Herringman,* at the *Bell* in St. *Pauls* Church- | yard, and at the *Anchor* in the Lower | Walk of the *New Exchange,* 1678.

Title-page Part II: HUDIBRAS. | [rule] | *The Second Part.* | [rule] | By the Author of the First. | [rule] | CORRECTED & AMENDED, | With | Several Additions and Annotations. | [rule] | *LONDON:* | Printed by *T.N.* for *John Martyn* and *Henry* | *Herringman,* at the *Bell* in St. *Pauls* Church- | yard, and at the *Anchor* in the Lower | Walk of the *New Exchange,* 1678.

Collation: 8°. A–2C⁸ [T3 unsigned], 208 leaves, pp. [*2*] 1–220 [*2*] 221–412 [numbering 24–26 in inner margin, misnumbering 84 as 85, 85 as 15, 207–20 as 189–202, 229 as 329, 319 as 316].

Contents: arrangement identical with C1.

Catchword p. 21 misprints 'A' for 'As' in some copies; catchword p. 47 misprints 'Do' for 'To'. No running-title p. 389.

Copies collated: British Museum; Bodleian (two copies); Harvard (three copies); Yale (three copies).

THE THIRD AND LAST PART

D1 *Title-page*: HUDIBRAS. | [rule] | THE | Third and last | PART. | [rule] | Written by the AUTHOR | OF THE | FIRST and SECOND PARTS. | [rule] | *LONDON*, | Printed for *Simon Miller*, at the Sign of the *Star* | at the West End of St. *Pauls*. 1678.

> *Collation*: 8°. A–S⁸T₁, 145 leaves, pp. [2] 1–285 [*286–8*] [misprinting 157 as 175].
> *Contents*: title-page A1ʳ; blank A1ᵛ; Canto I pp. 1–92; Canto II pp. 93–192; Canto III pp. 193–240; Epistle of Hudibras pp. 241–62; Ladies Answer pp. 263–85; blank p. 286; errata p. *286*; blank p. *288*.
> Catchwords misprinted: p. 61 'For' for '*For*', p. 67 '*Tho*' for 'The' in some copies, p. 93 'So,' for 'So', p. 151 'In' for '*In*', p. 211 'Quoth' for '*Quoth*', p. 224 '*What*,' for '*What*'. Running-title pp. 274–5 misprinted '*The Ladies Answer*' (274), '*Answer to the Knight*.' (275).
> *Copies collated*: British Museum; Bodleian; Bristol University; Harvard (two copies); Yale (two copies); Princeton.

D2 *Title-page*: identical with D1.

> *Collation*: 8°. A–S⁸, 144 leaves, pp. [2] 1–285 [286].
> *Contents*: title-page A1ʳ; licence A1ᵛ: [rule] | *Licensed and Entred, according to the* | *Act of Parliament for Printing*. | [rule]; text arranged as in D1; no errata.
> The errata noted on p. 287 of D1 have been corrected. Misprinted catchwords pp. 67 and 224 have been corrected; misprinted running-title and other misprinted catchwords remain.
> *Copies collated*: British Museum; Bodleian; Harvard; Yale.

D3 *Title-page*: identical with D1 and D2.

> *Collation*: 8°. A–Q⁸ [mis-signing L3 as L2 and O3 as O4], 128 leaves, pp. [2] 1–254.
> *Contents*: title-page A1ʳ; blank A1ᵛ; Canto I pp. 1–83; Canto II pp. 84–173; Canto III pp. 173–215; Epistle of Hudibras pp. 215–34; Lady's Answer pp. 235–54.
> Catchwords misprinted: p. 127 '*And*' for '*Trepann'd*', p. 155 '*T*' for '*To*': p. 173 '*And*' for '*And*', p. 189 'Quoth' for '*Quoth*'.
> *Copies collated*: Bodleian; Yale (two copies).

D4 *Title-page*: HUDIBRAS. | [rule] | THE | Third and last | PART. | [rule] | Written by the AUTHOUR | OF THE | FIRST and SECOND PARTS. | [rule] | *LONDON*, | Printed for *Robert Horne*, at the South Entrance | of the *Royal-Exchange*. 1679.

> *Collation*: identical with D3, including mis-signings.
> *Contents*: title-page A1ʳ; licence A1ᵛ: [rule] | *Licensed and Entred according to the* | *Act of Parliament for Printing*. | [rule]; text arranged as in D3.
> Catchwords misprinted as in D3.
> *Copies collated*: British Museum; Bodleian; Cambridge; Harvard (two copies); Princeton.

D5 *Title-page*: identical with D4 apart from the date '1680'.

Collation: identical with D3 and D4, including mis-signings.
Contents: identical with D4.
Copies collated: Bodleian; Harvard.

III. *The Text*

The First Part of *Hudibras* was entered in the *Stationers' Register* on 11 November 1662, when it was assigned to the bookseller Richard Marriot.[1] The Printing Act, passed earlier that year,[2] required all books to be approved by the official licenser before publication, to ensure that their contents were neither blasphemous nor seditious. *Hudibras* was accordingly licensed by Sir John Birkenhead and his imprimatur printed before the title-page. Although Marriot's first edition (A1) was dated 1663, it was on sale by 26 December of the previous year, when a copy was purchased by Samuel Pepys.[3] The poem rapidly became popular:[4] before the end of 1662 it had been pirated, and in January 1663 advertisements were placed in *The Kingdom's Intelligencer*[5] and *Mercurius Publicus*[6] warning their readers against an unauthorized edition. Four pirated editions were printed (A6–A9), all dated 1663.[7] The errata noted in A1 were corrected in the first pirated edition (A6) which itself contained a list of errors, later corrected in A7. Variations in the texts of these editions are confined almost entirely to accidentals, but by the time the last of the four (A9) had been set up, a number of misprints had been admitted.

The poor quality of the paper and narrow spacing of the type indicate that the pirated editions were sold more cheaply than Marriot's large octavo volume. He himself, probably by way of retort to the pirates, published two cheap editions, one in duo-decimo, of which there are three distinct issues (A2–A4), and one in small octavo (A5), all of which have identical title-pages bearing the date 1663. The three duodecimo issues are very similar. Page by page arrangement of the text is identical in all

---

[1] *Transcript of the Registers*, 1913–14, ii. 319.   [2] 14° Car. II, c. 33.
[3] *Diary*.   [4] Ibid., 6 February 1663.
[5] No. i, 29 Dec. 1662–5 Jan. 1663.   [6] No. i, 1–8 Jan. 1663.
[7] The fact that all the pirated editions contain an imprimatur similar to those published in Marriot's editions is no evidence that they were issued by Marriot himself. Cf. Beverly Chew, 'Some Notes on the Three Parts of *Hudibras*', *The Bibliographer*, 1 (New York, 1902), iv. 123–4.

three, and variants are confined almost entirely to accidentals. Their order of publication and the descent of the text is therefore difficult to establish beyond doubt, but close examination suggests that they appeared in the order in which they are listed above. A useful piece of evidence is Butler's use of two alternative spellings for the words 'squire' and 'brethren', which he varied according to the requirements of the metre. The normal spelling 'squire' was used when the metre required a monosyllable, but the alternative form 'squier' was employed to make two syllables when necessary. Similarly the trisyllabic 'bretheren' was substituted for the disyllabic 'brethren' to meet metrical requirements. These idiosyncratic spellings are found more frequently in A2 than in any of Marriot's other editions apart from the first. This feature, together with a closer similarity in accidentals, indicates that A2 was the first of the duodecimo issues and was set up from A1. The compositor of A2 also introduced a number of errors[1] which were carried over into A3 and A4, suggesting that the two latter issues were set up directly or indirectly from A2, and not from the first edition. A3 was reset only partially: the last two sheets, signed E and F, are identical with those of A2 in every detail, including damaged type. A4 was again only partially reset, sheet A and most of sheet B having been printed from the same formes as those used for A3. The text printed on the remaining sheets of A4 contains a number of variants in common with A3 which are not to be found in A2, suggesting that A3 was the compositor's copy-text for A4. Since A4 has, moreover, several peculiarities of spelling and punctuation not to be found in the other issues, it was probably the last of the three. The text of Marriot's small octavo edition (A5) has a greater number of distinctive readings, both of substantives and accidentals, than any of the duodecimo editions. It has most in common with A4 and was therefore probably the last of Marriot's editions, set up by the compositor from A4. In short, the evidence, though not conclusive, points to a simple, vertical line of descent from A1 through the duodecimo issues (A2–A4) to the small octavo (A5).

The Second Part of *Hudibras* was licensed on 5 November 1663 and assigned in the *Stationers' Register* to John Martyn and James

---

[1] The most notable is an error in the division of ll. 1235–6 of Canto III. A1 prints (correctly) 'And Manners; can pronounce a *Saint* | Idolatrous, or ignorant'. A2–A4 print 'And Manners; can pronounce | A Saint Idolatrous, or ignorant'.

Allestry.[1] Their edition (B1), which in size and appearance resembles A1, was dated 1664, but a licence which gave Butler sole control over the publication of his poem describes the Second Part as being in print by 23 November 1663.[2] Pepys bought a copy on 28 November.[3] The Second Part was not pirated, but Martyn and Allestry brought out a second, cheaper edition (B2), also dated 1664, in which several misprints were corrected, including some of those noted in the errata to B1, and a number of slight changes, largely of punctuation, were introduced into the text.

In 1669 the right to publish the First Part was transferred to Henry Herringman.[4] The rights to the Second Part, having been held for a time by another bookseller, Sir Thomas Davies, were acquired again by John Martyn in 1672.[5] A revised version of both parts 'with several additions and annotations' was issued jointly by Martyn and Herringman in 1674 (C1). The text of this edition varies considerably from that of earlier versions. While there is little evidence to suggest that Butler had hitherto intervened to correct his text, there is every sign that C1 was revised by the poet. Many short passages have been deleted and new ones added, the 'Heroical Epistle to Sidrophel' appears for the first time, and explanatory notes are appended to each of the two parts. These annotations, often similar in content to entries in Butler's commonplace books, are undoubtedly the work of the poet. A second edition of the two parts (C2), set up from the first, came out under the same imprint in 1678.

The Third Part of *Hudibras* was assigned on 22 August 1677 to the bookseller Simon Miller.[6] He published three editions with identical title-pages, all dated 1678, though the first (D1) was on sale by 6 November 1677.[7] The punctuation of D1, which was erratic in places, was improved in Miller's second edition (D2), and a number of misprints were corrected, including those noted in the errata to D1. The type was also entirely reset and an attempt made to distinguish typographically between passages of dialogue and passages of narrative by the alternate use of italic and roman type. This device had already been used in D1 to differentiate between alternate speakers in the dialogues. The italicization was

[1] *Transcript*, ii. 332.
[2] *Cal. State Papers, Ireland, 1663–1665*, p. 298.   [3] *Diary*.
[4] *Transcript*, ii. 404.   [5] Ibid. ii. 452.   [6] Ibid. iii. 41.
[7] H. M. C., *Marquis of Bath at Longleat*, ii. 159.

carried still further in Miller's third edition (D3), with the result that several of the dialogues were printed entirely in italic type and the original distinction obscured.

After the publication of D3, the rights to publish the Third Part were acquired by Robert Horne.[1] Horne's first edition (D4), dated 1679, was, however, merely a reissue of D3 with a new title-page. It was issued for a third time (D5) in 1680, the year of the poet's death, the only alteration being the new date. Hence, though at first sight five editions of the Third Part may appear to have been published by 1680, there were, in fact, only three. Variants between the three editions, apart from those already mentioned, are confined to accidentals and were probably the work of the compositor. Certainly Butler could have had no hand in the resetting of D3 with its unfortunate italicization, though he may have been responsible for the improved punctuation of D2.

The text of the first two parts of *Hudibras*, having been revised by the poet for the edition of 1674, presents a slightly more complex editorial problem than the text of the Third Part. Errors common to the first editions (A1 and B1) and the first revised edition (C1) show that the copy-text used for the latter was not an entirely fresh manuscript but copies of the first editions themselves, to which Butler had added his revisions. The copy-text for the present edition is therefore basically the first editions (A1 and B1), but where the revised edition differs from these substantively and in such a way as to suggest a revision by the poet, the new reading has generally been incorporated into the text and the original reading recorded in the apparatus. It has been assumed that Butler had no responsibility for the pirated editions of the First Part, variants in which have therefore been ignored. Variants in Marriot's editions (A2–A5) are, as has been said, largely confined to accidentals, but by the time the last of these editions had been set up, a few substantive changes had been introduced into the text. These are all of a kind which could be the work of the compositor or could have been made by the poet in an attempt to improve unsatisfactory passages. In order to differentiate between the two possible sources, comparison has been made between these variants and the text of the revised edition (C1). Substantive variants occurring in A2–A5 which reappear in C1, and variants in passages which were again revised for C1 have therefore been recorded in the apparatus on the assumption that they could be the work of the author. Substantive variants in passages where C1 reverts to the original reading have been omitted.

The Third Part presents no difficulties of this kind. The copy-text used is the first edition of 1678 (D1). Where editorial emendations are supported by D2, however, I have recorded the fact in the apparatus. No use has been made of Miller's third edition (D3) or its reissues (D4–D5), on the grounds that all the variants appearing for the first time in this edition are apparently the work of the compositor and almost always result in obscuring the meaning of the text. The extensive use of italics, which is the principal feature of D3, is confusing and unnecessary.

I have attempted whenever possible to retain all the features of the first editions. Accidentals—spelling, capitalization, and use of italics—are those of the first editions or, in the case of revised passages, those of the revised edition. Obvious misprints, turned letters, and wrong founts have been silently corrected; long 's' has been discarded, standard contractions have been expanded, and the typography of titles made uniform. Italic punctuation after italicized words in passages printed otherwise in roman type has been replaced by roman punctuation. Butler's punctuation, in accordance with the practice of his time, is rhetorical rather than grammatical: it is a guide to the reading of the poem rather than the structure of the sentences. For this reason I have tampered with it as little as possible. Idiosyncratic punctuation must, however, be distinguished from actual misprints. I have endeavoured to correct the latter, recording the original punctuation in the apparatus. Butler's own annotations, first published in the 1674 edition, are printed below the text, since many of them are satirical or enlarge upon ideas contained in the text, and may therefore be regarded as an integral part of the poem.

In the preparation of this edition, I have used the copies of the first editions of each of the three parts in the library of Bristol University, and a copy of the 1674 edition of the First and Second Parts lent to me by Mr. Esmond de Beer.

IV. *Later Editions*

At the time of Butler's death, in 1680, no complete edition of *Hudibras* in all its three parts had been published. The first edition of the whole poem was issued in 1684, the title-page announcing 'Printed, and are to be sold by *W. Rogers*, at the *Sun* against St. *Dunstan*'s Church'. The three parts were not, however, printed consecutively, but the Third Part, 'Printed for *Robert Horne*', was set up as a separate unit, some copies being sold separately and others sewn together and sold with the first two parts. This was the first of a great many issues of the complete poem, of which only the most significant will be mentioned here.

The next edition of note appeared in 1704. Of the three parts, the First was 'Printed by *E.P.* for *Geo. Sawbridge*', the Second for '*R. Chiswel*, *G. Sawbridge*, *R. Wellington*, and *G. Wells*', and the Third 'for *Thomas Horne*'. This is an interesting volume, for it contains the first biography of the poet to be published with his work.[1] The text, moreover, is not a mere reprint, but one which shows signs of some editorial care. The text of the first two parts is an eclectic one, derived from a collation of the first editions (A1 and B1) with the first revised edition (C1). Miller's last edition (D3) appears to have been the copy-text for the Third Part. In addition to the author's annotations, it contains additional notes to the First Part, presumably the work of the anonymous biographer.

The first of several illustrated editions of *Hudibras* appeared in 1710, 'Printed for JOHN BAKER at the *Black-Boy* in *Paternoster-Row*'. The text and accompanying biography were reprinted from the 1704 edition, but there is an index to the poem and some annotations to the Third Part (attributed by Oldys to D'Urfey the dramatist) which had not previously been published. The eighteen illustrations were engraved by an unknown artist, probably a refugee Walloon named Le Pipre.[2] They are unremarkable in themselves, but have some interest in that they provided a model for the better-known illustrations of Hogarth. Hogarth engraved two sets of illustrations for *Hudibras*, one for an edition of the poem and one independent set which was sold separately without the text. The former appeared in the edition of 1726 published both by 'B. MOTTE, at the *Middle Temple-Gate*' and by '*T.W.* for *D. Browne, J. Walthoe*' and others. In this set Hogarth follows Le Pipre very closely, both in his choice of subjects and in their treatment. The independent set consists of much larger

---

[1] See p. xiii, note 4.
[2] See Frederick Antal, *Hogarth and his Place in European Art*, 1962, p. 87.

engravings which are freer and more elaborate in design. Although
these were almost certainly designed later than the others, they
actually appeared in the same year as Motte's edition, 1726, and
were subsequently reproduced many years later in T. R. Nash's
edition of 1793.[1]

By the middle of the eighteenth century Butler's literary and
political allusions had become obscure, even to so learned a reader
as Samuel Johnson,[2] and the need arose for a scholarly commentary on the poem. This was supplied by Zachary Grey with his
two-volume edition, 'corrected and amended with large illustrations and a preface', first published in 1744. Grey prepared an
eclectic text, taking what he considered the best readings from
the revised and unrevised versions of the first two parts, and
noting some variant readings. He was not acquainted with all
the early editions, however, and unnecessarily recorded a number
of variants from editions published after the poet's death. He also
exercised a free hand in the printing of accidentals. The principal
feature of his edition is the commentary, which is extremely full
and informative. Although Grey is verbose and could seldom
resist the temptation to comment, even when he had little of
relevance to say, his copious and erudite remarks have left all
subsequent commentators on *Hudibras* in his debt. His text was
also reprinted by several later editors, including Samuel Johnson
(1779).

Butler's next commentator was T. R. Nash, the historian of
Worcestershire and rector of Butler's native parish of Strensham,
whose de luxe edition appeared in 1793. It was first printed in
three volumes on fine paper, with many illustrations, most of
them after Hogarth. His commentary, as he acknowledged, was
derived largely from Grey's, and though it is less obtrusive it is
also much less thorough. Nash's edition, like Grey's, has been
republished many times, generally in two volumes.

Robert Bell's text (1855) was ostensibly 'founded upon a careful
examination of former editions, from the earliest to the last reprint by Dr. Nash'. 'The edition of 1674, containing the First
and Second Parts revised by Butler' was, he wrote, 'with few
exceptions followed throughout, and wherever any variances

---

[1] See Ronald Paulson, *Hogarth's Graphic Works*, 2 vols., New Haven, 1965,
i. 116, 125.
[2] *Idler* lix.

occur they are explained'. Spelling and punctuation were, however, modernized, and the whole text printed in roman type.
Editing of a different kind was carried out by Alfred Milnes,
whose annotated edition (1881–3) was 'rigidly expurgated by
the omission, whenever possible, of the whole passage in which
anything objectionable occurs, no exception being allowed in
favour even of such indecent passages as are directly quoted from
Scripture'.

Our knowledge of Butler and his work was advanced considerably with the appearance of Reginald Brimley Johnson's edition
of the *Poetical Works* (2 vols., 1893). The value of Johnson's
edition lies not so much in the text as in the extensive introductory
matter, which was the first attempt to compile a complete biblio-
graphy of *Hudibras*, including many of the early editions, trans-
lations, spurious editions, and imitations. Johnson also gathered
together all the known material relating to Butler's life. Although
he worked within the limits of the bibliographical scholarship
of his time, his work has in some respects not been superseded.

The only twentieth-century edition which deserves attention
is that of A. R. Waller (Cambridge, 1905). This is the first of three
volumes comprising Butler's collected works. The second volume
(1908), also edited by Waller, includes the prose *Characters* and
the text of two of the commonplace books; and the third volume
(1928), edited by René Lamar, contains the minor poems and
miscellaneous writings. Waller was certainly familiar with some,
if not all, of the early editions and was careful to reproduce the
accidentals of his copy-texts. He selected one of the revised editions
as the copy-text for the first two parts, but chose the edition of
1678 (C2) rather than the more authoritative one of 1674 (C1). His
text of the Third Part was, similarly, Horne's edition of 1679
(Đ4) rather than Miller's earliest edition of 1678 (D1). Thus,
although Waller came closer than any of his predecessors to
realizing the poet's intentions, his choice of texts was faulty and
necessitated the editing of *Hudibras* yet again for the present edition.

HUDIBRAS

THE FIRST PART

CANTO I

THE ARGUMENT

Sir Hudibras *his passing worth,*
The manner how he sally'd forth:
His Arms and Equipage are shown;
His Horse's Vertues, and his own.
Th' Adventure of the Bear *and* Fiddle
Is sung, but breaks off in the middle.

WHEN *civil* Fury first grew high,
And men fell out they knew not why;
When hard words, *Jealousies* and *Fears*,
Set Folks together by the ears,
And made them fight, like mad or drunk,
For Dame *Religion* as for Punk,
Whose honesty they all durst swear for,
Though not a man of them knew wherefore:
When *Gospel-trumpeter*, surrounded
With long-ear'd rout, to Battel sounded,   10
And Pulpit, Drum Ecclesiastick,
Was beat with fist, instead of a stick:
Then did Sir *Knight* abandon dwelling,
And out he rode a Colonelling.

A wight he was, whose very sight wou'd
Entitle him *Mirrour of Knighthood*;
That never bent his stubborn knee
To any thing but Chivalry,
Nor put up blow, but that which laid
Right Worshipfull on shoulder-blade: 20

1 Fury *C*: *Dudgeon A*   8 know *C*   14 a Colonelling *A2–A5*, *C*: rode
Colonelling *A1*   17 bent *C*: bow'd *A*

Chief of Domestick Knights and Errant,
Either for Chartel or for Warrant:
Great on the Bench, Great in the Saddle,
That could as well bind o're, as swaddle:
Mighty he was at both of these,
And styl'd of *War* as well as *Peace*.
(So some Rats of amphibious nature,
Are either for the Land or Water.)
But here our Authors make a doubt,
Whether he were more wise, or stout.   30
Some hold the one, and some the other:
But howsoe're they make a pother,
The difference was so small, his Brain
Outweigh'd his Rage but half a grain:
Which made some take him for a tool
That Knaves do work with, call'd a Fool.
And offer to lay wagers, that
As *Mountaigne*, playing with his Cat,
Complaines she thought him but an Ass,
Much more she would Sir *Hudibras*. *   40
(For that's the Name our valiant Knight
To all his Challenges did write.)
But they'r mistaken very much,
'Tis plain enough he was no such.
We grant, although he had much wit,
H' was very shie of using it,
As being loath to wear it out,
And therefore bore it not about,
Unless on Holy-dayes, or so,
As men their best Apparel do.   50
Beside 'tis known he could speak *Greek*,
As naturally as Pigs squeek:
That *Latin* was no more difficile,
Then to a Blackbird 'tis to whistle.

24 Bind over to the Sessions, as being a Justice of the Peace in his County, as well
as Colonel of a Regiment of Foot, in the Parliaments Army, and a Committee-man.
38 *Mountaign* in his Essays supposes his Cat thought him a Fool, for loosing his
time, in playing with her.

22 Chartel *A1* (*errata*), *A2–A5*, C: Chastel *A1*   37 And . . . wagers C:
For't has been held by many *A*   41–42 *added in* C   48 about. C
Note 24 County] Countrey C

Being rich in both he never scanted
His Bounty unto such as wanted;
But much of either would afford
To many that had not one word.
For *Hebrew* Roots, although th' are found
To flourish most in barren ground,   60
He had such plenty, as suffic'd
To make some think him circumcis'd:
And truly so perhaps, he was
'Tis many a Pious Christians case.

He was in *Logick* a great Critick,
Profoundly skill'd in Analytick.
He could distinguish, and divide
A hair 'twixt South and South-west side:
On either which he would dispute,
Confute, change hands, and still confute.   70
He'd undertake to prove by force
Of Argument, a Man's no Horse.
He'd prove a Buzzard is no Fowl,
And that a *Lord* may be an Owl;
A Calf an *Alderman*, a Goose a *Justice*,
And Rooks *Committee-men* and *Trustees*.
He'd run in Debt by Disputation,
And pay with Ratiocination.
All this by Syllogism, true
In mood and figure, he would doe.   80

For *Rhetorick*, he could not ope
His mouth, but out there flew a Trope:
And when he hapned to break off
I'th' middle of his speech, or cough,
H' had hard words ready, to shew why,
And tell what Rules he did it by.
Else when with greatest Art he spoke,
You'd think he talk'd like other foke.

66 *Analitique* is a part of *Logick* that teaches to Decline and Construe *Reason*, as
Grammar does *Words.*

63–64 perhaps, ... case. *C*: he was perhaps, | Not as a *Proselyte*, but for *Claps. A*
85 words, ready to *C*

For all a Rhetoricians Rules
Teach nothing but to name his Tools.   90
His ordinary Rate of Speech
In loftiness of sound was rich,
A *Babylonish* dialect,
Which learned Pedants much affect.
It was a particolour'd dress
Of patch'd and pyball'd Languages:
'Twas *English* cut on *Greek* and *Latin*,
Like Fustian heretofore on Sattin.
It had an odde promiscuous Tone,
As if h' had talk'd three parts in one.   100
Which made some think, when he did gabble,
Th' had heard three Labourers of *Babel*;
Or *Cerberus* himself pronounce
A Leash of Languages at once.
This he as volubly would vent,
As if his stock would ne're be spent.
And truly to support that charge
He had supplies as vast and large.
For he could coyn or counterfeit
New words, with little or no wit: 110
Words so debas'd and hard, no stone
Was hard enough to touch them on.
And when with hasty noise he spoke 'em,
The Ignorant for currant took 'em.
That had the Orator who once,
Did fill his Mouth with Pebble stones
When he harangu'd; but known his Phrase
He would have us'd no other ways.

In *Mathematicks* he was greater
Then *Tycho Brahe* or *Erra Pater*:   120
For he by *Geometrick* scale
Could take the size of *Pots of Ale*;

93 A confusion of Languages, such, as some of our Modern *Virtuosi* use to express themselves in.
115 *Demosthenes*, who is said to have a defect in his Pronunciation, which he cur'd by using to speak with little stones in his mouth.

89–90 *added in* C   90 Tools.] Tools, C   91 His . . . Speech C: But when he pleas'd to shew't, his speech A   115–18 *added in* C

Resolve by Sines and Tangents straight,
If *Bread* or *Butter* wanted weight;
And wisely tell what hour o'th' day
The Clock does strike, by *Algebra*.

Beside he was a shrewd *Philosopher*,
And had read every Text and gloss over:
What e're the crabbed'st Author hath
He understood b'implicit Faith,   130
What ever *Sceptick* could inquere for;
For every *why* he had a *wherefore*:
Knew more then forty of them do,
As far as words and termes could goe.
All which he understood by Rote,
And as occasion serv'd, would quote;
No matter whether right or wrong:
They might be either said or sung.
His Notions fitted things so well,
That which was which he could not tell;   140
But oftentimes mistook the one
For th'other, as Great Clerks have done.
He could reduce all things to Acts
And knew their Natures by Abstracts,
Where Entity and Quiddity,
The Ghosts of defunct Bodies, flie;
Where Truth in Person does appear,
Like words congeal'd in Northern Air.

---

143 The old Philosophers thought to extract Notions out of Natural things, as
Chymists do Spirits and Essences, and when they had refin'd them into the nicest
subtleties, gave them as insignificant Names, as those Operators do their Extractions:
But (as *Seneca* says) the subtler things are render'd, they are but the nearer to Nothing.
So are all their definitions of things by Acts, the nearer to Nonsense.
147 Some Authors have mistaken Truth for a Real thing, when it is nothing but
a right Method of putting those Notions, or Images of things (in the understanding
of Man) into the same state and order, that their Originals hold in Nature, and
therefore *Aristotle* says, *unum quodque sicut se habet secundum esse ita se habet secundum
veritatem.* Met. L.2.
148 Some report that in *Nova Zembla*, and *Greenland*, Mens words are wont to be
Frozen in the Air, and at the Thaw may be heard.

129–30 *added in C*   143–4 *added in C*   145 Where Entity *C*: He'd tell
where Entity *A1–A4*: He'd tell where *Ens A5*   147 Person *A1* (*errata*), *A2–*
A5, C: Prison *A1*   Note *148* Zembla] Zemble *C*

He knew *what's what*, and that's as high
As *Metaphysick* wit can flie.   150
In *School-Divinity* as able
As he that hight *Irrefragable*;
Profound in all the Nominal
And real ways beyond them all,
And with as delicate a Hand
Could twist as tough a Rope of Sand.
And weave fine Cobwebs, fit for skull
That's empty when the Moon is full;
Such as take lodgings in a Head
That's to be let unfurnished.   160
He could raise Scruples dark and nice,
And after solve 'em in a trice:
As if Divinity had catch'd
The Itch, of purpose to be scratch'd;
Or, like a Mountebank, did wound
And stab her self with doubts profound,
Onely to shew with how small pain
The sores of faith are cur'd again;
Although by woful proof we find,
They alwayes leave a Scar behind.   170
He knew the seat of Paradise,
Could tell in what degree it lies:
And, as he was dispos'd, could prove it,
Below the Moon, or else above it:
What *Adam* dreamt of when his Bride
Came.from her Closet in his side:
Whether the Devil tempted her
By a *high Dutch* Interpreter:

171 There is nothing more ridiculous then the various opinions of Authors about the
Seat of Paradise; Sir *Walter Rawleigh* has taken a great deal of pains to collect them,
in the beginning of his *History of the World*; where those who are unsatisfied, may
be fully inform'd.
178 *Goropius Becanus* endeavors to prove that High-Dutch was the Language that
Adam and *Eve* spoke in *Paradise*.

153-4 Profound ... all, *C*: A second *Thomas*, or, at once | To name them all, an-
other *Dunce. A*   155-6 And with ... Sand. *C*: For he a Rope of sand could
twist, | As tough as learned *Sorbonist*; *A*   173-4 *added in C*   174 it:]
it *C*

If either of them had a Navel;
Who first made Musick malleable: 180
Whether the Serpent at the Fall
Had cloven Feet, or none at all.
All this, without a Gloss or Comment,
He would unriddle in a moment
In proper terms, such as men smatter
When they throw out and miss the matter.

For his *Religion* it was fit
To match his Learning and his Wit:
'Twas *Presbyterian* true blew,
For he was of that stubborn Crew   190
Of Errant Saints, whom all men grant
To be the true Church *Militant*:
Such as do build their Faith upon
The holy Text of *Pike* and *Gun*;
Decide all Controversies by
Infallible *Artillery*;
And prove their Doctrine Orthodox
By Apostolick *Blows* and *Knocks*;
Call Fire and Sword and Desolation,
A *godly-thorough-Reformation*,   200
Which alwayes must be carry'd on,
And still be doing, never done:
As if Religion were intended
For nothing else but to be mended.
A Sect, whose chief Devotion lies
In odde perverse Antipàthies;
In falling out with that or this,
And finding somewhat still amiss:
More peevish, cross, and spleenatick,
Then Dog distract, or Monky sick: 210
That with more care keep holy-day
The wrong, then others the right way:

179 *Adam* and *Eve* being Made, and not Conceiv'd, and Form'd in the Womb, had
no Navels, as some Learned Men have suppos'd, because they had no need of them.
180 Musick is said to be invented by *Pythagoras*, who first found out the Proportion
of Notes, from the sounds of Hammers upon an Anvil.

Compound for Sins, they are inclin'd to,
By damning those they have no mind to;
Still so perverse and opposite,
As if they worshipp'd God for spight.
The self-same thing they will abhor
One way, and long another for.
Free-will they one way disavow,
Another, nothing else allow.   220
All Piety consists therein
In them, in other men all Sin.
Rather then faile, they will defie
That which they love most tenderly,
Quarrel with *minc'd Pies*, and disparage
Their best and dearest friend, *Plum-porredge*;
Fat *Pig* and *Goose* it self oppose,
And blaspheme *Custard* through the *nose*.
Th'Apostles of this fierce Religion,
Like *Mahomet*'s, were Ass and Widgeon,   230
To whom our Knight by fast instinct
Of wit and temper was so linkt,
As if Hypocrisie and non-sense
Had got th'Advouson of his Conscience.

Thus was he gifted and accouter'd
We mean on th'inside, not the outward:
That next of all we shall discuss;
Then listen Sirs, It followeth thus.

His tawny *Beard* was th'equall grace
Both of his wisdome and his face;   240
In Cut and Dy so like a tile,
A sudden view it would beguile:
The upper part thereof was Whey,
The nether Orange mixt with Gray.
This hairy Meteor did denounce
The fall of Scepters and of Crowns;

---

230 *Mahomet* had a tame Dove that used to pick Seeds out of his Ear, that it might
be thought to whisper and Inspire him. His Ass was so intimate with him, that the
Mahometans believe it carry'd him to Heaven, and stays there with him to bring
him back again.

213–14 *added in* C

With grizly type did represent
Declining Age of Government;
And tell with Hieroglyphick Spade,
Its own grave and the State's were made.   250
Like *Sampson*'s Heart-breakers, it grew
In time to make a nation rue;
Though it contributed its own fall,
To wait upon the publick downfall.
It was Canonick, and did grow
In holy Orders, by strict vow;
Of Rule as sullen and severe,
As that of rigid *Cordeliere*.
'Twas bound to suffer Persecution
And Martyrdome with resolution;   260
T'oppose it self against the hate
And vengeance of th'incensed State:
In whose defiance it was worn,
Still ready to be pull'd and torn,
With red-hot Irons to be tortur'd,
Revil'd, and spit upon, and martyr'd.
Maugre all which, 'twas to stand fast,
As long as Monarchy should last.
But when the State should hap to reel,
'Twas to submit to fatal steel,   270
And fall, as it was consecrate
A Sacrifice to fall of State;
Whose thred of life the fatal Sisters
Did twist together with its whiskers,
And twine so close, that time should never,
In life or death, their fortunes sever;
But with his rusty Sickle mow
Both down together at a blow.

So learned *Taliacotius* from
The brawny part of Porter's Bum,   280

255–6 He made a Vow never to cut his *Beard*, until the Parliament had subdued the
King, of which Order of Phanatique Votaries, there were many in those times.
279 *Taliacotius* was an *Italian* Chirurgeon, that found out a way to repair lost and
decay'd Noses.

255 Canonick *C*: monastick *A*

Cut supplementall Noses, which
Would last as long as Parent breech:
But when the Date of *Nock* was out,
Off dropt the Sympathetick Snout.

His *Back*, or rather Burthen, show'd
As if it stoop'd with its own load.
For as *Æneas* bore his Sire
Upon his shoulders through the fire:
Our Knight did bear no less a Pack
Of his own Buttocks on his back: 290
Which now had almost got the upper-
Hand of his Head, for want of Crupper.
To poize this equally, he bore
A *Paunch* of the same bulk before:
Which still he had a speciall care
To keep well cramm'd with thrifty fare;
As White-pot, Butter-milk, and Curds,
Such as a Countrey house affords;
With other Victual, which anon
We further shall dilate upon,   300
When of his Hose we come to treat,
The Cup-bord where he kept his meat.

His *Doublet* was of sturdy Buff,
And though not Sword- yet Cudgel-proof;
Whereby 'twas fitter for his use,
That fear'd no blows but such as bruise.

His *Breeches* were of rugged woollen,
And had been at the Siege of *Bullen*;
To old King *Harry* so well known,
Some writers held they were his own.   310
Through they were lin'd with many a piece
Of Ammunition-Bread and Cheese,
And fat Black-puddings, proper food
For Warriers that delight in bloud.
For, as we said, He alwayes chose
To carry Vittle in his hose.

308 **Siege** *C*: siege *A*

That often tempted Rats, and Mice,
The Ammunition to surprize:
And when he put a Hand but in
The one or th'other Magazine,   320
They stoutly in defence on't stood
And from the wounded Foe drew bloud
And till th' were storm'd, and beaten out
Ne'r left the Fortify'd Redoubt;
And though Knights Errant, as some think,
Of old did neither eat nor drink,
Because when thorough Deserts vast
And Regions desolate they past,
Where Belly-timber above ground
Or under was not to be found,   330
Unless they graz'd, there's not one word
Of their Provision on Record:
Which made some confidently write,
They had no stomachs, but to fight,
'Tis false: For *Arthur* wore in Hall
Round-Table like a Farthingal,
On which, with shirt pull'd out behind,
And eke before, his good Knights din'd.
Though 'twas no Table, some suppose,
But a huge pair of round Trunk-hose;   340
In which he carry'd as much meat
As he and all his Knights could eat,
When laying by their swords and truncheons,
They took their Breakfasts or their Nuncheons.
But let that pass at present, lest
We should forget where we digrest;
As learned Authors use, to whom
We leave it, and to th' purpose come.
His puissant *Sword* unto his side
Near his undaunted heart was ty'd,   350
With Basket-hilt, that would hold broth,
And serve for fight and dinner both.
In it he melted lead for Bullets,
To shoot at Foes; and sometimes Pullets,

To whom he bore so fell a Grutch,
He ne're gave quarter t'any such.
The trenchant blade, *Toledo* trusty,
For want of fighting was grown rusty,
And ate into it self, for lack
Of somebody to hew and hack.   360
The peacefull *Scabbard* where it dwelt,
The Rancour of its Edge had felt:
For of the lower end two handfull
It had devoured, 'twas so manfull;
And so much scorn'd to lurk in case,
As if it durst not shew its face.
In many desperate Attempts,
Of Warrants, Exigents, Contempts,
It had appear'd with Courage bolder
Then Sergeant *Bum*, invading shoulder.   370
Oft had it ta'ne possession,
And Pris'ners too, or made them run.

This Sword a *Dagger* had his Page,
That was but little for his age:
And therefore waited on him so,
As Dwarfs upon Knights Errant do.
It was a serviceable Dudgeon,
Either for fighting or for drudging.
When it had stabb'd, or broke a head,
It would scrape Trenchers, or chip Bread,   380
Toast Cheese or Bacon, though it were
To bait á Mouse-trap, 'twould not care.
'Twould make clean shooes, and in the earth
Set Leeks and Onions, and so forth.
It had been Prentice to a Brewer,
Where this and more it did endure.
But left the Trade, as many more
Have lately done on the same score.

In th'Holsters, at his saddle-bow,
Two aged *Pistolls* he did stow,   390

387–8 *Oliver Cromwel* and Colonel *Pride* had been both Brewers.

360 some body *C*   368 Warrants] Wars *C*

Among the surplus of such meat
As in his hose he could not get.
They were upon hard Duty still,
And every night stood sentinel,
To guard the magazine i'th' hose
From two-legg'd and from four-legg'd foes.

Thus clad and fortify'd, Sir Knight
From peaceful home set forth to fight.
But first with nimble active force
He got on th'outside of his *Horse*. 400
For having but one stirrup ty'd
T'his saddle, on the further side,
It was so short, h' had much ado
To reach it with his desperate toe.
But after many strains and heaves,
He got up to the saddle eaves.
From whence he vaulted into th' seat
With so much vigour, strength, and heat,
That he had almost tumbled over
With his own weight, but did recover, 410
By laying hold on tail and mane,
Which oft he us'd instead of Reyn.

But now we talk of mounting Steed,
Before we further do proceed,
It doth behove us to say something,
Of that which bore our valiant *Bumkin*.
The Beast was sturdy, large and tall,
With mouth of meal and eyes of wall:
I would say eye, for h' had but one,
As most agree, though some say none. 420
He was well stay'd, and in his Gate
Preserv'd a grave, majestick state.
At Spur or Switch no more he skipt,
Or mended pace, then *Spaniard* whipt:

392–3 get. | They *C* : get | These would inveigle Rats with th' sent, | To forrage
when the Cocks were bent, | And sometime catch 'em with a snap | As cleverly
as th'ablest trap. | They *A*

And yet so fiery, he would bound,
As if he griev'd to touch the Ground:
That *Cæsar*'s Horse, who, as fame goes,
Had Corns upon his feet and toes,
Was not by half so tender-hooft,
Nor trod upon the ground so soft.   430
And as that Beast would kneel and stoop,
(Some write) to take his rider up:
So *Hudibras* his ('tis well known)
Would often doe, to set him down.
We shall not need to say what lack
Of Leather was upon his back:
For that was hidden under pad,
And breech of Knight gall'd full as bad.
His strutting Ribs on both sides show'd
Like furrows he himself had plow'd: 440
For underneath the skirt of Pannel,
'Twixt every two there was a Channel.
His dragling Tail hung in the Dirt,
Which on his Rider he would flurt
Still as his tender side he prickt,
With arm'd heel or with unarm'd kickt:
For *Hudibras* wore but one Spur,
As wisely knowing, could he stir
To active trot one side of's Horse,
The other would not hang an Arse.   450

A *Squire* he had whose name was *Ralph*,
That in th'adventure went his half.
(Though writers, for more stately tone,
Do call him *Ralpho*; 'tis all one:
And when we can with Meeter safe,
We'l call him so, if not plain *Raph*.
For Rhyme the Rudder is of Verses,
With which like Ships they stear their courses.)
An equal stock of Wit and Valour
He had laid in, by birth a Taylor.   460

427-8 *Julius Cæsar* had a Horse with Feet like a Man's. *Utebatur equo insigni, pedibus prope Humanis, et in modum Digitorum ungulis fissis.* Sueton *in* Jul. Cap.61.

450 an Arse *C*: an-Arse *A*   458 courses.)] courses. *C*

The mighty *Tyrian* Queen that gain'd
With subtle shreds a Tract of Land,
Did leave it with a Castle fair
To his great Ancestor, her Heir:
From him descended cross-legg'd Knights,
Fam'd for their faith and warlike fights
Against the bloudy Caniball,
Whom they destroy'd both great and small.
This sturdy Squier had as well
As the bold *Trojan* Knight, seen hell,   470
Not with a counterfeited Pass
Of Golden Bough, but true gold-lace.
His *Knowledge* was not far behind
The Knight's, but of another kind,
And he another way came by't:
Some call it *Gifts*, and some *New light*;
A Liberal Art, that costs no pains
Of Study, Industry, or Brains.
His wits were sent him for a Token,
But in the Carriage crackt and broken.   480
Like Commendation Nine-pence, crookt
With to and from my Love, it lookt.
He ne're consider'd it, as loath
To look a gift-horse in the mouth;
And very wisely would lay forth
No more upon it then 'twas worth.
But as he got it freely, so
He spent it frank and freely too.
For Saints themselves will sometimes be
Of Gifts that cost them nothing, free.   490
By means of this, with *hem* and *cough*,
Prolongers to enlightned Snuff,
He could deep Mysteries unriddle,
As easily as thread a Needle;

461–2 *Dido* Queen of *Carthage*, who bought as much Land as she could compass
with an Oxes Hide, which she cut into small Thongs, and cheated the owner of so
much ground, as serv'd her to build *Carthage* upon.
470 *Æneas* whom *Virgil* reports to use a Golden Bough, for a Pass to Hell, and
Tailors call that place Hell, where they put all they steal.

469 Squier *A1*, *A2*: Squire *A3–A5*, C   477 liberal C   490 nothing,
A2–A5, C: nothing *A1*   494 Needle; C: Needle *A1*: Needle. *A2–A5*

For as of Vagabonds we say,
That they are ne're beside their way:
Whate're men speak by this *new Light*,
Still they are sure to be i'th' right.
'Tis a *dark-Lanthorn* of the Spirit,
Which none see by but those that bear it: 500
A Light that falls down from on high,
For Spiritual Trades to cousen by:
An *Ignis Fatuus*, that bewitches,
And leads men into Pools and Ditches,
To make them *dip* themselves, and sound
For Christendome in Dirty pond;
To dive like Wild-foul for Salvation,
And fish to catch Regeneration.
This Light inspires, and playes upon
The nose of Saint, like Bag-pipe-drone,   510
And speaks through hollow empty soul,
As through a Trunk, or whisp'ring hole,
Such language as no mortall ear
But spiritual Eaves-droppers can hear.
So *Phœbus* or some friendly Muse
Into small Poets song infuse;
Which they at second-hand reherse
Through reed or bag-pipe, verse for verse.

Thus *Ralph* became infallible,
As three or four-legg'd Oracle,   520
The ancient Cup, or modern Chair;
Spoke truth point-blank, though unaware:
For mystick Learning, wondrous able
In Magick, *Talisman*, and *Cabal*,

---

524 Talisman is a Device to destroy any sort of Vermin by casting their Images in
Metal, in a precise minute, when the Stars are perfectly inclin'd to do them all the
mischief they can. This has been experimented by some modern *Virtuosi*, upon Rats,
Mice, and Fleas, and found (as they affirm) to produce the Effect with admirable
success.

    Raymund Lully interprets *Cabal* out of the *Arabick*, to signify *Scientia superabundans*,
which his Comentator *Cornelius Agrippa*, by over magnifying, has render'd a very
superfluous Foppery.

---

524 Magick,] Magick *C*

Whose primitive tradition reaches
As far as *Adam*'s first green breeches:
Deep-sighted in Intelligences,
Idea's, Atomes, Influences;
And much of *Terra Incognita*,
Th'Intelligible world could say: 530
A deep occult Philosopher,
As learn'd as the *Wild Irish* are,
Or Sir *Agrippa*, for profound
And solid Lying much renown'd:
He *Anthroposophus*, and *Floud*,
And *Jacob Behmen* understood;
Knew many an Amulet and Charm,
That would do neither good nor harm:
In *Rosy-Crucian* Lore as learned,
As he that *Verè adeptus* earned.   540
He understood the speech of Birds
As well as they themselves do words:
Could tell what subtlest *Parrots* mean,
That speak and think contrary clean;
What *Member* 'tis of whom they talk
When they cry *Rope*, and *Walk, Knave, walk*.
He'd extract numbers out of matter,
And keep them in a Glass, like water,
Of sov'raign pow'r to make men wise;
For dropt in blere, thick-sighted eyes,   550
They'd make them see in darkest night,
Like Owls, though pur-blind in the light.
By help of these (as he profest)
He had *First Matter* seen undrest:

526 The Author of *Magia Adamica* indeavors to prove the Learning of the antient
Magi, to be deriv'd from that knowledge which God himself taught *Adam* in *Paradise*, before the Fall.
529–30 The Intelligible world, is a kind of *Terra del Fuego*, or *Psittacorum Regio*,
discover'd only by the Philosophers, of which they talk, like Parrots, what they do
not understand.
532 No Nation in the World is more addicted to this occult Philosophy, then the
Wild Irish, as appears by the whole practice of their Lives, of which see *Cambden*
in his description of *Ireland*.
539–40 The Fraternity of the *Rosy Crucians* is very like the Sect of the antient
Gnostici who call'd themselves so, from the excellent Learning they pretended to,
although they were really the most ridiculous Sots of all Mankind.
Vere Adeptus, is one that has Commenc'd in their Fanatique extravagance.

He took her naked all alone,
Before one Rag of *Form* was on.
The *Chaos* too he had descry'd,
And seen quite through, or else he ly'd:
Not that of Past-board which men shew
For Groats at *Fair of Bartholmew*;   560
But its great Grandsire, first o'th' name,
Whence that and *Reformation* came:
Both Cousin-germans, and right able
T'inveigle and draw in the Rabble.
But *Reformation* was, some say,
O'th' younger house to *Puppet-play*.
He could foretell whats'ever was
By consequence to come to pass.
As Death of Great men, Alterations,
Diseases, Battels, Inundations.   570
All this without th'eclipse of Sun,
Or dreadful Comet, he hath done,
By inward light, a way as good,
And easy to be understood.
But with more lucky hit then those
That use to make the Stars depose,
Like Knights o'th' Post, and falsely charge
Upon themselves what others forge:
As if they were consenting to
All Mischief in the World men do: 580
Or like the Dev'l, did tempt and sway 'em
To Rogueries, and then betray 'em.
They'l search a Planet's house, to know
Who broke and robb'd a house below:
Examine *Venus*, and the *Moon*,
Who stole a thimble or a spoon:
And though they nothing will confess,
Yet by their very looks can guess,
And tell what guilty Aspect bodes,
Who stole, and who receiv'd the goods.   590
They'l question *Mars*, and by his look
Detect who 'twas that nimm'd a Cloke:
Make *Mercury* confess and peach
Those thieves which he himself did teach.

They'l find i'th' Physiognomies
O'th' Planets all mens destinies:
Like him that took the Doctor's Bill,
And swallow'd it instead o'th' Pill.
Cast the Nativity o'th' Question,
And from Positions to be guest on, 600
As sure as if they knew the Moment
Of Natives birth, tell what will come on't.
They'l feel the Pulses of the Stars,
To find out Agues, Coughs, Catarrhs;
And tell what *Crisis* does divine
The Rot in Sheep, or Mange in Swine:
In men what gives or cures the Itch,
What makes them Cuckolds, poor or rich:
What gains or loses, hangs or saves;
What makes men great, what fooles or knaves; 610
But not what wise, for onely of those
The Stars (they say) cannot dispose,
No more then can the Astrologians.
There they say right, and like true *Trojans.*
This *Ralpho* knew, and therefore took
The other Course, of which we spoke.

Thus was th'accomplish'd Squire endu'd
With Gifts and Knowledge, per'lous shrewd.
Never did trusty Squire with Knight,
Or Knight with Squier jump more right. 620
Their Arms and Equipage did fit,
As well as Vertues, parts, and wit.
Their Valours too were of a Rate,
And out they sally'd at the Gate.
Few miles on horseback had they jogged,
But fortune unto them turn'd Dogged.
For they a sad Adventure met,
Of which we now prepare to treat:
But ere we venture to unfold
Atchievements so resolv'd and bold, 630

619 Squire *A2–A5*, C: Squier *A1*   620 Squire *A, C*   628 we now prepare C: anon we mean *A*

We should, as learned Poets use,
Invoke th'assistance of some *Muse*;
However Criticks count it sillier
Then Juglers talking t'a Familiar.
We think 'tis no great matter which:
They'r all alike: yet we shall pitch
On one that fits our purpose most,
Whom therefore thus do we accost.

Thou that with Ale, or viler Liquors,
Didst inspire *Withers*, *Pryn*, and *Vickars*,   640
And force them, though it were in spight
Of nature and their stars, to write;
Who, as we find in sullen Writs,
And cross-grain'd Works of modern wits,
With Vanity, Opinion, Want,
The wonder of the Ignorant,
The praises of the Author, penn'd
By himself, or wit-ensuring friend,
The Itch of Picture in the Front,
With Bays, and wicked Rhyme upon't,   650
All that is left o'th' forked Hill
To make men scribble without skill,
Canst make a Poet, spight of fate,
And teach all people to translate;
Though out of Languages in which
They understand no part of speech:
Assist me but this once, I 'mplore,
And I shall trouble thee no more.

In Western Clime there is a Town
To those that dwell therein well known;   660
Therefore there needs no more be sed here,
We unto them refer our Reader:

639–40 This *Vickars* was a Man of as great Interest and Authority in the late Reformation, as *Pryn*, or *Withers*, and as able a Poet; He Translated *Virgils Æneides* into as horrible Travesty in earnest, as the French *Scaroon* did in Burlesque, and was only out-done in his way by the Politique Author of *Oceana*.

634 t'a *C* : to *A*   638 do we *C*: we do *A*

For brevity is very good,
When w' are, or are not understood.
To this Town People did repair
On dayes of Market or of Fair,
And to crack'd Fiddle and hoarse Tabor
In merriment did drudge and labour:
But now a sport more formidable
Had rak'd together Village rabble.   670
'Twas an old way of Recreating,
Which learned Butchers call *Bear-baiting*:
A bold advent'rous exercise,
With ancient *Hero's* in high prize;
For Authors do affirm it came
From *Isthmian* or *Nemean* game.
Others derive it from the *Bear*
That's fixt in Northern Hemisphere,
And round about the Pole does make
A circle, like a Bear at stake,   680
That at the Chain's end wheels about,
And overturns the Rabble-rout.
For after solemn proclamation
In the Bear's name (as is the fashion,
According to the Law of Arms,
To keep men from inglorious harms)
That none presume to come so near
As forty foot of stake of Bear;
If any yet be so fool-hardy,
T'expose themselves to vain Jeopardy;   690
If they come wounded off and lame,
No honour's got by such a maim.
Although the Bear gain much, b'ing bound
In honour to make good his ground,
When he's engag'd, and take no notice,
If any press upon him, who 'tis,
But let them know at their own cost
That he intends to keep his post.
This to prevent, and other harms,
Which always wait on feats of Arms,   700
(For in the hurry of a Fray
'Tis hard to keep out of harm's way)

Thither the *Knight* his course did stear,
To keep the peace 'twixt *Dog* and *Bear*;
As he believ'd h' was bound to doe
In Conscience and Commission too.
And therefore thus bespoke the Squire;

We that are wisely mounted higher
Then Constables, in Curule wit,
When on Tribunal bench we sit,   710
Like Speculators, should foresee,
From *Pharos* of Authority,
Portended Mischiefs farther then
Low Proletarian Tithing-men.
And therefore being inform'd by bruit,
That *Dog* and *Bear* are to dispute;
For so of late men fighting name,
Because they often prove the same;
(For where the first does hap to be,
The last does *coincidere*)   720
Quantum in nobis, have thought good,
To save th'expence of Christian bloud,
And try if we by mediation
Of Treaty and accommodation
Can end the Quarrel, and compose
The bloudy Duell without blows.
Are not our Liberties, our Lives,
The Lawes, Religion, and our Wives
Enough at once to lye at stake,
For *Cov'nant* and the *Cause*'s sake;   730
But in that quarrel *Dogs* and *Bears*,
As well as we, must venture theirs?
This Feud by *Jesuits* invented,
By *evil Counsel* is fomented.
There is a *Machiavilian* Plot,
(Though ev'ry *nare olfact* it not)

708 This Speech is set down as it was deliver'd by the Knight in his own words: but
since it is below the Gravity of Heroical Poetry, to admit of Humor, but all men are
oblig'd to speak wisely alike. And too much of so extravagant a Folly would become
tedious, and impertinent, the rest of his Harangues have only his Sense exprest in other
words, unless in some few places where his own words could not be so well avoided.

736 *nare olfact A1* (errata), *A2–A5, C*: *Nero* effect *A1*

A deep design in't, to divide
The well-affected that confide,
By setting Brother against Brother,
To claw and curry one another.   740
Have we not enemies *plus satis*,
That *Cane et angue pejus* hate us?
And shall we turn our fangs and claws
Upon our own selves, without cause?
That some occult design doth ly
In bloudy *Cynarctomachy*,
Is plain enough to him that knows
How Saints lead brothers by the nose.
I wish my self a Pseudo-prophet,
But sure some mischief will come of it: 750
Unless by providential wit
Or force we averruncate it.
For what design, what interest
Can Beast have to encounter Beast?
They fight for no espoused *Cause*,
Frail *Priviledge, Fundamentall Laws*;
Nor for a *thorough Reformation*,
Nor *Covenant*, nor *Protestation*;
Nor *Liberty of Consciences*,
Nor Lords and Commons *Ordinances*;   760
Nor for the *Church*, nor for *Church Lands*,
To get them in their own no hands;
Nor *evil Counsellours* to bring
To Justice that seduce the King;
Nor for the worship of us men,
Though we have done as much for them.
Th'*Ægyptians* worshipp'd *Dogs*, and for
Their faith made fierce and zealous war.

746 Cynarctomachy signifies nothing in the World, but a Fight between *Dogs* and *Bears*, though both the Learned and Ignorant agree, that in such words very great Knowledge is contained: and our Knight as one, or both of those, was of the same opinion.
752 Another of the same kind, which though it appear ever so Learned, and Profound, means nothing else but the weeding of Corn.

---

759 Nor *Liberty of Consciences C*: Nor for free *Liberty of Conscience A*   761 *Church Lands A1* (errata), *A2–A5, C*: *Church-land A1*   762 hands *A1* (errata), *A2–A5, C*: hand *A1*   768 fierce and zealous *C*: internecine *A*

Others ador'd a *Rat*, and some
For that Church suffer'd martyrdome.   770
The *Indians* fought for the truth
Of th'*Elephant*, and *Monkey*'s tooth:
And many, to defend that faith,
Fought it out *mordicus* to death.
But no Beast ever was so slight,
For man, as for his God, to fight.
They have more wit, alas! and know
Themselves and us better then so.
But we, we onely do infuse
The Rage in them like *Boute-feus*.   780
'Tis our example that instills
In them th'infection of our ills.
For, as some late Philosophers
Have well observ'd, Beasts that converse
With Man, take after him, as Hogs
Get Pigs all th'year, and Bitches Dogs.
Just so by our example Cattel
Learn to give one another Battel.
We read in *Nero*'s time, the Heathen,
When they destroy'd the *Christian brethren*,   790
They sow'd them in the skins of Bears,
And then set Dogs about their ears:
From whence, no doubt, th'invention came
Of this lewd, Antichristian Game.

To this, quoth *Ralpho*, Verily,
The Point seems very plain to me.
It is an Antichristian Game,
Unlawful both in thing and name.

771-2 The History of the White Elephant, and the Monkeys Tooth, which the
Indians ador'd, is written by Monsieur *Le Blanc*. This Monkey's Tooth was taken
by the Portuguese from those that worship't it, and though they offer'd a vast
Ransom for it, yet the Christians were perswaded by their Priests, rather to burn it.
But as soon as the Fire was kindled, all the People present were not able to indure the
horrible stink that came from it, as if the Fire had been made of the same Ingredients,
with which Seamen use to compose that kind of Granado's, which they call *Stinkards*.
780 *Boute-feus* is a French word, and therefore it were uncivil to suppose any English
Person (especially of Quality) ignorant of it, or so ill-bred as to need an Exposition.

796 me] be *C*

First for the *name*, The word *Bear-baiting*
Is carnal, and of man's creating :   800
For certainly there's no such word
In all the *Scripture* on record.
Therefore unlawful and a sin.
And so is (secondly) the *thing*.
A vile *Assembly* 'tis, that can
No more be prov'd by Scripture than
Provincial, Classick, National;
Mere humane Creature-cobwebs all.
Thirdly, it is Idolatrous.
For when men run a-whoring thus   810
With their Inventions, whatsoe're
The thing be, whether *Dog* or *Bear*,
It is Idolatrous and Pagan,
No less then worshipping of *Dagon*.

Quoth *Hudibras*, I smell a *Rat*;
Ralpho, thou dost prevaricate.
For though the *Thesis* which thou lay'st
Be true *ad amussim* as thou say'st :
(For that *Bear-baiting* should appear
Jure Divino lawfuller   820
Then *Synods* are, thou dost deny,
Totidem verbis so do I)
Yet there's a fallacy in this :
For if by sly *Homæosis*,
Thou wouldst Sophistically imply
Both are unlawfull, I deny.

And I (quoth *Ralpho*) do not doubt
But *Bear-baiting* may be made out
In Gospel-times, as lawfull as is
Provincial or *Parochial Classis* :   830
And that both are so near of kin,
And like in all, as well as sin,
That put them in a bag and shake 'em,
Your self o'th' sudden would mistake 'em,

824–5 *Homæosis*, | Thou C : *Homæosis*, (*Tussis pro crepitu*, an Art | Under a Cough
to slur a Fart | Thou *A*

And not know which is which, unlesse
You measure by their Wickedness:
For 'tis not hard t'imagine whether
O'th' two is worst, though I name neither.

Quoth *Hudibras*, Thou offer'st much,
But art not able to keep touch.   840
Mira de lente, as 'tis i'th' Adage,
Id est, to make a Leek a Cabbage.
Thou canst at best but overstrain
A Paradox, and th' own hot brain.
For what can *Synods* have at all
With *Bears* that's analogicall?
Or what relation has debating
Of Church-Affaiers with *Bear-baiting*?
A just comparison still is,
Of things *ejusdem generis*.   850
And then what *Genus* rightly doth
Include, and comprehend them both?
If *Animal*, both of us may
As justly pass for Beares as they.
For we are Animals no less,
Although of different *Specieses*.
But, *Ralpho*, this is no fit place
Nor time to argue out the Case:
For now the Field is not far off,
Where we must give the world a proof   860
Of Deeds, not Words, and such as suit
Another manner of Dispute.
A Controversie that affords
Actions for Arguments, not Words:
Which we must manage at a rate
Of Prowess and Conduct adæquate
To what our place and fame doth promise,
And all the *Godly* expect from us.
Nor shall they be deceiv'd, unless
W' are slurr'd and outed by success: 870

843–4 canst . . . brain *C*: wilt at best but *suck a Bull*, | Or *shear Swine, All Cry, and
no Wooll. A*   848 Affaiers *A1*: Affaires *A2*: Affairs *A3–A5, C*   852 Include,
and comprehend them *C*: Compr'hend them *inclusivè A*   854 justly *C*:
likely *A*

Success, the mark no mortal wit,
Or surest hand, can alwayes hit:
For whatsoe're we perpetrate,
We do but row, w' are stear'd by Fate,
Which in success oft disinherits,
For spurious causes, noblest merits.
Great Actions are not always true sons
Of great and mighty Resolutions:
Nor do the bold'st attempts bring forth
Events still equal to their worth;   880
But sometimes fail, and in their stead
Fortune and Cowardise succeed.
Yet we have no great cause to doubt,
Our actions still have born us out.
Which though th' are known to be so ample,
We need not copy from example,
We're not the onely person durst
Attempt this Province, nor the first.
In Northern Clime a valorous Knight
Did whilom kill his Bear in fight,   890
And wound a Fidler: we have both
Of these the objects of our wroth,
And equal fame and glory from
Th'Attempt or Victory to come.
'Tis sung, There is a valiant *Mamaluke*
In forrain Land, yclep'd ——
To whom we have been oft compar'd,
For Person, Parts, Address, and Beard;
Both equally reputed stout,
And in the same Cause both have fought.   900
He oft in such Attempts as these
Came off with glory and success.
Nor will we fail in th'execution,
For want of equal Resolution.
Honour is, like a Widow, won
With brisk Attempt and putting on;
With entring manfully, and urging;
Not slow approaches, like a Virgin.

886 not] no *C*   887 durst *C2*: durst, *A, C1*

This said, as once the *Phrygian* Knight,
So ours with rusty steel did smite   910
His *Trojan* horse, and just as much
He mended pace upon the touch;
But from his empty stomach gron'd
Just as that hollow beast did sound,
And angry answer'd from behind,
With brandish'd Tail and blast of wind.
So have I seen with armed heel,
A Wight bestride a *Common-weal*;
While still the more he kick'd and spurr'd,
The less the sullen Jade has stirr'd.   920

909 once *C* : yerst *A*

THE FIRST PART

CANTO II

THE ARGUMENT

The Catalogue and Character
Of th' Enemy's best men of War;
Whom in a bold Harangue, the Knight
Defy's, and challenges to fight:
H' incounters Talgol, *routs the* Bear,
And takes the Fidler *Prisoner;*
Conveys him to enchanted Castle,
There shuts him fast in Wooden Bastile.

THERE was an ancient sage *Philosopher*,
That had read *Alexander Ross* over,
Añd swore the world, as he could prove,
Was made of *Fighting* and of *Love* :
Just so *Romances* are, for what else
Is in them all, but *Love* and *Battels* ?
O'th' first of these w' have no great matter
To treat of, but a world o'th' later:
In which to doe the Injur'd Right
We mean, in what concerns just fight.   10
Certes our Authors are to blame,
For to make some well-sounding name
A Pattern fit for modern Knights,
To copy out in Frays and Fights,
(Like those that a whole street do raze,
To build a Palace in the place.)
They never care how many others
They kill, without regard of mothers,

The Argument. 3–5 *Whom . . . H' incounters* C : *To whom the* Knight *does make a speech,*
And they defie him: after which | *He fights with* A

Or wives, or children, so they can
Make up some fierce, dead-doing man,   20
Compos'd of many ingredient Valours,
Just like the Manhood of nine Taylors.
So a wild *Tartar* when he spies
A man that's handsome, valiant, wise,
If he can kill him, thinks t'inherit
His Wit, his Beauty, and his Spirit:
As if just so much he enjoy'd
As in another is destroy'd.
For when a Giant's slain in fight,
And mow'd orethwart, or cleft downright,   30
It is a heavy case, no doubt,
A man should have his Brains beat out,
Because he's tall, and has large Bones;
As men kill Beavers for their stones.
But as for our part, we shall tell
The naked Truth of what befell;
And as an equal friend to both
The Knight and Bear, but more to Troth,
With neither faction shall take part,
But give to each his due desert: 40
And never coyn a formal lye on't,
To make the *Knight* o'recome the *Giant*.
This b'ing profest, we hope's enough,
And now go on where we left off.

They rode, but Authors having not
Determin'd whether Pace or Trot,
(That is to say, whether *Tollutation*,
As they do tearm't, or *Succussation*)
We leave it, and go on, as now
Suppose they did, no matter how.   50
Yet some from subtle hints have got
Mysterious light, it was a Trot.
But let that pass: they now begun
To spur their living Engines on.
For as whipp'd Tops and bandy'd Balls,
The learned hold, are Animals:
So Horses they affirm to be

Mere Engines, made by Geometry,
And were invented first from Engins,
As *Indian Britans* were from *Penguins*.   60
So let them be; and, as I was saying,
They their live Engines ply'd, not staying
Untill they reach'd the fatal champain,
Which th'Enemy did then incamp on,
The dire *Pharsalian* Plain, where Battel
Was to be wag'd 'twixt puissant Cattel,
And fierce Auxiliary men,
That came to aid their Bretheren:
Who now began to take the Field
As from his Steed the Knight beheld.   70
For as our modern wits behold,
Mounted a Pick-back on the Old,
Much further off; much further he
Rais'd on his aged Beast could see:
Yet not sufficient to descry
All postures of the enemy.
And therefore orders the bold Squire
T'advance, and view their Body nigher
That when their motions he had known,
He might know how to fit his own.   80
Meanwhile he stopp'd his willing Steed,
To fit himself for martial deed:
Both kinds of mettle he prepar'd,
Either to give blows, or to ward,
Courage within, and Steel without,
To give, or to receive a Rout.
His Death-charg'd Pistols he did fit well,
Drawn out from life-preserving vittle.

60 The *American Indians* call a great Bird they have, with a white head a *Penguin*; which signify's the same thing in the *Brittish* Tongue: From whence (with other words of the same kind) some Authors have indeavour'd to prove, That the *Americans* are originally deriv'd from the *Brittains*.

69–70 take . . . Knight *C*: draw in field, | As Knight from ridge of Steed *A*
74 Rais'd on *C*: From off *A*   77–78 And therefore . . . nigher *C*: Wherefore he bids the Squire ride further, | T'observe their numbers, and their order; *A*
85–86 within . . . Rout *C*: and Steel, both of great force, | Prepar'd for better or for worse *A*

These being prim'd, with force he labour'd
To free Sword from retentive Scabbard: 90
And after many a painfull pluck,
He clear'd at length the rugged Tuck.
Then shook himself, to see that Prowess
In Scabbard of his Arms sate loose;
And rais'd upon his desperate foot
On stirrup side he gaz'd about,
Portending Bloud, like Blazing Star,
The Beacon of approaching War.
The Squire advanc'd with greater speed
Then could b'expected from his Steed;   100
But far more in returning made,
For now the Foe he had survey'd
Rang'd, as to him they did appear,
With *Van, main Battel, Wings,* and *Rear.*

In th'head of all this Warlike Rabble
Crowdero march'd, expert and able:
Instead of Trumpet and of Drum,
That makes the Warrier's stomach come,
Whose noise whets Valour sharp, like Beer
By thunder turn'd to Vineger,   110
(For if a Trumpet sound or Drum beat,
Who has not a month's mind to combat?)
A squeaking Engine he apply'd
Unto his neck, on North-east side,
Just where the Hangman does dispose
To special friends the fatal Noose:
For 'tis *great Grace* when *Statesmen* straight
Dispatch a friend, let others wait.
His warped *Ear* hung o're the strings,
Which was but *Souce* to *Chitterlings*:   120
For Guts, some write, e're they are sodden,
Are fit for Musick, or for Pudden:
From whence men borrow ev'ry kind
Of Minstrelsy, by string or wind.

90 free's *C*   92 He . . . rugged *C*: From rusty Durance he bayl'd *A*
99 The Squire advanc'd *C*: *Ralpho* rode on *A*   greater *C*: no less *A*
100–1 could . . . made *C*: *Hugo* in the Forrest did; | But with a great deal more
return'd *A*   102 survey'd *C*: discern'd, *A*   116 fatal *C*: Knot of *A*

His grizly *Beard* was long and thick,
With which he strung his Fiddle-stick:
For he to Horse-tail scorn'd to owe,
For what on his own chin did grow.
Chiron, the four-legg'd Bard, had both
A Beard and Tail of his own growth;   130
And yet by Authors 'tis averr'd,
He made use onely of his Beard.
In *Staffordshire,* where Vertuous worth
Does raise the Minstrelsy, not Birth;
Where Bulls do chuse the Boldest King
And Ruler, o're the men of string;
(As once in *Persia,* 'tis said,
Kings were proclaim'd by a Horse that neigh'd)
He bravely vent'ring at a Crown,
By chance of War was beaten down,   140
And wounded sore: his *Leg* then broke,
Had got a Deputy of Oke:
For when a shin in fight is cropt,
The knee with one of timber's propt;
Esteem'd more honourable then the other,
And takes place, though the younger Brother.

Next march'd brave *Orsin,* famous for
Wise Conduct, and success in War:
A skilful Leader, stout, severe,
Now Marshall to the Champion Bear.   150
With Truncheon tipp'd with Iron-head,
The Warrior to the lists he led;
With solemn march and stately pace,
But far more grave and solemn face:
Grave as the Emperour of *Pegu,*
Or *Spanish* Potentate *Don Diego.*
This Leader was of knowledge great,
Either for Charge or for Retreat.
Knew when t'engage his *Bear* Pel-mel
And when to bring him off as well.   160

147 march'd brave *C*: follow'd *A*   159–60 Knew ... off *C*: He knew when
to fall on pell-mell, | To fall back and retreat *A*

G

So Lawyers, lest the *Bear* defendant,
And Plaintiff *Dog*, should make an end on't,
Do stave and tail with *Writs of Error*,
Reverse of Judgement, and *Demurrer*,
To let them breath awhile, and then
Cry whoop, and set them on agen.
As *Romulus* a Wolf did rear,
So he was dry-nurs'd by a Bear,
That fed him with the purchas'd prey
Of many a fierce and bloudy fray;   170
Bred up, where Discipline most rare is,
In Military *Garden-Paris*.
For Souldiers heretofore did grow
In Gardens, just as Weeds do now;
Untill some splay-foot Politicians
T'*Apollo* offer'd up Petitions,
For licensing a new invention
Th' had found out, of an antique engine
To root out all the Weeds that grow
In Publick Garden at a blow,   180
And leave th'Herbs standing. Quoth Sir *Sun*,
My friends, that is not to be done.
Not done? quoth Statesmen; yes, an't please ye,
When 'tis once known you'l say 'tis easy.
Why then let's know it, quoth *Apollo*.
We'l beat a Drum, and they'l all follow.
A Drum (quoth *Phœbus*) troth that's true,
A pretty invention, quaint and new.
But though of Voice and Instrument
We are ('tis true) chief President;   190
We such loud Musick do not profess,
The Devil's Master of that office,
Where it must pass, if't be a Drum,
He'l sign it with *Cler. Parl. Dom. Com.*
To him apply your selves, and he
Will soon dispatch you for his fee.
They did so, but it prov'd so ill,
Th' had better have let them grow there still.

190 ('tis true) chief *C*: th'undoubted *A*

But to resume what we discoursing
Were on before, that is stout *Orsin*: 200
That which so oft by sundry writers
Has been apply'd t'almost all fighters,
More justly may b'abscrib'd to this,
Then any other Warrior (*viz.*)
None ever acted both parts bolder,
Both of a Chieftain and a Souldier.
He was of great descent and high,
For Splendor and Antiquity,
And from Celestial origine
Deriv'd himself in a right line. 210
Not as the Ancient *Hero's* did,
Who, that their base births might be hid,
(Knowing they were of doubtful gender,
And that they came in at a Windore)
Made *Jupiter* himself and others
O'th' Gods Gallants to their own mothers,
To get on them a Race of Champions,
(Of which old *Homer* first made *Lampoons*.)
Arctophylax in Northern Sphere
Was his undoubted Ancestor: 220
From him his Great Fore-fathers came,
And in all Ages bore his name.
Learned he was in Medc'nal Lore,
For by his side a Pouch he wore
Replete with strange Hermetick Powder,
That Wounds nine miles point-blank would solder,
By skilfull *Chymist* with great cost
Extracted from a rotten Post;
But of a heav'nlier influence
Then that which Mountebanks dispense; 230
Though by *Promethean* fier made,
As they do quack that drive that trade.
For as when Slovens doe amiss
At others doors by Stool or Piss,
The Learned write, a Red-hot Spit,
B'ing prudently apply'd to it,

218 (Of] Of *A*, *C*   226 nine] 6 *C*   solder,] solder *C*

Will convey mischief from the Dung
Unto the part that did the wrong:
So this did healing, and as sure
As that did mischief, this would cure.   240

Thus vertuous *Orsin* was endu'd
With Learning, Conduct, Fortitude,
Incomparable: and as the Prince
Of Poets, *Homer*, sung long since,
A Skilful Leech is better far
Then half a hundred men of War;
So he appear'd, and by his skill,
No less then Dint of Sword, could kill.

The Gallant *Bruin* marcht next him,
With Visage formidably grim,   250
And rugged as a *Saracen*,
Or *Turk* of *Mahomet*'s own kin;
Clad in a Mantle *della Guer*
Of rough impenetrable Fur;
And in his Nose, like *Indian* King,
He wore for ornament a Ring;
About his Neck a three-fold Gorget,
As tough as trebled leathern Target;
Armed, as Heraulds cant, and *langued*,
Or, as the Vulgar say, *sharp-fanged*.   260
For as the Teeth in Beasts of Prey
Are Swords, with which they fight in Fray;
So Swords in men of War are teeth,
Which they do eat their Vittle with.
He was by birth, some Authors write,
A *Russian*, some a *Muscovite*,
And 'mong the *Cossacks* had been bred,
Of whom we in *Diurnals* read,
That serve to fill up Pages here,
As with their Bodyes Ditches there.   270
Scrimansky was his Cousin-german,
With whom he serv'd, and fed on Vermin:

And when these fail'd he'd suck his claws,
And quarter himself upon his paws.
And though his Country-men, the *Huns*,
Did use to stew between their Bums
And their warm Horses backs, their meat
And every man his Saddle eat:
He was not half so nice as they,
But eat it raw, when't came in's way.   280
He had trac'd Countreys far and near,
More then *Le Blanc* the Traveller;
Who writes, He Spous'd in *India*
Of noble house a Lady gay,
And got on her a Race of Worthyes
As stout as any upon earth is.
Full many a fight for him between
Talgol and *Orsin* oft had been;
Each striving to deserve the Crown
Of a sav'd Citizen: the one   290
To guard his Bear, the other fought
To aid his Dog; both made more stout
By sev'ral spurs of neighborhood,
Church fellow-membership, and bloud:
But *Talgol*, mortal foe to Cows,
Never got ought of him but blows;
Blows hard and heavy, such as he
Had lent, repay'd with Usury.

Yet *Talgol* was of Courage stout,
And vanquish'd oftner then he fought: 300
Inur'd to labour, sweat, and toyl,
And, like a Champion, shone with Oyl.

---

275 This custom of the *Huns* is describ'd by *Ammianus Marcellinus*. *Hunii Semicruda cujusvis Pecoris carne vescuntur, quam inter femora sua et equorum terga subsertam, fotu calefaciunt brevi.* Pag.686.
283–4 This story in *Leblanc*, of a *Bear* that married a Kings Daughter, is no more strange then many others in most Travellers, that pass with allowance, for if they should write nothing but what is possible, or probable, they might appear to have lost their labor, and observed nothing, but what they might have done as well at home.

---

275 Country-men *A2–A5*, C2: Coutrey-men *A1, C1*   276 use to stew C: stew
their meat *A*   277 their warm Horses backs, their meat C: th'Horses backs
o're which they straddle, *A*   278 his Saddle eat C: eat ιp his Saddle *A*

Right many a Widow his keen blade,
And many Fatherless, had made.
He many a Bore and huge *Dun Cow*
Did, like another *Guy*, o'rethrow.
But *Guy* with him in fight compar'd,
Had like the Bore or Dun Cow far'd.
With greater Troops of Sheep h' had fought
Then *Ajax*, or bold *Don Quixot*:   310
And many a Serpent of fell kind,
With wings before and stings behind,
Subdu'd; as Poets say, long agon
Bold *Sir George Saint George* did the *Dragon*.
Nor Engine, nor Device Polemick,
Disease, nor Doctor Epidemick,
Though stor'd with Deletery Med'cines,
(Which whosoever took is dead since)
E're sent so vast a Colony
To both the under worlds as he.   320
For he was of that noble Trade
That *Demi-gods* and *Heroes* made,
Slaughter, and knocking on the head;
The Trade to which they all were bred;
And is, like others, glorious when
'Tis great and large, but base if mean.
The former rides in Triumph for it;
The later in a two-wheel'd Chariot,
For daring to profane a thing
So sacred, with vile bungleing.   330

Next these the brave *Magnano* came,
Magnano great in Martial fame.
Yet when with *Orsin* he wag'd fight,
'Tis sung he got but little by't.
Yet he was fierce as forrest-Bore,
Whose Spoils upon his Back he wore,
As thick as *Ajax* sev'n-fold Shield,
Which o're his brazen Arms he held.
But Brass was feeble to resist
The fury of his armed fist;   340

304 many] many a *C*

Nor could the hardest Ir'n hold out
Against his Blows, but they would through't.

In *Magick* he was deeply read,
As he that made the *Brazen-head*;
Profoundly skill'd in the black Art,
As *English Merlin* for his heart;
But far more skilfull in the Spheres
Then he was at the Sieve and Shears.
He could transform himself in Colour
As like the Devil as a Collier;   350
As like as Hypocrites in shew
Are to true Saints, or Crow to Crow.

Of warlike Engines he was Author,
Devis'd for quick dispatch of slaughter:
The *Cannon, Blunderbuss,* and *Saker,*
He was th'inventer of and maker:
The *Trumpet* and the *Kettle-Drum*
Did both from his Invention come.
He was the first that e're did teach
To make, and how to stop a breach.   360
A Lance he bore with Iron-pike,
Th'one half would thrust, the other strike:
And when their forces he had joyn'd,
He scorn'd to turn his Parts behind.

He *Trulla* lov'd, *Trulla* more bright
Then burnish'd Armour of her Knight:
A bold *Virago,* stout and tall
As *Joan* of *France,* or *English Mall.*
Through Perils both of Wind and Limb,
Through thick and thin she follow'd him,   370
In ev'ry Adventure h' undertook,
And never him or it forsook.
At Breach of Wall, or Hedge-surprize,
She shar'd in th'hazard and the prize:
At beating quarters up, or forrage,
Behav'd her self with matchless courage;
And laid about in fight more busily,
Then th'*Amazonian* Dame, *Penthesile.*

And though some Criticks here cry shame,
And say our Authors are to blame,   380
That (spight of all Philosophers,
Who hold no females stout, but Bears,
And heretofore did so abhor
Their Women should pretend to War,
They would not suffer the stout'st Dame
To swear by *Hercules* his Name)
Make feeble Ladies, in their Works,
To fight like *Termagants* and *Turks*;
To lay their native Arms aside,
Their modesty, and ride a-stride;   390
To run a-tilt at men, and wield
Their naked tools in open field;
As stout *Armida*, bold *Thalestris*,
And she that would have been the Mistriss
Of *Gundibert*, but he had grace,
And rather took a Countrey Lass:
They say 'tis false, without all sense,
But of pernicious consequence
To Government, which they suppose
Can never be upheld in prose: 400
Strip Nature naked to the skin,
You'l find about her no such thing.
It may be so, yet what we tell
Of *Trulla*, that's improbable,
Shall be depos'd by those have seen't,
Or, what's as good, produc'd in print:
And if they will not take our word,
We'l prove it true upon record.

The upright *Cerdon* next advanc't,
Of all his Race the Valiant'st;   410

385–6 The old *Romans* had particular Oaths for Men and Women to swear by, and
therefore *Macrobius* says, *Viri per Castorem non jurabant antiquitus, nec Mulieres per
Herculem, Ædepol autem juramentum erat tam mulieribus quam viris commune*, &c.
393 Two formidable Women at Arms in Romances, that were cudgell'd into Love
by their Gallants.

381 (spight] spight *C*   382 Bears, *C*: Bears,) *A*   383–6 *added in* C
386 Name)] Name, *C*

Cerdon the Great, renown'd in Song,
Like *Herc'les*, for repair of wrong:
He rais'd the low, and fortify'd
The weak against the strongest side.
Ill has he read, that never hit
On him in Muses deathless writ.
He had a weapon keen and fierce,
That through a Bull-hide-shield would pierce,
And cut it in a thousand pieces,
Though tougher then the Knight of *Greece* his;　420
With whom his black-thumb'd ancestor
Was Comrade in the ten years war:
For when the restless *Greeks* sate down
So many years before *Troy* Town,
And were renown'd, as *Homer* writes,
For *well-sol'd Boots*, no lesse then Fights;
They ow'd that Glory onely to
His Ancestor, that made them so.
Fast friend he was to *Reformation*,
Untill 'twas worn quite out of fashion.　430
Next Rectifier of Wry *Law*,
And would make three, to cure one flaw.
Learned he was, and could take note,
Transcribe, collect, translate and quote.
But *Preaching* was his chiefest Talent,
Or Argument, in which b'ing valiant,
He us'd to lay about and stickle,
Like Ram or Bull, at *Conventicle*:
For Disputants, like *Rams* and *Bulls*,
Do fight with *Arms* that spring from *Skulls*.　440

Last *Colon* came, bold man of war,
Destin'd to blows by fatal Star;
Right expert in Command of horse,
But Cruel, and without remorse.
That which of *Centaure* long ago
Was said, and has been wrested to
Some other Knights, was true of this,
He and his *Horse* were of a piece.
One Spirit did inform them both,

The self-same Vigor, Fury, Wroth: 450
Yet he was much the rougher part,
And alwayes had a harder heart;
Although his Horse had been of those
That fed on Man's flesh, as fame goes.
Strange food for Horse! and yet, alas!
It may be true, for *flesh is grass.*
Sturdy he was, and no less able
Then *Hercules* to clense a Stable;
As great a Drover, and as great
A Critick too in hog or neat.   460
He ripp'd the womb up of his mother,
Dame *Tellus*, 'cause she wanted fother
And Provender wherewith to feed
Himself and his less-cruel Steed.
It was a question whether He
Or's Horse were of a Family
More Worshipful: till Antiquaries,
(After th' had almost por'd out their eys,)
Did very learnedly decide
The bus'ness on the Horse's side,   470
And prov'd not onely Horse, but Cows,
Nay Pigs, were of the elder house:
For Beasts, when man was but a piece
Of earth himself, did th'earth possess.

These Worthies were the Chief that led
The Combatants, each in the head
Of his Command, with Arms and Rage,
Ready and longing to engage.
The numerous Rabble was drawn out
Of several Countries round about;   480
From Villages remote, and Shires,
Of East and Western Hemispheres:
From forain Parishes and Regions,
Of different manners, speech, Religions,
Came men and Mastives; some to fight
For fame and honour, some for sight.

And now the field of Death, the lists,
Were entred by Antagonists,
And bloud was ready to be broached;
When *Hudibras* in haste approached,   490
With Squire and weapons to attack them:
But first thus from his *Horse* bespake them.

What Rage, O Citizens, what fury
Doth you to these dire actions hurry?
What *Oestrum*, what phrenetick mood
Makes you thus lavish of your bloud,
While the proud *Vies* your Trophies boast,
And unreveng'd walks —— ghost?
What Towns, what Garrisons might you
With hazard of this bloud subdue,   500
Which now y' are bent to throw away
In vain, untriumphable fray?
Shall *Saints* in Civil bloudshed wallow
Of *Saints*, and let the *Cause* lie fallow?
The *Cause*, for which we fought and swore
So boldly, shall we now give o're?
Then because Quarrels still are seen
With Oaths and Swearing to begin,
The *Solemn League and Covenant*
Will seem a meer *God-dam-me* Rant;   510
And we that took it, and have fought,
As lewd as Drunkards that fall out.
For as we make War *for the King
Against himself*, the self-same thing
Some will not stick to swear we doe
For *God*, and for *Religion* too.
For if *Bear-baiting* we allow,
What good can *Reformation* doe?
The bloud and treasure that's laid out,
Is thrown away, and goes for nought.   520
Are these the fruits o'th' *Protestation*,
The Prototype of *Reformation*,
Which all the *Saints*, and some since *Martyrs*,

Wore in their hats, like Wedding-garters,
When 'twas resolv'd by either House
Six Members quarrel to espouse?
Did they for this draw down the Rabble,
With Zeal and Noises formidable;
And make all *Cries* about the Town
Joyn throats to cry the *Bishops* down?   530
Who having round begirt the Palace,
(As once a month they do the *Gallows*)
As Members gave the sign about,
Set up their throats with hideous shout.
When *Tinkers* bawl'd aloud, to settle
Church-Discipline, for patching *Kettle*.
No *Sow-gelder* did blow his horn
To geld a Cat, but cry'd *Reform*.
The *Oyster-women* lock'd their fish up,
And trudg'd away, to cry *No Bishop*.   540
The *Mousetrap-men* laid *Save-alls* by,
And 'gainst *Ev'l Counsellors* did cry.
Botchers left old cloaths in the lurch,
And fell to turn and patch the *Church*.
Some cry'd the *Covenant* instead
Of *Pudding-pies* and *Ginger-bread*:
And some for *Broom*, *old Boots and Shoes*,
Baul'd out to *purge the Common's House*:
Instead of *Kitchin-stuff*, some cry
A *Gospel-preaching-Ministry*;   550
And some for *Old Suits*, *Coats*, or *Cloak*,
No *Surplices*, nor *Service-book*.
A strange harmonious inclination
Of all degrees to *Reformation*.
And is this all? is this the end
To which these *carr'ings on* did tend?
Hath *Publick Faith* like a young heire
For this tak'n up all sorts of Ware,

524 Some few days after the King had accus'd the Five Members of Treason in the
House of Commons; great crouds of the Rabble came down to *Westminster-Hall*,
with Printed Copies of the Protestation, ty'd in their Hats like Favors.

548 Baul'd *C*: Cry'd *A*   555 And is this] And this is *Cr*

And run int' ev'ry Tradesman's book,
Til both turn'd Bankrupts, and are broke?   560
Did *Saints* for this bring in their *Plate*,
And crowd as if they came too late?
For when they thought the *Cause* had need on't,
Happy was he that could be rid on't.
Did they coyn *Piss-pots*, *Bouls* and *Flaggons*,
Int' Officers of Horse and Dragoons;
And into Pikes and Musketiers
Stamp *Beakers*, *Cups* and *Porringers*?
A *Thimble*, *Bodkin*, and a *Spoon*
Did start up living men, as soon   570
As in the Furnace they were thrown,
Just like the *Dragons teeth* b'ing sown.
Then was the *Cause* all Gold and Plate,
The *Brethrens* off'rings, consecrate
Like th'*Hebrew-calf*, and down before it
The *Saints* fell prostrate, to adore it.
So say the *Wicked*—and will you
Make that Sarcasmous Scandal true,
By running after Dogs and Bears,
Beasts more unclean then Calves or Steers?   580
Have *pow'rful Preachers* ply'd their tongues,
And *laid* themselves *out* and their lungs;
Us'd all means, both direct and sinister,
I'th' power of *Gospel-preaching Minister*?
Have they invented *Tones*, to win
The *Women*, and make them draw in
The men, as *Indians* with a female
Tame Elephant enveigle the male?
Have they told *Prov'dence* what it must do,
Whom to avoid, and whom to trust to?   590
Discover'd th'*Enemy*'s design,
And which way best to countermine;
Prescrib'd what wayes it hath to work,
Or it will ne're advance the *Kirk*;
Told it the *News* o'th' last express,
And after good or bad success

---

578 Abusive, or insulting had been better, but our Knight believ'd the Learned
Languages, more convenient to understand in, then his own Mother-tongue.

Made Prayers, not so like *Petitions*,
As *Overtures* and *Propositions*,
(Such as the *Army* did present
To their Creator th' *Parliament*)   600
In which they freely will confess,
They will not, cannot *acquiesce*,
Unless the *Work* be carry'd on
In the same way they have begun,
By setting Church and Common-weal
All on a flame bright as their zeal,
On which the Saints were all a-gog,
And all this for a *Bear* and *Dog*?

The Parliament drew up *Petitions*
To't self, and sent them, like Commissions,   610
To *Well-affected* Persons down,
In ev'ry City and great Town;
With pow'r to leavy horse and men,
Onely to bring them back agen:
For this did many, many a mile,
Ride manfully in Rank and file,
With *Papers* in their hats, that show'd
As if they to the *Pillory* rode.
Have all these courses, these efforts,
Been try'd by people of all sorts,   620
Velis et Remis, omnibus Nervis,
And all t'advance the *Cause*'s service?
And shall all now be thrown away
In petulant intestine fray?
Shall we that in the *Cov'nant* swore,
Each man of us to run before
Another still in *Reformation*,
Give Dogs and Bears a Dispensation?
How will *dissenting Brethren* relish it?
What will *Malignants* say? *Videlicet*,   630
That each man swore to doe his best,
To damn and perjure all the rest;
And bid *the Devil take the hinmost*,
Which at this Race is like to win most.
They'l say our bus'ness to *reform*

The Church and State is but a worm;
For to subscribe, unsight unseen,
T'an unknown Churches Discipline
What is it else, but before-hand
T'ingage, and after understand? 640
For when we swore to carry on
The present *Reformation,*
According to the Purest mode
Of Churches, best Reform'd abroad,
What did we else but make a vow
To doe we know not what, nor how?
For no three of us will agree
Where, or what Churches these should be.
And is indeed the self-same case
With theirs that swore *Et cæteras*; 650
Or the *French League,* in which men vow'd
To fight to the last drop of bloud.
These slanders will be thrown 'upon
The *Cause* and *Work* we carry on,
If we permit men to run headlong
T'exorbitancies fit for Bedlam,
Rather then *Gospel-walking* times,
When slightest Sins are greatest Crimes.
But we the matter so shall handle,
As to remove that odious scandal. 660
In name of King and Parliament,
I charge ye all, no more foment

649-50 The Convocation in one of the short Parliaments that usher'd in the long
one (as Dwarfs are wont to do Knights Errant) made an Oath to be taken, by the
Clergy, for observing of Canonical obedience; in which they injoyn'd their Brethren,
out of the abundance of their Consciences, to swear to Articles with *&c.*
651-2 The Holy League in *France,* design'd and made for the Extirpation of the
Protestant Religion, was the Original, out of which the Solemn League and Covenant
here, was (with difference only of Circumstances) most faithfully Transcrib'd. Nor
did the success of both differ more then the Intent and Purpose; for after the
destruction of vast numbers of People of all sorts, both ended with the Murthers of
two Kings, whom they had both sworn to defend: and as our Covenanters swore
every Man, to run one before another in the way of Reformation, So did the French
in the Holy League, to fight to the last drop of Bloud.

637-40 subscribe . . . understand? *C*: transcribe a Church invisible, | As we have
sworn to doe, it is *a bull*: | For when we swore to doe it after | *The best-reformed
Churches* that are, *A*   641-4 *added in C*

This feud, but keep the peace between
Your Brethren and your Countrey-men;
And to those places straight repair
Where your respective dwellings are.
But to that purpose first surrender,
The *Fidler*, as the prime offender,
Th'Incendiary vile, that is chief
Author and Enginier of mischief;   670
That makes division between friends,
For prophane and malignant ends.
He and that Engine of vile noyse,
On which illegally he playes,
Shall (*dictum factum*) both be *brought*
To condigne Punishment, as th' ought.
This must be done, and I would fain see
Mortal so sturdy as to gain-say:
For then I'le take another course,
And soon *Reduce* you all by force.   680
This said, he clapt his hand on Sword,
To shew he meant to keep his word.

But *Talgol*, who had long supprest
Enflamed wrath in glowing breast,
Which now began to rage and burn as
Implacably as flame in furnace,
Thus answer'd him. Thou Vermin wretched,
As e're in Meazel'd Pork was hatched;
Thou Tail of Worship, that dost grow
On Rump of Justice, as of Cow;   690
How dar'st thou with that sullen Luggage
O' thy self, old Ir'n, and other Baggage,
With which thy Steed of Bones and Leather
Has broke his Wind in halting hither;
How durst th', I say, adventure thus
T'oppose thy Lumber against us?
Could thine Impertinence find out
No work t'employ it self about,
Where thou secure from wooden blow
Thy busie vanity might'st show?   700

694 Has broke his Wind *C*: Is lam'd and tir'd *A*

Was no dispute afoot between
The *Catterwauling Bretheren*?
No subtle Question rais'd among
Those *out-o'-their-wits* and those i'th' wrong?
No prize between those Combatants
O'th' times, the Land and Water-*Saints*;
Where thou might'st *stickle without hazard*
Of outrage to thy hide and mazzard,
And not for want of bus'ness come
To us to be thus troublesome,   710
To interrupt our better sort
Of Disputants, and spoil our sport?
Was there no Felony, no Bawd,
Cut-purse, nor Burglary abroad?
No *Stollen Pig*, nor *Plunder'd Goose*,
To tie thee up from breaking loose?
No Ale unlicenc'd, broken hedge,
For which thou Statute might'st alledge,
To keep thee busie from foul evil,
And shame due to thee from the Devil?   720
Did no Committee sit, where he
Might cut out Journey-work for thee;
And set th' a task, with subornation,
To stitch up *sale* and *sequestration*;
To *cheat* with *Holiness* and *Zeal*
All Parties, and the Common-weal?
Much better had it been for thee,
H' had kept thee where th' art us'd to be;
Or sent th' on bus'ness any whither,
So he had never brought thee hither.   730
But if th' hast Brain enough in Skull
To keep within it's lodging whole,
And not provoke the rage of Stones
And Cudgels to thy Hide and Bones;
Tremble, and vanish while thou may'st,
Which I'le not promise if thou stay'st.
At this the *Knight* grew high in wroth,
And *lifting* hands and *eyes up* both,

732 within it's *C*: it self in *A*

Three times he smote on stomack stout,
From whence at length these words broke out.   740

Was I for this entitled *Sir*,
And girt with trusty sword and spur,
For fame and honour to wage battel,
Thus to be brav'd by foe to Cattel?
Not all that Pride that makes thee swell
As big as thou dost blown-up Veal;
Nor all thy tricks and slights to cheat,
And sell thy Carrion for good meat;
Not all thy Magick to repair
Decay'd old age in tough lean ware,   750
Make Natural Death appear thy work,
And stop the Gangrene in stale Pork;
Not all that force that makes thee proud,
Because by Bullock ne're withstood;
Though arm'd with all thy clevers, knives,
And Axes made to hew down lives;
Shall save or help thee to evade
The hand of Justice, or this blade
Which I her Sword-bearer do carry,
For civil deed and military.   760
Nor shall these words of Venom base,
Which thou hast from their native place,
Thy stomack, pump'd to fling on me,
Go unreveng'd, though I am free.
Thou down the same throat shalt devour 'em,
Like tainted Beef, and pay dear for 'em.
Nor shall it e're be said, that wight
With Gantlet blew and Bases white,
And round blunt Dudgeon by his side,
So great a man at Arms defy'd   770
With words far bitterer then wormwood,
That would in *Job* or *Grizel* stir mood.
Dogs with their tongues their wounds do heal;
But men with hands, as thou shalt feel.

739 he smote] smote *C*   745 that Pride *A2–A5, C*: the Pride *A1*
751 Make Natural Death appear *C*: Turn Death of Nature to *A*

This said, with hasty rage he snatch'd
His Gun-shot, that in holsters watch'd;
And bending Cock, he level'd full
Against th'outside of *Talgol*'s Skull;
Vowing that he should ne're stir further,
Nor henceforth Cow or Bullock murther.   780
But *Pallas* came in shape of Rust,
And 'twixt the Spring and Hammer thrust
Her *Gorgon*-shield, which made the Cock
Stand stiff as if 'twere turn'd t'a stock.
Meanwhile fierce *Talgol* gath'ring might,
With rugged Truncheon charg'd the *Knight*.
And he his rusty Pistol held
To take the blow on, like a Shield;
The Gun recoyl'd, as well it might,
Not us'd to such a kind of fight,   790
And shrunk from its great Master's gripe,
Knock'd down and stunn'd with mortal stripe.
Then *Hudibras* with furious haste
Drew out his sword; yet not so fast,
But *Talgol* first with hardy thwack
Twice bruiz'd his head, and twice his back.
But when his nut-brown Sword was out,
Couragiously he laid about,
Imprinting many a wound upon
His mortal foe the Truncheon.   800
The trusty Cudgel did oppose
It self against dead-doing blows,
To guard its Leader from fell bane,
And then reveng'd it self again.
And though the sword (some understood)
In force had much the odds of Wood;
'Twas nothing so, both sides were ballanc't
So equal, none knew which was valiant'st.
For Wood with Honour b'ing engag'd,
Is so implacably enrag'd,   810

784 if 'twere turn'd t'a *C*: 'twere transform'd to *A*   786 charg'd the *C*: smote
at *A*   787–8 And he . . . Shield; *C*: But he with Petronel up-heav'd, | Instead
of shield, the blow receiv'd. *A*   797 nut-brown *C*: rugged *A*   798 Couragiously *C*: With stomack huge *A1–A4*: With stomack stout *A5*

Though Iron hew and mangle sore,
Wood wounds and bruises honour more.
And now both *Knights* were out of breath,
Tir'd in the hot pursuit of Death;
While all the rest amaz'd stood still,
Expecting which should take, or kill.
This *Hudibras* observ'd, and fretting
Conquest should be so long a getting,
He drew up all his force into
One Body, and that into one Blow.   820
But *Talgol* wisely avoided it
By cunning sleight; for had it hit,
The Upper part of him the Blow
Had slit, as sure as that below.

Mean while th'incomparable *Colon*,
To aid his Friend began to fall on,
Him *Ralph* encountred, and straight grew
A fierce Dispute betwixt them two:
Th'one arm'd with Metal, th'other Wood;
This fit for bruise, and that for bloud.   830
With many a stiff thwack, many a bang,
Hard Crab-tree and old Iron rang;
While none that saw them could divine
To which side Conquest would encline:
Until *Magnano*, who did envy
That two should with so many men vye,
By subtle stratagem of brain
Perform'd what force could ne're attain.
For he, by foul hap having found
Where Thistles grew on barren ground,   840
In haste he drew his weapon out
And having crop'd them from the Root
He clapp'd them under th'Horses Tail
With prickles sharper then a Nail.

825–6 Mean while . . . fall on, *C*: But now fierce *Colon* 'gan draw on, | To aid the
distrest Champion. *A*   828 fierce Dispute betwixt *C*: dismal Combat 'twixt *A*
829 Wood] with Wood *C*   841–2 *added in C*   843–4 under th'Horses
Tail | With prickles sharper then a Nail *C*: underneath the Tail | Of Steed, with
pricks as sharp as nail. *A*

The angry Beast did straight resent
The wrong done to his Fundament,
Begun to kick, and fling, and wince,
As if h' had been beside his sense,
Striving to disengage from Smart,
And raging Pain, th'afflicted Part.   850
Instead of which he threw the pack
Of *Squire* and baggage from his back;
And blundring still, with smarting rump,
He gave the Champions Steed a thump,
That staggar'd him. The *Knight* did stoop,
And sate on further side aslope.
This *Talgol* viewing, who had now
By flight escap'd the fatal blow,
He rally'd, and again fell to't;
For catching him by nearer foot,   860
He lifted with such might and strength,
As would have hurl'd him thrice his length,
And dash'd his brains (if any) out.
But *Mars*, that still protects the stout,
In Pudding-time came to his aid,
And under him the *Bear* convey'd;
The *Bear*, upon whose soft fur-gown
The *Knight* with all his weight fell down.
The friendly rug preserv'd the Ground,
And headlong *Knight* from bruise or wound: 870
Like feather-bed betwixt a Wall,
And heavy brunt of Cannon-ball.
As *Sancho* on a blanket fell,
And had no hurt; ours far'd as well
In body, though his mighty Spirit,
B'ing heavy, did not so well bear it.
The *Bear* was in a greater fright,
Beat down and worsted by the *Knight*.
He roar'd, and rag'd, and flung about,
To shake off bondage from his snout.   880

846 The wrong done to his *C*: And feel regret on *A*   849–50 Smart, | And
raging Pain, th'afflicted Part *C*: Thistle, | That gall'd him sorely under his tail. *A*
853 still,] still *C*   854–5 Champions Steed a thump, | That staggar'd him *C*:
Knight's Steed such a thump, | As made him reel *A*   860 him *C*: foe *A*

His wrath enflam'd boil'd o're, and from
His Jaws of Death he threw the fome.
Fury in stranger postures threw him,
And more, then ever Herauld drew him.
He tore the Earth, which he had sav'd
From squelch of *Knight*, and storm'd, and rav'd;
And vext the more, because the harms
He felt were 'gainst the *Law of Arms*:
For Men he always took to be
His friends, and Dogs the enemy: 890
Who never so much hurt had done him,
As his own side did falling on him.
It griev'd him to the Guts, that they
For whom h' had fought so many a fray,
And serv'd with loss of bloud so long,
Should offer such inhumane wrong;
Wrong of unsouldier-like condition:
For which he flung down his Commission,
And laid about him, till his Nose
From thrall of Ring and Cord broke loose.   900
Soon as he felt himself enlarg'd,
Through thickest of his foes he charg'd,
And made way through th'amazed crew.
Some he o'reran, and some o'rethrew,
But took none; for by hasty flight
He strove t'avoid the conquering *Knight*,
From whom he fled with as much haste
And dread as he the Rabble chac'd.
In haste he fled, and so did they,
Each and his fear a sev'ral way.   910

Crowdero onely kept the field,
Not stirring from the place he held,
Though beaten down and wounded sore
I'th' Fiddle, and a Leg that bore
One side of him, not that of bone,
But, much its betters, th' wooden one.
He spying *Hudibras* lye strow'd
Upon the ground, like log of wood,

906 t'avoid the conquering *C*: t'escape pursuit of *A*

With fright of fall, supposed wound,
And loss of Urine, in a swound,   920
In haste he snatch'd the wooden limb
That hurt in th'ankle lay by him,
And fitting it for sudden fight,
Straight drew it up, t'attack the *Knight*.
For getting up on stump and huckle,
He with the foe began to buckle,
Vowing to be reveng'd for breach
Of Crowd and Shin upon the wretch,
Sole author of all Detriment
He and his Fiddle underwent.   930
But *Ralpho* (who had now begun
T'adventure resurrection
From heavy squelch, and had got up
Upon his legs with sprained Crup)
Looking about beheld the Bard
To charge the *Knight* intranc'd prepard.
He snatch't his Whiniard up, that fled
When he was falling off his Steed,
(As Rats do from a falling house,)
To hide it self from rage of blows;   940
And wing'd with speed and fury, flew
To rescue *Knight* from black and blew.
Which e're he could atchieve, his Sconce
The Leg encounter'd twice and once;
And now 'twas rais'd, to smite agen,
When *Ralpho* thrust himself between.
He took the blow upon his arm,
To shield the *Knight* from further harm;
And joining wrath with force, bestow'd
On th' wooden member such a load,   950
That down it fell, and with it bore
Crowdero, whom it propp'd before.
To him the *Squire* right nimbly run,
And setting his bold foot upon

920 in a swound *C*: cast in sownd *A*   923 fitting *C*: lifting *A*   924 t'attack
the *C*: to fall on *A*   928 Shin *C*: skin *A*   935–6 about . . . prepard, *C*:
about, beheld pernicion | Approaching *Knight* from fell Musician. *A*   944 Leg
C: Skin *A1*: Shin *A2–A5*   947 upon his *C*: on side and *A*   948 from
further *C*: entraunc'd from *A*   954 his bold *C*: conquering *A*

His trunk, thus spoke: What *desp'rate Frenzie*
Made thee (thou whelp of Sin) to fancy
Thy self and all that Coward Rabble
T'encounter us in battel able?
How durst th', I say, oppose thy Curship
'Gainst Arms, Authority and Worship?   960
And *Hudibras*, or me provoke,
Though all thy Limbs were heart of Oke,
And th'other half of thee as good
To bear out blows as that of Wood?
Could not the whipping-post prevail
With all its rhet'rick, nor the Gaol,
To keep from flaying scourge thy skin,
And ankle free from Iron gin?
Which now thou shalt—but first our care
Must see how *Hudibras* doth fare.   970
This said, He gently rais'd the *Knight*,
And set him on his Bum upright:
To rouze him from Lethargick dump,
He tweak'd his Nose with gentle thump,
Knock'd on his breast, as if't had been
To raise the Spirits lodg'd within.
They wakened with the noise, did flye
From inward Room to Window eye,
And gently op'ning lid, the Casement,
Lookt out, but yet with some amazement.   980
This gladded *Ralpho* much to see,
Who thus bespoke the *Knight*: quoth he,
Tweaking his nose, You are, great Sir,
A *self-denying* Conqueror;
As high, victorious and great,
As e're fought for the Churches yet,
If you will give your self but leave
To make out what y' already have;
That's Victory. The foe, for dread
Of your Nine-worthiness, is fled,   990
All save *Crowdero*, for whose sake
You did th'espous'd *Cause* undertake:

964 out *A1, A4, A5, C*: our *A2, A3*

And he lies pris'ner at your feet,
To be dispos'd as you think meet,
Either for life, or death, or sale,
The Gallows, or perpetual Jayl.
For one wink of your pow'rful eye
Must sentence him to live, or dye.
His Fiddle is your proper purchace,
Wone in the Service of the *Churches*;　　　　1000
And by your doom must be allow'd
To be, or be no more, a *Crowd*.
For though success did not confer
Just Title on the Conquerer;
Though *dispensations* were not strong
Conclusions whether right or wrong;
Although *Out-goings* did not confirm,
And *Owning* were but a meer term:
Yet as the *wicked* have no *right*
To th' *Creature*, though usurp'd by might,　　　　1010
The property is in the *Saint*,
From whom th' injuriously detain't;
Of him they hold their Luxuries,
Their Dogs, their Horses, Whores and Dice,
Their Riots, Revels, Masks, Delights,
Pimps, Buffoons, Fidlers, Parasites:
All which the *Saints* have *title* to,
And ought t'enjoy, if th' had their due.
What we take from them is no more
Then what was ours by right before.　　　　1020
For we are their true *Landlords* still,
And they our *Tenants* but at will.

At this the *Knight* begun to rouse,
And by degrees grow valorous.
He star'd about, and seeing none
Of all his foes remain but one,
He snatch'd his weapon that lay near him,
And from the ground began to rear him;
Vowing to make *Crowdero* pay
For all the rest that ran away.　　　　1030

But *Ralpho* now in colder bloud,
His fury mildly thus withstood:
Great Sir, quoth he, your mighty Spirit
Is rais'd too high, this Slave does merit
To be the Hangman's bus'ness, sooner
Then from your hand to have the honour
Of his Destruction. I that am
So much below in deed and name,
Did scorn to hurt his forfeit Carcass,
Or ill intreat his Fiddle or Case.   1040
Will you, Great Sir, that glory blot
In cold bloud which you gain'd in hot?
Wil you employ your Conqu'ring Sword,
To break a Fiddle and your Word?
For though I fought, and overcame,
And quarter gave, 'twas in your name.
For great Commanders alwayes own
What's prosperous by the Souldier done.
To save, where you have pow'r to kill,
Argues your Pow'r above your Will;   1050
And that your will and pow'r have less
Then both might have of selfishness.
This pow'r which now alive with dread
He trembles at, if he were dead,
Would no more keep the slave in awe
Then if you were a Knight of Straw:
For death would then be his Conqueror,
Not you, and free him from that terror.
If danger from his life accrew,
Or honour from his death to you;   1060
'Twere Policy, and honour too,
To doe as you resolv'd to doe.
But, Sir, 'twould wrong your Valor much,
To say it needs or fears a Crutch.
Great Conquerors greater glory gain
By foes in Triumph led, then slain:
The Lawrells that adorn their brows
Are pull'd from living, not dead boughs,

1038 So much below *C*: A Nothingness *A*

And living foes; the greatest fame
Of Cripple slain can be but lame.   1070
One half of him's already slain,
The other is not worth your pain.
Th'Honour can but on one side light,
As Worship did, when y' were dub'd *Knight*.
Wherefore I think it better far,
To keep him Prisoner of War;
And let him fast in bonds abide,
At *Court of Justice* to be try'd:
Where if h' appear so bold or crafty,
There may be danger in his safety;   1080
If any Member there dislike
His Face, or to his Beard have pike;
Or if his death will save, or yield,
Revenge, or fright, it is *reveal'd*,
Though he has quarter, ne'retheless
Y' have pow'r to hang him when you please.
This hath been often done by some
Of our great Conquerors, you know whom:
And has by most of us been held
Wise Justice, and to some *reveal'd*.   1090
For Words and promises that yoke
The Conquerour, are quickly broke,
Like *Sampson*'s Cuffs, though by his own
Direction and advice put on.
For if we should fight for the *Cause*
By rules of military Lawes,
And onely doe what they call just,
The *Cause* would quickly fall to dust.
This we among our selves may speak,
But to the *Wicked* or the Weak   1100
We must be cautious to declare
Perfection-truths, such as these are.

This said, the high outragious mettle
Of *Knight* began to cool and settle.
He lik'd the *Squire*'s advice, and soon
Resolv'd to see the bus'ness done:

1069 foes; *As*: foes *A1–A4, C*

And therefore charg'd him first to bind
Crowdero's hands on rump behind,
And to its former place and use
The Wooden member to reduce: 1110
But force it take an *Oath* before,
Ne're to bear arms against him more.

Ralpho dispatch'd with speedy haste,
And having ty'd *Crowdero* fast,
He gave Sir *Knight* the end of Cord,
To lead the Captive of his sword
In triumph, while the Steeds he caught,
And them to further service brought.
The *Squire* in state rode on before,
And on his nut-brown Whiniard bore   1120
The Trophee-*Fiddle* and the *Case*,
Plac'd on his shoulder like a Mace.
The *Knight* himself did after ride,
Leading *Crowdero* by his side,
And tow'd him, if he lagg'd behind,
Like Boat against the Tide and Wind.
Thus grave and solemn they march on,
Until quite through the Town th' had gone:
At further end of which there stands
An ancient Castle, that commands   1130
Th'adjacent parts; in all the fabrick
You shall not see one stone nor a brick,
But all of Wood, by pow'rfull Spell
Of Magick made impregnable.
There's neither Iron-bar, nor Gate,
Port-cullis, Chain, nor Bolt, nor Grate:
And yet men durance there abide,
In Dungeon scarce three inches wide;
With Roof so low, that under it
They never stand, but lie, or sit: 1140
And yet so foul, that whoso is in,
Is to the middle-leg in prison,
In Circle Magical confin'd,
With walls of subtle Air and Wind,

1122 Plac'd on his *C*: Leaning on *A*   1136 nor Bolt, nor *C*: or Bolt, or *A*

Which none are able to break thorough,
Until th' are freed by head of Burrough.
Thither arriv'd, th'advent'rous *Knight*
And bold *Squire* from their Steeds alight,
At th'outward wall, near which there stands
A Bastile, built t'imprison hands;   1150
By strange enchantment made to fetter
The lesser parts, and free the greater.
For though the Body may creep through,
The Hands in Grate are fast enough.
And when a circle 'bout the wrist
Is made by Beadle Exorcist,
The Body feels the Spur and Switch,
As if 'twere ridden Post by Witch
At twenty miles an houer pace,
And yet ne're stirs out of the place.   1160
On top of this there is a Spire,
On which Sir *Knight* first bids the *Squire*
The *Fiddle*, and its Spoils, the *Case*,
In manner of a Trophee, place.
That done, they ope the Trap-dore-gate,
And let *Crowdero* down thereat.
Crowdero making doleful face,
Like Hermit poor in pensive place,
To Dungeon they the wretch commit,
And the survivor of his feet: 1170
But th'other, that had broke the peace,
And head of Knighthood, they release,
Though a *Delinquent* false and forged,
Yet b'ing a Stranger, he's enlarged;
While his Comrade, that did no hurt,
Is clapt up fast in prison for't.
So Justice, while she winks at Crimes,
Stumbles on Innocence sometimes.

1158 'witch *A, C*   1159 houer *A1–A4*: hours *A5*: hour *C*

THE FIRST PART

CANTO III

THE ARGUMENT

The scatter'd Rout return and rally,
Surround the Place; the Knight *does sally,*
And is made Pris'ner: then they seize
Th'Inchanted Fort by storm, release
Crowdero, *and put the* Squire *in's place.*
I should have first said, Hudibras.

AY me! what perils do inviron
The man that meddles with cold Iron!
What plaguy mischiefs and mishaps
Do dog him still with after-claps!
For though Dame Fortune seem to smile
And leer upon him for a while;
She'l after shew him, in the nick
Of all his Glories, a Dog-trick.
This any man may sing or say
I'th' Ditty call'd, *What if a Day.*   10
For *Hudibras,* who thought h' had won
The Field as certain as a Gun,
And having routed the whole troop,
With Victory was Cock-a hoop;
Thinking h' had done enough to purchase
Thanksgiving-day among the *Churches,*
Wherein his Mettle and brave Worth
Might be explain'd by *Holder-forth,*
And register'd by fame eternal,
In Deathless Pages of *Diurnal*;   20
Found in few minutes, to his Cost,
He did but *Count without his Host*;

12 certain C: suer A   15 Thinking] Think C1: Thinks C2

And that a *Turn-stile* is more certain,
Then in events of War Dame Fortune.

For now, the late-faint-hearted Rout
O'rethrown and scatter'd round about,
Chac'd by the horrour of their fear
From bloudy fray of *Knight* and *Bear*,
(All but the *Dogs*, who in pursuit
Of the *Knight*'s Victory stood to't,　　　30
And most ignobly sought to get
The Honour of his bloud and sweat)
Seeing the coast was free and clear
O'th' Conquer'd and the Conquerer,
Took heart again, and fac'd about,
As if they meant to stand it out:
For now the half-defeated *Bear*
Attack'd by th'enemy i'th' rear,
Finding their number grew too great
For him to make a safe retreat,　　　40
Like a bold Chieftain fac'd about;
But wisely doubting to hold out,
Gave way to fortune, and with haste
Fac'd the proud foe, and fled, and fac'd,
Retiring still, until he found
H' had got th'advantage of the Ground;
And then as valiantly made head,
To check the foe, and forthwith fled;
Leaving no Art untry'd, nor Trick
Of Warrior stout and Politick.　　　50
Until in spight of hot pursuit,
He gain'd a Pass, to hold dispute
On better terms, and stop the course
Of the proud foe. With all his force
He bravely charg'd, and for a while
Forc'd their whole Body to recoil:
But still their numbers so encreast,
He found himself at length opprest,

---

35 again *C*: of grace *A1*: at grasse *A2–A5*　　37 now the half-defeated *C*:
by this time, the routed *A*

And all evasions so uncertain,
To save himself for better fortune,   60
That he resolv'd, rather then yield,
To die with honour in the field,
And sell his hyde and carcase at
A price as high and desperate
As e're he could. This Resolution
He forthwith put in execution,
And bravely threw himself among
The enemy i'th' greatest throng.
But what could single valour doe
Against so numerous a foe?   70
Yet much he did, indeed too much
To be believ'd, where th'odds was such:
But one against a multitude,
Is more then mortal can make good.
For while one party he oppos'd,
His Rear was suddenly enclos'd,
And no room left him for retreat,
Or fight against a foe so great.
For now the Mastives charging home
To blows and handy-gripes were come;   80
While manfully himself he bore,
And setting his right-foot before,
He rais'd himself, to shew how tall
His Person was, above them all.
This equal shame and envy stirr'd
In th'enemy, that one should beard
So many Warriors and so stout
As he had done, and stand it out,
Disdaining to lay down his Arms,
And yield on honourable terms.   90
Enraged thus some in the rear
Attack'd him, and some ev'ry where;
Till down he fell, yet falling fought,
And being down still laid about;
As *Widdrington* in doleful Dumps
Is said to fight upon his stumps.

88 stand *A2–A4*, *C*: stav'd *A1*, *A5*

But all, alas! had been in vain,
And he inevitably slain,
If *Trulla* and *Cerdon* in the nick
To rescue him had not been quick.   100
For *Trulla*, who was light of foot,
As shafts which long-field *Parthians* shoot,
(But not so light as to be born
Upon the ears of standing Corn,
Or trip it o're the Water quicker
Then Witches when their staves they liquor,
As some report) was got among
The foremost of the Martial throng;
Where pittying the vanquisht *Bear*,
She call'd to *Cerdon*, who stood near   110
Viewing the bloudy fight, to whom,
Shall we (quoth she) stand still *hum drum*,
And see stout *Bruin* all alone
By numbers basely overthrown?
Such feats already h' has atchiev'd,
In story not to be believ'd:
And 'twould to us be shame enough,
Not to attempt to fetch him off.

I would (quoth he) venture a Limb
To second thee, and rescue him: 120
But then we must about it straight,
Or else our aid will come too late.
Quarter he scorns, he is so stout,
And therefore cannot long hold out.
This said, they wav'd their weapons round
About their heads, to clear the ground;
And joyning forces laid about
So fiercely, that th'amazed rout
Turn'd tail again, and straight begun,
As if *the Devil drove*, to run.   130
Meanwhile th' approach'd the place where *Bruin*
Was now engag'd to mortal ruine:
The conquering foe they soon assail'd;
First *Trulla* stav'd, and *Cerdon* tail'd,

134 Staving and Tayling are terms of Art usd in the *Bear-Garden*, and signify there

Until the Mastives loos'd their hold:
And yet, alas! doe what they could,
The worsted *Bear* came off with store
Of bloudy wounds, but all before.
For as *Achilles* dipt in Pond,
Was *anabaptiz'd* free from wound,   140
Made proof against dead-doing steel
All over but the Pagan heel:
So did our Champion's Arms defend
All of him but the other end,
His head and ears, which in the Martial
Encounter lost a leathern parcel.
For as an *Austrian Archduke* once
Had one ear (which in *Ducatoons*
Is half the Coin) in Battel par'd
Close to his head; so *Bruin* far'd: 150
But tugg'd and pull'd on th'other side,
Like *Scrivener* newly crucify'd;
Or like the late-corrected Leathern
Ears of the *circumcised Brethren.*
But gentle *Trulla* into th' ring
He wore in's nose convey'd a string,
With which she marcht before, and led
The Warrior to a grassy Bed,
As Authors write, in a cool shade,
Which Eglentine and Roses made,   160
Close by a softly-murm'ring stream
Where Lovers us'd to loll and dream.
There leaving him to his repose,
Secured from pursuit of foes,
And wanting nothing but a Song,
And a well-tun'd *Theorbo* hung
Upon a Bough, to ease the pain
His tugg'd ears suffer'd, with a strain.

only the parting of *Dogs* and *Bears*: though they are us'd Metaphorically in several
other Professions, for moderating, as Law, Divinity, Hectoring, *&c.*
153-4 *Prynn, Bastwyck,* and *Burton,* who laid down their Ears as Proxies for three
Professions of the Godly Party, who not long after maintain'd their Right and Title
to the Pillory, to be as good and lawful, as theirs, who first of all took possession of
it in their Names.

135 the] their *C*

They both drew up, to march in quest
Of his great Leader, and the rest.   170

For *Orsin* (who was more renown'd
For stout maintaining of his ground
In standing fights then for pursuit,
As being not so quick of foot)
Was not long able to keep pace
With others that pursu'd the Chace,
But found himself left far behind,
Both out of heart and out of wind;
Griev'd to behold his *Bear* pursu'd
So basely by a multitude,   180
And like to fall, not by the prowess,
But numbers of his Coward foes.
He rag'd and kept as heavy a coil as
Stout *Hercules* for loss of *Hylas*,
Forcing the Vallies to repeat
The Accents of his sad regret.
He beat his breast, and tore his hair,
For loss of his dear Crony *Bear*:
That Echo from the hollow ground
His doleful wailings did resound   190
More wistfully, by many times,
Then in small Poets splay-foot rimes,
That make her, in their ruthful stories,
To answer to inter'gatories,
And most unconscionably depose
To things of which she nothing knows:
And when she has said all she can say,
'Tis wrested to the Lover's fancy.
Quoth he, O whether, wicked *Bruin*,
Art thou fled to my—Echo, *ruine*?   200
I thought th' hadst scorn'd to budge a step,
For fear. (Quoth Echo) *Marry guep*.
Am not I here to take thy part?
Then what has quail'd thy stubborn heart?
Have these bones rattled, and this head
So often in thy quarrel bled?
Nor did I ever winch or grudge it,

For thy dear sake. (Quoth she) *Mum budget.*
Think'st thou 'twill not be laid i'th' dish,
Thou turn'dst thy back? Quoth Echo, *Pish.* 210
To run from those th' hadst overcome
Thus cowardly? Quoth Echo, *Mum.*
But what a-vengeance makes thee flie
From me too, as thine enemy?
Or if thou hast no thought of me
Nor what I have endur'd for thee,
Yet shame and honour might prevail
To keep thee thus from turning tail:
For who would grutch to spend his bloud in
His honor's cause? Quoth she, *a Puddin.* 220
This said, his grief to anger turn'd,
Which in his manly stomack burn'd;
Thirst of Revenge and Wrath, in place
Of Sorrow, now began to blaze.
He vow'd the Authors of his woe
Should equal vengeance undergo;
And with their bones and flesh pay dear
For what he suffer'd and his Bear.
This b'ing resolv'd, with equal speed
And rage he hasted to proceed 230
To action straight, and giving o're
To search for *Bruin* any more,
He went in quest of *Hudibras,*
To find him out, where e're he was:
And if he were above ground, vow'd
He'd ferret him, lurk where he wou'd.

But scarce had he a furlong on
This resolute adventure gone,
When he encounter'd with that Crew
Whom *Hudibras* did late subdue. 240
Honour, Revenge, Contempt and Shame,
Did equally their breasts enflame.
'Mong these the fierce *Magnano* was,
And *Talgol* foe to *Hudibras*;

227 their *C*: his *A*

Cerdon and *Colon*, Warriors stout
And resolute as ever fought:
Whom furious *Orsin* thus bespoke,

Shall we (quoth he) thus basely brook
The vile affront, that paultry Ass
And feeble *Scoundrel Hudibras*,   250
With that more paultry *Ragamuffin*
Ralpho, with vapouring and huffing
Have put upon us, like tame Cattel,
As if th' had routed us in battel?
For my part, it shall ne're be sed,
I for the washing gave my head:
Nor did I turn my back for fear
Of them, but loosing of my *Bear*,
Which now I'm like to undergo;
For whether these fell wounds, or no,   260
He has receiv'd in fight are mortal,
Is more then all my skill can fortel.
Nor do *I know* what is become
Of him, *more then the Pope of Rome.*
But if I can but find them out
That caus'd it, (as I shall no doubt,
Where e're th' in Hugger-mugger lurk)
I'le make them rue their handy-work;
And wish that they had rather dar'd,
To *pull the Devil by the Beard.*   270

Quoth *Cerdon*, Noble *Orsin*, th' hast
Great reason to doe as thou say'st;
And so has ev'ry body here
As well as thou hast or thy Bear.
Others may doe as they see good;
But if this Twig be made of wood
That will hold tack, I'le make the fur
Flie 'bout the eares of that old Cur,
And th'other mungrel Vermin, *Ralph*,
That brav'd us all in his behalf.   280

Thy Bear is safe and out of peril,
Though lugg'd indeed, and wounded very ill.
My self and *Trulla* made a shift
To help him out at a dead lift;
And having brought him bravely off,
Have left him where he's safe enough.
There let him rest; for if we stay,
The Slaves may hap to get away.

This said, they all engag'd to joyn
Their forces in the same design: 290
And forthwith put themselves in search
Of *Hudibras* upon their march.
Where leave we them a while, to tell
What the Victorious *Knight* befell:
For such, *Crowdero* being fast
In Dungeon shut, we left him last.

Triumphant Laurels seem'd to grow
No where so green as on his brow:
Laden with which, as well as tir'd
With conquering toil, he now retir'd   300
Unto a neighb'ring Castle by,
To rest his body, and apply
Fit med'cines to each glorious bruise
He got in fight, *Reds*, *blacks*, and *blews*;
To mollifie th'uneasie pang
Of ev'ry honourable bang.
Which b'ing by skilful Midwife drest,
He laid him down to take his rest.

But all in vain. H' had got a hurt
O'th' inside, of a deadlier sort,   310
By *Cupid* made, who took his stand
Upon a Widow's joynture-land,
(For he, in all his amorous battels,
No 'dvantage finds like goods and chattels)
Drew home his Bow, and aiming right,
Let fly an Arrow at the *Knight*:

315 Drew . . . Bow *C*: As now he did *A*   316 Let . . . the *C*: An Arrow
he let flie at *A*

The shaft against a rib did glance,
And gall him in the *Purtenance.*
But time had somewhat swag'd his pain,
After he found his suit in vain.   320
For that proud Dame, for whom his soul
Was burnt in's belly like a coal,
(That Belly that so oft did ake
And suffer griping for her sake,
Till purging Comfits and Ants eggs
Had almost brought him off his leggs)
Us'd him so like a base *Rascallion,*
That old *Pyg-* (what d'y' call him?) *malion,*
That cut his Mistress out of stone,
Had not so hard-a-hearted one.   330
She had a thousand jadish tricks,
Worse then a Mule that flings and kicks:
'Mong which one cross-grain'd freak she had,
As insolent as strange and mad:
She could love none but onely such
As scorn'd and hated her as much.
'Twas a strange Riddle of a Lady;
Not love, if any lov'd her? ha day!
So Cowards never use their might,
But against such as will not fight.   340
So some diseases have been found
Onely to seize upon the sound.
He that gets her by heart must say her
The back-way, like a Witche's prayer.
Meanwhile the *Knight* had no small task,
To compass what he durst not ask.
He loves, but dares not make the motion;
Her *ignorance* is his *devotion.*
Like Caitiff vile, that for misdeed
Rides with his face to rump of Steed,   350
Or rowing Scull, he's fain to love,
Look one way, and another move;
Or like a Tumbler that does play
His game, and look another way,
Until he seize upon the Coney:
Just so does he by Matrimony.

But all in vain: her subtle snout
Did quickly wind his meaning out;
Which she return'd with too much scorn,
To be by man of Honour born.   360
Yet much he bore, until the distress
He suffer'd from his spightful Mistress
Did stir his stomack, and the Pain
He had endur'd from her disdain
Turn'd to regret, so resolute,
That he resolv'd to wave his suit,
And either to renounce her quite,
Or for a while play least in sight.
This Resolution b'ing put on,
He kept some months, and more had done;   370
But being brought so nigh by fate,
The Victory he atchiev'd so late
Did set his thoughts agog, and ope
A dore to discontinu'd hope,
That seem'd to promise he might win
His Dame too now his hand was in;
And that his valour and the honour
H' had newly gain'd might work upon her.
These reasons made his mouth to water
With amorous longings to be at her.   380

Thought he unto himself, Who knows
But this brave Conquest o're my foes
May reach her heart, and make that stoop,
As I but now have forc'd the Troop?
If nothing can oppugne love,
And Vertue invious wayes can prove,
What may not he confide to doe
That brings both love and vertue too?
But thou bring'st Valour too and wit,
Two things that seldome fail to hit.   390
Valour's a mouse-trap, wit a gin,
Which women oft are taken in.
Then, *Hudibras*, why shouldst thou fear
To be, that art a Conquerer?

381 Thought *C*: Quoth *A*

Fortune th'audacious doth *juvare*,
But lets the timidous miscarry.
Then while the honour thou hast got
Is spick and span-new, piping hot,
Strike her up bravely thou hadst best,
And trust thy fortune with the rest.   400

Such thoughts as these the *Knight* did keep,
More then his bangs or fleas, from sleep.
And as an Owl that in a Barn
Sees a Mouse creeping in the Corn,
Sits still, and shuts his round blew eyes,
As if he slept, until he spies
The little beast within his reach,
Then starts, and seizes on the wretch:
So from his Couch the *Knight* did start,
To seize upon the Widow's heart;   410
Crying with hasty tone and hoarse,
Ralpho, dispatch, To horse, to horse.
And 'twas but time, for now the Rout
We left engag'd to seek him out,
By speedy marches werc advanc'd
Up to the fort where he ensconc'd,
And had all th'avenues possest
About the place, from East to West.

That done, awhile they made a halt,
To view the Ground, and where t'assault: 420
Then call'd a Councel, which was best,
By siege or onslaught, to invest
The enemy: and 'twas agreed,
By storm and onslaught to proceed.
This b'ing resolv'd, in comely sort,
They now drew up t'attack the fort.
When *Hudibras*, about to enter
Upon another gate's adventure,
To *Ralpho* call'd aloud to arm,
Not dreaming of approaching storm.   430
Whether Dame Fortune, or the care
Of Angel bad, or Tutelar,

Did arm, or thrust him on a danger,
To which he was an utter stranger;
That Foresight might, or might not blot
The glory he had newly got;
Or to his shame it might be sed,
They took him napping in his bed:
To them we leave it to expound,
That deal in Sciences profound.　　　　440

His Courser scarce he had bestrid,
And *Ralpho* that on which he rid,
When setting ope the Postern gate,
To take the Field and sally at,
The Foe appear'd, drawn up and drill'd,
Ready to charge them in the field.
This somewhat startled the bold *Knight*,
Surpriz'd with th'unexpected sight.
The bruises of his bones and flesh
He thought began to smart afresh:　　　　450
Till recollecting wonted Courage,
His fear was soon converted to rage.
And thus he spoke: The Coward Foe,
Whom we but now gave quarter to,
Look, yonder's rally'd, and appears,
As if they had outrun their fears.
The Glory we did lately get,
The fates command us to repeat.
And to their wills we must succumb,
Quocunque trahunt, 'tis our doom.　　　　460
This is the same numerick Crew
Which we so lately did subdue,
The self-same individuals that
Did run, as Mice do from a Cat,
When we couragiously did wield
Our martial weapons in the field,
To tug for Victory: and when
We shall our shining blades agen
Brandish in terrour o're our heads,
They'l straight resume their wonted dreads.　　　　470

444 To ... and *C*: Which they thought best to *A*

Fear is an Ague, that forsakes
And haunts by fits those whom it takes.
And they'l opine they feel the pain
And blows, they felt to day, again.
Then let us boldly charge them home,
And make no doubt to overcome.

This said, his Courage to enflame,
He call'd upon his *Mistress* name.
His Pistol next he cockt anew,
And out his nut-brown whiniard drew.   480
And placing *Ralpho* in the front,
Reserv'd himself to bear the brunt;
As expert Warriors use: then ply'd
With Iron-heel his Courser's side,
Conveying Sympathetick speed
From heel of *Knight* to heel of Steed.

Meanwhile the foe with equal rage
And speed advancing to engage,
Both Parties now were drawn so close,
Almost to come to handiblows.   490
When *Orsin* first let flie a stone
At *Ralpho*; not so huge a one
As that which *Diomed* did maul
Æneas on the Bum withall:
Yet big enough, if rightly hurl'd,
T'have sent him to another world;
Whether above-ground, or below,
Which *Saints twice dipt* are destin'd to.
The danger startled the bold *Squire*,
And made him some few steps retire.   500
But *Hudibras* advanc'd to's aid,
And rouz'd his spirits half dismayd.
He, wisely doubting lest the shot
Of th'enemy, now growing hot,
Might at a distance gall, prest close,
To come, pell-mell, to handiblows:

472 fits *C*: turns *A*

And that he might their aim decline,
Advanc'd still in an oblique line;
But prudently forbore to fire,
Till breast to breast he had got nigher: 510
As expert Warriors use to doe,
When hand to hand they charge the foe.
This order the advent'rous *Knight*
Most Souldierlike observ'd in fight:
When Fortune (as she's wont) turn'd fickle
And for the foe began to stickle.
The more shame for her *goody-ship*,
To give so near a friend the slip.
For *Colon* chusing out a stone,
Levell'd so right, it thumpt upon   520
His manly panch with such a force,
As almost beat him off his horse.
He loos'd his weapon, and the reyn;
But laying fast hold on the mane,
Preserv'd his seat: And as a Goose
In death contracts his talons close;
So did the *Knight*, and with one claw
The tricker of his Pistol draw.
The Gun went off: and as it was
Still fatal to stout *Hudibras*,   530
In all his feats of Arms, when least
He dreamt of it, to prosper best;
So now he far'd: the Shot let flie
At randome 'mong the enemy,
Pierc'd *Talgol*'s Gabberdine, and grazing
Upon his shoulder, in the passing
Lodg'd in *Magnano*'s brass Habergeon,
Who straight *A Surgeon* cry'd, *a Surgeon*.
He tumbled down, and as he fell,
Did *Murther, murther, murther* yell.   540
This startled their whole body so,
That if the *Knight* had not let go
His Arms, but been in warlike plight,
H' had won (the second time) the fight.

As if the *Squire* had but faln on,
He had inevitably done:
But he, diverted with the care
Of *Hudibras* his wound, forbare
To press th'advantage of his fortune,
While danger did the rest dishearten.   550
He had with *Cerdon* been engag'd
In close encounter, which both wag'd
So desp'rately, 'twas hard to say
Which side was like to get the day.
And now the busie work of death
Had tir'd them so, th' agreed to breath,
Preparing to renew the fight;
When the disaster of the *Knight*
And th'other party did divert
And force their sullen Rage to part.   560
Ralpho prest up to *Hudibras*,
And *Cerdon* where *Magnano* was;
Each striving to confirm his party
With stout encouragements and hearty.
Quoth *Ralpho*, Courage, valiant Sir,
And let revenge and honour stir
Your spirits up, once more fall on,
The shatter'd foe begins to run:
For if but half so well you knew
To use your Victory as subdue,   570
They durst not, after such a blow
As you have giv'n them, face us now;
But from so formidable a Souldier
Had fled like Crows when they smel powder.
Thrice have they seen your Sword aloft
Wav'd o're their heads, and fled as oft.
But if you let them recollect
Their spirits, now dismay'd and checkt,
You'l have a harder game to play,
Then yet y' have had, to get the day.   580

545 As . . . on, *C*: As *Ralpho* might; but he with care *A*   546–7 *added in C*
548 wound, *C*: hurt *A*   551 He . . . been *C*: For he with *Cerdon* b'ing *A*
552 which *C*: they *A*   553 So desp'rately *C*: The fight so well *A*
558 When the] When th' hard th' *C*   560 And . . . to *C*: Their fell intent,
and forc'd them *A*

Thus spoke the stout *Squire*; but was heard
Of *Hudibras* with small regard.
His thoughts were fuller of the bang
He lately took, then *Ralph*'s harangue;
To which he answer'd, Cruel fate
Tells me thy Counsel comes too late.
The knotted bloud within my hose,
That from my wounded body flows,
With mortal *Crisis* doth portend
My dayes to appropinque an end.   590
I am for action now unfit,
Either of fortitude or wit.
Fortune my foe begins to frown,
Resolv'd to pull my stomack down.
I am not apt upon a wound,
Or trivial basting, to despond:
Yet I'd be loth my dayes to curtal.
For if I thought my wounds not mortal,
Or that we'd time enough as yet
To make an honourable retreat,   600
'Twere the best course: but if they find
We flie, and leave our Arms behind,
For them to seize on, the dishonour
And danger too is such, I'le sooner
Stand to it boldly, and take quarter,
To let them see I am no starter.
In all the trade of War, no feat
Is nobler then a brave retreat.
For those that Run away, and fly,
Take Place at least of th'enemy.   610

This said, the *Squire* with active speed
Dismounted from his bony Steed,
To seize the Arms which by mischance
Fell from the bold *Knight* in a trance.
These being found out, and restor'd
To *Hudibras*, their natural Lord,
The active *Squire* with might and main

Prepar'd in haste to mount again.
Thrice he assay'd to mount aloft;
But by his weighty bum as oft   620
He was pull'd back: till having found
Th'advantage of the rising ground,
Thither he led his warlike steed,
And having plac'd him right, with speed
Prepar'd again to scale the beast.
When *Orsin*, who had newly drest
The bloudy scar upon the shoulder
Of *Talgol* with *Promethean* powder,
And now was searching for the shot
That laid *Magnano* on the spot,   630
Beheld the sturdy *Squire* aforesaid
Preparing to climb up his horse-side.
He left his Cure, and laying hold
Upon his Arms, with Courage bold
Cry'd out, 'Tis now no time to dally,
The enemy begins to rally:
Let us that are unhurt and whole
Fall on, and happy man be's dole.

This said, like to a thunderbolt
He flew, with fury, to th'assault,   640
Striving the enemy to attack
Before he reacht his horse's back.
Ralpho was mounted now, and gotten
O'rethwart his Beast with active vauting,
Wrigling his body to recover
His seat, and cast his right leg over;
When *Orsin* rushing in, bestow'd
On horse and man so heavy a load,
The Beast was startled, and begun
To kick and fling like mad, and run,   650
Bearing the tough *Squire* like a Sack,
Or stout King *Richard*, on his back:
Till stumbleing he threw him down,
Sore bruis'd, and cast into a sown.

Meanwhile the *Knight* began to rouse
The sparkles of his wonted prowess;
He thrust his hand into his hose,
And found both by his eyes and nose,
'Twas onely Choler, and not bloud,
That from his wounded body flow'd.   660
This, with the hazard of the *Squire*,
Inflam'd him with despightful ire;
Courageously he fac'd about,
And drew his other Pistol out,
And now had half-way bent the Cock,
When *Cerdon* gave so fierce a shock,
With sturdy truncheon, thwart his arm,
That down it fell, and did no harm;
Then stoutly pressing on with speed,
Assay'd to pull him off his Steed.   670
The *Knight* his Sword had onely left,
With which he *Cerdon*'s head had cleft,
Or at the least cropt off a limb,
But *Orsin* came and rescu'd him.
He with his Launce attack'd the *Knight*
Upon his quarters opposite.
But as a Bark that in foul weather,
Toss'd by two adverse winds together,
Is bruis'd, and beaten to and fro,
And knows not which to turn him to: 680
So far'd the *Knight* between two foes,
And knew not which of them t'oppose.
Till *Orsin* charging with his Launce
At *Hudibras*, by spightful chance
Hit *Cerdon* such a bang, as stunn'd
And laid him flat upon the ground.
At this the *Knight* began to chear up,
And raising up himself on stirrup;
Cry'd out *Victoria*; lie thou there,
And I shall straight dispatch another,   690
To bear thee company in death:
But first I'le halt awhile and breath.

679 bruis'd,] bruis'd *C*

As well he might: for *Orsin* griev'd
At th' wound that *Cerdon* had receiv'd,
Ran to relieve him with his lore,
And cure the hurt he made before.
Meanwhile the *Knight* had wheel'd about,
To breath himself, and next find out
Th'advantage of the ground, where best
He might the ruffled foe infest.   700
This b'ing resolv'd, he spurr'd his Steed,
To run at *Orsin* with full speed,
While he was busie in the care
Of *Cerdon*'s wound, and unaware:
But he was quick, and had already
Unto the part apply'd remedy;
And seeing th'enemy prepar'd,
Drew up, and stood upon his guard.
Then like a Warrior right expert
And skilful in the martial art,   710
The subtle *Knight* straight made a halt,
And judg'd it best to stay th'assault,
Until he had reliev'd the *Squire*,
And then (in order) to retire;
Or, as occasion should invite,
With forces joyn'd renew the fight.
Ralpho by this time disentranc'd,
Upon his Bum himself advanc'd,
Though sorely bruis'd; his limbs all o're
With ruthless bangs were stiff and sore.   720
Right fain he would have got upon
His feet again, to get him gone;
When *Hudibras* to aid him came.

Quoth he, (and call'd him by his name)
Courage, the day at length is ours,
And we once more as Conquerours,
Have both the field and honour won,
The Foe is profligate and run:
I mean all such as can, for some
This hand hath sent to their long home;   730

And some ly spralling on the ground,
With many a gash and bloudy wound.
Cæsar himself could never say
He got two victories in a day,
As I have done, that can say, Twice I
In one day, *Veni, vidi, vici.*
The foe's so numerous, that we
Cannot so often *vincere*
As they *perire*, and yet enough
Be left to strike an after-blow.   740
Then lest they rally, and once more
Put us to fight the bus'ness o're,
Get up, and mount thy Steed, dispatch,
And let us both their motions watch.

Quoth *Ralph*, I should not, if I were
In case for action, now be here;
Nor have I turn'd my back, or hang'd
An Arse, for fear of being bang'd:
It was for you I got these harms,
Advent'ring to fetch off your Arms.   750
The blows and drubs I have receiv'd,
Have bruis'd my body, and bereav'd
My Limbs of strength: unless you stoop,
And reach your hand to pull me up,
I shall lie here, and be a prey
To those who now are run away.

That shalt thou not (quoth *Hudibras*:)
We read, the Ancients held it was
More honourable far *Servare*
Civem, then slay an adversary.   760
The one we oft to day have done;
The other shall dispatch anon.
And though th' art of a diff'rent Church,
I will not leave thee in the lurch.
This said, he jogg'd his good steed nigher,
And steer'd him gently toward the *Squier*:
Then bowing down his body stretcht
His hand out, and at *Ralpho* reacht;

When *Trulla*, whom he did not mind,
Charg'd him like Lightening behind.   770
She had been long in search about
Magnano's wound, to find it out:
But could find none, nor where the shot
That had so startled him was got.
But having found the worst was past,
She fell to her own work at last,
The Pillage of the Prisoners,
Which in all feats of Arms was hers:
And now to plunder *Ralph* she flew,
When *Hudibras* his hard fate drew   780
To succour him; for as he bow'd
To help him up, she laid a load
Of blows so heavy, and plac'd so well,
On th'other side, that down he fell.

Yield, *Scoundrel* base, (quoth she) or die;
Thy life is mine and liberty.
But if thou think'st I took thee tardy,
And dar'st presume to be so hardy,
To try thy fortune o're afresh,
I'le wave my title to thy flesh,   790
Thy Arms and baggage, now my right:
And if thou hast the heart to try't,
I'le lend thee back thy self awhile,
And once more for that carcase vile
Fight upon tick—Quoth *Hudibras*,
Thou offer'st nobly, valiant Lass,
And I shall take thee at thy word.
First let me rise, and take my sword;
That sword which has so oft this day
Through Squadrons of my foes made way,   800
And some to other worlds dispatcht,
Now with a feeble Spinster matcht,
Will blush with bloud ignoble stain'd,
By which no honour's to be gain'd.
But if thou'lt take m' advice in this,
Consider while thou may'st, what 'tis

778 in all feats] all in feat *C*

To interrupt a Victor's course,
B'opposing such a trivial force.
For if with Conquest I come off,
(And that I shall do sure enough)   810
Quarter thou canst not have nor grace,
By law of Arms, in such a case;
Both which I now do offer freely.

I scorn (quoth she) thou Coxcomb silly,
(Clapping her hand upon her breech,
To shew how much she priz'd his speech)
Quarter or Counsel from a foe:
If thou canst force me to it, do.
But lest it should again be sed,
When I have once more won thy head,   820
I took thee napping unprepar'd,
Arm, and betake thee to thy guard.

This said, she to her tackle fell,
And on the *Knight* let fall a peal
Of blows so fierce, and prest so home,
That he retir'd and follow'd 's bum.
Stand to't, quoth she, or yield to mercy;
It is not fighting *Arsie-versie*
Shall serve thy turn—This stirr'd his spleen
More then the danger he was in,   830
The blows he felt, or was to feel,
Although th' already made him reel.
Honour, despight, revenge and shame,
At once unto his stomack came;
Which fir'd it so, he rais'd his arm
Above his head, and rain'd a storm
Of blows so terrible and thick,
As if he meant to hash her quick.
But she upon her truncheon took them,
And by oblique diversion broke them;   840
Waiting an opportunity
To pay all back with usury.

820 won *A5, C*: wore *A1–A4*   827 mercy; *A2–A5*: mercy *A1, C*

Which long she fail'd not of, for now
The *Knight* with one dead-doing blow
Resolving to decide the fight,
And she with quick and cunning slight
Avoiding it, the force and weight
He charg'd upon it was so great,
As almost sway'd him to the ground.
No sooner she th'advantage found,   850
But in she flew, and seconding
With home-made thrust the heavy swing,
She laid him flat upon his side,
And mounting on his trunk a-stride,
Quoth she, I told thee what would come
Of all thy vapouring, base Scum.
Say, will the Law of Arms allow
I may have Grace, and Quarter now?
Or wilt thou rather break thy word,
And stain thine Honor, then thy Sword.   860
A Man of War to damn his Soul,
In basely breaking his Parole.
And when before the Fight, th' hadst vow'd
To give no Quarter in cold bloud:
Now thou hast got me for a *Tartar*,
To make m' against my will take quarter,
Why dost not put me to the sword?
But cowardly flie from thy word?

Quoth *Hudibras*, the day's thine own;
Thou and thy stars have cast me down: 870
My Laurels are transplanted now,
And flourish on thy conqu'ring brow:
My loss of honour's great enough,
Thou need'st not brand it with a scoff:
Sarcasmes may eclipse thine own,
But cannot blur my lost renown:
I am not now in Fortune's power,
He that is down can fall no lower.

857–60 Say ... Sword. *C:* Shall I have quarter now? You Ruffin; | Or wilt thou
be worse then thy huffing? | Thou saidst th'woud'st kill me, marry woud'st thou: |
Why dost thou not, thou *Jack-a-Nods* thou? *A*   861–6 *added in C*

The ancient *Hero's* were illustrious
For b'ing benigne, and not blustrous,   880
Against a vanquisht foe: their swords
Were sharp and trencheant, not their words;
And did in fight but cut work out
T'employ their Courtesies about.

Quoth she, Although thou hast deserv'd,
Base *Slubberdegullion*, to be serv'd
As thou didst vow to deal with me,
If thou hadst got the Victory;
Yet I shall rather act a part
That suits my fame, then thy desert.   890
Thy Arms, thy Liberty, beside
All that's on th'outside of thy hide,
Are mine by military law,
Of which I will not bate one straw:
The rest, thy life and limbs, once more,
Though doubly forfeit, I restore.

Quoth *Hudibras*, It is too late
For me to treat or stipulate;
What thou command'st I must obey:
Yet those whom I expugn'd to day,   900
Of thine own party, I let go,
And gave them life and freedome too,
Both *Dogs* and *Bear*, upon their parol,
Whom I took pris'ners in this quarrel.

Quoth *Trulla*, Whether thou or they
Let one another run away,
Concerns not me; but was't not thou
That gave *Crowdero* quarter too?
Crowdero, whom in Irons bound,
Thou basely threw'st into *Lob's pound*:   910
Where still he lies, and with regret
His generous bowels rage and fret.
But now thy carcase shall redeem,
And serve to be exchange for him.

This said, the *Knight* did straight submit,
And laid his weapons at her feet.

Next he disrob'd his Gaberdine,
And with it did himself resign.
She took it, and forthwith devesting
The mantle that she wore, said jesting,   920
Take that, and wear it for my sake;
Then threw it o're his sturdy back.
And as the *French* we conquer'd once,
Now give us Laws for Pantaloons,
The length of Breeches, and the gathers,
Port-canons, Perriwigs, and Feathers;
Just so the proud insulting Lass
Array'd and dighted *Hudibras.*

Meanwhile the other Champions, yerst
In hurry of the fight disperst,   930
Arriv'd, when *Trulla*'d won the day,
To share in th'honour and the prey,
And out of *Hudibras* his hide
With vengeance to be satisfy'd;
Which now they were about to pour
Upon him in a wooden showre.
But *Trulla* thrust her self between,
And striding o're his back agen,
She brandisht o're her head his sword,
And vow'd they should not break her word;   940
Sh' had given him quarter, and her bloud
Or theirs should make that quarter good.
For she was bound by Law of Arms,
To see him safe from further harms.
In Dungeon deep *Crowdero* cast
By *Hudibras* as yet lay fast,
Where to the hard and ruthless stones
His great heart made perpetual mones.
Him she resolv'd that *Hudibras*
Should ransome, and supply his place.   950

This stopt their fury, and the basting
Which toward *Hudibras* was hasting.

942 that] their *C*   948 mones. *A2–A5*: mones *A1, C*

They thought it was but just and right,
That what she had atchiev'd in fight,
She should dispose of how she pleas'd:
Crowdero ought to be releas'd;
Nor could that any way be done
So well as this she pitcht upon:
For who a better could imagine?
This therefore they resolv'd t'engage in.   960
The *Knight* and *Squier* first they made
Rise from the ground where they were laid;
Then mounted both upon their Horses,
But with their faces to the *Arses.*
Orsin led *Hudibras*'es beast,
And *Talgol* that which *Ralpho* prest;
Whom stout *Magnano,* valiant *Cerdon*
And *Colon* waited as a guard on,
All ush'ring *Trulla,* in the reer
With th'Arms of either prisoner.   970
In this proud order and array
They put themselves upon their way,
Striving to reach th'*inchanted Castle,*
Where stout *Crowdero* in durance lay still.
Thither with greater speed, then shows
And triumphs over conquer'd foes
Do use t'allow, or then the *Bears*
Or *Pageants* born before *Lord Mayors*
Are wont to use, they soon arriv'd,
In order Souldierlike contriv'd,   980
Still marching in a warlike posture,
As fit for Battel as for Muster.
The *Knight* and *Squire* they first unhorse,
And bending 'gainst the Fort their force,
They all advanc'd, and round about
Begirt the *Magical Redoubt.*
Magnan' led up in this adventure,
And made way for the rest to enter.
For he was skilfull in *Black Art*
No less then he that built the Fort;   990

984 the] their *C*

And with an Iron Mace laid flat
A breach, which straight all enter'd at,
And in the wooden Dungeon found
Crowdero laid upon the ground.
Him they release from durance base,
Restor'd t'his *Fiddle* and his *Case*,
And liberty, his thirsty rage
With lushious vengeance to asswage.
For he no sooner was at large,
But *Trulla* straight brought on her charge,   1000
And in the self-same *Limbo* put
The *Knight* and *Squire* where he was shut.
Where leaving them i'th' wretched hole,
Their bangs and durance to condole,
Confin'd and conjur'd into narrow
Enchanted mansion, to know sorrow;
In the same order and array
Which they advanc'd, they marcht away.

But *Hudibras*, who scorn'd to stoop
To Fortune, or be said to droop,   1010
Chear'd up himself with ends of verse,
And sayings of Philosophers.
Quoth he, Th'one half of man, his mind,
Is *Sui juris*, unconfin'd,
And cannot be laid by the heels,
What e're the other moity feels.
'Tis not Restraint or Liberty
That makes men prisoners or free;
But perturbations that possess
The Mind or Æquanimities.   1020
The whole world was not half so wide
To *Alexander*, when he cri'd
Because he had but one to subdue,
As was a paultrie narrow tub to
Diogenes, who is not sed
(For ought that ever I could read)
To whine, put finger i'th' eye, and sob
Because h' had ne're another *Tub*.

1003 i'th' wretched hole *C*: in *Hockly i'th' hole A*

The Ancients make two several kinds
Of Prowess in heroick minds,   1030
The *Active*, and the *Passive* valiant;
Both which are *pari librâ* gallant:
For both to give blows and to carry,
In fights are equenecessary;
But in defeats, the passive stout
Are alwayes found to stand it out
Most desp'rately, and to outdoe
The Active, 'gainst a conqu'ring foe.
Though we with blacks and blews are suggill'd,
Or, as the Vulgar say, are *cudgell'd*:   1040
He that is valiant, and dares fight,
Though drubb'd can lose no honour by't.
Honour's *a lease for Lives to come*,
And cannot be *extended* from
The legal Tenant: 'tis a Chattel,
Not to be forfeited in battel.
If he that in the field is slain,
Be in the *Bed of Honour* lain;
He that is beaten may be sed
To lye in Honour's *Truckle-bed*.   1050
For as we see th'eclipsed Sun
By mortals is more gaz'd upon,
Then when adorn'd with all his light
He shines in serene skie most bright:
So Valour in a low estate
Is most admir'd and wonder'd at.

Quoth *Ralph*, How great I do not know
We may by being beaten grow;
But none that see how here we sit,
Will judge us overgrown with wit.   1060
As *gifted Brethren* preaching by
A *Carnal Hour-glass*, do imply
Illumination can convey
Into them what they have to say,
But not how much: so well enough
Know you to charge, but not draw off.

1043 *Lives C: time A*   1047 in . . . is *C*: is in Battel *A*

For who without a *Cap* and *Bauble*,
Having subdu'd a *Bear* and *Rabble*,
And might with honour have come off,
Would put it to a second proof: 1070
A politick exploit, right fit
For *Presbyterian zeal* and *wit*.

Quoth *Hudibras*, That Cuckow's tone,
Ralpho, thou alwayes harp'st upon:
When thou at any thing wouldst rail,
Thou mak'st *Presbytery* thy scale
To take the height on't, and explain
To what degree it is profane.
Whats'ever will not with thy (*what d'y' call*)
Thy *light* jump right thou call'st *Synodicall.*   1080
As if *Presbytery* were a standard
To size whats'ever's to be slander'd.
Dost not remember how this day
Thou to my beard wast bold to say,
That thou could'st prove, *Bear-baiting* equal
With *Synods*, orthodox and legal?
Do if thou can'st, for I deny't,
And dare thee to't with all thy *light*.

Quoth *Ralpho*, Truly that is no
Hard matter for a man to doe   1090
That has but any *guts in's brains*,
And could believe it worth his pains.
But since you dare and urge me to it,
You'l find I've *light* enough to doe it.

Synods are mystical *Bear-gardens*,
Where *Elders*, *Deputies*, *Church-wardens*,
And other Members of the Court,
Manage the *Babylonish* sport.
For *Prolocutor*, *Scribe*, and *Bearward*,
Do differ onely in a mere word.   1100
Both are but sev'ral Synagogues
Of *carnal Men*, and *Bears* and *Dogs*:
Both *Antichristian Assemblies*,
To mischief bent as far's in them lies:

Both stave and tail, with fierce contests,
The one with men, the other beasts.
The diff'rence is, The one fights with
The Tongue, the other with the Teeth;
And that they bait but *Bears* in this,
In th'other *Souls* and *Consciences*;   1110
Where *Saints* themselves are brought to stake
For *Gospel-light* and *Conscience* sake;
Expos'd to *Scribes* and *Presbyters*,
Instead of *Mastive-dogs* and *Curs*;
Then whom th' have less humanity,
For these at souls of men will flie.
This to the *Prophet* did appear,
Who in a Vision saw a *Bear*,
Prefiguring the beastly rage
Of *Church-rule* in this later Age: 1120
As is demonstrated at full
By him that baited the *Pope's Bull*.
Bears naturally are beasts of Prey,
That live by rapine, so do they.
What are their *Orders, Constitutions,*
Church-censures, Curses, Absolutions,
But sev'ral mystick chains they make,
To tie poor Christians to the stake?
And then set heathen *Officers*,
Instead of *Dogs*, about their ears.   1130
For to prohibit and dispence,
To find out or to make offence,
Of hell and heaven to dispose,
To play with souls at fast and loose;
To set what Characters they please,
And mulcts on Sin or Godliness;
Reduce the Church to *Gospel-order*,
By *Rapine, Sacriledge,* and *Murther*;
To make *Presbyterie* supreme,
And *Kings* themselves submit to them;   1140
And force all people, though against
Their Consciences, to turn *Saints*,

1122 A Learned Divine in King *James*'s time wrote a Polemick Work against the
Pope, and gave it that unlucky Nick-Name, of *The Popes Bull Baited*.

Must prove a pretty thriving trade,
When *Saints* Monopolists are made.
When *pious* frauds and *holy* shifts
Are *dispensations* and *gifts*,
There *Godliness* becomes mere ware,
And ev'ry *Synod* but a Fair.

Synods are whelps of th'*Inquisition*,
A mungrel breed of like pernicion,   1150
And growing up became the Sires
Of *Scribes, Commissioners,* and *Triers*;
Whose bus'ness is, by cunning sleight
To cast a figure for mens *Light*;
To find in lines of beard and face,
The Physiognomy of *Grace*;
And by the sound and *twang of Nose*,
If all be *sound* within disclose,
Free from a crack or flaw of sinning,
As men try *Pipkins* by the ringing.   1160
By *black-caps*, underlaid with *white*,
Give certain guess at inward *Light*;
Which *Serjeants at the Gospel* wear,
To make their *spiritual Calling* clear.
The *hand-kercher* about the neck
(Canonical *Crabat* of *Smeck*,
From whom the Institution came,
When Church and State they set on flame,
And worn by them as badges then
Of *Spiritual Warfaring* men)   1170
Judge rightly if *Regeneration*
Be of the *newest Cut* in fashion.
Sure 'tis an Orthodox opinion
That *Grace is founded in dominion.*
Great *Piety* consists in Pride;
To *rule* is to be *sanctifi'd*:

1166 *Smectymnuus* was a Club of Parliamentary Holders-forth, The Characters of
whose Names and Talents were by themselves exprest, in that senseless and insignificant word; They wore Handkerchers about their Necks for a Note of Distinction,
(as the Officers of the Parliament Army then did) which afterwards degenerated
into Carnal Crabats.

1164 their] the *C*

To domineer and to controul
Both o're the body and the soul,
Is the most perfect *discipline*
Of Church-rule, and by *right divine*.   1180
Bel and the *Dragon*'s Chaplains were
More moderate then these by far:
For they (poor Knaves) were glad to cheat,
To get their Wives and Children meat;
But these will not be fobb'd off so,
They must have wealth and power too,
Or else with bloud and desolation
They'l tear it out o'th' heart o'th' Nation.

Sure these themselves from Primitive
And Heathen Priesthood do derive,   1190
When *Butchers* were the onely *Clerks*,
Elders and *Presbyters* of *Kirks*,
Whose *Directorie* was to *kill*;
And some believe it is so still.
The onely diff'rence is, that then
They slaughter'd onely *beasts*, now *men*.
For then to sacrifice a Bullock,
Or now and then a child to *Moloch*,
They count a vile Abomination,
But not to slaughter a whole *Nation*.   1200
Presbyterie does but translate
The Papacy to a *Free State*,
A *Common-wealth of Poperie*,
Where ev'ry Village is a *See*
As well as *Rome*, and must maintain
A *Tithe-pig-Metropolitan*:
Where ev'ry *Presbyter* and *Deacon*
Commands the *Keies* for Cheese and Bacon;
And ev'ry Hamlet's governed
By's *Holiness*, the *Churche's head*,   1210
More haughty and severe in's place
Then *Gregorie* and *Boniface*.
Such Church must (surely) be a Monster
With many heads: for if we conster
What in th'*Apocalyps* we find,

According to th'Apostle's mind,
'Tis that the *Whore of Babylon*
With many heads did ride upon;
Which Heads denote the sinful tribe
Of *Deacon, Priest, Lay-elder, Scribe.*   1220

Lay-elder, Simeon to *Levi,*
Whose little finger is as heavy
As loyns of Patriarchs, Prince-Prelate,
And Bishop-secular. This Zelot
Is of a mungrel, diverse kind,
Clerick before, and *Lay* behind;
A Lawless *linsie-woolsie brother,*
Half of one Order, half another;
A Creature of amphibious nature,
On land a Beast, a Fish in water;   1230
That alwayes preys on Grace, or Sin;
A Sheep without, a Wolf within.
This fierce Inquisitor has chief
Dominion over mens Belief
And Manners; can pronounce a *Saint*
Idolatrous, or ignorant,
When superciliously he sifts
Through coursest boulter others *gifts.*
For all men live and judge amiss
Whose *Talents* jump not just with his.   1240
He'l lay on *Gifts* with hands, and place
On dullest noddle *light* and *grace,*
The manufacture of the *Kirk;*
Those Pastors are but th'Handiwork
Of his mechanick Pawes, instilling
Divinity in them by feeling,
From whence they start up *chosen vessels,*
Made by Contact, as men get *Meazles.*
So *Cardinals,* they say, do grope
At th'other end the new-made *Pope.*   1250

Hold, hold, quoth *Hudibras, Soft fire,*
They say, *does make sweet mault.* Good *Squire,*
Festina lente, not too fast;

For *hast* (the Proverb sayes) *makes waste*.
The Quirks and Cavils thou dost make
Are false, and built upon mistake.
And I shall bring you, with your pack
Of *Fallacies*, *t'Elenchi* back;
And put your Arguments in mood
And figure, to be understood.   1260
I'le force you by right ratiocination
To leave your *Vitilitigation*,
And make you keep to th' question close,
And argue *Dialecticŵs*.

The Question then, to state it first,
Is which is *better*, or which *worst*,
Synods or *Bears*. *Bears* I avow
To be the worst, and *Synods* thou.
But to make good th'Assertion,
Thou say'st th' are really *all one*.   1270
If so, not *worst*; for if th' are *idem*,
Why then, *Tantundem dat tantidem*.
For if they are the *same*, by course
Neither is *better*, neither *worse*.
But I deny they are the *same*,
More then a *Maggot* and *I* am.
That both are *Animalia*,
I grant, but not *Rationalia*:
For though they do agree in kind,
Specifick difference we find,   1280
And can no more make *Bears* of these,
Then prove *my horse is Socrates*.

That *Synods* are *Bear-gardens* too,
Thou dost affirm; but I say no:
And thus I prove it, in a word,
Whats'ever *Assembly*'s not impowr'd
To *censure*, *curse*, *absolve*, and *ordain*,

1262 Vitilitigation is a word the Knight was passionately in love with, and never
fail'd to use it upon all possible occasions, and therefore to omit it, when it fell in the
way, had argu'd too great a Neglect of his Learning, and Parts, though it means no
more then a perverse humour of wrangling.

Can be no *Synod*: but *Bear-garden*
Has no such pow'r, *Ergo* 'tis none.
And so thy Sophistry's o'rethrown.   1290

But yet we are beside the Question
Which thou didst raise the first Contest on;
For that was, Whether *Bears* are *better*
Then *Synod-men*; I say, *Negatur.*
That *Bears* are *Beasts*, and *Synods Men*,
Is held by all: They'r *better* then.
For *Bears* and *Dogs* on *four* legs go,
As Beasts, but *Synod-men* on *two.*
'Tis true, they all have *teeth* and *nails*;
But prove that *Synod-men* have *tails*;   1300
Or that a rugged, shaggie *fur*
Growes o're the hide of *Presbyter*;
Or that his *snout* and *spacious ears*
Do hold proportion with a *Bear*'s.
A *Bear*'s a savage Beast, of all
Most ugly and unnatural,
Whelpt without form, until the Dam
Have lickt him into shape and frame:
But all thy *light* can ne're evict
That ever *Synod-man* was *lickt*;   1310
Or brought to any other fashion
Then his own will and inclination.

But thou dost further yet in this
Oppugne thy self and sense, that is,
Thou wouldst have *Presbyters* to go
For *Bears* and *Dogs* and *Bearwards* too.
A strange *Chimæra* of Beasts and Men,
Made up of pieces Heterogene,
Such as in Nature never met
In eodem Subjecto yet.   1320

Thy other Arguments are all
Supposures, Hypothetical,
That do but beg, and we may chuse
Either to grant them, or refuse.

Much thou hast said, which I know when,
And where, thou stol'st from other men,
(Whereby 'tis plain thy *light* and *gifts*
Are all but plagiary shifts;)
And is the same that *Ranter* sed,
That arguing with me, broke my head,   1330
And tore a handful of my Beard:
The self-same Cavils then I heard,
When b'ing in hot dispute about
This Controversie, we fell out;
And what thou know'st I answer'd then,
Will serve to answer thee agen.

Quoth *Ralpho*, Nothing but th'abuse
Of *Humane Learning* you produce;
Learning that Cobweb of the Brain,
Profane, erroneous, and vain;   1340
A trade of knowledge as repleat
As others are with fraud and cheat;
An Art t'incumber *Gifts* and wit,
And render both for nothing fit;
Makes *light* unaçtive, dull and troubled,
Like little *David* in *Saul*'s doublet;
A cheat that Scholars put upon
Other mens reason and their own;
A fort of Errour, to ensconce
Absurdity and ignorance;   1350
That renders all the avenues
To Truth impervious and abstruse,
By making plain things, in debate,
By Art, perplext and intricate:
For nothing goes for sense or *Light*
That will not with old rules jump right.
As if Rules were not in the Schools
Deriv'd from Truth, but Truth from Rules.

This *Pagan, Heathenish invention*
Is good for nothing but Contention.   1360
For as in Sword-and-Buckler fight,
All blows do on the Target light:

So when men argue, the great'st part
O'th' Contest falls on tearms of Art,
Until the fustian stuff be spent,
And then they fall to th'Argument.

Quoth *Hudibras*, Friend *Ralph*, thou hast
Out-run the Constable at last;
For thou art fallen on a new
Dispute, as senseless as untrue,   1370
But to the former opposite,
And *contrary as black to white*;
Mere *Disparata*, that concerning
Presbyterie, this, *Humane Learning*;
Two things s'averse, they never yet
But in thy rambling fancy met.
But I shall take a fit occasion
T'evince thee by Ratiocination,
Some other time, in place more proper
Then this w' are in: Therefore let's stop here,   1380
And rest our weary'd bones awhile,
Already tir'd with other toile.

1370 as untrue *C*: and untrue *A*

HUDIBRAS

THE SECOND PART

CANTO I

THE ARGUMENT

The Knight being clapp'd by th'heels in prison,
The last unhappy Expedition,
Love *brings his Action on the Case,*
And layes it upon Hudibras.
How he receives the Ladies visit,
And cunningly sollicit's his sute,
Which Shee deferres: yet on Parole,
Redeems him from th'inchanted Hole.

Bᴜᴛ now t'observe *Romantique* Method,
Let rusty Steel a while be sheathed;
And all those harsh and rugged sounds
Of Bastinado's, Cuts, and Wounds
Exchang'd to Love's more gentle stile,
To let our Reader breathe a while:
In which, that we may be as brief as
Is possible, by way of *Preface.*

1 The beginning of this Second Part may perhaps seem strange and abrupt to those who do not know, that it was written of purpose, in imitation of *Virgil,* who begins the IV Book of his *Æneides* in the very same manner, *At Regina gravi, &c.* And this is enough to satisfy the curiosity of those who believe that Invention and Fancy ought to be measur'd (like Cases in Law) by Precedents, or else they are in the power of the Critique.

The Argument. 1–2 *Knight . . . Expedition,* C: *Knight, by Damnable* Magician, | *Being cast illegally in Prison;* B   5 *receives* C: *revi's* B   Canto I.   2 rusty C: bloody B   3–4 *added in* C   5 Exchang'd . . . gentle C: And unto *Love* turn we our B   6 while: C: while | By this time tyr'd with th'horrid sounds | Of blows, and cutts, and bloud, and wounds: B

Is't not enough to make one strange,
That some mens fancies should ne'r change?   10
But make all People do, and say,
The same things still the self-same way?
Some Writers make all *Ladies* perloynd,
And *Knights* pursuing like a whirlwind:
Others make all their *Knights*, in fits
Of Jealousie, to lose their wits;
Til drawing bloud o'th' Dames, like witches,
Th' are forthwith cur'd of their Capriches.
Some always thrive in their *Amours*,
By pulling plaisters off their sores;   20
As Cripples do to get an Almes,
Just so do they, and win their Dames.
Some force whole Regions, in despight
O' *Geography*, to change their site:
Make former times shake hands with latter,
And that which was before, come after.
But those that write in *Rhime*, still make
The one *Verse*, for the others sake:
For, one for *Sense*, and one for *Rhime*,
I think's sufficient at one time.   30

But we forget in what sad plight
We lately left the Captiv'd *Knight*,
And pensive *Squire*, both bruis'd in body,
And conjur'd into safe Custody:
Tyr'd with Dispute, and speaking *Latin*,
As well as basting, and *Bear-bayting*;
And desperate of any course,
To free himself by wit or force,
His onely Solace was, That now
His dog-bolt Fortune was so low,   40
That either it must quickly end,
Or turn about again, and mend:
In which he found th'event, no less
Then other times, beside his guess.

10 some mens fancies *C*: a mans fancy *B*   12 way?] way: *C*   32 lately *C*:
whilom *B*

There is a Tall Long-sided Dame,
(But wondrous light) ycleped *Fame*,
That like a thin *Camelion* Bourds
Her self on Ayr, and eats your words:
Upon her shoulders wings she wears,
Like hanging-sleeves, lin'd through with ears   50
And eys, and ⁺ongues, as *Poets* list,
Made good by deep *Mythologist.*
With these, she through the Welkin flyes,
And sometimes carries *Truth*, oft *Lyes*;
With letters hung like *Eastern* Pidgeons,
And *Mercuries* of furthest Regions;
Diurnals writ for Regulation
Of Lying, to enform the Nation:
And by their Publick use to bring down
The rate of *Whetstones* in the Kingdome.   60
About her neck a Pacquet-*Male*,
Fraught with Advice, some fresh, some stale;
Of men that walk'd when they were dead,
And *Cows* of *Monsters* brought to bed:
Of *Hailstones* big as *Pullets* egs,
And *Puppies* whelp'd with twice two legs:
A *Blazing-Star* seen in the *West*,
By six or seven men at least.
Two Trumpets she does sound at once,
But both of clean contrary tones.   70
But whether both with the same wind,
Or one before, and one behind,
We know not; onely this can tell,
The one sounds vilely, th'other well.
And therefore Vulgar *Authors* name
Th'one Good, the other Evil *Fame*.

This tatling *Gossip* knew too well
What mischief *Hudibras* befell,
And streight the spightful tydings bears,
Of all, to th'unkind Widow's ears.   80
Democritus ne'r laugh'd so loud
To see *Bauds* carted through the crowd,

48 your B1 (*errata*): her B1, B2, C   77 tatling *C*: twatling *B*

Or Funerals with stately Pomp,
March slowly on in solemn dump;
As she laugh'd out, until her back
As well as sides, was like to crack.
She vow'd she would go see the sight,
And visit the distressed *Knight*,
To do the office of a Neighbour,
And be a *Gossip* at his Labour: 90
And from his wooden Jayl the Stocks
To set at large his Fetter-locks,
And by Exchange, Parole, or Ransome,
To free him from th'Inchanted Mansion.
This b'ing resolv'd, she call'd for hood
And Usher, Implements abroad,
Which *Ladies* wear, beside a slender
Young waiting *Damsel* to attend her.
All which appearing, on she went,
To find the *Knight* in *Limbo* pent: 100
And 'twas not long, before she found
Him, and his stout *Squire*, in the Pound;
Both coupled in Inchanted Tether,
By further leg behind together:
For as he sate upon his Rump,
His head like one in doleful dump,
Between his knees, his hands appli'd
Unto his ears on either side.
And by him, in another hole,
Afflicted *Ralpho*, cheek by Joul;   110
She came upon him in his wooden
Magicians Circle, on the sudden,
As *Spirits* do t'a Conjurer,
When in their dreadful shapes th' appear.
No sooner did the *Knight* perceive her,
But streight he fell into a feaver,
Inflam'd all over with disgrace,
To be seen by her in such a place;
Which made him hang the head, and scoul,
And wink, and goggle like an Owl.   120

91–92 And . . . Fetter-locks, *C*: That is, to see him deliver'd safe | Of's wooden
burthen, and *Squire Raph*; *B*   114 dreadful *C* : dreadfulst *A*

He felt his brains begin to swim,
When thus the Dame accosted him;
This place (quoth she) they say's Inchanted,
And with *Delinquent Spirits* haunted;
That here are ty'd in Chains, and scourg'd,
Until their guilty Crimes be purg'd;
Look, there are two of them appear
Like Persons I have seen somewhere:
Some have mistaken Blocks and Posts,
For *Spectres, Apparitions, Ghosts*   130
With Sawcer-eyes, and Horns; and some
Have heard the Devil beat a Drum:
But if our eyes are not false Glasses,
That give a wrong account of faces;
That *Beard* and I should be acquainted,
Before 'twas conjur'd and inchanted.
For though it be disfigur'd somewhat
As if 't had lately been in Combat;
It did belong t'a worthy *Knight*,
How e're this *Goblin* is come by't.   140

When *Hudibras* the *Lady* heard
To take kind notice of his *Beard*,
And speak with such respect and honour,
Both of the *Beard*, and the *Beard*'s owner,
He thought it best to set as good
A face upon it as he cou'd,
And thus he spoke; *Lady*, your bright
And radiant eyes are in the right:
The *Beard*'s th'Identique *Beard* you knew,
The same numerically true: 150
Nor is it worn by Fiend or Elf,
But its Proprietor himself.

O Heavens! quoth she, can that be true?
I do begin to fear 'tis you:
Not by your Individual Whiskers,
But by your Dialect and Discourse;
That never spoke to Man or Beast,

142 To take kind notice of *C*: Discoursing thus upon *B*

In notions vulgarly exprest.
But what malignant Star, alas,
Has brought you both to this sad pass?   160

Quoth he, the fortune of the War,
Which I am less afflicted for,
Then to be seen with *Beard* and *Face*,
By you, in such a homely case.

Quoth she, those need not be asham'd,
For being honourably maym'd;
If he that is in battel conquer'd,
Have any Title to his own *Beard*,
Though yours be sorely lugg'd, and torn,
It does your visage more adorn,   170
Then if 'twere prun'd, and starch'd, and landerd,
And cut square by the *Russian* Standerd.
A torn *Beard*'s like a tatterd Ensign,
That's bravest which there are most rents in.
That Petticoat about your shoulders,
Does not so well become a Souldiers,
And I'm afraid they are worse handled,
Although i'th' rere, your *Beard* the Van led.
And those uneasie Bruises make
My heart for company to ake,   180
To see so worshipful a friend
I'th' Pillory set, at the wrong end.

Quoth *Hudibras*, this thing call'd *Pain*,
Is (as the Learned *Stoicks* maintain)
Not bad *simpliciter*, nor good,
But meerly as 'tis understood.
Sense is Deceitful, and may feign,
As well in counterfeiting Pain
As other gross *Phænomena*'s,
In which it oft mistakes the Case.   190
But since th'Immortal Intellect
(That's free from Error and Defect,
Whose objects still persist the same)

164 a homely *C*: elenctique *B*

Is free from outward bruise or maim,
Which nought external can expose
To gross material bangs or blows:
It follows, we can ne'r be sure,
Whether we pain or not endure:
And just so far are sore and griev'd,
As by the Fancy is believ'd.   200
Some have been wounded with conceit,
And dy'd of meer opinion streight;
Others, though wounded sore, in reason
Felt no contusion nor Discretion.

A *Saxon* Duke did grow so fat,
That *Mice* (as Histories relate)
Eat Grots and Labyrinths to dwell in
His Postique parts, without his feeling:
Then how is't possible a kick
Should e're reach that way to the quick?   210

Quoth she, I grant it is in vain,
For one that's basted, to feel pain;
Because the *Pangs* his bones endure,
Contribute nothing to the Cure:
Yet *Honor* hurt, is wont to rage
With *Pain* no med'cine can asswage.

Quoth he, That *Honor*'s very squeemish
That takes a basting for a blemish:
For what's more honorable then *scarrs*,
Or skin to tatters rent in *Warrs*?   220
Some have been beaten, till they know
What wood a *Cudgel*'s of by th' blow;
Some kick'd, until they can feel whether
A shoo be *Spanish* or *Neats*-Leather:
And yet have met, after long running,
With some whom they have taught that cunning.
The furthest way about, t'orecome

205 This History of the Duke of *Saxony*, is not altogether so strange as that of
a Bishop his Countrey-man, who was quite eaten up with Rats, and Mice.

203 sore, in reason] sore in reason, *B, C*

In th'end does prove the nearest home;
By *Laws* of learned *Duellists*
They that are bruis'd with *wood,* or *fists*,   230
And think one beating may for once
Suffice, are *Cowards,* and *Pultroons* :
But if they dare engage t'a second,
They'r *stout* and *gallant* fellows reckond.
Th'old *Romans,* freedom did bestow;
Our *Princes* worship, with a blow :
King *Pyrrhus* cur'd his splenatick
And testy Courtiers with a kick.
The *Negus,* when some mighty *Lord*
Or *Potentate*'s to be restor'd   240
And Pardon'd for some great offence
With which he's willing to dispence,
First has him layd upon his *Belly,*
Then beaten *back,* and *side,* t'a *Jelly,*
That done, he rises, humbly bows,
And gives thanks for the gracious blows;
Departs not meanly proud, and boasting,
Of his magnificent *Rib-roasting.*
The Beaten *Souldier* proves most manfull,
That, like his *Sword,* endur's the Anvile :   250
And justly's held more formidable,
The more his Valour's malleable.
But he that fears a *Bastinadoe,*
Will run away from his own shadow.
And though I'm now in *durance* fast,
By our own *Party,* basely cast,
Ransome, Exchange, Parole, refus'd,
And worse then by the *Enemy* us'd;
In close *Catasta* shut, past hope

237-8 *Pyrrhus* King of *Epirus,* who as *Pliny* says, had this occult Quality in his Toe, *Pollicis in dextro Pede tactu Lienosis medebatur.* L.7. C.ii.
259 *Catasta* is but a pair of Stocks in English, But Heroical Poetry must not admit of any vulgar word (especially of paultry signification) and therefore some of our Modern Authors are fain to import forrain words from abroad, that were never before heard of in our Language.

241-2 And Pardon'd . . . dispence, *C* : To his good *Grace,* for some offence, | Forfeit before, and pardond since : *B*   246 gracious *C* : *Princely B*

Of *Wit*, or *Valour*, to elope.   260
As *Beards*, the nearer that they tend
To th'*Earth*, still grow more reverend :
And *Cannons* shoot the higher pitches,
The lower we let down their breeches :
I'le make this low dejected *fate*
Advance me to a greater height.

Quoth she, Y' have almost made m' in love
With that, which did my pitty move,
Great *Wits* and *Valours*, like great *States*,
Do sometimes sink with their own weights :   270
Th'extreams of *Glory*, and of *Shame*,
Like *East* and *West*, become the same :
No *Indian-Prince* has to his *Pallace*
More follow'rs then a Thief to th' *Gallows*.
But if a *beating* seem so brave,
What *Glories* must *a Whipping* have?
Such great *Atchievements* cannot fayl,
To cast salt on a *Womans* Tayl.
For if I thought your *nat'ral Talent*
Of *Passive Courage*, were so Gallant;   280
As you strain hard, to have it thought
I could grow *Amorous*, and *dote*.

When *Hudibras* this language heard,
He prick'd up's ears, and strok'd his *Beard* :
Thought he, this is the *Lucky hour*,
Wines work, when *Vines* are in the flour;
This *Crisis* then I'l set my rest on,
And put her boldly to the *Question*.

Madam, what you would seem to doubt,
Shall be to all the world made out,   290
How I've been *Drubd*, and with what *Spirit*,
And *Magnanimity*, I bear it.
And if you doubt it to be true,
I'l stake my *self* down against you :
And if I fayl in *Love*, or *Troth*,

Be you the *Winner*, and take both.

Quoth She, I've heard old cunning *Stagers*
Say, Fools for *Arguments* use wagers.
And though I prays'd your *Valour*, yet
I did not mean to baulk your *Wit*,   300
Which if you have, you must needs know
What I have told you before now,
And you b'experiment have prov'd,
I cannot *Love* where I'm *belov'd*.

Quoth *Hudibras*, 'tis a *Caprich*
Beyond th'infliction of a *Witch*;
So Cheats, to play with those still aime,
That do not understand the Game.
Love in your heart as idely burns,
As fire in antique *Roman*-Urns,   310
To warm the *Dead*, and vainly light,
Those only, that see nothing by't.
Have you not power to *entertain*,
And render *Love* for *love* again?
As *no man* can draw in his *breath*,
At once, and force out *Air* beneath?
Or do you *love* your self so much,
To bear all *Rivals* else a Grutch?
What *Fate* can lay a greater Curse,
Then you upon your self would force?   320
For *Wedlock* without *love*, some say,
Is but a *Lock* without a *Key*.
It is a kind of *Rape* to *marry*
One, that neglects, or cares not for yee:
For, what does make it *Ravishment*,
But b'ing against the *Mind's Consent*?
A *Rape*, that is the more inhumane,
For being acted by a *Woman*.
Why are you *fair*, but to entice us
To *love* you, that you may despise us?   330
But though you cannot *love*, you say,
Out of your own *Fanatique* way,

Why should you not, at least, allow,
Those that *love* you, to do so too?
For, as you fly mee, and pursue
Love more averse, so I do you:
And am by your own *Doctrine* taught,
To practise what you call a *fault*.

Quoth she, If what you say be true,
You must fly mee, as I do you,   340
But 'tis not what we do, but say,
In *Love*, and *Preaching*, that must sway.

Quoth he, to bid me not to *love*,
Is to forbid my *Pulse* to move,
My *Beard* to grow, my *Ears* to prick up,
Or (when I'm in a fit) to hickup;
Command me to piss out the Moon,
And 'twill as easily be done.
Loves power's too great to be withstood,
By feeble humane *flesh* and *blood*.   350
'Twas he, that brought upon his knees
The *Hect'ring* Kill-Cow *Hercules*;
Reduc'd his *Leager-lions* skin
T'a *Petticoat*, and made him spin:
Seiz'd on his *Club*, and made it dwindle
T'a feeble *Distaff*, and a *Spindle*.
'Twas he made *Emperours* Gallants
To their own *Sisters*, and their *Aunts*;
Set *Popes*, and *Cardinals* agog,
To play with *Pages*, at Leap-frog;   360
'Twas he, that gave our *Senate* purges,
And fluxt the *House*, of many a *Burgess*;
Made those that represent the *Nation*
Submit, and suffer *amputation*:
And all the *Grandees* o'th' *Cabal*
Adjorn to *Tubs*, at *spring* and *fall*.
He mounted *Synod-men* and rod 'em
To *Durty-lane*, and *little-Sodom*;
Made 'em Corvet, like *Spanish* Jenets

353 Reduc'd *C*: Transform'd *B*

And take the Ring at Madam ——   370
'Twas he, that made Saint *Francis* do
More then the Dev'l could tempt him to;
In cold and frosty weather, grow
Inamourd of a wife of *Snow*;
And though she were of *rigid* temper,
With melting *flames* accost, and tempt her:
Which after in *enjoyment* quenching,
He hung a *Garland* on his *Engine*.

Quoth she, if *Love* have these effects,
Why is it not forbid our *Sex*?   380
Why is't not damn'd, and interdicted,
For *Diabolical*, and wicked?
And song, as out of tune, against,
As *Turk* and *Pope* are by the Saints?
I find, I've greater reason for it,
Then I believ'd before, t'abhor it.

Quoth *Hudibras*, These sad effects
Spring from your *Heathenish* neglects
Of *Love*'s great pow'r, which he returns
Upon your selves, with equal scorns;   390
And those who worthy *Lovers* slight,
Plague's with prepost'rous Appetite;
This made the beauteous *Queen* of *Crete*
To take a *Town-Bull* for her *Sweet*;
And from her greatness stoop so low,
To be the Rival of a Cow.
Others to prostitute their great *hearts*,
To be *Baboons*, and *Munkeys* sweet-hearts.
Some with the Dev'l himself in league grow,

371 The antient Writers of the Lives of Saints, were of the same sort of People, who
first writ of Knight-Errantry, and as in the one, they rendred the brave Actions of
some very great Persons ridiculous, by their prodigious Lies, and sottish way of
describing them: So they have abus'd the Piety of some very devout Persons, by
imposing such stories upon them, as this upon *St. Francis*.
393 The History of *Pasiphaë* is common enough, only this may be observ'd, That
though she brought the Bull a Son and Heir; yet the Husband was fain to father it,
as appears by the Name, perhaps because the Countrey being an Island, he was
within the four Seas, when the Infant was begotten.

372 More *C2*: More, B, *C1*   383 song *B1*, C: sung *B2*

By's Representative a *Negro*.   400
'Twas this made *Vestal*-Maids love-sick,
And venture to be bury'd Quick.
Some by their *Fathers*, and their *Brothers*,
To be made *Mistresses*, and *Mothers*:
'Tis this that Proudest *Dames* enamours
On Laquies, and *Varlets des-Chambres*:
Their haughty *Stomachs* overcomes,
And makes 'em stoop to Durty *Grooms*,
To slight the *World*, and to disparage
Claps, Issue, Infamy, and *Marriage*.   410

Quoth She, these Judgments are severe,
Yet such, as I should rather bear,
Then trust men with their *Oaths*, or prove
Their *faith*, and *secresie* in *love*.

Says he, There is a weighty reason,
For secresie in *Love* as *Treason*.
Love is a *Burglarer*, a *Felon*,
That at the *Windore*-eye do's steal in
To rob the *Heart*, and with his prey
Steals out again a closer way,   420
Which whosoever can discover,
He's sure (as he deservs) to suffer.
Love is a fire, that burns and sparcles,
In *Men*, as nat'rally as in Char-coals,
Which sooty *Chymists* stop in holes,
When out of wood, they extract Coles;
So *Lovers* should their *Passions* choak,
That though they burn, they may not smoak.
'Tis like that sturdy *Thief*, that stole,
And drag'd Beasts backwards, into's hole: 430
So *Love* does *lovers*; and us men
Draws by the Tayls into his Den; ·
That no *impression* may discover,
And trace t'his *Cave*, the wary *Lover*.
But if you doubt I should reveal
What you entrust me under seal,

406 *Chambres*:] *Chambres* B, C   426 Coles; C: Coles B   429 *Thief*,] *Thief* C

I'l prove my self as close, and vertous,
As, your own *Secretary*, *Albertus*.

Quoth she, I grant, you may be close
In hiding what your aims propose: 440
Love-passions are like *Parables*,
By which men still mean something else:
Though *Love* be all the worlds pretence,
Mony's the *Mythologique* sence,
The real substance of the shadow,
Which all Address and Courtship's made to.

Thought he, I understand your *Play*,
And how to quit you your own way;
He that will win his *Dame*, must do,
As *Love* do's, when he bends his *Bow*:   450
With one hand thrust the *Lady* from,
And with the other pull *her* home.
I grant, quoth he, *Wealth* is a great
Provocative, to am'rous heat;
It is all *Philters*, and high Diet
That makes *Love* Rampant, and to fly out:
'Tis *Beuty* always in the flower,
That buds and blossoms at fourscore:
'Tis that by which the *Sun*, and *Moon*,
At their own weapons, are out-done;   460
That makes *Knights Errant* fall in trances,
And lay about 'm in *Romances*.
'Tis *virtue*, *wit*, and *worth*, and all
That men *divine* and *sacred* call.
For what is *worth* in any thing,
But so much *money* as 'twill bring?
Or what but *Riches* is there known,
Which man can solely call his own;
In which, no Creature goes his half,
Unless it be to *squint* and *laugh*?   470

438 *Albertus Magnus* was a Swedish Bishop, who wrote a very Learned Work, *De Secretis Mulierum*.
470 *Pliny* in his *Natural History* affirms that *Uni animalium homini oculi depravantur, unde Cognomina Strabonum et Pætorum*. Lib. 2.

461 *Knights* B2, C: *Knight* B1

I do confess, with *goods* and *land*,
I'd have a wife, at second hand;
And such you are: Nor is't your person,
My stomach's set so *sharp*, and *fierce* on,
But 'tis (your better part) your *Riches*,
That my enamour'd heart bewitches;
Let me your *fortune* but possess,
And settle your person how you please,
Or make it o're in *trust* to th' *Devil*,
You'l find me *reasonable* and *civil*.   480

Quoth she, I like this plainness better,
Then false *mock-passion*, *speech*, or *letter*,
Or any feat of *qualm* or *sowning*,
But *hanging* of your self, or *drowning*;
Your only way with me, to *break*
Your minde, is *breaking* of your Neck:
For as when *Merchants* break, orethrown
Like *Nine-pins*, they strike others down;
So, that would break my *heart*, which done,
My tempting *fortune* is your own.   490
These are but trifles, ev'ry *Lover*
Will damn himself, over and over,
And greater matters undertake,
For a less worthy *Mistress* sake;
Yet th' are the only ways to prove
Th'unfeign'd *realities* of *Love*;
For he that hangs, or beats out's brains
The *Devil*'s in him if he feigns.

Quoth *Hudibras*, this way's too rough,
For meer *experiment*, and *proof*;   500
It is no jesting, trivial matter,
To swing in th'*Air*, or plunge in.water
And like a Water-witch, try *love*,
That's to destroy and not to prove:
As if a man should be dissected,
To find what part is disaffected:

472 at *B1* (*errata*), *C2*: a *B1, B2, C1*   502 plunge *C*: douce *B1, B2*: dive
B1 (*errata*)

Your better way, is to make over
In *trust*, your fortune to your *Lover*;
Trust is a *Tryal*, if it break,
'Tis not so desp'rate, as a *Neck*:   510
Beside, th'*experiment*'s more certain,
Men venture *necks* to gain a fortune;
The Soldier do's it ev'ry day
(Eight to the week) for sixpence pay:
Your Pettifoggers damn their Souls,
To share with Knaves in Cheating Fools:
And Merchants ventring through the Main,
Slight Pirats, Rocks, and Horns for gain.
This is the way I advise you to,
Trust me, and see what I will do.   520

Quoth she, I should be loath to run
My self all th'hazard, and you none,
Which must be done, unless some *deed*
Of yours, aforesaid do precede;
Give but your self one gentle *swing*,
For tryal, and I'l cut the *string*:
Or give that Reverend *Head*, a maul,
Or two, or three, against a wall;
To shew you are a man of mettle,
And I'l engage my self, to *settle*.   530

Quoth he, my *Head*'s not made of *brass*
As Frier *Bacon*'s noddle was:
Nor (like some *Indians* scull) so tough,
That *Authors* say, 'twas *Musket-proof*:
As it had need to be, to enter
As yet, on any new *Adventure*;

---

532 The Tradition of Frier *Bacon* and the Brazen-Head, is very commonly known, and considering the times he liv'd in, is not much more strange then what another great Philosopher of his Name, has since deliver'd up of a Ring, that being ty'd in a string, and held like a Pendulum in the middle of a Silver Bowl, will vibrate of it self, and tell exactly against the sides of the Divining Cup, the same thing with, *Time is, Time was, &c.*
533-4 *American Indians*, among whom (the same Authors affirm) that there are others, whose Sculls are so soft, to use their own words, *Ut Digito perforari possunt.*

513-18 *added in* C   533 some C *1* (some copies): the A, C

You see what *bangs* it has endur'd,
That would, before new *feats*, be cur'd:
But if that's all you stand upon,
Here, strike me *luck*, it shall be done. 540

Quoth she, The matter's not so far gone
As you suppose, *Two words t'a Bargain*.
That may be done, and time enough,
When you have given down-right proof;
And yet 'tis no *Fantastique* pike,
I have to *love*, nor coy *dislike*;
'Tis no implicite, nice *Aversion*
T'your *Conversation, Meine*, or *Person*:
But a just fear lest you should prove
False, and perfidious in *Love*; 550
For if I thought you could be *true*,
I could *love* twice as much as you.

Quoth he, My faith as *Adamantine*
As Chains of *Destiny*, I'l maintain;
True as *Apollo* ever spoke,
Or *Oracle* from heart of Oak.
And if you'l give my *flame* but vent,
Now in close hugger-mugger pent,
And shine upon me but benignly,
With that one, and that other *Pigsney*, 560
The *Sun* and *Day* shall sooner part,
Then *love*, or you, shake off my heart.
The *Sun* that shall no more dispence
His own, but *your* bright influence;
I'l carve your name on *Barks* of *Trees*,
With *true-loves knots*, and *flourishes*;
That shall infuse eternal *spring*,
And ever-lasting flourishing:
Drink every letter on't, in *Stum*;
And make it brisk *Champaign* become; 570
Where ere you tread your foot shall set
The *Primrose* and the *Violet*;

556 *Jupiters* Oracle in *Epirus*, near the City of *Dodona*. *Ubi Nemus erat Jovi sacrum, Querneum totum in quo Jovis Dodonæi Templum fuisse narratur.*

542 *Bargain*. B2: *Bargain*, B1, C   560 *Pigsney*, C: *Pigsney*. B

All *spices*, *perfumes*, and *sweet powders*,
Shall borrow from your breath their *Odors*;
Nature her *Charter* shall renew,
And take all *lives* of things from you;
The *World* depend upon your *eye*,
And when you frown upon it, die.
Only our *loves*, shall still survive,
New worlds and natures to out-live;   580
And, like to *Heraulds* Moons, remain
All *Crescents*, without *change* or *wane*.

Hold, hold, Quoth she, no more of this,
Sir *Knight*, you take your aim amiss;
For you will find it a hard *Chapter*,
To catch me with *Poetique Rapture*,
In which your *Mastery* of *Art*
Doth shew it self, and not your *Heart*:
Nor will you raise in mine *combustion*,
By dint of high *Heroique* fustian: 590
Shee that with *Poetry* is won,
Is but a *Desk* to write upon;
And what men say of her, they mean,
No more, then that on which they *lean*.
Some with *Arabian spices* strive
T'embalm her, cruelly alive;
Or *season* her, as *French* Cooks use,
Their *Haut-gusts*, *Boullies*, or *Ragusts*;
Use her so barbarously ill,
To grind her Lips upon a *Mill*,   600
Until the *Facet Doublet* doth
Fit their *Rhimes* rather then her mouth;
Her mouth compar'd t'an *Oyster's*, with
A Row of *Pearl* in't, stead of *Teeth*;
Others, make *Posies* of her *Cheeks*,
Where *red*, and *whitest* colours mix;
In which the *Lilly*, and the *Rose*
For *Indian* Lake, and Ceruse goes.
The *Sun*, and *Moon* by her bright eys,
Eclips'd, and darkned in the *Skies*;   610

594 that on which *C*: on the thing *B*   598 *Buollies B, C*

Are but *black-patches*, that she wears,
Cut into *Suns*, and *Moons*, and *Stars*.
By which *Astrologers*, as well
As those in *Heav'n* above, can tell
What strange Events they do foreshow
Unto her Under-world below.
Her voyce the *Musique* of the *Spheres*
So loud, it deafens mortal ears;
As wise *Philosophers* have thought,
And that's the cause we hear it not.   620
This has been done by some, who those
Th' ador'd in *Rhime* would kick in *Prose*;
And in those *Ribbins* would have hung,
Of which melodiously they sung.
That have the hard *fate*, to write best
Of those still, that deserve it least;
It matters not how *false*, or *forc'd*,
So the *best* things be said o'th' *worst*;
It goes for nothing when 'tis sed
Only the *Arrow*'s drawn to th'head,   630
Whether it be a *Swan* or *Goose*
They level at: So *Shepherds* use
To set the same *mark* on the *hip*
Both of their *sound* and *rotten Sheep*.
For *Wits* that carry *low* or *wide*,
Must be aim'd *higher*, or *beside*,
The *mark*, which else they ne'r come *nigh*,
But when they take their aim awry.
But I do wonder you should chuse
This way t'attack me with your *Muse*,   640
As one cut out to pass your tricks on,
With *Fulhams* of *Poetique fiction*:
I rather hop'd, I should no more
Hear from you, oth' *Gallanting* score:
For hard *dry-bastings* use to prove
The readiest Remedies of *Love*,
Next a *dry-diet*: But if those fayl,
Yet this uneasie Loop-hold *Jail*

613–16 *added in* C

In which y' are *hamperd* by the *fet-lock*,
Cannot but put y' in mind of *Wedlock*:   650
Wedlock, that's worse then any hole here,
If that may serve you for a *Cooler*;
T'allay your *Mettle*, all agog
Upon a *Wife*, the heavy'r clog.
Nor rather thank your gentler *Fate*,
That, for a bruis'd or broken *Pate*,
Has freed you from those *knobs*, that grow
Much harder, on the marry'd *Brow*:
But if no dread can cool your Courage,
From vent'ring on that *Dragon*, Marriage;   660
Yet give me *Quarter*, and advance
To nobler aims, your Puissance:
Level at *Beauty*, and at *Wit*,
The fairest *mark* is easiest hit.

Quoth *Hudibras*, I'm before hand
In that already, with your command:
For where does *Beauty*, and high *Wit*,
But in your *Constellation* meet?

Quoth she, What does a *Match* imply
But *likeness* and *equality*?   670
I know you cannot think mee fit,
To be the *Yoke-fellow* of your *Wit*:
Nor take one of so mean *Deserts*,
To be the *Partner* of your *Parts*;
A *Grace*, which if I could believe,
I've not the Conscience to receive.

That *Conscience*, quoth *Hudibras*,
Is misinform'd; I'l state the *Case*.
A man may be a *Legal Doner*
Of any thing, whereof he's *Owner*;   680
And may confer it where he lists,
I'th' Judgment of all *Casuists*:
Then, *Wit*, and *Parts*, and *Valour* may
Be ali'nated, and made away,

672 the] th' *C*

By those that are *Proprietors*;
As I may give, or sell my *Horse*.

Quoth she, I grant the *Case* is true,
And proper 'twixt your *Horse* and you;
But whether I may *take*, as well
As you may *give* away, or sell?   690
Buyers you know are bid beware;
And worse then Thieves *Receivers* are.
How shall I answer *Hue* and *Cry*,
For a *Roan-Guelding*, twelve hands high,
All spur'd and switch'd, a *Lock* on's hoof,
A *sorrel-mane*; can I bring proof,
Where, when, by whom, and what y' were sold for,
And in the open *Market* toll'd for?
Or should I take you for a stray,
You must be kept a year, and day,   700
(Ere I can own you) here i'th' *Pound*,
Where if y' are sought you may be found:
And in the mean time I must pay
For all your *Provender* and *Hey*.

Quoth he, It stands me much upon,
T'*enervate* this *Objection*,
And prove my self, by *Topique* clear,
No *Guelding* as you would infer.
Loss of *Virility's* aver'd
To be the cause of loss of *Beard*,   710
That does (like *Embryo* in the Womb)
Abortive on the *Chin* become.
This first a *Woman* did invent,
In envy of *Mans* ornament.
Semiramis of *Babylon*,
Who first of all cut men 'oth' *Stone*:

715 *Semiramis*, Queen of *Assyria*, is said to be the first that invented *Eunuches*.
Semiramis teneros mares castravit omnium Prima. Am. Marcel. L.14.p.22. Which is
something strange in a Lady of her Constitution, who is said to have receiv'd Horses
into her embraces (as another Queen did a Bull). But that perhaps may be the reason,
why she after thought Men not worth the while.

To marr their *Beards*, and lay'd foundation
Of *Sow-geldering* operation.
Look on this *Beard*, and tell me whether,
Eunuchs wear such, or *Gueldings* either.   720
Next it appears, I am no *Horse*,
That I can argue, and discourse,
Have but two *legs*, and ne're a *tayl*.

Quoth she, That nothing will avayl;
For some *Philosophers* of late here,
Write, Men have fower legs by *Nature*,
And that 'tis *Custom* makes them go
Erroneously upon but two;
As 'twas in *Germany* made good,
B'a Boy, that lost himself in a *Wood*;   730
And growing down t'a man, was wont
With *Wolves* upon all four to hunt.
As for your reasons drawn from *tayls*,
We cannot say, th' are true, or false
Till you explain your self, and show
B'experiment 'tis so, or no.

Quoth he, if you'l joyn *Issue* on't,
I'l give you satisfactory account;
So you will promise, if you loose,
To settle all, and be my *Spouse*.   740

That never shall be done (Quoth she)
To one that wants a *Tayl*, by me:
For *Tayls* by Nature sure were meant
As well as *Beards*, for ornament:
And though the *Vulgar* count them homely,
In *man* or *beast*, they are so comely,
So *Gentee*, *Allamode*, and handsom,
I'l never marry *man* that wants one:
And till you can demonstrate plain,
You have one equal to your *Mane*,   750

725 *S. K.D.* in his Book of *Bodies*; who has this story of the *German-Boy*, which he
indeavors to make good, by several Natural Reasons; By which those who have the
Dexterity to believe what they please, may be fully satisfied of the probability of it.

743 **Nature** Br (*errata*), B2: Natures Br, C

I'l be torn piece-meal by a *Horse*,
Ere I'l take you *for better or worse*.
The *Prince* of *Cambays* dayly food,
Is *Aspe*, and *Basilisque*, and *Toad*,
Which makes him have so strong a breath,
Each night he stinks a *Queen* to death;
Yet I shall rather ly'n his *Arms*
Then yours, on any other *tearms*.

Quoth he, What *Nature* can afford,
I shall produce upon my word,   760
And if she ever gave that *boon*
To man, I'l prove that I have one;
I mean, by *postulate Illation*,
When you shall offer just occasion;
But since y' have yet deny'd to give
My *Heart*, your *Pris'ner*, a Reprieve,
But made it sink down to my heel,
Let that at least your Pitty feel,
And for the sufferings of your *Martyr*,
Give it's poor entertainer *quarter*;   770
And by *Discharge*, or *Main-prize* grant
Deliv'ry from this base *Restraint*.

Quoth she, I grieve to see your *Leg*
Stuck in a hole here like a *Peg*,
And if I knew which way to do't
(Your *Honor* safe) I'de let you out.
That *Dames* by *Jail-delivery*
Of *Errant Knights* have been set free,
When by *Enchantment* they have been,
And sometimes for it too, lay'd in;   780
Is that which *Knights* are bound to do
By *Order*, *Oath*, and *Honor* too:
For what are they *renown'd* and *famous* else
But aiding of distressed *Damosels*?
But for a *Lady* no ways *Errant*
To free a *Knight*, we have no warrant

In any Authentical *Romance*,
Or *Classique Author* yet of *France* :
And I'de be loath to have you break
An Ancient *Custom* for a freak,   790
Or *Innovation* introduce
In place of things of *antique* use;
To free your heels by any Course
That might b'unwholsom to your *Spurs·*
Which if I should consent unto,
It is not in my power to do;
For 'tis a service must be done yee,
With solemn previous Ceremony.
Which always has been us'd t'untie
The *Charms* of those who here do lie;   800
For as the *Ancients* heretofore
To *Honor's Temple* had no dore,
But that which thorough *Virtues* lay;
So, from this *Dungeon*, there's no way
To *honor'd freedom*, but by passing
That other *Virtuous* School of *Lashing*,
Where *Knights* are kept in narrow lists,
With wooden *Lockets* 'bout their wrists,
In which they for a while are *Tenants*
And for their *Ladies* suffer *Penance* :   810
Whipping that's *Virtues* Governess,
Tutress of *Arts* and *Sciences*;
That mends the gross mistakes of *Nature*,
And puts new life into dull matter;
That lays foundation for *Renown*,
And all the *honors* of the *Gown* :
This suffer'd, they are set at large
And *free'd* with honorable discharge,
Then in their *Robes* the *Penitentials*,
Are streight presented with *Credentials*,   820
And in their way attended on
By *Magistrates* of ev'ry Town;
And all respect, and charges pay'd,
They'r to their ancient *Seats* convey'd.
Now if you'l venture for my sake,
To try the toughness of your *back*,

And suffer (as the rest have done)
The laying of a *Whipping* on,
(And may you prosper in your suit,
As you with equal Vigour do't)   830
I here engage to be your Bayl,
And free you from the Unknightly *Jayle*.
But since our *Sexe*'s modesty
Will not allow I should be by,
Bring me on *Oath*, a fair account,
And *honor* too, when you have don't;
And I'l admit you to the place,
You claim as *due* in my good grace.
If *Matrimony*, and *Hanging* go
By *Dest'ny*, why not *Whipping* too?   840
What med'cine else can cure the *fits*
Of *Lovers*, when they lose their *Wits*?
Love is a *Boy*, by *Poets* styl'd,
Then *Spare the rod, and spill the Child.*
A *Persian* Emp'rour whip'd his Grannum
The Sea, his Mother *Venus* came on;
And hence some Rev'rend men approve
Of *Rosemary* in making *Love*.
As skilful *Coopers* hoop their Tubs,
With *Lydian* and with *Phrygian* Dubs;   850
Why may not *Whipping* have as good
A Grace, perform'd in time and mood;
With comely movement, and by *Art*,
Rayse Passion in a *Ladies* heart?
It is an easier way, to make
Love by, then that which many take.
Who would not rather suffer *Whipping*,
Than swallow *Toasts* of bits of *Ribbin*?
Make wicked *Verses*, *Treats*, and *Faces*,
And spell names over, with *Bere-glasses*?   860
Be under Vows to *hang* and *dy*
Loves Sacrifice, and all a *lie*?

845 *Xerxes* who us'd to whip the Seas and Winds. *In corum, atque Eurum solitus sevire
Flagellis.* Juven. Sat. 10.

831–2 to be . . . *Jayle C*: my self to loose yee, | And free your *heels* from *Caperdewsie B*

With *China-Orenges*, and *Tarts*,
And whining *Plays*, lay baits for Hearts?
Bribe *Chamber-maids* with *love* and *money*,
To break no Roguish *jeasts* upon yee?
For Lillyes limn'd on *Cheeks*, and Roses,
With painted perfumes, hazard noses?
Or vent'ring to be brisk and wanton,
Do penance in a *Paper-lanthorn*?   870
All this you may compound for, now
By suffering what I offer you:
Which is no more then has been done,
By *Knights* for *Ladies* long agone:
Did not the Great *La Mancha* do so
For the *Infanta Del Taboso*?
Did not th'Illustrious *Bassa* make
Himself a *Slave* for *Misse's* sake?
And with Buls-pizzle, for her *love*
Was taw'd as gentle as a Glove?   880
Was not Young *Florio* sent (to cool
His flame for *Biancafiore*) to School,
Where *Pedant* made his *Pathick* Bum
For her sake suffer *Martyrdom*?
Did not a certain *Lady* whip,
Of late, her husband's own Lordship?
And though a Grandee of the *House*,
Claw'd him with *Fundamental* blows,
Ty' d him stark-naked to a Bed-post
And firk'd his Hide, as if sh' had rid post;   890
And after in the *Sessions-Court*
Where *Whipping*'s Judg'd, had *honor* for't?
This *swear* you will perform, and then
I'l set you from th'inchanted *Den*,
And the *Magician*'s Circle clear.

Quoth he, I do *profess* and *swear*,
And will perform what you enjoyn,
Or may I never see you *mine*.

Amen (quoth she;) Then turn'd about
And bid her *Squier* let him out.   900
But e're an *Artist* could be found
T'undo the *Charms* another bound,
The *Sun* grew low, and left the Skies,
Put down (some write) by *Ladies* eys.
The *Moon* pul'd off her Vail of Light,
That hides her Face by day from sight,
(Mysterious Vail, of brightness made,
That's both her luster, and her shade)
And in the Night as freely shon,
As if her Rays had been her own: 910
For Darkness is the proper Sphere,
Where all false Glories use t'appear.
The twinckling *Stars* began to muster
And glitter with their borrow'd luster,
While Sleep the weary'd *World* reliev'd,
By counterfeiting *Death* reviv'd.
Our *Vot'ry* thought it best t'adjorn
His *Whipping*-penance till the morn,
And not to carry on a *Work*
Of such *importance* in the Dark   920
With erring haste, but rather stay,
And do't in th'open face of *Day*;
And in the mean time, go in quest
Of next *Retreat* to take his Rest.

900 *Squier* B2 : *Squire B1, C2* : *Squirer B1 (errata), C1*   909–10 **Night . . . own**
C : *Lanthorn* of the Night | With shining *Horns,* hung out her light *B*   911–12 *added*
in C

THE SECOND PART

CANTO II

THE ARGUMENT

The Knight *and* Squire *in hot Dispute,*
Within an Ace of falling out,
Are parted with a sudden fright
Of strange Alarm, and stranger sight;
With which adventuring to stickle,
They'r sent away in nasty pickle.

'T is strange how some mens Tempers suit
(Like *Bawd*, and *Brandee*) with Dispute,
That for their own *opinions* stand fast,
Only to have them claw'd and canvast.
That keep their *Consciences* in Cases
As *Fidlers* do their *Crowds* and *Bases*.
Ne'r to be us'd but when they'r bent
To play a fit for *Argument*.
Make *true* and *false*, *unjust* and *just*,
Of no use but to be discust.   10
Dispute and set a *Paradox*
Like a streight Boot upon the Stocks
And stretch it more unmercifully
Then *Helmont*, *Mountaygn*, *White*, or *Tully*.
So th'Ancient *Stoicks* in their Porch
With fierce dispute maintain'd their *Church*
Beat out their Brains in fight and study,
To prove that *Virtue* is a *Body*,

---

15 *In Porticu (Stoicorum Scholâ Athenis) Discipulorum seditionibus, mille Quadringenti triginta Cives interfecti sunt.* Diog. Laert. *in vita Zenonis.* p.383. Those old *Virtuoso's* were better Proficients in those Exercises, then the Modern, who seldom improve higher then Cuffing, and kicking.

That *Bonum* is an *Animal*,
Made good with stout *Polemique* Braul   20
In which, some Hundreds on the Place
Were slain outright, and many a face
Retrencht of *Nose*, and *Eys*, and *Beard*
To maintain what their *Sect* aver'd,
All which, the *Knight* and *Squire* in wrath
Had like t'have suffer'd for their faith,
Each striving to make good his own,
As by the *Sequel* shall be shown.
The Sun had long since in the Lap
Of *Thetis*, taken out his *Nap*,   30
And like a *Lobster* boyl'd, the *Morn*
From *black* to *red* began to turn.

When *Hudibras*, whom thoughts and aking
'Twixt sleeping kept, all night, and waking,
Began to rub his drowsie eys,
And from his Couch prepar'd to rise;
Resolving to dispatch the Deed
He vow'd to do, with trusty speed.
But first with knocking lowd and bauling,
He rows'd the *Squire*, in *Truckle* lolling,   40
And, after many Circumstances,
Which vulgar *Authors* in *Romances*
Do use to spend their *time*, and *wits* on
To make impertinent Description;
They got (with much ado) to *horse*,
And to the *Castle* bent their Course,
In which, he to the *Dame* before
To suffer *whipping* duty swore:
Where now arriv'd, and half unharnest
To carry on the *work* in earnest,   50
He stop'd and paws'd upon the sudden,
And with a serious forehead plodding,

19 *Bonum* is such a kind of Animal, as our Modern *Virtuosi* from Don *Quixot*, will
have Windmils under sail to be. The same Authors are of opinion, That all Ships
are Fishes while they are afloat, but when they are run on ground, or laid up in the
Dock, become Ships again.

48 duty *B1 (errata)*, *B2*: duely *B1*: Duty *C*

Sprung a new Scruple in his head,
Which first he scratch'd, and after sed,
Whether it be direct *infringing*
An *Oath*, if I should wave this *swinging*,
And what I've sworn to bear, forbear
And so b'*equivocation* swear;
Or whether 't be a lesser *Sin*
To be forsworn then act the thing,   60
Are deep and subtle *points*, which must,
T'inform my conscience, be discust.
In which to *err* a tittle, may
To *errors* infinite make way:
And therefore I desire to know
Thy *Judgment*, e're we further go.

Quoth *Ralpho*, since you do injoyn't
I shall inlarge upon the *Point*.
And for my own part do not doubt
Th'*Affirmative* may be made out.   70
But first to *state* the *Case* aright,
For best advantage of our light;
And thus 'tis: Whether 't be a *Sin*
To *Claw* and *Curry* your own *skin*
Greater, or less, then to forbear,
And that you are forsworn, forswear.
But first, 'oth' first: The *Inward Man*,
And *Outward*, like a *Clan*, and *Clan*,
Have always been at Daggers-drawing,
And one another Clapper-clawing: 80
Not that they really cuff, or fence,
But in a Spiritual *Mystique* sence,
Which to mistake, and make 'm squabble,
In literal fray, 's abhominable;
'Tis heathenish, in frequent use
With *Pagans*, and *Apostate Jews*,
To offer sacrifice of *Bridewells*:
Like modern *Indians* to their *Idols*,
And mungrel *Christians* of our times,
That expiat less, with greater *Crimes*,   90

53 head, C: head; B   54 Which . . . scratch'd C: He scratch'd it first B

And call the foul *Abhomination*,
Contrition, and *Mortification*.
Is't not enough w' are bruis'd, and kicked,
With sinful members of the wicked,
Our vessels, that are *sanctifi'd*,
Profan'd, and *Curry'd*, back and side;
But we must claw our selves, with shameful,
And Heathen stripes, by their example?
Which (were there nothing to forbid it)
Is *Impious*, because they did it.   100
This therefore may be justly reckon'd
A *heinous* sin. Now to the second,
That *Saints* may claim a *Dispensation*
To *swear* and *forswear*, on occasion;
I doubt not, but it will appear,
With pregnant light. The *point* is clear.
Oaths are but *words*, and *words* but *wind*,
Too feeble implements to *bind*;
And hold with *deeds* proportion, so
As *shadows* to a *substance* do.   110
Then when they strive for *place*, 'tis fit
The *weaker Vessel* should submit:
Although your *Church* be opposite
To ours, as *Black-Friers*, are to *White*,
In *Rule* and *Order*: Yet I grant
You are a *Reformado Saint*,
And what the *Saints* do claim as due,
You may pretend a Title to:
But *Saints* whom *Oaths*, or *Vows* oblige,
Know little of their *Priviledge*;   120
Further (I mean) then carrying on
Some self-advantage of their own.
For if the *Dev'l*, to serve his turn,
Can tell *Truth*; why the *Saints* should scorn
When it servs theirs, to *swear*, and *lie*,
I think, there's little reason why:
Else h' has a greater pow'r then they,
Which 'twere *impiety* to say.

106 light. B2, C: light, Br

W' are not commanded to forbear,
Indefinitely, at all to *swear*,   130
But to *swear* idly, and in vain,
Without self-interest, or gain.
For, breaking of an *Oath* and *Lying*,
Is but a kind of *Self-denying*,
A *Saint-like virtue*, and from hence,
Some have broke *Oaths*, by *Providence*:
Some, to the *Glory of the Lord*,
Perjur'd themselves, and broke their word:
And this the constant *Rule* and *practice*,
Of all our late *Apostles Acts* is.   140
Was not the *Cause* at first begun
With *Perjury*, and carry'd on?
Was there an *Oath* the *Godly* took,
But, in due time and place, they broke?
Did we not bring our *Oaths* in first,
Before our *Plate*, to have them burst,
And cast in fitter *models*, for
The present use of *Church* and *War*?
Did not our *Worthies* of the *House*,
Before they broke the *Peace*, break *Vows*?   150
For having free'd us, first from both
Th'*Allegeance*, and *Supremacy-Oath*;
Did they not, next, compel the *Nation*,
To take, and break the *Protestation*?
To *swear*, and after to *recant*
The *Solemn League and Covenant*?
To take th'*Engagement*, and disclaim it,
Enforc'd by those, who first did frame it?
Did they not swear at first, to *fight*
For the KING's *safety*, and his *Right*?   160
And after march'd to find him out,
And charg'd him home with *Horse* and *Foot*?
And yet still had the confidence,
To swear, it was in His *defence*?
Did they not swear to *live* and *die*
With *Essex*, and streight lay'd him by?

If that were all, for some have *swore*
As false as they, if th' did no more.
Did they not *swear* to maintain *Law*,
In which, that *swearing* made a *Flaw*?   170
For *Protestant Religion* Vow,
That did that *Vowing* disallow?
For *Priviledg* of *Parliament*,
In which that *swearing* made a *Rent*?
And, since, of all the *three*, not one
Is left in being, 'tis well known.
Did they not *swear*, in express words,
To prop and back the *House of Lords*?
And after turn'd out the whole *House-ful*
Of *Peers*, as dang'rous, and unuseful?   180
So *Crumwel* with deep *Oaths*, and *Vows*,
Swore all the *Commons* out 'oth' *House*,
Vow'd that the *Red-coats* would disband,
I marry would they, at their Command.
And trol'd 'em on, and *swore*, and *swore*,
Till th'*Army* turn'd 'em out of *Dore*;
This tells us plainly, what they thought,
That *Oaths* and *swearing* go for nought.
And that by them th' were only meant,
To serve for an *Expedient*.   190
What was the *Publick Faith* found out for,
But to slur men of what they fought for.
The *Publick Faith*, which ev'ry one
Is bound t'observe, yet kept by none;
And if that go for nothing, why
Should *Private faith* have such a tye?

Oaths were not purpos'd more then *Law*,
To keep the *Good* and *Just* in awe,
But to confine the *Bad* and *Sinful*
Like Moral Cattle in a *Pinfold*.   200
A *Saint*'s of th'heavenly Realm a *Peer*:
And as no *Peer* is bound to *swear*,
But on the *Gospel* of his *Honor*,
Of which he may dispose, as *Owner*;
It follows, though the thing be *forgery*,

And false, th' affirm, it is no *perjury*,
But a meer *Ceremony*, and a breach
Of nothing, but a form of speech,
And goes for no more when 'tis took,
Then meer *saluting* of the *Book*.   210
Suppose the *Scriptures* are of force,
They'r but *Commissions* of Course,
And *Saints* have freedom to digress,
And vary from 'em, as they please;
Or misinterpret them, by *private*
Instructions, to all *Aims* they drive at.
Then why should we our selves *abridg*,
And *Curtail* our own *Priviledg*?
Quakers (that, like to *Lanthorns*, bear
Their light within 'em) will not *swear*.   220
Their *Gospel* is an *Accidence*,
By which they construe *Conscience*,
And hold no *sin* so deeply *red*,
As that of breaking *Priscian*'s head
(The *Head* and *Founder* of their *Order*,
That stirring *Hats* held worse then murder)
These thinking th' are oblig'd to *Troth*
In *swearing*, will not take an *Oath*;
Like Mules, who if th' have not their will,
To keep their own pace, stand stock still;   230
But they are weak, and little know
What Free-born *Consciences* may do.
'Tis the *temptation* of the Devill,
That makes all humane actions evill:
For *Saints* may do the same things by
The *Spirit*, in *sincerity*,
Which other men are tempted to,
And at the Devils instance do;
And yet the Actions be contrary,
Just as the *Saints* and *Wicked* vary.   240
For as on land there is no *Beast*,
But in some *Fish* at Sea's exprest,
So in the *Wicked* there's no *Vice*,
Of which the *Saints* have not a spice;

206 false, *C*: false *B*   210 Then *C*: But *B*

And yet that thing that's *pious* in
The one, in th'other is a *Sin*.
Is't not *Ridiculous*, and *Nonsence*,
A *Saint* should be a slave to *Conscience*?
That ought to be above such Fancies,
As far, as above *Ordinances*.   250
She's of the *Wicked*, as I guess,
B'her *looks*, her *language*, and her *dress*;
And though, like *Constables*, we search
For false Wares, one anothers *Church*:
Yet all of us hold this for true,
No Faith is to the wicked due;
For *Truth* is *Pretious*, and *Divine*,
Too rich a *Pearl* for *Carnal Swine*.

Quoth *Hudibras*, All this is true,
Yet 'tis not fit, that all men knew   260
Those *Mysteries*, and *Revelations*;
And therefore *Topical* Evasions
Of subtle *Turns*, and *Shifts* of sence,
Serve best with th' *Wicked* for pretence,
Such as the learned *Jesuits* use,
And *Presbyterians*, for excuse,
Against the *Protestants*, when th' happen
To find their *Churches* taken napping.
As thus: A breach of *Oath* is *Duple*,
And either way admits a *scruple*,   270
And may þe *ex parte* of the *Maker*,
More criminal, then th'injur'd *Taker*.
For he that strains too far a *Vow*,
Will break it like an o're-bent *Bow*:
And he that made, and forc'd it, broke it,
Not he that for convenience took it:
A broken Oath is, *quatenus Oath*,
As sound t'all purposes of *Troath*,
As broken *Laws* are ne're the worse,
Nay till th' are broken, have no force,   280
What's *Justice* to a man, or *Laws*,
That never comes within their Claws?
They have no pow'r, but to admonish,

Cannot control, coerce, or punish,
Until they'r broken, and then touch
Those only that do make them such.
Beside, no *Engagement* is allow'd,
By men in *Prison* made, for Good;
For when they'r set at *liberty*,
They'r from th'*Engagement* too, set free ·   290
The *Rabbins* write, when any *Jew*
Did make to *God*, or *Man*, a *Vow*,
Which afterward he found untoward,
And stubborn to be kept, or too hard;
Any three other *Jews* 'oth' *Nation*,
Might free him from the *Obligation*:
And have not two *Saints* pow'r to use,
A greater *Priviledge* then three *Jews*?
The *Court* of *Conscience*, which in *Man*
Should be *supream* and *soveraign*;   300
Is't fit, should be *subordinate*,
To ev'ry petty *Court* i'th' *State*,
And have less Power then the *lesser*,
To deal with *Perjury* at pleasure?
Have it's proceedings disallow'd, or
Allow'd, at fancy of *Py-powder*?
Tell all it does, or does not know,
For swearing *ex Officio*?
Be forc'd t'empeach a broken hedg,
And *Pigs* un-ring'd at *Vis.Franc.Pledge*.   310
Discover *Thieves*, and *Bawds*, *Recusants*,
Priests, *Witches*, *Eves-droppers*, and *Nusance*;
Tell who did play at Games unlawful,
And who fill'd *Pots* of *Ale* but half-ful.
And have no pow'r at all, nor shift,
To help it self at a dead lift?
Why should not *Conscience* have *Vacation*
As well as other Courts 'oth' *Nation*?
Have equal power to adjorn
Appoint *Appearance* and *Retorn*?   320
And make as nice distinctions serve
To split a Case; as those that carve
Invoking Cookolds names, hit joynts,

Why should not tricks as slight, do points?
Is not th'*High-Court of Justice* sworn
To just that Law, that serves their *turn*?
Make their own Jealousies High-Treason,
And fix 'em whomsoe're they please on?
Cannot the *Learned Councel* there
Make Laws in any shape appear?   330
Mould 'em, as *Witches* do their clay,
When they make *Pictures* to destroy?
And vex 'em into any form,
That fits their purpose to do harm?
Rack 'em until they do confess,
Impeach of Treason, whom they please,
And most perfidiously condemn,
Those that engag'd their *Lives* for them?
And yet do nothing in their own sense,
But what they ought by *Oath* and *Conscience*!   340
Can they not juggle, and with slight
Conveyance, play with *wrong* and *right*;
And sell their blasts of *wind* as dear,
As *Lapland Witches* bottled *Air*?
Will not *Fear*, *Favour*, *Bribe*, and *Grutch*,
The same Case sev'ral ways adjudge;
As Seamen, with the self-same *Gale*
Will sev'ral different Courses sayl?
As when the *Sea* breaks o're its bounds,
And overflows the level grounds;   350
Those *Banks* and *Dams*, that like a *Screen*,
Did keep it out, now keep it in:
So when *Tyrannical Usurpation*
Invades the Freedom of a *Nation*,
The *Laws* 'oth' Land that were entended
To keep it out, are made defend it.
Do's not in *Chanc'ry* ev'ry man *swear*,
What makes best for him, in his Answer?
Is not the winding up *Witnesses*,
And nicking, more then half the buis'ness?   360
For *Witnesses*, like *Watches*, go
Just as they'r set, too fast or slow.

326 just *B1* (*errata*): judg *B1*: judge *B2, C*

And where in *Conscience*, th' are streit-lac'd;
'Tis ten to one, that side is cast.
Do not your *Juries* give their *Verdict*
As if they felt the *Cause*, not heard it?
And as they please make *Matter of Fact*
Run all on one side, as th' are pack't?
Nature has made Mans breast no *Windores*,
To publish what he does within dores;   370
Nor what dark secrets there inhabit,
Unless his own rash folly blab it.
If *Oaths* can do a man no good,
In his own buis'ness, why they shou'd
In other matters, do him hurt,
I think there's little reason for't.
He that imposes an *Oath*, makes it,
Not he, that for convenience takes it:
Then how can any man be said,
To break an *Oath* he never made?   380
These *Reasons* may perhaps look odly
To th' *Wicked*, though they evince the *Godly*;
But if they will not serve to clear
My *Honor*, I am ne're the near.
Honor is like that glassy Bubble
That finds *Philosophers* such trouble,
Whose least part crackt, the whole does fly
And *Wits* are crack'd, to find out why.

Quoth *Ralpho*, Honor's but a Word
To swear by only, in a *Lord*:   390
In other men 'tis but a Huff,
To vapour with, instead of proof,
That like a *Wen*, looks big, and swels,
Is senseless, and just nothing else.

Let it (quoth he) be what it will
It has the *World*'s opinion still.
But as men are not *Wise* that run
The slightest *hazard*, they may shun:
There may a *Medium* be found out
To clear to all the *World* the doubt;   400

And that is, if a man may do't
By *Proxy* whipt, or Substitute.

Though nice, and dark the *Point* appear,
(Quoth *Ralph*) it may hold up, and clear.
That *Sinners* may supply the place
Of suff'ring *Saints*, is a plain *Case*.
Justice gives *Sentence*, many times,
On one man for another's *Crimes*,
Our Brethren of *New-England* use
Choice *Malefactors* to excuse,   410
And *hang* the *Guiltless* in their stead,
Of whom the *Churches* have less need.
As lately't happen'd: In a Town,
There liv'd a *Cobler*, and but one,
That out of *Doctrine* could cut *Use*,
And mend mens *lives*, as well as *shoos*.
This pretious *Brother* having slain,
In times of *Peace*, an *Indian*,
(Not out of *Malice*, but meer *Zeal*
Because he was an *Infidel*)   420
The mighty *Tottipottymoy*
Sent to our *Elders* an *Envoy*,
Complaining sorely of the *Breach*
Of *League*, held forth by Brother *Patch*,
Against the *Articles* in force
Between both *Churches*, his, and ours,
For which he crav'd the *Saints*, to render
Into his hands, or hang th'*Offender*:
But they maturely having weigh'd,
They had no more but him 'oth' Trade,   430
(A man, that serv'd them in a double
Capacity to *Teach*, and *Cobble*)
Resolv'd to spare him, yet to do
The *Indian Hoghgan Moghgan* too
Impartial justice; in his stead did
Hang an old *Weaver* that was Bed-rid.

413-14 This History of the Cobler has been attested by Persons of good credit, who were upon the place when it was done.

Then wherefore may not you be skip'd,
And in your room another *whip'd*:
For all *Philosophers*, but the *Sceptick*,
Hold *Whipping* may be *Sympathetick*.   440

It is enough quoth *Hudibras*,
Thou hast resolv'd, and clear'd the *Case*,
And canst in *Conscience*, not refuse,
From thy own *Doctrine*, to raise *Use*:
I know thou wilt not (for my sake)
Be tender-Conscienc'd of thy back:
Then strip thee of thy Carnal-*Jerkin*,
And give thy *outward-fellow* a ferking.
For when thy *Vessel*, is new *hoop'd*,
All Leaks of *sinning* will be stop'd.   450

Quoth *Ralpho*, You mistake the matter,
For in all *Scruples* of this Nature,
No man includes himself, nor turns
The *Point* upon his own Concerns.
As no man of his own self catches,
The *Itch*, or amorous *French-aches*:
So no man does himself convince
By his own *Doctrine* of his *Sins*.
And though all cry down *Self*, none means
His own self in a *literal sense*.   460
Beside, it is not only *Foppish*,
But *Vile*, *Idolatrous*, and *Popish*,
For one man, out of his own Skin,
To firk and whip another's *Sin*:
As *Pedants* out of School-boys breeches
Do claw and curry their own Itches.
But in this Case it is profane,
And sinful too, because in Vain:
For we must take our *Oaths* upon it,
You did the *deed*, when I have done it.   470

Quoth *Hudibras*, That's answer'd soon;
Give us the *Whip*, wee'l lay it on.

Quoth *Ralpho*, That we may swear true,
'Twere properer that I whip'd you:
For when with your consent 'tis done,
The *Act* is really your own.

Quoth *Hudibras*, It is in vain
(I see) to argue 'gainst the grain,
Or, like the *Stars*, encline men to
What they'r averse themselves to do.   480
For when *Disputes* are wearyed out
'Tis *interest* still resolves the doubt;
But since no reason can confute yee,
I'l try to force you to your *Duty*;
For so it is, how e're you mince it,
As e're we part, I shall evince it;
And *curry* (if you stand out) whether
You will, or no, your *stubborn Leather*.
Canst thou refuse to bear thy part,
I'th' publick *Work*, base as thou art?   490
To higgle thus, for a few blows,
To gain thy *Knight* an opulent *Spouse*?
Whose *wealth*, his *Bowels* yearn to purchase
Meerly for th'Interest of the *Churches*,
And when he has it in his Claws,
Will not be hide-bound to the *Cause*;
Nor shalt thou find him a *Curmudgin*,
If thou dispatch it without grudging;
If not, resolve before we go,
That you and I must pull a Crow.   500

Y' had best (quoth *Ralpho*) as the *Ancients*
Say wisely, *have a care 'oth' main chance*,
And look before you, e're you leap;
For, as you sow, y' are like to reap.
And were y' as good as *George a Green*,
I shall make bold to turn agen;
Nor am I doubtful of the *Issue*
In a just *Quarrel*; and mine is so.

478 'gainst *C*: against *B*   485 you *C*: ye *B*

Is't fitting for a man of *Honor*
To whip the *Saints* like *Bishop Bonner*?   510
A *Knight* t'usurp the *Beadles* office,
For which y' are like to raise brave *Trophees*:
But I advise you (not for fear,
But for your own sake) to forbear,
And for the *Churches*, which may chance
From hence, to spring a variance;
And raise among themselves new *Scruples*,
Whom common *Danger* hardly couples.
Remember how in *Arms* and *Politicks*,
We still have worsted all your holy Tricks,   520
Trapan'd your Party with *Intregue*,
And took your *Grandees* down a peg.
New-modell'd th' *Army*, and *Cashier'd*
All that to *Legion-SMEC* adher'd,
Made a mere Utensill o' your *Church*,
And after left it in the lurch
A Scaffold to build up our own,
And when w' had done with't, pul'd it down.
O're reach'd your *Rabbins* of the *Synod*,
And snap'd their *Canons* with a *Why-not*.   530
(Grave *Synod-men*, that were rever'd
For solid face and depth of *Beard*)
Their *Classique-model* prov'd a Maggot,
Their *Directory* an *Indian Pagod*.
And drown'd their *Discipline* like a Kitten,
On which th' had been so long a sitting;
Decry'd it as a *Holy Cheat*,
Grown out of Date, and Obsolete,
And all the *Saints* o' the first Grass,
As Castling *Foles* of *Balams Ass*.   540

At this the *Knight* grew high in Chafe,
And staring furiously on *Raph*,
He trembled and look'd pale with Ire,
Like Ashes first, then Red as Fire.
Have I (quoth he) been ta'ne in fight,

529 O're reach'd *C*: Capoch'd *B*   533 Maggot, *B2*, *C2*: Maggot *B1*, *C1*
543–4 *added in* C

And, for so many *Moons* lay'n by't;
And when all other means did fail,
Have been exchang'd for *Tubs* of *Ale*:
Not but they thought me worth a *Ransom*,
Much more considerable, and handsom,   550
But for their own sakes, and for fear,
They were not safe, when I was there?
Now to be baffled by a *Scoundrel*,
An upstart *Sect'ry* and a *Mungrel*,
Such as breed out of peccant humours,
Of our own *Church*, like Wens, or Tumours:
And like a *Maggot* in a *Sore*,
Would that which gave it life, devour.
It never shall be done, or said:
With that he seiz'd upon his *Blade*.   560
And *Ralpho* too as quick, and bold,
Upon his *Basket-hilt* laid hold,
With equal readiness prepar'd,
To draw and stand upon his Guard.
When both were parted on the sudden,
With hideous *Clamour*, and a lowd one,
As if all sorts of *Noyse* had been
Contracted into one lowd *Din*;
Or that some Member to be chosen,
Had got the *odds* above a *Thousand*;   570
And by the greatness of his noyse
Prov'd fittest for his *Countryes* choice.
This strange surprisal put the *Knight*,
And wrathful *Squire*, into a fright,
And though they stood prepar'd, with fatall,
Impetuous rancour, to joyn *Battel*;
Both thought it was their wisest course,
To wave the Fight, and mount to *Horse*;
And to secure, by swift retreating,
Themselves from Danger of worse *beating*.   580
Yet neither of them would disparage
By utt'ring of his mind, his Courage,

548 The Knight was kept prisoner in *Exeter*, and after several exchanges propos'd,
but none accepted of, was at last releas'd for a Barrel of Ale, as he often us'd upon
all occasions to declare.

Which made 'em stoutly keep their ground
With horror and disdain, wind-bound.
And now the cause of all their *fear*,
By slow degrees approach'd so near,
They might distinguish diff'rent noyse
Of *Horns*, and *Pans*, and *Dogs*, and *Boyes*;
And *Kettle-Drums*, whose sullen *Dub*
Sounds like the hooping of a *Tub*:   590
But when the sight appear'd in view,
They found it was an *antique* Show,
A *Triumph*, that for *Pomp*, and *State*,
Did proudest *Romans* emulate;
For as the *Aldermen* of *Rome*
For foes at training overcome,
And not enlarging *Territory*,
(As some mistaken write in *Story*)
Being mounted in their best Aray,
Upon a *Carre*, and who but they?   600
And follow'd with a world of Tall-Lads,
That merry *Ditties* trol'd, and *Ballads*;
Did ride, with many a Good morrow,
Crying, *hey for our town* through the *burrough*.
So when this *Triumph* drew so nigh,
They might particulars descry,
They never saw two things so Pat,
In all respects, as this, and that.
First, He that led the *Cavalcate*,
Wore a Sowgelder's *Flagellate*,   610
On which he blew as strong a *Levet*,
As well-fee'd *Lawyer* on his *Breviate*,
When over one anothers Heads,
They charge (three Ranks at once) like Sweads.
Next *Pans*, and *Kettles* of all keys,
From *Trebles* down to *double-Base*,
And after them upon a *Nag*,
That might pass for a forehand Stag,
A *Cornet* rod, and on his Staff,
A Smock display'd, did proudly wave.   620

587 distinguish diff'rent *C*: discern respective *B*   604 *burrough.* B2:
burrough B1, C1   613–14 *added in C*   615 *Pans* B2, *C*: *Pan* B1

Then *Bagpipes* of the lowdest Drones,
With snuffling broken winded tones;
Whose blasts of air in pockets shut,
Sound filthier then from the Gut,
And make a viler noyse then *Swine*
In windy weather, when they whine.
Next, one upon a pair of *Panniers*
Full fraught with that, which for good manners
Shall here be nameless, mixt with *Grains*
Which he dispenc'd among the *Swains*,   630
And buisily upon the Crowd,
At random round about bestow'd.
Then mounted on a Horned *Horse*,
One bore a *Gaunilet* and *Guilt-spurs*,
Ty'd to the *Pummel* of a long *Sword*,
He held reverst the point turn'd downward.
Next after, on a Raw-bon'd Steed,
The Conqueror's *Standard-bearer* rid,
And bore aloft before the *Champion*
A *Petticoat* displaid, and Rampant;   640
Near whom the *Amazon* triumphant
Bestrid her *Beast*, and on the *Rump* on't
Sate *Face* to *Tayl*, and *Bum* to *Bum*,
The *Warrier* whilome overcome;
Arm'd with a *Spindle* and a *Distaff*,
Which as he rod, she made him twist off;
And when he loyter'd, o're her shoulder,
Chastiz'd the *Reformado* Souldier.
Before the *Dame*, and round about,
March'd *Whifflers*, and *Staffiers* on foot,   650
With *Lacquies*, *Grooms*, *Valets*, and *Pages*,
In fit and proper equipages;
Of whom, some Torches bore, some Links,
Before the Proud *Virago-Minx*,
That was both *Madam*, and a *Don*
Like *Nero*'s *Sporus*, or *Pope Jone*;
And at fit Periods the whole Rout
Set up their throats, with clamorous shout.
The *Knight* transported, and the *Squire*
Put up their Weapons, and their Ire,   660

And *Hudibras,* who us'd to ponder
On such Sights, with judicious wonder,
Could hold no longer to impart
His *Animadversions,* for his Heart.

Quoth he, In all my life till now
I ne'r saw so profane a *Show.*
It is a *Paganish* Invention,
Which *Heathen* Writers often mention:
And he that made it, had read *Goodwine*
(I warrant him) and understood him: 670
With all the Grecian Speeds and Stows:
That best describe those Antient Shows
And has observ'd all fit *Decorums,*
We find describ'd by old *Historians.*
For as a *Roman Conqueror,*
That put an end to forrain *War,*
Ent'ring the *Town* in Triumph for it,
Bore a Slave with him, in his Chariot:
So this insulting *Female Brave,*
Carries behind her here, a *Slave,*   680
And as the *Ancients* long ago,
When they in field defi'd the foe,
Hung out their *Mantles Della Guer;*
So her proud *Standard-bearer* here,
Waves, on his Spear, in dreadful manner,
A *Tyrian-Petticoat* for a *Banner:*
Next Links, and Torches, heretofore
Still borne before the *Emperor:*
And as in *Antique Triumphs, Eggs*
Were borne for mystical intregues;   690
There's one in Truncheon, like a Ladle,
That carries *Eggs* too, fresh or adle;

678   —— *Et sibi Consul*
        Ne placeat, curru servus portatur eodem. Juven. Sat. 10.
683 *Tunica Coccinea solebat pridie quam dimicandum esset, supra Prætorium poni quasi*
admonitio et indicium futuræ Pugnæ. Lipsius in Tacit. p. 56.
687 That the *Roman* Emperors were wont to have Torches born before them (by
day) in publick, appears by *Herodian* in *Pertinace.* Lip. in *Tacit* p. 16.

666 I ne'r B2: I, ne'r B1, C   669 he that] he, who C   670 (I . . . him:
C: Or *Ross,* or *Cælius Rodogine,* B   671–2 *added in* C
811844   O

And still at random, as he goes,
Among the Rabble-rout bestows.

Quoth *Ralpho*, you mistake the matter;
For, all th'*Antiquity* you smatter,
Is but a *Riding*, us'd of Course,
When the *Grey Mare's the better Horse*.
When o're the Breeches greedy *Women*
Fight, to extend their vast *Dominion*,   700
And in the cause Impatient *Grizel*
Has drub'd her Husband, with *Bulls pizzel*,
And brought him under *Covert-Baron*,
To turn her *Vassail* with a *Murrain*;
When *Wives* their Sexes shift, like *Hares*,
And ride their *Husbands*, like *Night-mares*,
And they in mortal *Battle* vanquish'd,
Are of their *Charter* dis-enfranchiz'd,
And by the Right of *War* like *Gills*
Condemn'd to *Distaff*, *Horns*, and *Wheels*;   710
For when Men by their *Wives* are Cow'd,
Their *Horns* of course are understood.

Quoth *Hudibras*, Thou still giv'st sentence
Impertinently, and against sense.
'Tis not the least disparagement,
To be defeated by th'event;
Nor, to be beaten by main *force*,
That does not make a *man* the worse,
Although his shoulders, with *batoon*,
Be claw'd and cudgeld to some tune :   720
A *Taylers* Prentice has no hard
Measure, that's bang'd with a true yard :
But to turn *Tayl*, or run away,
And without blows give up the Day;
Or to surrender e're the *Assault*,
That's no mans fortune but his fault :
And renders men of *Honor* less,
Then all th'*Adversity* of Success.
And only unto such, this Shew

Of *Horns* and *Petticoats* is due.   730
There is a lesser *Profanation*,
Like that the *Romans* call'd *Ovation*.
For as *Ovation* was allow'd
For *Conquest*, purchas'd without bloud,
So men decree those lesser Shows,
For *Vict'ry* gotten without Blows.
By dint of hard sharp *words*, which some
Give *Battle* with, and overcome;
These mounted in a *Chair Curule*,
Which *Moderns* call a *Cucking-stool*,   740
March proudly to the River's side,
And o're the *Waves* in *Triumph* ride.
Like *Dukes* of *Venice*, who are sed
The *Adriatique Sea* to wed,
And have a Gentler *Wife*, then those,
For whom the *State* decrees those Shows.
But both are *Heathenish*, and come
From th' Whores of *Babylon* and *Rome*,
And by the *Saints* should be withstood,
As *Antichristian* and *Lewd*,   750
And we, as such, should now contribute
Our utmost *struglings* to prohibite.

This said, They both advanc'd, and *rod*,
A *Dog-trot* through the bawling Crowd,
T'attack the *Leader*, and still prest,
Till they approach'd him *breast* to *breast*.
Then *Hudibras* with face, and hand,
Made signs for *Silence*, which obtain'd:
What means (quoth he) this dev'ls *procession*
With men of *Orthodox* Profession?   760
'Tis *Ethnique* and *Idolatrous*,
From *heathenism* deriv'd to us.
Does not the Whore of *Babylon* ride
Upon her *Horned-Beast* astride,
Like this proud *Dame*, who either is
A *Type* of her, or she of this?
Are things of Superstitious *function*,
Fit to be us'd in *Gospel Sunshine*?

It is an *Antichristian Opera*,
Much us'd in midnight-times of *Popery*,   770
A running after self-Inventions
Of wicked and profane *Intentions*,
To scandalize that *Sex*, for scoulding,
To whom the *Saints* are so beholding,
Women, that were our first *Apostles*,
Without whose aid w' had all been lost else,
Women, that left no stone unturn'd,
In which the *Cause* might be concern'd :
Brought in their childrens *spoons*, and *whistles*,
To purchase *Swords, Carbines* and *Pistols*:   780
Their Husbands *Cullies*, and *Sweet-hearts*,
To take the *Saints* and *Churches* Parts,
Drew several guifted *Brethren* in,
That for the *Bishops* would have been,
And fixt 'em constant to the *Party*,
With motives *powerful*, and *hearty*:
Their Husbands rob'd and made hard shifts,
T'administer unto their *Guifts*,
All they could rap and run and pilfer,
To scraps, and ends of Gold and Silver;   790
Rub'd down the *Teachers*, tyr'd and spent,
With holding forth for *Parliament*,
Pamper'd and edifi'd their *Zeal*,
With *Marrow-puddings*, many a meal;
Enabled them, with store of meat,
On controverted *Points* to eat.
And cram'd 'em till their *Guts* did ake
With *Cawdle, Custard*, and *Plum-cake*.
What have they done, or what left undone,
That might advance the *Cause* at *London*?   800
March'd, rank and file, with *Drum* and *Ensign*,
T'entrench the *City*, for defence in;
Rais'd *Rampiers*, with their own soft hands,
To put the enemy to stands;
From *Ladies* down to *Oyster-wenches*,
Labour'd like *Pioners* in *Trenches*,

---

775 that] who *C*   782 Parts,] parts; *C*   788 *Guifts*,] *Guifts*; *C*
792 *Parliament*,] *Parliament*; B2, *C*   794 meal; B2, *C*: Meal Br

Fell to their *Pick-axes*, and *Tools*,
And help'd the men to dig like *moles*?
Have not the *Handmaids* of the *City*,
Chosen of their members a *Committee*   810
For raysing of a *Common-Purse*,
Out of their wages to raise *Horse*?
And do they not as *Tryers* sit,
To judg what *Officers* are fit?
Have they ——? At that an *Egg*, let fly,
Hit him directly o're the eye,
And running down his Cheek, besmear'd
With Orenge-Tawny-slime, his *Beard*;
But *Beard*, and slime being of one Hue,
The *wound* the less appear'd in view.   820
Then he that on the *Panniers* rod,
Let fly on th'other side a load;
And quickly charg'd again, gave fully
In *Ralpho*'s face, another *Volley*.
The *Knight* was startled with the smell,
And for his *sword* began to feel:
And *Ralpho* smoother'd with the stink,
Grasp'd his; when one that bore a *Link*,
'Oth' sudden, clap'd his flaming Cudgel,
Like *linstock* to the Horse's *touch-hole*;   830
And streight another with his *Flambeux*
Gave *Ralpho*'s, o're the eys, a damn'd blow,
The *Beasts* began to kick, and fling,
And forc'd the Rout to make a Ring.
Through which, they quickly broke their way
And brought them off, from further fray;
And though disorderd in Retreat,
Each of them stoutly kept his seat:
For quitting both their *swords*, and *rains*,
They grasp'd with al their strength the *manes*;   840
And to avoyd the *Foe's* pursuit,
With spurring put their Cattle to't,
And till all four were out of wind,
And danger too, ne'r look'd behind.

807 Fell *C*: Falne *B*   810 *Committee*] Committee? *B, C*   811 *Purse, B2, C*:
Purse? B1   812 wages] Wages, *C*   813 they not *C*: not they *B*

After th' had paws'd awhile, supplying
Their *Spirits*, spent with fight and flying,
And *Hudibras* recruited force,
Of Lungs, for *Action*, or *discourse*:

Quoth he, that man is sure to lose,
That fowls his *hands* with durty foes: 850
For where no *honor*'s to be gain'd,
'Tis thrown away in b'ing maintain'd.
'Twas ill for us, we had to do
With so dishonorable a Foe:
For though the *Law of Arms* does bar
The use of venom'd shot in *War*,
Yet by the nauseous smell, and noysom,
Their *Case-shot* savours strong of *Poyson*;
And doubtless have been chew'd with teeth
Of some that had a *stinking breath*:   860
Else when we put it to the push,
They had not giv'n us such a brush.
But as those *Pultroons* that fling Durt,
Do but defile, but cannot hurt;
So all the *Honor* they have won,
Or we have lost, is much at one.
'Twas well we made so resolute
A brave Retreat, without Pursuit;
For if we had not, we had sped
Much worse, to be in Triumph led;   870
Than which the *Ancients* held no state
Of Man's life more unfortunate.
But if this bold *Adventure* e're
Do chance to reach the *Widdows* ear,
It may, b'ing destin'd to assert
Her *Sexe's honor*, reach her Heart:
And as such homely treats (they say)
Portend good *fortune*, so this may.
Vespasian being dawb'd with durt,

879 C. Cæsar *succensens, propter curam verrendis viis non adhibitam, Luto jussit oppleri, congesto per milites in prætextæ sinum.* Sueton in Vespas. Ca.5.

853 do B2, C: do, B1   868 without C: to avoyd B   869–70 sped
Much worse, B2, C: sped, | Much worse B1   879–84 *added in C*

Was destin'd to the Empire for't:
And from a Scavinger, did come
To be a mighty Prince in *Rome*:
And why may not this foul Address
Presage in Love the same success?
Then let us streight, to cleanse our wounds.
Advance in quest of nearest *Ponds*;
And after (as we first *design'd*)
Swear I've perform'd what she *enjoyn'd*.

THE SECOND PART

CANTO III

THE ARGUMENT

The Knight *with various doubts possest*
To win the Lady, goes in Quest
Of Sidrophel *the* Rosy-crucian,
To know the Dest'nies resolution;
With whom being met, they both chop Logick,
About the Science Astrologick.
Till falling from Dispute, to Fight,
The Conjurer's *worsted by the Knight.*

DOUBTLESS, The pleasure is as great,
Of being *cheated*, as to *cheat*.
As lookers-on feel most delight,
That least perceive a *Juglers* slight;
And still the less they understand,
The more th' admire his slight of hand.

Some with a noyse, and greasie light,
Are snapt, as men catch *Larks* by night;
Ensnar'd and hamper'd by the *Soul*,
As noozes by the *Legs* catch *Foul*.   10

Some with a *Med'cine*, and *Receit*,
Are drawn to nibble at the *Bait*;
And though it be a two-foot *Trout*,
'Tis with a single hair pull'd out.

Others believe no *Voice* t'an *Organ*;
So sweet as *Lawyers* in his *Bar-gown*.

The Argument. 3 *Of C: To B*   7 *Fight, C: Fight B*

Until, with subtle Cobweb-Cheats,
Th' are catch'd in knotted *Law,* like *Nets:*
In which when once they are imbrangled,
The more they stir the more th' are tangled   20
And while their *Purses* can dispute,
There's no end of th'immortal Suit.

Others still gape t'anticipate
The Cabinet-designs of *Fate,*
Apply to *Wisards* to foresee
What shall, and what shall never be.
And, as those *Vultors* do foreboad,
Believe events prove *bad,* or *good.*
A flamm more senseless then the Roguery
Of old *Aruspicy* and *Augury.*   30
That out of *Garbages* of *Cattle,*
Presag'd th'events of *Truce,* or *Battle,*
From flight of *Birds,* or *Chickens pecking,*
Success of great'st *Attempts* would reckon,
Though *cheats,* yet more intelligible,
Then those that with the *Stars* do fribble;
This *Hudibras* by proof, found true,
As in due time, and place wee'l shew.
For He, with *Beard* and *Face* made clean,
Being mounted on his *Steed* agen,   40
(And *Ralpho* got a Cock-horse too
Upon his *Beast,* with much adoe)
Advanc'd on for the *Widdows* House,
T'acquit himself, and pay his *Vows;*
When various *thoughts* began to bustle,
And with his inward man to justle.
He thought what *danger* might accrue,
If she should find he *swore* untrue:
Or, if his *Squire,* or he should fail,
And not be punctual in their *Tale;*   50
It might at once the ruine prove
Both of his *Honour, Faith,* and *Love.*
But if He should forbear to go,
She might conclude h' had broke his *Vow;*

25 Apply to *C:* Run after *B*

And that he durst not now for shame
Appear in *Court* to try his *Claim*.
This was the Pen'worth of his *thought*,
To pass *time*, and uneasie *trot*.

Quoth he, In all my past *Adventures*,
I ne'r was set so on the Tenters,   60
Or taken tardy with *Dilemma*
That, ev'ry way I turn, does hem me;
And with inextricable doubt,
Besets my puzzeld *Wits* about:
For though the *Dame* has been my Bail,
To free me from enchanted *Jail*:
Yet as a *Dog* committed close
For some offence, by chance breaks loose,
And quits his *Clog*; but all in vain,
He still draws after him his Chain.   70
So though my *Ancle* she has quitted,
My *Heart* continues still committed.
And like a *Bayl'd* and *Mainpriz'd Lover*,
Although at large, I am bound over.
And when I shall appear in *Court*,
To plead my *Cause*, and answer for't,
Unless the *Judg* do partial prove,
What will become of *Me* and *Love*?
For, if in our accompt we vary,
Or but in *Circumstance* miscarry;   80
Or if she put me to strict proof,
And make me pull my *Dublet* off
To shew by evident Record,
Writ on my skin, I've kept my word;
How can I e're expect to have her,
Having demur'd unto her favour?
But *Faith*, and *Love*, and *Honour* lost,
Shall be reduc'd t'a *Knight oth' Post·*
Beside, that *Stripping* may prevent
What I'm to prove by *Argument*;   90
And justifie I have a *Tayle*,
And that way too, my *proof* may faile.

O that I could enucleate,
And solve the *Problems* of my *Fate*;
Or find by *Necromantick* art,
How farr the *Dest'nies* take my part;
For if I were not more then certain,
To *win*, and *wear* her, and her *Fortune*,
I'de go no further in this *Courtship*,
To hazzard *Soul*, *Estate*, and *Worship*.   100
For though an *Oath* obliges not,
Where any *thing* is to be got,
(As thou hast prov'd) yet 'tis *profane*,
And *sinful*, when men *swear* in *Vain*.

Quoth *Ralph*, Not far from hence doth dwell
A cunning man, hight *Sidrophel*,
That deals in *Destinies* dark *Counsels*,
And sage *Opinions* of the *Moon* sells;
To whom all *People* far and near,
On deep importances repair.   110
When *Brass* and *Pewter* hap to stray,
And *Linnen* slinks out of the way;
When *Geese*, and *Pullen* are seduc'd,
And *Sows* of sucking *Pigs* are chews'd;
When *Cattle* feel Indisposition,
And need th'opinion of *Physitian*;
When *Murrain* reigns in *Hogs*, or *Sheep*,
And *Chicken* languish of the *Pip*;
When *Yeast* and outward means do fail,
And have no pow'r to work on *Ale*;   120
When Butter does refuse to come,
And *Love* proves *Cross* and *Humoursom*:
To him with *Questions*, and with *Urine*,
They for discov'ry flock, or *Curing*.

Quoth *Hudibras*, This *Sidrophel*
I've heard of, and should like it well,
If thou canst prove, the *Saints* have freedom,
To go to *Sorc'rers* when they need 'em.

Says *Ralpho*, There's no doubt of that:
Those *Principles* I quoted late,   130
Prove that the *Godly* may alleadge
For any thing their *Priviledge*;
And to the Dev'l himself may go,
If they have *motives* thereunto.
For as there is a *War* between
The *Dev'l* and *them*, it is no *Sin*,
If they, by subtle Stratagem,
Make use of *him*, as he does *them*.
Has not this present *Parliament*
A *Ledger* to the *Devil* sent,   140
Fully impower'd to treat about
Finding revolted *Witches* out?
And has not he with in a year,
Hang'd threescore of 'em in one *Shire*?
Some only for not being *drown'd*,
And some for sitting above ground,
Whole *days* and *nights*, upon their breeches
And feeling pain, were hang'd for *Witches*.
And some, for putting *Knavish* tricks
Upon *Green-Geese*, and *Turkey-Chicks*,   150
Or *Pigs*, that suddenly deceast,
Of griefs unnatural, as he guest;
Who after prov'd himself a *Witch*,
And made a *Rod* for his own *breech*.
Did not the Dev'l appear to *Martin*
Luther in *Germany*, for certain;
And would have gull'd him with a Trick,
But *Mart.* was too too *Politick*?
Did he not help the *Dutch* to purge
At *Antwerp*, their *Cathedral* Church?   160

139–40 The Witchfinder in *Suffolk*, who in the Presbyterian times had a Commission
to discover Witches, of whom (right or wrong) he caus'd 60 to be hang'd within the
compass of one year, and among the rest an old Minister, who had been a painful
Preacher for many years.
159–60 In the beginning of the Civil Wars of *Flanders*, the common people of
Antwerp in a tumult, broke open the Cathedral Church, to demolish Images and
Shrines: and did so much mischief in a small time, that *Strada* writes, There were
several Devils seen very busy among them, otherwise it had been impossible.

142 out?] out: C

Sing Catches to the *Saints* at *Mascon*,
And tell them all they came to ask him?
Appear in divers shapes to *Kelly*?
And speak 'ith' *Nun* of *Loudon's* Belly?
Meet with the *Parliament's Committee*
At *Woodstock*, on a Pars'nal Treaty?
At *Sarum* take a *Cavallier*
'Ith' *Cause's* service, *Prisoner*;
As *Withers* in Immortal Rime
Has registerd, to after-time?   170
Do not our great *Reformers* use
This *Sidrophel* to foreboad *News*?
To write of *Victories* next year,
And *Castles* taken yet in th'*Air*?
Of Battles fought at *Sea*, and Ships
Sunk, two years hence, the last Eclips?
A Total Overthrow giv'n the *King*
In *Cornwal*, *Horse* and *Foot*, next Spring?
And has not he point-blanck foretold
Whats'ere the close *Committee* would?   180
Made *Mars* and *Saturn* for the *Cause*,
The *Moon* for fundamental *Laws*?
The *Ram*, and *Bull*, and *Goat* declare
Against the Book of *Common-Pray'r*?

161 This Devil of *Mascon* deliver'd all his Oracles, like his Forefathers, in Verse,
which he sung to Tunes: He made several Lampoones upon the Hugonots, and
foretold them many things, which afterwards came to pass; as may be seen in his
Memoires, written in *French*.
163–4 The History of Dr. *Dee* and the Devil, published by *Mer. Causabon, Isac. Fil.*
Prebend of *Canterbury*, has a large accompt of all those Passages; in which the stile
of the true and false Angels appears to be penn'd by one and the same person. The
Nun of *Loudon* in *France*, and all her tricks have been seen by many Persons of
Quality of this Nation yet living, who have made very good observations upon the
French Book written upon that occasion.
165–6 A Committee of the long Parliament sitting in the Kings House in *Woodstock-Park*, were terrify'd with several Apparitions, the particulars whereof were then the
News of the whole Nation.
167 *Withers* has a long story in Doggerel, of a Soldier of the Kings Army, who
being a Prisoner at *Salisbury*, and drinking a health to the Devil upon his knees,
was carried away by him through a single pane of Glass.

164 of *Loudon's*] at *Londons* B, C   168 *Prisoner*; B2: *Prisoner?* B1, C
174 *Air?*] *Air!* B, C1   183 declare B2, C2: declare? B1, C1

The *Scorpion* take the *Protestation*,
And *Bear* engage for *Reformation*?
Made all the *Royall Stars* recant,
Compound, and take the *Covenant*?

Quoth *Hudibras*, The case is cleer,
The *Saints* may 'mploy a *Conjurer*;   190
As thou hast prov'd it by their *practice*.
No *Argument* like matter of fact is,
And we are best of all led to
Mens *Principles*, by what they do.
Then let us streit advance in quest
Of this Profound *Gymnosophist*:
And as the *Fates*, and *He* advise,
Pursue, or wave this *Enterprise*:
This said, he turn'd about his Steed,
And forthwith on th'adventure rid.   200
Where, leave we *Him* and *Ralph* awhile,
And to the *Conjurer* turn our stile:
To let our *Reader* understand
What's useful of him, before hand.

He had been long t'wards *Mathematicks*,
Opticks, *Philosophy*, and *Staticks*,
Magick, *Horoscopie*, *Astrologie*,
And was *old Dog* at *Physiologie*:
But, as a *Dog* that turns the spit,
Bestirs himself, and plys his feet,   210
To clime the *Wheel*; but all in vain,
His own weight brings him down again:
And still he's in the self same place,
Where at his setting out he was.
So in the *Circle* of the *Arts*,
Did he advance his nat'rall Parts;
Till falling back still, for retreat,
He fell to *Juggle*, *Cant*, and *Cheat*;
For, as those *Fowls* that live in Water
Are never wet, he did but smatter;   220

191 *practice*.] *practice* C   200 forthwith *C1 (some copies)*: eftsoons B, C

What ere he labour'd to appear,
His Understanding still was clear.
Yet none a deeper knowledg boasted,
Since old *Hodg Bacon*, and *Bob Grosted*.
Th'*Intelligible world* he knew,
And all, men dream on't, to be true:
That in this *World*, there's not a *Wart*,
That has not there a Counterpart;
Nor can there on the *face* of Ground,
An Individuall *Beard* be found,   230
That has not, in that Forrain *Nation*,
A fellow of the self-same fashion;
So *cut*, so *colour'd*, and so *curl'd*,
As those are, in th'*Inferior World*.
H' had read *Dee's* Prefaces before
The *Dev'l*, and *Euclide* o're and o're.
And, all th'*Intregues*, 'twixt him and *Kelly*,
Lescus and th'*Emperor*, would tell yee.
But with the *Moon* was more familiar
Then e're was *Almanack-well-willer*.   240
Her Secrets understood so clear,
That some believ'd he had been there.
Knew when she was in fittest mood,
For cutting *Corns* or letting *blood*,
When for anoynting *Scabs* or *Itches*,
Or to the *Bum* applying *Leeches*;
When *Sows*, and *Bitches* may be spade,
And in what Sign best *Sider*'s made,
Whether the *Wane* be, or *Increase*,
Best to sett *Garlick*, or sow *Pease*.   250

---

224 *Roger Bacon*, commonly called *Frier Bacon*, liv'd in the Reign of our *Edward* the I. and for some little skill he had in the *Mathematicks*, was by the Rabble accompted a Conjurer, and had the sottish story of the *Brazen Head* father'd upon him, by the ignorant Monks of those days. *Robert Grosthead* was Bishop of *Lincoln* in the Reign of *Hen.* III. He was a Learned Man for those times, and for that reason, suspected by the Clergy to be a Conjurer, for which crime being degraded by Pope *Innocent* the IV. and summon'd to appear at *Rome*, he appeal'd to the Tribunal of Christ; which our Lawyers say is illegal, if not a *Praemunire*, for offering to sue in a Forraign Court.

---

224 *Bob*] Bod C   238 would] would not C

Who first found out the *Man 'ith' Moon*,
That to the *Ancients* was unknown;
How many *Dukes*, and *Earls*, and *Peers*,
Are in the *Planetary Spheres*:
Their *Aiery Empire* and Command,
Their sev'ral strengths by Sea and Land;
What factions th' have, and what they drive at
In publique Vogue, and what in private;
With what designs and Interests,
Each Party manages Contests.   260
He made an *Instrument* to know
If the *Moon* shine at full, or no,
That would as soon as e're she shon, streit
Whether 'twere Day or Night demonstrate;
Tell what her *D'ameter* t'an inch is,
And prove she is not made of *Green Cheese*.
It would demonstrate, that the *Man in*
The Moon's a *Sea Mediterranean*.
And that it is no *Dog*, nor *Bitch*,
That stands behind him at his breech;   270
But a huge *Caspian Sea*, or *Lake*,
With *Arms* which men for *Legs* mistake.
How large a *Gulph* his Tayl composes,
And what a goodly *Bay* his Nose is;
How many *German* leagues by'th' scale,
Cape-Snout's from *Promontory-Tayl*:
He made a *Planetary Gin*
Which *Rats* would run their own heads in,
And come of purpose to be taken,
Without th'expence of Cheese or Bacon;   280
With *Lute-strings* he would counterfeit
Maggots, that crawl on dish of meat,
Quote Moles and Spots, on any place
'Oth' body, by the *Index-face*:
Detect lost *Maidenheads*, by sneezing,
Or breaking wind, of *Dames*, or pissing.
Cure *Warts* and *Corns*, with application
Of Med'cines, to th'*Imagination*.
Fright *Agues* into Dogs, and scare
With *Rimes*, the *Tooth-ach* and *Catarrh*.   290

Chase evil *spirits* away by dint
Of *Cickle, Horse-shoo, Hollow-flint.*
Spit fire out of a *Walnut-shell,*
Which made the *Roman* Slaves rebel.
And fire a Mine in *China,* here
With Sympathetick *Gunpowder.*
He knew whats'ever's to be known,
But much more then he knew, would own.
What *Med'cine* 'twas that *Paracelsus*
Could make a man with, as he tells us.   300
What figur'd *Slats* are best to make,
On wat'ry surface, *Duck* or *Drake.*
What *Bowling-stones,* in running race
Upon a *Board,* have swiftest pace.
Whether a *Pulse* beat in the black
List, of a Dappled *Louse's* back:
If *Systole* or *Diastole* move
Quickest, when hee's in wrath, or love:
When two of them do run a race,
Whether they *gallop, trot,* or *pace.*   310
How many scores a *Flea* will jump,
Of his own length, from head to rump;
Which *Socrates,* and *Chærephon*
In vain, assaid so long agon;
Whether his *Snout* a perfect *Nose* is,
And not an Elephants *Proboscis,*
How many different *Specieses*
Of Maggots breed in Rotten Cheese,
And which are next of kin to those,
Engendred in a *Chaundler's* nose.   320
Or those not seen, but understood,
That live in *Vineger* and *Wood.*

A paultry Wretch he had, half-starv'd,
That him in place of *Zany* serv'd;
Hight *Whachum,* bred to dash and draw,
Not *wine,* but more unwholsom *Law:*

313–14 *Aristophanes* in his Comedy of the Clouds, brings in *Socrates* and *Chærephon,*
measuring the Leap of a Flea, from the ones Beard to the others.

322 *Wood.* B2: *Wood,* B1, C1   323 *Editor's paragraph*

To make 'twixt words and lines, huge gaps,
Wide as *Meridians* in Maps.
To squander Paper, and spare Ink,
Or cheat men of their words, some think;   330
From this, by merited degrees,
He to more high Advancement rise:
To be an Under-*Conjurer*,
Or Journey-man *Astrologer*:
His bus'ness was to pump and whedle,
And men, with their own keys, unriddle.
To make them to themselves give answers,
For which they pay the *Necromancers*.
To fetch and carry *Intelligence*,
Of whom, and what, and where, and whence   340
And all *Discoveries* disperse,
Among th' whole *pack* of *Conjurers*;
What *Cutpurses* have left with them,
For the right owners to redeem;
And, what they dare not vent, find out,
To gain Themselves, and th'*Art*, repute.
Draw *Figures*, *Schemes*, and *Horoscopes*,
Of *Newgate*, *Bridewell*, *Brokers* Shops.
Of Thieves *ascendent* in the *Cart*,
And find out all by rules of *Art*.   350
Which way a Serving-man, that's run
With Cloaths or Money away, is gone:
Who pick'd a *Fob*, at *Holding-forth*,
And where a *Watch*, for half the worth,
May be redeem'd; or Stollen Plate
Restor'd, at Conscionable rate.
Beside all this, He serv'd his *Master*,
In quality of *Poetaster*:
And *Rimes* appropriate could make,
To ev'ry month, in th'*Almanack*, ·   360
When *Termes* begin, and end, could tell,
With their *Returns*, in *Doggerel*.
When the *Exchequer* opes and shuts,
And *Sowgelder* with safety cuts.
When men may eat, and drink, their fill,
And when be temp'rate, if they will.

When use, and when abstain from vice,
Figgs, Grapes, Phlebotomy, and *Spice*.
And as in *Prisons*, mean Rogues beat
Hemp, for the service of the *Great*;   370
So *Whachum* beat his durty brains,
T'advance his Master's fame and gains;
And, like the Devil's *Oracles*,
Put into *Dogrel-Rimes* his *Spells*,
Which over ev'ry Month's blank-page
In th'*Almanack*, strange *Bilks* presage.
He would an *Elegie* compose
On Maggots squeez'd out of his Nose;
In *Lyrick* numbers, write an *Ode* on
His Mistress, eating a Black-pudden: 380
And when imprison'd Aire escap'd her,
It puft him with *Poetick Rapture*;
His *Sonnets* charm'd th'attentive Crowd,
By wide-mouth'd Mortal trol'd aloud,
That, circled with his long ear'd Guests,
Like *Orpheus* look'd, among the Beasts,
A *Carman's* Horse could not pass by,
But stood ty'd up to *Poetry*;
No Porter's *Burthen* past along,
But serv'd for *Burthen* to his Song.   390
Each Windore like a *Pill'ry* appears,
With heads thrust through, nail'd by the ears;
All Trades run in as to the sight
Of Monsters, or their dear delight,
The *Gallow-tree*, when cutting Purse,
Breeds bus'ness for *Heroick* Verse,
Which none does hear, but would have hung
T'have been the *Theme* of such a *Song*.

Those two together long had liv'd,
In *Mansion* prudently contriv'd;   400
Where neither Tree, nor House could bar
The free detection of a *Star*;

382 *Rapture*; *B2* : *Rapture*, *B1, C1*   392 ears; *B2*: ears *B1, C1*
394 delight, *B2*: delight; *B1, C*   399 *Editor's paragraph*

And nigh an *Antient Obelisk*
Was rais'd by him, found out by *Fisk*,
On which was written, not in words,
But *Hieroglyphick* Mute of *Birds*,
Many rare pithy Saws concerning
The worth of *Astrologick* Learning:
From top of this there hung a *rope*,
To which he fastned *Telescope*;   410
The *Spectacles* with which the *Stars*
He reads in smallest *Characters*.
It hapned as a *Boy*, one night,
Did fly his *Tarsel* of a *Kite*,
The strangest long-wing'd *Hauk* that flies,
That like a *Bird* of *Paradise*,
Or *Heraulds* Martlet, has no *legs*,
Nor hatches young ones, nor lays *Eggs*;
His *Train* was six yards long, milk-white,
At th'end of which, there hung a *Light*,   420
Enclos'd in *Lanthorn* made of *Paper*,
That far off like a *Star* did appear.
This, *Sidrophel* by chance espi'd,
And with Amazement staring wide,
Bless us, quoth he! What dreadful wonder
Is that, appears in *heaven* yonder?
A *Comet*, and without a *Beard*?
Or *Star*, that ne'r before appear'd?
I'm certain, 'tis not in the *Scrowl*,
Of all those Beasts, and Fish, and Fowl,   430
With which, like *Indian Plantations*,
The Learned stock the *Constellations*;
Nor those that drawn for *Signs* have bin,
To th'*Houses*, where the *Planets* Inn.
It must be supernaturall,
Unless it be that Cannon-Ball,

404 This *Fisk* was a late famous Astrologer, who flourish'd about the time of Subtle, and Face, and was equally celebrated by *Ben. Johnson*.
436 This experiment was try'd by some Forreign *Virtuoso*'s, who planted a Piece of Ordnance point-blanc against the *Zenith*, and having fir'd it, the Bullet never rebounded back again, which made them all conclude, that it sticks in the mark; but *Des-Cartes* was of opinion, That it does but hang in the Air.

436 that *C*: the *B*

That, shot in th'aire, point-blank, upright,
Was borne to that prodigious height,
That learn'd *Philosophers* maintain,
It ne'r came backwards, down again;   440
But in the *Aery region* yet,
Hangs like the Body of *Mahomet*.
For if it be above the Shade,
That by the *Earths* round bulk is made,
'Tis probable, it may from far,
Appear no Bullet but a Star.

This said, He to his Engine flew,
Plac'd near at hand, in open view,
And rais'd it, till it level'd right,
Against the *Glow-worm* Tayl of *Kite*.   450
Then peeping through, *Bless* us! (quoth he)
It is a *Planet* now I see;
And if I err not, by his proper
Figure, that's like *Tobacco-Stopper*,
It should be *Saturn*; yes, 'tis clear,
'Tis *Saturn*, But what makes he there?
He's got between the *Dragons* Tayl,
And further leg behind, 'oth' *Whale*;
Pray *Heaven*, divert the fatal Omen,
For 'tis a *Prodigie* not common,   460
And can no less then the *World's* end,
Or *Natures* funeral portend.
With that, He fell again to pry,
Through *Perspective*, more wistfully,
When by mischance, the fatal string
That kept the *Tow'ring Fowl* on wing,
Breaking, down fell the Star: Well shot,
Quoth *Whachum*, who right wisely thought
H' had level'd at a Star, and hit it:
But *Sidrophel* more subtle-witted,   470
Cry'd out, What horrible and fearful
Portent is this, to see a Star fall;
It threatens *Nature*, and the doom
Will not be long, before it come.

451 (*Bless* us ! quoth *B*: (*Bless* us quoth *C*   471 fearful *B2*: fearful, *B1, C*

When Stars do fall, 'tis plain enough,
The *Day of Judgment*'s not far off:
As lately 'twas reveal'd to *Sedgwick*,
And some of us find out by *Magick*.
Then, since the time we have to live,
In this *world's* shortned, Let us strive,   480
To make our best advantage of it,
And pay our losses with our profit.

This Feat fell out, not long before
The *Knight* upon the forenam'd score,
In quest of *Sidrophel* advancing,
Was now in prospect of the *Mansion*:
Whom he discovering, turn'd his *Glass*,
And found far off, 'twas *Hudibras*.

Whachum (quoth he) look yonder; some
To try, or use our Art, are come: 490
The one's the Learned *Knight*; seek out,
And pump 'em, what they come about.
Whachum advanc'd, with all submisness,
T'accost 'em, but much more, their bus'ness.
He held the Stirrup, while the *Knight*
From *Leathern Bare-bones* did alight,
And taking from his hand, the Bridle,
Approach'd, the dark *Squire* to unriddle,
He gave him first the time 'oth' day,
And welcom'd him, *as he might say*:   500
And ask'd him whence they came, and whither
Their bus'ness lay? Quoth *Ralpho*, hither;
Did you not lose—? Quoth *Ralpho*, nay;
Quoth *Whachum*, Sir, I meant your *way*,
Your *Knight*—Quoth *Ralpho*, is a *Lover*,
And pains intolerable doth suffer,

---

477 This *Sedgwyck* had many Persons (and some of Quality) that believ'd in him,
and prepar'd to keep the day of Judgment with him, but were disappointed; for
which the false Prophet was afterwards call'd by the name of *Doomesday Sedgwyck*.

---

501 him] them *C*

For *Lovers* hearts are not their own hearts,
Nor lights, nor lungs, and so forth downwards.
What time—Quoth *Ralpho*, Sir too long,
Three years it off and on, has hung—   510
Quoth He, I meant what time 'oth' day 'tis.
Quoth *Ralpho*, between seven and eight 'tis.
Why then (quoth *Whachum*) my smal *Art*,
Tells me, the *Dame* has a hard *Heart*,
Or great *Estate*—Quoth *Ralph*, a *Joynter*,
Which makes him have so hot a mind t'her.
Mean while the *Knight* was making water,
Before he fell upon the matter;
Which having done, the *Wizard* steps in,
To give him suitable Reception;   520
But kept his bus'ness at a *Bay*,
Till *Whachum* put him in the way.
Who having now by *Ralpho's* light,
Expounded th'Errand of the *Knight*,
And what he came to know, drew near,
To whisper in the *Conj'rers* ear,
Which he prevented thus: What was't
Quoth he, that I was saying last,
Before these *Gentlemen* arriv'd?
Quoth *Whachum*, *Venus* you retriv'd,   530
In opposition with *Mars*,
And no benigne friendly Stars
T'allay th'effect. Quoth *Wizard*, So!
In *Virgo*? Ha! quoth *Whachum*, No.
Has *Saturn* nothing to do in it?
One tenth of 's *Circle* to a minute.
'Tis well quoth he—Sir you'l excuse
This Rudeness, I am forc'd to use,
It is a *Scheme*, and *face* of *Heaven*
As th'*Aspects* are dispos'd, this *Even*,   540
I was contemplating upon,
When you arriv'd: but now I've done.

Quoth *Hudibras*, If I appear
Unseasonable in coming here
At such a time, to interrupt

Your *Speculations*, which I hop'd
Assistance from, and come to use,
'Tis fit that I ask your Excuse.

By no means Sir, quoth *Sidrophel*,
The Stars your coming did foretel: 550
I did expect you here, and know,
Before you speak, your bus'ness too.

Quoth *Hudibras*, Make that appear,
And I shall credit whatsoe're
You tell me after, on your word,
How e're unlikely, or absurd.

You are in *Love*, Sir, with a *Widdow*,
Quoth he, that does not greatly heed you;
And for three years has rid your *Wit*
And *Passion* without drawing *Bit*:   560
And now your bus'ness is, to know
If you shall carry her, or no.

Quoth *Hudibras*, you'r in the right,
But how the *Devil* you come by't,
I can't imagine; for the *Stars*
I'm sure, can tell no more then a *Horse*,
Nor can their *Aspects* (though you pore
Your eys out on 'em) tell you more
Then th'*Oracle* of *Sive* and *Sheers*,
That turns as certain as the *Spheres*.   570
But if the *Devil*'s of your Counsel,
Much may be done, my noble *Donzel*,
And 'tis on his Accompt I come,
To know from you my fatal Doom.

Quoth *Sidrophel*, If you suppose,
Sir *Knight*, that I am one of those,
I might suspect, and take the *Alarm*,
Your Bus'ness is, but to enform,

551-2 know, | Before you speak C: knew, | Before you spake B   563 *Editor's*
paragraph

But if it be; 'tis ne'r the near,
You have a *wrong Sow by the ear*,   580
For I assure you, for my part,
I only deal by *Rules* of *Art*,
Such as are lawful, and judg by
Conclusions of *Astrology*:
But for the *Devil*, know nothing by him,
But only this, that I defie him.

Quoth he, What ever others deem yee
I understand your *Metonymie*;
Your words of second hand intention,
When things by wrongful names you mention,   590
The Mystick sense of all your *Terms*,
That are indeed but *Magick Charms*,
To raise the Devil, and mean one thing,
And that is, down-right *Conjuring*:
And in it self's more warrantable,
Then *Cheat*, or *Canting* to a *Rabble*,
Or putting *Tricks* upon the *Moon*,
Which by confederacy are done.
Your Ancient *Conjurers* were wont
To make her from her Sphere dismount,   600
And to their *Incantations* stoop,
They scorn'd to pore through *Telescope*,
Or idly play at bo-peep with her,
To find out cloudy, or fair weather,
Which ev'ry *Almanack* can tell,
Perhaps, as learnedly, and well,
As you your self—Then friend I doubt
You go the furthest way about.
Your Modern *Indian Magician*
Makes but a hole in th'earth to piss in,   610
And streit resolves all Questions by't,
And seldom fails to be 'ith' right.
The *Rosy-crucian* way's more sure,
To bring the Devil to the Lure,

609–10 This compendious new way of Magick is affirm'd by Monsieur *Le Blanc* (in his Travels) to be us'd in the *East-Indies*.

595 it self's *B2*: it's self *B1*: its self *C*

Each of 'em has a sev'ral Gin,
To catch *Intelligences* in.
Some by the *Nose* with fumes trapan 'em,
As *Dunstan* did the *Devil*'s *Grannum*.
Others with *Characters* and *Words*,
Catch 'em as men in *Nets* do *Birds*.   620
And some with *Symbols*, *Signs*, and *Tricks*,
Engrav'd in *Planetary* nicks.
With their own influences, will fetch 'em,
Down from their Orbs, arrest and catch 'em;
Make 'em depose, and answer to
All *Questions*, e're they let them go.
Bumbastus, kept a *Devil*'s *Bird*
Shut in the Pummel of his Sword,
That taught him all the cunning Pranks,
Of past, and future *Mountebanks*.   630
Kelly did all his Feats upon
The Devil's *Looking-glass*, a *Stone*.
Where playing with him at *Bo-peep*
He solv'd all *Problems* ne'r so deep.
Agrippa kept a *Stygian-Pug*,
I'th' garb and habit of a *Dog*,
That was his *Tutor*; and the *Curr*
Read to th'Occult *Philosopher*,
And taught him subtly to maintain
All other *Sciences are vain*.   640

To this, quoth *Sidrophello*, Sir,
Agrippa was no *Conjurer*,
Nor *Paracelsus*, no nor *Behman*;
Nor was the Dog a *Cacodæmon*,

627 *Paracelsus* is said to have kept a small Devil pris'ner in the Pummel of his
Sword, which was the reason, perhaps, why he was so valiant in his Drink; Howso-
ever it was to better purpose then *Annibal* carry'd poyson in his, to dispatch himself,
if he should happen to be surpriz'd in any great extremity, for the Sword would
have done the Feat alone, much better, and more Soldier-like. And it was below the
Honor of so great a Commander, to go out of the World like a Rat.
635 *Cornelius Agrippa* had a Dog, that was suspected to be a Spirit, for some tricks
he was wont to do, beyond the capacity of a Dog, as it was thought; but the Author
of *Magia Adamica* has taken a great deal of pains to vindicate both the Doctor and
the Dog, from that aspersion, in which he has shown a very great respect and
kindness for them both.

635 B *and* C *start new paragraph*

But a true Dog, that would shew tricks,
For th'*Emperor*, and leap o're sticks;
Would *fetch* and *carry*, was more civil
Then other *Dogs*, but yet no Devil;
And whatsoe'r he's sayd to do,
He went the self-same way we go.　　　650
As for the *Rosie-cross Philosophers*,
Whom you will have to be but *Sorcerers*;
What they pretend to, is no more,
Then *Trismegistus* did before,
Pythagoras, old *Zoroaster*,
And *Appollonius* their Master;
To whom they do confess they owe,
All that they do, and all they know.

Quoth *Hudibras*, Alas What is't to us,
Whether't were sayd by *Trismegistus*:　　　660
If it be *nonsense*, *false*, or *mystick*,
Or not *intelligible*, or *sophistick*.
'Tis not *Antiquity*, nor *Author*,
That makes *truth truth*, altho *time's daughter*;
'Twas he that put her in the *Pit*,
Before he pul'd her out of it.
And as he eats his *Sons*, just so
He feeds upon his *Daughters* too.
Nor do's it follow, cause a *Herauld*
Can make a *Gentleman*, scarce a year old,　　　670
To be descended of a Race,
Of ancient *Kings* in a small space;
That we should all Opinion hold
Authentick, that we can make old.

Quoth *Sidrophel*, It is no part
Of prudence, to cry down an *Art*;
And what it may perform deny,
Because you understand not Why.
(As *Averrhois* play'd but a mean trick,
To damn our whole *Art* for *Excentrick*)　　　680

679 Averrhois *Astronomiam propter Excentricos contempsit.* Phil. Melancton in Elem.
Phys. p.781.

For who knows all that knowledg contains?
Men dwell not on the *Tops* of *Mountains*,
But on their sides, or rising's seat;
So 'tis with knowledge's vast height.
Do not the Hist'ries of all *Ages*
Relate miraculous presages,
Of strange turns, in the *World's* affairs,
Foreseen b'*Astrologers*, *Southsayers*,
Chaldeans, Learn'd *Genethliacks*,
And some that have writ *Almanacks*?   690
The *Median* Emp'rour dreamt, his Daughter
Had pist all *Asia* under water,
And that a *Vine*, sprung from her *hanches*,
O'respread his *Empire*, with its branches;
And did not *Southsayers* expound it,
As after by th'event he found it?
When *Cæsar* in the Senate fell,
Did not the Sun eclips'd fortel,
And in resentment of his slaughter,
Look'd pale, for almost a year after?   700
Augustus having, b'oversight,
Put on his *left*-shoo, 'fore the *right*,
Had like to have been slain that day,
By *Souldiers* mutining for pay.
Are there not myriads of this sort,
Which Stories of all times report?
Is it not ominous in all *Countrys*,
When *Crows* and *Ravens* croak upon trees?
The *Roman Senate*, when within
The City-walls an *Owl* was seen,   710
Did cause their *Clergy* with *Lustrations*
(Our *Synod* calls *Humiliations*)

691 *Astyages* King of *Media* had this Dream of his Daughter *Mandane*, and the
Interpretation from the *Magi*, wherefore he married her to a *Persian* of mean quality,
by whom she had *Cyrus*, who conquer'd all *Asia*, and translated the Empire from the
Medes to the *Persians*. Herodot. L.2.
697 *Fiunt aliquando Prodigiosi, et longiores Solis Defectus, quales occiso Cæsare Dictatore
et Antoniano Bello, totius Anni Pallore continuo.* Plin.
701 *Divus Augustus Lævum sibi prodidit calceum præpostere indutum, quo die seditione
Militum propè afflictus est.* Idem. Lib.2.
709-10 *Romani L. Crasso et C. Mario Coss. Bubone viso urbem lustrabant.*

702 the] his *C*   705 not] no *C*   Note 709 urbem] orbem *C*

The round-fac'd *Prodigie* t'avert
From doing *Town* or *Countrey* hurt.
And if an *Owl* have so much pow'r,
Why should not *Planets* have much more?
That in a *Region*, far above
Inferior fowls of the *Air*, move,
And should see further, and fore-know,
More then their *Augury* below,   720
Though that once serv'd the *Politie*
Of mighty States to govern by;
And this is that we take in hand,
By pow'rful *Art* to understand.
Which how we have perform'd, all Ages
Can speak th'*Events* of our Presages.
Have we not lately in the *Moon*
Found a *New World* to th'*Old* unknown?
Discover'd *Sea* and *Land*, *Columbus*
And *Magellan* could never compass?   730
Made Mountains, with our *Tubes*, appear
And Cattle grazing on 'em there?

Quoth *Hudibras*, You lie so ope,
That I, without a *Telescope*,
Can find your Tricks out, and descry
Where you tell truth, and where you lie.
For *Anaxagoras*, long agon,
Saw *Hills*, as well as you i'th' *Moon*;
And held the *Sun* was but a piece
Of *Red-hot-Ir'n*, as big as *Greece*;   740
Believ'd the Heavens were made of *Stone*,
Because the *Sun* had voyded one;
And, rather then he would recant
Th'*Opinion*, suffer'd Banishment.

But what, alas, is it to us,
Whether in the *Moon*, men thus, or thus,

737 Anaxagoras *affirmabat Solem Candens Ferrum esse, et Peloponesso majorem*: Lunam *Habitacula in se Habere, et Colles, et valles. Fertur dixisse Cælum omne ex Lapidibus esse Compositum; Damnatus et in exilium pulsus est, quod impie, Solem Candentem laminam esse dixisset.* Diogen. Laert. in Anaxag. p. 11.13.

Note 737 *Candentem* C2 : *Candensem* C1

Do eat their *Porredg*, cut their Corns,
Or whether they have Tayls or Horns?
What *Trade* from thence can you advance
But what we nearer have from *France*?   750
What can our *Travellers* bring home
That is not to be learnt at *Rome*?
What *Politicks*, or strange *Opinions*,
That are not in our own *Dominions*?
What *Science* can be brought from thence,
In which we do not here Commence?
What Revelations, or Religions,
That are not in our Native *Regions*?
Are sweating *Lant-horns*, or Screen-*Fans*
Made better there, then th' are in *France*?   760
Or do they teach to *sing* and *play*
O'th' *Gittarr* there, a newer way?
Can they make *Plays* there, that shall fit
The *Publick Humour*, with less *Wit*?
Write *wittier Dances*, quainter Shows,
Or fight with more ingenious *Blows*?
Or does the *Man* i'th' *Moon* look big,
And wear a huger *Perewig*,
Shew in his gate, or face, more tricks
Then our own *Native Lunaticks*?   770
But if w' out-do him here at home,
What good of your design can come?
As *wind* in th'*Hypocondries* pent
Is but a blast if downward sent;
But if it upwards chance to fly
Becoms new *Light* and *Prophecy*:
So when your Speculations tend
Above their just and useful end,
Although they promise strange and great
Discoveries of things far fet,   780
They are but idle *Dreams* and *Fancies*
And savour strongly of the *Ganzas*.
Tell me but what's the nat'ral cause,
Why on a *Sign*, no *Painter* draws
The *Full-Moon* ever, but the *Half*,
Resolve that with your *Jacobs-staff*;

Or why *Wolves* raise a Hubbub at her,
And *Dogs* howle when she shines in water;
And I shall freely give my *Vote*,
You may know something more remote.   790

At this deep *Sidrophel* look'd wise,
And staring round with *Owl-like* eys:
He put his face into a posture
Of *Sapience*, and began to bluster,
For having three times shook his Head
To stir his wit up, thus he said.

Art has no mortal enemies
Next *Ignorance*, but *Owls* and *Geese*;
Those Consecrated Geese in Orders,
That to the *Capitol* were *Warders*:   800
And being then upon *Petrol*
With noyse alone beat off the *Gaul*.
Or those *Athenian Sceptick Owls*,
That will not credit their own *Souls*;
Or any *Science* understand,
Beyond the reach of eye, or hand:
But meas'ring all things by their own
Knowledg, hold, Nothing's to be known.
Those wholesale *Criticks*, that in *Coffee-
Houses*, cry down all *Philosophy*.   810
And will not know, upon what ground
In Nature, we our *doctrine* found;
Although with pregnant evidence,
We can demonstrate it to sence.
As I just now have done to you,
Fore-telling what you came to know.
Were the *Stars* only made to light
Robbers and Burglarers by night?
To wait on *Drunkards*, *Thievs*, *Gold-finders*,
And *Lovers* solacing behind Dores?   820
Or giving one another Pledges
Of *Matrimony* under Hedges?
Or Witches *Simpling*, and on *Gibbets*
Cutting from *Malefactors* snippets?

Or from the *Pillory* tips of ears
Of Rebel-Saints, and Perjurers?
Only to stand by and look on,
But not know what is said, or done?
Is there a *Constellation* there,
That was not born, and bred up here?   830
And therefore cannot be to learn,
In any inferiour Concern.
Were they not, during all their lives,
Most of 'em Pirates, Whores, and Thieves?
And is it like they have not still
In their old *Practices* some skill?
Is there a *Planet* that by *Birth*
Does not derive its *House* from *Earth*?
And therefore probably must know
What is, and hath been, done below?   840
Who made the *Ballance*; or whence came
The *Bull*, the *Lion*, and the *Ram*?
Did not we here, the *Argo* rigg;
Make *Berenice's Periwig*?
Whose *Liv'ry* does the *Coach-man* wear?
Or who made *Cassiopæa's* Chair?
And therefore, as they came from hence,
With us may hold *Intelligence*.
Plato deny'd, The *World* can be
Govern'd without *Geometree*,   850
(For money b'ing the common Scale
Of things by measure, weight, and tale;
In all th'affairs of *Church* and *State*,
'Tis both the *Ballance* and the *Weight*:)
Then much less can it be without
Divine *Astrology* made out,
That puts the other down in worth,
As far as *Heaven's* above *Earth*.

These reasons (quoth the *Knight*) I grant
Are something more significant   860
Then any that the *Learned* use,
Upon this *subject* to produce;

843 rigg;] rigg B, C

And yet, th' are far from satisfactory
T'establish, and keep up your *Factory*.
The *Ægyptians* say, The *Sun* has twice
Shifted his *setting*, and his *rise*;
Twice has he risen in the *West*,
As many times, sett in the *East*;
But whether that be true, or no,
The *Devil* any of you know.   870
Some hold, the *Heavens* like a *Top*
Are kept by *Circulation* up;
And 'twere not for their wheeling round,
They'd instantly fall to the ground:
As sage *Empedocles* of old,
And from him *Modern* Authors hold.
Plato believ'd the *Sun* and *Moon*,
Below all other *Planets* run.
Some *Mercury*, some *Venus* seat
Above the *Sun* himself in height.   880
The learned *Scaliger* complain'd
'Gainst what *Copernicus* maintain'd,
That in Twelve hundred years, and odd,
The *Sun* had left his antient Road,
And nearer to the Earth, is come
'Bove Fifty thousand miles from home:
Swore 'twas a most notorious Flam,
And he that had so little Shame
To vent such *Fopperies* abroad,
Deserv'd to have his *Rump* well claw'd,   890

865–6 *Ægyptii Decem millia Annorum, et amplius, recensent; et observatum est in hoc tanto Spatio, bis mutata esse Loca Ortuum et Occasuum solis; ita ut Sol bis ortus sit ubi nunc occidit, et bis descenderit ubi nunc oritur.* Phil. Melanct. Lib. I. p.60.
871–2 *Causa quare Cælum non Cadit,* (secundum *Empedoclem*) *est velocitas sui motus.* Comment *in* L.2. Aristot. de Cælo.
877–8 *Plato Solem et Lunam Cæteris Planetis inferiores esse putavit.* G. Cunnin. *in* Cosmogr. L.I.p.11.
881 *Copernicus in Libris Revolutionum, deinde Reinholdus, post etiam Stadius Mathematici nobiles perspicuis Demonstrationibus docuerunt, solis Apsida Terris esse propiorem, quam Ptolomæi ætate duodecim partibus, id est uno ac triginta terræ semidiametris.* Jo. Bod. Met.Hist. p.455.

883–4 That . . . Road, *C*: About the *Suns* and *Earths* approach; | And swore, that he, that dar'd to broach *B*   885–8 added in *C*   889 To vent such *C*:
Such paultry *B*   Note 881 StadiusC2: Staduis C1

Which *Mounsier Bodin* hearing, swore,
That he deserv'd the *Rod* much more,
That durst upon a *truth* give doom,
He knew less then the *Pope of Rome*.
Cardan believ'd, Great States depend
Upon the tip o'th' *Bears* Tayls end;
That as she whisk'd it t'wards the Sun,
Strow'd Mighty *Empires* up and down;
Which others say must needs be false,
Because your true *Bears* have no Tayls.   900
Some say, the *Zodiack-Constellations*
Have long since chang'd their antique Stations
Above a *Sign*; and prove the same,
In *Taurus* now, once in the *Ram*;
Affirm the *Trigons* chop'd and chang'd,
The *Watry* with the *Firy* rang'd;
Then how can their *effects* still hold
To be the same they were of old?
This, though the *Art* were true, would make
Our Modern *Southsayers* mistake;   910
And is one cause they tell more lies,
In *Figures* and *Nativities*,
Then th'old *Chaldean* Conjurers,
In so many hundred thousand years;
Beside their Nonsence in translating,
For want of *Accidence* and *Latin*.
Like *Idus* and *Calendæ* Englisht
The *Quarter-days*, by skilful Linguist.
And yet with *Canting*, *slight*, and *cheat*
'Twill serve their turn to do the feat;   920
Make Fools believe in their fore-seeing
Of things, before they are in Being;
To swallow *Gudgeons*, e're th' are catch'd,
And count their *Chickens*, e're th' are hatch'd,

---

895 *Putat Cardanus, ab extrema Cauda, Helices seu Majoris ursæ omne magnum Imperium pendere.* Ide. p.325.
913–14 *Chaldæi jactant se quadraginta septuaginta Annorum millia in periclitandis, experiundisque Puerorum Animis posuisse.* Cicero.

---

894 less *C*: no more *B*   901–3 the . . . a *Sign C*: The Stars ith' *Zodiack*, | Are
more then a whole *Signe* gone back, | Since *Ptolomy B*   904 once *C*: then *B*

Make them the *Constellations* prompt,
And give 'em back their own accompt:
But still the Best to him that gives,
The best price for't, or best believes.
Some *Towns* and *Cities*, some for brevity,
Have cast the Versal World's *Nativity*;   930
And make the Infant-Stars confess,
Like Fools or Children, what they please:
Some calculate the hidden fates
Of *Monkeys*, *Puppy-dogs*, and *Cats*,
Some *Running-Nags*, and *Fighting-Cocks*;
Some *Love*, *Trade*, *Law-suits*, and the *Pox*;
Some take a measure of the lives
Of Fathers, Mothers, Husbands, Wives,
Make *Opposition*, *Trine*, and *Quartile*;
Tell who is barren, and who fertile.   940
As if the *Planet's* first aspect
The tender Infant did infect
In *Soul*, and *Body*, and instill
All future good, and future ill:
Which, in their dark fatalities lurking,
At destin'd Periods fall a working;
And break out like the hidden seeds
Of long diseases into deeds,
In Friendships, enmities, and strife,
And all th'emergencies of Life: 950
No sooner does he peep into
The *World*, but he has done his doe,
Catch'd all Diseases, took all *Physick*,
That cures, or kills a man that is Sick;
Marri'd his punctual dose of Wives,
Is Cookolded, and Breaks, or Thrives.
There's but the twinckling of a *Star*
Between a Man of *Peace* and *War*,
A *Thief* and *Justice*, *Fool* and *Knave*,
A huffing *Officer* and a *Slave*,   960
A crafty-*Lawyer* and *Pick-pocket*,
A great *Philosopher* and a *Block-head*,
A formal *Preacher* and a *Player*,
A Learn'd *Physitian* and *Man-slayer*.

As if men from the Stars did suck
Old-age, Diseases, and *ill-luck,*
Wit, Folly, Honor, Virtue, Vice,
Trade, Travel, Women, Claps and *Dice,*
And draw with the first Air they breathe,
Battle, and *Murther, sudden Death.*   970
Are not these fine Commodities,
To be imported from the Skies?
And vended here among the Rabble,
For staple goods, and warrantable?
Like money by the *Druids* borrow'd,
In th'other *World* to be restor'd.

Quoth *Sidrophel,* to let you know
You wrong the *Art,* and *Artists* too:
Since Arguments are lost on those
That do our *Principles* oppose;   980
I will (although I've don't before)
Demonstrate to your sense once more,
And draw a *Figure* that shall tell you
What you perhaps forget, befel you;
By way of *Horary* inspection,
Which some accompt our worst erection.
With that, He *Circles* draws, and *Squares*
With *Cyphers, Astrall Characters;*
Then looks 'em o're, to understand 'em,
Although set down *Hab-nab,* at random.   990

Quoth he, This *Scheme* of th'Heavens set
Discovers how in fight you met
At *Kingston* with a *May-pole Idol,*
And that y' were bang'd, both back and side wel
And though you overcame the *Bear,*
The *Dogs* beat You at *Brentford Fair;*
Where sturdy *Butchers* broke your Noddle,
And handled you like a *Fop-doodle.*

975 *Druidæ pecuniam mutuo accipiebant in Posteriore vita redituri.* Patricius Tom.2.p.97.

---

991 he, *C*2: He | B, *C*1

Quoth *Hudibras*, I now perceive,
You are no *Conj'rer*, by your leave, 1000
That *Paultry story* is untrue,
And forg'd to cheat such *Gulls* as you.

Not true, quoth he? how e're you vapour,
I can, what I affirm, make appear;
Whachum shall justifie't t'your face,
And prove he was upon the place:
He play'd the *Saltinbanco*'s part,
Transform'd t'a *Frenchman* by my *Art*.
He stole your Cloke, and pick'd your pocket,
Chews'd, and Caldes'd ye like a Block-head: 1010
And what you lost, I can produce
If you deny it, here i'th' House.

Quoth *Hudibras*, I do believe,
That Argument's *Demonstrative*;
Ralpho, bear witness, and go fetch us
A *Cunstable* to seize the Wretches:
For though th' are both false *Knaves*, and *Cheats*,
Impostors, *Juglers*, *Counterfets*,
I'l make them serve for perpendiculars,
As true, as e're were us'd by *Brick-layers*, 1020
They're *guilty*, by their own Confessions,
Of *Felony*; and at the *Sessions*
Upon the *Bench*, I will so handle 'em,
That the *Vibration* of this *Pendulum*

1001-2 There was a notorious Ideot (that is here describ'd by the Name and
Character of *Whachum*) who counterfeited a Second Part of *Hudibras*, as untowardly
as Captain *Po*, who could not write himself, and yet made a shift to stand on the
Pillory, for Forging other Mens Hands, as his Fellow *Whachum*, no doubt deserv'd;
in whose abominable Doggerel, This story of *Hudibras* and a French Mountebank
at *Brentford*-Fair, is as properly describ'd.
1024-6 The device of the Vibration of a Pendulum, was intended to settle a certain
Measure of Ells and Yards, &c. (that should have its foundation in Nature) all the
world over: For by swinging a weight at the end of a string, and calculating (by the
motion of the Sun, or any Star) how long the Vibration would last, in proportion to
the length of the String, and weight of the Pendulum; they thought to reduce it
back again, and from any part of time, compute the exact length of any string, that
must necessarily vibrate in so much space of time: So that if a man should ask in
China for a Quarter of an Hour of Satin or Taffeta, they would know perfectly what
it meant. And all Mankind learn a new way to measure things no more by the Yard,
Foot, or Inch, but by the Hour, Quarter, and Minute.

Shall make all *Taylers* yards, of one
Unanimous Opinion:
A thing he long has vapour'd of,
But now shall make it out by proof.

Quoth *Sidrophel*, I do not doubt,
To find Friends, that will bear me out: 1030
Nor have I hazarded my *Art*,
And Neck, so long on the *State's* part,
To be expos'd in th'end to suffer,
By such a *Braggadochio* Huffer.

Huffer, quoth *Hudibras*? This *Sword*
Shall down thy false throat, Cram that word.
Ralpho, make haste, and call an Officer
To apprehend this *Stygian* Sophister;
Mean while I'l hold 'em at a *Bay*,
Lest He and *Whachum* run away.   1040

But *Sidrophel*, who from th'*Aspect*
Of *Hudibras*, did now erect
A *Figure* worse portending far,
Then that of most malignant Star:
Believ'd it now the fittest moment,
To shun the danger that might come on't,
While *Hudibras* was all alone,
And he and *Whachum*, two to one;
This being resolv'd, He spi'd by chance,
Behind the Dore, an Iron-Lance,   1050
That many a sturdy Limb had gor'd,
And Legs, and Loyns, and shoulders bor'd.
He snatch'd it up, and made a Pass,
To make his way through *Hudibras*.
Whachum had got a Fier-fork,
With which he vow'd to do his Work.
But *Hudibras* was well prepar'd,
And stoutly stood upon his Guard.
He put by *Sidrophello's* thrust

1036 word. B2: word, B1 C

And in, right manfully, he rusht,   1060
The Weapon from his gripe he wrung,
And lay'd him on the earth along.
Whachum his seacole-Prong threw by,
And basely turn'd his back to fly.
But *Hudibras* gave him a twitch
As quick as Lightning, in the Breech.
Just in the Place, where *Honor*'s lodg'd,
As wise *Philosophers* have judg'd;
Because a kick in that part more
Hurts *Honor*, then deep wounds before.   1070

Quoth *Hudibras*, The Stars determine
You are my Prisoners, Base Vermine.
Could they not tell you so, as wel
As what I came to know, foretel?
By this, what *Cheats* you are, we find,
That in your own Concerns are blind:
Your Lives are now at my dispose,
To be redeem'd by fine, or blows:
But who his Honor would defile,
To take, or sell, two lives so Vile?   1080
I'l give you *Quarter*, but your *Pillage*
The Conqu'ring Warrier's *Crop* and *Tillage*,
Which with his Sword he reaps, and plows;
That mine, the *Law* of *Arms* allows.

This said in haste, in haste he fell
To romaging of *Sidrophel*.
First, He expounded both his Pockets,
And found a *Watch*, with *Rings* and *Lockets*,
Which had been left with him, t'erect
A *Figure* for, and so detect.   1090
A *Copper-Plate*, with *Almanacks*
Engrav'd upon't, with other knacks,
Of *Booker*'s, *Lilly*'s, *Sarah Jimmers*,
And *Blank-Schemes* to discover *Nimmers*;
A *Moon-Dial*, with *Napiers* bones,
And severall *Constellation*-stones,

1093 *Booker*'s, B2, C: *Booker*'s B1

Engrav'd in *Planetary hours*,
That over *Mortals* had strange powers
To make 'em thrive in *Law*, or *Trade*;
And stab, or poyson, to evade;   1100
In *Wit*, or *Wisdom* to improve,
And be victorious in *Love*.
Whachum had neither *Cross*, nor *Pile*,
His *Plunder* was not worth the while;
All which the *Conqu'rer* did discompt,
To pay for curing of his Rump.

But *Sidrophel*, as full of tricks,
As *Rota-men* of *Politicks*,
Streight cast about to over-reach
Th'unwary Conqu'rer with a fetch,   1110
And make him glad, (at least) to quit
His *Victory*, and fly the *Pit*,
Before the *Secular Prince* of *Darkness*
Arriv'd to seize upon his Carcass.
And, as a *Fox*, with hot pursuit,
Chac'd through a *Warren*, cast about
To save his credit, and among
Dead *Vermine* on a *Gallows* hung;
And while the *Dogs* ran underneath,
Escap'd (by counterfeiting Death)   1120
Not out of Cunning, but a *Train*
Of *Atoms* justling in his Brain,
As learn'd *Philosophers* give out:
So *Sidrophello* cast about,
And fell to's wonted *Trade* again,
To feign himself in earnest slain.
First, stretch'd out one leg, then another,
And seeming in his Breast to smother
A broken Sigh; Quoth He, Where am I,
Alive, or Dead? Or which way came I   1130

1113 As the Devil is the spiritual Prince of Darkness, so is the Constable the
Secular, who governs in the night with as great Authority as his Colleague, but far
more imperiously.

1128 smother] smother, *B, C*

Through so immense a space so soon?
But now, I thought my self in th' *Moon*;
And that a *Monster* with huge *Whiskers*,
More formidable then a *Switzers*,
My body through, and through, had dril'd,
And *Whachum* by my side, had kill'd,
Had cross-examin'd both our Hose,
And plundred all we had to lose;
Look there he is, I see him now,
And feel the Place I am run through.   1140
And there lies *Whachum* by my side,
Stone-dead, and in his own blood di'd.
Oh! Oh! With that he fetch'd a *Grone*,
And fell again into a swoun.
Shut both his eys, and stop'd his breath,
And to the *Life*, out-acted *Death*.
That *Hudibras*, to all appearing,
Believ'd him to be dead as *Herring*.
He held it now, no longer safe,
To tarry the return of *Raph*;   1150
But rather leave him in the *Lurch*:
Thought he, He has abus'd our *Church*,
Refus'd to give himself one firk,
To carry on the *Publick work*.
Despis'd our *Synod-men* like Durt,
And made their *Discipline* his Sport;
Divulg'd the secrets of their *Classes*,
And their *Conventions* prov'd *High-Places*;
Disparag'd their *Tith-pigs*, as *Pagan*,
And set at nought, their *Cheese* and *Bacon*;   1160
Rayl'd at their *Covenant*, and jear'd
Their rev'rend Persons to my *Beard*:
For all which *Scandals* to be quit,
At once, this *Juncture* falls out fit.
I'l make him henceforth, to beware,
And tempt my fury, if he dare:
He must (at least) hold up his hand,
By twelve *Free-holders* to be scan'd,

1151 *Lurch*: B2: *Lurch*, B1, C1   1162 Persons] Parsons *C*

Who by their skill in *Palmistry*
Will quickly read his *Destiny*;   1170
And make him glad to read his *Lesson*,
Or take a turn for't at the *Session*:
Unless his *Light*, and *Gifts* prove truer,
Then ever yet they did, I'm sure;
For if he scape with *Whipping* now,
'Tis more then he can hope to do.
And that will disengage my *Conscience*,
Of th'*Obligation*, in his own sense.
I'l make him now by force abide,
What he by gentle means deny'd,   1180
To give my *Honor* satisfaction,
And right the *Brethren* in the *Action*.
This being resolv'd with equal speed,
And *Conduct*, he approach't his *Steed*;
And with *Activity* unwont,
Assay'd the lofty *Beast* to mount;
Which once atchiev'd, he spur'd his *Palfry*,
To get from th'*Enemy*, and *Ralph*, free;
Left Danger, Fears, and Foes behind
And beat, at least three lengths, the Wind.   1190

An Heroical Epistle of Hudibras
to Sidrophel

Ecce iterum Crispinus ——

WELL! *Sidrophel,* though 'tis in vain
To tamper with your Crazy Brain,
Without Treppanning of your Scull,
As often as the *Moon*'s at *Full*:
'Tis not amiss, e're y' are giv'n o're,
To try one desp'rate Med'cine more:
For where your Case can be no worse,
The desp'rat'st is the wisest course.
Is't possible, that you, whose Ears
Are of the Tribe of *Issachars*   10
And might (with equal Reason) either
For Merit, or extent of Leather,
With *William Pryn*'s, before they were
Retrench'd, and Crucify'd, compare,
Should yet be deaf against a noise
So roaring as the Publick voice?
That speaks your Virtues free, and loud,
And openly in ev'ry croud.
As loud as one that sings his part
T'a Wheelbarrow, or Turnip Cart, ——   20
Or your New Nicknam'd old Invention
To cry Green-Hastings with an Engine.
(As if the vehemence had stun'd,
And torn your Drum-heads with the Sound)
And 'cause your Folly's now no news
But over grown and out of use,
Perswade your self there's no such matter,
But that 'tis vanish'd out of Nature,
When Folly, as it grows in years
The more extravagant appears.   30

26 use,] use. *C*

For who but you could be possest
With so much Ignorance, and Beast,
That neither all mens Scorn, and Hate,
Nor being Laugh'd and Pointed at,
Nor bray'd so often in a Morter,
Can teach you wholesome Sense, and Nurture?
But (like a Reprobate) what course
Soever's us'd, grow worse and worse?
Can no Transfusion of the Bloud,
That makes Fools Cattle, do you good?   40
Nor putting Pigs t'a Bitch to Nurse
To turn 'em into Mungrel-Curs,
Put you into a way, at least,
To make your self a better Beast?
Can all your critical Intrigues
Of trying sound from rotten Eggs,
Your several Newfound Remedies,
Of curing Wounds, and Scabs in Trees,
Your Arts of *Fluxing* them for *Claps*,
And Purging their infected *Saps*,   50
Recov'ring Shankers, Chrystalines,
And Nodes and Botches in their Rindes
Have no effect to operate
Upon that duller Block, your Pate,
But still it must be lewdly bent
To tempt your own due punishment? ——
And like your whimsey'd Chariots draw
The Boys to course you without Law?
As if the Art you have so long
Profest, of making old *Dogs* young,   60
In you had Virtue to renew
Not only Youth, but Childhood too.
Can you, that understand all Books
By Judging only with your Looks,
Resolve all Problems with your Face
As others do with *B's*, and *A's*,
Unriddle all that Mankind knows
With solid bending of your Brows,
All Arts and Sciences advance,
With screwing of your Countenance,   70

And with a penetrating Eye,
Into th'abstrusest Learning pry,
Know more of any Trade b'a Hint,
Then those that have been bred up in't,
And yet have no Art true, or false
To help your own bad Naturals?
But still the more you strive t'appear,
Are found to be the wretcheder.
For Fools are known by looking wise.
As Men find Woodcocks by their Eies.   80
Hence 'tis, that 'cause y' have gain'd, o'th' *Colledge*,
A Quarter-share (at most) of Knowledge,
And brought in none, but spent Repute,
Y' assume a Pow'r as absolute
To Judge and Censure, and Controll,
As if you were the sole Sir *Poll*
And saucily pretend to know
More then your Dividend comes to.
You'l find the thing will not be done,
With Ignorance, and Face alone: 90
No though y' have purchas'd to your Name,
In History so great a Fame,
That now your Talent's so well known,
For having all Belief outgrown;
That ev'ry strange Prodigious Tale
Is measur'd by your *German* Scale, ——
By which the *Virtuosi* try
The Magnitude of ev'ry Ly,
Cast up to what it does amount:
And place the big'st to your account.   100
That all those stories that are lai'd
Too truly to you, and those made,
Are now still charg'd upon your score,
And lesser Authors nam'd no more.
Alas that Faculty destroys
Those soonest, it designes to raise.
And all your vain Renown will spoil,
As Guns o're-charg'd the more recoyl.

88 to.] to, C

Though he that has but Impudence
To all things has a fair Pretence   110
And put among his wants, but shame,
To all the world may lay his claim:
Though you have try'd that nothing's born
With greater ease then Publique Scorn;
That all affronts do still give Place
To your Impenetrable Face;
That makes your way through all affairs,
As Pigs through Hedges creep with theirs:
Yet as 'tis Counterfeit and Brass
You must not think 'twill always pass: 120
For all Impostors, when they'r known,
Are past their Labor, and undone.
And all the best that can befall
An Artificial Natural,
Is that which Madmen find, as soon
As once th' are broke loose from the Moon
And proof against her Influence,
Relaps to ere so little Sense
To turn stark Fools, and Subjects fit
For sport of Boys, and Rabble-wit.   130

120 pass:] pass *C*

HUDIBRAS

THE THIRD AND LAST PART

CANTO I

THE ARGUMENT

The Knight and Squire resolve, at once,
The one, the other, to renounce;
They both approach the Ladies Bower,
The Squire t'inform, the Knight to wooe her;
She treats them with a Masquerade,
By Furies, and Hobgoblins made,
From which the Squire conveys the Knight,
And steals him, from himself, by Night.

'Tis true, no Lover has that Pow'r,
T'enforce a desperate Amour,
As he that has two *Strings* t'his *Bow*
And burns for *Love*, and *Money* too:
For then he's Brave, and Resolute,
Disdains to render in his Suit,
H'as all his *Flames* and *Raptures* double,
And *Hangs* or *Drowns*, with half the trouble.
While those who sillily pursue
The simple downright way and true,   10
Make as unlucky Applications,
And steer, against the Stream, their passions:
Some forge their *Mistresses* of *Stars*
And when the Ladyes prove averse
And more untoward to be won,
Then by *Caligula*, the *Moon*,
Cry out upon the *Stars*, for doing
Ill Offices, to cross their *Wooing*,

When only by themselves, they're hindred
For trusting *those they made her kindred*:   20
And still the Harsher, and Hide-bounder
The Damsels prove, become the Fonder.
For what Mad Lover ever dy'd,
To gain a soft, and gentle *Bride*?
Or for a Lady tender-hearted,
In *Purling Streams*, or *Hemp* departed?
Leap't headlong int'*Elizium*,
Through th' Windows of a *Dazeling Room*?
But for some cross Ill-natur'd Dame,
The Am'rous Fly burnt in his *flame*.   30
This to the *Knight* could be no *News*,
With all Mankind, so much in use;
Who therefore took the wiser course,
To make the most of his *Amours*,
Resolv'd to try all sorts of ways,
As follows in due *Time* and *Place*.

No sooner was the bloody Fight,
Between the *Wizard*, and the *Knight*,
With all th'Appurtenances over,
But he relaps'd again t'a *Lover*:   40
As he was always wont to do,
When h' had discomfited a Foe,
And us'd as only *Antick Philters*,
Deriv'd from old *Heroick Tilters*.
But now Triumphant, and Victorious,
He held th'Atchievement was too glorious
For such a Conquerour, to meddle
With *Petty Constable*, or *Beadle*:
Or fly for Refuge, to the *Hostess*
Of th'Ins of Court, and Chanc'ry, *Justice*:   50
Who might, perhaps, reduce his Cause
To th'*Ordeal Tryal* of the Laws;
Where none escape, but such as branded
With red-hot Irons have past *Bare-handed*:
And if they cannot read one *Verse*
Ith' Psalms, must sing it, and that's worse.

He therefore judging it below him,
To tempt a shame, the *Dev'l might owe him*,
Resolv'd to leave the Squire for *Bail*
And *Mainprize* for him, to the *Gaol*,   60
To answer, with his Vessel, all
That might disastrously befall.
He thought it now the fittest juncture,
To give the Lady a Rencounter;
T'acquaint her with his Expedition,
And Conquest, o're the *fierce Magician.*
Describe the manner of the Fray,
And shew the spoils he brought away.
His bloody *Scourging* aggravate,
The Number of the Blows, and Weight;   70
All which might probably, succeed,
And gain belief, h' had done the deed.
Which he resolv'd to enforce, and spare
No pawning of his Soul, to swear;
But rather then produce his Back,
To set his Conscience on the Rack:
And in pursuance of his urging
Of Articles perform'd, and scourging:
And all things else, upon his part,
Demand delivery of her Heart,   80
Her Goods, and Chattels, and good Graces,
And Person, up to his embraces.

Thought he, the Ancient *Errant Knights,*
Won all their Ladies Hearts, in *Fights,*
And cut whole Gyants into fitters,
To put them into amorous twitters:
Whose stubborn Bowels scorn'd to yield,
Until their *Gallants* were half kill'd:
But when their Bones were drub'd so sore
They durst not *wooe one Combat* more;   90
The Ladies Hearts began to melt,
Subdu'd with Blows their Lovers felt.

57 it] it, *D*   60 *Gaol, D2*: *Gaol. D1*   62 befall.] befall, *D*   73 spare]
spare, *D*   77 urging] urging, *D*   89 sore] sore, *D*
811844   R

So *Spanish Heroes*, with their Lances,
At once wound *Bulls*, and *Ladies fancies*:
And he acquires the noblest Spouse,
That Widdow's greatest Herds of Cows,
Then what may I expect to do,
Wh' have quel'd so vast a *Buffalo*?

Mean while, the Squire was on his way,
The Knight's *late Orders* to obey;   100
Who sent him for a *Strong Detachment*
Of *Beadles*, *Constables*, and *Watchmen*;
T'attach the *Cunning-man*, for Plunder
Committed falsly on his Lumber,
When he, who had so lately sack'd
The Enemy, had done the Fact,
Had rifled all his Pokes, and Fobs,
Of *Gimcracks*, *Whims*, and *Jiggumbobs*;
Which He, by Hook, or Crook, had gather'd;
And for his own Inventions, father'd: 110
And when they should, at *Gaol-delivery*,
Unriddle one another's Thievery,
Both might have evidence, enough,
To render neither Halter-proof.
He thought it desperate, to tarry,
And venture to be *Accessary*:
But rather wisely slip his Fetters,
And leave them for the Knight, his *Betters*.
He call'd to mind th'unjust foul play
He would have offer'd him, that day;   120
To make him curry his own Hide,
Which no Beast ever did beside,
Without all possible evasion,
But of the *Riding Dispensation*.
And therefore much about the hour,
The Knight (for reasons told before)
Resolv'd, to leave him, to the Fury,
Of *Justice*, and an *unpackt Jury*:
The *Squire* concur'd t'abandon him,
And serve him in the self-same Trim.   130

T'acquaint the *Lady* what h' had done,
And what he meant to carry on;
What *Project* 'twas he went about,
When *Sidrophel* and he fell out:
His firm, and stedfast Resolution,
To swear her to an *Execution*:
To pawn his inward Ears, to marry her,
And Bribe the Dev'l himself to carry her.
In which both dealt, as if they meant
Their *Party Saints* to represent,   140
Who never fail'd, upon their sharing
In any Prosperous *Arms-bearing*,
To lay themselves out, to supplant
Each other *Cousin-German Saint*.
But e're the Knight could do his Part,
The Squire had got so much the Start,
H' had to the Lady done his Errand,
And told her all his tricks afore-hand.
Just as he finish'd his Report,
The *Knight* alighted in the Court;   150
And having ty'd his Beast t'a Pale,
And taken time, for both to stale,
He put his Band, and Beard in Order,
The Sprucer, to accost, and board her.
And now began t'approach the Door,
When she, wh' had spy'd him out before,
Convey'd th'*Informer* out of sight,
And went to entertain the *Knight*.
With whom encountring, After *Longees*
Of *humble*, and *submissive Congees*,   160
And all *Due Ceremonies* paid,
He strok'd his Beard, and thus he said,
Madam, I do, as is my Duty,
Honour the Shadow of your Shoo-tye.
And now am come, to bring your Ear
A Present, you'l be glad to hear;
At least I hope so, *The thing*'s done,
Or may I never see the Sun;

152 stale,] stale *D*

For which I humbly now demand
Performance, at your gentle Hand: 170
And that you'ld please to do your part
As I have done mine, to my smart.
With that he shrug'd his sturdy back,
As if he felt his Shoulders ake:
But she who well enough, knew what
(Before he spoke) he would be at,
Pretended not to apprehend
The Mystery, of what he mean'd:
And therefore wish'd him to expound
His dark expressions, *less profound*.   180

Madam, quoth he, I come to prove
How much, I've suffer'd for your Love:
Which (like your *Votary*) to win,
I have not spar'd my tatter'd skin:
And for those meritorious Lashes,
To claim your favour, and good Graces.

Quoth she, I do remember, once
I freed you, from th'Inchanted Sconce;
And that you promis'd, for that favour,
To bind your Back to th' *good Behaviour*,   190
And for my Sake, and Service, vow'd,
To lay upon't a heavy Load,
And what 'twould bear, t'a scruple, prove,
As other Knights do oft make love:
Which whether you have done or no,
Concerns your self, not me, to know.
But if you have, I shall confess
Y' are honester, then I could guess.

Quoth he, if you suspect my troth,
I cannot prove it, but by Oath;   200
And if you make a question on't:
I'le pawn my Soul, that I have don't.

172 smart.] smart, *D*   181 *Editor's paragraph*   187 *Editor's paragraph*
198 guess.] guess; *D*   199 *Editor's paragraph*

And he that makes his Soul, his Surety
I think, does give the best security.

Quoth she, some say, the *Soul's secure,*
Against Distress, and *Forfeiture;*
Is free from Action, and exempt
From Execution, and Contempt;
And to be summon'd to appear
In th'other world, 's illegal here: 210
And therefore few make any account,
Int' what incumbrances they run't.
For most Men carry things so even
Between this *World,* and *Hell,* and *Heaven;*
Without the least offence to either,
They freely deal in all together:
And equally abhor to quit
This *World,* for both, or both for it.
And when they pawn, and damn their Souls,
They are but *Pris'ners* on *Parols.*   220

For that, quoth he, 'tis rational
They may be accomptable, in all;
For when there is that intercourse,
Between *Divine, and Humane Pow'rs;*
That all that we determine here,
Commands Obedience every where;
When penalties may be commuted,
For Fines, or Ears, and Executed,
It follows, nothing binds so fast
As Souls in Pawn, and Mortgage past: 230
For Oaths are th'only *Tests,* and *Seals,*
Of *Right,* and *Wrong,* and *True,* and *False.*
And there's no other way to try
The Doubts of Law, and Justice by.

Quoth She, what is it you would Swear?
There's no believing till I hear:

For till th' are understood, all Tales
(Like Nonsense) are nor *True*, nor *False*.

Quoth he, when I resolv'd t'obey
What you commanded th'other day;   240
And to perform my Exercise,
(As Schools are wont) for your fair eyes:
T'avoid all Scruples in the Case,
I went to do't upon the Place:
But as the *Castle* is inchanted,
By *Sidrophel the Witch*, and haunted
With evil Spirits as you know,
Who took my Squire and me for two:
Before I'd hardly time to lay
My weapons by, and disarray,   250
I heard a Formidable Noise
Loud as the *Stentrophonick Voice*
That Roar'd far off; Dispatch and Strip,
I'm ready with th'Infernal Whip,
That shall divest thy Ribs of Skin,
To expiate thy lingring Sin:
Th' hast broke perfidiously thy *Oath*,
And not perform'd thy plighted Troth:
But spar'd thy Renegado Back,
Where th' hadst so great a Prize at Stake.   260
Which now the Fates have order'd me
For *Penance* and *Revenge* to Flea.
Unless thou presently make hast,
Time is, Time was, and there it ceas'd.
With which though startled I confess
Yet th'Horror of the thing was less
Than th'other Dismal apprehension,
Of *Interruption* or *Prevention*,
And therefore snatching up the Rod,
I laid upon my back a load;   270
Resolv'd to spare no Flesh and Blood,
To make my Word and Honour good:

239 *Editor's paragraph*   252 *Voice*] Voice. D   253–64 Dispatch *&c.*
D2 prints ita ics   264 there it ceas'd] *there it ceas'd D1*   266 less *D2:*
less; *D1*

Till tyr'd, and taking Truce at length,
For new Recruits of Breath and Strength,
I felt the *Blows*, still ply'd as fast,
As if th' had been by *Lovers* Plac'd,
In *Raptures of Platonique Lashing,*
And *chast Contemplative Bardashing.*
When facing hastily about,
To stand upon my Guard, and Scout,   280
I found th'Infernal Cunning-man,
And th'Under-witch his *Caliban*,
With Scourges (like the Furies) Arm'd,
That on my outward Quarters storm'd:
In hast, I snatch'd my weapon up,
And gave their Hellish Rage a stop.
Call'd thrice upon your Name, and fell
Couragiously, on *Sidrophel.*
Who now transform'd himself t'a Bear,
Began to Roar aloud, and tear,   290
When I as furiously prest on,
My weapon down his Throat to run,
Laid hold on him, but he broke loose,
And turn'd himself into a Goose:
Div'd under *Water*, in a Pond,
To hide himself from being found:
In vain I sought him, but as soon
As I perceiv'd him fled and gone;
Prepar'd with equal Hast and Rage,
His *Under Sorcerer* t'ingage;   300
But bravely Scorning to defile
My Sword with feeble blood and vile;
I judg'd it better from a *Quick-*
Set-Hedge to cut a knotted Stick,
With which, I furiously laid on,
Till in a Harsh and Doleful tone,
It Roar'd, *Oh Hold for pity Sir,*
I am too great a Sufferer,
Abus'd, as you have been b'a Witch,
But conjur'd into a worse Caprich   310

301 defile] defile, D

Who sends me out, on many a Jaunt,
Old Houses in the Night to haunt:
For opportunities t'Improve
Designs of Thievery or Love:
With Drugs convey'd in Drink, or Meat,
All *Feats* of *Witches* counterfeit,
Kill *Pigs* and *Geese* with *Poudered Glass,*
And make it for *Inchantments* Pass.
With *Cowitch* meazle like a Leper
And choak with Fumes of *Guiny-Pepper,*   320
Make *Leachers,* and their *Punks* with *Dewtry,*
Commit Phantastical Advowtry,
Bewitch *Hermetique-men* to Run
Stark staring mad with *Manicon,*
Believe *Mechanick Virtuosi*
Can raise 'em *Mountains* in *Potosi;*
And sillier than the *Antick Fools,*
Take *Treasure* for a *Heap of Coals:*
Seek out for Plants with *Signatures*
To Quack of *Universal Cures:*   330
With Figures ground on *Panes* of *Glass,*
Make People on their Heads to pass;
And mighty heaps of Coyn increase,
Reflected from a single piece:
To Draw in Fools whose Nat'ral Itches
Incline perpetually to Witches;
And keep me in continual Fears
And Danger of my Neck and Ears:
When less Delinquent have been scourg'd
And Hemp on wooden Anvils forg'd,   340
Which others for Cravats have worn,
About their Necks and took a Turn.

I pity'd the sad Punishment,
The *wretched Caitiffe* underwent,
And Held my Drubbing of his Bones,
Too great an honour for *Pultrones;*
For Knights are bound to feel no Blows
From Paltry and unequal Foes,

311–42 *D2 prints italics*   335 Itches] Itches; *D1*   342 Turn.] Turn: *D*
343 *Editor's paragraph*

Who when they slash and cut to pieces,
Do all with civilest addresses;   350
Their Horses never give a blow,
But when they make a Leg and Bow:
I therefore Spar'd his Flesh, and Prest him
About the Witch with man' a Question.
Quoth he, For many years he drove
A kind of Broking-Trade in Love,
Employed in all th'*Intrigues* and *Trust*,
Of feeble *Speculative Lust*:
Procurer to th'Extravagancy,
And crazy Ribaldry of Fancy;   360
By those the Devil had forsook
As things below him to provoke,
But b'ing a virtuoso, able
To *Smatter*, *Quack*, and *Cant*, and *Dabble*,
He held his *Talent* most Adroyt
For any *Mystical Exploit*;
As others of his Tribe had done,
And rais'd their Prices Three to One;
For *one Predicting Pimp* has th'Odds
Of *Chauldrons*, of plain downright Bauds: 370
But as an *Elf* (*the Devils Valet*)
Is not so slight a thing to get,
For those that do his Business best,
In Hell, are us'd the Ruggedest:
Before so meriting a Person
Could get a *Grant*, *but in Reversion*:
He serv'd two Prenticeships and longer,
I'th' Myst'ry of a *Lady-Monger*.
For (as some write) A *Witches Ghost*,
As soon as from the Body loos'd,   380
Becomes a *Puiney-Imp* it self,
And is another *Witches Elf*.
He after searching far and near,
At length found one in *Lancashire*,
With whom he bargain'd before hand,
And after Hanging, entertain'd:

355-402 For many &c. D2 *prints italics*   362 him to provoke,] him, to
provoke D

Since which, H' has playd a thousand Feats,
And Practis'd all Mechanick Cheats:
Transform'd himself, to th'ugly Shapes
Of *Wolves*, and *Bears*, *Baboons*, and *Apes*;   390
Which he has vary'd more than Witches,
Or *Pharaoh*'s *Wizards* could their *Switches*:
And all with whom H' has had to do,
Turn'd to as Monstrous Figures too.
Witness my self whom h' has abus'd
And to this Beastly shape Reduc'd;
By feeding me on *Beans* and *Pease*,
He Cram's in *Nasty Crevices*,
And turns to Comfits by his Arts,
To make me relish for *Disserts*,   400
And one by one with Shame and Fear,
Lick up the Candid Provender.
Beside —— But as h' was running on,
To tell what other Feats h' had done,
The Lady stopt his full Carier,
And told him, Now 'twas time to hear.

If half those things (said she) be true,
(*Th' are all (Quoth he) I swear by you:*)
Why then (said she) that *Sidrophel*
Has Damn'd himself to th' Pit of Hell: 410
Who mounted on a Broom, the *Nag*
And Hackney of a Lapland Hag,
In Quest of you came hither Post,
Within an Hour (I'm sure) at most,
Who told me all you swear and say,
Quite contrary another way:
Vow'd that you came to him to know
If you should carry me or no;
And would have hir'd him and his Imps,
To be your Match-makers and Pimps,   420
T'ingage the Devil on your side,
And steal (like *Proserpine*) your Bride.
But he disdaining to embrace

406 hear.] hear, *D1*   407 *Editor's paragraph*   407–78 *D2 prints*
italics

So filthy a Design and Base,
You fell to vapouring and Huffing,
And drew upon him like a Ruffin,
Surpriz'd him meanly, unprepar'd,
Before h' had time to mount his Guard;
And left him dead upon the Ground,
With many a Bruise and desperate wound.   430
Swore you had broke, and Rob'd his House
And stole his *Talismanique Louse*,
And all his New-*found Old Inventions*,
With Flat Felonious Intentions:
Which he could bring out where he had,
And what he bought 'em for and Paid.
His *Flea*, his *Morpion*, and *Punese*,
H' had gotten for his Proper ease,
And all in perfect Minutes made,
By th'Ablest Artists of the Trade: 440
Which (he could prove it) since he lost,
He has been eaten up almost:
And all together, might amount
To many hundreds on account:
For which h' had got sufficient warrant,
To scize the Malefactors Errand;
Without capacity of Bail,
But of a *Carts*, or *Horses Tail*:
And did not doubt to bring the Wretches,
To serve for *Pendulums to Watches*:   450
Which modern Vertuoso's say,
Incline to Hanging every way.
Beside he swore, and swore 'twas true,
That e're he went in Quest of you,
He set a Figure to Discover
If you were fled to *Rye*, or *Dover*,
And found it clear that to betray
Your selves and me, you fled this way,
And that he was upon pursuit
To take you somewhere hereabout.   460
He vow'd h' had had Intelligence,
Of all that past before and since:

433 *Inventions,*] *Inventions* D   454 you,] you. D

And found that e're you came to him,
Y' had been Ingaging Life and Limb,
About a case of tender Conscience,
Where both abounded in your own Sense:
Till *Ralpho* by his Light and Grace,
Had clear'd all Scruples in the Case:
And prov'd that you might swear and own
Whatever's by the Wicked done: 470
For which most basely to requite
The Service of his *Gifts* and *Light*,
You strove t'oblige him by main force
To scourge his Ribs instead of yours,
But that he stood upon his Guard,
And all your vapouring outdar'd,
For which between you both, the Feat
Has never been perform'd as yet.

While thus the Lady talk'd, the Knight
Turn'd th'Outside of his eyes to white,   480
(*As men of Inward light are wont*
To turn their Opticks in upon't)
He wonder'd how she came to know,
What he had done and meant to do:
Held up his *Affidavit hand*,
As if h' had been to be arraign'd:
Cast t'wards the Door a Ghastly look,
In Dread of *Sidrophel*, and spoke.
Madam, if but one word be true,
Of all the Wizard has told you,   490
Or but one single Circumstance
In all th'*Apocryphal Romance*:
May dreadful Earthquakes swallow down,
This Vessel, *that is all your own*:
Or may the Heavens fall and cover,
These Relicks of your Constant Lover.

You have provided well, quoth She,
(I thank you) for your self and me:

And shewn your *Presbyterian* wits
Jump punctual with the *Jesuites*.   500
A most compendious way and civil,
At once to cheat the *World*, the *Devil*,
And *Heaven* and *Hell, your Selves* and *Those*,
On whom you vainly think t'impose.
Why then (Quoth He) may *Hell surprize* ——
That trick (said she) will not pass twice,
I've learn'd how far I'm to believe
Your Pinning Oaths upon your Sleeve.
But there's a better way of Clearing
What you would prove than downright Swearing,   510
For if you have perform'd the Feat,
The Blows are visible as yet:
Enough to serve for satisfaction
Of Nicest scruples in the Action:
And if you can produce those *Knobs*
Although th' are but the *Witches* Drubs;
I'le pass them all upon account,
As if your Natural Self had don't.
Provided that they pass th'opinion,
Of Able Juries of old Women: 520
Who us'd to judge all *matt'r of Facts*
For *Bellies*, may do so, for *Backs*.

Madam (quoth he) *your Love's a Million,*
To do is less, than to be willing,
As I am, were it in my Pow'r,
T'obey what you command and more:
But for performing what you bid,
I thank you as much, as if I did:
You know I ought to have a care
To keep my wounds, from taking Air: 530
For wounds in those that are all Heart,
Are dangerous in any Part.

I find (quoth she) my *Goods and Chattels*
Are like to prove, but meer *drawn Battels*;
For still the longer we contend,
We are but farther off the end.

But granting now, we should agree,
What is it you expect from me?
Your plighted Faith (quoth he) and Word
You past in Heaven, on Record.   540
Where all Contracts, to have, and t'hold
Are everlastingly inrol'd,
And if 'tis counted Treason, here
To *race Records*, 'tis much more there.

Quoth she, there are no *Bargains driv'n*
Nor *Marriages* clap'd up in *Heaven*,
And that's the reason as some guess,
There is no Heav'n in Marriages:
Two things, that naturally press
Too narrowly, to be at ease: 550
Their bus'ness there is only *Love*
Which Marriage is not like t'improve.
Love, that's too generous, t'abide
To be against its Nature, ty'd;
For where 'tis of it self inclin'd
It breaks loose, when it is confin'd:
And like the Soul its harbourer,
Debar'd the freedom of the Air;
Disdains, against its will, to stay,
But struggles out, and flies away.   560
And therefore, never can comply,
T'indure the Matrimonial tye:
That binds the Female, and the Male,
Where th'one is but the others Bail.
Like Roman Gaolers, when they slept,
Chain'd to the Prisoners they kept.
Of which the True, and *Faithful'st* Lover
Gives best security, to *suffer*.

Marriage is but a Beast, some say,
That *carries double in foul way*,   570
And therefore 'tis not to be admir'd,
It should so suddenly be tyr'd:
A bargain, at a venture made,
Between two Part'ners in a *Trade*,

545 *Editor's paragraph*

(For what's infer'd by *T'have, and t'hold*,
But something past away, and sold?)
That as it makes but one, of two,
Reduces all things else, as low:
And at the best is but a *Mart*
Between the one, and th'other part,   580
That on the Marriage-day is paid,
Or, hour of Death, the Bet it laid
And all the rest of *Bett'r or worse*:
Both are but losers, out of Purse.
For when upon their ungot Heirs
Th' intail themselves, and all that's theirs,
What blinder Bargain e're was driven,
Or Wager laid at *six and seven*?
To pass themselves away, and turn
Their Children's Tenants, e're th' are born?   590
Beg one another *Idiot*,
To *Guardians* e're they are begot;
Or ever shall, perhaps, by th'one,
Who's bound to vouch 'em for his own,
Though got b'*Implicite Generation*,
And *General Club* of all the Nation;
For which she's fortify'd no less
Than all the Island, with four *Seas*:
Exacts the Tribute of her Dow'r
In ready Insolence, and Pow'r;   600
And makes him pass away, to *Have*
And *Hold*, to her, himself, her slave,
More wretched than an *Ancient Villain*,
Condemn'd to *Drudgery*, and *Tilling*,
While all he does upon the By,
She is not bound to justifie;
Nor at her proper cost, and charge
Maintain the Feats, he does at large.
Such hideous Sots, were *those obedient*
Old Vassals, to their *Ladies Regent*;   610
To give the Cheats, the *Eldest hand*
In *Foul Play*, by the Laws o'th' Land,
For which so many a *legal Cuckold*
Has been run down in Courts, and truckled.

A Law that most unjustly yokes,
All *Johns* of *Stiles*, to *Joans* of *Nokes*,
Without distinction of degree,
Condition, Age, or Quality,
Admits no *Pow'r* of *Revocation*,
Nor *valuable Consideration*,   620
Nor *Writ* of *Error*, nor *Reverse*,
Of *Judgement* past, *For better, or worse*.
Will not allow the Priviledges
That Beggers challenge under Hedges,
Who when th' are griev'd can make dead Horses
Their Spiritual Judges of Divorces;
While nothing else, but *Rem* in *Re*,
Can set the proudest Wretches free.
A slavery, beyond induring,
But that 'tis of their own procuring.   630
As Spiders never seek the Fly,
But leave him, of himself, t'apply:
So Men are by themselves betray'd
To quit the freedom they injoy'd,
And run their Necks into a Noose,
They'ld break 'em after, to break loose.
As some, whom *Death would not depart*,
Have done the Feat themselves, by Art.
Like *Indian Widdows* gone to Bed
In *Flaming Curtains*, to the Dead,   640
And Men as often dangled for't,
And yet will never leave the Sport.

Nor do the Ladies want excuse,
For all the *Stratagems* they use
To gain th'advantage of *the Set*,
And lurch the Amorous Rook, and Cheat,
For as a *Pythagorean Soul*,
Runs through all Beasts, and Fish, and Fowl,
And has a smack of ev'ry one:
So Love do's, and has ever done.   650
And therefore, though 'tis ere so fond,
Takes strangely to the Vagabond.

635 run *D1* (*errata*), *D2*: runs *D1*   644 use] use. *D*

'Tis but an Ague that's reverst,
Whose hot fit takes the Patient first,
That after burns with cold as much,
As Ir'n in *Greenland*, does the touch,
Melts in the Furnace of desire,
Like Glass, that's but the Ice of Fire,
And when his heat of Fancy's over
Becomes as hard, and frail a Lover,   660
For when he's with Love-powder laden,
And Prim'd, and Cock'd by *Miss*, or *Madam*,
The smallest sparkle of an Eye
Gives Fire to his Artillery;
And off the loud Oaths go, but while
Th' are in the very Act, recoyl:
Hence 'tis, so few dare take their chance
Without a sep'rate maintenance,
And Widdows, who have try'd one Lover,
Trust none again, 'till th' have made over;   670
Or if they do, before they marry,
The Foxes weigh the Goose they carry:
And e're they venture o're a stream,
Know how to size themselves, and them.
Whence witty'st Ladies always choose
To undertake the heavyest Goose.
For now the World is grown so wary,
That few of either Sex dare marry,
But rather trust, on tick, t'Amours
The *Cross* and *Pile*, for *Bett'r* or *Worse*;   680
A Mode, that is held honourable,
As well as French, and fashionable.
For when it falls out for the best,
Where both are incommoded least;
In Soul, and Body too, unite,
To make up one *Hermaphrodite*;
Still Amorous, and Fond, and Billing,
Like *Philip* and *Mary*, *on a Shilling*;
Th' have more Punctilio's, and Capriches
Between th' Petticoat, and Breeches,   690
More petulant extravagancies,

672 Goose] Geese D2   691 petulant] potulant D

Than Poets make 'em in Romances.
Though, when *their Heroes*, *'spouse the Dames*,
We hear no more of *Charms* and *Flames*:
For then their late attracts decline
And turn as eager, as *Prik'd Wine*.
And all their Catterwauling tricks
In earnest, to as jealous Piques,
Which th'Ancients wisely signify'd
By th' *yellow Manto's* of the Bride.   700
For jealousie is but a kind
Of *Clap*, and *Grincam* of the mind,
The Natural effect of Love,
As other Flames, and Aches prove;
But all the mischief is, the doubt,
On whose account, they first broke out:
For though *Chineses* go to Bed,
And lye in, in their Ladies stead,
And for the pains they took before,
Are nurs'd, and pamper'd to do more: 710
Our *Green-men* do it worse, when th' hap
To fall in labour of a Clap,
Both lay the Child to one another,
But who's the *Father*, who the *Mother*,
'Tis hard to say in multitudes,
Or who imported the *French Goods*:
But Health, and Sickness, b'ing all one,
Which both ingag'd before to own;
And are not with their Bodies bound
To Worship, only when th' are sound,   720
Both give, and take their equal shares,
Of all they suffer by false Wares:
A Fate, no Lover can divert
With all his caution, Wit, and Art,
For 'tis in vain, to think to guess
At Women, by *Appearances*,
That Paint, and Patch their *Imperfections*
Of *Intellectual Complexions*:
And daub their Tempers o're, *with Washes*,

719 bound] bound, *D*   720 are sound,] art sound. *D*

As Artificial, as their Faces;   730
Wear, under Vizard-Masks, *their Talents*
And Mother Wits, before their Gallants;
Until th' are hampered in the Nooze,
Too fast, to dream of breaking loose.
When all the Flaws they strove to hide
Are made unready, with the Bride
That with her Wedding-clothes undresses
Her Complaisance, and Gentilesses;
Try's all her Arts, to take upon her
The Government, from th'easie owner,   740
Until the Wretch is glad to wave
His lawful Right, and turn her Slave;
Finds all his *Having, and his Holding*,
Reduc'd t'Eternal *Noise*, and *Scolding*,
The *Conjugal Petard*, that tears
Down all *Portcullices of Ears*,
And makes the Volly of one Tongue,
For all their Leathern Shields too strong,
When only arm'd with Noise, and Nails,
The Female Silk-worms ride the Males.   750
Transform 'em into Rams, and Goats,
Like *Syrens* with their charming Notes:
Sweet as a Screech-Owl's *Serenade*,
Or those inchanting murmurs made
By th'Husband *Mandrake*, and the *Wife*,
Both bury'd (like themselves) alive.

Quoth he, these Reasons are but strains
Of wanton, over-heated Brains,
Which Ralliers in their *Wit*, or *Drink*,
Do rather wheedle with, than think: 760
Man was not Man, in *Paradise*,
Until he was Created twice,
And had his better half, his *Bride*,
Carv'd from th'Original, his side.
T'amend his Natural defects
And perfect his recruited Sex,
Inlarge his Breed, at once, and lessen
The *Pains and labour of increasing*,

By changing them, for other cares,
As by his *dry'd-up Paps* appears.   770
His Body, that stupendious Frame
Of all the World *The Anagram*,
Is of two equal parts compact
In Shape, and Symmetry, exact.
Of which the Left, and Female side,
Is to the Manly Right, a Bride,
Both joyn'd together, with such Art,
That nothing else but Death can part:
Those heavenly Attracts of yours, your Eyes
And Face, that all the World surprize,   780
That dazle all that look upon ye,
And scorch all other Ladies Tawny:
Those Ravishing, and charming Graces,
Are all made up, of *two Half faces*,
That in a *Mathematick Line*,
Like those in other Heavens, joyn.
Of which if either grew alone
'Twould fright as much, to look upon:
And so would that *sweet Bud, your Lip*,
Without the others fellowship.   790
Our Noblest Senses act by Pairs,
Two Eyes to see, to hear, two Ears,
Th'Intelligencers of the mind,
To wait upon the Soul design'd,
But those, that serve the Body alone,
Are single and confin'd to one:
The World is but two Parts, that meet,
And close at th'Æquinoctial fit;
And so are all the works of Nature,
Stamp'd *with her signature* on matter: 800
Which all her Creatures, to a Leaf,
Or smallest Blade of Grass, receive.
All which sufficiently declare
How intirely *Marriage* is her care,
The only method that she uses,
In all the wonders she produces:
And those that take their rules from her
Can never be deceiv'd, nor err.

For what secures the *Civil Life*
But pawns of *Children, and a Wife*?　　　810
That lie, like *Hostages*, at stake,
To pay for all, Men undertake;
To whom it is as necessary,
As to be born, and breath, to marry.
So Universal, all Mankind
In nothing else, is of one mind:
For in what stupid Age, or Nation,
Was Marriage ever out of Fashion?
Unless among the *Amazons*,
Or *Vestal Fryers*, and *Cloyster'd Nuns*,　　　820
Or *Stoicks*, who to bar the *Freaks*,
And loose Excesses of the *Sex*;
Prepostrously would have all Women,
Turn'd up, to all the World, in common:
Though Men would find such mortal *Fewds*,
In sharing of their *publick Goods*,
'Twould put them to more charge of Lives,
Then th' are supply'd with now, by Wives.
Until they Graze, and wear their Cloaths,
As Beasts do, of their *Native Growths*,　　　830
For simple wearing of their *Horns*,
Will not suffice to serve their turns.
For what can we pretend to inherit,
Unless the *Marriage-deed* will bear it?
Could claim no Right to Lands, or Rents,
But for our Parents settlements:
Had been but younger *Sons o' th' Earth*,
Debar'd it all, but for our Birth.
What Honours, or Estates of *Peers*
Could be preserv'd but by their Heirs?　　　840
And what security maintains
Their Right, and Title, but the *Banes*?
What Crowns could be Hereditary,
If greatest *Monarchs did not marry*?
And with their *Consorts*, consummate
Their weightyest *Interests of State*?

846 *State?*] *State* D

For all the Amours of Princes, are
But *Garranties* of Peace, or War.
Or what but Marriage has a Charm,
The *Rage of Empires* to disarm?   850
Make Blood, and Desolation cease,
And Fire, and Sword, unite in Peace?
When all their fierce contests *for Forrage*,
Conclude in Articles of *Marriage*?
Nor does the Genial Bed provide
Less, for the interests of the *Bride*:
Who else had not the least pretence
T'as much, as *Due Benevolence*,
Could no more Title take upon her
To *Virtue, Quality, and Honour*   860
Then *Ladies Errant*, unconfin'd,
And *Feme-Coverts* to all Mankind.
All Women would be of one piece,
The virtuous *Matron*, and the *Miss*.
The Nymphs of *chast Diana's Train*,
The same with those in *Lewkners-lane*;
But for the difference Marriage makes
'Twixt *Wives*, and *Ladies of the Lakes*.
Besides the joys of *Place* and *Birth*,
The Sexes Paradise on Earth,   870
A priviledge so sacred held
That none will to their Mothers yield,
But rather then not go before,
Abandon Heaven at the Door.
And if the Indulgent Law allows,
A greater freedom, to the Spouse;
The reason is, because the Wife
Runs greater hazards of her Life.
Is trusted with the *Form*, and *Matter*
Of all Mankind, by careful Nature: 880
Where Man brings nothing, but the Stuff,
She frames the wondrous Fabrick of.
Who therefore, in a strait, may freely
Demand the *Clergy of her Belly*,
And make it save her, the same way,
It seldom misses to betray.

Unless both parties wisely enter
Into the Liturgy-Indenture.
And though some fits of small contest
Sometimes fall out among the *Best,*   890
That is no more, then every Lover
Does, from his *Hackney Lady* suffer.
That makes no Breach of Faith, and Love,
But rather (sometime) serves t'improve.
For as in running, *ev'ry Pace*
Is but between two Legs a Race,
In which, both do their uttermost,
To get before, and win the *Post* :
Yet when th' are at their races ends,
Th' are still as kind, and constant friends;   900
And to relieve their weariness,
By turns give one another ease :
So all those false Allarms of strife,
Between the *Husband,* and the *Wife* :
And little quarrels, often prove
To be but new recruits of Love :
When those, wh' are always kind, or coy,
In time, must either Tire, or Cloy.
Nor are their loudest clamours, more
Then as th' are relish'd, *Sweet,* or *Sour,*   910
Like *Musick,* that proves bad, or good,
According as 'tis understood.
In all Amours, a Lover burns,
With *Frowns,* as well as *Smiles* by turns,
And hearts have been as oft, with sullen,
As charming looks, surprized, and stollen,
Then why should more bewitching clamour,
Some Lovers not as much enamour?
For Discords make the sweetest Airs,
And Curses are a kind of Prayers.   920
Too slight Alloys, for all those grand
Felicities, by Marriage gain'd.
For nothing else has Pow'r to settle
Th'interests of Love, perpetual.
An *Act* and *Deed,* that makes one Heart,
Become another's counter-part,

And *passes Fines* on Faith and Love
Inrol'd, and Registred above,
To seal the slippery knot of Vows,
Which nothing else but Death can lose :   930
And what security's too strong,
To guard that gentle Heart from wrong,
That to its Friend is glad to pass,
It self away, and all it has :
And, like an *Anchorite*, gives over
This World, for *th'Heaven of a Lover*?

I grant (quoth she) there are some few
Who take that course, and find it true :
But Millions, whom the same does sentence
To Heaven, b'another way, repentance.   940
Love's Arrows are but shot at Rovers,
Though all they hit, they turn to Lovers,
And all the weighty consequents
Depend upon more blind events
Then Gamesters when they play a set
With greatest cunning at Piquet,
Put out with caution, but take in
They know not what, unsight-unseen.
For what do Lovers, when th' are fast
In one another's Arms imbrac't;   950
But strive, to plunder; and convey
Each other, *like a Prize*, away?
To change the property of selves,
As sucking Children are, by *Elves*?
And if they use their *Persons* so,
What will they to their *Fortunes* do?
Their Fortunes! the perpetual aims
Of all their Extasies, and Flames :
For when the Money's on the Book,
And *all my Worldly Goods* —— but spoke :   960
(The Formal *Livery, and Seasin*,
That puts a Lover in possession)
To that alone the Bridegroom's wedded,
The Bride a flam, that's superseded;

952 away?] away! *D*   964 superseded;] superseded *D*

To that, their Faith is still made good,
And all the Oaths to us they vow'd.
For when we once resign our Pow'rs,
W' have nothing left, we can call ours.
Our Money's now become the *Miss*,
Of all your *Lives* and *Services*:   970
And we forsaken, and Postpon'd,
But Bawds to what before we own'd;
Which as it made y' at first Gallant us,
So now hires others to supplant us,
Until 'tis all turn'd out of doors,
(As we had been) for *New Amours*.
For what did ever *Heiress* yet
By being born to *Lordships*, get?
When the more *Ladies sh' is of Mannors*,
She's but expos'd to more Trepanners,   980
Pays for their Projects, and Designs,
And for her own destruction Fines.
And does but tempt them, with her Riches,
To use her, as the Dev'l does Witches,
Who takes it for a special Grace,
To be their Cully for a space
That when the time's expir'd, the Drazels
For ever, may become his Vassals.
So she bewitch'd by *Rooks* and *Spirits*,
Betrays her self, and all sh' inherits   990
Is bought and sold, like stollen goods,
By *Pimps*, and *Match-makers*, and *Bawds*:
Until they force her to convey,
And steal the Thief himself away.
These are the Everlasting Fruits
Of all your passionate Love-suits,
The effects of all your *amorous Fancies*,
To *Portions*, and *Inheritances*.
Your Love-sick Raptures, *for Fruition*
Of Dowry, Joynture, and Tuition;   1000
To which you make Address, and Courtship,
And with your Bodies, strive to Worship:
That th'Infants Fortunes may partake
Of Love too, for the Mothers sake.

For these, you play at *Purposes*,
And love your Loves with *A's*, and *B's*,
For these, at *Beast*, and *L'hombre*, wooe,
And play for *Love*, and *Money* too.
Strive who shall be the ablest Man,
At right *Gallanting of a Fan*:   1010
And who the most Gentilely bred,
At sucking of a *Vizard Bead*;
How best t'accost us, in all Quarters
T'our *question*-and-*command New Garters*,
And solidly discourse upon
All sorts of dresses, *Pro* and *Con*.
For there's no Mystery, nor Trade,
But in the Art of Love is made.
And when you have more Debts to pay
Then *Michaelmas* and *Lady-day*,   1020
And no way possible to do't
But *Love* and *Oaths*, and *restless Suit*,
To us y' apply, to pay the Scores
Of all your cully'd past Amours:
Act o're your *Flames*, and *Darts*, again,
And charge us with your wounds and pain,
Which other's influences, long since
Have charm'd your *Noses* with, and *Shins*.
For which, the *Surgeon* is unpaid,
And like to be, without our aid.   1030
Lord! what an Amorous thing is want,
How *Debts*, and *Mortgages* inchant,
What Graces must that Lady have,
That can from *Executions* save!
What Charms! that can *reverse extent*,
And *Null Decree, and Exigent*!
What *Magical Attracts*, and *Graces*
That can redeem from *Scire Facias*!
From Bonds, and Statutes can discharge,
And from contempts of Courts inlarge!   1040
These are the highest excellencies
Of all our true, or false pretences;

And you would Damn your selves, and swear,
As much, t'an *Hostess Dowager*;
Grown Fat, and Pursy, by Retail
Of Pots of Beer, and Bottled Ale;
And find her fitter for your turn,
For fat is wondrous apt to burn.
Who at your Flame would soon take Fire,
Relent, and melt to your desire: 1050
And, like a Candle in the Socket,
Dissolve her Graces int' your Pocket.

By this time, 'twas grown dark, and late,
When th' heard a knocking, at the Gate
Laid on in hast, with such a powder,
The blows grew louder, still, and louder:
Which *Hudibras*, as if th' had been
Bestow'd, as freely on his Skin,
Expounded by his inward Light,
Or rather more Prophetick fright,   1060
To be the *Wizard*, come to search,
And take him napping, in the lurch.
Turn'd pale as Ashes, or a Clout,
But why, or wherefore, is a doubt:
For Men will tremble, and turn paler
With too much, or too little Valour;
His Heart laid on, as if it try'd
To force a passage through his side,
Impatient (as he vow'd) to wait 'em,
But in a Fury, to fly at 'em: 1070
And therefore beat, and laid about,
To find a cranny, to creep out.
But she, who saw in what a taking
The Knight was, by his *Furious Quaking*,
Undaunted, cry'd, *Courage! Sir Knight,*
Know I'm resolv'd to break no Rite
Of Hospitality, t'a Stranger,
But to secure you out of danger,
Will here my self stand Sentinel,
To guard this Pass, 'gainst Sidrophel: 1080

1049 Flame] Flames *D2*   1066 *Valour*; *D2*: *Valour*, *D1*

Women, you know, do seldom fail,
To make the stoutest Men turn tail:
And bravely scorn to turn their Backs
Upon the desperat'st Attacks.

At this the Knight grew resolute,
As *Iron-side*, or *Hardy-knute*;
His fortitude began to rally,
And out he cry'd aloud, to sally:
But she besought him, to convey
His courage rather out oth' way,   1090
And lodge in Ambush on the Floor,
Or fortify'd behind a Door,
That if the enemy should enter
He might relieve her in th'Adventure.

Mean while, they knock'd against the door
As fierce as at the Gate, before,
Which made the Renegado Knight
Relapse again t'his former fright;
He thought it desperate to stay
Till th'Enemy had forc'd his way,   1100
But rather post himself, to serve
The Lady, for a *fresh Reserve*;
His Duty was not to dispute,
But what sh' had order'd, execute;
Which he resolv'd in hast t'obey,
And therefore stoutly march'd away:
And all h' encountred fell upon,
Though in the dark, and all alone.
Till fear, that braver Feats performs,
Then ever Courage dar'd in Arms: 1110
Had drawn him up, before a Pass,
To stand upon his Guard, and Face.
This he couragiously invaded,
And having enter'd *Barricado'd*:
Insconc'd himself as formidable,
As could be, underneath a Table:

1102 *Reserve*;] *Reserve*, D

Where he lay down in ambush close,
T'expect the arrival of his Foes;
Few minutes, had he lain pordue,
To guard his desp'rate Avenue,   1120
Before he heard a dreadful shout,
As loud as putting to the Rout,
With which impatiently Alarm'd,
He fancy'd, th'Enemy had storm'd,
And after entring *Sidrophel*
Was fall'n upon the Guards pell-mell,
He therefore sent out all his sences,
To bring him in, Intelligences,
Which vulgars out of ignorance,
Mistake, for falling in a Trance: 1130
But those, that Trade in *Geomancy*,
Affirm to be the strength of fancy:
In which the *Lapland-Magi* deal
And things incredible reveal.
Mean while, the Foe beat up his Quarters
And storm'd the out-works of his Fortress,
And as another of the same
Degree, and Party, in Arms, and Fame,
That in the same Cause, had ingag'd,
And War with equal conduct wag'd,   1140
By vent'ring only but to thrust
His Head, a Span beyond his Post:
B'a *Gen'ral* of the *Cavalliers*
Was drag'd, through a window by th'Ears:
So he was serv'd in his Redoubt,
And by the other end pull'd out.

Soon as they had him, at their mercy,
They put him to the Cudgel fiercely,
As if they scorn'd to Trade and Barter,
By giving or by taking Quarter: 1150
They stoutly on his Quarters Laid,
Until his Scouts came in t'his Aid:
For when a *Man is past his Sense*,
There's no way to Reduce him thence,

1143 *Cavalliers*] *Cavalliers; D1*

But twinging him by th'*Ears*, or *Nose*,
Or laying on of *heavy Blows*,
And if that will not do the Deed,
To burning with *Hot Irons* proceed.

No sooner was he come t'himself,
But on his Neck, a Sturdy Elf   1160
Clap'd in a Trice, his Cloven Hoof,
And thus attack'd him with Reproof.
Mortal; Thou art betraid to us,
B'our Friend, thy evil Genius,
Who for thy horrid Perjuries,
Thy Breach of Faith, and Turning Lyes,
(The Brethrens Priviledge, against
The Wicked) on themselves the Saints,
Has here thy wretched Carcass sent,
For just Revenge, and Punishment;   1170
Which thou hast now, no way to lessen
But by an open, free Confession,
For if we catch thee failing once,
'Twill fall the heavyer on thy Bones.
What made thee venture to betray,
And filch the Ladies Heart away?
To Spirit her to Matrimony —— ?
That which contracts all Matches, Money.
It was th'Inchantment of her Riches,
That made m' apply t' your *Croney Witches*,   1180
That in return, would pay th'expence,
The *Wear-and-tear* of Conscience.
Which I could have patch'd-up, and turn'd,
For th'Hundredth-part of what I earn'd.
Didst thou not love her then? Speak true.
No more (quoth he) then I love you.
How would'st th' have us'd her, and her Money?
First, turn'd her up, to Alimony,
And laid her Dowry out in Law,
To null her Joynture with a Flaw,   1190
Which I before-hand had agreed,
T'have put, of purpose, in the Deed.

1167 (*The*] The *D*   *against*] (*against D2*

And bar her Widows-making-over
T'a Friend in Trust, or private Lover.
What made thee pick and choose her out
T'imploy their Sorceries about?
That, which makes Gamesters play with those,
Who have least Wit, and most to lose.
But didst thou scourge thy Vessel thus
As thou hast damn'd thy self to us?   1200
I see, you take me for an Ass,
'Tis true! I thought the trick would pass
Upon a woman well enough,
As 't has been often found by Proof.
Whose Humours are not to be won
But when they are Impos'd upon:
For Love approves of all they do,
That stand for Candidates and woo.
Why didst thou forge those shameful Lyes,
Of Bears and Witches in Disguise?   1210
That is no more than Authors give
The Rabble credit to Believe:
A Trick of *Following their Leaders,*
To entertain their *Gentle Readers.*
And we have now no other way
Of Passing all we do, or say,
Which when 'tis Natural and True,
Will be believ'd b'a very Few.
Beside the danger of offence
The Fatal enemy of Sense.   1220
Why didst thou chuse that cursed Sin
Hypocrisie, to set up in?
Because it is the Thrivingst Calling
The only *Saints Bell* that Rings all in.
In which all Churches are concern'd,
And is the Easiest to be learn'd.
For no Degrees, unless th' Imploy't,
Can ever gain much or injoy't.
A *Gift,* that is not only able
To Domineer among the *Rabble*   1230

But by the Laws impowr'd, to Rout
And awe the greatest that stand out.
Which few hold forth against, for fear
Their Hands should slip and come too near,
For no sin else among the Saints,
Is taught so tenderly against.
What made thee break thy Plighted Vows?
That which makes others break a House.
And hang, and scorn ye all, before
Indure the Plague of being poor.   1240
Quoth he, I see you have more tricks
Then all our doting Politicks
That are grown old, and out of fashion;
Compar'd with your new Reformation:
That we must come to School to you,
To learn your more refin'd, and New.
Quoth he, if you will give me leave
To tell you, what I now perceive,
You'ld find your self an arrant Chouse
If y' were but at a *Meeting-House*.   1250
'Tis true, quoth he, we ne're come there,
Because, w' have let them out by th' year.
Truly, quoth he, you can't imagine
What wondrous things they will engage in,
That as your Fellow Fiends in Hell,
Were Angels all before they fell:
So you are like to be agen,
Compar'd with th'Angels of us Men.
Quoth he, I am resolv'd to be
Thy Scholar, in this Mystery,   1260
And therefore first desire to know,
Some Principles, on which you go;
What makes a Knave, a Child of God,
And one of us? —— A Livelyhood.
What renders beating-out of Brains,
And murther Godliness? —— Great gains.
What's tender Conscience? —— 'Tis a Botch,
That will not bear the gentlest touch,

1250 *House.*] *House*, D

But breaking out, dispatches more,
Then th'Epidemical'st Plague-Sore.   1270
What makes y' encroach upon our Trade,
And damn all others? —— To be paid.
What's Orthodox, and true Believing
Against a Conscience? —— A good living.
What makes Rebelling against Kings
A Good Old Cause? Administrings.
What makes all Doctrines Plain and Clear?
About two Hundred Pounds a Year.
And that which was prov'd true before,
Prove false again? Two Hundred more.   1280
What makes the Breaking of all Oaths
A Holy Duty? Food, and Cloaths.
What Laws, and Freedom, Persecution?
B'ing out of Pow'r and Contribution.
What makes a Church a Den of Thieves?
A Dean, a Chapter, and white Sleeves.
And what would serve if those were gone,
To make it Orthodox? Our own.
What makes Morality a Crime,
The most Notorious of the Time?   1290
Morality, which both the Saints,
And wicked too, Cry out against?
'Cause Grace and Virtue are within
Prohibited Degrees of Kin:
And therefore no true Saint allows,
They should be suffered to espouse.
For Saints can need no Conscience
That with Morality dispense;
As vertue's impious, when 'tis Rooted
In Nature onl' and not Imputed.   1300
But why the wicked should do so,
We neither know nor care to do.
What's Liberty of Conscience,
I'th' Natural and Genuine Sense?
'Tis to restore with more security,
Rebellion to its ancient Purity:

And Christian Liberty Reduce,
To th'Elder Practice of the *Jews*.
For a large Conscience is all one,
And signifies the same with none.   1310

It is enough (quoth he) for once,
And has repriev'd thy forfeit bones:
Nick Machiavel had ne're a trick,
(*Though he gave his Name to our Old Nick*)
But was below the least of these,
That pass i'th' World, for Holiness.

This said, the Furies, and the Light,
In th'instant vanish'd out of sight;
And left him in the dark alone,
With stinks of Brimstone, and his own.   1320

The *Queen of Night*, whose large command
Rules all the Sea, and half the Land;
And over moist, and crazy Brains,
In high Spring-tides, at Midnight, Reigns,
Was now declining to the West,
To go to Bed, and take her rest.
When *Hudibras*, whose stubborn blows
Deny'd his Bones, that soft repose;
Lay still expecting worse, and more,
Stretch'd out at length, upon the Floor: 1330
And though he shut his Eyes as fast,
As if h' had been to sleep his last:
Saw all the shapes, that Fear, or Wizards,
Do make the Devil wear for Vizards.
And pricking up his Ears, to heark,
If he could hear too, in the dark;
Was first invaded with a groan,
And after, in a feeble Tone,
These trembling words. *Unhappy Wretch,*
What hast thou gotten by this Fetch?   1340
Or all thy tricks in this New Trade,
The Holy Brother-hood o'th' Blade?

1324 Reigns,] Reigns. *D*   1334 Devil *D2*: Devil, *D1*

By Santring still on some Adventure,
And Growing to thy Horse a Centaure?
To stuff thy Skin with Swelling Knobs,
Of Cruel and hard wooded Drubs?
For still th' hast had the worst on't yet,
As well in Conquest as defeat.
Night is the Sabbath of Mankind
To rest the Body and the Mind.   1350
Which now thou art deny'd to keep,
And cure thy labour'd Corps with Sleep.
The Knight who heard the words, explain'd
As meant to him, this Reprimand
Because the Character did hit
Point Blank upon his Case so fit
Believ'd it was some Drolling Sprite
That staid upon the Guards that Night,
And one of those h' had seen and felt
The Drubs he had so freely dealt.   1360
When after a short pause and Grone,
The Doleful Spirit thus went on.
This 'tis t'ingage with Dogs and Bears,
Pelmel together by the Ears.
And after Painful Bangs and Knocks,
To lye in Limbo in the Stocks:
And from the Pinacle of Glory,
Fall Headlong into Purgatory.
(Thought he, This Devil's full of Malice,
That on my late Disasters Rallies)   1370
Condemn'd to Whipping but declin'd it,
By being more Heroick-minded,
And at a Riding handled worse,
With Treats more Slovenly and course.
Ingag'd with Fiends in Stubborn Wars,
And hot Disputes with Conjurers.
And when th' hadst bravely won the day,
Wast fain to steal thy self away.
I see, thought he, this Shameless Elf,
Would fain steal me too from my self   1380

1349 *Sabbath* D2: *Sabaoth* D1   1379 I] (I D   1380 self] self) D

That impudently dares to own
What I have suffer'd for and done.
And now but vent'ring to betray,
Hast met with Vengeance the same way.
Thought he, how does the Devil know
What 'twas that I design'd to do?
His *Office of Intelligence*
His *Oracles* are ceast long since:
And he knows nothing of the Saints,
But what some treacherous Spy acquaints: 1390
This is some Pettifogging Fiend,
Some under door-keepers Friends Friend.
That undertakes to understand,
And Juggles at the Second Hand:
And now would pass for *Spirit Po,*
And all Mens Dark Concerns foreknow.
I think I need not fear him for't,
These *Rallying Devils do no hurt.*
With that He rouz'd his drooping Heart
And hastily cry'd out, *What art?*   1400
A Wretch (Quoth he) whom want of Grace,
Has brought to this unhappy Place.
I do believe thee, Quoth the Knight,
Thus far, I'm sure, Th' art in the Right:
And know what 'tis that troubles thee,
Better than thou hast guest of me.
Thou art some Paultry *Black-Guard Sprite*
Condemn'd to Drudg'ry in the Night,
That hast no work to do in th'House,
Nor *Half-penny to drop in Shooes,*   1410
Without the Raising of which Sum,
You dare not be so Troublesome,
To Pinch the Slatterns black and blew,
For leaving you their Work to do.
This is your Business Good *Pug Robin,*
And your Diversion, dull *Dry Bobbing:*
T'intice *Fanaticks* in the Dirt,
And wash 'em clean in Ditches for't.

1405 thee, *D2*: thee. *D1*

Of which conceit you are so proud,
At ev'ry Jest you laugh aloud.   1420
As now you would have done by me,
But that I bar'd your Rallery.

Sir, (Quoth the Voice) Y' are no such Sophy,
As You would have the World judge of Ye,
If You design to weigh our Talents,
I'th' Standard of Your own false Ballance:
Or think it possible to know,
Us Ghosts, as well as we do you.
We, who have been the everlasting
Companions of Your Drubs and Basting: 1430
And never left you in Contest
With Male or Female, Man or Beast,
But prov'd as true t' ye, and intire
In all adventures as your Squire.
Quoth he, that may be said as true,
By th'Idlest *Pug* of all your Crew:
For none could have betraid us worse,
Than those Allyes of ours and yours.
But I have sent him for a Token
To your Low Countrey *Hogen Mogen*,   1440
To whose Infernal Shores I hope
He'l swing like Skippers in a Rope.
And if y' have been more just to me,
(As I am apt to think) than he;
I am afraid it is as true,
What th'Ill-affected say of you:
Y' have spous'd the *Covenant* and *Cause*
By holding up your *Cloven Paws*:
Sir, Quoth the voice, *'Tis true I grant,*
We made and took the Covenant.   1410
But that no more concerns the Cause
Than other Perj'ries do the Laws:
Which when th' are prov'd in open Court
Wear wooden Peccadilio's for't.
And that's the Reason Cov'nanters
Held up their Hands, like Rogues at Bars.

1449 Quoth the voice,] *D prints italics*

I see, Quoth Hudibras, from whence
These scandals of the Saints commence:
That are but Natural Effects
Of Satans Malice and his Sects.   1460
Those Spider Saints, that hang by Threads
Spun out of th'Entrails of their Heads.
Sir, Quoth the Voice, *that may as true*
And properly be said of you:
Whose Talents may compare with either,
Or both the other put together.
For all the Independents do,
Is only what you forc'd them to.
You who are not content alone,
With Tricks to put the Devil down: 1470
But must have Armies rais'd to back
The Gospel work you undertake.
As if Artillery, and Edge Tools,
Were th'only Engines to save Souls.
While He, poor Devil, has no Pow'r
By Force to Run down and Devour.
Has nere a Classis, cannot sentence
To Stools, or Poundage of Repentance.
Is ty'd up only to design,
T'Intice, and Tempt, and Undermine;   1480
In which you all his Arts out-do,
And prove your selves his Betters too.
Hence 'tis Possessions do less evil
Than mere Temptations of the Devil:
Which all the Horridst Actions done,
Are charg'd in Courts of Law upon;
Because unless you help the Elf,
He can do little of himself:
And therefore where he's best Possest,
Acts most against his Interest.   1490
Surprises none, but those wh' have Priests,
To turn him out, and Exorcists,
Supply'd with Spiritual Provision,
And Magaz'nes of Ammunition:

1463 Quoth the Voice] *D prints italics*

With Crosses, Relicks, Crucifixes,
Beads, Pictures, Rosaries and Pixes:
The Tools of working out Salvation,
By meer Mechanick Operation.
With Holy Water, like a Sluce,
To overflow all Avenues. 1500
But those, wh' are utterly unarm'd,
T'oppose his Entrance if he storm'd,
He never offers to surprise,
Although his falsest Enemies.
But is content to be their Drudge,
And on their Errands glad to Trudge.
For where are all your Forfeitures,
Intrusted in safe hands but ours?
Who are but Jaylors of the Holes,
And Dungeons, where you clap up Souls. 1510
Like Under-keepers, turn the Keys,
T' your Mittimus Anathemas:
And never Boggle to Restore
The Members you deliver o're
Upon Demand, with fairer Justice,
Than all your Covenanting Trustees:
Unless to punish them the worse,
You put them in the secular Pow'rs,
And pass their Souls, as some demise,
The same Estate in Mortgage twice, 1520
When to a Legal Utlegation
You turn your Excommunication,
And for a Groat unpaid, that's due,
Distrain on Soul and Body too.

Thought He, 'Tis no mean part of Civil,
State Prudence, to Cajol the Devil,
And not to handle him too Rough,
When h' has us in his Cloven Hoof.
'Tis true, Quoth He, that intercourse
Has past between your Friends and ours, 1530
That as you trust us in our way,
To raise your Members and to lay:

1502 *storm'd,*] *storm'd.* D   1520 *twice,*] *twice.* D   1528 Hoof.] Hoof, D

We send you others of our own,
Denounc'd to hang themselves, or Drown.
Or frighted with our Oratory,
To leap down headlong many a story.
Have us'd all means to propagate
Your mighty interests of State,
Laid out our Spiritual Gifts, to further
Your great designs of Rage and Murther.   1540
For if the Saints are Nam'd from Blood,
We onl' have made that Title good,
And if it were but in our Power,
We should not scruple to do more.
And not be half a Soul behind,
Of all Dissenters of Mankind.
Right, Quoth the Voice, *And as I scorn*
To be ungrateful in return,
Of all those kind good Offices,
I'll free you out of this Distress: 1550
And set you down in safety, where
It is no time to tell you here.
The Cock crows and the Morn draws on,
When 'tis Decreed I must be gone,
And if I leave you here till Day,
You'l find it hard to get away.
With that the Spirit grop'd about
To find th'Inchanted Hero out.
And try'd with hast to lift him up,
But found his *Forlorn Hope*, his *Croop*,   1560
Unserviceable with Kicks and Blows,
Receiv'd from hardned-hearted Foes:
He thought to drag him by the Heels,
Like Gresham Carts, with Legs for Wheels.
But fear that soonest cures those Sores,
In danger of Relapse to worse;
Came in t'assist him with its Aid,
And up his sinking Vessel weigh'd.
No sooner was he fit to trudge,
But both made ready to dislodge: 1570

The Spirit hors'd him like a Sack,
Upon the *Vehicle*, his Back.
And bore him headlong into th'Hall,
With some few Rubs against the Wall:
Where finding out the Postern lock'd
And th'*Avenues* as strongly block'd,
H' attacked the Window, storm'd the Glass,
And in a Moment gain'd the Pass.
Through which he drag'd the worsted Soldier's
Fore quarters out by th'Head and Shoulders: 1580
And cautiously began to Scout,
To find their Fellow-Cattle out.
Nor was it half a Minutes Quest,
Ere he retriev'd the Champions Beast,
Ty'd to a Pale instead of Rack,
But ne're a Saddle on his Back;
Nor Pistols at the Saddle-bow,
Convey'd away the Lord knows how.
He thought it was no time to stay,
And let the Night too steal away,   1590
But in a trice advanc'd the Knight,
Upon the *Bare Ridge*, Bolt upright,
And groping out for Ralpho's Jade,
He found the Saddle too was straid:
And in the place a Lump of Sope,
On which he speedily leap'd up:
And turning to the Gate the Rein,
He Kick'd and Cudgel'd on amain.
While Hudibras with equal hast,
On both sides, laid about as fast,   1600
And spur'd as Jockies use, to break,
Or Padders to secure a Neck.
Where let us leave them for a time,
And to their *Churches* turn our *Rhyme*:
To hold forth their Declining State,
Which now come near an Even Rate.

1579 Soldier's] Soldier's, *D*

THE THIRD AND LAST PART

CANTO II

THE ARGUMENT

The Saints engage in Fierce Contests,
About their Carnal Interests:
To share their Sacrilegious Preys,
According to their Rates of Grace,
Their various Frenzies to Reform,
When Cromwel *left them in a Storm;*
Till in th' Effigie of Rumps, the Rabble,
Burns all their Grandees of the Cabal.

THE Learned Write, *An Insect Breeze,*
Is but a Mungrel Prince of *Bees,*
That Falls, before a Storm, on Cows,
And stings the Founders of his House;
From whose Corrupted Flesh, that Breed
Of Vermine, did at first proceed:
So ere the Storm of war broke out
Religion spawn'd a various Rout,
Of Petulant Capricious Sects,
The Maggots of Corrupted Texts,   10
That first Run all Religion down,
And after every swarm its own.
For as the *Persian Magi* once,
Upon their *Mothers,* got their *Sons,*
That were incapable t'injoy,
That Empire any other way;
So *Presbyter* begot the other,
Upon the *Good Old Cause* his Mother.
That bore them like the Devils Dam,
Whose *Son* and *Husband* are the same.   20

And yet no Nat'ral Tye of Blood,
Nor Int'rest for their common good,
Could when their Profits interfer'd
Get Quarter for each others Beard.
For when they thriv'd they never fag'd
But only by the ears engag'd:
Like Dogs that snarl about a Bone,
And play together when th' have none.
As by their truest Characters
Their Constant Actions plainly appears.　　30

Rebellion now began for lack
Of *Zeal* and *Plunder* to grow slack,
The *Cause* and *Covenant* to lessen,
And Providence to b'out of Season:
For now there was no more to purchase
O'th' Kings Revenue and the Churches,
But all divided, shar'd, and gone,
That us'd to urge the Brethren on.
Which forc'd the Stubbornst for the Cause,
To cross the Cudgels to the Laws:　　40
That what by breaking them, th' had gain'd
By their Support, might be maintain'd
Like Thieves, that in a *Hemp-plot* lye,
Secur'd against the *Huon-cry*.
For *Presbyter* and *Independent*,
Were now turn'd *Plaintiff* and *Defendant*:
Laid out their Apostolick Functions,
On Carnal Orders and *Injunctions*,
And all their Precious Gifts and Graces,
On outlawries, and *Scire facias*.　　50
At *Michaels Term* had many a Tryal,
Worse than the *Dragon* and St. *Michael*:
Where thousands fell in shape of Fees,
Into the *Bottomless Abyss*.
For when, like Bretheren and Friends,
They came to share the Dividends,
And ev'ry Partner to Possess,
His Church and State Joynt-Purchaces,

22 their *D1* (*errata*), *D2*: the *D1*　　55 Bretheren] Brethren *D*

In which the Ablest Saint and Best,
Was Nam'd in Trust by all the Rest,   60
To pay their Money, and instead
Of ev'ry Brother pass the Deed:
He streight converted all his Gifts,
To pious Frauds and holy Shifts,
And setled all the others Shares,
Upon his *outward Man* and's *Heirs*.
Held all they claim'd as Forfeit Lands,
Deliver'd up into his hands,
And past upon his Conscience,
By *Pre-intail of Providence*.   70
Impeach'd the Rest for Reprobates,
That had no Titles to Estates;
But by their Spiritual Attaints,
Degraded from the Right of Saints.
This being reveal'd; They now begun
With Law and Conscience to fall on,
And laid about as hot and Brain-sick,
As th'*Utter Barrister of Swanswick*.
Ingag'd with Money-bags, as bold
As men with Sand-bags did of Old: 80
That brought the Lawyers in more fees,
Than all th'unsanctify'd Trustees:
Till he who had no more to show
I'th' Case, receiv'd the overthrow:
Or both sides having had the worst,
They Parted as they met at first.

Poor *Presbyter* was now Reduc'd
Secluded, and Cashier'd, and Chews'd,
Turn'd out, and Excommunicate,
From all Affairs of Church and State.   90
Reform'd t'a Reformado Saint,
And glad to turn Itinerant.
To strowl and teach from Town to Town,
And those he had taught up, Teach down,
And make those uses serve agen,
Against the New-inlightned Men.

82 all th'] al' *D*

As fit, as when at first, they were
Reveal'd against the *Cavalier*:
Damn *Anabaptist*, and *Fanatick*,
As Pat as *Popish*, and *Prelatick*,   100
And with as little variation,
To serve for any Sect i'th' Nation.

The good old Cause, which some believe
To be the Dev'l that tempted *Eve*,
With Knowledge, and does still invite
The World to Mischief with new light,
Had store of Money in her Purse,
When he took her for bett'r or worse.
But now was grown Deform'd and Poor,
And fit to be turn'd out of Door.   110

The *Independents* whose first station,
Was in the *Rere of Reformation*,
A Mungrel kind of *Church-Dragoons*,
That serv'd for Horse and Foot at once:
And in the Saddle of one Steed,
The *Sarazen and Christian rid.*
Were Free of ev'ry Spiritual Order,
To *Preach*, and *Fight*, and *Pray*, and *Murther*.
No sooner got the Start to lurch,
Both Disciplines of *War* and *Church*,   120
And Providence enough to Run
The Chief Commanders of 'em down:
But carried on the War against
The Common Enemy oth' Saints:
And in a while, Prevail'd so far,
To win of them the Game of War;
And be at Liberty once more,
T'Attack themselves as th' had before.

For now there was no Foe in Arms,
T'unite their Factions with Alarms,   130
But all Reduc'd and overcome
Except their worst, themselves at home:
Wh' had compast all they Praid and swore;
And Fought, and Preach'd, and Plunder'd for.

Subdu'd the Nation, Church and State,
And all things, but their Laws and Hate.
But when they came to treat and transact,
And share the spoils of all th' had ransackt,
To Botch up what th' had torn and rent,
Religion, and the *Government*,   140
They met no sooner, but Prepar'd
To pull down all the War had spar'd:
Agreed in Nothing, but t'Abolish,
Subvert, Extirpate, and *Demolish*.
For Knaves and Fools being near of Kin,
As *Dutch-Boors* are t'a *Sooter-Kin*,
Both Parties joyn'd to do their best,
To Damn the Publick Interest.
And Hearded only in consults,
To put by one anothers Bolts.   150
T'outcant the Babylonian Labourers,
At all their Dialects of Jabberers.
And tug at both ends of the Saw,
To tear down Government and Law.
For as two Cheats that play one Game,
Are both defeated of their Aim:
So those who play a *Game of State*,
And only *Cavil* in Debate,
Although there's nothing lost nor won,
The Publick Business is undone,   160
Which still the longer 'tis in doing,
Becomes the surer way to Ruine.
This when the *Royallists* perceiv'd,
Who to their Faith as firmly cleav'd:
And own'd the Right, they had paid down
So Dearly for, *The Church and Crown*,
Th' united Constanter, and Sided,
The more, the more their Foes divided.
For though out-number'd, overthrown,
And by the Fate of War, Run down: 170
Their Duty never was defeated,
Nor from their Oaths and Faith Retreated:

138 ransackt,] ransackt. *D*   158 Debate,] Debate. *D*   166 *Crown,*]
Crown. D

For Loyalty is still the same,
Whether it win or lose the Game:
True as a Dyal to the Sun,
Although it be not shin'd upon.
But when these Bretheren in evil,
Their *Adversaries*, and the *Devil*,
Began once more, to shew them Play,
And Hopes, at least to have a day,   180
They Rallied in Parades of Woods,
And unfrequented Solitudes:
Conven'd at midnight in out-Houses,
T'Appoint New-*Rising Rendevouzes*,
And with a Pertinacy unmatch'd,
For new Recruits of Danger watch'd.
No sooner was one Blow diverted,
But up another Party started
And as if Nature too in hast,
To furnish out Supplies as fast,   190
Before her time had turn'd Destruction,
T'a New and Numerous Production:
No sooner those were overcome,
But up rose others in their Room,
That like the Christian Faith, increast
The more, the more they were Supprest.
Whom neither *Chains* nor *Transportation*,
Proscription, *Sale*, nor *Confiscation*,
Nor all the desperate events,
Of Former try'd Experiments,   200
Nor wounds could terrifie, nor Mangling,
To leave off *Loyalty* and *Dangling*:
Nor Death with all his Bones affright
From vent'ring to maintain the Right,
From staking Life and Fortune down,
'Gainst all together for the Crown:
But kept the Title of their Cause,
From *Forfeiture*, like Claims in Laws,
And prov'd no Prosp'rous Usurpation
Can ever settle on the Nation: 210

177 Bretheren] Brethren *D*   191 Destruction *D1* (*errata*), *D2*: Destructions *D1*
205 down, *D2*: down. *D1*

Until in spight of Force and Treason
They put their Loy'lty in Possession,
And by their Constancy and Faith,
Destroyed the Mighty Men of *Gath*.

Toss'd in a Furious *Hurricane*,
Did *Oliver* give up his *Reign*:
And was believ'd as well by Saints,
As Moral Men and Miscreants,
To Founder in the Stygian Ferry.
Until he was retriev'd by *Sterry*: 220
Who in a false Erroneous Dream,
Mistook the *New Jerusalem*:
Prophanely, for th'*Apochryphal*,
False Heaven, at the *End o'th' Hall*:
Whither, it was decreed by Fate,
His Pretious Relicks to Translate,
So *Romulus* was seen before,
B'as Orthodox a *Senator*;
From whose Divine Illumination,
He stole the Pagan Revelation. 230

Next him, his Son and *Heir Apparent*,
Succeeded, though a *Lame Vicegerent*:
Who first laid by the *Parliament*,
The only Crutch on which *he leant*,
And then Sunk underneath the *State*,
That Rode him above *Horsemans Weight*.

And now the Saints began their *Reign*,
For which th' had yearn'd so long in vain,
And felt such Bowel-Hankerings,
To see an *Empire all of Kings*: 240
Deliver'd from th'*Ægyptian Awe*,
Of Justice, Government, and Law.
And free t'erect what *Spiritual Cantons*,
Should be reveal'd, Or *Gospel Hans-Towns*,
To Edify upon the Ruines
Of *John* of *Leidens old out-goings*,

233 first] first, D   236 *Weight*. D2: *Weight*, D1

Who for a Weather-Cock hung up,
Upon their *Mother Churches* Top,
Was made a Type by Providence,
Of all their Revelations since: 250
And now fulfill'd by his Successors,
Who equally mistook their measures;
For when they came to shape the *Model*,
Not one could fit anothers Noddle.
But found their Light and Gifts more wide
From Fadging, than th'unsanctified.
While ev'ry Individual Brother
Strove hand to fist against another.
And still the Maddest and most Crackt,
Were found the busiest to Transact.   260
For though most Hands dispatch'd apace,
And *make light work* (the Proverb says)
Yet many different Intellects,
Are found t'have contrary Effects:
And many Heads t'obstruct Intrigues,
As slowest Insects have most Leggs.

Some were for setting up a King,
But all the rest for no such thing,
Unless King *Jesus*; others tamper'd
For *Fleetwood, Desborough,* and *Lambard,*   270
Some for the *Rump*, and some more crafty,
For *Agitators*, and *the Safety*:
Some for the Gospel, and Massacres,
Of *Spiritual Affidavit makers*
That swore to any Humane Regence
Oaths of Supremacy and *Allegiance.*
Yea though the Ablest swearing Saint,
That vouch'd the Bulls oth' Covenant.
Others for Pulling down th'High Places
Of *Synods*, and *Provincial Classes,*   280
That us'd to make such Hostile Inroads,
Upon the Saints, like Bloody *Nimrods,*
Some for Fulfilling Prophecies,
And th'Extirpation of th'Excise;

And some against th'*Ægyptian Bondage*,
Of *Holy-days*, and *Paying Poundage*,
Some for the Cutting down of *Groves*,
And Rectifying Bakers Loaves:
And some for finding out Expedients,
Against the Slav'ry of Obedience: 290
Some were for *Gospel-Ministers*,
And some for *Red-Coat Seculars*:
As Men most fit t'hold forth the Word,
And wield the one, *and th'other Sword*,
Some were for carrying on the Work,
Against the *Pope*, and some the *Turk*.
Some for engaging to suppress,
The *Camisado of Surplices*,
That Gifts and Dispensations hinder'd,
And turn'd to th'*Outward Man the Inward*;   300
More proper for the Cloudy Night,
Of *Popery*, than *Gospel Light*.
Others were for Abolishing
That Tool of Matrimony, *a Ring*,
With which th'unsanctify'd *Bridegroom*,
Is marry'd only to a *Thumb*;
(As wise as Ringing of a Pig,
That is to break up ground and Dig)
The *Bride* to nothing but her Will,
That Nuls the After marriage still.   310
Some were for th'utter Extirpation
Of *Linsy-Woolsy* in the Nation.
And some against all Idolizing
The *Cross* in *Shop-Books*, or *Baptizing*;
Others to make all things Recant
The *Christian, or Sirname* of Saint.
And force all *Churches, Streets*, and *Towns*,
The *Holy Title* to Renounce;
Some 'gainst a *Third Estate of Souls*,
And bringing down the Price of Coals: 320
Some for Abolishing Black-Pudding,
And eating nothing with the Blood in:
To Abrogate them, Roots and Branches,
While others were for *Eating Haunches*,

Of *Warriors*, and *now* and *then*,
The *Flesh of Kings*, and *Mighty Men* :
And some for Breaking of their Bones,
With Rods of Ir'n, by *Secret ones.*
For Thrashing Mountains, and with Spels,
For Hallowing Carriers Packs, and Bells.   330
Things that the *Legend* never heard of,
But made the wicked sore afeard of.
The Quacks of Government, who sate
At th'unregarded *Helm of State*;
And understood, this wild Confusion
Of Fatal Madness, and Delusion,
Must sooner than a Prodigie,
Portend Destruction to be nigh;
Consider'd timely, how t' withdraw,
And save their Wind-pipes from the Law :   340
For one Rencounter at the Bar,
Was worse than all, th' had scap'd in War :
And therefore met in Consultation,
To *Cant* and *Quack* upon the Nation :
Not for the sickly Patients sake,
Nor what to give, but what to take.
To feel the Pulses of their Fees,
More wise than fumbling Arteries :
Prolong the snuff of Life in pain,
And from the Grave Recover —— *Gain.*   350

'Mong these there was a *Politician*,
With more heads than a *Beast in Vision*,
And more Intrigues in ev'ry one,
Than all the *Whores of Babylon* :
So politick, as if one eye
Upon the other were a Spy;
That to trapan the one to think
The other Blind, both strove to blink :
And in his dark Pragmatick Way,
As Busie as a Child at Play.   360
H' had seen three Governments Run down,
And had a Hand in ev'ry one,

---

332 afeard *D1 (errata)*, *D2*: afraid *D1*   351 *Editor's paragraph*

Was for 'em, and against 'em all,
But Barb'rous when they came to fall:
For by *Trapanning* th'old to Ruine,
He made his Int'rest with the New one.
· Plaid true and faithful, though against
His Conscience, and was still advanc'd:
For by the Witch-craft of Rebellion,
Transform'd t'a feeble *State Camelion*,   370
By giving aim from side, to side,
He never fail'd to save his Tide,
But got the start of ev'ry State,
And at a Change, ne're came too late.
Could turn his Word, and Oath, and Faith,
As many ways, as in a Lath,
By turning, wriggle, like a Screw
Int' highest Trust, and out, for New;
For when h' had happily incur'd
Instead of Hemp, to be prefer'd,   380
And past upon a Government,
He play'd his trick and out he went,
But being out, and out of hopes,
To mount his Ladder (more) of Ropes,
Would strive to raise himself, upon
The publick ruine, and his own;
So little did he understand
The Desp'rate Feats he took in hand,
For when h' had got himself a Name
For Fraud, and Tricks, He spoyld his Game;   390
Had forc'd his Neck into a Noose,
To shew his Play, at fast and loose,
And when he chanc'd t'escape, mistook
For Art, and Subtlety, His Luck,
So right his Judgment was cut fit,
And made a Tally to his wit,
And both together most Profound
At Deeds of Darkness under ground:
As th'Earth is easiest undermin'd
By vermine Impotent and Blind.   400

381 Government,] Government *D*   390 Tricks, He spoyld his Game;]
Tricks; He spoyld his Game *D*

By all these Arts, and many more
H' had practic'd long and much before,
Our *State-Artificer* foresaw,
Which way the World began to draw:
For as *Old Sinners* have all Poynts
O'th' Compass in their Bones and Joynts,
Can by their Pangs and Aches find
All Turns and Changes of the wind:
And better than by *Napiers Bones*,
Feel in their own the Age of Moons: 410
So guilty Sinners in a State,
Can by their Crimes Prognosticate
And in their Consciences feel Pain,
Some days before a Show'r of Rain.
He therefore wisely cast about,
All ways he could, t'*insure his Throat*;
And hither came t'observe and smoke
What Courses other Riscers took:
And to the utmost do his Best
To Save himself and Hang the Rest.   420

To match this Saint, there was another,
As busie, and perverse a Brother,
An Haberdasher of small Wares,
In Politicks, and State-affairs:
More Jew then *Rabbi Achitophel*,
And better gifted to Rebel:
For when h' had taught his Tribe, to Spouse
The Cause, aloft, upon one House,
He scorn'd to set his own in Order
But try'd another, and went further,   430
So Sullenly addicted still
To's only principle, *His Will*:
That whatsoe're it chanc'd to prove,
No force of Argument could move:
Nor *Law*, nor *Cavalcade of Ho'burn*,
Could render half a grain less stubborn;
For he, at any time would hang,
For th'opportunity t'*harangue*

431 So Sullenly *D1* (*errata*), *D2*: Suddenly *D1*

And rather on a Gibbet dangle,
Then miss his dear delight, to wrangle,   440
In which his Parts were so accomplisht
That right, or wrong, he ne're was non-plust.
But still his Tongue ran on, the less
Of weight it bore, with greater ease:
And with it's Everlasting Clack,
Set all Mens Ears upon the Rack.
No sooner could a hint appear,
But up he started to Pickere,
And made the stoutest yield to mercy,
When he engag'd in *Controversie*:   450
Not by the force of carnal reason,
But indefatigable teazing;
With Volleys of Eternal Babble,
And clamour, more unanswerable.
For though his *Topiques* Frail and Weak,
Could nere amount above a Freak:
He still maintain'd 'em like his Faults,
Against the Desperat'st Assaults;
And back'd their Feeble want of Sense,
With greater Heat and Confidence: 460
As Bones of *Hectors* when they differ,
The more th' are *Cudgel'd*, grow the *Stiffer*.
Yet when his Profit moderated,
The fury of his Heat abated:
For nothing but his Interest,
Could lay his Devil of Contest.

It was his *Choice*, or *Chance*, or *Curse*,
T'espouse the Cause, for *Bett'r or Worse*:
And with his worldly Goods and wit,
And *Soul* and *Body* worship'd it: 470
But when he found the sullen *Trapes*
Possest with th' *Devil, Worms and Claps*;
The *Trojan Mare* in Fole with *Greeks*,
Not half so full of *Jadish Tricks*;
Though Squemish in her outward woman,
As loose and Rampant as *Dol common*:

He still resolv'd to mend the matter,
T'Adhere, and Cleave the Obstinater:
And still the skittisher and looser,
Her Freaks appear'd, to sit the Closer: 480
For *Fools are Stubborn in their way*:
As *Coyns are hardned by th' Allay*:
And obstinacy's ne're so stiff,
As when 'tis in a wrong Belief.

These two, with others, being met
And close in Consultation set:
After a discontented pause
And not without sufficient cause,
The Oratour we mention'd late,
Less troubled with the pangs of State: 490
Then with his own impatience,
To give himself first Audience.
After he had a while look'd wise,
At last broke silence, and the *Ice*.

Quoth he, there's nothing makes me doubt,
Our last *Out-goings* brought about,
More then to see, the Characters,
Of real *Jealousies* and *Fears*,
Not feign'd, as once, but sadly horrid,
Scor'd upon ev'ry Members Forehead: 500
Who, cause the Clouds are drawn together,
And threaten sudden change of Weather,
Feel Pangs, and Aches, of *State-turns*,
And *Revolutions* in their *Corns*.
And since our *workings-out* are crost,
Throw up the Cause, before 'tis lost.
Was it to run away, we meant,
Who taking of the *Covenant*,
The lamest Cripples of the Brothers,
Took Oaths, to run before all others;   510
But in their own sense only swore
To strive to run away before?
And now would prove, the *Words*, and *Oath*,
Ingage us to renounce them both?

'Tis true! the cause is in the lurch,
Between a right, and Mungrel-Church:
The *Presbyter*, and *Independent*,
That stickle, which shall make an end on't.
As 'twas made out to us, *the last*
Expedient —— I mean *Margrets Fast*:   520
When Providence had been suborn'd,
What answer was to be return'd:
Else why should Tumults fright us now,
We have so many times gone through?
And understand as well to *Tame*,
As when they serve our turns t'*inflame*.
Have prov'd how inconsiderable
Are all Engagements of the Rabble,
Whose Frenzies must be Reconcil'd,
With *Drums* and *Rattles* like a Child.   530
But never prov'd so prosperous,
As when they were led on by us:
For all our *Scouring of Religion*,
Began with Tumults and Sedition:
When *Hurricanes* of Fierce Commotion,
Became strong Motives to *Devotion*:
(As Carnal Sea-men in a Storm,
Turn Pious Converts, and Reform.)
When Rusty weapons with chalk'd Edges,
Maintain'd our Feeble Priviledges: 540
And brown Bills, Levied in the City,
Made Bills to pass the Grand Committee:
When Zeal with Aged Clubs and Gleaves,
Gave chase to *Rochets* and *White Sleeves*,
And made the Church, and State, and Laws,
Submit t'old Iron and the Cause.
And as we thriv'd by Tumults then,
So might we better now agen,
If we know how as then we did,
To use them rightly in our need.   550
Tumults, by which the Mutinous,
Betray themselves instead of us;
The Hollow Hearted *Disaffected*,
And *Close Malignant* are detected:

Who lay their Lives and Fortunes down,
For Pledges to secure our own,
And freely sacrifice their Ears,
T'appease our Jealousies, and Fears.
And yet for all these Providences,   560
W' are offer'd, if we had our senses,
We idly sit, like stupid Blockheads,
Our hands committed to our Pockets.
And nothing, but our Tongues, at large,
To get the Wretches a discharge.
Like Men condemn'd to *Thunderbolts*
Who, e're the Blow, become meer Dolts;
Or Fools besotted with their Crimes,
That know not how to shift betimes.
And neither have the hearts to stay,
Nor wit enough to run away.   570
Who, if we could resolve on either
Might stand, or fall (at least) together.
No mean, nor trivial solaces,
To Partners, in extreme distress:
Who use to lessen their Despairs,
By parting them int' equal shares:
As if the more there were to bear,
They felt the weight the easier:
And ev'ry one the gentler hung,
The more, he took his turn among.   580

But 'tis not come to that, as yet,
If we had Courage left, or wit.
Who, when our *Fate* can be no worse,
Are fitted for the bravest course;
Have time to Rally, and Prepare
Our last, and best defence, *Despair*,
Despair, by which the gallant'st Feats,
Have been atchiev'd in greatest straits:
And horridst dangers safely wav'd,
By b'ing Couragiously out-brav'd.   590
As wounds, by wider wounds are heal'd,
And Poysons, by themselves, expel'd.

566 become *D1 (errata)*, *D2*: became *D1*

And so they might be now agen,
If we were, what we should be, *Men*;
And not so dully desperate,
To side, against our selves, with Fate.
As Criminals condemn'd to suffer,
Are blinded first, and then, turn'd over.

This comes of *Breaking Covenants*,
And setting up *Exauns of Saints*,   600
That Fine, like Aldermen, for *Grace*,
To be excus'd the *Efficace*;
For Spiritual Men are too *Transcendent*,
That mount their Banks, for *Independent*.
To hang like *Mahomet*, in *th' Air*,
Or St. *Ignatius*, at his Prayer,
By Pure *Geometry*, and hate
Dependence, upon *Church, or State*,
Disdain the *Pedantry o'th' Letter*,
And since obedience is better,   610
(The *Scripture* says) then *Sacrifice*,
Presume the less on't, will suffice.
And scorn, to have the moderat'st stints,
Prescrib'd their peremptory *Hints*:
Or any opinion, true or false,
Declar'd as such, in *Doctrinals*:
But left at large to make their best on,
Without being call'd to account, or question.

Interpret all the Spleen reveals,
As *Whittington* explain'd the Bells;   620
And bid themselves, turn back agen
Lord May'rs of New-Jerusalem,
But look so big, and *Over-grown*,
They scorn their Edifiers t'own.
Who taught them all their *sprinkling Lessons*,
Their Tones, and sanctify'd expressions,
Bestow'd their Gifts upon a Saint,
Like Charity, on those, that want.
And learn'd th'*Apocryphal Bigots*,
T'inspire themselves with *Short-hand Notes*,   630

For which they scorn, and hate them worse,
Than Dogs and Cats do Sowgelders.
For who first bred them up to *Pray*,
And teach the House of Commons way?
Where had they all their *gifted Phrases*,
But from our *Calamy*'s and *Cases?*
Without whose *Sprinkling* and *Sowing*,
Who e're had heard of *Ny* or *Owen?*
Their dispensations had been stifled,
But for our *Adoniram Bifield*,   640
And had we not begun the War,
Th' had ne're been Sainted as they are.
For Saints in Peace degenerate,
And dwindle down to Reprobate:
Their Zeal corrupts like standing Water,
In th'Intervals of war and slaughter:
Abates the sharpness of its Edge,
Without the *Pow'r of Sacriledge*:
And though th' have Tricks to cast their Sins,
As easie as Serpents do their Skins,   650
That in a while grow out agen,
In Peace they turn mere Carnal Men,
And from the most Refin'd of Saints,
As Naturally grow Miscreants,
As *Barnacles* turn *Soland-Geese*,
In th'Islands of *the Orcades*.
Their Dispensation's but a Ticket,
For their conforming to the Wicked.
With whom, their greatest difference,
Lies more in words, and shew, then sense: 660
For as the *Pope*, that *keeps the Gate*
Of *Heaven*, wears three Crowns in state;
So he that keeps the *Gate of Hell*,
Proud *Cerberus*, wears three Heads, as well.
And, if the World has any troth,
Some have been Canoniz'd in both.
But that which does them greatest harm,
Their *Spiritual Gizzards* are too warm,

Which puts the over-heated Sots
In Feavers still, like other Goats,   670
For though the Whore bends Hereticks,
With Flames of Fire, like crooked sticks,
Our Schismaticks so vastly differ,
Th'hotter th' are, they grow the stiffer:
Still setting off their spiritual goods,
With fierce and pertinatious feuds,
For Zeal's a dreadful *Termagant*,
That teaches Saints to *Tear, and Rant.*
And *Independents*, to profess
The Doctrine, of *Dependences*:   680
Turns meek, and sneaking *Secret ones*,
To *Raw-heads fierce*, and *Bloody Bones*:
And not content with endless quarrels
Against the Wicked, and their Morals;
The *Gibellins*, for want of *Guelfs*,
Divert their rage upon themselves:
For now the War is not between
The Brethren, and the Men of sin:
But *Saint, and Saint*, to spill the Blood,
Of one anothers Brotherhood;   690
Where neither side can lay pretence
To *Liberty of Conscience*,
Or zealous *suffring for the Cause*,
To gain one Groats-worth of Applause.
For though endur'd with *Resolution*,
'Twill ne're amount to *Persecution*.
Shall Precious Saints and *Secret ones*,
Break one anothers outward Bones?
And eat the Flesh of Brethren,
Instead of Kings and Mighty men?   700
When Fiends agree among themselves,
Shall they be found the greater Elves?
When *Bell*'s at union with the *Dragon*,
And *Baal-Peor* Friends with *Dagon*,
When Savage Bears agree with Bears,
Shall *Secret ones* lug *Saints by th' Ears*?

675 setting off *D2*: setting-of, *D1*   696 *Persecution.*] *Persecution*, D
699 Bretheren] Brethren *D*

And not Atone their Fatal wrath,
When common Danger threatens both?
Shall Mastives by the Collars pull'd,
Ingag'd with Bulls, let go their hold?   710
And Saints whose Necks are pawn'd at stake,
No notice of the Danger take?
But though no Pow'r of *Heaven or Hell*,
Can Pacifie *Phanatick Zeal*:
Who would not guess there might be hopes,
The Fear of *Gallowses and Ropes*,
Before *their Eyes* might Reconcile
Their Animosities a while?
At least until th' had a *Clear Stage*,
And equal Freedom to Ingage: 720
Without the Danger of Surprise,
By both our common Enemies?

This none but we alone could doubt,
Who understand their *Workings-out*,
And know 'em both in *Soul* and *Conscience*,
Giv'n up t'as *Reprobate a Non-sence*,
As Spiritual Out-laws whom the Pow'r
Of Miracle can ne're Restore.
We whom, at first, they set up under,
In Revelation only of *Plunder*,   730
Who since have had so many Tryals
Of their encroaching *Self-denyals*,
That rook'd upon us with design
To *Out-Reform, and Undermine*:
Took all our Interests and Commands
Perfidiously, out of our hands,
Involv'd us in the *Guilt of Blood*,
Without the *Motive-gains* allow'd,
And made us serve as *Ministerial*,
Like younger Sons of *Father Belial*.   740

And yet for all th'inhumane wrong,
Th' had done us, and the Cause, so long,
We never fail'd, to carry on
The work still, as we had begun;

But true and faithfully obey'd,
And neither *Preach'd them hurt, nor Pray'd*:
Nor troubled them to crop our Ears,
Nor hang us like the *Cavaliers*:
Nor put them to the charge of *Gaols*,
To find us *Pillories*, and *Carts-tails*,   750
Or *Hangmans Wages*, which the *State*
Was forc'd (before them) to be at,
That cut like *Tallies*, to the *Stumps*
Our Ears for keeping true accounts:
And burnt our Vessels, like a *New-*
Seal'd Peck, or Bushel, for *b'ing true*.
But hand in hand, like faithful Brothers,
Held forth the Cause, against all others,
Disdaining equally to yield
One Syllable, of what we held: 760
And though we differ'd now and then,
'Bout outward things, and outward Men:
Our inward Men and *Constant Frame*
Of Spirit, still were near the same.
And till they first began to *Cant*,
And *Sprinkle down the Covenant*;
We ne're had *Call* in any Place,
Nor Dream'd of Teaching down *Free-grace*.
But joyn'd our Gifts perpetually,
Against the Common Enemy: 770
Although 'twas ours and their Opinion,
Each others Church was but a *Rimmon*,
And yet for all this *Gospel Union*,
And outward shew of *Church Communion*,
They'ld ne're admit us to our shares,
Of Ruling *Church* or *State Affairs*:
Nor give us leave t'*absolve, or sentence*
T'our own Conditions of Repentance.
But shar'd our *Dividend o'th' Crown*,
We had so painfully *Preach'd down*.   780
And forc'd us though against the Grain,
T'have Calls to teach it up again.

753 *Stumps D2*: *Stamps D1*   758 others, *D2*: others *D1*

For 'twas but Justice to Restore
The Wrongs we had receiv'd before,
And when 'twas held forth in our way,
W' had been ungrateful not to pay:
Who for the Right w' have done the Nation,
Have earn'd our *Temporal Salvation*:
And put our Vessels in a way,
Once more to come again in Play: 790
For if the turning of us out,
Has brought this Providence about.
And that our only Suffering,
Is able to bring in the King:
What would our Actions not have done,
Had we been suffer'd to go on?
And therefore may pretend t'a share,
At least in *Carrying on* th'Affair:
But whether that be so, or not,
W' have done enough, to have it thought   800
And that's as good, as if w' had don't,
And easier past upon account.
For if it be but half deny'd,
'Tis half as good as justify'd.
The World is Nat'rally averse
To all the truth, it Sees or Hears,
But swallows Non-sense, and a Lie,
With Greediness, and Gluttony;
And though it have the Picque, and long,
'Tis still for something in the wrong: 810
As Women long, when th' are with Child
For things extravagant and wild:
For Meats ridiculous, and fulsome,
But seldom, any thing that's wholesome;
And like the World, *Mens Jobbernoles*,
Turn round upon their *Ears, the Poles*;
And what th' are confidently told,
By no sense else, can be controul'd.

And this, perhaps, may prove the means,
Once more, to *Hedge-in Providence*,   820
For as *Relapses* make Diseases

More desp'rate then their first Accesses,
If we but get again in Pow'r,
Our work is easier then before,
And we more *Ready and Expert*,
I'th' Mystery, to do our Part.
We, who did rather undertake
The *First War* to create, then make:
And when of Nothing 'twas begun,
Rais'd *Funds*, as strange to carry't on;   830
Trepan'd the State, and fac'd it down,
With Plots, and Projects of our own:
And if we did such Feats at first,
What can we now w' are better vers'd?
Who have a Freer Latitude,
Then Sinners give themselves allow'd:
And therefore likeliest to bring in
On fairest Terms our Discipline.
To which it was Reveal'd long since,
We were ordain'd by Providence: 840
When Three Saints Ears, our Predecessors,
The Causes Primitive Confessors,
B'ing Crucified, The Nation stood
In just so many years of Blood:
That multiply'd by Six, exprest
The Perfect Number of the Beast.
And Prov'd that we must be the Men,
To bring this work about agen:
And those who laid the first Foundation
Compleat the thorow Reformation: 850
For who have Gifts to carry on,
So great a work but we alone?
What Churches have such *Able Pastors?*
And Precious, Powerful, *Preaching Masters?*
Possest with absolute Dominions,
O're *Brethrens Purses, and Opinions?*
And trusted with the *Double Keys*
Of Heaven, and their Ware-Houses:
Who when the Cause is in distress,
Can furnish out what Sums they Please,   860
That Brooding lye in *Bankers* hands,

To be Dispos'd at their Commands:
And daily increase and Multiply,
With Doctrine, Use, and Usury.
Can fetch in Parties (as in War,
All other Heads of Cattle are)
From th'Enemy of all Religions,
As well as High and Low Conditions,
And share them from *Blew Ribands* down,
To all *Blew Aprons in the Town.*   870
From Ladies hurried in *Calleches,*
With Cornets at their Footmens Breeches,
To Bawds as fat as *Mother Nab,*
All Guts and Belly like a Crab.
Our Party's great, and better ty'd,
With *Oaths* and *Trade* than any side:
Has one considerabl' Improvement,
To double Fortifie the Cov'nant:
I mean our Covenants to Purchase
Delinquents Titles and the Churches: 880
That Pass in Sale, from *Hand to Hand,*
Among our Selves, *for Current Land.*
And Rise or Fall, *like Indian Actions,*
According to the Rate of Factions:
Our best *Reserve* for Reformation,
When *New-outgoings* give occasion:
That keeps the Loyns of Brethren Girt,
Their Covenant (*their Creed*) t'assert:
And when th' have Pack'd a *Parliament,*
Will once more try th'Expedient,   890
Who can already Muster Friends
To serve for Members to our Ends:
That Represent no part o'th' Nation,
But *Fishers Folly Congregation:*
Are only Tools to our Intrigues,
And sit like Geese, to hatch our Eggs:
Who by their Precedents of Wit,
T'*out-fast, out-loiter and out-sit:*
Can order Matters under hand
To put all Bus'ness to a stand: 900

879 Covenants *D1* (errata), *D2*: Covenant *D1*   899 hand] hand. *D*

Lay *Publick Bills* aside, for *Private*,
And make 'em one another *Drive out*,
Divert the *Great and Necessary*,
With Trifles to contest and vary
And make the Nation *Represent*,
And serve for us, in *Parliament*,
Cut out more work then can be done,
In *Plato's Year*, but finish none
Unless it be the *Bulls of Lenthall*
That always past for *Fundamental*.   910
Can set up *Grandee*, against *Grandee*
To squander *Time away*, and *Bandy*.
Make *Lords and Commoners* lay sieges
To one another's *Priviledges*;
And rather then compound the quarrel
Ingage, to th'inevitable peril,
Of both their ruines; th'only scope
And consolation of our hope;
Who though we do not play the Game,
Assist as much, by giving aim.   920
Can introduce our ancient Arts,
For Heads of Factions, t'act their parts,
Know what a Leading-Voice is worth,
A *Seconding*, a *Third*, or *Fourth*,
How much a *Casting-Vote* comes to
That turns up Trump, of I, or No;
And by adjusting all, at th'end,
Share ev'ry one his *Dividend*,
An Art, that so much study cost
And now's in danger to be lost;   930
Unless our ancient *Virtuoso's*,
That found it out, *get into th'Houses*.
These are the Courses, that we took
To carry things, by *Hook, or Crook*:
And practic'd down from *Forty four*,
Until they turn'd us *out of Door*,
Besides the Herds of *Boutefeus*,
We set on work, without the House.

When ev'ry *Knight,* and *Citizen*
Kept *Legislative Journey-men,*   940
To bring them in Intelligence,
From all Points of the Rabbles Sense:
And fill the Lobbys of both Houses,
With Politick Important Buzzes:
Set up Committees of *Cabals,*
To pack designs without the Walls:
Examine and draw up all News,
And fit it to our present use.
Agree upon the Plot *o'th' Farce,*
And every one *his Part Rehearse.*   950
Make Q's of Answers, to way-lay
What th'other Parties like to say:
What *Repartees* and *smart Reflections,*
Shall be return'd to all Objections.
And who shall break the *Master-jest,*
And *what,* and *how, upon the Rest:*
Help Pamphlets out, *with safe Editions,*
Of Proper Slanders and Seditions:
And Treason for a Token send,
By Letter to a Country Friend.   960
Disperse *Lampoons,* the only wit,
That Men, like *Burglary Commit:*
Wit, falser than a *Padders Face,*
That all its owner does, betrays:
Who therefore dare not trust it, when
He's in his *Calling,* to be seen.
Disperse the Dung on Barren Earth,
To bring new Weeds of Discord forth.
Be sure to keep up *Congregations*
In Spight of *Laws and Proclamations,*   970
For *Chiarlatans* can do no good,
Until th' are Mounted in a Crowd:
And when th' are Punish'd; All the Hurt,
Is but to fare the better for't:
As long as Confessors are sure
Of double Pay for all th' endure:
And what they earn in *Persecution,*
Are paid t'a Groat in *Contribution.*

Whence some *Tub-holders-forth* have made
In *Powdring-Tubs*, their richest Trade :   980
And while they kept their Shops in Prison,
Have found their Prices strangely risen.
Disdain to own the least regret
For all the *Christian Blood*, w' have let;
'Twil save our credit, and maintain
Our Title, to do so again :
That needs not cost one *Dram of Sense*,
But *Pertinacious Impudence* :
Our constancy t'our Principles
In time, will wear out all things else,   990
Like Marble Statues, rub'd to pieces,
With *Gallantry* of Pilgrim's kisses :
While those who turn, and wind their Oaths,
Have swelld, and sunk like other *Froths*.
Prevail'd a while : but 'twas not long,
Before from *World to World* they swung :
As they had turn'd from side, to side,
And as the Changelings lived they died.

This said; the impatient *States-Monger*
Could now contain himself no longer,   1000
Who had not spar'd to shew his Piques,
Against th'*Haranguers Politicks*
With smart remarks of *Leering Faces*
And Annotations of Grimashes,
After h' had ministred a Dose
Of *Snuff-Mundungus*, to his Nose :
And Powder'd th'inside of his Soul,
Instead of th'outward Jobbernoll :
He shook it, with a scornful look
On th'Adversary, and thus he spoke.   1010

In Dressing a Calves Head, Although
The *Tongue and Brains* together go,
Both keep so great a distance here,
'Tis strange, if ever they come near :

For who did ever play his Gambols,
With such unsufferable Rambles?
To make the Bringing in the King,
And keeping of him out, *One Thing*?
Which none can do, but those who swore
T'as *Point-Blank Nonsense* heretofore: 1020
That to *Defend was to Invade*,
And to *Assassinate, to Aid*:
Unless because you drove him out,
(And that was never made a Doubt)
No Pow'r is able to Restore
And bring him in but on your Score.
A *Spiritual Doctrine*, that Conduces
Most properly, *to all your Uses*.
'Tis true, *A Scorpions Oyl is said*
To cure the Wounds the Vermine made;   1030
And Weapons drest with Salves, Restore;
And heal the hurts they gave before:
But whether *Presbyterians* have
So much *Good Nature* as the *Salve*:
Or *Virtue* in them as the *Vermine*,
Those who have try'd 'em can Determine.
Indeed, 'Tis pity you should miss
Th'*Arrears* of all your *Services*,
And for th'Eternal Obligation,
Y' have laid upon th'Ungrateful Nation: 1040
Be us'd s'unconscionable Hard,
As not to find a Just Reward.
For letting Rapin loose, and Murther,
To Rage just so far, *but no further*:
And setting all the Land on Fire,
To burn t'a Scantling, *but no higher*:
For ventring to *Assassinate*,
And cut the Throats of *Church and State*:
And not be allow'd the fittest Men,
To take the charge of both agen.   1050
Especially, that have the *Grace*,
Of Self-denying, *Gifted Face*;
Who when your Projects have miscarry'd,
Can lay them with undaunted Fore-head,

On those you painfully trepan'd,
And sprinkled in at second hand.
As we have been, to share the guilt
Of Christian Blood devoutly spilt;
For so our Ignorance was flam'd
To damn our selves, t'avoid being damn'd: 1060
Till finding your old Foe, the Hangman,
Was like to lurch you at *Back-gammon*;
And win your Necks, *upon the Set,*
As well as Ours, *who did but Bet*:
(For he had drawn *your Ears before,*
And Nick'd *'em,* on the self-same score:)
We threw the Box, and Dice away,
Before y' had lost us, at *foul Play*:
And brought you down to *Rook, and Lye,*
And Fancy, only on the By.   1070
Redeem'd your forfeit Jobbernolls,
From perching upon lofty Poles:
And rescued all your *Outward Traytors*
From hanging up like *Alegators*:
For which ingeniously y' have shew'd
Your *Presbyterian* gratitude:
Would freely have paid us home in kind,
And not have been one *Rope* behind.
Those were your motives, to divide,
And scruple, on the other side,   1080
To turn your zealous Frauds, and Force,
To·Fits of Conscience, and Remorse.
To be convinc'd they were in vain,
And face about for New again:
For Truth no more unveil'd your Eyes,
Than *Maggots are convinc'd to Flies*:
And therefore all your *Lights* and *Calls,*
Are but *Apocryphal and Fals,*
To charge us with the Consequences,
Of all your Native insolences.   1090
That to your own *Imperious Wills,*
Laid *Law and Gospel Neck and Heels*:

Corrupted the Old Testament,
To serve the New for Precedent:
T'amend its Errors and Defects,
With Murther and Rebellion Texts:
Of which there is not any one,
In all the Book to sow upon:
And therefore from (your Tribe) the Jews
Held Christian Doctrine forth and Use: 1100
As *Mahomet* (your Chief) began,
To mix them in the *Alchoran*:
Denounc'd, and Pray'd, *with Fierce Devotion,*
And bended Elbows on the Cushion:
Stole from the Beggars, *All your Tones,*
And Gifted Mortifying *Groans*:
Had Lights where better Eyes were blind,
As Pigs are said to see the Wind:
Fill'd *Bedlam* with *Predestination,*
And *Knights-Bridge* with *Illumination*:   1110
Made Children with your Tones to *Run for 't,*
As bad as *Bloody Bones or Lunsford.*
While women great with Child, Miscarri'd,
For being to Malignants marry'd:
Transform'd all Wives to *Dalilahs,*
Whose Husbands were not *For the Cause*:
And turn'd the Men to Ten-Horn'd Cattle,
Because they came not out to Battle:
Made Taylors Prentices *turn Heroes,*
For fear of being *transform'd to Meroz*;   1120
And rather forfeit their Indentures
Then not espouse the Saints Adventures.

Could *Transubstantiat, Metamorphose,*
And charm whole Herds of Beasts, like *Orpheus.*
Inchant the *Kings, and Churches Lands,*
T'obey, and follow, your Commands:
And settle on a *New Free-hold,*
As *Marcley-hill* had done of Old.
Could turn *The Covenant, and Translate*
The *Gospel, into Spoons, and Plate,*   1130

Expound upon all *Merchants Cashes,*
And open th'*Intricatest Places:*
Could *Catechise* a Money-Box,
And prove all Powches *Orthodox,*
Until the Cause became a *Damon,*
And *Pythias, the wicked Mammon.*

And yet in spight of all your Charms
To conjure *Legion up,* in Arms,
And raise more Devils in the Rout,
Then e're y' were able to cast out: 1140
Y' have been reduc'd, and by those Fools,
Bred up (you say) in your own Schools,
Who though but gifted at *your Feet,*
Have made it plain; they have more Wit.
By whom you have been so oft trepan'd,
And Held-forth out of all command:
Out-gifted, out-impuls'd, out-done,
And out-reveal'd, at carryings-on,
Of all your Dispensations Worm'd,
Out-Providenc'd, and out-Reform'd.   1150
Ejected out of Church, and State,
And all things, but the Peoples hate:
And spirited out of th'enjoyments
Of precious, edifying employments;
By those who lodg'd their Gifts, and Graces
Like better Bowlers in your Places;
All which you bore, with Resolution
Charg'd on th'Accompt of Persecution;
And though, most righteously opprest,
Against your Wills, still Acquiest: 1160
And never *Hum'd, and Hah'd* Sedition,
Nor *snuffled Treason, nor Misprision.*
That is because you never durst,
For had you *Preach'd, and Pray'd your worst:*
Alas, you were no longer able
To raise your *Posse of the Rabble:*
One single *Red-Coat Sentinel*
Out-charm'd the *Magick of the Spell,*

1156 *Places;* D2: *Places* D1

And with his *Squirt-fire*, could disperse
Whole Troops, with Chapter rais'd, and Verse: 1170
We knew too well those tricks of yours,
To leave it ever in your powers:
Or trust our *Safeties, or Undoings,*
To your *Disposing, of Outgoings;*
Or to your *ordering Providence,*
One Farthings-worth of Consequence.

For had you pow'r, to undermine,
Or wit to carry a design,
Or correspondence, to Trepan,
Inveagle, or betray one Man,   1180
There's nothing else, that intervenes,
And bars your zeal, to use the means.
And therefore wondrous like, no doubt,
To bring in Kings, or keep them out:
Brave Undertakers to *Restore,*
That could not keep your selves in Pow'r:
T'advance the *Intrests of the Crown,*
That wanted Wit to keep your own.

'Tis true, you have (*for I'ld be loth*
To wrong ye) done your Parts, in *Both*;   1190
To keep him out, and bring him in,
As *Grace is introduc'd by Sin,*
For 'twas your *zealous want of sense,*
And Sanctify'd Impertinence:
Your carrying business in a Huddle
That forc'd our Rulers, to *New-model,*
Oblig'd the State to tack about
And turn you Root, and Branch, all out
To Reformado One, and All,
T'your *Great Croysado General*:   1200
Your greedy slav'ring to devour
Before, 'twas in your Clutches, *Pow'r.*
That sprung the Game you were to set,
Before y' had time to draw the Net:
Your spight to see the Churches Lands
Divided into other hands.

And all your *Sacrilegious ventures*
Laid out on *Tickets, and Debentures*;
Your envy to be sprinkled down,
By Under Churches, in the Town.   1210
And no course us'd to stop their Mouths
Nor th'*Independents* spreading Growths:
All which consider'd, 'tis most true
None bring him in so much as you.
Who have prevail'd, beyond *their Plots,*
Their Midnight Juntos, and seal'd knots,
That thrive more by your zealous Piques
Then all their own rash Politicks.
And this way you may claim a share,
In carrying (as you brag) *Th'affair,*   1220
Else Frogs, and Toads, that croak'd the Jews
From *Pharo, and his Brick-kills* loose:
And Flies, and Mange, that set them free,
From Task-Masters, and slavery:
Were likelyer to do the Feat,
In any indifrent Man's conceit;
For who e're heard of *Restoration,*
Until your *thorough Reformation,*
That is the Kings, and Churches Lands
Were Sequestred int'other hands?   1230
For only then, and not before,
Your eyes were opened to restore.
And when the work was carrying on,
Who crost it, but your selves alone?
As by a World of hints, appears,
All plain, and extant, as your Ears:
But first o'th' first; *The Isle of Wight*
Will rise up, if you should deny't;
Where *Hinderson, and th'other Masses*
Were sent to Cap Texts, and Put Cases: 1240
To pass for deep, and *Learned Scholars,*
Although but Paltry, *Ob-and-Sollers*:
As if th'unseasonable Fools,
Had been a *Coursing in the Schools*;

1222 *kills*-loose D

Until th' had prov'd, *The Devil Author*
O'th' Covenant, and the Cause his Daughter:
For when they charg'd him, with the guilt
Of all the Blood, that had been spilt:
They did not mean, He *wrought th'effusion*,
In Person, like Sir Pride, and Hughson: 1250
But only those, who first begun
The Quarrel, were by him set on.
And who could those be, but the Saints,
Those *Reformation-Termegants*?
But e're *This* past; the wise Debate
Spent so much time it grew too late:
For Oliver had gotten ground,
T'enclose them, with his Warriers, round.
Had brought his Providence about,
And turn'd the untimely Sophists out.   1260
Nor had the *Uxbridge bus'ness* less
Of Non-sence in't, and sottishness,
When from a *Scoundrel Holder forth,*
The Scum, as well as Son o' th' Earth,
Your *Mighty Senators* took Law
At his Command, were forc'd t' withdraw;
And sacrifice the Peace o'th' Nation,
To *Doctrine, Use, and Application.*
So when *the Scots, your constant Cronyes,*
Th' Espousers of your Cause, and Monies: 1270
Who had so often, in your Aid,
So many ways been soundly paid;
Came in at last, for better ends,
To prove themselves your trusty Friends,
You basely left them, and the Church,
Th' had train'd you up to, *in the lurch*:
And suffer'd your *own Tribe of Christians,*
To fall before as true Philistines.
This shews, what Utensils y' have been;
To bring the King's concernments in;   1280
Which is so far from being true,
That none but *He,* can bring in you.
And if he take you into trust,
Will find you most exactly just:

Such as will punctually *Repay*
With double Interest, and Betray.

Not that I think those *Pantomimes,*
Who vary Action, with the Times:
Are less ingenious in their Art,
Then those, who dully *Act one Part,*   1290
Or those who turn from Side, to Side,
More guilty, then the Wind, and Tide.
All Countries are a Wise-mans home,
And so are Governments to some
Who change them for the same Intrigues,
That States-Men use in breaking Leagues:
While others in *Old Faiths, and Troths,*
Look odd, as *Out-of-Fashion'd Cloaths:*
And Nastier, in an *Old Opinion,*
Then those, who never shift *their Linnen.*   1300

For True and Faithful's sure to lose,
Which way soever the Game goes:
And whether Parties loose or win,
Is always *Nick'd, or else hedg'd in.*
While Pow'r usurp'd like stoln delight,
Is more bewitching then the right.
And when the Times begin *to Alter,*
None rise so high as *from the Halter.*

And so may we, if w' have but sense
To use the necessary means   1310
And not your usual *Stratagems,*
On one another, Lights, and Dreams.
To stand on terms as positive,
As if we did not take, but give:
Set up the Covenant, on Crutches
'Gainst those, who have us in their Clutches,
And dream of pulling Churches down,
Before w' are sure, to prop our own:
Your constant *Method of Proceeding,*
Without the *Carnal means of Heeding:*   1320

1289 ingenious *D2*: ingenuous *D1*   1302 soever] soever, *D*
1303 Parties] Parties, *D*

Who 'twixt your *Inward sense, and Outward,*
Are worse, then if y' *had none,* Accoutred.

I grant, all courses are in vain,
Unless we can get in, again :
The only way that's left us now,
But all the difficulty's, How ?
'Tis true ! w' have Money, th'*only Pow'r,*
That all Mankind falls down before;
Money, that like the Swords of Kings,
Is the last reason of all things;   1330
And therefore, need not doubt our Play
Has all advantages, that way
As long as Men have *Faith to sell,*
And meet with those that can *Pay well.*
Whose half-starv'd *Pride, and Avarice,*
One *Church, and State* will not suffice,
T'expose to Sale; Beside the Wages,
Of storing Plagues to after Ages.
Nor is our Money less our own,
Then 'twas, before we laid it down :   1340
For 'twil return, and turn t'account,
If we are brought in Play upon't :
Or but by *Casting Knaves* get in,
What pow'r can hinder us to win ?
We know the Arts, we us'd before,
In *Peace and War,* and something more :
And by the unfortunate events,
Can mend our next experiments.
For when w' are taken into trust,
How easie, are the wisest choust ?   1350
Who see but th'out-sides of our Feats,
And not their secret Springs and Weights,
And while th' are *busie at their Ease,*
Can carry what designs, we please :
How easie is't to serve for *Agents,*
To prosecute our old Engagements!
To keep the good Old Cause on Foot
And present Power from taking root!

1356 *Engagements!*] *Engagements?* D   1358 *root!*] *root?* D

Inflame them both, with false Alarms,
Of Plots, and Parties, taking Arms: 1360
To keep the Nations wounds too wide,
For healing up of Side to Side.
Profess the passionat'st *Concerns*,
For both their Interests by *Turns*.
The only way t'improve our own
By dealing faithfully with none.
(As Bowls Run true, by being made
Of Purpose False, and to be sway'd)
For if we should be true to either,
T'would turn us out of both together: 1370
And therefore have no other means,
To stand upon our own Defence;
But keeping up our *Antient Party*
In Vigor, Confident, and Hearty:
To Reconcile our late Dissenters,
Our Brethren, though by other venters,
Unite them, and their Different Maggots,
As long, and Short Sticks, are in Faggots.
And make them Joyn again, as Close,
As when they first began t'Espouse;   1380
Erect them into Separate,
New Jewish Tribes, in Church and State;
To Joyn in *Marriage and Commerce*,
And only among themselves, *Converse*.
And all, that are not of their Mind,
Make Enemies to All Mankind:
Take All Religions in, and Stickle,
From *Conclave down to Conventicle*
Agreeing still, or dis-agreeing,
According to the Light in Being.   1390
Sometimes, for *Liberty of Conscience*
And *Spiritual Mis-rule, in one Sense.*
But in another quite contrary,
As Dispensations chance to vary:
And stand for, as the times will bear it,
All contradictions of the Spirit:

1377 *Maggots*, D2: *Maggots.* D1   1383 *Commerce*, D2: *Commerce.* D1
1386 Mankind: D2: Mankind D1

Protect *their Emissaries,* Impower'd
To *Preach Sedition, and the Word,*
And when th' are hamper'd by the Laws,
Release the Lab'rers for the Cause,   1400
And turn the Persecution back,
On those, that made the first Attack.

To keep them equally in awe,
From *breaking, or maintaining Law*;
And when they have their Fits too soon,
Before the *Full-tides* of the Moon:
Put off their zeal, t'a fitter season,
For sowing Faction in, and Treason:
And keep them hooded and their Churches,
Like Hawks from bating *on their Perches.*   1410
That when the blessed time shall come
Of quitting *Babylon, and Rome,*
They may be ready to restore
Their own *Fift-Monarchy,* once more;
Mean while, be better Arm'd to Fence
Against *Revolts of Providence*;
By watching narrowly, and snapping
All blind-sides of it, as they happen:
For if success could make us Saints,
Our Ruine turn'd us *Miscreants*:   1420
A scandal that would fall to hard
Upon *A Few,* and unprepard.

These are the courses we must run,
Spight of our Hearts, or be undone:
And not to stand on Tearms, and Freaks,
Before we have secur'd our Necks.
But do our work, as out of sight,
As Stars by Day, and Suns by Night:
All Licence of the people own,
In opposition, to the Crown.   1430
And for the Crown, as fiercely side,
The *Head* and *Body,* to divide,
The end of all we first design'd,
And all that yet remains behind:

Be sure to spare no *Publick Rapine*,
On all emergencies, that happen;
For 'tis as easie to supplant
Authority, as Men in want:
As some of us, in trusts, have made
The one hand, with the other Trade;   1440
Gain'd vastly, by their *Joynt-endeavour*,
The Right a Thief, *the Left* Receiver;
And what the one, by tricks *Fore-stal'd*;
The other, by as sly, *Retail'd*.
For Gain has wonderful effects
T'improve the Factory of Sects:
The Rule of Faith in all Professions,
And great *Diana* of the Ephesians:
Whence turning of Religion's made,
The means, to *Turn, and wind a Trade*.   1450
And though some change it for the worse,
They put themselves into a Course:
And draw in store of Customers
To thrive the better in Commerce
For all Religions, flock together,
Like *Tame*, and *Wild-Fowl* of a Fether,
To nab the Itches of their Sects:
As Jades do one anothers Necks.
Hence 'tis; Hypocrisie, as well,
Will serve t'improve a Church, as zeal: 1460
As Persecution, or Promotion,
Do equally advance devotion.

Let Business like Ill watches, go,
Some time too fast, sometime too slow,
For things in order, are put out
So easie, *Ease it self, will do't*.
But when the Feat's design'd, and meant,
What Miracle can bar th'event?
For 'tis more easie to betray,
Then ruine any other way.   1470

All possible occasions start,
The weighty'st matters to divert:

1441 Gain'd *D2*: Gam'd *D1*

Obstruct, Perplex, Distract, Intangle,
And lay Perpetual Trains to wrangle:
But in affairs of less import,
That neither do us good, nor hurt,
And they receive as little by,
Out-fawn as much, and out-comply:
And seem as scrupulously just,
To bait our Hooks for greater Trust.   1480

But still be careful *to cry down*
All publick Actions, though our own,
The least miscarriage aggravate
And charge it all, *upon the State:*
Express the horridst detestation,
And pitty the distracted Nation.
Tell stories, *Scandalous, and False,*
I'th' proper Language of *Cabals:*
Where all a subtle States-man says,
Is half in Words, and half in Face: 1490
(As Spaniards talk in *Dialogues*
Of Heads, and Shoulders, Nods, and Shrugs)
Entrust it under solemn vows
Of *Mum,* and *Silence,* and the *Rose*
To be Re-tail'd again in whispers
For th'easie credulous, to disperse.

Thus far the States-man. When a Shout,
Heard at a distance, put him out,
And strait another all agast,
Rush'd in with equal Fear, and Hast: 1500
Who star'd about, as pale as death,
And for a while, *as out of Breath,*
Till having gather'd up his Wits,
He thus began his Tale by fits.

That beastly Rabble, —— that came down
From all the Garrets —— in the Town,
And Stalls, and Shop-boards —— in vast swarms,
With new-chalk'd Bills —— and rusty Arms,

1491 Spaniards *D2*: Spaniard *D1*   *Dialogues*] Dialogues, D
811844   Y

To cry the Cause —— up, heretofore,
And Baul the Bishops —— out of Door,   1510
Are now drawn up, —— in greater Shoals,
To Roast —— and Broil us on the Coals:
And all the Grandees —— of our Members
Are Carbonading on —— the Embers;
Knights, Citizens, and Burgesses ——
Held-forth by Rumps —— of Pigs, and Geese.
That serve for Characters —— and Badges,
To represent their Personages.
Each Bone-fire is a *Funeral Pile*,
In which, they *Roast, and Scorch, and Broil*;   1520
And ev'ry Representative
Have vow'd to *Roast* —— *and Broil alive*,
And 'tis a miracle, we are not
Already, sacrific'd Incarnate.
For while we wrangle here, and Jar,
W' are Grilly'd all at *Temple-Bar*,
Some, on the Sign-Post of an Ale-house,
Hang in Effigy, on the Gallows,
Made-up of Rags, to personate
Respective Officers of State;   1530
That henceforth, they may stand reputed,
Proscrib'd in Law, and Executed,
And while the work is carrying on,
Be ready listed under *Dun*,
That worthy Patriot, *once the Bellows*,
And Tinder-box of all his Fellows.
The activ'st Member of the *Five*,
As well as the most Primitive,
Who for his faithful service, then;
Is chosen for a *Fift* agen,   1540
(For since the State has made a *Quint*
Of Generals, he's listed in't)
This Worthy, as the World will say,
Is paid in specie, his own way;
For moulded to the Life in Clouts,
Th' have pick'd from Dunghils hereabouts:
He's mounted on a *Hazel Bavin*,
A Cropt malignant Baker gave 'em.

And to the largest Bonefire, riding
Th' have Roasted *Cook* already, and *Pride* in,   1550
On whom in Equipage, and State,
His scare-crow fellow-Members wait,
And march in order, two and two,
As at *Thanksgivings*, *th' us'd to do*
Each in a tatter'd *Talismane*,
Like Vermine in *Effigie slain*.

But (what's more dreadful then the rest)
Those Rumps are but the *Tayl o'th' Beast*,
Set up by *Popish Engineers*,
As by the *Crackers* plainly appears: 1560
For none, but Jesuits, have a Mission,
To Preach the Faith with Ammunition;
And propagate the Church with Powder,
Their Founder was a blown-up Souldier:
These *Spiritual Pioneers* o'th' *Whores,*
That have the charge of all her stores;
Since first they fail'd in their Designs,
To take in Heav'n, by springing Mines;
And with unanswerable Barrels
Of Gun-powder dispute their quarrels: 1570
Now take a course more practicable,
By laying trains to fire the Rabble,
And blow us up, in th'open streets;
Disguis'd in Rumps, like *Sambenites*,
More like to ruine, and confound,
Then all their Doctrines *under-ground*.

Nor have they chosen Rumps amiss
For Symbols of State-mysteries;
Though some suppose, 'twas but to shew,
How much they scorn'd the Saints, *The Few*,   1580
Who, 'cause th' are wasted to the Stumps
Are represented best by Rumps:
But Jesuits have *deeper reaches*
In all their *Politick Far-fetches*,

And from their *Coptick-Priest, Kirkerus,*
Found out this Mystick way to jeer us.

For as the *Ægyptians us'd by Bees,*
T'express their Antick Ptolomies,
And by their Stings, the Swords they wore
Held-forth Authority and Pow'r: 1590
Because these subtile Animals
Bear all their Intrests in their *Tails,*
And when th' are once impair'd in that,
Are banish'd their well order'd State:
They thought, all Governments were best
By *Hieroglyphick Rumps,* exprest.

For as in *Bodies Natural,*
The Rump's the Fundament of all,
So in a *Common-wealth, or Realm,*
The Government is call'd the *Helm,*   1600
With which, like Vessels under Sail,
Th' are turn'd and winded by the Tail.
The Tail, which Birds and Fishes steer
Their courses with, through Sea and Air
To whom, the *Rudder of the Rump,* is
The same thing with the *Stern, and Compass,*
This shews, how perfectly, the Rump,
And Common-wealth in Nature jump;
For as a Fly, that goes to Bed,
Rests with his Tail above his Head: 1610
So in this Mungril *State of ours,*
The Rabble are the Supream Powers.
That Hors'd us on their Backs to show us
A Jadish trick at last, and throw us.

The Learned *Rabins of the Jews,*
Write there's a Bone, which they call *Luez,*
I'th' Rump of Man, of such a virtue,
No force in Nature can do hurt to,
And therefore, at the last great Day,
All th'other Members shall, *they say,*   1620

Spring out of this, as from a Seed,
All sorts of Vegetals proceed,
From whence, the *Learned Sons of Art*
Os Sacrum, justly stile that part.

Then what can better represent,
Than this Rump-bone, *the Parliament*?
That after several *Rude Ejections*,
And as *Prodigious Resurrections*,
With new Reversions of nine Lives
Starts up, and like a Cat Revives? 1630

But now, alas, th' are all expir'd,
And *Th'House*, as well as *Members*, fir'd;
Consum'd in Kennels, by the Rout,
With which they other Fires put out:
Condemn'd t'un-governing distress,
And Paultry, Private wretchedness.
Worse than the *Devil to Privation*,
Beyond all hopes of Restoration;
And parted like the Body, and Soul,
From all Dominion, and Controul. 1640

We, who could lately, with a look,
Enact, Establish, or Revoke;
Whose *Arbitrary Nods* gave Law,
And frowns kept multitudes in awe;
Before the bluster of whose huff,
All Hats, as in a Storm flew off.
Ador'd and bow'd to, by the Great,
Down to the Foot-man, and valet.
Had more bent knees, then *Chappel-Mats*,
And *Prayers, then the Crowns of Hats.* 1650
Shall now be scorn'd as wretchedly,
For *Ruines just as low, as high*,
Which might be suffer'd, were it all
The horrour, that attends our fall:
For some of us, have scores more large,
Then *Heads and Quarters* can discharge.

1652 *Ruines*] *Rume's* D

And others who by *Restless scraping*
With *Publick Frauds,* and *Private Rapine,*
Have mighty heaps of Wealth amass't
Would gladly lay down all, at last,   1660
And to be but undone, Entail
Their Vessels on perpetual Jayl,
And bless the Devil to let them Farms
Of forfeit Souls, on no worse terms.

This said, *A near and louder shout*
Put all th'Assembly to the Rout,
Who now begun t'out-run their fear,
As Horses do, from those they bear:
But crouded on, with so much hast,
Until th' had block'd the passage fast,   1670
And Barricadoed it with *Haunches,*
Of *outward Men, and Bulks, and Paunches:*
That with their Shoulders, strove to squeeze,
And rather save a *Cripled piece*
Of all their crush'd, *and broken Members,*
Then have them *Grillied on the Embers:*
Still pressing-on, with heavy packs,
Of one another, on their Backs,
The Van-guard could no longer bear
The charges, of the *Forlorn-Rere,*   1680
But born down head-long by the Rout,
Were trampled sorely under-foot.
Yet nothing prov'd so formidable,
As the *horrid Cookery of the Rabble:*
And fear that keeps all feeling out,
As lesser pains are, *by the Gout,*
Reliev'd 'em with a fresh supply
Of rallied Force, enough to fly;
And beat a *Tuscan running Horse,*
Whose Jocky-Rider is *all Spurs.*   1690

1674 *piece*] *piece*; D

THE THIRD AND LAST PART

CANTO III

THE ARGUMENT

The Knight and Squire's Prodigious flight,
To quit th'Inchanted Bow'r, by Night,
He plods to turn his amorous Suit,
T'a Plea in Law, and prosecute:
Repairs to Counsel, to advise
'Bout managing the Enterprise,
But first resolves to try by Letter,
And once more, fair Address, to get her.

WHO would believe, what strange *Bug-bears*
Mankind creates it self, of *Fears*?
That spring like Fern, that Insect-weed
Equivocally, without seed;
And have no possible Foundation,
But merely in th'Imagination:
And yet can do more Dreadful Feats,
Than Hags with all their *Imps and Teats*:
Make more bewitch and haunt themselves,
Than all their *Nurseries of Elves.*   10
For fear do's things so like a Witch,
'Tis hard t'unriddle which is which:
Sets up communities of Senses,
To chop and change Intelligences,
As *Rosi-crusian Virtuoso's,*
Can see with *Ears,* and hear with *Noses*;
And when they neither see nor hear,
Have more than Both supply'd by Fear.
That makes 'em in the dark *see Visions,*
And hag themselves with *Apparitions:*   20

13 **Senses,** D2: Senses. D1

And when their eyes discover least,
Discern the subtlest Objects best.
Do things not contrary alone
To th' course of Nature but its own:
The courage of the Bravest Daunt
And turn Pultroons as valiant;
For men as Resolute appear,
With too much as too little Fear:
And when th' are out of hopes of Flying,
Will run away from death by dying: 30
Or turn again to stand it out,
And those they fled like Lions, Rout.
This *Hudibras* had prov'd too true,
Who by the Furies left Perdue,
And haunted with Detachments, sent
From *Marshal-Legions Regiment,*
Was by a *Fiend,* as Counterfeit,
Reliev'd and Rescu'd with a Cheat:
When nothing but himself and fear
Was both the *Imps and Conjurer*:   40
As by the Rules o'th' *Virtuosi,*
It follows in due *Form of Poesie.*

Disguis'd in all the Masks of Night,
We left our Champion on his flight:
At *Blind Mans Buff,* to grope his way,
In equal fear, of *Night and Day*:
Who took his dark and desp'rate course,
He knew no better than his Horse,
And by an unknown Devil led,
(He knew as little whither) fled.   50
He never was in greater need,
Nor less capacity of Speed:
Disabled both in Man and Beast,
To fly, and run away, *his best,*
To keep the Enemy, and fear,
From equal falling on his Rere.
And though with kicks, and bangs, he ply'd
The further, and the nearer side,

34 Perdue,] Perdue. D

(As *Seamen* ride with all their force,
And *Tug* as if they *Rowed the Horse*,   60
And when the Hackney Sails most swift,
Believe they *lag*, or *run a drift*)
So though he posted e're so fast,
His fear was greater then his *hast*:
For fear, though fleeter then the Wind,
Believes 'tis always left behind.
But when the Morn began to appear,
And shift *t'another Scene* his fear;
He found his new officious *shade*,
That came so timely to his Aid: 70
And forc'd him from the Foe t'escape,
Had turn'd it self, to *Ralpho's shape*.
So like in *Person, Garb, and Pitch*,
'Twas hard t'interpret *which was which*.

For *Ralpho* had no sooner told
The Lady all he had t'unfold,
But she convoy'd him out of sight,
To entertain the Approaching Knight.
And while he gave himself Diversion,
T'accomodate his *Beast and Person*,   80
And put his *Beard* into a posture,
At best advantage to accost her,
She order'd th'*Antimasquerade*,
(For his Reception) *aforesaid*,
But when the *Ceremony* was done,
The *Lights put out, and furies gone*,
And *Hudibras* among the Rest,
Convey'd away as *Ralpho* guest,
The wretched Caitiff all alone,
(As he believ'd) began to moan,   90
And tell his Story to himself;
The Knight mistook him for an Elf,
And did so still till he began,
To scruple at *Ralphs* outward man:
And thought because they oft agreed,
T'appear in one anothers stead,

And act the *Saints* and *Devils* part,
With undistinguishable Art,
They might have done so now perhaps,
And put on one anothers Shapes,   100
And therefore to resolve the doubt,
He star'd upon him and cry'd out.
What art? My Squire or that bold Sprite,
That took his Place and Shape to Night?
Some Busie Independent Pug,
Retainer to his Synagogue?

Alas, quoth he, *I'm none of those,*
Your Bosom Friends, as you suppose,
But Ralph himself, your trusty Squire,
Wh' has drag'd your Dun-ship out o'th' Mire,   110
And from the Inchantments of a Widow
Wh' has turn'd you int' a Beast, have freed you.
And though a Prisoner of War,
Have brought you safe, where now you are.
Which you would gratefully Re-pay,
Your constant Presbyterian way.
That's stranger (*quoth the Knight*) and stranger,
Who gave thee notice of my danger?
Quoth he, *Th' Infernal Conjurer*
Pursu'd, and took me Prisoner,   120
And knowing you were here about,
Brought me along, to find you out
Where I in hugger-mugger hid,
Have noted all they said and did:
And, though they lay to him, the Pageant:
I did not see him, nor his Agent,
Who plaid their Sorceries out of sight
T' avoid a fiercer, second Fight.

But didst thou see no Devils then?
Not one (quoth he) *but carnal Men.*   130
A little worse then Fiends in Hell
And that she-Devil Jezabel,
That Laugh'd, and Tee-he'd with derision,

To see them take your Deposition.
What then (quoth *Hudibras*) was he,
That plaid the Dev'l to examine me?
A Rallying Weaver, in the Town,
That did it in a Parsons Gown,
Whom all the Parish takes for gifted,
But for my part I ne're believ'd it.   140
In which you told them all your Feats,
Your Consciencious Frauds and Cheats,
Deny'd your whipping and confest
The naked truth of all the rest,
More plainly than the Reverend writer
That to our Churches veil'd his Miter.
All which they took in Black and White,
And cudgel'd me to under-write;
What made thee, when they all were gone
And none, but thou, and I alone,   150
To Act the Devil, and forbear
To rid me, of my *hellish Fear?*
Quoth he, *I knew your constant Rate*
And Frame of Sp'rite, too obstinate,
To be, by me prevayl'd upon,
With any motives, of my own:
And therefore strove to Counterfit,
The Dev'l awhile, to Nick your wit.
The Devil, that is your constant Crony,
That only can prevail upon ye,   160
Else we might still have been disputing,
And they with weighty drubs confuting.

The Knight who now began to find
Th' had left the Enemy behind;
And saw no farther harm remain,
But feeble weariness and pain;
Perceiv'd by losing of their way,
Th' had gain'd th'Advantage of the Day,
And by declining of the Rode,
They had by chance their Rere made good.   170
He ventur'd to dismiss his *Fear,*

That parting's wont to *Rant and Tear*.
And gives the desperat'st Attack,
To danger still behind its Back.
For having paws'd to recollect,
And on his past success reflect,
T'examine and consider why,
And whence, and how, he came to fly,
And when no Dev'l had appear'd,
What else, it could be said, he fear'd;   180
It put him in so fierce a Rage,
He once resolv'd to re-ingage,
Tost like a Foot-ball back again,
With *shame, and vengeance, and disdain.*

Quoth he, It was thy Cowardise,
That made me from this Leaguer rise;
And when I had half-reduc'd the place,
To quit it infamously base.
Was better cover'd, by thy New-
Arriv'd Detachment then I knew: 190
To slight my new-Acquests, and run
Victoriously, from Battles won.
And reck'ning all I gain'd or lost,
To sell them cheaper then they cost.
To make me put my self to flight:
And Conqu'ring, run away, by Night.
To drag me out, which th'haughty Foe,
Durst never have presum'd to do.
To mount me in the dark, by force,
Upon the bare Ridge of my Horse.   200
Expos'd in Querpo to their Rage,
Without my Arms, and Equipage,
Lest if they ventur'd to pursue,
I might the unequal Fight renew.
And, to preserve thy outward Man,
Assum'd my Place, and led the Van.

All this, quoth Ralph, *I did, 'tis true,*
Not to preserve my self, but you.

180 fear'd;] fear'd? D   184 disdain.] disdain; D   185-206 It was &c.
D prints in italics

You, who were damn'd to baser drubs,
Then Wretches feel in Powd'ring Tubs 210
To mount two wheel'd Carroches, worse
Then managing a wooden Horse:
Drag'd out through straiter Holes, by th' Ears,
Eras'd, or Coup'd, for Perjurers.
Who though the Attempt had prov'd in vain
Had had no reason to complain,
But since it prosper'd 'tis unhandsome
To blame the hand that paid your Ransome.
And rescued your obnoxious Bones,
From unavoidable Batoons. 220
The Enemy was Re-inforc'd,
And we disabled, and unhors'd:
Disarm'd, unqualified for fight
And no way left, but hasty flight.
Which, though as desperate in th' attempt,
Has giv'n you freedom to condemn't.

But were our Bones in fit condition,
To re-inforce the Expedition,
'Tis now unseasonable, and vain,
To think of falling on, again: 230
No Martial project to surprize;
Can ever be attempted twice,
Nor cast design serve afterwards,
As Gamesters tear their loosing Cards.
Beside, our bangs of Man, and Beast,
Are fit for nothing now but rest.
And for a while will not be able
To rally, and prove serviceable.
And therefore I with reason chose
This stratagem, t'amuse our Foes. 240
To make an honourable Retreat,
And wave a total sure defeat:
For those that fly, may fight again,
Which he can never do that's slain.
Hence timely Running's no mean part
Of conduct, in the Martial Art.

By which some glorious Feats atchieve,
As Citizens, by breaking, thrive.
And Cannons conquer Armies, while
They seem to draw-off, and recoyl.   250
Is held the gallantest course, and bravest,
To great exploits, as well as safest:
That spares the expence of time, and pains,
And dangerous beating out of Brains.
And in the end prevails; as certain
As those that never trust to fortune.
But make their Fear do execution,
Beyond the stoutest Resolution,
As Earth-quakes kill, without a blow,
And only trembling overthrow.   260
If th' Ancients crown'd their bravest Men,
That only sav'd a Citizen,
What Victory could e're be won
If ev'ry one would save but one?
Or fight indanger'd to be lost
Where all resolve to save the most?
By this means when a Battle's won,
The War's as far from being done:
For those that save themselves, and fly,
Go half's at least in the Victory: 270
And sometime, when their loss is small,
And danger great, they challenge all:
Print new Additions to their Feats,
And Emendations in Gazets;
And when for furious hast to run,
They durst not stay to fire a Gun:
Have don't with Bonefires, and at home
Made Squibs, and Crackers overcome;
To set the Rabble on a Flame,
And keep their Governours from blame,   280
Disperse the News, the Pulpit tells,
Confirm'd with Fire-works, and with Bells,
And though reduc'd to that extream,
They have been forc'd to sing Te Deum,

278 *overcome;*] *overcome.* D   279 *D has new paragraph*

Yet with Religious Blasphemy
By flattering Heaven, with a Lie,
And for their Beating, giving thanks,
Th' have rais'd recruits, and fill'd their Banks.
For those who run from the Enemy,
Ingage them equally, to fly,   290
And when the fight becomes a chace,
Those win the day, that win the Race;
And that which would not pass in Fights,
Has done the Feat with easie slights.
Recover'd many a desp'rate Campain,
With Burdeaux, Burgundy, and Champaign.
Restor'd the fainting High and Mighty
With Brandy-Wine, and Aqua-vitæ.
And made them stoutly overcome,
With Bacrack, Hocamore, and Mum,   300
Whom, the uncontroul'd decrees of Fate
To Victory necessitate.
With which although they run or burn,
They unavoidably return:
Or else, their Sultan-Populaces
Still strangle all their routed Bassa's.

Quoth *Hudibras*, I understand
What Fights thou mean'st at Sea, and Land
And who those were that run away,
And yet gave out th' had won the day: 310
Although the Rabble souc'd them for't,
O're Head, and Ears, in Mud and Dirt.
Tis true, our Modern way of War
Is grown more politick by far,
But not so resolute, and bold,
Nor ty'd to Honour, as the old.
For now they laugh, at giving Battle
Unless it be to Herds of Cattle:
Or fighting convoys of Provision,
The whole design of the Expedition.   320
And not with down-right blows to rout
The Enemy, but eat them out:

307–72 *D prints in italics*

As Fighting in all Beasts of Prey,
And Eating, are perform'd one way,
To give defiance to their teeth,
And fight their stubborn Guts to Death,
And those atchieve the high'st renown,
That bring the other Stomachs down.
There's now no Fear of wounds nor maiming,
All dangers are reduc'd to Famine.   330
And Feats of Arms, to Plot, Design,
Surprize, and Stratagem, and Mine.
But have no need, nor use of courage,
Unless it be for Glory, or Forrage:
For if they fight, 'tis but by chance,
When one side vent'ring to advance,
And come uncivilly too near,
Are charg'd unmercifully i'th' Rere:
And forc'd with terrible resistance,
To keep hereafter at a distance.   340
To pick out ground to incamp upon
Where store of largest Rivers run,
That serve instead of peaceful Barriers
To part th'engagements of their Warriors,
Where both from side to side may skip,
And only encounter at Bo-peep.
For Men are found the stouter-hearted,
The certainer th' are to be parted.
And therefore post themselves in bogs,
As the ancient Mice attack'd the Frogs,   350
And made their mortal Enemy,
The Water-Rat, their great Allie.
For 'tis not now, who's stout and bold,
But who bears hunger best, and cold:
And he's approv'd the most deserving
Who longest can hold out at starving:
But he that routs most Pigs, and Cows,
The formidablest Man of Prowess.
So, the Emperour *Caligula*,
That triumph'd o're the British Sea;   360
Took Crabs, and Oysters Prisoners,
And Lobsters, 'stead of Curasiers,

Ingag'd his Legions in fierce bustles,
With Perywinkles, Prawns, and Muscles:
And led his Troops with furious gallops,
To charge whole Regiments of Scallops.
Not like their ancient way of War,
To wait on his triumphal Carr:
But when he went to dine or sup,
More bravely eat his Captives up;   370
And left all Wars by his example,
Reduc'd to vict'ling of a Camp well.

Quoth *Ralph*, by all that you have said
And twice as much that I could add,
'Tis plain, you cannot now do worse,
Then take this out-of-fashion'd course:
To hope by stratagem to wooe her,
Or waging Battle to subdue her.
Though some have done it in *Romances*,
And *bang'd* them into *Amorous Fancies*,   380
As those, who won the *Amazons*,
By wanton drubbing of their bones:
And stout *Rinaldo* gain'd his Bride,
By courting *of her back, and side.*
But since those times and Feats are over,
They are not for a *Modern Lover*:
When *Mistresses* are too cross-grain'd,
By such addresses, to be gain'd:
And if they were, would have it out,
With many another kind of bout.   390
Therefore I hold no course s'infesible
As this of force to win the *Jesabel*.
To storm her heart, by th'Antick charms
Of Ladies Errant, force of Arms,
But rather strive by Law to win her,
And try the Title you have in her.
Your Case is clear, you have her word,
And me to witness the accord.
Besides two more of her retinue
To testifie what past between you.   400

More probable, and like to hold,
Then Hand or Seal, or breaking Gold:
For which so many that renounc'd
Their plighted Contracts have been trounc'd.
And Bills upon Record been found,
That forc'd the Ladies to compound:
And that unless I miss the matter,
Is all the business you look after,
Besides, *Encounters at the Bar,*
Are braver now, then those in War.   410
In which the Law does execution,
With less Disorder and Confusion:
Has more of Honour in't some hold,
Not like the *New way,* but the *Old.*
When those the *Pen* had drawn together,
Decided quarrels with *the Feather,*
And winged Arrows kill'd as dead,
And more then Bullets now of Lead.
So all their Combats now, as then,
Are manag'd chiefly by the Pen.   420
That does the Feat, with braver vigours,
In words at length, as well as Figures.
Is Judge of all the World performs,
In voluntary Feats of Arms.
And whatso'ere's atchiev'd in Fight
Determines which is wrong or right;
For whether you *Prevail,* or *lose,*
All must be try'd there in the close.
And therefore 'tis not wise to shun,
What you must trust to, ere y' have done.   430

The Law, that settles all you do,
And marries where you did but wooe.
That makes the most perfidious Lover,
A Lady, that's as false, recover:
And if it judge upon your side,
Will soon *extend her* for your *Bride:*
And put her *Person, Goods, or Lands,*
Or which you like best int' your hands.

426 right; *D2*: right *D1*   438 hands.] hands, *D1*: hands; *D2*

For *Law's* the Wisdom of all Ages
And manag'd by the ablest Sages,   440
Who though their *bus'ness at the Bar*
Be but a kind of *civil War*,
In which th' ingage with *fiercer Dudgeons*
Then e're the *Grecians did, and Trojans.*
They never manage the contest,
T'impair their publick interest,
Or by their controversies, lessen
The dignity of their *Profession*:
Not like us Brethren, who divide
Our Common-wealth, *The Cause*, and side,   450
And though w' are all as near of kindred
As th'*outward Man is to the inward*;
We agree in nothing but to wrangle
About the slightest fingle fangle,
While Lawyers have more sober sense,
Then to argue at their own expence.
But make their best advantages,
Of other quarrels, like the *Swiss*,
And out of Foraign controversies,
By aiding both sides, *fill their Purses.*   460
But have no int'rest in the Cause,
For which, th' *ingage, and wage the Laws*:
Nor further Prospect then their *Pay.*
Whether they loose or win the *Day.*
And though th' abounded in all Ages,
With sundry Learned *Clerks, and Sages.*
Though all their business be dispute,
With which they canvass every suit;
Th' have no disputes about their *Art*
Nor in *Polemicks controvert.*   470
While all *Professions* else are found,
With nothing but *Disputes* t'abound:
Divines af all sorts, and *Physicians*,
Philosophers, Mathematicians,
The *Gallenist*, and *Paracelsian*,
Condemn the way, each other deals in.
Anatòmists Dissect and *Mangle*
To cut themselves out work to *wrangle.*

Astrologers dispute their *Dreams*:
That in their sleeps they talk of, *Schemes*.   480
And *Heralds stickle*, who got who,
So many hundred years ago.

But Lawyers are too wise a Nation,
T'expose their Trade to Disputation:
Or make the busie Rabble Judges,
Of all their secret Piques, and grudges:
In which whoever wins the day,
The whole Profession's sure to Pay.

Beside, no *Mountebanks*, nor *Cheats*
Dare undertake to do their *Feats*,   490
When in all other *Sciences*,
They swarm, like *Insects*, and *Increase*.
For what *Bigot* durst ever draw
By *Inward Light, a Deed in Law*?
Or could Hold forth, by *Revelation*,
An *Answer to a Declaration*?
For those that meddle with their Tools
Will Cut their Fingers, if th' are Fools.
And if you follow their Advice,
In Bills, and Answers, and Reply's: 500
They'l write a Love-letter in *Chancery*
Shall bring her upon Oath to *Answer ye*.
And soon Reduce her to b' your Wife,
Or make her weary of her Life.

The *Knight*, who us'd with *tricks* and *shifts*,
To Edifie, by *Ralphos gifts*:
But in Appearance, cry'd him down,
To make them better seem his own
(All *Plagiary's* Constant Course
Of *sinking*, when they *take a purse*)   510
Resolv'd to follow his advice,
But kept it from him, in Disguise:
And after stubborn Contradiction,
To Counterfeit his own Conviction,

508 own] own. D

And by Transition, fall upon
The Resolution, as his own

Quoth he; *This Gambol thou Advisest,*
Is, of all others, the unwisest;
For if I think by Law to gain her,
There's nothing Sillier, nor Vainer.   520
'Tis but to hazard my Pretence,
Where nothing's certain, but th' Expence.
To Act against my self, and Traverse
My Suit, and Title, to her favors.
And if she should, which heav'n forbid,
O'rethrow me, as the Fidler did,
What after-course have I to take,
'Gainst loosing all I have at stake?
He that with injury is griev'd,
And go's to Law, to be Reliev'd;   530
Is Syllier then a sottish Chews,
Who when a thief has Rob'd his house,
Apply's himself to Cunning-men
To help him to his goods agen.
When all he can expect to gain,
Is but to squander more, in vain.
And yet I have no other way,
But is as difficult, to play.
For to reduce her, by main force,
Is now in vain, by Fair means, worse: 540
But worst of all, to give her over,
Till she's as Desp'rat to recover.
For bad games are thrown-up too soon,
Until th' are never to be won.
But since I have no other course,
But is as bad t'attempt, or worse:
He that complies against his Will,
Is of his own opinion still,
Which he may adhere to, yet disown,
For Reasons to himself best known,   550
But 'tis not to be avoided now,
For Sidrophel *resolves to sue:*

526 *did,] did.* D   547 *Will,* D2: *Will.* D1

Whom I must answer, or begin
Inevitably, first with him.
For I've receiv'd advertisement,
By-times enough, of his intent;
And knowing, he that first complains,
Th' advantage of the business gains.
For Courts of Justice understand
The Plaintiff, to be eldest hand;   560
Who what he pleases may aver,
The other nothing till he swear:
Is freely admitted to all grace,
And lawful Favor by his place:
And for his bringing custom in,
Has all advantages to win;
I who Resolve, to oversee
No Lucky opportunity,
Will go to Counsel, to Advise
Which way t'incounter, or surprise.   570
And after long consideration:
Have found out one to fit th' occasion,
Most apt, for what I have to do,
As Counsellor, and Justice, too.
And truly so, no doubt, he was,
A Lawyer fit for such a Case.

An *Old Dul Sot*; wh' had told the Clock,
For many years, at *Bridewel-Dock,*
At *Westminster,* and *Hickses-hall,*
And *Hiccius-Dockius* play'd in all;   580
Where in all *governments, and times,*
H' had been both *friend,* and *fo* to Crimes,
And us'd two equal ways of gaining,
By *hindring justice,* or maintaining:
To many a Whore *gave Priviledge,*
And whip'd, for *want of Quarteridge,*
Cart-loads of Bawd's, to Prison sent
For b'ing behind a Fortnights Rent.
And many a trusty *Pimp,* and *Croney,*
To *Puddle-dock,* for want of Money.   590

578 *Dock,*] *Dock.* D

Ingag'd the *Constable* to cease
All those, that would not break the Peace.
Nor give him back his own foul words,
Though sometimes *Commoners, or Lords*:
And kept 'em Prisoners, of Course,
For being *sober at ill hours*.
That in the Morning he might Free,
Or Bind 'em over, for his Fee.
Made *Monsters Fine*, and *Puppet-plays*,
For leave to practice, in their ways: 600
Farm'd out all Cheats, and went a Share,
With th'*Head-burrow*, and *Scavenger*
And made the Durt i'th' Streets Compound,
For taking up the Publick Ground:
The *Kennel*, and *the Kings High-way*,
For being unmolested, Pay.
Let out *the Stocks*, and *Whipping Post*,
And Cage, to those that gave him most.
Impos'd a Tax on *Bakers Ears*,
And for *False Weights* on *Chandellers*.   610
Made *Victuallers*, and *Vintners Fine*
For Arbitrary *Ale*, and *Wine*.
But was a kind and Constant Friend,
To all that *Regularly* offend:
As *Residentiary Bawds*,
And *Brokers, that receive stoln Goods*;
That cheat in *Lawful Mysteries*,
And pay *Church-duties*, and *his Fees*,
But was Implacable, and Auker'd
To all that *Interlop'd, and Hawker'd*.   620

To this brave Man, the Knight repairs
For Counsel, in his *Law-affairs*,
And found him mounted, *in his Pew*,
With *Books*, and *Money* plac'd, for shew,
Like *Nest-eggs*, to make *Clients lay*
And for his false Opinion, pay:
To whom the Knight, with comely grace,
Put off his Hat, to put his Case,
Which he as proudly entertain'd,
As the other courteously strain'd: 630

And to assure him, 'twas not that,
He look'd for; Bid him put on's Hat.

Quoth he, there is one *Sidrophel*
Whom I have cudgel'd —— *Very well.*
And now he brags, t'have beaten me.
Better, and better still, quoth he,
And vows to stick me, to a Wall
Where e're he meets me —— *best of all.*
'Tis true, the Knave has taken's Oath,
That I rob'd him —— *Well done in troth.*   640
When h' has confest, he stole my Cloak,
And pick'd my Fob, and what he took,
Which was the cause, that made me bang him,
And take my Goods again —— *marry hang him:*
Now whether I should, before hand
Swear he rob'd me? —— *I understand*
Or bring my *Action of conversion*
And Trover for my Goods? *Ah Whorson.*
Or if 'tis better to Indite,
And bring him to his Trial? —— *Right,*   650
Prevent what he designs to do,
And swear for th' state against him? —— *True.*
Or whether he that is Defendant
In this Case, has the better end on't;
Who putting in a new cross-bill,
May traverse th'Action? —— *better still.*
Then there's a Lady too. —— *I marry,*
That's easily prov'd accessary.
A Widow, who by solemn Vows,
Contracted, to me, for my Spouse,   660
Combin'd with him to break her word,
And has abetted all —— *Good Lord,*
Suborn'd the aforesaid *Sidrophel,*
To tamper with the *Dev'l of Hell.*
Who put m' into a horrid fear,
Fear of my Life. —— *Make that appear.*
Made an assault, with Fiends and Men
Upon my body. —— *Good agen.*

667 Men] Men. D

And kept me in a deadly fright
And false Imprisonment all Night,   670
Mean while, they rob'd me, and my Horse,
And stole my Saddle, —— *worse and worse;*
And made me mount upon the bare-ridge,
T'avoid a wretcheder miscarriage:

Sir, quoth the Lawyer, not to flatter ye,
You have as *Good, and Fair a Battery,*
As heart can wish, and need not shame,
The proudest Man alive to claim.
For if th' have us'd you, as you say,
Marry, quoth I, *God give you joy,*   680
I would it were my Case, I'd give,
More then Ile say, or you'l believe.
I would so trounce her, and her Purse,
I'ld make her kneel for *bett'r or worse;*
For Matrimony, and Hanging here;
Both go by Destiny so clear,
That you as sure, may *Pick and Choose,*
As *Cross I win,* and *Pile you loose.*
And if I durst, I would advance
As much, in *Ready Maintenance*   690
As upon any Case I've known,
But we that practice dare not own,
The Law severely *contrabands,*
Our taking business, of *Mens hands;*
Tis *Common barratry,* that *bears*
Point blank an Action 'gainst our *Ears*
And crops them, till there is not Leather,
To stick a Pen in, left of either;
For which, some do the *Summer-sault*
And ore the Bar, like *Tumblers, vault.*   700
But you may swear at any rate
Things not in Nature, *for the State:*
For in all *Courts of Justice* here
A Witness is not said *to swear,*
But *make Oath,* that is, in plain terms,
To forge whatever he affirms:

690 *Maintenance*] Maintenance; D

(I thank you, quoth the Knight, for that,
Because 'tis to my purpose pat ——)
For Justice, though she's painted blind,
Is to the weaker side, enclin'd   710
Like *charity*, else *right, and wrong*,
Could never hold it out so long;
And like *blind Fortune*, with a slight,
Conveys Mens *Interest, and Right*,
From *Stile's Pocket, into Nokeses*;
As easily, as *Hocus Pocus.*
Plays fast, and loose, makes *Men Obnoxious*,
And *Clear again, like Hiccius-Doctius.*
Then whether you would *take her life*,
Or but recover her *for your wife*:   720
Or be content, with what she has,
And let all other matters Pass,
The Business to the Law's alone,
The Proof is all it look's upon.
And you can want no witnesses,
To Swear to any thing you please:
That hardly get their mere *Expences*
By *th' Labor of their Consciences*,
Or letting out to hire, *their Ears*,
To *Affidavit-customers*:   730
At inconsiderable values,
To *serve for Jury-men, or* Tales
Although Retain'd in th'*hardest matters*,
Of Trustees, and Administrators.

For that, *Quoth he*, Let me alone,
W' have store of such, and all our own;
Bred-up and tutor'd, *by our Teachers*,
The Ablest of all Conscience-stretchers.

That's well! Quoth he, But I should Guess:
By weighing all Advantages.   740
Your surest way is first to Pitch
On *Bongey*, for a *Water-witch*:

712 long;] long *D1* : long, *D2*   718 *Doctius. D2* : *Doctius D1*
735 *Editor's paragraph*   739 *Editor's paragraph*

And when y' have hang'd the Conjurer,
Y' have time enough, to deal with her.
In th'Intrim; Spare for *No Trepans*,
To draw her Neck, into the *Banes*:
Ply her with *Love-letters*, and *Billets*,
And Bait 'em well, for *Quirks*, and *Quillets*
With Trains t'inveagle, and surprise,
Her Heedless *Answers*, and *Reply's*:   750
And if she Miss the *Moustrap-Lines*,
They'l serve for other *by-Designs*:
And make an *Artist* understand,
To Copy out *her Seal, or Hand*:
Or find voy'd Places in the *Paper*,
To steal in something to *Intrap her*.
Till with her worldly *Goods*, and *Body*,
Spight of her Heart, she has indow'd ye.

Retain all sorts of *Witnesses*,
That Ply ith' Temples, *under trees*,   760
Or *walk the Round*, with *Knights oth' Posts*,
About the *Cross-leg'd Knights, their hosts*
Or wait for *Customers*, between
The *Piller-Rows* in *Lincolns-Inn*.
Where *Vowchers*, *Forgers*, *Common-bayl*,
And *Affidavit-men*, ne're fayl
T'expose to Sale, all *sorts of Oaths*,
According to *their Ears, and Cloaths*.
Their only *Necessary Tools*,
Besides the *Gospel*, and *their Souls*.   770
And when y' are furnish'd with all *Purveys*
I shall be ready, *at your service*.

I would not give, *quoth Hudibras*,
A straw, to understand *a Case*,
Without the admirabler skill
To *Wind, and Manage it at Will*:
To *Vere*, and *Tack*, and stear a *Cause*,
Against the *Weather-gage of Laws*;
And Ring the Changes upon *Cases*,
As plain, as Noses upon Faces.   780

As you have well instructed me
For which you have earn'd (here 'tis) *your Fee*,
I long to practice your advice,
And try the subtle Artifice:
To bait a Letter, as you bid,
As not long after, thus he did,
For having pump'd-up all his Wit,
And hum'd upon it, thus he Writ.

An Heroical Epistle of Hudibras
to his Lady

I WHO was once as great as *Cæsar*,
Am now reduc'd to *Nebuchadnezar*.
And from as fam'd a Conquerour,
As ever took degree in War,
Or did his *Exercise*, in *battle*,
By you turn'd out to *Grass with Cattle*.
For since I am deny'd access
To all my Earthly happiness
Am fallen from the *Paradise*
Of your good *Graces*, and fair *Eyes*,   10
Lost to the World, and you, I'me sent
To Everlasting Banishment
Where all the *Hopes* I had, t'*have won*
Your Heart, being dash'd, will break my own:
Yet if you were not so severe
To pass your doom, before you hear,
You'ld find, upon my just defence,
How much y' have wrong'd my Innocence.
That once I made a *Vow to you*,
Which yet is unperform'd '*tis true*;   20
But not, because it is unpaid,
'Tis *Violated*, though *delay'd*:
Or if it were, it is no fault
So hainous, as you'ld have it thought,
To undergo the loss of Ears,
Like vulgar *Hackney Perjurers*,
For there's a difference in the case
Between the *Noble*, and the *Base*:
Who always are observ'd t'have don't
Upon a different account: 30
The one for *great, and weighty Cause*,
To salve in Honour *ugly Flaws*.

For none are like to do it sooner,
Then those, who are nicest of their Honour.
The other, for *base Gain*, and *Pay*,
Forswear, and *Perjure, by the Day*;
And make th'exposing, and retailing
Their Souls, and Consciences, a Calling.

It is no *Scandal*, nor *Aspersion*,
Upon a *Great, and noble Person*,   40
To say, he Nat'rally abhor'd
Th'old fashion'd trick, to keep his Word.
Though 'tis perfidiousness, and shame,
In meaner Men, to do the same.
For to be able to *Forget*,
Is found more useful, to *the Great*:
Then *Gout*, or *Deafness*, or *bad Eyes*,
To make 'em pass for wondrous wise.
But though the *Law*, on Perjurers,
Inflicts, the *Forfeiture of Ears*;   50
It is not *just*, that does exempt
The *Guilty, and punish the Innocent*,
To make the Ears repair the wrong,
Committed by th'*ungovern'd Tongue*
And when one Member is forsworn,
Another to be cropt, or torn.
And if you should, as you design,
By course of Law recover mine,
You're like, if you consider right,
To Gain but little Honour by't.   60
For he that for his Ladies sake
Lays down his Life, or Limbs, at *Stake*,
Does not so much deserve her Favour,
As he, *that Pawns his Soul* to have her.
This y' have acknowledg'd I have done,
Although you now disdain to own:
But sentence, what you rather ought
T'esteem *good Service*, then a *Fault*.
Besides, Oaths are not bound to bear
That *Literal Sense*, the words infer;   70

53 Ears] Ears, *D*   58 mine,] mine. *D*

But by the practice of the Age,
Are to be judg'd how far th' engage.
And where the Sense by Custom's checkt,
Are found *void, and of none effect.*
For no Man takes, or keeps a vow,
But just as he sees others do.
Nor are th' oblig'd to be so brittle,
As not to yield, and bow a little,
For as best temper'd Blades are found
Before they break, to bend quite round,   80
So truest Oaths are still most tough,
And though they *bow, are breaking-proof.*
Then wherefore should they not b'allow'd
In Love a greater Latitude?
For as the Law of Arms approves
All ways to Conquest, so *should Loves*;
And not be ty'd to true, or false,
But make that justest, that prevails.

For how can that which is above
All Empire, *High and Mighty Love*,   90
Submit it's great Prerogative,
To any other power alive?
Shall Love, that to no Crown gives place
Become the subject of a Case?
The *Fundamental Law of Nature*,
Be over-rul'd! by those made after?
Commit the censure of *its Cause*
To any, but it's own *Great Laws*?
Love, that's the Worlds preservative,
That keeps all Souls of things alive,   100
Controuls the *Mighty pow'r of Fate*,
And gives, *Mankind*, a longer date.
The Life of Nature, that restores,
As fast as *Time*, and *Death* devours,
To whose free gift, the World does owe
Not only Earth but Heav'n too:
For Love's the only Trade that's driven
The *Interest of State in Heaven*,

89 above] above, D   100 alive,] alive? D   104 fast as] fast and D

Which nothing but the Soul of Man,
Is capable to entertain.   110
For what can Earth produce, but *Love*
To represent the *Joys above*?
Or who, *but Lovers, can converse,*
Like Angels, by the Eye Discourse?
Address, and complement by vision,
Make Love, and Court, by intuition?
And burn in amorous Flames as fierce,
As those Celestial Ministers?
Then how can any thing offend
In order, to so *great an end*?   120
Or Heav'n it self a Sin resent,
That for its own supply was meant?
That merits in a kind mistake,
A Pardon for the offences sake.
Or if it did not, but the *Cause*
Were left to th'injury *of Laws*,
What tyranny can disapprove
There should be *Equity* in Love?
For Laws, that are Inanimate
And feel no sense of Love, or Hate: 130
That have no Passion of their own
Nor pity to be wrought upon,
Are only proper to inflict
Revenge, on criminals, as strict:
But to have *Power to forgive,*
Is Empire, and Prerogative;
And 'tis in *Crowns, a nobler Jem,*
To grant a Pardon, then condemn.
Then since so few do what they ought,
'Tis great, t'indulge a well meant fault.   140
For why should he, who made address
All humble ways, without success:
And met with nothing in return, ·
But Insolence, Affronts, and Scorn,
Not strive by Wit to counter-mine
And bravely carry his Design?
He who was us'd so unlike a Soldier,
Blown up with *Philters of Love-Powder*?

And after *letting Blood, and Purging,*
Condemn'd to *voluntary Scourging?*   150
Alarm'd with many a horrid fright,
And claw'd, by *Goblins,* in the Night?
Insulted on, Revil'd, and Jear'd,
With rude Invasion of his Beard?
And when your Sex was fouly scandal'd,
As fouly by the Rabble handled?
Attack'd by despicable Foes,
And drub'd with mean and vulgar blows,
And after all, to be debar'd,
So much as standing on his Guard?   160
When Horses, being *Spur'd,* and *Prick'd,*
Have leave to *kick,* for being *kick'd?*

Or why should you, whose *Mother Wits,*
Are furnish'd with all Perquisits,
That with your *Breeding Teeth* begin,
And *Nursing Babies,* that *Lye in,*
B'allow'd to put all tricks upon
Our *Cully-Sex,* and we use none?
We, who have nothing, but frail vows,
Against your stratagems t'oppose?   170
Or Oaths, more feeble then your own,
By which, we are no less put down?
You wound, like *Parthians,* while you fly,
And kill, with a *Retreating Eye,*
Retire the more, the more we press,
To draw us into Ambushes.
As *Pyrates* all false colours wear,
T'intrap th'unwary Mariner:
So Women to surprize us, spread
Their *borrowed Flags, of White and Red.*   180
Display 'em thicker on their Cheeks,
Then their old Grandmothers, *the Picts*:
And raise more Devils, *with their looks,*
Then *Conjurers less subtle Books.*
Lay Trains of *Amorous Intriegues,*
In *Towrs, and Curls, and Perriwigs.*

164 Perquisits,] Perquisits? *D*   166 *in,*] *in? D*

With greater Art, and cunning rear'd,
Then *Philip Ny's Thanks-giving-beard.*
Prepost'rously t'intice, and Gain,
Those to adore 'em they disdain: 190
And only draw 'em in, to clog
With idle Names, a Catalogue.

A Lover is, the more he's brave,
T'his Mistress, but the more a Slave,
And whatsoever she commands
Becomes a favour from her hands
Which he's oblig'd to obey, and must,
Whether it be unjust, or just.
Then when he is compel'd by her
T'Adventures, he would else forbear,   200
Who with his Honour, can withstand,
Since force is greater then command?
And when Necessity's obey'd
Nothing can be unjust, or bad
And therefore, when the mighty Pow'rs
Of Love, *your great Allie, and yours*;
Joyn'd Forces, not to be withstood,
By frail enamoured Flesh, and Blood,
All I have done unjust, or ill,
Was in obedience to your will: 210
And all the blame that can be due
Falls to your cruelty, and you.

Nor are those scandals I confest,
Against my Will, and Interest,
More then is daily done of course
By all Men, when th' are under force
Whence some, upon the Rack, confess
What th'*Hangman, and their Prompters please.*
But are no sooner out of pain
Then they deny it all again.   220
But when the Devil turns Confessor,
Truth is a Crime, he takes no pleasure,
To Hear, or Pardon, like the *Founder*
Of Lyars, whom they all claim under.

And therefore, when I told him none,
I think it was the wiser done.
Nor am I without Precedent,
The first that on th'Adventure, went:
All Mankind ever did of course,
And daily does the same, or worse.   230
For what *Romance* can shew a Lover,
That had a *Lady to recover*,
And did not steer a nearer course,
To fall aboard in his Amours?
And what at first was held a crime,
Has turn'd to Honourable in time.

To what a height did *Infant Rome*,
By Ravishing of Women come?
When Men upon their Spouses seiz'd,
And freely Marry'd where they pleas'd: 240
They ne're *Forswore* themselves nor *Ly'd*,
Nor in the Minds they were in, *Dy'd*:
Nor took the pains, *t'address, and sue*,
Nor *plaid the Masquerade* to wooe.
Disdain'd to stay for Friends consents,
Nor juggled about settlements:
Did need no *License*, nor no *Priest*,
Nor Friends, nor Kindred to assist;
Nor Lawyers, to *joyn Land, and Money*,
In th'*Holy State of Matrimony*:   250
Before they settled Hands and Hearts:
Till *Alimony*, or *Death departs*:
Nor would indure to stay, until
Th' had got the very *Brides* good will.
But took a wise, and shorter course,
To win the Lady's, *Down-right Force*.
And justly made 'em Prisoners then
As they have often since us Men,
With *Acting Plays* and *Dancing Jiggs*,
The Luckiest of all Loves Intrigues: 260
And when they had them at their Pleasure,
Then talk'd of *Love, and Flames*, at Leisure.

232 *recover,*] *recover.* D   258 often] often, D

For after *Matrimony's* over,
He that Holds out, but *Half a Lover*;
Deserv's for evry *Minute*, more
Then *half a year* of Love before:
For with the Dames, in Contemplation
Of that best way of Application,
Proved Nobler wives, then ere were known
By *Suite*, or *treaty*, to be won: 270
And such as all Posterity,
Could never equal nor come nigh.

For Women first were made for Men,
Not Men for them. —— It follows then,
That Men have right to every one,
And they no freedom of their own:
And therefore Men have pow'r to chuse,
But they no Charter to refuse:
Hence 'tis apparent, that what course
So e're we take, to *your Amours*,   280
Though by the Indirectest way
'Tis no *Injustice*, nor *Foul Play*.
And that you ought to take that course,
As we take you *for Bett'r or worse*,
And Gratefully submit to those,
Who you, before another chose:
For why should every Savage Beast
Exceed his *Great Lord's Interest*?
Have freer Pow'r, then he, in *Grace*,
And Nature, o're the Creature has?   290
Because the Laws, he since has made,
Have cut off all the Pow'r he had,
Retrench'd the absolute Dominion
That Nature gave him, over Women.
When all his Pow'r will not extend,
One *Law of Nature* to suspend:
And but to offer to repeal
The smallest clause, is to rebel.
This, if Men rightly understood
Their Priviledge, they would make good,   300

291 since has made,] since, has made *D*   292 had,] had *D*

And not, like Sots, permit their Wives
T'encroach, on their Prerogatives.
For which Sin, they deserve to be
Kept, as they are, in slavery.
And this, some precious *Gifted Teachers*,
Unrev'rently reputed *Leachers*,
And disobey'd in making Love
Have vow'd to all the World, to prove
And make ye suffer, as you ought,
For that uncharitable fault.   310

But, I forget my self, and rove,
Beyond th'Instructions of my Love:
Forgive me (*Fair*) and only blame,
Th'extravagancy of my *Flame*,
Since 'tis too much, at once, to show
Excess of Love, and temper too:
All I have said, that's *bad, and true*,
Was never meant to aim *at you*:
Who have so Sov'raign a controul,
O're that Poor Slave of yours, *my Soul*:   320
That rather then to forfeit you,
Has ventur'd *loss of Heaven* too.
Both with an equal Pow'r possest
To render all, that serve ye blest
But none like him, who's destin'd, either
To *have*, or *loose* you, both together.
And if you'l but this fault release,
(For so it must be, since you please,)
I'le pay down all that vow, and more
Which you *commanded*, and I *swore*.   330
And expiate upon my Skin,
The Arreers in full of all my Sin.
For 'tis but just, that I should pay,
Th'accrewing penance, for delay,
Which shall be done, until it move
Your equal pity, and your Love.

The *Knight*, perusing *this Epistle*,
Believ'd, h' had brought her to *his Whistle*,

And read it, like a jocund Lover,
With great applause, t'himself, twice over,   340
Subscrib'd his *Name*, but at a Fit,
And humble distance, *to his wit*:
And dated it with wondrous Art,
Giv'n from the bottom of his heart:
Then seal'd it, with *his coat of Love*
A smoaking Faggot —— and above
Upon a Scrol —— *I burn, and weep*,
And near it —— *For her Ladyship*,
Of all her Sex, most excellent,
These to her gentle hands present.   350
Then gave it to his faithless Squire
With Lessons, how t'observe, and eye her.

She first consider'd which was better,
To send it back or burn the Letter:
But guessing that it might import
Though nothing else, at least, her sport
She open'd it and read it out,
With many a smile, and learing flout:
Resolv'd to answer it in kind
And thus perform'd what she design'd.   360

349–50 *Of . . . present*] D *prints in roman*

The Ladies Answer to the Knight

THAT you'r a *Beast*, and turn'd to *Grass*,
Is no strange News, nor ever was,
At least, to me, who once you know
Did from the Pound, *Replevin you*.
When both your *Sword, and Spurs*, were won
In Combat, by an *Amazon*;
That Sword, that did (like Fate) determine
Th'Inevitable Death of Vermine:
And never dealt its furious blows,
But cut the threds of *Pigs, and Cows*,   10
By *Trulla*, was in *single Fight*,
Disarm'd, and wrested *from its Knight*:
Your Heels *Degraded* of your Spurs,
And in the Stocks, Close Prisoners.
Where still th' had Layn, in base Restraint,
If I, in Pitty'of your Complaint,
Had not on Honorable Conditions,
Release 'em from the worst of Prisons,
And what Return that favour met,
You cannot (though you would) forget   20
When being free, you strove t'evade
The Oaths you had in Prison made:
Forswore your self, and first deny'd it,
But after own'd, and justify'd it:
And when y' had falsely broke one *Vow*:
Absolv'd your self, by *breaking two*.
For while you sneakingly submit,
And beg for Pardon, at our feet:
Discourag'd by your guilty fears,
To hope for Quarter, for your *Ears*,   30
And doubting 'twas in vain, to sue,
You claim us boldly as your due.
Declare that Treachery, and Force,
To deal with us, is th'only course.

26 Absolv'd] Absolv'd, *D*   30 *Ears,*] *Ears. D*   31 sue,] sue. *D*

Who have no Title, nor Pretence,
To *Body, Soul, or Conscience* :
But ought to fall to that Man's share,
That claims us, for his proper Ware :
These are the motives, which t'induce,
Or fright us into Love, you use,   40
A pretty new way of *Gallanting*,
Between *Soliciting*, and *Ranting*,
Like sturdy Beggers, that intreat,
For *Charity*, at once, and *threat*,
But since you undertake to Prove
Your own Propriety, in Love
As if we were but *Lawful Prize*
In *War*, between two Enemies;
Or *Forfeitures*, which ev'ry Lover
That would but sue for, might Recover;   50
It is not Hard to understand
The *Mystr'y* of this Bold Demand :
That cannot at our Persons aim;
But something capable of Claim.

Tis not, *Those Paultry counterfeit*
French Stones, which in our Eyes, you set :
But our *Right Diamonds*, that Inspire,
And set your Amo'rous Hearts on fire.
Nor can those False *Saint Martins beads*
Which on our Lips, you lay *for Reds*   60
And make us wear, like *Indian Dames*,
Add Fewel, to your Scorching Flames.
But those true Rubies of the Rock,
Which in our Cabinets, we lock.

'Tis not those Orient Pearls our Teeth,
That you are so transported with.
But those we wear about our Necks,
Produce those Amorous Effects.
Nor is't those Threads of Gold, our *Hair*
The *Perewigs you make us wear*   70

50 Recover;] Recover D   55 *counterfeit*] *counterfeit,* D

But those bright Guinneys in our Chests
That light the wild fire in your Brests.
These Love-tricks I've been vers't in so,
That all their sly *Intrigues*, I know.
And can unriddle, by *their Tones*;
Their *Mystique Cabals*, and *Jargones*.
Can tell what Passions, by their Sounds,
Pine for the Beauties, of my Grounds:
What Raptur's Fond, and Amorous,
O'th' *Charms*, and *Graces* of my House.   80
What *Exstacy*, and *Scorching Flame*
Burns for my *Money*, *in my Name*.
What from th'unnatural Desire
To *Beasts*, and Cattle, takes it's fire.
What *Tender Sigh*, and *Trickling tear*,
Longs for a *Thousand Pound a year*.
And Languishing Transports, are Fond
Of *Statute, Mortgage, Bill, and Bond*.

These are th'Attracts, which most men fall
Inamour'd, at first sight, with all: 90
To these th' Address with *Serenades*
And Court with *Balls*, and *Maskerades*
And yet, For all the yearning Pain
Y' have suffer'd for their Loves, in vain:
I fear they'l prove so nice and Coy
To *have and t'Hold*, and *to Injoy*:
That all *your Oaths*, and *labor lost*
They'l ne're turn *Ladys of the Post*.
This is not meant, to Disapprove
Your Judgment, in your Choice of Love   100
Which is so wise, The greatest Part
Of Mankind, study't as an Art,
For Love should, *like a Deodand*,
Still fall to th'*owner of the Land*:
And where there's Substance, for it's Ground,
Cannot but be more Firm, and Sound,
Then that which has the slighter Bassis,
Of *Airey virtue, wit, and graces*:

Which is of such thin Subtlety,
It Steal's, and Creep's in at the eye.   110
And as it can't indure to stay,
Steals out again, *as nice a way.*

But Love, that its extraction owns
From solid *Gold, and precious Stones*
Must, like its shining Parents prove,
As *solid*, and as *Glorious Love*:
Hence 'tis, you have no way, t'express
Our *Charms*, and *Graces*, but by these:
For what are *Lips*, and *Eyes*, and *Teeth*,
Which *Beauty* invades, and *conquers* with?   120
But *Rubies, Pearls*, and *Diamonds*
With which a *Philter Love commands?*

This is the way all Parents prove,
In managing their Childrens Love
That force 'em t'*inter-marry and wed,*
As if th' were *Bur'ing of the Dead.*
Cast *Earth, to Earth*, as in the *Grave*,
To Joyn in Wedlock all they have.
And when the settlement's in Force,
Take all the rest, *For Better or worse*,   130
For Money has a Power, above
The *Stars, and Fate*, to manage *Love*:
Whose Arrows, Learned Poets hold,
That never miss, *are Tip't with Gold.*
And though some say the Parents claims,
To make Love in their Childrens Names,
Who, many times, at once, Provide,
The *Nurse, the Husband, and the Bride,*
Feel *Darts, and Charms; Attracts, and Flames,*
And *woo, and contract, in their Names,*   140
And as they *Christen*, use to marry 'em,
And, like their *Gossips*, answer for 'em,
Is not to give in Matrimony,
But Sell, and *Prostitute*, for Money,

Tis better then their own Betrothing,
Who often do't for worse then Nothing.
And when th' are at their own Dispose;
With greater Disadvantage, choose.
All this is Right! But for the Course,
You take to do't, by Fraud, or Force: 150
'Tis so Ridiculous, As soon,
As told, 'tis never to be done.
No more then *Setters can Betray*,
That tell what *Tricks* they are to Play.
Marriage, at best is but a Vow,
Which all men, either *Break*, or *Bow*,
Then what will those forbear to do,
Who *Perjure*, when they do but *Woo*?
Such as before hand, *Swear, and lye*,
For *Earnest* to their Treachery: 160
And rather then a Crime confess,
With greater strive to make it less.
Like Thieves, who after sentence past,
Maintain their Innocence to the last.
And when their Crimes were made appear,
As Plain as witnesses can swear.
Yet when the wretches come to Dy,
Will take upon their Deaths a Ly.
Nor are the virtues, you Confest,
T'your *Ghostly Father*, as you Guest,   170
So slight, as to be Justify'd,
By being, as shamefully, Deny'd.
As if you thought your word would Pass:
Poynt-blanc, on both sides, of a Case,
Or Credit were not to be lost,
B'a *Brave Knight Errant of the Post*.
That *Eats*, perfidiously, his *Word*,
And *swears his Ears, through a two Inch Board*,
Can own the same thing, and Disown,
And Perjure booty, *Pro and Con*.   180
Can make the *Gospel* serve his turn,
And help him out, to be forsworn.

175 not] not, D

When 'tis *lay'd hands upon, and kist.*
To be betray'd, and sold, like Christ.

These are the virtues, in whose name,
A Right to all the World, you claim:
And boldly challenge a Dominion,
In *Grace,* and *Nature,* o're all Women.
Of whom no less will satisfie,
Then all the Sex, your Tyranny.   190
Although you'l find it, a Hard Province,
With all your Crafty Frauds, and Covins,
To Govern such a num'rous Crew,
Who one by one now governs you,
For if you all were *Solomons,*
And *Wise* and *Great* as he was once,
You'l find Th' are able to subdue,
(*As they did him*) and baffle you.

And if you are impos'd upon,
'Tis by your own Temptation done: 200
That with your Ignorance invite,
And teach us how to use the slight.
For when we find y' are still most taken,
With false Attracts of our own making,
Swear that's a *Rose* and that a *Stone,*
Like Sots to us that laid it on,
And what we did but slightly prime,
Most ignorantly daub in Rhime:
You force us in our own defences,
To *Copy Beams* and *Influences,*   210
To lay *Perfections* on and *Graces,*
And draw *Attracts* upon our faces:
And in compliance to your wit,
Your own false Jewels counterfeit.
For by the Practice of those Arts,
We gain the greater share of Hearts,
And those deserve in reason most,
That greatest pains and study cost,
For great Perfections are like Heav'n,
Too rich a Present to be given: 220

Nor are those *Master-strokes of Beauty*,
To be perform'd, without *hard duty*.
Which when th' are nobly done and well,
The simple Natural excell.

How fair and sweet, *the Planted Rose*,
Beyond the *Wild* in Hedges grows!
For without Art the Noblest Seeds
Of Flow'rs, degenerate to Weeds:
How Dul and Rugged, e're 'tis Ground,
And Polish'd looks a Diamond!   230
Though *Paradise* were ere so fair,
It was not kept so, without Care.
The whole World without *Art*, and *Dress*,
Would be but one great *Wilderness*.
And Mankind but a Savage Heard,
For all that Nature has Conferd.
That do's but *Rough-hew*, and *Design*,
Leave *Art* to *Polish*, and *Refine*.

Though Women first were made for Men,
Yet Men were made for them agen: 240
For when (*out witted by his Wife*)
Man first turn'd *Tenant*, but, *for life*,
If Women had not Interven'd,
How soon had Mankind had an end?
And that it is in *Being* yet,
To us alone, you are *in Debt*.
Then where's your Liberty of Choyce,
And our unnatural No-voyce?
Since all the *Priviledge* you *Boast*,
And Falsly *usurp'd*, or *vainly lost*:   250
Is now our Right, to *whose Creation*,
You ow your *Happy Restoration*.
And if we had not weighty Cause
To not Appear, in making Laws,
We could, in spight of all your *Tricks*,
And *shallow, Formal, Politicks*;

Force you our *Managements* t'obey,
As we to yours (in shew) give way.
Hence 'tis, that while you vainly strive,
T'advance your *high Prerogative*,   260
You basely, after all your Braves,
Submit, and own your selves, our Slaves.
And cause we do not make it known
Nor Publickly our Intrests own
Like Sots, suppose we have no shares
In *Ordring you*, and *your Affairs*:
When all your Empire, and Command
You have from us, at *Second Hand*.
As if a *Pilot*, that appears
To sit still only, while he stear's: 270
And does not make a Noyse, and stir,
Like every Common *Mariner*:
Knew nothing of the *Card*, nor *Star*,
And did not Guide the *Man of war*:
Nor we, because we don't appeare
In *Councils*, do not govern there.
While like the Mighty *Prester John*
Whose Person, none dare's look upon:
But is Preserv'd in *Close Disguise*,
From being made *cheap* to *vulgar eye* :   280
W' Injoy as large a Pow'r, unseen,
To *Govern him*, as *He do's* men.
And in the Right of our *Pope Jone*,
Make *Emp'rors*, at our Feet, fall down.
Or *Jone the Pucel's* Braver Name,
Our Right to *Arms*, and *Conduct claime*
Who, though a *Spinster*, yet was Able
To serve *France*, for a *Grand Constable*.

We make and Execute *all Laws*,
Can *Judge the Judges*, and the *Cause*.   290
Prescribe all Rules, of *Right*, or *Wrong*,
To th' *Long-Robe*, and the *Longer Tongue*:
'Gainst which the world *has no Defence*,
But our more *Pow'rful Eloquence*.

257 Force] Force, *D*   260 *Prerogative*,] *Prerogative. D*

We Manage things of Greatest weight,
In all the world's *Affairs of State.*
Are Ministers in War, and Peace,
That sway *all Nations* how we Please,
We rule *all Churches,* and *their Flocks,*
Heretical, and Orthodox.   300
And are the *Heavenly vehicles,*
O'th' *Spirit, in all conventicles.*
By us is all *Commerce,* and *Trade,*
Improv'd, and *Manag'd,* and *Decay'd.*
For nothing can go of, so well,
Nor bears that Price, *as what we Sell.*
We Rule in ev'ry *Publique Meeting,*
And make Men do, what we Judge Fitting
Are Magistrates, in all great *Towns,*
Where Men do nothing, but *wear Gowns.*   310
We make the *Man of War strike Sail,*
And to our Braver Conduct *vail.*
And, when H' has chac'd his Enemies,
Submit to us, upon his Knees.
Is there an *Officer of State,*
Untimely Rais'd; or *Magistrate,*
That's *Haughty, and Imperious?*
He's but a *Jorny-man* to us.
That as he gives us Cause to Do't,
Can *keep him in,* or *turn him out.*   320

We are your *Guardians,* that *increase,*
Or *wast* your Fortunes, how we Please.
And as you Humour us, can Deal,
In all your Matters, *ill or well.*

Tis wee, that can Dispose alone,
Whether your *Heirs* shall be your *own.*
To whose Integrity, you must,
In spight of all your Caution, trust.
And 'less you *Fly beyond the Seas*:
Can fit you with what Heirs we Please.   330

313 has] ha's D   327 must,] must. D

And force you t'own 'em; Though Begotten
By *French Valets*, or *Irish Footmen*.
Nor can the Rigorousest Course,
Prevail, unless to make us worse.
Who still the harsher we are us'd,
Are Further off from being Reduc'd:
And scorn t'Abate, for any Ills,
The least *Puntillio of our Wills*.
Force do's but whet our wits to Apply
Arts, born with us, for Remedy: 340
Which all your Politicks as yet,
Have ne're been Able to Defeat:
For when y' have Try'd *all sorts of ways*
What Fools D'we make of you in Plays?
While all the Favors we Afford
Are but to Girt you with the Sword,
To Fight our Battels, in our steads
And have your Brains beat out o' your Heads,
Incounter in despite of Nature,
And fight at once, with Fire, and Water,   350
With Pyrats, Rocks, and Storms, and Seas,
Our Pride, and vanity t'appease.
Kill one another, and cut throats,
For our Good Graces, and best Thoughts,
To do your Exercise for Honor
And have your Brains beat out, the sooner,
Or crackt, as Learnedly, upon
Things that are never to be known,
And still appear the more Industrious
The more your Projects, are Prepostrous.   360
To Square the Circle of the Arts,
And Run stark-mad, to shew your Parts.
Expound the Oracle of Laws,
And turn 'em, which way, we see Cause.
To be our Solicitors, and Agents,
And stand for us, in all Ingagements.
And these are all the *Mighty Powers*,
You vainly Boast, to cry down ours

And what in real Value's wanting,
Supply with vapouring and Ranting: 370
Because your selves are Terrifyd,
And Stoop to one anothers Pride:
Believe we have as little Wit,
To be *Out-Hector'd*, and *Submit*:
By your *Example* Loose that Right,
In *Treatys*, which we Gain'd *in Fight*.
And Terrify'd into an Awe,
Pass on our selves a *Salique Law*:
Or, as some Nations use, Give Place,
And Truckle, to *your Mighty* Race: 380
Let Men usurp Th'unjust Dominion,
As if they were *the Better Women*.

FINIS

COMMENTARY

THE FIRST PART

CANTO I

THE ARGUMENT 1. *Hudibras*. The name is taken from Spenser, *Faerie Queene*, II. ii. 17:

> He that made Love unto the eldest Dame,
> Was hight Sir *Huddibras*, an hardy man;
> Yet not so good of deedes, as great of name,
> Which he by many rash adventures wan,
> Since errant armes to sew he first began;
> More huge in strength, then wise in workes he was,
> And reason with foole-hardize over ran;
> Sterne melancholy did his courage pas,
> And was for terrour more, all armd in shyning bras.

Butler's Hudibras, like Spenser's, is rash, foolhardy, and severe in temperament, and is subject to extremes of emotion. See Ian Jack, *Augustan Satire*, Oxford, 1952, p. 15. The existence of a legendary British king of the same name is coincidental (*Faerie Queene*, II. x. 25), though his name, with its suggestions of 'hubris' and 'brazen' may have come to Spenser's mind as he created an allegorical character who was partially the embodiment of these qualities.

CANTO I 3. *hard words*: (i) harsh words; (ii) cant words, used by the Puritans, of which 'jealousies and fears' are examples. Cf. Hobbes, *Leviathan*, II. xxix: 'When the spiritual power, moveth the members of a commonwealth. . . and by strange, and hard words suffocates their understanding, it must needs thereby distract the people, and either overwhelm the commonwealth with oppression, or cast it into the fire of a civil war.'

Jealousies: suspicions. 'Fears and jealousies were the new words which served to justify all indispositions and to excuse all disorders' (Clarendon, iv. 167). For further examples of this usage, see Clarendon, iv. 172, 239, 244.

4. *by the ears*: a proverbial phrase, originally used of animals fighting (*ODEP* 576; Tilley, E23).

10. *long-ear'd rout*. The Puritans were popularly described as having long ears. Cf. 'The Character of a Roundhead', *Rump*, i. 42:

> What Creature's this with his short hairs,
> His little band and huge long ears,
> That this new faith hath founded?

See also Cleveland, 'Character of a London Diurnal', 1644, 3–4.

14. *a Colonelling.* See Butler's note to I. i. 24.

16. *Mirrour of Knighthood*: the English title of a Spanish romance, *Espejo de Principes y Cavalleros*, by Diego Ortuñez de Calahorra, Pedro de la Sierra, and Marcos Martinez. The translation, which appeared between 1578 and 1601, was apparently popular among servants and country folk. Overbury writes of 'a Chamber-maide' that she 'is so carried away with the *Mirror of Knighthood*, she is many times resolv'd to runne out of her selfe, and become a lady errant' (*Miscellaneous Works*, 1890, p. 101). See also Beaumont and Fletcher, *Knight of the Burning Pestle*, II. ii. 50.

19. *put up*: submit to, suffer quietly.

22. *Chartel*: 'In such places as publique Combats were permitted by Princes, the custome was that the parties agreed to fight, should challenge one the other by some instrument in writing, which they commonlie call a *Cartel*' (Segar, *Booke of Honor and Armes*, 1590, I. xiii. 16).

24. *swaddle*: (i) to bind (an infant) in swaddling clothes; (ii) to beat soundly.

38. *Mountaigne, playing with his Cat, etc.* See Montaigne, 'Apologie de Raymond Sebond', *Essais*, II. xii, ed. Leclerc, 2 vols. Paris, 1908, i. 416.

51. *speak Greek.* Cf. *Notebooks*, p. 286.

60. *To flourish most in barren ground.* A gibe at the stupidity of scholars, and an allusion to the idea that Hebrew was the first and natural language of men. It was thought that a child, growing up away from human society, would naturally speak Hebrew. See Browne, *Pseudodoxia*, v. xxiii. 2.

65–186. The knight's learning is described under the headings of Logic, Rhetoric, Mathematics, and Philosophy, which correspond roughly to the Trivium, the Quadrivium, and Philosophies which were the basis of education in the universities of the time. Hudibras is typical of the early Presbyterians, many of whom were university men. Ralpho resembles the unlettered independent sectarians of the mid-seventeenth century who laid claim to divine inspiration.

65. *Logick.* Cf. *Notebooks*, p. 293: 'Logitians cannot teach men solid, and substantiall Reason, but only little Tricks and evasions, that are worse then nothing.' The knight demonstrates his skill in logic in the debate on Presbyterian synods (I. iii. 1251 ff.).

72. *a Man's no Horse, etc.* Aristotle uses this proposition to demonstrate relative properties (*Topica*, v. 1). The lines that follow (ll. 72–76) satirize the kind of topics set for disputation in the universities. A commonplace book in the library of St. John's College, Cambridge, formerly belonging to a sizar who entered the college in 1685, contains a list of themes for disputation, including 'Which is preferable, an ignorant or a learned wife' and 'Whether the eloquence or wisdom of the emperor Caesar ought to be preferred' (K. M. Burton, 'Cambridge Exercises in the Seventeenth Century', *The Eagle*, January 1951, 251). A disputation took place at Cambridge in the presence of

James I on the proposition, derived from Empiricus, 'Whether dogs could make syllogisms' (Thomas Ball, *Life of the Renowned Dr. Preston*, 1885, p. 23).

73. *Buzzard*: a worthless or ignorant person (colloquial).

74. *Owl*: a stupid person who appears wise (colloquial).

75. *Calf*: a stupid person, a dolt; *Goose*: a simpleton (colloquial).

76. *Committee-men and Trustees*: men appointed by Parliament for the sequestration and sale of lands owned by the Church and by royalist 'delinquents'. Many such committees were set up during the interregnum. For example, in July 1651 'estates forfeited to the Commonwealth for treason' were transferred into the possession of parliamentary trustees, and later sold to produce revenue for Parliament (Firth and Rait, II. 520–45). The trustees were frequently accused of abusing their authority to their own pecuniary advantage. See note to III. ii. 60.

80. *In mood and figure*: in due logical form.

89. *For all a Rhetoricians Rules, etc.* Cf. 'A Mathematician' (*Characters*, p. 79): 'All the Figures he draws are no better, for the most Part, than those in Rhetoric, that serve only to call certain Rotines and Manners of Speech by insignificant Names, but teach nothing.'

91. *His ordinary Rate of Speech, etc.* In the following lines, Butler satirizes both the scholastic manner of preaching, in vogue chiefly among the Anglicans (ll. 93–106), and the style used by the Puritans (ll. 109–14). The Anglican style was often highly formal and included a great many Greek, Latin, and Hebrew terms, while the Puritan style, though less academic, included a characteristic jargon of compound English words. Robert South castigates both in a sermon preached in 1660: 'Wit in divinity is nothing else, but sacred truths suitably expressed. It is not shreds of Latin or Greek, nor a *Deus dixit*, and a *Deus benedixit*, nor those little quirks, or divisions into the ὅτι, the διότι, and the καθότι, or the *egress*, *regress*, and *progress*, and other such stuff, (much like the style of a lease,) that can properly be called wit . . . so neither can the whimsical cant of *issues*, *products*, *tendencies*, *breathings*, *indwellings*, *rollings*, *recumbencies*, and scriptures misapplied, be accounted divinity' ('The Scribe Instructed', *Sermons*, 1823, iii. 33–35).

98. *Like Fustian heretofore on Sattin*. In the reign of Henry VIII the fashion was introduced of decorating doublet and hose with slashings lined with brightly coloured satin. Apart from the slashings, the garments were made of fustian, a tougher, cheaper cloth. The fashion began to disappear in the reign of James I (C. H. Ashdown, *British Costume*, 1929).

104. *A Leash*: a set of three. Cerberus, the dog who guarded the gate of Hades, was said to have three heads.

115. *the Orator*. See Plutarch, *Demosthenes*, xi. For another version of this passage, see *Satires*, p. 455.

120. *Tycho Brahe*: the Danish astronomer (1546–1601) and collaborator with

Kepler. He discovered a new star in the constellation of Cassiopeia and drew up the 'Tychonic' system of the universe.

Erra Pater. An almanac appeared early in the sixteenth century under the title *The Pronostycacion for ever of Erra Pater, a Jewe borne in Jewery, a doctour in Astronomye and Physicke, Profytable to kepe the bodye in health.* It contained predictions for the future, mainly concerning the weather, and medical advice based on astrological observations. Such books continued to appear until the end of the seventeenth century. They were sold as chapbooks and were extremely popular.

121. *For he by Geometrick scale, etc.* One of the duties of a Justice of the Peace was the inspection of weights and measures. 'A Justice of the Peace . . . is most expert in the Cases of light Bread, Highways, and getting of Bastards' (*Characters*, pp. 83–84).

130. *implicit Faith*: a term of scholastic theology (*fides implicita*), used in contradistinction to 'explicit faith'. The latter implies acceptance of a doctrine with full knowledge of all that is logically involved in it. Implicit faith implies acceptance of a doctrine on the authority of another person and without question; doctrine so accepted generally rests on the authority of the Church. See Aquinas, *Summa Theologica*, 1911–25, II. ii. ii. 5. 39.

132. *For every why he had a wherefore.* Proverbial (*ODEP* 707; Tilley, W331).

134. *words and termes.* Cf. *Notebooks*, p. 340: 'Those who imploy their Studies upon Fancy and words, do commonly abate as much in their Reason, and Judgments, as they improve the other way.'

139. *His Notions fitted things, etc.* 'Notions are but Pictures of things in the Imagination of Man, and if they agree with their originals in Nature, they are true, and if not False. And yet some Men are so unwary in their Thoughts, as to confound them and mistake the one for the other, as if the Picture of a Man were really the Person for whom it was drawn' (*Notebooks*, p. 284).

143. *Acts*: used in the philosophical sense of 'essences' (Latin *actus*). The notion is derived through the schoolmen from Aristotle, who believed that an object had 'accidents' (quantity, qualities, extention in space and time) and a more profound reality or 'essence' without which its accidents could not exist (Aristotle, *Categories* v). For the source of Butler's note see Seneca, *Epist. Morales*, lxxxii. 24: 'Quaedam inutilia et inefficacia ipsa subtilitas reddit.'

147. *Where Truth in Person does appear.* For the source of Butler's note see Aristotle, *Metaphysica*, II. i. 993ᵇ30.

148. *Like words congeal'd, etc.* See Plutarch's essay on Progress in Virtue (*Moralia*, 1927, i. 421); Castiglione, *Cortegiano* (Florence, 1929, II. lv. 222); Rabelais, *Pantagruel* IV. lvi (*Œuvres*, 6 vols. Paris, 1868–1903, II. 466); *NQ*, 5th ser. iii. 505; iv. 313, 475.

152. *Irrefragable*: Alexander of Hales (?1175–1245), who was known as the *Doctor Irrefragabilis*. He was born in Gloucestershire and studied in Paris,

where he became famous as a teacher. His most celebrated work, the *Summa Theologiæ*, was a compilation of his own writings and those of his fellow Franciscan theologians of Paris.

156. *Rope of Sand*: an incoherent argument (*ODEP* 548; Tilley, R174).

157. *fit for skull, etc.* Cf. the proverbial expression 'his cockloft is unfurnished' (*ODEP* 101; Tilley, C500).

161. *He could raise Scruples, etc.* Cf. Bacon, *Advancement of Learning*: 'This same unprofitable subtilty or curiosity is . . . in the manner or method of handling of a knowledge; which amongst them [the schoolmen] was this; upon every particular position or assertion to frame objections, and to those objections, solutions' (*Works*, 1857–74, iii. 286).

163. *As if Divinity had catch'd, etc.* Cf. 'A Zealot': 'He is always troubled with small Scruples, which his Conscience catches like the Itch, and the rubbing of these is both his Pleasure and his Pain: But for Things of greater Moment he is unconcerned' (*Characters*, p. 178). 'Catched' was formerly in normal use for 'caught'.

165. *like a Mountebank, etc.* Cf. 'The Case of King Charles I': 'Thus, like right Mountebanks, you are fain to wound and poison your selves to cheat others, who cannot but wonder at the Confidence of your Imposture' (*Satires*, p. 370).

170. *alwayes leave a Scar behind.* Cf. Bacon, loc. cit.: 'And such is their [the schoolmen's] method, that rests . . . upon particular confutations and solutions of every scruple, cavillation, and objection; breeding for the most part one question as fast it solveth another.'

171. *He knew the seat of Paradise, etc.* For the source of Butler's note see Raleigh, *History of the World*, 1614, I. i. iii. vii. 43.

178. *high Dutch Interpreter.* It was generally held that Adam and Eve spoke Hebrew (see note to l. 60, above), but Johannes Goropius Becanus (1519–72), the physician to Queen Maria of Hungary, maintained that the original language was High Dutch or Teutonic. See Goropius, *Origines Antuerpianæ*, Antwerp, 1569; *Hermathena* (*Opera*, Antwerp, 1580, 204); Jonson, *Alchemist*, II. i. 84.

179. *If either of them had a Navel.* See Browne, *Pseudodoxia*, v. v.

180. *Who first made Musick malleable.* For the source of Butler's note see Macrobius, *Somnium Scipionis*, II. ii.

182. *cloven Feet, or none at all.* God's words to the serpent after the Fall of Adam, 'Upon thy belly shalt thou go' (Gen. iii. 14), raised the question as to how the serpent had propelled itself before the Fall. See Browne, *Religio Medici*, i. 10; *Pseudodoxia*, v. xxii. 19.

189. *Presbyterian true blew.* Blue was proverbially the colour of constancy (*ODEP* 672; Tilley, T542–3); hence the expression 'true blue' came to mean 'unwavering'. Butler may also allude to the colour adopted by the Scottish Presbyterian Covenanters, who wore it in opposition to the Royalist red.

There are many allusions to this custom in the ballads of the period, for example *Sir John Berkenhead Reviv'd, or a Satyr Against the late Rebellion*, 1681, p. 1:

> Then down went *King* and *Bishops* too;
> On goes the holy *Wirk*,
> Betwixt them and the *Brethren blew*,
> T'advance the *Crown* and *Kirk*.

191. *Errant*: (i) arrant, thoroughgoing; (ii) 'wandering', as in 'knight errant'. The term 'Saints' was applied to Puritans of nearly all sects, since they claimed to be the elect of God: 'The Saints, Brethren, godly, wel-affected, rod[e] out to meet thee' ('John Audland's Letter', *Satires*, p. 333).

192. *true Church Militant*. As well as punning on the word 'militant', Butler here alludes to the fundamental controversy between Presbyterians and Anglicans as to which church could be regarded as 'true', or justifiable in doctrine and government by the word of the Gospels. See Neal, ii. 44.

199. *Call Fire and Sword and Desolation, etc.* Cf. Tacitus, *Agricola*, 30: 'Ubi solitudinem faciunt, pacem appellant.' 'The word *Thorough* as defining the policy of the government from 1633 onwards, appears first in the correspondence between Laud and Wentworth. "As for the State," says Laud, writing to Wentworth, Sept. 9, 1633, "indeed, my Lord, I am for *Thorough* . . . and it is impossible for me to go Thorough alone." ' (Masson, *Life of Milton*, 1881, i. 668).

201. *Which alwayes must be carry'd on.* 'Carrying on the work' was a phrase used by the Puritans to describe the furtherance of their religious plans. '[They] humbly sue for the Trust, and beg for the Honour *to carry on the Work*' ('Speeches in the Rump Parliament', *Satires*, p. 319).

211. *That with more care keep holy-day, etc.* Cf. 'An Hypocritical Nonconformist', *Characters*, p. 22: '[He] makes his Devotions rather Labours than Exercises, and breaks the Sabbath by taking too much Pains to keep it.' In Laud's time the Anglican clergy encouraged the people to take part in recreations after evening prayer on Sundays, lest they should 'go either into tipling houses, and there upon their Ale-benches talke of matters of the Church or State, or else into Conventicles' (Bishop of Bath and Wells, letter to Laud, quoted in Prynne, *Canterburies Doome*, 1646, p. 151). The Puritans, however, prohibited the traditional recreations on Sundays and declared certain occupations illegal. See Firth and Rait, ii. 1162.

213. *Compound for Sins, etc.* Cf. 'A Zealot', *Characters*, p. 178.

219. *Free-will they one way disavow, etc.* '[He] is really made up of nothing but Contradictions; denies free Will, and yet will endure Nothing but his own Will in all the Practice of his Life' ('An Hypocritical Nonconformist', *Characters*, p. 22).

225. *Quarrel with minc'd Pies, etc.* The Puritans condemned the traditional celebration of Christmas. Their efforts to abolish this and other festivals culminated in a Parliamentary Ordinance of 1647, in which they were declared

illegal (Firth and Rait, i. 954). The passing of this ordinance gave rise to riots (Gardiner, iv. 45–46) and was lamented in popular ballads, such as 'The World is Turned Upside Down', Anon., 1646 (reprinted in Rollins, *Cavalier and Puritan*, N.Y., 1923, p. 161).

228. *through the nose.* The Puritan clergy adopted a characteristic nasal tone of voice which they used especially when preaching. Robert South complains in 1660 that this 'speaking through the nose . . . cannot so properly be called *preaching*, as *toning* of a sermon' ('The Scribe Instructed', *Sermons,* 1823, iii. 37).

230. *Like Mahomet's, were Ass and Widgeon.* Mahomet was said to have been taken to heaven on a kind of mule known as an alborak (Topsel, *Four-footed Beasts,* 1658, p. 26). The legend of the pigeon that would 'pick a pease out of his eare' is told by Scot (XII. xv. 252). Butler substitutes 'Ass and Widgeon' for 'alborak and pigeon', since the former were both colloquialisms for 'fools'.

251. *Heart-breakers*: long, curled locks of hair, otherwise known as 'love-locks'.

255. *It was Canonick, etc.* The custom of allowing the hair or beard to remain uncut until the defeat of an enemy is common among primitive tribes. See Tacitus, *Germania* xxxi; *Historiae* iv. 61; Suetonius, *Julius,* 67.

258. *Cordeliere*: a Franciscan friar of the strict rule; so called from the knotted cord which they wear round the waist.

279. *Taliacotius*: Gaspare Tagliacozzo (1545–99), Professor of Anatomy at Bologna, and the first person to practise plastic surgery scientifically. He described his methods in 1586, in a letter to Gerolamo Mercuriale, published a year later in the second edition of Mercuriale's *De Decoratione.* Tagliacozzo published a more detailed account of them in his *De Curtorum Chirurgia per Insitionem*, Venice, 1597.

283. *Nock*: the cleft in the buttocks. The 'Key to *Hudibras*' (*Posth. Works,* ii. 289) erroneously explains this word as an allusion to Cromwell.

284. *Off dropt the Sympathetick Snout.* 'There was a certaine Lord, or Nobleman of Italy, that by chance lost his nose in a fight or combate, this party was counselled by his Physicians to take one of his slaves, and make a wound in his arme, and immediately to ioyne his wounded nose to the wounded arme of the slave, and to binde it fast, for a season, untill the flesh of the one was united and assimulated unto the other. The Noble Gentleman got one of his slaves to consent, for a large promise of liberty and reward; the double flesh was made all one, and a collop or gobbet of flesh was cut out of the slaves arme, and fashioned like a nose unto the Lord, and so handled by the Chirur-gion, that it served for a naturall nose. The slave being healed and rewarded, was manumitted or set at liberty, and away he went to Naples. It happened, that the slave fell sicke and dyed, at which instant, the Lords nose did gangre-nate and rot' (*Doctor Fludds Answer unto M. Foster,* 1631, II. vii. 132). Butler again satirizes beliefs in sympathetic magic in I. ii. 223–38.

287. *as Æneas bore his Sire, etc.* Virgil, *Aeneid,* ii. 705–29.

297. *White-pot*: a milk pudding, formerly eaten in Devonshire, made from eggs, flour, raisins, and sugar, spiced and boiled with milk or cream.

303. *Buff*: a stout kind of leather made of ox-hide, generally used for military dress.

308. *siege of Bullen, etc.* At the siege of Boulogne Henry VIII led the British troops in person. There may also be an allusion to Henry VIII's courtship of Anne Boleyn.

313. *Black-puddings.* The eating of black pudding was implicitly forbidden by Levitical law. See note to III. ii. 321.

325. *And though Knights Errant, etc.* Cf. *Don Quixote*, I. II. ii: 'For though I passed over many [bookes], yet did I never finde recorded in any, that Knights errant did ever eate, but by meere chance and adventure, or in some costly banquets that were made for them, and all the other daies they past over with hearbes and rootes: and though it is to be understood that they could not live without meate . . . it is likewise to bee understood, that spending the greater part of their lives in Forrests and desarts, and that too without a Cook, that their most ordinary meats were but course and rusticall.'

327. *Deserts*: a favourite word among writers of chivalric romance. Ralph, in *The Knight of the Burning Pestle*, instructs his squire to 'call all forests and heaths "deserts" ' (I. iii. 79). See also note to l. 325 above.

329. *Belly-timber*: food, provisions (a term formerly in normal use).

340. *Trunk-hose*: a kind of breeches, covering the hips and upper thighs. They were extremely full and were often stuffed with wool and other padding.

344. *Nuncheons*: a light refreshment originally taken in the afternoon; a lunch.

368. *Warrants.* Warrants for arrest and search warrants were issued by Justices of the Peace (Blackstone, IV. xxi. 289).

Exigents: 'a writ commanding the sheriff to summon the defendant to appear and deliver up himself upon pain of outlawry' (*OED*).

370. *Sergeant Bum*: a bailiff employed in arrests, generally known as the bum-bailiff or bum. He was so called because he was always at the debtor's back or caught him in the rear. Butler describes a similar officer as 'laying his authority, like a knighthood on the shoulder' ('A Catchpole', *Characters*, p. 204).

371. *ta'ne possession.* Cf. Jonson, *Epicoene*, IV. v. 99:

Daw: But is he arm'd, as you say?
True: Arm'd? did you ever see a fellow, set out to take possession?
Daw: I, sir.
True: That may give you some light, to conceive of him.

Gifford comments on this passage: 'When estates were litigated, or, as was too frequently the case formerly, transferred to a hungry favourite, this was

330 *Commentary*

a service of some danger; and the new owner set forth with his attendants and friends well armed' (Jonson, *Works*, 1875, iii. 435).

377. *Dudgeon*: originally a kind of wood (ash or box) used to make the handles of knives and daggers; hence a dagger made of dudgeon.

385. *It had been Prentice to a Brewer, etc.* The association of Cromwell or his parents with brewing, for which there is no known evidence, is frequently mentioned by hostile propagandists and ballad writers (Heath, *Flagellum*, 1665, p. 8; Dugdale, *Short View*, 1681, p. 459). The *Second Narrative of the late Parliament*, 1658 (*Harleian Miscellany*, 1808–13, iii. 481), describes Pride as 'some time an honest brewer in London'.

424. *Spaniard whipt.* 'A *Spaniard*, under the Lash, made a Point of Honour of it not to mend his pace for the Saving of his Carcass: and so march'd his Stage out, with as much Gravity as if he had been upon a Procession' (L'Estrange, *Fables and Storyes Moralized . . . Second Part*, 1699, cxlii. 132). See also John Taylor, 'Bull, Beare and Horse' (*Works*, 3rd Coll. 1876, p. 41).

426. *griev'd to touch the Ground.* Cf. Cervantes, *Don Quixote*, I. 1. iv: 'Rozinante . . . began to trot on with so good a will, as she seemed not to touch the ground.'

431. *as that Beast would kneel and stoop, etc.* Butler confuses Caesar's horse with Bucephalus, the horse of Alexander the Great, which, according to Diodorus Siculus, would kneel down for its master to mount (Diodorus, XVII. lxxvi). Butler was familiar with this legend (*Satires*, p. 427).

439. *strutting*: protruding, standing out.

441. *Pannel*: a piece of cloth placed under the saddle to prevent the horse's back from being galled.

447. *For Hudibras wore but one Spur, etc.* Cf. *Gratiae Ludentes: Jests from the Universitie*, by H. L., *Oxen*, 1628, p. 84: 'A Scholler beeing jeer'd on the way for wearing but one Spurre, said that if one side of his horse went on, it was not likely that the other would stay behinde.' See *NQ*, 1st ser. ii. 68.

450. *Hang an Arse*: 'hold back' (*OED*).

451. *A Squire he had whose name was Ralph, etc.* The squire's name may have been taken from that of the hero of *The Knight of the Burning Pestle*. The 'Key to *Hudibras*' identifies Ralph as '*Isaac Robinson*, Squire to *Hudibras*; and a zealous Botcher in *Moorfields*, who, in the time of the Rebellion in Forty One, was always contriving some new Quirpo-cut of Church-Government' (*Posth. Works*, i, n.p.). This identification is almost certainly erroneous, since Butler himself describes the original Ralpho as the clerk to a West Country knight. See Appendix A and Quintana, 'The Butler–Oxenden Correspondence', *MLN* xlviii (1933), 4. Several of Ralpho's characteristics are also attributed to Butler's Characters of 'A Taylor', 'An Hypocritical Nonconformist', 'An Hermetic Philosopher', 'An Anabaptist', and 'A Fanatic'. It is significant that, while Hudibras is a knight and an educated man, Ralpho is a tailor.

The Presbyterian leaders were generally men of learning, whereas many of the sectarian preachers were illiterate tradesmen.

457. *Rhyme the Rudder is of Verses, etc.* Cf. 'A Small Poet', *Characters*, p. 51.

461. *The mighty Tyrian Queen, etc.* See Virgil, *Aeneid*, i. 367–8.

465. *cross-legg'd Knights.* It was a popular belief that the figures on the tombs of Crusaders were always depicted with their legs crossed. Tailors used to sit cross-legged at their work. See 'A Taylor', *Characters*, p. 123.

466. *Fam'd for their faith.* Cf. 'A Taylor', loc. cit.: 'He lives much more by his Faith than good Works; for he gains more by trusting and believing in one that pays him at long Running, than six that he works for, upon an even Accompt, for ready Money.'

470. *the bold Trojan Knight, etc.* See Virgil, *Aeneid*, vi. 187 ff. 'Hell' was the colloquial term for the waste-box under the tailor's counter, into which he threw the pieces of cloth which remained after the process of cutting out clothes (cf. 'A Taylor', *Characters*, p. 123).

472. *Golden Bough.* See Virgil, *Aeneid*, vi. 136–41.

476. *Gifts*: a term used by the sectarians to signify 'divine inspiration', taken originally from 1 Cor. xii. 1, 4. See also 'A Fanatic', *Characters*, p. 85.

New light: i.e. divine revelation. Brian Walton writes of 'those who bragg of their *new Lights*, and daily increase amongst us, to reject all Scripture as uselesse' (*The Considerator Considered*, 1659, p. 168).

477. *A Liberal Art, etc.* 'His Interest has always obliged him to decry human Learning, Reason, and Sense; he and his Brethren have with long and diligent Practice found out an Expedient to make that Dullness . . . pass for *Dispensations, Light, Grace*, and *Gifts*' ('An Hypocritical Nonconformist', *Characters*, p. 19).

479. *Token*: (i) an act to demonstrate divine power; (ii) 'a stamped piece of metal, having the general appearance of a coin, issued as a medium of exchange by a private company or person' (*OED*). A writer in 1638 alludes to 'Retailers of victuals and small wares . . . using their owne tokens', and records that 'in and about London there are above three thousand that one with another cast yearely five pound a piece of leaden tokens' (Sir Robert Cotton, *Abstract of the records of the tower*, p. 25).

481. *Like Commendation Nine-pence, etc.* Ninepenny pieces were formerly bent and given to a sweetheart as a love token. See Gay, *Shepherd's Week*, v. 129.

487. *as he got it freely, etc.* Cf. 'A Small Poet', *Characters*, p. 48.

491. *hem and cough, etc.* Cf. 'John Audland's Letter', *Satires*, p. 332; 'A Factious Member', *Characters*, p. 124.

492. *Snuff*: a candle-end.

495. *For as of Vagabonds, etc.* Proverbial (*ODEP* 30; Tilley, B228).

502. *For Spiritual Trades to cousen by.* 'His false Lights are a Kind of *Deceptio visus*, with which he casts a Mist . . . before the Eyes of his Customers, that they may take no Notice of the Imperfections and Infirmities of his spotted and stained Stuffs, until it is too late' ('A Shopkeeper', *Characters*, p. 149).

505. *To make them dip themselves, etc.* Ralpho, as a Baptist, believes in the efficacy only of adult baptism by immersion in water, as practised by the primitive Church. Featley claimed that the Baptists 'have rebaptised hundreds of men and women together in the twilight, in Rivelets, and some armes of the Thames, dipping them over head and elsewhere ears' (*The Dippers Dipt*, 1645, 'To the Reader').

506. *Dirty pond.* 'He does not like the use of Water in his Baptism, as it falls from Heaven in Drops, but as it runs out of the Bowels of the Earth, or stands putrefying in a dirty Pond' ('An Anabaptist', *Characters*, p. 163).

510. *Bag-pipe-drone.* Probably an allusion to Hobbes's Answer to Davenant's Preface to *Gondibert* (1651): 'A man, enabled to speak wisely from the principles of nature and his own meditation, loves rather to be thought to speak by inspiration, like a Bagpipe' (Spingarn, *Critical Essays*, ii. 59). There is also an allusion to the nasal tone of voice adopted by the Puritan preachers (see note to 1. i. 228).

512. *Trunk*: a speaking-tube.

520. *three or four-legg'd Oracle.* The priestess of Apollo at Delphi sat on a three-legged stool, placed over the hole in the earth from which the oracle issued. The 'four-legg'd oracle' is the chair occupied by the Pope when making *ex cathedra* pronouncements.

523. *For mystick Learning, wondrous able, etc.* The following lines (523–64), describing Ralpho's addiction to the hermetic philosophy, have many similarities with Butler's Character of 'An Hermetic Philosopher' (*Characters*, pp. 97–108). Although the latter has been seen by some critics as a portrait of Thomas Vaughan (see *DNB*), it is more probably a satire on the hermetic philosophers generally, of whom Vaughan was a prominent follower. They take their name from Hermes Trismegistus, a legendary figure who was supposed to have been a contemporary of Moses and the author of the *Hermetica*, a collection of mystical writings composed in the form of Platonic dialogues. The *Hermetica* are in fact the work of many hands, and were composed at various times during the first three centuries A.D. They contain a mixture of neo-Platonism, the mysticism of the *Cabala*, and Judaism. They enjoyed a considerable vogue during the Renaissance, when they were welcomed as a relief from the prevailing Aristotelianism, and were revered for the occult wisdom they appeared to embody. Ficino translated the hermetic writings into Latin in 1471, Pico della Mirandola preached their doctrines with enthusiasm, and they became widely known through Cornelius Agrippa's *De Occulta Philosophia* and the mystical writings of Paracelsus and Jacob Boehme. The chief exponents of these doctrines in England were Robert Fludd and Thomas Vaughan. See Frances A. Yates, *Giordano Bruno and the Hermetic Tradition*, 1964.

524. *Talisman.* Talismans were made in an attempt to embody the spiritual power of the stars in material objects. They were manufactured from metals, stones, or other materials thought to contain the influence of particular stars, and were often imprinted with symbols representing the stars whose influence was to be invoked. See Yates, pp. 45 ff.

Cabal. The *Cabala* (meaning literally 'tradition') is the name given to a literature which appeared in the Middle Ages and which was thought to be a record of Jewish wisdom handed down orally from the time of Moses. One of the chief works of the *Cabala*, the *Zohar*, was written in Spain in the thirteenth century. Like the *Hermetica*, it was revered for its apparent antiquity. Its mysticism and concern with magic have similarities with hermetic beliefs, and the two were brought together by Pico della Mirandola. Subsequently hermetic and cabalistic doctrines were frequently amalgamated, notably by Cornelius Agrippa. See Yates, pp. 84 ff.; J. L. Blau, *Christian Interpretation of the Cabala*, New York, 1944.

526. *As far as Adam's first green breeches.* Both the *Hermetica* and the *Cabala* were thought to originate from the time of Moses. Thomas Vaughan describes them as 'an Art wherein the physics of Adam and the patriarchs consisted' (*Magia Adamica, Works*, p. 152). The phrase 'green breeches' is taken from the Geneva version of Gen. iii. 7, where Adam and Eve are said to have 'sowed figge tree leaves together, and made themselves breeches'. See also 'An Hermetic Philosopher', *Characters*, p. 97.

527. *Intelligences*: the spirits who were thought to preside over and rotate the planets. Ficino and his followers developed the notion (ultimately Aristotelian) that each planet was the domain of a good or bad angel, and that, through the use of spells and incantations, these intelligences could be used to influence human temperament and actions. See D. P. Walker, *Spiritual and Demonic Magic*, 1958, pp. 34–35, 45–47. Agrippa describes an intelligence as 'an intelligible substance, free from all gross and putrifying mass of a body, immortall, insensible, assisting all, having Influence over all; and the nature of all intelligencies, spirits and Angels is the same' (*Occult Philosophy*, trans. J. F., 1651, III. xvi. 390).

528. *Idea's*: Platonic ideas, found in the 'intelligible world' (see note to I. i. 530). These were identified by the hermetic philosophers with the good and evil angels (see Yates, p. 334).

Atomes. One of the many traditions of thought introduced into hermeticism was the atomism of Democritus, which became familiar through Lucretius' *De Rerum Natura*. See Yates, pp. 224–5, 319.

Influences: the power of the stars over human character and conduct. 'Every power and vertue is above, from God, from the Intelligences and Stars, who can neither erre nor do evill' (Agrippa, III. xxxix. 469).

530. *Th' Intelligible world.* 'There is a three-fold World, Elementary, Celestiall, and Intellectuall, and every inferior is governed by its superior, and receiveth the influence of the vertues thereof, so that the very original, and chief

Worker of all doth by Angels, the Heavens, Stars, Elements, Animals, Plants, Metals, and Stones convey from himself the vertues of his Omnipotency upon us, for whose service he made, and created all these things' (Agrippa, 1. i. 1). See also Yates, p. 121; note to 11. iii. 225 below.

532. *As learn'd as the Wild Irish are.* See Butler's note. Camden describes in some detail the superstitions of the Irish (*Britannia*, 1610, pp. 145–6).

533. *Sir Agrippa*: Heinrich Cornelius Agrippa von Nettesheim (1486–1535), hermetic philosopher and cabalist. His *De Occulta Philosophia* was a popular work which did much to disseminate hermetic beliefs. It was completed in 1510, but remained unpublished until 1533, appearing after the publication of his *De Incertitudine et Vanitate Scientiarum* (1530), a work in which he renounced his former faith in magic and professed a kind of scepticism. An English translation of the *De Occulta Philosophia* by 'J. F.' appeared in 1651. See D. P. Walker, *Spiritual and Demonic Magic*, pp. 90 ff.; J. L. Blau, *Christian Interpretation of the Cabala*, pp. 79–85.

535. *Anthroposophus*: Thomas Vaughan (1622–66), author of *Anthroposophia Theomagica*. He was the twin brother of the poet and mystic Henry Vaughan, and author of a number of mystical works in the hermetic tradition, most of which appeared under the pseudonym of Eugenius Philalethes. He practised alchemy and died from the fumes of mercury while engaged in an alchemical projection. See E. K. Chambers, Introduction to *Poems of Henry Vaughan*, 2 vols., 1896, 11. xxxiii–lvi.

Floud: Robert Fludd (1574–1637), English physician and hermetic philosopher. His major work was a vast mystical interpretation of creation, *Utriusque cosmi, maioris scilicet et minoris, metaphysica, physica atque technica historia* (1617–19). He also wrote two lesser works defending the Rosicrucians. See Thorndike, *Magic and Experimental Science*, 8 vols. New York, 1923–58, vii. 439 ff.; Yates, pp. 403 ff.

536. *Jacob Behmen*: Jacob Boehme (1575–1624), German philosopher, mystic, and alchemist. His major works were translated into English by John Sparrow in the middle of the seventeenth century. J. J. Stoudt's *Sunrise to Eternity* gives a full account of Boehme's life and ideas (Philadelphia, 1957).

537. *Amulet and Charm.* 'In what things therefore there is an excess of any quality, or property, as heat, cold, boldness, fear, sadness, anger, love . . . these things do very much move, and provoke to such a quality, passion or Vertue. . . . It is said, that the right eye of a Frog helps the soreness of a mans right eye, and the left eye thereof, helps the soreness of his left eye, if they be hanged about his neck in a Cloth' (Agrippa, 1. xv. 34–35).

539. *Rosy-Crucian Lore.* The occult wisdom, said to be guarded by the members of the secret society of the Rosicrucians, closely resembles the beliefs of the hermetic philosophers. The society was supposedly founded in the fifteenth century by one Christian Rosenkreuz, and is first mentioned in a manifesto, the *Fama Fraternitatis*, published in Germany in 1614. Since its members were forbidden to reveal either their beliefs or their membership, very

little is known of them, and it has even been thought that they did not exist as an organized brotherhood. Thomas Vaughan describes their knowledge as 'an art that is a perfect, entire map of the creation, that can lead me directly to the knowledge of the true God, by which I can discover those universal essences which are subordinate to Him—an Art that is no way subject to evil and by which I can attain to all the secrets and mysteries in Nature' (*Magia Adamica, Works*, p. 152). See P. Arnold, *Histoire des Rose-Croix*, Paris, 1955, pp. 166–7; Yates, pp. 407–16.

540. *Verè adeptus.* Many of the hermetic philosophers were also alchemists, since their claims were not purely religious but also practical. 'Adept' was the term applied to one who had penetrated into their secret wisdom.

541. *understood the speech of Birds.* The Rosicrucians were thought to understand the languages of birds and beasts ('An Hermetic Philosopher', *Characters*, p. 100).

543. *Parrots*: i.e. the hermetic philosophers, who 'talk, like Parrots, what they do not understand' (Butler's note to 1. i. 530).

545. *Member*: i.e. of the secret fraternity of Rosicrucians.

546. *Rope, and Walk, Knave, walk*: words commonly taught to parrots. See Lyly, *Midas*, 1. ii (*Works*, 1902, iii. 120); *NQ*, 9th ser. vii. 292.

547. *extract numbers out of matter.* '*Severinus Boethius* saith, that all things which were first made by the nature of things in its first Age, seem to be formed by the proportion of numbers ... Numbers therefore are endowed with great and sublime vertues' (Agrippa, II. ii. 170). See also 'An Hermetic Philosopher', *Characters*, p. 102.

548. *keep them in a Glass, etc.* Cf. 'An Hermetic Philosopher', *Characters*, p. 107.

554. *First Matter*: the universal substance, according to Hermetic beliefs, out of which all things were originally created. Thomas Vaughan describes a vision in which he beheld first matter (*Lumen de Lumine, Works*, p. 247).

557. *The Chaos.* Thomas Vaughan describes the chaos as 'that limbus or huddle of matter wherein all things were so strangely contained' before the creation of the universe (*Anthroposophia Theomagica, Works*, p. 18).

559. *Not that of Past-board, etc.* Cycles of religious plays depicting the creation of the world were presented in the Middle Ages by the trade guilds on sacred festivals. Such performances were no longer given in the late seventeenth century, but the plays survived in the repertoire of the puppet-showmen and were performed in the puppet-theatres at Bartholomew Fair. The pasteboard 'chaos' was presumably a scene from such performances. A playbill of Queen Anne's reign advertises, 'during the time of Bartholomew Fair', 'a little opera, called the Old Creation of the World, yet newly revived; with the addition of Noah's Flood' (Joseph Strutt, *Sports and Pastimes*, ed. Cox, 1903, pp. 144–7).

577. *Knights o'th'Post*: notorious perjurers; men who earned a living by giving false evidence.

579. *As if they were consenting, etc.* Cf. 'An Hermetic Philosopher', *Characters*, p. 107; Shakespeare, *King Lear*, i. ii. 121 ff.

583. *a Planet's house*: a sign of the zodiac, regarded as the seat of greatest influence of a particular planet.

584. *Who broke and robb'd a house below.* One of the most popular astrological books of Butler's time, William Lilly's *Christian Astrology*, includes a chapter 'Of Servants fled, Beasts strayed, and things lost', containing instructions on how to discover the identity of a thief by astrological observations (*Christian Astrology*, 1647, pp. 319 ff.).

591. *They'l question Mars, etc.* Both Mars and Mercury, according to Lilly, are planets with special influence over thieves (*Christian Astrology*, pp. 67, 78).

597. *Like him that took the Doctor's Bill, etc.* 'The learned Astrologers, observing the Impossibility of knowing the exact Moment of any Man's Birth, do use very prudently *to cast the Nativity of the Question* (like him, that swallowed the Doctor's Bill instead of the Medicine) and find the Answer as certain and infallible, as if they had known the very Instant, in which the Native, as they call him, crept into the World' ('An Hermetic Philosopher', *Characters*, p. 103).

599. *Nativity*: horoscope.

602. *Native*: the subject of a horoscope.

605. *Crisis*: a conjunction of the planets which determines the outcome of a disease.

611. *But not what wise, etc.* Cf. 'An Hermetic Philosopher', *Characters*, p. 108.

614. *true Trojans*: good fellows (colloquial).

620. *jump*: agree completely, coincide. Cf. i. iii. 1240.

633. *However Criticks count it sillier, etc.* 'And as he [Homer] often interrogates his Muse, not as his rational Spirit, but as a *Familiar*, separated from his body, so her replys bring him where he spends time in immortal conversation' (Davenant, Preface to *Gondibert* (1650), in Spingarn, *Critical Essays*, ii. 2).

640. *Withers*: George Wither (1588–1667), a Puritan poet and pamphleteer, chiefly remembered for his *Abuses Stript and Whipt* (1613), a series of satires on contemporary vices. Wither was a supporter of Parliament and, in 1642, sold his estate in order to raise a troop of horse on their behalf.

Pryn: William Prynne (1600–69), the Puritan pamphleteer, described by Clarendon as 'a barrister of Lincoln's Inn . . . not unlearned in the profession of the law, as far as learning is acquired by the mere reading of books; but, being a person of great industry, had spent more time in reading divinity, and, which marred that divinity, in the conversation of factious and hot-headed divines: and so, by a mixture of all three with the rudeness and arrogancy of his own nature, had contracted a proud and venomous dislike against the discipline of the Church of England, and so by degrees . . . an equal irreverence to the government of the State too; both which he vented in several absurd, petulant, and supercilious discourses in print' (Clarendon, iii. 58–59).

Aubrey, in his life of Prynne, sees Butler's reference to ale as an allusion to Prynne's habit of drinking ale while studying (*Brief Lives*, 1898, ii. 174).

Vickars: John Vickars (? 1580–1652), a Presbyterian poetaster and author of attacks in verse and prose upon the bishops, Catholics, and sectarians. His chief writings in verse include *England's Hallelujah; or Great Brittaines . . . deliverances since the halcyon dayes of Elizabeth* (1631) and a translation of the *Aeneid*. Butler's note refers to James Harrington (1611–77), the author of the political romance *Oceana*, who also translated some of Virgil's *Eclogues* and six books of the *Aeneid* into English. For Harrington, see G. P. Gooch and H. J. Laski, *English Democratic Ideas in the Seventeenth Century*, 1927, pp. 241–57.

647. *The praises of the Author, etc.* 'There are some, that drive a Trade in writing in praise of other Writers . . . not at all to celebrate the learned Author's Merits, as they would shew, but their own Wits, of which he is but the Subject' ('A Small Poet', *Characters*, p. 52).

681. *That at the Chain's end wheels about.* 'Both bulls and bears were chained to a staple in the arena or pit by a chain of about fifteen feet in length, so that the defending animal had relative freedom of movement over a circle of thirty feet. . . . The dog, attended by his owner, was held in front of the chained animal by the ears until he was wild with fury, and then let go' (W. B. Boulton, *Amusements of Old London*, 1901, i. 6–7).

685. *According to the Law of Arms.* An ironical comparison between the customs followed at bear-baitings and those practised at jousts and tournaments. At the latter, 'an *Herehault* by commandment of the *Conestable* and *Marshall*, did make proclamation at foure corners of the Lists thus *Oiez, Oiez*. We charge and command in the name of the King, the *Conestable* and *Marshal*, that no man . . . shall approach the Lists neerer than foure foote in distance' (Segar, *Booke of Honor and Armes*, 1590, viii. 79). A similar proclamation was made at the bull-running at Tutbury in Staffordshire, with which Butler was familiar (i. ii. 133–6), that 'all manner of persons give way to the *Bull*, none being to come near him by 40 foot . . . but to attend his or their own *safeties*, every one at his perill' (Robert Plot, *Natural History of Staffordshire*, 1686, p. 439).

706. *In Conscience and Commission too.* Before their rise to power the Puritans denounced bear-baiting for its cruelty and for the vices that flourished at bear-gardens (see Stubbes, *Anatomie of Abuses*, 1877–9, p. 177; John Field, *A godly exhortation by occasion of the late judgement of God shewed at Paris Garden*, 1583; Prynne, *Histrio-Mastix*, 1633, i. 556). Bear-baiting was declared illegal by order of Parliament in 1642 (*Commons Journals*, ii. 885).

709. *Curule*: civic. The Curule Chair was the seat used by the highest magistrate in Rome.

711. *Speculators*: watchmen.

712. *Pharos*: a lighthouse; originally an island off Alexandria on which a famous lighthouse stood.

C C

714. *Tithing-men*: parish officers, petty constables; originally the head man of the community known as a tithing.

727. *Are not our Liberties, our Lives, etc.* These ideals were very frequently appealed to in the Ordinances and political tracts of the early part of the Civil War. In 1643, for example, Parliament issued an Ordinance for the levying of money to maintain the army 'for the saving of the whole Kingdome, our Religion, Lawes, and Liberties from utter ruine and destruction' (Firth and Rait, i. 85).

730. *Cov'nant*: the 'Solemn League and Covenant' between England and Scotland (1643), in which the parties agreed to preserve 'the reformed religion in the Church of Scotland' and to reform religion in England 'according to the Word of God, and the example of the best reformed Churches' (*Const. Docs.* lviii. 267–71).

the Cause: the Puritan term for their own religious cause. Cf. i. ii. 504–5.

733. *by Jesuits invented.* Parliament frequently accused the Jesuits of attempting to subvert the established religion and government, and of influencing Charles I (see 'The Grand Remonstrance', *Const. Docs.* xliii. 206).

734. *evil Counsel.* 'The common soldiers of the army were generally persuaded . . . that the King was in truth little better than imprisoned by *evil counsellors, malignants, delinquents,* and *cavaliers,* (the terms applied to his whole party)' (Clarendon, vi. 31).

738. *well-affected that confide.* 'Well-affected' was a term commonly used by the Puritans to describe men sympathetic to their cause. Such people were also known as persons in whom they could 'confide' (Clarendon, vi. 143, iv. 214).

740. *claw and curry*: beat and thrash. Cf. ii. ii. 74.

742. *Cane et angue pejus*: 'worse than dog or snake' (proverbial). See Erasmus, *Adagia*, II. ix. lxiii.

752. *averruncate*: a word originally derived from the Latin *averruncare*, 'to ward off'. Butler presumably imagines the Latin root to be *ab-eruncare*, 'to weed out'. Henry Cockeram (*English Dictionarie*, 1623) also defines 'averruncate' as 'to weede'.

756. *Priviledge.* Breach of parliamentary privilege was the chief complaint made against Charles I by the five members of Parliament whom he accused of high treason in January 1642 (Clarendon, iv. 164). Later it became a political slogan: 'It is not to be believed how many sober, well-minded men . . . had their understandings confounded, and so their wills perverted, by the mere mention of *privilege of Parliament*' (Clarendon, iv. 233).

Fundamentall Laws: another political slogan. 'The root of all this mischief we find to be a malignant and pernicious design of subverting the fundamental laws and principles of government' ('The Grand Remonstrance', *Const. Docs.* xliii. 206).

757. *thorough Reformation.* See i. i. 199 and note.

758. *Covenant.* See 1. i. 730 and note.

Protestation. After rumours of an army plot in May 1641 Pym proposed 'for the better evidence of their union and unanimity . . . that some protestation might be entered into by members of both Houses' (Clarendon, iii. 184). In the Protestation they vowed to defend 'the true reformed Protestant religion . . . as also the power and privilege of Parliaments' (*Const. Docs.* xxviii. 156).

759. *Liberty of Consciences.* 'Liberty of conscience was now the common argument and quarrel [1647], whilst the Presbyterian party proceeded with equal bitterness against the several sects as enemies to all godliness' (Clarendon, x. 80).

760. *Ordinances.* 'Ordinance of Parliament, as they called it . . . is . . . a determination of those members who sat in the Houses' (Clarendon, viii. 206).

763. *evil Counsellours.* See note to 1. i. 734.

767. *Th'Ægyptians worshipp'd Dogs, etc.* Cf. Juvenal, *Satires,* xv. 1–8. The worship by the Egyptians of the god Anubis, represented as a man with the head of a dog, was described by several classical writers and Elizabethan travellers. See Diodorus, i. 87; Lucan, viii. 831–3; Purchas, *Pilgrimes,* 1625, II. vi. viii. iii. 911.

769. *Others ador'd a Rat.* The Egyptians were said to worship the ichneumon, a species of mongoose, found on the banks of the Nile (Purchas, *Pilgrimage,* 1626, VI. iii. ii. 635).

771. *The Indians fought for the truth, etc.* See Vincent le Blanc, *The World Surveyed,* trans. F. B., 1660, I. xx. 69, xxv. 103, xxvii. 112–19.

774. *mordicus*: 'with the teeth'; tenaciously. *Mordicus tenere* is included in Erasmus, *Adagia,* I. iv. xxii.

783. *some late Philosophers, etc.* Socrates, in Xenophon's *Memorabilia* (1. iv. 12), remarks that man, unlike the animals, has no fixed season for procreation.

789. *We read in Nero's time, etc.* Tacitus, *Annales,* xv. xliv.

799. *First for the name, etc.* A satire on the rigorous fundamentalism of some of the Puritan theologians. Grey compares this passage with the anonymous tract *Accommodation Discommended: as Incommodious to the Commonwealth* (n.d., pp. 3–4): 'First *Accommodation* is not the Language of *Canaan,* and therefore cannot conduce to the Peace of *Jerusalem* . . . It is no Scripture word. Now to strive to vilifie the Ordinances, which are in Scripture; And to set up *Accommodation,* which is not in Scripture, no, not so much as in the Apocrypha, is to relinquish the word, and follow the inventions of man, which is plaine Popery.'

805. *A vile Assembly 'tis, etc.* As a sectarian, Ralpho attacks the Presbyterian plan for Church government by synods, on the principle that 'every Companie, Congregation or Assemblie of men, ordinarilie joyneing together in the true worship of God, is a true *visible church* of Christ, and that the same title is

improperlie attributed to any other Convocations, Synods, Societies, combinations, or assemblies whatsoever' (William Bradshaw, *English Puritanisme*, 1605, p. 5).

807. *Provincial.* The Presbyterians proposed that each county should have a Provincial Assembly, consisting of delegates from the various 'classes' within the province or county.

Classick. 'Classical Presbyteries . . . are Assemblies made up of Ministers of the Word, and other Ruling Officers belonging unto several neighbouring Congregations' ('An Ordinance for the Form of Church Government', 1648, Firth and Rait 1. 1199).

National. 'The National Assembly shall be constituted of Members chosen by, and sent from, the several Provincial Assemblies' (ibid., 1. 1197).

810. *when men run a-whoring thus, etc.* Ps. cvi. 39.

814. *Dagon*: a god worshipped among the Philistines of the Old Testament. The name was used by the Puritans to describe anything they considered idolatrous. Busy, in Jonson's *Bartholomew Fair* (v. v), condemns the puppet-show with the words 'Down with *Dagon*' (*Works*, vi. 133).

818. *ad amussim*: *amussis* is a carpenter's rule; hence, according to the rule; exactly. See Erasmus, *Adagia*, I. v. xc.

820. *Jure Divino*: a phrase frequently used by the Presbyterian divines, who held that their form of Church government was founded upon divine laws revealed through the Scriptures. Cf. Rushworth III. i. 165 : 'Then Part of the Ministers *Remonstrance* concerning the Government of the Church was read; in the Debate whereof, some smart Repartees pass'd . . . Mr. *Grimston* arguing thus; That *Bishops are* Jure Divino, *is a Question*; *That Archbishops are not* Jure Divino *is out of question. Now that Bishops that are question'd whether* Jure Divino, *or Archbishops which out of Question are not* Jure Divino, *should suspend Ministers that are* Jure Divino, *I leave you to be considered.*'

824. *Homœosis*: 'a making like. The substitution of a similar thing for the thing itself' (Milnes).

839. *offer'st*: propoundest.

840. *keep touch*: remain true.

841. *Mira de lente*: an obscure proverbial expression, the original meaning of which was probably 'to serve a pea as if it were a feast'. See Erasmus, *Adagia*, IV. v. xxx.

851. *And then what Genus, etc.* Cf. I. iii. 1279 and note.

868. *the Godly*: a Puritan expression, used to denote the members of their own party. See note to I. i. 191.

870. *slurr'd*: cheated, cozened. Cf. II. ii. 192. Originally a term used in dice-play: 'to slip or slide a die out of the box so that it will not turn' (*OED*).

success: the outcome.

889. *In Northern Clime a valorous Knight, etc.* There are several records of the killing of bears by Puritan officers as a result of the prohibition of bear-baiting by Parliament. The most notorious episode of this kind was the killing of some bears by Colonel Pride when he was High Sheriff of Surrey. See *The last Speech and dying Words of Thomas . . . Pride; being touched in Conscience for his inhuman Murder of the Bears* (*Harleian Miscellany*, 1808–13, iii. 136). Two similar events are mentioned in this document: 'Did not the Lord-Deputy Ireton kill a bear? Did not another lord of ours kill five bears, and five fidlers?' Several bears are said to have been shot at Uppingham in Rutland by Cromwell's officers (see *A Perfect Diurnall of some Passages in Parliament*, 24–31 July 1643).

895. *Mamaluke*: a member of the band of Caucasian slaves who seized the throne of Egypt in 1254, and from then until the early nineteenth century formed the Egyptian ruling class.

896. *In forrain Land, yclep'd* ——. 'The Author means by this Person Sir Samuel Luke, the chief Hero of his Poem' ('Key to *Hudibras*', *Posth. Works*, i). For Luke see Appendix B.

897. *To whom we have been oft compar'd, etc.* In his description of Luke, in *Mercurius Menippeus*, Butler dwells at length on his hunch back: 'He looks like a Snail with his House upon his back, or the Spirit of the *Militia* with a Natural Snapsack . . . He looks like the visible type of *Æneas* boulstring up his Father' (*Satires*, 357; cf. I. i. 287–8).

905. *Honour is, like a Widow, etc.* 'He told me that I must observe the old Proverb, I enquired of him what that was, then he told me, *That he that would woe a Maid, must fain, lye, and flatter*; but he, *That Wooes a Widdow . . . must down with his britches and at her*' (Nathaniel Smith, *Quakers Spiritual Court Proclaim'd*, n.d., p. 13). See also Tilley, M18.

909. *the Phrygian Knight*: Laocoon, who attempted to warn the Trojans of the danger of the wooden horse (Virgil, *Aeneid*, ii. 50–53).

918. *A Wight*. Grey suggests that the allusion is to Richard Cromwell, but it is more probably to Oliver Cromwell, who rose to power and ruled the country with the help of the 'armed heel' of the army.

CANTO II

1. *an ancient sage Philosopher*: Empedocles of Acragas, who held that matter was composed of four 'roots', earth, air, fire, and water. These roots were set in motion, and united or divided, by two other substances which he called respectively 'love' and 'strife'. See Burnet, *Early Greek Philosophy*, 1908, pp. 241–3.

2. *Alexander Ross*: a prolific writer of theological and historical works (1590–1654). His writings include an abridgement of Raleigh's *History of the*

World (1652), criticisms of Hobbes, Browne, and Sir Kenelm Digby, and *Pansebeia, or a View of All Religions in the World* (1653).

20. *dead-doing*: murderous.

22. *the Manhood of nine Taylors*. An allusion to the proverb 'Nine tailors make but one man' (*ODEP* 453; Tilley, T23).

23. *So a wild Tartar, etc.* '[The Tartars] used, that when any Stranger which seemed of good presence and parts lodged with them, they slue him by night, supposing that those good parts of that man might abide afterwards in that house: and this was the death of many' (Purchas, *Pilgrimes*, 1625, III. i. iv. 92).

34. *As men kill Beavers for their stones*. An oily substance known as castoreum was formerly extracted from the testicles of beavers for use as a medicine. See Pliny, *Nat. Hist.* XXXII. iii. 13.

37. *as an equal friend to both, etc.* An allusion to the proverbial expression *amicus Plato, amicus Socrates, sed magis amica veritas*. It is included in some editions of Erasmus's *Adagia* (Hanover, 1617, pp. 48, 453) and is mentioned in *Don Quixote* (II. li; 1896 edn., iv. 109).

47. *whether Tollutation, etc.* An allusion to Browne, *Pseudodoxia*, IV. vi: '[Animals] move *per latera*, that is, two legs of one side together, which is Tollutation or ambling; or *per diametrum*, lifting one foot before, and the cross foot behind, which is succussation or trotting.'

55. *For as whipp'd Tops, etc.* Possibly an allusion to the opening words of Hobbes's *Leviathan*: 'Nature . . . is by the *Art* of man, as in many other things, so in this also imitated, that it can make an Artificial Animal. For seeing life is but a motion of Limbs, the beginning whereof is in some princi-pall part within; why may we not say, that all *Automata* (Engines that move themselves by springs and wheeles as doth a watch) have an artificiall life?'

57. *So Horses they affirm to be, etc.* Possibly an allusion to Descartes's *Discours de la méthode*, v.: 'Je m'estois icy particulierement aresté a faire voir que, s'il y avoit de telles machines, qui eussent les organes et la figure d'un singe, ou de quelque autre animal sans raison, nous n'aurions aucun moyen pour reconnoistre qu'elles ne seroient pas en tout de mesme nature que ces ani-maux' (*Œuvres*, Paris, 1897–1910, vi. 56).

60. *As Indian Britans were from Penguins*. There was a popular legend that America had been discovered in the twelfth century by a Welsh prince, Madoc ap Owen Gwyneth. The only remaining evidence of his discovery was said to be a number of Welsh words which had survived in America, one of which was the word 'penguin'. See Sir Humphrey Gilbert, *True Reporte of the Late Discoveries . . . of the New-found Landes*, 1583, iii; David Powel, *Historie of Cambria*, 1584, p. 229. For the complex problem of the word 'penguin' see *OED*.

65. *The dire Pharsalian Plain*. Lucan, i. 38:

> diros Pharsalia campos
> inpleat et Poeni saturentur sanguine manes.

71. *as our modern wits behold, etc.* Possibly an ironic reference to Alexander Ross. In the Preface to his abridgement of Raleigh's *History of the World* Ross compares himself to Raleigh: 'for though hee was a giant in knowledg; and saw far, yet a pigmie set on his shouldiers [*sic*] may see a little further' (*Marrow of Historie*, 1650). The simile was frequently used, however, especially when comparing the relative achievement of the ancients and the moderns. See F. E. Guyer, 'The Dwarf on the Giant's Shoulders', *MLN* xlv (1930), 398–402.

92. *Tuck*: a slender sword or rapier.

99. *The Squire advanc'd with greater speed, etc.* In the original unrevised version of this passage, Ralpho is compared to Hugo, the lieutenant of Gondibert (Davenant, *Gondibert*, I. ii. 66–67).

106. *Crowdero*: a fiddler; so called because he plays on a 'crowd' or fiddle. The names of the bear-baiters are all derived from their professions, and may have been coined after the example of *The Knight of the Burning Pestle*, whose hero, Ralph, instructs his followers to call the servants at an inn Ostlero, Tapstero, and Chamberlino (Act II, Scene vi). The 'Key to *Hudibras*' identifies Crowdero as 'one *Jackson* a Milliner in the *New-Exchange* in the Strand; who falling to decay, by losing a Leg in the *Roundheads* Service, he was oblig'd to scrape upon a Violin from one Alehouse to another, for his Bread' (*Posthumous Works*, i). The Key is, however, unreliable.

110. *By thunder turn'd to Vineger.* 'Now that Beer, Wine, and other Liquors, are spoiled with lightning and thunder, we conceive it proceeds not onely from noise and concussion of the air, but also noxious spirits, which mingle therewith, and draw them to corruption' (Browne, *Pseudodoxia*, II. vi. 6). Vinegar, as its name suggests, was originally made from sour ale or wine (Thomas Coghan, *Haven of Health*, 1584, p. 165).

112. *a month's mind*: a strong desire (*ODEP* 431; Tilley, M1109).

114. *North-east side.* An allusion to 'the Geography of Paracelsus, who according to the Cardinal points of the World, divideth the body of man . . . making the face the East, but the posteriours the America or Western part of his Microcosm' (Browne, *Pseudodoxia*, II. iii).

119. *warped*: shrivelled.

121. *sodden*: boiled.

133. *In Staffordshire, where Vertuous worth, etc.* 'During the time of which ancient Earls and Dukes of *Lancaster* . . . had their abode, and kept a liberal *hospitality* here, at their *Honor* of *Tutbury*, there could not but be a general concourse of people from all parts hither; for whose diversion all sorts of *Musicians* were permitted likewise to come, to pay their *services*: amongst whom (being numerous) some quarrels and disorders now and then arising, it was found necessary after a while they should be brought under rules . . . and a *Governour* appointed them by the name of a *King*' (Plot, *Natural History of Staffordshire*, 1686, pp. 435–6). The bull-running alluded to in ll. 135–6 had no

connexion with the appointment of the minstrel king, but was held after his election, on the morning after the feast of the Assumption (Plot, pp. 439–40).

137. *As once in Persia, etc.* Darius conspired with six other Persian noblemen to destroy the usurper Smerdis. They agreed, after the death of Smerdis, that the man whose horse was the first to neigh at sunrise should be king (Herodotus, iii. 85–86).

146. *place*: precedence.

147. *Orsin*: a bear-warden, from the Latin *ursus*, Italian *orso*, a bear. The bear-warden in Jonson's *Masque of Augurs* is called John Urson. The 'Key to *Hudibras*' comments: 'This fictitious Name seems to hint at one *Joshua Goslin*, who kept Bears at *Paris-Garden* on *Southwark* side; however, he stood hard and fast for the Rump Parliament' (*Posthumous Works*, i).

151. *With Truncheon tipp'd with Iron-head, etc.* When tournaments were held according to the laws of chivalry, knights were led into the lists by the marshall or constable, who carried a truncheon of office. See Andrew Favine, *Theater of Honour*, 1623, x. iv. 448.

155. *Emperour of Pegu.* Pegu is a town and district north-east of Rangoon. Elizabethan travellers returned from the East with tales of the great wealth, power, and cruelty of the kings of Pegu (Purchas, *Pilgrimage*, v. iv. 498–9).

156. *Don Diego*: a colloquial term for any foreigner, particularly a Spaniard (e.g. Nashe, *Strange Newes of the Intercepting certaine Letters, Works*, 1910, i. 305). Cf. modern 'dago'.

163. *stave and tail*: terms used in bear-baiting. To stave is to hold back the bear or dog with a staff; to tail is to pull the dog by the tail. Cf. I. iii. 134 and Butler's note.

Writs of Error: a writ brought to procure the reversal of a judgement on the ground of error.

164. *Demurrer*: A pleading which, admitting for the moment the facts as stated by the opponent, denies that he is legally entitled to relief, and thus stops the action until this point can be determined by the court.

172. *Military Garden-Paris*: Paris Garden was an arena in Southwark used for bull- and bear-baitings. A military garden was a place where soldiers were trained. Cf. *A Letter from Mercurius Civicus to Mercurius Rusticus*, 1643, p. 4: 'You may well remember when the *Puritans* here did as much abominate the *Military-yard* or *Artillery-Garden*, as *Paris-Garden* it self.'

175–98. Grey notes that these lines refer to a passage in Trajano Boccalini's *Ragguagli di Parnaso*, published in Venice in 1612 and translated into English several times by various hands from 1622 onwards.

Ambassadors from all the Gardners of the world, are come to this Court, who have acquainted his Majestie [Apollo] that . . . so great abundance of weeds grew up in their Gardens, as not being any longer able to undergoe the charges they were at in weeding them out . . . they should be forced either to give them over, or else to inhaunce the price of their Pompions, Cabiges, and other hearbs, unless his Majestie would help them to some Instrument, by means whereof they might not be at such excessive charge in keeping their Gardens. . . . The Ambassadors did then couragiously reply, that they made this request, being moved thereunto by the great benefit which they saw his Majestie had been pleased to grant to Princes, who to purge their States from evil weeds, and seditious plants . . . had obtained the miraculous Instruments of Drum and Trumpet, at the sound whereof . . . pernitious plants of unusefull persons, doe of themselves willingly forsake the ground, to make room for . . . useful hearbs of Artificers and Citizens. . . . To this *Apollo* answered, That . . . the Instruments of Drum and Trumpets were granted for publick peace-sake to Princes, the sound whereof was chearfully followed by such plants as took delight in dying, to the end, that by the frequent use of gibbets, wholsom herbs should not be extirpated instead of such as were venemous (*Advertisements from Parnassus*, trans. Henry, Earl of Monmouth, 1657, Cent. 1, Adv. xvi, 27).

Butler appears to draw a parallel between this fable and a situation in the Civil War, probably the petitioning of the King by the Lower House and the citizens of various counties 'that the kingdom might be put into a posture of defence' (Clarendon, iv. 238, 244, 247). The King would not accede, and later refused to approve an Ordinance drawn up by Parliament for the raising of a militia (ibid. 307). Finally, Parliament claimed that 'his majesty . . . did by several messages invite them to settle the same by Act of Parliament', and on this authority a militia was raised (ibid. v. 118).

177. For *licensing a new invention*. Inventors were granted a patent by the king, allowing them sole use of their inventions for a certain period.

188. *quaint*: skilful.

194. *Cler. Parl. Dom. Com.*: the abbreviation of the title of the Clerk to the House of Commons, who signed Ordinances and correspondence published in the name of the Commons.

213. *gender*: birth.

214. *came in at a Windore*: i.e. were illegitimate. Proverbial (*ODEP* 103; Tilley, W456).

219. *Arctophylax*: Greek Ἀρκτοφύλαξ, bear-keeper. The name of the northern constellation of Boötes or the Waggoner, situated at the tail of the Great Bear.

225. *Hermetick Powder, etc.* An allusion to the belief that wounds could be cured by sympathy. Robert Fludd describes a sympathetic ointment which will cure wounds when applied to a cloth dipped in the blood of a wounded man (*Doctor Fludds Answer unto M. Foster*, 1631, p. 131). Nathaniel Highmore writes of a sympathetic powder with similar properties (Supplement to *History of Generation*, 1651, pp. 115 ff.). Sir Kenelm Digby discusses sympathetic effects generally in his *Late Discourse . . . Touching the Cure of Wounds by the Powder of Sympathy*, 1658.

233. *For as when Slovens doe amiss, etc.* 'If it happens that there be a Farmer . . . who keeps more neatly the approaches to his house than his neighbours do,

the boyes use to come thither . . . when it begins to be dark, to discharge their bellies there . . . but they who are acquainted with this trick go presently and fire red-hot a broach or fire-shovel, and then thrust it into the excrements all hot, and heat it again oftentimes to the same purpose; In the mean time the boy which made the ordure feels a kind of pain, and collick in his bowells, with an inflammation in his fundament' (Digby, *Late Discourse*, 1658, pp. 126–7).

245. *A Skilful Leech, etc.* See Homer, *Iliad*, xi. 514–15.

251. *rugged*: (i) coarse; (ii) rough with hair.

And rugged as a Saracen, etc. Nicholas Breton describes a Saracen's face as having 'his nose too long for his lips, his cheekes like the jawes of a horse, his eyes like a Smiths forge, and his haire all besprinckled with a whore frost' (*Wonders Worth the Hearing, Works*, 1879, ii. 7). George Sandys reports of the Turks that 'there lives not a race of ill-favoureder people' (*Travels*, 1673, i. 50).

255. *like Indian King, etc.* Purchas describes how the Mexican king Ticocic had his nostrils pierced 'and for an ornament put an Emerald therein; and for this reason in the *Mexican* Bookes, this King is noted by his nosthrils pierced' (*Pilgrimes*, III. v. iv. ii. 1016).

259. *Armed, as Heraulds cant, and langued.* 'When any beast of prey has teeth and claws . . . of a tincture different from its body, it is said to be armed of such a tincture' (*Glossary of Terms Used in Heraldry*, Oxford, 1894, p. 16). 'Langued . . . is used with reference to the tongue of a lion, or other quadruped, when of a different tincture' (ibid. 364).

270. *As with their Bodyes Ditches there.* George Sandys (*Travels*, 1673, 39) mentions the Azapi, one of the tribes who formed part of the army of the Grand Turk, and 'whose dead bodies do serve the *Janizaries* to fill up Ditches, and to mount the Walls of assaulted Fortresses'.

271. *Scrimansky*: possibly the name of a well-known bear, or a name coined in imitation of those given to bears. Nash notes that *scrimatur* is late Latin usage for *rugit* or *bucinat*, 'roars or bellows'. See Du Cange, *Glossarium*.

273. *he'd suck his claws, etc.* Young bears were popularly supposed to feed themselves by sucking their paws (Pliny, *Nat. Hist.* VIII. xxxvi. 54).

275. *his Countrey-men, the Huns, etc.* See Ammianus Marcellinus, xxxi. ii. The page reference in Butler's note suggests that he used the edition published 'apud Seb. Gryphium' in Leyden, 1552.

282. *Le Blanc the Traveller. Les Voyages Fameux du Sieur V. Leblanc . . . le tout recueilly de ses mémoires par le Sieur Coulon* was published in Paris in 1648. The book was translated into English by Francis Brook as *The World Surveyed: Or, The Famous Voyages . . . of Vincent le Blanc*, 1660.

283. *He Spous'd in India, etc.* According to Le Blanc, a princess named Agarida was carried off by a bear to a remote cave, and was kept there for many years. Agarida had five sons by the bear, 'all gallant men, without the least shape

or resemblance of the beast', who 'made themselves so Formidable that none
durst meddle with them' (*The World Surveyed*, 1660, pp. 78–79).

288. *Talgol*: a name coined from Italian *tagliare* (to cut) and *gola* (throat).
'He was a Butcher in *Newgate-Market*, his Name was Jackson; and obtain'd a
Captain's Commission for his rebellious Bravery at *Naseby* Fight' ('Key to
Hudibras', *Posth. Works*, i).

289. *Each striving to deserve the Crown, etc.* The *corona civica* was the most
distinguished military decoration of ancient Rome. It was awarded to men
who had saved the life of a fellow-citizen in war. See Pliny, *Nat. Hist.* xvi. iv.

306. *another Guy*: Guy of Warwick, whose exploits were recounted in popular
ballads and romances. Grey cites the anonymous *Plesante songe of the valiant
actes of Guy of Warwick*, which was published many times between 1592 and
the middle of the eighteenth century, and includes the episodes of the boar
and 'dun-cow':

> In *Windsor*-Forest I did slay
>   a Boar of passing Might and Strength,
> The like in *England* never was,
>   for Hugeness both in Breadth and Length,
> On *Dunsmore*-Heath I also slew
>   a monstrous wild and cruel Beast,
> Call'd the Dun-Cow of *Dunsmore-Heath*,
>   which many People had opprest.

See *The Noble and Renowned History of Guy Earl of Warwick*, 1736, p. 155.

310. *Ajax.* Ajax contended with Ulysses for the armour of Achilles and,
when he failed to win it, went mad with anger. He slaughtered a flock of sheep,
imagining them to be the Greeks, who had awarded the prize to Ulysses.
See Sophocles, *Ajax*, ll. 1–70; Harington, *Metamorphosis of Ajax*, 1596,
Prologue.

Don Quixot. Don Quixote mistook a flock of sheep for two contending
armies, and charged into the midst of them, killing those which he imagined
to be the enemy soldiers (*Don Quixote*, I. iii. iv).

314. *Sir George Saint George*: a man of this name was given the command of a
company of foot in 1628, and in 1632 became Deputy Vice-Admiral of
Connaught (*Cal. State Papers, Ireland (Charles I) 1625–32*, pp. 309, 662).

327. *The former rides in Triumph for it, etc.* Cf. Seneca, *Epistolae Morales*, lxxxvii.
23: 'nam sacrilegia minuta puniuntur, magna in triumphis feruntur.' The
cart in which prisoners were carried from gaol to the gallows was popularly
known as a 'two-wheeled chariot' (see Shirley, *The Wedding*, iv. iii, *Works*,
1833, i. 425).

331. *Magnano*: Italian, *magnano*, a locksmith. '*Magnano* here is put for *Simeon
Wait*, a Tinker, as famous an Independant Preacher as *Burroughs*; who, with
equal Blasphemy to his *Lord of Hosts*, would stile *Oliver Cromwel* the Arch-
angel giving Battle to the Devil' ('Key to *Hudibras*', *Posth. Works*, i).

336. *Whose Spoils upon his Back he wore.* The itinerant tinker used to carry his tools in a leather bag, slung over his back. See Overbury, 'A Tinker', *Miscellaneous Works*, 1890, pp. 89–91.

337. *Ajax sev'n-fold Shield.* Ajax carried a shield of bronze, backed with seven layers of bull's-hide (Homer, *Iliad*, vii. 222–3).

344. *he that made the Brazen-head*: Roger Bacon, the thirteenth-century philosopher, who was said in popular legend to have made a head of brass that could speak. See *The Famous Historie of Fryer Bacon*, 1624; Greene, *Friar Bacon and Friar Bungay*, Scene xi (A. W. Ward, *Old English Drama*, Oxford, 1901, clii, pp. 93–96).

346. *English Merlin*: the pseudonym of William Lilly (1602–81), the astrologer and author of *England's propheticall Merline* (1644), a book of astrological predictions. Lilly produced a series of almanacs annually from 1647 until his death, under the title *Merlini Anglici ephemeris*.

348. *the Sieve and Shears*: a method of divination. A sieve was suspended from a pair of shears, held up by the middle fingers of two assistants. In order to identify a thief or other criminal, a spell was spoken over the sieve, which would then turn at the mention of the name of the guilty person. See Petro de Albano, *De speciebus Magiae Cæremonialis*, xxi, supplement to Agrippa, *De Occulta Philosophia* (*Opera*, Leyden, 1600, ii. 472).

350. *As like the Devil as a Collier.* The devil was thought to be black in colour and was associated with colliers in several proverbs (*ODEP* 369; Tilley, L287).

355. *Saker*: a small cannon, used in sieges and on board ship.

365. *Trulla*: a name coined from 'trull', a prostitute. The 'Key to *Hudibras*' identifies her as 'The Daughter of *James Spencer*, a Quaker, debauch'd first by her Father; and then by *Magnano* the Tinker above mention'd' (*Posth. Works*, i).

368. *Mall*: probably Mary Ambree, the Amazonian heroine of a popular English ballad, who was said to have been one of the volunteers who helped in the attempt to recapture the city of Ghent from the Spaniards in 1584:

> When captain's courageous, whom death cold not daunte,
> Did march to the siege of the citty of Gaunt,
> They mustred their souldiers by two and by three,
> And the formost in battle was Mary Ambree.

See *Percy's Reliques of Ancient English Poetry*, ed. Wheatley, 3 vols. 1910, ii. 232. The ballad was well known in the early seventeenth century. See Jonson, *Fortunate Isles*, pp. 393–9; *Epicoene*, iv. ii. 123; Marston, *Antonio and Mellida*, i. i; Beaumont and Fletcher, *Scornful Lady*, v. iv. Milnes, alternatively, suggests an allusion to one Mary Frith (1584–1659), known as Moll Cutpurse, the central character in Middleton and Dekker's *Roaring Girl* (1611). For allusions to Moll Cutpurse, see Dyce's Introduction to *The Roaring Girl* (Middleton, *Works*, 1840, ii. 427 ff.).

378. *Penthesile*: Penthesilea, Queen of the Amazons, who fought on the side of Priam in the Trojan War (*Aeneid*, i. 490–3).

379. *some Criticks here cry shame, etc.* In his remarks on 'propriety' of character Aristotle declares that 'there is a type of manly valour; but valour in a woman, or unscrupulous cleverness, is inappropriate' (*Poetics*, xv, trans. Butcher, 1911, p. 53). Aristotle's view was developed by several neo-classical critics, including Scaliger (*Poetices*, iii. 13), La Mesnardière (*Poétique*, Paris, 1640, p. 137), and Le Bossu (*Traité du poème épique*, iv. 2).

382. *Who hold no females stout, but Bears.* 'In all living creatures whatsoever, the males be stronger than the females, setting aside the race of Panthers and Beares' (Pliny, *Nat. Hist.* XL. xlix. 109, trans. Holland, 1634, p. 352).

385. *They would not suffer, etc.* Butler's note erroneously attributes this statement to Macrobius. It is to be found in Aulus Gellius, XI. vi.

393. *stout Armida, bold Thalestris.* Armida, the enchantress in Tasso's *Gerusalemme Liberata*, fought for the King of Egypt against the Christians. Thalestris was a Queen of the Amazons (see Quintus Curtius, VI. v; Strabo, xi).

394. *she that would have been the Mistriss, etc.* Gondibert, the hero of Davenant's poem, is first a suitor for the hand of Rhodalind, the heir to the throne, but later falls in love with the 'Countrey Lass' Birtha.

400. *Can never be upheld in prose.* An allusion to Davenant's Preface to *Gondibert* (1650): 'Thus we have first observ'd the Four chief aids of Government, *Religion, Armes, Policy,* and *Law,* defectively apply'd, and then we have found them weak by an emulous war amongst themselves: it follows next we should introduce to strengthen those principal aids . . . some collateral help, which I will safely presume to consist in Poesy' (Spingarn, *Critical Essays*, 2 vols. Oxford, 1908, ii. 44).

401. *Strip Nature naked.* An allusion to Davenant's Postscript to *Gondibert* (1651, p. 244): 'I intended in this POEM to strip Nature naked, and clothe her again in the perfect shape of Vertue.'

409. *The upright Cerdon*: Latin, *cerdo*, a craftsman. The word is used specifically of a cobbler in Martial, *Epigrams*, iii. 59. There is also a pun on the word 'upright', formerly the name for a type of shoe which could fit either foot. In the most plausible of its identifications, the 'Key to *Hudibras*' notes that 'By *Cerdon* is meant one-ey'd *Hewson* the Cobler, who, from a private Centinel in the Parliament Army was made a Colonel'. Hewson's humble origins were the theme of popular ballads. See 'The *Cobler's* Last Will and Testament: or the Lord *Hewson's* translation', a ballad of 1659, reprinted in *Rump,* 1662, ii. 145.

420. *the Knight of Greece*: Ajax. See note to I. ii. 337.

421. *black-thumb'd.* Cobblers were proverbially said to have black thumbs (*ODEP* 295; Tilley, P441).

426. *well-sol'd Boots.* Homer refers to the Greeks as ἐϋκνήμιδες Ἀχαιοί. The κνημίς was a piece of leg-armour.

437. *stickle*: be busy, energetic.

441. *Colon*: Latin, *colonus*, a farmer. The 'Key to *Hudibras*' identifies Colon as '*Ned Perry*, an Hostler' of whom nothing further is known, but the allusion is more probably to John Desborough, one of Cromwell's army officers who, after Richard Cromwell's death, became Major-General of the army. Wood (*Fasti*, ed. Bliss, 1820, p. 155) describes Desborough as 'a yeoman and a great lubberly clown, who by Oliver's interest became a colonel'. He is frequently made fun of as a farmer in the ballads of the time. See 'The GANG or the Nine Worthies and Champions', a ballad of 1659, reprinted in *Rump*, ii. 104; 'The Rump' (*Rump*, i. 370); and 'The Rump Carbonado'd' (*Rump*, ii. 83–84).

448. *He and his Horse were of a piece*. Cf. Shakespeare, *Hamlet*, iv. vii. 86–89.

454. *That fed on Man's flesh*: the horses of Diomedes, King of Thrace. He was killed by Hercules, who threw his body to be devoured by his own horses.

458. *Then Hercules to clense a Stable*. An allusion to the fifth labour of Hercules, which was to clean the stables of Augeas, where three thousand oxen had been confined.

459. *As great a Drover, etc.* The seventh labour of Hercules was to bring alive into Peloponnesus the wild bull which had laid waste the island of Crete. In his fourth labour, he brought back the wild boar which was ravaging the region of Erymanthus.

493. *What Rage, O Citizens, etc.* Cf. Lucan, i. 8–14, trans. Thomas May, 1627:

> What fury, Countreymen, what madnesse cou'd
> Moove you to feast your fooes with Roman blood?
> And choose such warres, as could no triumphs yeeld,
> Whilest yet proud Babylon unconquer'd held
> The boasting Trophæs of a Roman hoast,
> And unrevenged wander'd *Crassus* Ghost?
> Alas, what Seas, what Lands might you have tane,
> With what bloods losse, which civill hands had drawne?

495. *Oestrum*: Greek, οἶστρος, an insect which infests cattle, a gadfly; hence, an insane passion.

497. *the proud Vies your Trophies boast*. Devizes was formerly known as De Vies or The Vies (Camden, *Britannia*, 1695, 'Wiltshire', col. 88). The Royalists, under Sir Ralph Hopton, were besieged in Devizes by Waller's army. Waller summoned them to surrender, but they refused, and, reinforced by troops from Oxford, routed Waller's forces at the Battle of Roundway Down, 13 July 1643 (Clarendon, vii. 111–20).

498. *unreveng'd walks —— ghost?* The blank should probably be filled with the name 'Waller'. After the Battle of Roundway Down Waller blamed his defeat on the Earl of Essex, who, he said, had purposely neglected to bring help 'out of envy at the great things he had done, which seemed to eclipse his glories' (Clarendon, vii. 120).

502. *vain, untriumphable fray*. In a civil war, victorious Roman leaders were not awarded the customary triumph, since they had shed the blood of their

fellow-countrymen, and not that of foreign foes. See Valerius Maximus, ii. viii. 7.

509. *Solemn League and Covenant*: see note to i. i. 730.

513. *we make War for the King, etc.* In the early stages of the Civil War, recruits were raised by Parliament to fight 'for the defence of the kingdom, the Parliament and city, (with their other usual expressions of religion and the King's person)' (Clarendon, vi. 103). The Parliamentarian claim to be taking arms for the King against himself was justified by the doctrine that a distinction could be made between his royal authority and his personal will. The former could be exercised only through the proper channels, and when the separation came between the King and his Parliament, he continued to act merely as an individual person. This was St. John's argument in Hampden's case. See J. R. Tanner, *English Constitutional Conflicts*, 1937, p. 273.

516. *For God, and for Religion too.* Another justification given by Parliament for the raising of troops was 'the upholding of the true Protestant religion' (Clarendon, v. 120; vi. 103).

521. *Protestation*: see note to i. i. 758.

523. *Which all the Saints, and some since Martyrs, etc.* Early in 1642 the King accused Lord Kimbolton and five members of the House of Commons of high treason. When the Commons refused to hand over the accused members, the King went in person to demand their submission. Meanwhile the accused men took refuge in the City, and riots began to break out. Charles retired to Hampton Court for safety, and the accused members returned to Westminster in triumph. 'There was one circumstance not to be forgotten in the march of the city that day . . . that the pikemen had fastened to the tops of their pikes, and the rest in their hats or their bosoms, printed papers of the Protestation which had been taken . . . the year before for the defence of the privilege of Parliament' (Clarendon, iv. 199).

524. *Wedding-garters*: lengths of ribbon, sometimes made into rosettes, worn by guests at a wedding.

530. *Joyn throats to cry the Bishops down.* 'It was quickly understood abroad that the Commons liked well the visitation of their neighbours; so that the people assembled in greater numbers than before about the House of Peers, calling still out with one voice, "*No bishops, no popish lords*" ' (Clarendon, iv. 111).

531. *the Palace*: the royal palace at Whitehall. Clarendon describes how the people flocked there 'making a stand before Whitehall and crying out "*No bishops, no bishops, no popish lords*" ' (Clarendon, iv. 119).

535. *When Tinkers bawl'd aloud, etc.* Following the publication of the Grand Remonstrance, in 1641, the people of London rallied to the support of Parliament, and presented petitions to them demanding that the prelates might be extirpated root and branch. 'This and such stuff being printed and scattered amongst the people, multitudes of mean people flocked to Westminster Hall, and about the Lords' House, crying, as they went up and down, "*No bishops, no bishops*", that so they might carry on the refor.. tion' (Clarendon, iv. 106).

537. *No Sow-gelder did blow his horn.* The sow-gelder announced his arrival by blowing a characteristic tune on his horn. See Beaumont and Fletcher, *Beggar's Bush,* III. i (*Works,* Cambridge, 1905–12, ii. 234).

541. *Save-alls*: a type of candlestick which held the candle in such a way that it would burn to the end and leave no waste. The mousetrap-men also sold save-alls; the tinder-box man in Jonson's *Bartholomew Fair* (II. iv. 7) sells mousetraps (*Works,* vi. 47), and Bristle, the brush-man in *The London Chanticleers,* 1659, sells tinder-boxes and save-alls. See Charles Hindley, *History of the Cries of London,* 1881, p. 73.

542. *Ev'l Counsellors*: see note to I. i. 734.

543. *Botchers*: tailors or cobblers who repair clothes.

545. *the Covenant.* The Solemn League and Covenant (see note to I. i. 730) was not taken until 1643, whereas the demonstrations described here took place in 1641. Unless his memory fails him, Butler must be alluding to the Scottish Covenant of 1638, taken by the Scottish Presbyterians in defence of their Church against the attempts of Charles I and Laud to introduce the Anglican liturgy (*Const. Docs.* xxiii. 124).

548. *purge the Common's House.* 'Where they came near the two Houses, [the people] took out papers from their pockets, and . . . would read the names of several persons under the title of *"disaffected members of the House of Commons"* ' (Clarendon, iv. 119).

549. *Kitchin-stuff*: vegetables.

552. *No Surplices.* An allusion to the 'Vestiarian Controversy', in which the Puritans attacked the wearing of vestments by ministers of the Church, on the grounds that it was not enjoined in the Scriptures. See W. H. Frere, *English Church in the Reigns of Elizabeth and James I,* 1924, pp. 54–56.

   nor Service-book. The Presbyterians were opposed to the Anglican liturgy contained in the *Book of Common Prayer.* By an Ordinance of 1645 Parliament ordered it to be replaced by the *Directory for Public Worship* (Firth and Rait, i. 582; Clarendon, x. 162).

556. *carr'ings on*: see note to I. i. 201.

557. *Publick Faith.* In order to finance the militia Parliament published 'propositions for the bringing in of money, or plate, to maintain horse, horsemen and arms'. 'And they further declared that whosoever brought in money or plate . . . should be repaid their money with interest of 8 *per cent.,* for which they did engage the public faith' (Clarendon, v., 337). 'The free Loanes and Contributions upon the Publique Faith amounted to a vast incredible summe in Money, Plate, Horse, Armes, etc.' (Clement Walker, *Mysterie of the Two Junto's,* 1647, p. 9).

   like a young heire. 'The most observable thing was, to see this old Parliament like a young Prodigall, take up money upon difficult termes and intangle all they had for a security' (Clement Walker, op. cit. 12).

569. *A Thimble, Bodkin, and a Spoon, etc.* 'Not onely the wealthiest Citizens and Gentlemen who were neer-dwellers, brought in their large bags and goblets; but the poorer sort, like that widow in the Gospel, presented their mites also; insomuch that it was a common Jeer of men disaffected to the Cause, to call it the Thimble and Bodkin-Army' (Thomas May, *History of the Parliament of England*, 1647, II. vi. 97). See also note to II. ii. 779.

572. *like the Dragon's teeth b'ing sown.* See Ovid, *Metamorphoses*, iii. 95–114.

575. *Like th' Hebrew-calf, etc.* Cf. *History of the English and Scotch Presbytery*, Anon., 1659, p. 320: 'When it was commanded for every person through the Kingdome to bring in their plate and Jewells . . . the seditious Zealots contributed as freely as the Idolatrous Israelites to make a Golden Calfe.' See also note to II. ii. 779.

578. *Sarcasmous*: a nonce-word formed from Greek σαρκασμός (Latin *sarcasmos*), a taunt or gibe.

580. *Beasts more unclean then Calves or Steers.* An allusion to God's words to Moses and Aaron concerning clean and unclean meats: 'The carcases of every beast which divideth the hoof, and is not clovenfooted, nor cheweth the cud, are unclean unto you: every one that toucheth them shall be unclean' (Lev. xi. 26).

582. *laid themselves out*: expended themselves. An expression frequently used among the Puritans. Cf. Thomas Burton, *Diary*, 5 Dec. 1656 (ed. Rutt, 1828, i. 24): 'God's displeasure will be upon you if you do not lay out your especial endeavours in the things of God.'

585. *Have they invented Tones, etc.* See note to I. i. 228.

587. *as Indians with a female, etc.* 'Every Hunter carrieth out with him five or sixe of these females, and they say that they anoint the secret place with a certaine composition they have, that when the wilde Elephant doeth smell thereunto, they follow the females and cannot leave them' (Purchas, *Pilgrimes*, II. x. iv. 1714).

597. *Prayers, not so like Petitions, etc.* 'It is comely enough for them, to take a great chair, and at the end of the Table, and with their cock'd hats on their heads, to say: God; we thought it not amiss to call upon thee this evening; and to let thee know, how affairs stand: we have been very watchful, since we were last with thee; and things are in a very hopeful condition. . . . We do somewhat long to hear from thee; and if thou pleasest to give us such a thing (Victory) we shall be . . . as good to thee in something else' (Eachard, *Observations upon the Answer to an Enquiry*, 1671, p. 63).

599. *Such as the Army did present, etc.* In 1647 discontent was widespread in the Parliamentarian army because they had not been adequately paid and had been asked to volunteer for service in Ireland. They protested by drawing up a petition demanding payment of arrears, and the assurance that men who had already served in the army would be free from future conscription. See Gardiner, *Civil War*, iii. 225.

609. *The Parliament drew up Petitions, etc.* In their attempt to persuade Charles I to raise a militia Parliament arranged for petitions to be signed by the people, supporting their demands (Clarendon, iv. 244, 262).

620. *of all sorts.* The Solemn League and Covenant was drawn up in the name of the 'noblemen, barons . . . ministers of the Gospel, and commons of all sorts' (*Const. Docs.* lviii. 267).

621. *Velis et Remis, omnibus Nervis*: both proverbial phrases, meaning 'with might and main' (Erasmus, *Adagia*, I. iv. xvi; xviii).

626. *Each man of us to run before, etc.* The subscribers to the Solemn League and Covenant agreed to 'amend our lives, and each one to go before another in the example of a real reformation' (*Const. Docs.* lviii. 270–1).

629. *dissenting Brethren*: members of the independent Puritan sects.

630. *Malignants*: a term of abuse applied to the Royalists by the Puritans. See note to 1. i. 734.

636. *worm*: whim.

637. *to subscribe, unsight unseen, etc.* An allusion to the terms of the Solemn League and Covenant, in which the subscribers swore to undertake 'the reformation of religion . . . according to the Word of God, and the example of the best reformed Churches' (*Const. Docs.* lviii. 268).

650. *theirs that swore Et cæteras.* At the Convocation of Canterbury in 1640 the clergy agreed not to give their consent to the alteration of the government of the Church by 'archbishops, bishops, deans, and archdeacons, etc.' This oath was to be sworn by all the clergy, but the vagueness of the concluding 'etc.' was taken up by the Puritans and intentionally misinterpreted as a mandate for any sort of repression the Church might choose to introduce. See Clarendon, iii. 71; Cleveland, 'A Dialogue between two Zealots upon the &c. in the Oath' (*Minor Caroline Poets*, iii. 43–45).

651. *the French League, etc.* Butler is here quoting verbatim from an oath taken by adherents to the Sainte Ligue, formed by the Catholics against the Huguenots. Supporters of the Ligue swore to defend it 'jusques à la dernière goutte de mon sang' (Théodore Agrippa d'Aubigné, *Histoire Universelle*, 3 vols. 1616–20, 1. iii. 230). Many Anglicans were quick to see the parallel between Puritan and Catholic opposition to the monarchy in the name of religion. The anonymous author of the *History of the English and Scotch Presbytery*, 1659, draws an extended parallel between the Covenant and the Sainte Ligue, and, as late as 1682, Dryden introduces his play *The Duke of Guise* with the words

> Our Play's a Parallel: The Holy League
> Begot our Cov'nant: Guisards got the Whigg

(Dryden, *Poems*, ed. Kinsley, 4 vols. Oxford, 1958, i. 326).

656. *exorbitancies*: attacks of insanity.

669. *Incendiary*: another Puritan term of abuse. The subscribers to the Solemn League and Covenant agreed to expose all those who were 'incendiaries, malignants or evil instruments' (*Const. Docs.* lviii. 269).

671. *division*: (i) dissension; (ii) a musical descant.

675. *dictum factum*: 'no sooner said than done'. See Erasmus, *Adagia*, III. vi. lxxxv. 866.

676. *To condigne Punishment.* Cf. Solemn League and Covenant: 'they may be brought to public trial and receive condign punishment, as the degree of their offences shall require or deserve' (*Const. Docs*. lviii. 269).

688. *Meazel'd Pork.* In swine, the measles is a disease produced by the larvae tapeworms.

705. *prize*: dispute.

717. *Ale unlicenc'd.* Justices of the Peace were empowered to grant licences for the keeping of ale-houses and to 'put away common selling of ale and beer' in unlicensed houses. See Tanner, *Tudor Constitutional Documents*, Cambridge, 1922, p. 501.

broken hedge. By a statute of 1601 Justices of the Peace were empowered to seize any person found breaking a hedge or fence and to commit him to the constable to be whipped (43° Eliz. c. 7).

720. *shame due to thee.* See III. i. 58 and note.

724. *To stitch up sale and sequestration.* An Ordinance of 1643 appointed committees of sequestrators in each county to seize the lands of Royalist 'delinquents'. The estates were then sold in order to raise funds for the Parliamentarian forces. See Firth and Rait, i. 106, 254. Cleveland describes a sequestrator as 'one that fishes for the publick, but feeds himself' ('A Country Committee Man , *Works*, 1687, p. 77).

742. *sword and spur*: the distinctive marks of a knight. 'The Title of Knight is given . . . nearer the antient fashion when the girding with a Sword, and the putting on of Spurs were necessarily used in the giving it' (Selden, *Titles of Honor*, 1672, II. vii. iii. 703).

764. *free*: guiltless.

768. *Bases*: a pleated skirt, attached round the waist to the doublet, common in Tudor times; a skirt of mail. Talgol presumably wears a butcher's apron.

783. *Gorgon-shield*: the shield carried by Pallas Athene. It bore the head of the Gorgon Medusa and turned all who saw it to stone.

792. *stripe*: blow.

843. *He clapp'd them under th'Horses Tail.* Cf. *Don Quixote*, II. lxi.

865. *Pudding-time*: a lucky time (*ODEP* 523; Tilley, P634).

873. *As Sancho on a blanket fell.* For the episode in which Sancho Panza is pulled from his ass and tossed in a blanket, see *Don Quixote*, I. III. iii.

937. *Whiniard*: a short sword. See I. iii. 480.

939. *As Rats do from a falling house.* Proverbial (*ODEP* 533). 'It is the wisedome of Rats, that will be sure to leave a House somewhat before it fall' (Bacon, 'Of Wisedome for a Man's Selfe' (*Essays*, ed. West, Cambridge, 1931, p. 70).

944. *twice and once*: once or twice.

984. *A self-denying Conqueror.* An allusion to the Self-Denying Ordinance of 1645, by which it became unlawful 'for any member of either House of Parliament to hold any office or command in the army, or any place or employment of profit in the State' (*Const. Docs.* lxiii. 287; Clarendon, viii. 196).

999. *proper purchace*: rightful booty.

1005. *dispensations*: a Puritan term for the interventions of divine Providence.

1007. *Out-goings*: another Puritan term for the ordering of events by Providence. '[He] does not care to have anything founded in Right, but left at large to *Dispensations* and *Out-goings* of Providence, as he shall find Occasion to expound them to the best Advantage of his own Will and Interest' ('An Hypocritical Nonconformist', *Characters*, p. 18).

1010. *Creature*: a Puritan term for material comforts, based on New Testament usage. Cf. 1 Tim. iv. 4, and the expression 'creature comforts', which has survived.

1011. *in the Saint*: i.e. legally vested in the Saint. 'Their . . . Principle is, *That the Good things of this World belong onely to the Saints (that is, themselves) all others being usurpers thereof: and therefore they may rob, plunder, sequester, extort, cheat and confiscate . . . other mens goods and estates*' (Walker, iii. 22).

1040. *intreat*: treat.

1049. *To save, where you have pow'r to kill, etc.* An allusion to, and perversion of, Stoic principles. 'Whosoever, having been cast down from high estate at his enemy's feet, has awaited the verdict of another upon his life and throne, lives on to the glory of his preserver, and by being saved confers more upon the other's name than if he had been removed from the eyes of men' Seneca, *De Clementia*, i. xxi (*Moral Essays*, trans. Basore, 1928–35, i. 417).

1085. *Though he has quarter, etc.* An allusion to the fate of Lord Capel, who was captured by the Roundheads at Colchester and sent by Fairfax to the Tower, with the assurance that he would be well treated. He was tried by the High Court of Justice a year later, and condemned to death, in spite of the 'law of nations which exempted all prisoners, though submitting to mercy, from death, if it was not inflicted within so many days' (Clarendon, xi. 255).

1088. *our great Conquerors, you know whom.* Probably an allusion to Cromwell's notorious victory at Drogheda, where he 'put the whole garrison to the sword, not sparing those upon second thoughts to whom in the heat of the action they promised and gave quarter' (Clarendon, *View of the Affairs of Ireland*, 1849, lxxxii. 96).

1111. *force it take an Oath, etc.* Prisoners of war were sometimes released on condition that they swore not to bear arms for the enemy again. See Clarendon, vi. 140.

1168. *Like Hermit poor in pensive place*: the opening line of a popular lyric attributed to Raleigh, and printed in *The Phoenix Nest*, 1593.

1173. *forged*: manufactured.

1174. *Yet b'ing a Stranger, he's enlarged.* An allusion to Sir Bernard Gascoigne, a Florentine, originally named Guasconi, who fought with the Royalists until 1648, when he was captured at Colchester. Gascoigne's fellow-prisoners were executed and he 'had his doublet off, and expected the next salvo; but the officer told him he had order to carry him back to his friends. . . . The council had considered, that if they had in this manner taken the life of a foreigner . . . their friends or children who should visit Italy might pay dear for many generations' (Clarendon, xi. 107).

1177. *So Justice, while she winks at Crimes, etc.* Nash notes a parallel with Juvenal, *Satires*, ii. 63:

> dat veniam corvis, vexat censura columbas.

CANTO III

1. *what perils do inviron, etc.* Cf. Spenser, *Faerie Queene*, i. viii. 1:

> Ay me, how many perils doe enfold
> The righteous man, to make him daily fall?

2. *cold Iron*: a sword (colloquial).

8. *a Dog-trick*: an ill turn (colloquial).

10. *What if a Day*: the opening words of a song attributed to Thomas Campion:

> What if a day, or a month, or a yeare
> Crown thy delights with a thousand sweet contentings?
> Cannot a chance of a night or an howre
> Crosse thy desires with as many sad tormentings?

This lyric was extremely popular and appeared in many anthologies and songbooks, including Richard Alison's *An Howres Recreation in Musicke*, 1606.

12. *as certain as a Gun*: proverbial: 'beyond question' (*ODEP* 632; Tilley, G480).

16. *Thanksgiving-day.* After a military victory or other event favourable to their cause, Parliament would order a special day of thanksgiving to be held in the churches. After the discovery of Waller's plot in 1643, for example, 'the first thing they agreed on was a day of thanksgiving to God for this wonderful delivery' (Clarendon, vii. 67).

22. *Count without his Host.* Cf. the proverb 'He that reckons without his host must reckon again' (*ODEP* 535; Tilley, H726).

95. *Widdrington in doleful Dumps, etc.* An allusion to the ballad of Chevy Chase or 'The Hunting of the Cheviot':

> For Witherington needs must I wayle
> as one in dolefull dumpes,
> For when his leggs were smitten of,
> he fought upon his stumpes.

(*English and Scottish Popular Ballads*, ed. F. J. Child, 5 vols. Boston, 1882–98, iii, No. 162, st. 50).

Dumps: mournful songs.

103. *But not so light as to be born, etc.* An allusion to Virgil's description of Camilla (*Aeneid*, vii. 808–11).

106. *Witches when their staves they liquor.* Witches were believed to ride through the air on staves or broomsticks by means of a magical ointment, made from the flesh of newly born children, with which they anointed themselves and their sticks. See Kramer and Sprenger, *Malleus Maleficarum*, trans. Summers, 1928, 107; A. J. Clark, 'Flying Ointments', appendix to Margaret Murray, *Witch-Cult in Western Europe*, Oxford, 1921.

112. *hum drum*: undecided.

130. *As if the Devil drove.* Cf. the proverb 'He needs must go that the devil drives' (*ODEP* 447; Tilley, D278).

134. *First Trulla stav'd, etc.* See note to 1. ii. 163.

147. *an Austrian Archduke*: Cardinal the Archduke Albert, Archbishop of Toledo, later sovereign of the Low Countries. He led the Spanish forces against the States' army under Maurice of Nassau, at the Battle of Nieuport, 1600. During this battle, according to Grotius, he was wounded in the ear (*Annales et Historiæ de Rebus Belgicis*, Amsterdam, 1657, ix. 398). See also Bentivoglio, *History of the Warrs of Flanders*, trans. Henry, Earl of Monmouth, 1654, iii. vi. 397.

148–9. *one ear (which in Ducatoons, etc.* A ducatoon was a Venetian silver coin. 'This piece hath in one side the effigies of the Duke of Venice and the Patriarch, holding a staffe betweene them stamped thereon, with the Dukes name. And in the other, the figure of St. *Justina*' (Thomas Coryate, 'Observations of Venice', *Coryats Crudities*, 1611, p. 285). St. Justina is depicted carrying a large ear of corn which covers almost half the coin.

152. *crucify'd*: i.e. imprisoned in the pillory. By a Statute of Queen Elizabeth's time a man found guilty of forging legal documents was punished with standing in the pillory and having his ears cut off. This punishment for dishonest scriveners is often mentioned by seventeenth-century writers (Butler, 'A Scrivener', *Characters*, p. 256; Jonson, *Masque of Owls*, ll. 167–79, *Works*, vii. 786).

154. *the circumcised Brethren.*

William Pryn, a barrister of Lincoln's Inn, John Bastwick, a doctor of physic, and Henry Burton, a minister and lecturer in London . . . having been for several follies and libelling humours . . . severely censured and imprisoned, found some means in prison of correspondence . . . and to combine themselves in a more pestilent and seditious libel than they had ever before vented. . . . They were all three censured as scandalous, seditious, and infamous persons, to lose their ears in the pillory, and to be imprisoned in several gaols during the King's pleasure: all which was executed with rigour and severity enough (Clarendon, iii. 58, 62).

159. *As Authors write, etc.* Virgil, *Aeneid,* i. 691–4.

166. *Theorbo:* a large lute with two necks and two sets of tuning-pegs. The melody was played on the lower neck and the accompaniment on the upper.

172. *stout maintaining of his ground, etc.* Ajax is so described in Homer, *Iliad,* xiii. 324–5.

184. *Stout Hercules for loss of Hylas.* Hylas, who accompanied Hercules on his journeys, was drawn into a fountain by enamoured nymphs. Hercules, letting the Argonauts go on their way, stayed behind, searching for Hylas and lamenting his loss. See Valerius Flaccus, *Argonautica,* iii. 593–7.

194. *To answer to inter'gatories.* The echo-device, to which Butler alludes here, and which he parodies below (ll. 199–220), was used by Euripides in the *Andromeda,* now extant only in fragments, but familiar from Aristophanes' parody of the echo-device in his *Thesmophoriazusae* (ll. 1069–96). It was used by Latin poets, including Ovid (*Metamorphoses,* iii. 380–92) and became a characteristic device of the English masque (Jonson, *Cynthia's Revels,* i. ii. 1, *Masque of Blacknesse, Masque of Beautie*). Webster used it in *The Duchess of Malfi* (v. iii), Barnabe Barnes in *Parthenophil and Parthenope* (Sonnet lxxxix), and Sidney in the *Arcadia* (*Works,* Cambridge, 1912, ii. 352). Other examples can be found in poems by George Herbert and Lord Herbert of Cherbury.

195. *depose:* testify, swear.

202. *Marry guep:* an exclamation of surprise; originally the oath 'by Mary gypsy' or 'by St. Mary of Egypt'.

207. *winch:* flinch.

208. *Mum budget:* 'keep quiet!' Cotgrave's *Dictionarie,* 1611, defines the French expression *demeurer court* as 'to play at Mumbudget, or be at a Nonplus; not to have a word to throw at a dog'.

209. *laid i'th' dish:* held as a reproach against you.

252. *vapouring and huffing:* boasting. See I. iii. 856; II. ii. 391.

256. *for the washing gave my head:* yielded without resistance. Proverbial (*ODEP* 239; Tilley, H252).

277. *hold tack:* last out, be strong enough.

282. *lugg'd:* (i) baited; (ii) wounded in the ear.

284. *at a dead lift*: in an extremity (Tilley, L271).

311. *stand*: a place from which a hunter may shoot game.

312. *a Widow's joynture-land.* The 'Key to *Hudibras*' identifies the widow as 'The precious Relique of *Aminadab Wilmot*, an Independant, kill'd at the Fight of *Edge-hill*; and having Two hundred Pounds *per Annum* left her for a Jointure, *Hudibras* fell in Love with her, or did worse' (*Posth. Works*, i). The spurious 'Hudibras' Elegy', formerly attributed to Butler, identifies her as one widow Tomson (*Posth. Works*, 1719, iii. 236):

> Ill has he Read that never hear'd,
> How he wi' th' Widow *Tomson* far'd.

There is no evidence to support either claim.

318. *Purtenance*: the 'inwards', usually of an animal.

325. *Ants eggs.* 'Some again either through age or disease . . . have lost their generative power, that they cannot do the office of a husband if they would. Some authours commend to these oyl of Sesamum with Emmets egges bruised and set in the sun, if the yard and testicles were anointed with it' (Thomas Moffet, *Theater of Insects*, ii. xvi. 1080, appended to Topsel, *Four-footed Beasts*, 1658).

348. *Her ignorance is his devotion.* An allusion to the proverb 'Ignorance is the mother of devotion' (*ODEP* 313; Tilley, I17).

350. *Rides with his face to rump of Steed.* Ralpho and Hudibras are carried to the stocks in this way (I. iii. 963–4).

352. *Look one way, and another move.* Proverbial (*ODEP* 384; Tilley, W143).

353. *like a Tumbler, etc.* 'This sort of dogs . . . we Englishmen call "Tumblers;" because, in hunting, they turn and tumble, winding their bodies about in circle wise, and then fiercely and violently venturing upon the beast, doth suddenly gripe it' (John Caius, *Of English Dogs*, trans. Abraham Fleming, Arber, *English Garner*, 1877–96, iii. 240). 'Tumbler' may also be used with the secondary meaning of 'one who allures or inveigles persons into the hands of swindlers' (*OED*).

385. *oppugne*: overcome (Lat. *oppugnare*, to besiege).

386. *Vertue invious wayes can prove.* Cf. Horace, *Carmina*, iii. ii:

> Virtus, recludens immeritis mori
> caelum, negata temptat iter via.

invious: pathless.

395. *Fortune th'audacious doth juvare*: the Latin proverb *fortes fortuna adiuvat* (Erasmus, *Adagia*, I. ii. xlv. 88; *ODEP* 221; Tilley, F601)

428. *another gate's*: of a different kind.

460. *Quocunque trahunt.* An abbreviation of the Latin proverbial expression *quo fata trahunt*. See Virgil, *Aeneid*, v. 709; Lucan, ii. 287.

467. *tug*: strive.

478. *call'd upon his Mistress name.* Cf. III. i. 287; *Don Quixote*, I. i. 3.

493. *As that which Diomed did maul, etc.* See Homer, *Iliad*, v. 302–7.

498. *Saints twice dipt*: the Baptists, who believed in the efficacy of adult baptism, even of those who had already been baptized in childhood.

517. *goody-ship*: 'goody' was a term of civility applied to a woman, usually a married woman of low rank.

535. *Gabberdine*: a loose upper garment; a smock.

574. *Crows when they smel powder.* Grey suggests an allusion to the following custom: 'If the *Crows* toward *Harvest* are anything mischievous . . . destroying the *Corn* in the outer limits of the *Fields*, they dig a *hole* narrow at the bottom, and broad at the top, in the *green swarth* near the *Corn*, wherein they put *dust*, and *cinders* from the *Smiths* forge, mixt with a little *Gun-powder*, and in and about the *holes* stick *feathers* . . . which they find about *Burford* to have good success' (Robert Plot, *Natural History of Oxfordshire*, Oxford, 1677, ix. 98. 255).

602. *We flie, and leave our Arms behind.* 'If he did runne away, and abandoned the lists or field, where the fight was to be performed . . . this was the most base and dishonourable sort of vanquishment' (Sir William Segar, *Of Honor Military and Civill*, 1602, III. vii. 120).

606. *starter*: coward.

610. *Take Place*: (i) take precedence; (ii) precede. See I. ii. 146.

638. *happy man be's dole.* A proverbial expression (*ODEP* 277; Tilley, M158).

652. *Or stout King Richard, on his back.* 'Kyng Richardes body was brought naked over a horse backe, the hed and the armes hangyng on the one side and the legges on the other, and caried into the Grey Freres of Lecester, and surely it was but a miserable sight to looke upon' (Grafton, Continuation of Hardyng's *Chronicle*, ed. Ellis, 1812, p. 547).

728. *profligate*: overthrown.

747–8. *hang'd An Arse*: held back. See I. i. 450.

759. *More honourable far Servare, etc.* 'Multae res exstiterunt urbanae maiores clarioresque quam bellicae. . . . Sunt igitur domesticae fortitudines non inferiores militaribus; in quibus plus etiam quam in his operae studiique ponendum est' (Cicero, *De Officiis*, I. xxii).

778. *Which in all feats of Arms was hers.* Virgil's Camilla, of whom Trulla is in part a parody (see note to I. iii. 103), also plunders the dead for spoils (*Aeneid*, xi. 781–2).

804. *By which no honour's to be gain'd.* An allusion to Virgil, *Aeneid*, ii. 583–4:

> nullum memorabile nomen
> feminea in poena est nec habet victoria laudem.

865. *got me for a Tartar*: 'To catch a Tartar, in stead of catching, to be catcht in a Trap' (B.E., *Dictionary . . . of the Canting Crew*, 1699).

878. *He that is down can fall no lower*. A translation of the Latin proverb *Qui iacet in terra non habet unde cadat*. Charles I is said to have repeated this proverb when he was offered a means of escape, shortly before his execution (Louis du Four de Longuerue, *Longueruana*, Berlin, 1754, p. 23).

879. *The ancient Hero's were illustrious, etc.* To show mercy to a conquered enemy was one of the virtues upheld by the Stoics. Cicero praises the action several times, and it is a recurring theme in Seneca's *De Clementia* (see note to I. ii. 1049). Cf. Cleveland, 'Letter to the Protector after long and vile Durance in Prison', *Clievelandi Vindiciae*, 1677, p. 144: 'The most renown'd *Hero*'s have ever with such Tenderness cherished their Captives, that their Swords did but cut out work for their Courtesies.'

893. *Are mine by military law*: 'Whosoever was vanquished within the Lists, was the prisoner of him that did vanquish. To him also was due all Armes . . . garments and horse, with all furniture brought thither' (Sir William Segar, *Of Honor Military and Civill*, 1602, III. viii. 120).

900. *expugn'd*: vanquished.

910. *Lob's pound*: the stocks (colloquial).

912. *bowels*: feelings, 'heart'. Fuller describes Bishop Bonner as being 'full of guts and empty of bowels' (*Waltham Abbey*, ed. Nichols, 1840, vi. 274).

913. *now thy carcase shall redeem, etc.* Trulla's decision is in accordance with the code of chivalry: 'In case the Chalenger did not vanquish the Enemy, then ought he suffer the same paines that are due to the Defender, if he were vanquished. . . . The party vanquished should not be drawn unto the place of execution, but onely led thither to receive death or other punishment, according to the quality of the crime' (Segar, III. xvii. 136).

922. *threw it o're his sturdy back*. The 'Amazon' Radigund, having overcome Artegall, also makes him wear women's clothes as a mark of shame (Spenser, *Faerie Queene*, V. v. 20).

926. *Port-canons*: ornamental rolls sewn round the legs of breeches.

928. *dighted*: dressed.

1003. *i'th' wretched hole*. The unrevised version of this line reads 'Where leaving them in *Hockly i'th'hole*', 'meaning, by a low pun, the place where the hocks, or ankles were confined' (Nash). Hockley in the Hole was formerly an arena in Clerkenwell, used for bull- and bear-baiting (see W. B. Boulton, *Amusements of Old London*, 1901, i. 1-2). The town of Hockliffe in Bedfordshire was also known as Hockley in the Hole and is so called in a ballad (Rollins, *The Pepys Ballads*, Cambridge, Mass., 1929, I. xlv. 269).

1013. *Th'one half of man, his mind, etc.* The following lines (1013-38) are a parody of Stoic principles. 'Meanwhile, hampered by mortal limbs and encompassed by the heavy burden of the flesh, it [the mind] surveys, as best it can, the things of heaven in swift and winged thought. And so the mind can never suffer exile, since it is free, kindred to the gods, and at home in every world and every age. . . . The poor body, the prison and fetter of the soul, is tossed hither and thither. . . . But the soul itself is sacred and eternal, and upon it no hand can be laid' (Seneca, *Ad Helviam Matrem de Consolatione*, xi. 6–7, *Moral Essays*, trans. Basore, 1928–35, ii. 458–9).

1015. *laid by the heels*: put in the stocks.

1019. *perturbations*: a philosophical term used by the Stoics to signify a commotion of the mind, caused by some unreasoning impulse, which upsets the desirable state of equanimity. 'Perturbationes animorum, quae vitam insipientium miseram acerbamque reddunt . . . nulla naturae vi commoventur, omniaque ea sunt opiniones ac iudicia levitatis; itaque his sapiens semper vacabit' (Cicero, *De Finibus*, iii. x. 35).

1022. *Alexander, when he cri'd, etc.* On being told of Democritus' opinion that there were an infinite number of worlds, Alexander cried out in despair that he had only conquered one of them. See Valerius Maximus, viii. xiv; Plutarch, *De Tranquillitate Animi*, iv. 466.

1025. *Diogenes*. According to Cicero (*Tusculan Disputations*, v. xxxii. 92), Diogenes frequently told Alexander that he himself was superior to the King, for whereas he had no needs, Alexander was never satisfied.

1027. *put finger i'th'eye*: to cry (colloquial).

1031. *The Active, and the Passive valiant*. A distinction made by the Stoics: 'In duas partes virtus dividitur, in contemplationem veri, et actionem: contemplationem institutio tradit, actionem admonitio' (Seneca, *Epistolae Morales*, xciv. 45).

1039. *suggill'd*: beaten black and blue.

1044. *extended*: a legal term: to take possession by a writ of extent; hence, to seize upon, take possession of.

1050. *Truckle-bed*: a small, low bed, running on castors or truckles, usually pushed underneath a higher bed when not in use. There is also a play on the word 'truckle', which, as a derivative of 'truckle-bed', came to mean 'submit', or 'yield meanly', such beds being used by inferiors.

1080. *jump*: coincide, agree. See i. i. 620.

1091. *guts in's brains*: proverbial: 'sense' (*ODEP* 269; Tilley, G484).

1099. *Prolocutor*: the presiding officer or moderator of a church assembly.

1103. *Both Antichristian Assemblies, etc.* Ralpho is here voicing the chief objection of the independent sectarians against Presbyterian administration. Milton complained of the Westminster Assembly of Divines that their 'intents are clear to have been no better than Antichristian: setting up a Spiritual Tyranny by a Secular power' (*Character of the Long Parliament, Works*, New York, 1931–40, xviii. 252).

1117. *This to the Prophet did appear, etc.* Dan. vii. 5.

1122. *him that baited the Pope's Bull*: Henry Burton (see note to I. iii. 154), author of *The Baiting of the Popes Bull*, 1627.

1125. *Constitutions*: decrees made by ecclesiastical authority.

1126. *Church-censures*: the condemnation of spiritual offenders by the ecclesiastical power. This power was vested in the officers of the Presbyterian Church according to the Confession of Faith agreed upon by the Westminster Assembly of Divines, 1647. 'To these officers the keys of the kingdom of heaven are committed, by virtue whereof they have power respectively to retain and remit sins, to shut that kingdom against the impenitent . . . and to open it unto penitent sinners' (*Confession of Faith*, Edinburgh, 1855, p. 120).

1129. *set heathen Officers, etc.*: that is, to hand over spiritual offenders to the officers of the secular power, to be imprisoned or otherwise punished.

1134. *play with souls at fast and loose*: to bind or unbind them as they please. Butler uses the phrase in the old literal sense as an allusion to the game of 'fast and loose', in which an object, tied in a trick knot, appears to be held fast, but can be released when the conjuror wishes. The trick is explained in Scot, XIII. xxix. 336–7.

1136. *mulcts on Sin or Godliness.* In 1648 Parliament passed an 'Ordinance for the punishing of Blasphemies', specifying what were considered to be the major heresies and how those professing them should be punished (Firth and Rait, i. 1133).

1144. *Saints Monopolists are made.* This criticism was frequently made against the Presbyterians by their Anglican and sectarian opponents. Cf. Richard Overton, *Araignement of Mr Persecution*, 1645, p. 37: 'But for them hereupon to arogate Supremacy over the State and people, lay claime to an unerring spirit . . . and hereupon to compell all men to their Decrees, is most impudent presumption . . . 'tis a meere *Monopole of the Spirit*.'

1146. *dispensations and gifts*: actions done according to the will of God. See I. ii. 1005 and note; I. i. 476 and note.

1149. *Synods are whelps of th'Inquisition.* A comparison frequently made by anti-Presbyterian writers. Cf. Milton, *Observations on the Articles of Peace*: 'To require the fleshly arm of Magistracy in the execution of a spirituall Discipline . . . . we hold it no more to be *the hedg and bulwark of Religion*, then the Popish and Prelaticall Courts, or the *Spanish Inquisition*' (*Works*, New York, 1931–40, vi. 264).

1152. *Commissioners, and Triers.* In 1646 Parliament passed an 'Ordinance for keeping of Scandalous Persons from the Sacrament of the Lord's Supper and the enabling of Congregations for the Choice of Elders'. It decreed that 'Tryers of Elections' should be appointed to ensure that only men fitted for the office should be chosen to be Elders in each parish. They were to ensure that the Elders were properly qualified and to 'examine charges of undue election, scandal etc.' (Firth and Rait, i. 835). It was also declared that 'in every Province, persons shall be chosen by the Houses of Parliament that shall be Commissioners to judge of scandalous offences. . . . And if the said Commissioners after examination of all parties, shall determine the offence so presented and proved to be scandalous and the same shall certifie to the Congregation, the Eldership thereof may suspend such person from the Sacrament of the Lords Supper' (ibid. 836).

1154. *cast a figure*: draw up a horoscope.

1157. *sound and twang of Nose.* See note to 1. i. 228.

1161. *black-caps, underlaid with white*: the head-dress of Presbyterian ministers, consisting of a white skull-cap, covered by a slightly shorter black one. The edge of the white cap was turned up round the black one to form a border. See George Fox, *Journal*, Cambridge, 1952, p. 298.

1163. *Which Serjeants at the Gospel wear.* Sergeants at Law formerly wore a coif, closely resembling the Presbyterian minister's cap, as part of their robes of office. Celia Fiennes describes it as 'a black satten Cap wth a white Lace or Edge round ye bottom' (*Diary*, 1888, p. 261).

1166. *Canonical Crabat of Smeck.* 'Smectymnuus' was the name coined from the initials of five Presbyterian divines, Stephen Marshal, Edmund Calamy, Thomas Young, Matthew Newcomen, and William Spurstow. They were joint authors of *An Answer to a Book entituled An Humble Remonstrance*, 1640, an attack on episcopacy. Their attack was answered by Bishop Hall, the author of *An Humble Remonstrance*, and they were defended by Milton in his *Animadversions upon the Remonstrants Defence, against Smectymnuus*, 1641. Butler may have taken the abbreviation 'Smeck' from Cleveland who used it in his 'Smectymnuus, or the Club-Divines' (*Minor Caroline Poets*, iii. 45-48).

1174. *Grace is founded in dominion.* The concept that 'dominion is founded in grace' was probably first defined by Wycliffe in his *Of Civil Dominion*, written about 1371. Temporal power, according to Wycliffe, was held by kings because they were elected by God and stood in a state of grace. See R. L. Poole, *Illustrations of the History of Medieval Thought*, 1920, 255-9. The same defence was adopted both by the Presbyterians and the Independents during their period of power. Henry Cromwell writes to Fleetwood in 1658: 'Is it a dangerous error, that dominion is founded in grace, when it is held by the church of Rome, and a sound principle, when it is held by the fifth monarchy?' (*State Papers of John Thurloe*, ed. Birch, 1742, vii. 454). Here, however, the words are reversed, implying that, once in power, the Presbyterians could freely lay claim to grace: 'to rule is to be sanctifi'd'.

1179 *discipline*: (i) control; (ii) church administration.

1181. *Bel and the Dragon's Chaplains, etc.* Cf. Overton, *Araignement of Mr Persecution*, 1645, p. 36: 'This great gorbelly'd Idoll, called the *Assembly of Divines*, is not ashamed in this time of State necessity, to guzle up and devoure dayly more at an ordinary meale, then would make a Feast for *Bell and the Dragon*.' 'The History of the Destruction of Bel and the Dragon' is contained in the *Apocrypha*.

1193. *Directorie*: an allusion to the *Directory for the Public Worship of God*, 1644, with which the Presbyterians replaced the *Book of Common Prayer* (Firth and Rait, i. 582).

1203. *A Common-wealth of Poperie, etc.* The complaint that the new Presbyterian Elders were likely to be as dogmatic as the newly ejected Bishops, or the Pope himself, is to be found in many sectarian writings of the 1640's. Overton (*Mr Persecution*, p. 37) objected 'We did not suppresse the *High Commission*, to subject Our Selves to an *Assembly*, rase out Episcopall, to set up *Presbyterian Prelacy*', and Milton in his sonnet 'On the new forcers of Conscience' summed up anti-Presbyterian feelings in the words '*New Presbyter* is but *Old Priest* writ Large'.

1206. *Metropolitan*: Archbishop. In their attempt to introduce Presbyterianism into England, Parliament passed an Ordinance confirming that tithes should continue to be paid to ministers of the Church (Firth and Rait, i. 996).

1207. *Deacon*: an officer of the Presbyterian Church, appointed in each parish to attend to the secular affairs of the congregation, as distinct from the Elder, whose province is spiritual. This practice accords with the appointment of the first deacons, described in Acts vi. 1-6. The chapter-headings of the Geneva and Authorized Versions of this passage use the word 'Deacon' in this context.

1212. *Gregorie and Boniface.* Butler probably uses the names to signify the papacy in general, but if any specific reference is intended, it is probably to Gregory VII and Boniface VIII. The former, who was Pope from 1073 to 1085, attempted to enforce the sovereignty of the papal see over Corsica, Sardinia, Spain, and Hungary, and to increase the authority of the papacy over that of the higher prelates. Boniface VIII was Pope from 1294 to 1303. He was involved in controversies with the leading European powers, notably Philip IV of France, because of his attempts to exercise authority in temporal affairs.

1217. *'Tis that the Whore of Babylon, etc.* See Rev. xvii. 3-8. Cf. Milton, *Means to Remove Hirelings* (*Works*, vi. 81-83): 'The church then fell off and turnd whore sitting on that beast in the *Revelation*. . . . And for the magistrate in person of a nursing father to make the church his meer ward . . . transformes her oft-times into a beast of many heads and many horns.'

1221. *Simeon to Levi*: sons of Jacob and Leah. Together they massacred Hamor, Shechem, and the men of their city in revenge for the injury done to their sister Dinah. On his death-bed Jacob cursed them for their violence, saying 'Simeon and Levi are brethren; instruments of cruelty are in their habitations' (Gen. xlix. 5). The sons of Levi, or the Levites, were a sacred caste of priests, and guardians of the Temple service at Jerusalem. In England 'Levite' was formerly a contemptuous word for a member of the clergy.

1222. *Whose little finger is as heavy, etc.* On succeeding his father Solomon as king, Rehoboam was advised to say to his people 'My little finger shall be thicker than my father's loins. . . . My father hath chastised you with whips, but I will chastise you with scorpions' (1 Kings xii. 10-11). As a result, the ten tribes of Israel revolted against Rehoboam.

1227. *Lawless linsie-woolsie brother.* Linsey-woolsey was originally a material woven from a mixture of wool and flax; hence it was used figuratively to mean 'mixed' or 'confused'. By strict interpretation of the Bible, it was unlawful to wear linsey-woolsey: 'Thou shalt not wear a garment of divers sorts, as of woollen and linen together' (Deut. xxii. 11).

1237. *superciliously*: dogmatically, dictatorially.

1249. *So Cardinals, they say, do grope, etc.* 'John [VIII], of English Extraction, but born at *Mentz*, is said to have arrived at the Popedom by evil Arts; for disguising her self like a Man, whereas she was a Woman . . . upon the death of *Leo*, as *Martin* says, by common consent she was chosen Pope in his room. . . . Some say . . . that to avoid the like Error, when any Pope is first plac'd in the Porphyry Chair, which has a hole made for the purpose, his Genitals are handled by the youngest Deacon' (Baptista Platina, *Lives of the Popes*, trans. Paul Rycaut, 1688, p. 165).

1251. *Soft fire, etc.* Proverbial (*ODEP* 602; Tilley, F280).

1253. *Festina lente.* Proverbial (Erasmus, *Adagia*, II. i. i. 398).

1254. *hast (the Proverb sayes) makes waste.* See *ODEP* 281; Tilley, H189.

1258. *Elenchi*: Greek ἔλεγχος, an argument of disproof or refutation.

1259–60. *in mood and figure.* See i. i. 80 and note.

1279. *For though they do agree in kind, etc.* An allusion to the distinction between genus and species, as made by Aristotle. 'First of all we must define the number of senses borne by the term "Sameness". Sameness would be generally regarded as falling, roughly speaking, into three divisions. We generally apply the term numerically or specifically or generically—numerically in cases where there is more than one name but only one thing . . . specifically where there is more than one thing but they present no differences in respect of their species, as one man and another, or one horse and another: for things like this that fall under the same species are said to be "specifically the same". Similarly, too, those things are called generically the same which fall under the same genus, such as a horse and a man' (Aristotle, *Topica*, i. 7, trans. Pickard-Cambridge, Oxford, 1928, 103ª).

1282. *prove my horse is Socrates.* Aristotle often uses the name Socrates when indicating, for purposes of argument, a particular man. See, for example, *Topica*, viii. 10; *De Sophisticis Elenchis*, v. See also *Topica*, v. 1, where Aristotle shows the method of distinguishing 'relative' properties by the example of an argument comparing a man to a horse.

1297. *For Bears and Dogs on four legs go, etc.* An allusion to the definition of a man, proposed by Aristotle, as an animal that walks on two feet (*Topica*, v. 1; vi. 3).

1307. *Whelpt without form, etc.* 'The shee beare . . . bringeth forth commonly five whelps at a time. At the first, they seem to be a lump of white flesh without all form, little bigger than rattons, without eies, and wanting haire: only there is some shew and apparance of claws that put forth. This rude lumpe, with licking they fashion by little and little into some shape' (Pliny, *Nat. Hist.*, trans. Holland, 1634, VIII. xxxvi. 215–16).

1309. *evict*: evince; prove by argument.

1317. *Chimæra*: the beast slain by Bellerophon, according to Greek mythology. Hesiod describes the chimaera as having three heads, one of a lion, one of a goat, and one of a snake. Her forepart was a lion's, her tail a dragon's, and her waist a goat's. See Hesiod, *Theogony*, 319–25.

1329. *Ranter*: used either in the general sense of 'one who speaks bombastically', or with specific reference to the sect known as Ranters, who were, according to Baxter, 'full of horrid Oaths and Curses and Blasphemy, not fit to be repeated by the Tongue or Pen of Man' (*Reliquiae Baxterianae*, 1696, p. 77).

1343. *Gifts*: see I. i. 476 and note.

1346. *Like little David in Saul's doublet*. See 1 Sam. xvii. 38–39.

1368. *Out-run the Constable*: gone too far, beyond all bounds (*ODEP* 481; Tilley, C615).

1372. *contrary as black to white*. Proverbial (Tilley, B438).

THE SECOND PART

CANTO I

THE ARGUMENT 3. *brings his Action on the Case*: brings a writ against him. Actions of trespass on the case, or actions on the case, were so called 'because the plaintiff's whole case or cause of complaint is set forth at length in the original writ . . . formed according to the peculiar circumstances of his own particular grievance' (Blackstone, III. viii. 4. 122).

CANTO I 9. *strange*: wonder, be surprised.

17. *Til drawing bloud o'th' Dames, like witches, etc.* It was believed that a man held in the power of a witch could free himself by drawing her blood: Cleveland writes, in 'The Rebel Scot' (*Minor Caroline Poets*, iii. 57):

> Scots are like witches; do but whet your pen,
> Scratch till the blood come, they'll not hurt you then.

Accounts of this practice are given in George Giffard's *Dialogue concerning Witches and Witchcraftes*, 1593, E3ᵛ–E4ʳ.

18. *Capriches*: 'an humour, a fancy, a toy in ones head, a giddy thought' (Blount, *Glossographia*, 1674).

23. *Some force whole Regions, etc.* 'Some Critics are of Opinion, that Poets ought to apply themselves to the Imitation of *Nature*, and make a Conscience of digressing from her; but he is none of these. The antient Magicians could charm down the Moon, and force Rivers back to their Springs by the Power of Poetry only; and the Moderns will undertake to turn the Inside of the Earth outward . . . make *Nature* shew Tricks like an Ape, and the Stars run on Errands; but still it is by dint of Poetry' ('A Small Poet', *Characters*, pp. 53–54).

25. *Make former times shake hands with latter, etc.* 'He has no Respect to Decorum and Propriety of Circumstance; for the Regard of Persons, Times, and Places is a Restraint too servile to be imposed upon poetical Licence; like him that made *Plato* confess *Juvenal* to be a Philosopher' ('A Small Poet', *Characters*, p. 51).

38. *by wit or force.* 'Cum autem duobus modis, id est aut vi aut fraude, fiat injuria' (Cicero, *De Officiis*, I. xiii. 41).

40. *dog-bolt*: wretched.

41. *either it must quickly end, etc.* 'Dolor in longinquitate levis, in gravitate brevis soleat esse' (Cicero, *De Finibus*, I. xii. 40).

45. *There is a Tall Long-sided Dame, etc.* The description of Fame here is a parody of Virgil's description of Rumour (*Aeneid*, iv. 173 ff.). Chaucer partially follows Virgil in his account of Fame (*Hous of Fame*, iii. 1360 ff.).

47. *like a thin Camelion, etc.* 'Concerning the Chameleon there generally passeth an opinion that it liveth only upon air, and is sustained by no other aliment' (Browne, *Pseudodoxia*, III. xxi).

50. *lin'd through with ears, etc.* Cf. Virgil, *Aeneid*, iv. 181–3:

> monstrum horrendum, ingens, cui quot sunt corpore plumae,
> tot vigiles oculi subter (mirabile dictu),
> tot linguae, totidem ora sonant, tot subrigit auris.

The Prologue to *2 Henry IV* is spoken by Rumour 'in a Garment painted full of tongues'. Shakespearean commentators have noted other examples of Rumour's being presented in this way in Elizabethan entertainments. See Shakespeare, *2 Henry IV*, ed. Shaaber, Philadelphia, 1940, note to Induction.

53. *through the Welkin flyes.* Cf. *Aeneid*, iv. 184:

> nocte volat caeli medio terraeque per umbram
> stridens.

54. *sometimes carries Truth, oft Lyes.* Cf. *Aeneid*, iv. 188:

> tam ficti pravique tenax quam nuntia veri.

55. *like Eastern Pidgeons.* 'They which dwell heere [on the Persian Gulf], and travell from hence to Balsara, carrie with them Pigeons, whom they make their Letter-posts to Bagdad, as they doe likewise betweene Ormuz and Balsara' (Purchas, *Pilgrimage*, III. xiv. ii. 580). See also Heylyn, *Cosmographie*, 1670, iii. 786.

60. *The rate of Whetstones.* It was formerly the custom to hang a whetstone about the neck of notorious liars as they stood in the pillory; hence the proverbial expression 'He lies for the whetstone' (*ODEP* 704; Tilley, W298).

61. *Pacquet-Male*: mail-bag.

62. *Advice*: news.

64. *Cows of Monsters brought to bed, etc.* Events of this kind were presumably the source of widespread gossip and rumour among country folk. Stow records several 'monstrous births' in 1562, including the birth of a two-headed foal and a pig with legs 'like to the armes of a man child, with hands and fingers' (*Annales*, 1615, p. 647). Plot records several similar events, and also 'a storm of *Hail*, the stones near as big as *pullets eggs*', which took place in 1659 (*Natural History of Staffordshire*, 1686, vii. 262 and i. 23).

69. *Two Trumpets, etc.* Chaucer describes Aeolus as blowing on two trumpets, one of which is called Clere Laude, the other Sclaundre (*Hous of Fame*, iii. 1572–82).

79. *streight the spightful tydings bears, etc.* Cf. *Aeneid*, iv. 196–7:

> protinus ad regem cursus detorquet Iarban
> incenditque animum dictis atque aggerat iras.

81. *Democritus ne'r laugh'd so loud, etc.* See Juvenal, *Satires*, x. 33–37.

90. *be a Gossip at his Labour.* Neighbours and 'gossips' were accustomed to

visit women at the time of childbirth. Fuller writes of 'the midwife, and all the gossips present at their mother's labours' (*Worthies*, I. xx).

96. *Usher*: a male attendant on a lady.

100. *Limbo*: a prison (colloquial).

104. *further leg behind*: i.e. their right hind legs. The further side of a horse is the 'off' or right side. See *OED*, and cf. II. iii. 458.

124. *Delinquent Spirits*: see note to I. i. 734.

132. *Have heard the Devil beat a Drum*. An allusion to the ghostly drummer who, according to Glanvill, haunted the house of one John Mompesson in April 1662 (*Sadducismus Triumphatus*, 1681, ii. 89 ff.). See also Kittredge, 214.

150. *numerically*: precisely; an adverb used to emphasize the idea of identity.

172. *cut square by the Russian Standerd*. 'The Russe people . . . are for the most parte of a large sise and of very fleshly bodies, accounting it a grace to bee somewhat grosse and burley, and therefore they nourish and spread their beardes to have them long and broad' (Giles Fletcher, *Of the Russe Common Wealth*, ed. Bond, 1856, xxviii. 146).

183. *this thing call'd Pain, etc.* 'Quasi vero hoc didicisset a Zenone, non dolere cum doleret! Illud audierat nec tamen didicerat, malum illud non esse quia turpe non esset, et esse ferendum viro' (Cicero, *De Finibus*, v. xxxi. 94). See also Cicero, *Tusculan Disputations*, II. xii. 29 and II. xxv. 61.

186. *meerly as tis understood*. 'Qui doleat oportere opinetur se dolere. His autem perturbationibus, quas in vitam hominum stultitia quasi quasdam furias immittit atque incitat, omnibus viribus atque opibus, repugnandum est' (Cicero, *Tusc. Disp.* III. xi. 25).

204. *Discretion*: separation, dissolution.

205. *A Saxon Duke, etc.* John Frederick, Duke of Saxony (1503–54), was described by Roger Ascham as being 'so byg of personage as a very strong horse is scarce able to beare him' (*Report . . . of the affaires and state of Germany*, 1552, fo. 21). 'The Bishop his Countrey–man' mentioned in Butler's note is the notorious Archbishop Hatto of Mainz who, according to legend, massacred the poor people of his country and, as a punishment, was devoured by mice. See S. Baring-Gould, *Curious Myths of the Middle Ages*, 1872, p. 447.

208. *Postique*: posterior.

227. *The furthest way about, etc.* Proverbial (*ODEP* 192; Tilley, W158).

235. *Th'old Romans, freedom did bestow, etc.* It was a custom of the Romans to strike the face of a slave to mark his emancipation. The blow was known as an *alapa*.

237. *King Pyrrhus, etc.* 'Some men there be that have certaine members and parts of their bodies naturally working strange and miraculous effects, and in some cases medicinable. As for example, King *Pyrrhus*, whose great toe of his

right foot was good for them that had big, swelled, or indurate spleenes, if he did but touch the parties diseased, with that toe' (Pliny, *Nat. Hist.*, trans. Holland, 1634, VII. ii. 155).

239. *Negus*: the title of the ruler of Abyssinia.

when some mighty Lord, etc. 'If the Noble-man prove only guilty, the King leads him to his chamber, where being disrobed, prostrate on the ground, craving pardon, he receives from the Kings own hand certain stripes with a cudgell more or fewer, in proportion to the crime and services he hath done. Which done he revests, kisses the Kings feet, and with all humility thanks him for the favour received' (Vincent le Blanc, *The World Surveyed*, trans. F. B., 1660, II. iv. 190).

248. *Rib-roasting*: thrashing.

253. *Bastinadoe*: cudgelling. See II. i. 4.

259. *Catasta*: in Latin the word signifies a scaffold on which slaves were exposed for sale.

260. *elope*: escape, run away.

269. *Great Wits and Valours, etc.* Proverbial (Tilley, W579).

like great States, etc. Cf. Horace, *Epodes*, xvi. 2:

suis et ipsa Roma viribus ruit.

276. *What Glories must a Whipping have?* The proposal that Hudibras whip himself is probably derived from the advice given to Sancho Panza that he whip himself in order to release Dulcinea from enchantment (*Don Quixote*, II. xxxv).

278. *cast salt on a Womans Tayl.* An allusion to the notion that a bird may be caught by throwing salt on its tail (*ODEP* 560; Tilley, B401).

280. *Passive Courage*: i.e. stoical fortitude. See I. iii. 1031 and note.

286. *Wines work, when Vines are in the flour.* 'The Wine Marchants observe in this Country . . . that during the season that the Vines are in flower, the wine which is in the Cellar, makes a kind of fermentation . . . which continueth in a kind of disorder, untill the flowers of the Vines be fallen' (Sir Kenelm Digby, *Late Discourse . . . Touching the Cure of Wounds*, 1658, p. 79).

287. *set my rest on*: venture everything on.

300. *baulk*: overlook, ignore.

303. *experiment*: experience.

309. *idely*: uselessly.

310. *fire in antique Roman-Urns, etc.* The Romans were thought to have devised a sepulchral lamp which burned perpetually without fresh supplies of oil. See Fortunius Licetus, *De Lucernis Antiquorum Reconditis*, Venice, 1621; Montucla, *Philosophical Recreations*, trans. Hutton, 1803, iv. 496; John Wilkins, *Mathe-*

matical Magick, 1680, II. x. 232; Robert Plot, 'Discourse on the Sepulchral Lamps of the Ancients', 1684, *Philosophical Transactions*, Abridgement, iii. 100.

352. *Kill-cow*: swashbuckler, bully.

353. *Leager-lions skin*. A leaguer-coat was a military cloak used by soldiers in time of siege. Hercules is often represented as wearing the skin of the Nemean lion.

356. *T'a feeble Distaff, and a Spindle*. An allusion to the servitude of Hercules to Omphale, Queen of Lydia (Ovid, *Heroides*, ix. 55 ff.).

357. *made Emperours Gallants, etc.* The Emperor Caligula committed incest with his sister (Suetonius, *Caligula*, xxiv).

361. *gave our Senate purges, etc.* On his dissolution of Parliament in 1653 Cromwell told the House 'that they had sat long enough, unless they had done more good; that some of them were whoremasters . . . others of them were drunkards, and some corrupt and unjust men, and scandalous to the profession of the gospel' (Whitelock, *Memorials*, Oxford, 1853, iv. 5).

366. *Tubs*: sweating-tubs, used in the treatment of venereal disease. The patient was placed naked in a large barrel, in which hot stones were sprinkled with a mixture of vinegar and alcohol. The treatment is described in *The Workes of that famous Chirurgion Ambrose Parey*, trans. Thomas Johnson, 1649, XIX. xii. 480.

368. *Durty-lane, and little-Sodom*. Both notorious centres of prostitution. Dirty Lane, now Macklin Street, was in Long Acre. Little Sodom was Salisbury Court, off Fleet Street. See H. B. Wheatley, *London Past and Present*, 1891, i. 506 and ii. 206.

370. *Ring*: (i) 'the female pudend: low coll. verging on euphemistic. Standard English . . . C. 16–20' (Partridge, *Dictionary of Slang*, 1949); (ii) in horsemanship, a circle made of metal, hung from a post, which the rider attempted to carry off on the point of his lance.

Madam — : a certain Mrs. Bennett whom Pepys describes as 'a famous strumpet' (*Diary*, 22 Sept. 1660), and to whom Wycherley dedicated *The Plain Dealer*. There are references to her in Pepys, *Diary*, 30 May 1668 and Dryden, *Sir Martin Mar-all*, iv (*Works*, ed. Scott and Saintsbury, Edinburgh, 1882–93, iii. 55). The 'Key to *Hudibras*' identifies her as a Mrs. Stennet, to whom no other references have been found (*Posth. Works*, ii. 291).

371. *'Twas he, that made Saint Francis do, etc.* Bonaventure tells how the devil tempted Saint Francis with lustful desires, whereupon the saint plunged naked into a heap of snow and 'began to pile up therefrom with full hands seven mounds, the which he set before him, and thus addressed the outer man: "Behold, (saith he), this larger heap is thy wife, these four be two sons and two daughters, the other twain be a serving man and maid, that thou must needs have to serve these. Now bestir thee and clothe them, for they be perishing with cold. But if manifold cares on their behalf trouble thee, do thou be careful to serve the one Lord." Then the tempter departed, routed,

and the holy man returned to his cell victorious' (*Life of St. Francis*, v. 4, trans. E. Gurney Salter, 1904, 47–48).

383. *song*: sung. A form of the past tense of 'sing', now obsolete.

384. *As Turk and Pope are by the Saints*. An allusion to a hymn written by Robert Wisdom, appended to Sternhold and Hopkins's versions of the psalms and included in the seventeenth-century Bibles printed by Robert Barker:

> Preserve us Lord, by thy dear Word,
> From Turk and Pope defend us, Lord,
> Both which would thrust out of his throne
> Our Lord Christ Jesus, thy dear Son.

393. *the beauteous Queen of Crete, etc*. For an explanation of Butler's note, see note to III. i. 597. For the story of Pasiphaë, who conceived a passion for a bull sent from Poseidon, see Apollodorus, III. i. 3–4; Diodorus, iv. 77.

400. *By's Representative a Negro*. The devil was proverbially said to be black in colour (*ODEP* 47, 48; Tilley, D217, D255, D297).

402. *Quick*: alive. By an order of Tarquin the elder, vestal virgins who broke their vow of continence were buried in a small room and left to die of starvation (see Plutarch, *Life of Numa*, x).

425. *Which sooty Chymists stop in holes, etc*. 'When heated in the open air, [wood] burns completely away; but if the supply of air is limited, only the more volatile ingredients burn away, and the greater part of the carbon remains behind. This is the principle of *charcoal burning*. . . . A number of billets of wood are built up vertically in two or three rows into a large conical heap, which is covered over with turf or moistened charcoal-ash, holes being left at the bottom for the air to get in. . . . If a blue flame appears, it is a sign that the wood is burning away too fast, and the combustion must then be checked by partially stopping up the holes at the bottom' (Henry Watts, *Dictionary of Chemistry*, 1872, i. 759).

429. *that sturdy Thief*: the giant Cacus who stole oxen from Hercules. He dragged the animals into his cave backwards by their tails, so that they might leave no footprints (Virgil, *Aeneid*, viii. 193 ff.; Ovid, *Fasti*, i. 543; Livy, I. vii).

438. *Albertus*: Albertus Magnus (?1193–1280), Bishop of Ratisbon. Among the works formerly attributed to him is the *De Secretis Mulierum*, published in Leyden in 1596.

463. *'Tis virtue, wit, and worth, etc*. Cf. Horace, *Epistles*, I. vi. 36.

469. *goes his half*: shares with him; resembles him.

470. *Unless it be to squint and laugh*. See Pliny, XL. xxxvii. 55.

485–6. *break Your minde*: reveal your true thoughts.

487. *break*: go bankrupt.

503. *Water-witch*: i.e. a woman suspected of witchcraft who is subjected to the swimming test. See note to II. iii. 145.

532. *As Frier Bacon's noddle was.* For the source of Butler's note see Francis Bacon, *Sylva Sylvarum*, x. 957, and note to 1. ii. 344.

533. *Indians scull*. Purchas notes that the Indians 'have the bones of the sculs of their heads foure times thicker, and much stronger then ours, so that in comming to handstroakes with them, it shall be requisite not to strike them on the heads with swords, for so have many swords beene broken on their heads, with little hurt done' (*Pilgrimes*, III. v. iii. 993).

540. *strike me luck*: make a bargain. The phrase seems to have originated in the giving of a 'luck penny' as a pledge of good faith on making a bargain.

542. *Two words t'a Bargain*. Proverbial (*ODEP* 681; Tilley, W827).

547. *implicite*: vague, indefinite.

548. *Conversation*: way of life, behaviour.

555. *True as Apollo ever spoke*: i.e. through his oracle at Delphi.

556. *Oracle from heart of Oak*. See Herodotus, ii. 55; Pausanias, 1. xvii. The oracle delivered its messages through the rustling leaves of an oak tree.

560. *Pigsney*: 'dear little eye'. The word was also used as an endearing form of address.

566. *true-loves knots*: 'a kind of complicated and ornamental form of knot (usually either a double-looped bow, or a knot formed of two loops) used as a symbol of true love' (*OED*).

569. *Drink every letter on't, etc.* It was a Roman custom, when drinking the health of a mistress, to pour into the glass one cyathus (a twelfth part of a pint) for each letter in her name. See Martial, *Epigrams*, 1. lxxi.

598. *Haut-gusts, Boullies, or Ragusts*: an haut-goût is a highly seasoned dish; a bouilli is boiled or stewed meat; a ragoût is a heavily seasoned stew.

601. *Facet Doublet*: a counterfeit jewel, ground down so that it has many faces or sides.

608. *Indian Lake*: a red pigment, used as a cosmetic.

Ceruse: a cosmetic made from white lead.

618. *So loud, it deafens mortal ears.* The range and volume of the music of the spheres were thought to be so great that human ears were unable to hear it. See Censorinus, *De Die Natali*, xiii; Macrobius, *Somnium Scipionis*, 11. iv. 14.

642. *Fulhams*: dice loaded at the corner. There were two kinds of fulham, the 'high fulham', which was loaded to ensure a cast of 4, 5, or 6, and the 'low fulham' which produced a cast of 1, 2, or 3. See Charles Cotton, 'Complete Gamester', in Hartmann, *Games and Gamesters of the Restoration*, 1930, p. 6.

645. *dry-bastings*: beatings.

654. *clog*: 'Clogs, Pieces of Wood, or such like, fastened about the necks,

or to the legs of Beasts, that they run not away' (John Worlidge, *Systema Agriculturae*, 1668, p. 269).

684. *ali'nated*: transferred to the ownership of another person.

691. *Buyers you know, etc.* Proverbial (*ODEP* 73; Tilley, B788).

692. *worse then Thieves Receivers are.* Proverbial (*ODEP* 458; Tilley, R52).

698. *in the open Market toll'd for*: i.e. entered for sale in the toll-book of a cattle-market or fair. 'A horse . . . must be ridden two hours in the open market or fair, between ten and five of the clock and tolled for in the toll-book . . . or else the sale bindeth me not' (Bacon, *Use of the Law, Works*, vii. 500).

700. *You must be kept a year, and day.* 'By straying, property in live cattle is thus gotten. When they come into other men's grounds . . . then the party or lord into whose grounds or manor they come causeth them to be siezed . . . and to be cried in the markets adjoining . . . which done, if the true owner claim them not within a year and a day, then the property of them is in the lord of the manor' (Bacon, *Use of the Law, Works*, vii. 501).

703. *I must pay, etc.* 'He that takes an estray is bound, so long as he keeps it, to find it in provisions, and preserve it from damage' (Blackstone, I. VIII. XV. 298).

706. *enervate*: (i) destroy the grounds of an argument; (ii) cut the hamstrings of a horse.

707. *Topique*: argument.

715. *Semiramis of Babylon, etc.* The source of Butler's note is Ammianus Marcellinus, XIV. vi. 17. The page reference suggests that he again used the edition published in Leyden 'apud Seb. Gryphium' in 1552.

725. *some Philosophers of late here, etc.* See Sir Kenelm Digby, *Treatise of Bodies*, xxvii. 7, in *Two Treatises*, Paris, 1644, pp. 247–8. The story is also briefly told by John Webster: 'In the year 1543. there was in the parts of *Hesse* a Lad taken, who . . . was taken away, and afterwards nourished and brought up by Wolves. . . . They would make him go upon all four, and run with him, till by use and length of time, he could skip and run like a Wolf' (*Displaying of Supposed Witchcraft*, 1677, v. 91).

753. *The Prince of Cambays dayly food, etc.* 'This *Machamut* . . . so accustomed himselfe to poysons, that no day passed wherein hee tooke not some. . . . His Nature was transformed into so venemous a habit, that if hee did meane to put any of his Nobles to death, hee would cause them to be set naked before him, and chewing certaine fruits . . . by spitting upon him, in one halfe houre deprived him of life. . . . He had three or foure thousand Concubines, of whom, none lived to see a second Sunne, after hee had carnally knowne them' (Purchas, *Pilgrimage*, 1625, V. VIII. i. 537).

763. *Illation*: inference from premisses.

777. *Jail-delivery*: a pun on a legal term, meaning to clear a gaol of prisoners in order to bring them to trial.

794. *Spurs*. The distinguishing mark of a knight. See note to 1. ii. 742.

802. *To Honor's Temple had no dore, etc.* A temple dedicated to Honos was built by Fabius Cunctator. It was later enlarged and dedicated jointly to Honos and Virtus (Cicero, *De Natura Deorum*, 11. xxiii). Another temple to both deities was erected on the Capitol by Marius.

817. *This suffer'd, they are set at large, etc.* The following lines allude to the 'Act for Punishment of Rogues, Vagabonds and sturdy Beggars' (39° Eliz. c. iv). The offenders were stripped to the waist, whipped until they were bloody and escorted by the quickest route to the parish where they were born, 'after which Whipping, the same Person shall have a Testimonial subscribed with the Hand and sealed with the Seal of the same Justice of the Peace . . . testifying that the same Person hath been punished'.

839. *Matrimony, and Hanging, etc.* Proverbial (*ODEP* 276; Tilley, W232).

844. *Spare the rod, etc.* Proverbial (*ODEP* 609; Tilley, R155).

845. *A Persian Emp'rour, etc.* See Juvenal, *Satires*, x. 180; Herodotus, vii. 35. The sea is described as Cupid's grandmother, since his mother Venus was, according to some accounts, born from the sea. See Cicero, *De Natura Deorum*, 111. xxiii.

847. *some Rev'rend men approve, etc.* The Latin name for rosemary, *ros marinus*, means 'sea dew', which has been supposed to derive from the fact that it was grown close to the sea.

850. *Lydian and with Phrygian Dubs.* 'Coopers, like blacksmiths, give to their work alternately an heavy stroke and a light one; which our poet humorously compares to the Lydian and Phrygian measures' (Nash).

858. *bits of Ribbin.* 'In their frolicks, they spare not the externall ornaments of their Madams, they cannot at such seasons weare a piece of ferret ribbon but they will cut it to pieces, and swallow it in Urin to celebrate their better fortunes' (Anon., *A Character of France*, 1659, p. 13).

859. *Treats*: entreaties.

863. *China-Orenges*: the common sweet orange.

870. *Do penance in a Paper-lanthorn.* An allusion to one of the methods of treating syphilis. The patient's joints were anointed with a mixture of mercury and hog's grease, and were bound up in brown paper. See *The Workes of that famous Chirurgion Ambrose Parey*, trans. Thomas Johnson, 1649, XIX. xi. 472.

875. *Did not the Great La Mancha, etc.* See note to 11. i. 276.

877. *th'Illustrious Bassa*: the hero of Madeleine de Scudéry's romance *Ibrahim the Illustrious Bassa*, which was translated into English by Henry Cogan, 1652. As a result of his love for the Princess Isabella, Ibrahim became the slave of Solyman the Magnificent.

879. *Buls-pizzle*: the penis of a bull, dried and used as a whip.

880. *taw'd*: flayed; a word used of dressing leather.

881. *Young Florio*: the youthful lover of Biancofiore, whose story is told in Boccaccio's *Filocopo*. The boy is sent to school by his parents in order to distract his mind from Biancofiore (*Filocopo* ii, *Opere volgari*, Florence, 1827–34, vii. 77 ff.).

883. *Pathick*: (i) passive, suffering; (ii) pertaining to a catamite.

885. *Did not a certain Lady, etc.* Allusions in several popular ballads suggest that this is the wife of William Lord Monson, Lord Chief Justice of Common Pleas. He was one of the judges at the trial of Charles I, but refused to take part in the final proceedings. Grey claims that Monson was whipped by his wife because he forsook the Puritan cause, though the ballads give another reason:

> He there with the Buffle-Head,
>   Is called Lord, and of the same House,
> Who (as I have heard it said)
>   Was chastis'd by his Lady-Spouse.
> Because he run at Sheep,
>   She and her Maid gave him the Whip;
> And beat his Head so Addle;
>   You'd think he had a Knock in the Cradle,
> *Sing hi ho* Lord Mounson.

'A proper New Ballad of the Old Parliament', *Loyal Songs*, ii. xvii. 68. See also 'Chips of the Old Block', ibid. ii. xiv. 58.

888. *Claw'd*: thrashed.

890. *firk'd*: whipped.

919. *carry on a Work*. See i. i. 201 and note.

CANTO II

7. *bent*: determined.

8. *fit*: strain of music.

12. *streight*: tight.

14. *Helmont*: Jean Baptiste van Helmont (1577–1644), Belgian chemist and physician. He was an experimental scientist and the founder of the study of gases, but was also an alchemist and a mystic. His book *De Magnetica Vulnerum Curatione* incurred his condemnation for heresy by the Spanish Inquisition. He engaged in violent controversy with the theological faculties at Louvain and Cologne, and with his greatest enemy, a certain van Heer. See Thorndike, *Magic and Experimental Science*, New York, 1923–58, vii. 218–30.

14. *White*: Thomas White (1593–1676), Catholic theologian and philosopher. He was involved in continual controversy against the Protestants and earned the censure of his own Church (see *DNB*).

17. *Beat out their Brains, etc.* Cf. *Characters*, p. 104: 'This had been an excellent Course for the old Roundheaded *Stoics* to find out, whether *Bonum was Corpus*, or *Virtue an Animal*, about which they had so many fierce Encounters in their *Stoa*, that about one thousand four hundred and forty lost their Lives upon the Place.' This account is derived from a misreading of Diogenes Laertius, who writes that the philosopher Zeno used to discourse in the same colonnade where, at the time of the Thirty, 1,400 Athenian citizens had been put to death (*Zeno*, vi). The page reference in Butler's note suggests that he used the edition of Diogenes Laertius published in Paris 'apud Jacobum Nicole', 1585.

19. *That Bonum is an Animal.* 'Animum constat animal esse, cum ipse efficiat, ut simus animalia, cum ab illo animalia nomen hoc traxerint. Virtus autem nihil aliud est quam animus quodammodo se habens; ergo animal est' (Seneca, *Epistolae Morales*, cxiii. 2). Butler's note presumably refers to the ideas of Hobbes and Descartes (see notes to I. ii. 55, 57).

40. *Truckle*: a small bed. See note to I. iii. 1050.

44. *impertinent*: irrelevant.

50. *carry on the work.* See note to I. i. 201.

52. *plodding*: plotting, thinking hard.

56. *swinging*: thrashing.

58. *b'equivocation swear.* Cf. II. ii. 265 and note.

74. *Claw and Curry*: beat and thrash. Cf. I. i. 740.

80. *Clapper-clawing*: beating (colloquial).

87. *sacrifice of Bridewells*: i.e. whipping. The Bridewell was a house of correction in London, where prisoners were frequently whipped for offences. Its name became a general term for such institutions throughout the country. See H. B. Wheatley, *London Past and Present*, 1891, i. 241.

95. *vessels*: bodies; a Puritan term, taken from the Authorized and Geneva Versions of the Bible, for the body as a receptacle which contains the soul. Cf. 1 Thess. iv. 4.

103. *Saints may claim a Dispensation, etc.* As the control of Parliament passed from the Presbyterians to the Independent sectarians and the aims of the Puritan revolutionaries became more extreme, several of the oaths taken by Parliament, such as loyalty to the King and the preservation of both Houses of Parliament, were broken. Hence the Independents, and particularly Cromwell, were accused of perjury. In the following lines (ll. 103–258) Butler includes many of the principal accusations of perjury brought against the Puritan sectarians. 'Many are the publick Oaths, Protestations, Leagues, Covenants, which all English Subjects . . . by the Laws and Statutes of the

Land have formerly taken to their lawfull *Hereditary Kings, their Heirs and Successors*, to bind their *Souls*, Consciences, to bear constant Faith . . . and dutifull subjection to them . . . Which [have been] almost quite forgotten by those who have formerly taken, and as frequently violated them over and over, in the highest degree, if not abjured them by contrary late *Oaths* and *Ingagements*' (Prynne, *Concordia Discors*, 1659, 1).

107. *words but wind.* Proverbial (*ODEP* 729; Tilley, W833).

112. *weaker Vessel.* An allusion to 1 Pet. iii. 7: 'giving honour unto the wife, as unto the weaker vessel'.

116. *Reformado*: the name given to an officer who was left without a command, owing to the 'reforming' or disbanding of his company.

123. *the Dev'l, to serve his turn, etc.* Proverbial (*ODEP* 142; Tilley, D266).

131. *idly*: uselessly. An allusion to the third commandment, 'Thou shalt not take the name of the Lord thy God in vain' (Exod. xx. 7).

145. *Did we not bring our Oaths in first, etc.* Plate was brought in after the publication of 'Propositions for the bringing in of money or plate to maintain horse, horsemen and arms, for the preservation of the public peace', 1642 (Clarendon, v. 336). In these propositions reference was made to the 'Protestation', sworn in the previous year, to defend 'the true reformed Protestant religion' (Clarendon, v. 336; *Const. Docs.* xxviii. 156).

154. *break the Protestation.* The subscribers to the 'Protestation' swore to defend 'the true reformed Protestant religion expressed in the doctrine of the Church of England' and to 'defend His Majesty's royal person and estate' (*Const. Docs.* xxviii. 156).

155. *To swear, and after to recant, etc.* The terms of the 'Solemn League and Covenant' (1643) were contradicted by those of the 'Engagement' (1649). In the former the subscribers vowed to preserve the person and authority of the King, whereas in the latter they swore to defend the resolutions of Parliament 'concerning the settling of the government of this nation for the future in way of a Republic, without King or House of Lords' (*Const. Docs.* lviii. 269 and lxxxvii. 384).

160. *the KING's safety.* See 1. ii. 513 and note.

165. *Did they not swear to live and die, etc.* In 1642 both Houses voted 'That an army should be forthwith raised for the safety of the King's person . . . That the earl of Essex should be their general, and that they would live and die with him' (Clarendon, v. 388; *Const. Docs.* lvi. 261). Three years later Essex was compelled to surrender his commission by the 'Self-Denying Ordinance' (Clarendon, ix. 4; *Const. Docs.* lxiii. 287).

167. *for some have swore, etc.* Probably an allusion to the charge, made at the time of his death by some of Essex's friends, that he had been poisoned (Clarendon, x. 81).

169. *swear to maintain Law, etc.* In the 'Protestation', for example, Parliament swore to defend the Church of England, the privilege of Parliament, and 'the lawful rights and liberties of the subjects' (*Const. Docs.* xxviii. 156).

178. *prop and back the House of Lords.* 'The safety of the King's person and defence of both Houses of Parliament' were phrases very frequently included in the Parliamentary Ordinances at the beginning of the Civil War. See, for example, the 'Votes of the Houses for raising an Army', 1642 (*Const. Docs.* lvi. 261).

179. *turn'd out the whole House-ful, etc.* The House of Lords was abolished by the Commons in 1649, in the belief that it was 'useless and dangerous to the people of England to be continued' (*Const. Docs.* lxxxix. 387; Clarendon, xi. 247).

183. *Vow'd that the Red-coats would disband, etc.* During the disputes between the army and Parliament in 1647 Cromwell was accused of stirring up hostility towards the government among his troops, while at the same time assuring the House that the army would disband peaceably if they were so commanded. 'Cromwell hitherto carried himself with that rare dissimulation (in which sure he was a very great master,) that he seemed exceedingly incensed against the insolence of the soldiers. . . . He proposed that the general might be sent down to the army, who, he said, would conjure down this mutinous spirit quickly; and he was so easily believed that he himself was sent once or twice to compose the army' (Clarendon, x. 88).

185. *trol'd*: enticed; originally a fishing term, signifying to angle with a running bait.

186. *Till th' Army turn'd 'em out of Dore.* An allusion to Pride's Purge of 1648, in which the troops, commanded by Colonel Pride, blocked the entrance to the Commons and prevented the admission of those members who were known to be hostile to Cromwell's party (Clarendon, xi. 206).

191. *Publick Faith.* See i. ii. 557 and note.

192. *slur*: cheat. See i. i. 870 and note.

197. *Oaths were not purpos'd more then Law, etc.* 'The law is not made for a righteous man, but for the lawless and disobedient, for the ungodly and for sinners' (1 Tim. i. 9).

202. *no Peer is bound to swear, etc.* 'A peer sitting in judgment, gives not his verdict upon oath, like an ordinary juryman, but upon his honour: he answers also to bills in chancery upon his honour, and not upon his oath' (Blackstone, I. xii. 401).

213. *Saints have freedom, etc.* The Butler manuscripts include another version of this passage (*Satires*, p. 455).

219. *Quakers (that, like to Lanthorns, etc.* 'A Quaker . . . is the Link-Boy of the Sectaries, and talks much of his Light, but puts it under a Bushel, for nobody can see it but himself' (*Characters*, p. 149).

220. *will not swear.* The Quakers refused to take oaths, in obedience to Christ's words in the Sermon on the Mount, 'Swear not at all . . . but let your communication be Yea, yea; Nay, nay: for whatsoever is more than these cometh of evil' (Matt. v. 34, 37). See George Fox, *Journal*, ed. Nickalls, Cambridge, 1952, p. 244.

224. *breaking Priscian's head*: i.e. violating the rules of grammar (*ODEP* 500; Tilley, P595). Priscian was a celebrated Latin grammarian. This is an allusion to the Quakers' strict usage of 'thou' and 'thee', rather than 'you' for the second person singular. 'When the Lord sent me forth into the world, he forbade me to put off my hat to any, high or low; and I was required to 'thee' and 'thou' all men and women, without any respect to rich or poor, great or small' (George Fox, *Journal*, p. 36).

226. *That stirring Hats held worse then murder.* An allusion to the Quakers' refusal to remove their hats as a mark of respect. See note to l. 224 above. 'The poet humorously supposes that Priscian, who received so many blows on the head, was much averse to taking off his hat' (Nash).

235. *For Saints may do the same things, etc.* Cf. Walker, iii. 23: 'Their [the Independents'] fourth Principle is, *That they may commit any sin, and retain their Sanctity in the very Act of sinning: For what is sinfull in other men, is not so in the Saints; who may commit any crime against the Law of God, and yet it cannot be imputed to them for sin.*'

241. *as on land, etc.* 'That all Animals of the Land, are in their kind in the Sea, although received as a principle, is a tenent very questionable, and will admit of restraint. For some in the Sea are not to be matcht by any enquiry at Land, and hold those shapes which terrestrious forms approach not' (Browne, *Pseudodoxia*, iii. xxiv).

250. *above Ordinances*: Clarendon describes this phrase as 'peculiar to that time'. He applies it to the younger Vane, whom he describes as 'unlimited and unrestrained by any rules or bounds prescribed to other men by reason of his perfection. He was a perfect enthusiast and without doubt did believe himself inspired' (Clarendon, xvi. 88).

256. *No Faith is to the wicked due.* There was a proverbial expression, generally attributed to the Jesuits, that 'faith is not to be held with heretics' (*ODEP* 188; Tilley, F33).

262. *Topical*: based on probability rather than demonstration.

265. *such as the learned Jesuits use.* 'An oath, where the words according to their common signification are clear enough, but the party swearing having no will to oblige himself in that sense intendeth another, . . . is that *verball equivocation*, which amongst some other Casuists and Scholasticks, the Jesuites especially maintain and practise' (Robert Sanderson, *Obligation of Promissory Oathes*, 1655, vi. iii. 192).

287. *no Engagement is allow'd, etc.* 'If a man is under *duress of imprisonment* . . . he may allege this duress, and avoid the extorted bond' (Blackstone, i. i. 135-6).

291. *when any Jew, etc.* 'I have heard it was a Custom amongst the *Jews*, when any Man made a Vow to Almighty *God*, which afterward he found inconvenient to be kept, he might be by any three other *Jews* absolved of it' ('Two Speeches', *Satires*, p. 315). See also Selden, *Table Talk*, ed. Pollock, 1927, p. 86.

306. *Py-powder*: a summary court held at fairs and markets to deal with the offences committed among itinerant dealers; derived from Latin *pede pulverosus*, French *pied-poudreux*, a dusty-footed man, a wayfarer.

308. *swearing ex Officio.* The Court of High Commission revived the oath *ex officio mero* in Elizabeth's reign. 'The victim was bound to take the oath on pain of imprisonment for contempt, and to answer any questions, unless he wished silence to be accepted as confession' (A. F. Pollard, *Political History of England*, vi, 1910, p. 459). There was strong opposition to the use of this oath, especially from the Puritans; see Christopher Hill, *Society and Puritanism*, 1964, ch. xi.

316. *at a dead lift*: see i. iii. 284 and note.

322. *as those that carve, etc.* 'Our ancestors, when they found it difficult to carve a goose, a hare, or other dish, used to say in jest, they should hit the joint if they could think of the name of a cuckold' (Nash).

325. *High-Court of Justice.* The High Court of Justice was set up by Cromwell in 1649 for the purpose of trying Charles I. In the same year a second court was formed for the trial of such Royalists as were held prisoners. Both courts contained a large proportion of Cromwell's supporters. See Gardiner, *Commonwealth and Protectorate*, 1903, i. 10; Clarendon, xi. 218.

327. *Jealousies*: suspicions.

331. *Mould 'em, as Witches do their clay, etc.* Image magic, or *invultuacio*, was a form of witchcraft practised in many countries from classical times onwards. An effigy of clay, wax, or wood, made in the form of the victim, was tormented with nails or pins, or roasted, in the belief that the wounds would be transmitted to the victim by sympathetic magic. See Kittredge, *Witchcraft in Old and New England*, New York, 1956, pp. 73 ff.

333. *vex*: twist.

337. *most perfidiously condemn, etc.* The High Court of Justice condemned to death, among others, the Earl of Holland. A petition for mercy was presented to the court, supported by the Presbyterians, who pleaded that Holland had served Parliament against the King in the early days of the war. The petition was rejected, however, and Holland was executed. See Clarendon, xi. 259.

342. *Conveyance*: cunning; sleight of hand.

343. *blasts of wind*: 'That is, their breath, their pleadings, their arguments' (Nash).

344. *As Lapland Witches bottled Air.* '[The Laplanders], as *Zeiglers* relates it, tye three magical knots in this cord, when they untie the first, there blows a

favorable gale of wind; when the second, a brisket; when a third, the Sea and wind grow mighty stormy and tempestuous. This, that we have reported concerning the *Laplanders*, is by *Olaus Magnus*, and justly, related of the *Finlanders*, who border on the Sea, and sell winds to those Merchants that trafic with them' (John Sheffer, *History of Lapland*, Oxford, 1674, xi. 58). See also Purchas, *Pilgrimes*, III. III. i. 444.

360. *nicking*: used in the sense of 'corresponding' or 'resembling', with the suggestion that the witnesses are prepared in advance, so that their evidence is consistent and supports a certain case.

364. *cast*: convicted.

369. *Nature has made Mans breast no Windores*. Possibly an allusion to the fable told by Lucian, in which Hephaestus constructed a man, but was criticized by Momus for not making a window in the man's chest, through which his secret thoughts might be discerned (*Hermotimus*, xx, *Works*, Oxford, 1905, ii. 52).

382. *evince*: convince.

384. *ne're the near*: no nearer to my goal.

385. *glassy Bubble, etc.* 'These *Glass Drops* are small parcels of coarse green Glass taken out of the Pots that contain the *Metal* (as they call it) in fusion, upon the end of an Iron Pipe; and being exceeding hot, and thereby of a kind of sluggish fluid Consistence, are suffered to drop from thence into a Bucket of cold Water. . . . Some of these I broke in the open air, by snapping off a little of the small stem with my fingers . . . which I had no sooner done then the whole bulk of the drop flew violently, with a very brisk noise, into multitudes of small pieces' (Robert Hoöke, *Micrographia*, 1667, vii. 33).

390. *in a Lord*. See II. ii. 202 and note.

391. *Huff*: boast. Cf. I. iii. 252.

404. *hold up*: clear up (generally applied to rainy weather).

434. *Hoghgan Moghgan*: chieftain. 'A popular corruption or perversion of the Dutch *Hoogmogendheiden*, "High Mightinesses", the title of the States-General' (*OED*).

449. *Vessel*: see II. ii. 95 and note.

hoop'd: (i) supplied with hoops, like a barrel; (ii) whipped (colloquial).

468. *because in Vain*. See note to II. ii. 131.

475. *For when with your consent, etc.* 'As for those things which a servant may do on behalf of his master, they seem all to proceed upon this principle, that the master is answerable for the act of his servant, if done by his command, either expressly given, or implied: *nam, qui facit per alium, facit per se*' (Blackstone, I. xiv. 429).

479. *like the Stars, etc.* '[The stars] have a small precarious Empire, wholly at

the Will of the Subject; they can raise no Men but only Volunteers, for their Power does not extend to press any' ('An Hermetic Philosopher', *Characters*, p. 107).

485. *mince*: make light of; disparage.

491. *higgle*: cavil.

500. *pull a Crow*: settle the dispute. Cf. the proverbial expression 'I have a crow to pluck with you' (*ODEP* 120; Tilley, C855).

504. *as you sow, y' are like to reap*. Gal. vi. 7.

505. *George a Green*: a hero of ballad and romance, one of whose exploits was to fight a duel against Robin Hood. See *A Pleasant Conceyted Comedie of George a Greene*, 1599 (*Dodsley's Old Plays*, 1825–7, iii); 'The Pinder of Wakefield: Being the merry History of George a Greene', 1632; F. J. Child, *English and Scottish Popular Ballads*, Boston, 1888, iii. 129.

510. *Bishop Bonner*: Edmund Bonner, Bishop of London in the reign of Mary, who became notorious for his violent persecution of Protestants. He was said to have whipped two men, Thomas Hinshaw and John Willes, in his orchard in Fulham. See John Foxe, *Acts and Monuments*, 1596, pp. 1853–4.

523. *New-modell'd th' Army, etc.* The New Model Army, formed after the Self-Denying Ordinance of 1645, was commanded largely by Independents. See Gardiner, *Civil War*, ii. 190–4.

524. *Legion-SMEC*: i.e. the Presbyterians. See i. iii. 1166 and note.

530. *snap'd*: snapped at; defied.

533. *Maggot*: whim; fantastic notion.

534. *Directory*: the *Directory for Public Worship*. See note to i. iii. 1193.

Indian Pagod: pagan idol. A writer in 1634 alludes to the Indian 'Pagods (or Images of deformed demons)' (Sir Thomas Herbert, *Some Yeares Travels into Africa*, 1677, p. 50).

536. *On which th' had been so long a sitting.* 'The assembly of divines ... subsisted till February 22, 1648–9, about three weeks after the king's death, having sat five years, six months, and twenty-two days, in which time they had one thousand one hundred and sixty-three sessions' (Neal, iii. 413).

539. *o' the first Grass*: one year old. 'Grass' is used in the sense of 'the season when the grass grows' (*OED*).

540. *Castling*: abortive.

Foles of Balams Ass: i.e. totally outmoded. The ass of the prophet Balaam had a vision of the Lord. See Num. xxii.

557. *like a Maggot in a Sore.* Maggots were thought to be generated from the decomposition of flesh.

584. *wind-bound*: held, like a ship, by contrary winds.

F f

592. *They found it was an antique Show.* The procession which enters was known as a Skimmington, an English folk ceremony, now totally extinct. It was practised on unpopular members of the community, particularly shrewish or unfaithful wives. It generally consisted of a procession with drums and rough music, leading in two people on horseback, a woman impersonating the wife, seated in front and facing forwards, and a man, impersonating the husband, facing backwards and seated behind the woman. One of the fullest accounts, apart from Butler's, is in Marvell's 'Last Instructions to a Painter':

> From *Greenwich* . . .
> Comes news of Pastime, Martial and old:
> A Punishment invented first to awe
> Masculine Wives, transgressing Nature's Law.
> Where when the brawny Female disobeys,
> And beats the Husband till for peace he prays . . .
> . . . the just Street does the next House invade,
> Mounting the neighbour Couple on lean Jade.
> The Distaff knocks, the Grains from Kettle fly,
> And Boys and Girls in Troops run houting by.

See Marvell, *Poems and Letters*, ed. Margoliouth, 2 vols. Oxford, 1927, i. 150; E. K. Chambers, *Medieval Stage*, 2 vols. Oxford, 1903, i. 153. A Skimmington enters the stage in Heywood's *Witches of Lancashire* (*Works*, 1874, iv. 234).

596. *training*: military drill; hence, fighting.

597. *And not enlarging Territory.* A victorious Roman general was awarded an official triumph only if his success had been won after serious fighting. See Valerius Maximus, ii. viii. 1.

601. *Tall*: bold, brave.

610. *Sowgelder's Flagellate.* For the sow-gelder's 'flageolet' or horn, see note to i. ii. 537.

611. *Levet*: a trumpet-call to rouse soldiers in the morning.

612. *Breviate*: brief.

613. *over one anothers Heads.* Cf. Cleveland, 'Character of a Diurnal Maker': 'They write in the posture that the Swedes gave fire in, over one another's heads' (Morley, *Character Writings*, 1891, p. 305).

614. *They charge (three Ranks at once) like Sweads.* The tactics of the Swedish cavalry were reorganized by Gustavus Adolphus, who arranged them three or, at the most, four deep, and allowed them to charge at a gallop, independently of the infantry. Prince Rupert introduced these tactics into the Royalist army, and his methods were in turn adopted by Cromwell in the New Model Army. See C. R. L. Fletcher, *Gustavus Adolphus*, 1890, p. 123.

619. *Cornet*: carried the colours, and was the fifth commissioned officer, in a troop of cavalry.

620. *display'd*: spread out (a term of heraldry). Cf. ii. ii. 640.

626. *In windy weather, etc.* See note to iii. ii. 1108.

648. *Reformado.* See note to II. ii. 116.

650. *Whifflers*: attendants, employed to keep the way clear for a procession.

Staffiers: footmen.

656. *Sporus*: the boy whom Nero took as a wife. See Suetonius, *Nero*, xxviii.

Pope Jone: see note to I. iii. 1249.

669. *Goodwine*: Thomas Godwin (d. 1642), author of *Romanae Historiae Anthologia. An English Exposition of the Romane Antiquities, wherein many Romane and English Offices are paralleled*, Oxford, 1614.

671. *Speeds and Stows*: John Speed (?1552–1629), historian and cartographer, and author of *The Theatre of the Empire of Great Britain*, 1611; John Stow (?1525–1605), chronicler and antiquary.

683. *Hung out their Mantles Della Guer.* 'Vexillum . . . quod Tunicam etiam Isidorus [dixit]: *Russata, quam poeniceam vocant, nos coccineam. Hac sub consulibus Romani usi sunt milites, unde etiam Russati vocabantur. Solebant enim pridie quam dimicandum esset, ante principia poni* (vellem dixisset, *ante praetorium poni*, vel *supra praetorium*; id enim verius) *quasi admonitio et indicium futurae pugnae*' (Justus Lipsius, *Ad Annales Cornelii Taciti Liber Commentarius*, Leyden, 1585, p. 55).

687. *Next Links, etc.* For the sources of Butler's note see Herodianus, ii, Basle, 1535, p. 95; Lipsius, p. 13.

689. *as in Antique Triumphs, Eggs, etc.* Eggs were carried in procession at the ceremonial games held by the Greeks in honour of Ceres. See Joannes Rosinus, *Antiquitates Romanæ*, Paris, 1613, v. xiv. 363.

697. *of Course*: by custom.

698. *the Grey Mare's the better Horse.* Proverbial (*ODEP* 267; Tilley, M647).

703. *brought him under Covert-Baron*: i.e. made him act the wife. A married woman, under the protection of her husband, is said to be under covert-baron. See Blackstone, I. xv. 442.

705. *like Hares.* 'The common sort of people suppose, they are one year male, and another female. *Ælianus* also affirmeth . . . that a male Hare was once found almost dead, whose belly being opened, there were three young ones taken alive out of her belly' (Topsel, *Four-footed Beasts*, 1658, p. 209). See also Browne, *Pseudodoxia*, III. xvii.

709. *Gills*: wenches.

720. *to some tune*: considerably.

733. *Ovation was allow'd, etc.* A Roman general who had won a victory after little fighting was awarded an ovation, as a lesser form of triumph (Pliny, *Nat. Hist.* xv. xxix. 38).

739. *Chair Curule.* See note to 1. i. 709.

743. *Like Dukes of Venice, etc.* 'In this galley the Duke launceth into the sea some few miles off upon the Ascention day, being accompanied with the principall Senators and Patricians of the citie. . . . At the higher end there is a most sumptuous gilt Chaire for the Duke to sit in, at the backe whereof there is a loose boord to be lifted up, to the end he may looke into the Sea through that open space, and throw a golden ring into it, in token that he doth as it were betroth himselfe unto the sea, as the principall Lord and Commander thereof' (Thomas Coryat, 'Observations of Venice', *Coryats Crudities*, 1611, p. 219).

761. *Ethnique:* pagan.

763. *the Whore of Babylon, etc.* See Rev. xvii. 3.

766. *Type:* representation; symbol.

771. *running after self-Inventions.* See 1. i. 810 and note.

779. *Brought in their childrens spoons, and whistles.* An allusion to the time when Parliament appealed for money and plate to maintain the army. See 1. ii. 557 and note. 'Unusual voluntary collections were made both in Town and Country; the Seamstress brought in her silver Thimble, the Chamber-maid her Bodkin, the Cook his silver Spoon, the Vintner his Bowl into the common Tresury of War. . . . And observ'd it was, that some sorts of *Femalls* were freest in those contributions, as far as to part with their Rings and Ear-rings, as if some *Golden Calf* were to be molten and set up to be idoliz'd' (James Howell, *Phil Anglus*, 1660, pp. 125–6).

781. *Cullies:* dupes, gulls.

789. *rap and run:* snatch and steal.

796. *On controverted Points to eat:* 'That is, to eat plentifully of such dainties of which they would sometimes controvert the lawfulness to eat at all' (Nash). Cf. 1. i. 223–8 and notes.

798. *Cawdle:* a warm drink made from gruel, wine or ale, sugar, and spices, commonly given to invalids.

799. *done, or what left undone.* An allusion to the words of the General Confession, said at the services of Morning and Evening Prayer.

806. *Labour'd like Pioners in Trenches.* 'The parliament . . . order the trained bands to be in readiness, and fortify the passages about the city with posts, chains, and courts of guard; and it was wonderful to·see how the women and children and vast numbers of people would come to work, about digging and carrying of earth, to make their new fortifications' (Bulstrode Whitelock, *Memorials*, 9 Sept. 1642, Oxford, 1853, i. 184).

813. *Tryers.* See 1. iii. 1152 and note.

855. *the Law of Arms does bar, etc.* According to the laws of chivalry, combatants swore an oath before entering the lists, 'That they had not brought

into the Listes other Armour or weapon than was allowed, neither any engen, instrument, herbe, charme, or enchantment, and that neither of them should put affiance or trust in any thing other than God and their owne valours' (Sir William Segar, *Booke of Honor and Armes*, 1590, IV. viii. 79).

858. *Case-shot*: a collection of small projectiles, enclosed in a case and fired from a cannon.

861. *to the push*: to the test.

877. *such homely treats (they say), etc.* An allusion to the proverb 'shitten luck is good luck' (*ODEP* 582; Tilley, L581).

879. *Vespasian being dawb'd, etc.* When Vespasian was aedile, Caligula became angry with him for neglecting his duty of keeping the streets clean, and ordered him to be covered with mud. See Suetonius, *Vespasianus*, v. iii.

CANTO III

7. *with a noyse, and greasie light.* An allusion to a method of catching birds by means of a bell, a light, and a net. 'The sound of the *Low-Bell* causes the Birds to lie close, and not to stir while you lay the net over them, and the Light is so terrible to them, that it amazes them' (*Dictionarium Rusticum*, 1704, see *low bell*). The words may also be used to denote the Puritan clergy with the 'noise' of their preaching and their claims to divine 'light'.

27. *Vultors.* The word is applied colloquially to the rapacious astrologers, while at the same time alluding to the birds used for divination by the Romans.

29. *flamm*: trick, deception. Cf. II. iii. 887.

30. *Aruspicy*: divination by the inspection of entrails (Latin *haruspices*).

31. *out of Garbages of Cattle, etc.* The Roman soothsayers interpreted the will of the gods by examining the entrails of animals offered in sacrifice (Cicero, *De Divinatione*, I. xvi. 28).

33. *flight of Birds.* The Roman augurs foretold good or ill fortune by observing the flight of certain birds (Cicero, *De Divinatione*, I. xv. 26).

Chickens pecking. The auspices taken from the feeding of chickens was used particularly on military expeditions. If the birds refused to eat, the sign was unfavourable; if they ate eagerly the sign was good (Cicero, *De Divinatione*, I. xv. 27).

36. *fribble*: trifle.

50. *be punctual*: coincide exactly.

60. *on the Tenters*: on tenterhooks.

61. *taken tardy*: caught unawares.

69. *Clog.* See ii. i. 654 and note.

83. *evident Record*: written evidence.

88. *Knight oth' Post*: professional perjurer. Cf. i. i. 577 and note.

93. *enucleate*: lay open; discover.

98. *win, and wear*: possess and enjoy (*ODEP* 711; Tilley, W408).

104. *swear in vain.* See ii. ii. 131 and note.

106. *Sidrophel.* The name is formed from Latin *sidus*, a constellation, and Greek φίλος, lover. The character of Sidrophel embodies a general satire on astrology and experimental science rather than an attack on any particular individual. For evidence that Sidrophel may be a composite portrait derived from the characters of William Lilly, the astrologer, and Sir Paul Neile, the scientist, see Joseph Toy Curtiss, 'Butler's Sidrophel', *PMLA* xliv (1929), 1066 ff.

113. *Pullen*: poultry.

114. *chews'd*: tricked; deprived by trickery.

117. *Murrain*: a disease of cattle.

118. *Pip*: 'The Pippe is a white thin scale, growing on the tippe of the tongue, and will make poultry that they cannot feede' (Gervase Markham, *Cheape and Good Husbandry*, 1631, ii. ii. 149).

121. *Butter does refuse to come.* It was believed that witches had the power to enchant a farmer's cream so that it would not turn into butter. Similarly they could prevent the fermentation of ale. The astrologer would either reveal the identity of the witch or supply a charm to remove her spell. See Kittredge, pp. 167, 170; and cf. Jonson, *The Devil is an Ass*, i. i. 12–15.

127. *Saints have freedom, etc.* By a Parliamentary Ordinance of 1645, persons discovered consulting a 'Witch, Wizard or Fortune-teller' were to be suspended from the sacrament of the Lord's supper (Firth and Rait, i. 789). Such offenders were excepted from the general pardon of 1652 (ibid. ii. 569).

140. *A Ledger*: an agent, commissioner. This agent was the notorious Matthew Hopkins (d. 1647). Hopkins himself boasted that in one year he had brought sixty witches to the gallows, among whom was John Lowes, Vicar of Brandeston in Suffolk. See Matthew Hopkins, *Discovery of Witches*, 1647; Notestein, *History of Witchcraft in England*, Washington, 1911, pp. 164 ff.; Kittredge, p. 594.

145. *Some only for not being drown'd.* 'A woman, above the age of fiftie yeares, being bound hand and foote, hir clothes being upon hir, and laid downe softlie into the water, sinketh not in a long time; some saie not at all. By which experiment they were woont to trie witches' (Scot, xiii. ix. 303). 'The ordeal by swimming . . . was an old Germanic rite. The doctrine is, that the pure element of water will reject a criminal, not suffering him to sink—a notion originally pagan, but reinforced in Christian times by the use of water for baptism' (Kittredge, p. 232).

146. *some for sitting above ground.* '[Hopkins] having taken the suspected Witch, shee is placed in the middle of a room upon a stool, or Table, crosse legg'd, or in some other uneasie posture, to which if she submits not, she is then bound with cords, there is she watcht and kept without meat, or sleep for the space of 24. hours (for they say, within that Time, they shall see her Imp come and suck)' (John Gaule, *Select Cases of Conscience Touching Witches*, 1646, p. 78).

149. *putting Knavish tricks, etc.* Several of the witches brought before Hopkins were accused of having killed horses and cattle by occult means (Notestein, op. cit., pp. 169–70).

150. *Green-Geese*: goslings.

153. *after prov'd himself a Witch, etc.* 'The notion that Hopkins was "swum" and, since he floated, was subsequently hanged, most likely originated in a document criticising his performances which was brought before the Norfolk judges in 1646. . . . Hopkins printed a reply to this document shortly before his death,—*The Discovery of Witches: in Answer to severall Queries, lately delivered to the Judges of Assize for the County of Norfolk*' (Kittredge, p. 595).

155. *the Dev'l appear to Martin, etc.* 'As in the year 1521 I made in my journey a stay at Wartburg (said *Luther*), in the high castle in Pathmo, the devil many times plagued me there; but I resisted him in faith, and with this sentence I encountered him, God is my God, who hath created mankind, and hath put all things in subjection under their feet. Now if thou thinkest (Satan) that thou hast any power over me, so try it' (*Colloquia Mensalia or, the Familiar Discourses of Dr. Martin Luther . . .* translated by Captain Henry Bell, 1791, xxxv. 342).

159. *Did he not help the Dutch, etc.* See Famianus Strada, *De Bello Belgico*, Rome, 1640, I. v. 154).

161. *Sing Catches to the Saints at Mascon.* François Perreaud, a Calvinist minister of Mascon, describes the haunting of his house by a devil or unclean spirit, which 'chanta en mesme temps plusieurs chansons prophanes & lascives, notamment celle qu'on appelle *le filou*' (*L'Antidemon de Mascon*, p. 28, appended to Perreaud, *Demonologie, ou Traité des Demons et Sorciers*, Geneva, 1653). The account was translated into English by Peter du Moulin as *The Devill of Mascon*, Oxford, 1658.

163. *Appear in divers shapes to Kelly.* John Dee (1527–1608), the alchemist, astrologer, and mathematician, employed a certain Edward Kelly as a medium for making contact with the world of spirits. Dee kept a record of his conversations with the spirits, a large part of which was published, with a Preface by Meric Casaubon. See *A True and Faithful Relation of What passed for many Yeers Between Dr. John Dee . . . and Some Spirits*, 1659.

164. *And speak 'ith' Nun of Loudon's Belly.* In 1634 a certain Urbain Grandier, a priest of Loudun, was burned for witchcraft and diabolical possession. He was accused by the Ursuline nuns of Loudun of having caused them to be possessed of devils. Two years earlier, an attempt had been made to

exorcise the nuns, in the course of which conversations took place between the exorcists and the devils by whom the nuns were possessed. See Le R. P. Tranquille, *Véritable Relation des justes procédures observées au fait de la possession des Ursulines de Loudun*, Paris, 1634, reprinted in *Archives curieuses de l'histoire de France*, sér. ii, tom. v, Paris, 1838, pp. 183 ff.

165. *Meet with the Parliament's Committee, etc.* See Thomas Widows, *The just Devil of Woodstock; or a true narrative of the several apparitions, the frights and punishments, inflicted upon the Rumpish commissioners*, 1660; Anon., *The Woodstock Scuffle*, 1649, both reprinted as an appendix to Scott's *Woodstock*.

167. *At Sarum take a Cavallier, etc.* I have been unable to trace the poem by Wither mentioned in Butler's note.

171. *Do not our great Reformers, etc.* Butler here seems to identify Sidrophel with the astrologer William Lilly, who was employed by Parliament on several occasions, notably at the siege of Colchester in 1648, where he encouraged the Parliamentary forces with predictions of a speedy victory. See Sidney Lee's article on Lilly in *DNB*; Whitelock, *Memorials*, 4 vols., 1853, i. 444.

182. *fundamental Laws.* See I. i. 756 and note.

184. *Book of Common-Pray'r.* See I. ii. 552 and note.

185. *Protestation.* See I. i. 758 and note.

188. *Covenant.* See I. i. 730 and note.

196. *Gymnosophist*: a mystic. Originally the name given to a sect of ancient mystical philosophers who worshipped the Nile and lived in the open air. See Philostratus, *Life of Apollonius of Tyana*, vi. vi. ff.

224. *Hodg Bacon, and Bob Grosted.* For the legend of Bacon and the brazen head, see note to I. ii. 344. Grosseteste was several times engaged in controversy with Innocent IV, but not on charges of practising alchemy.

225. *Th'Intelligible world he knew, etc.* The hermetic philosophers adapted from Plato, through the *Hermetica*, the doctrine of the world of ideas, attributing to it the power of governing matter in the physical world. 'Every species hath its Celestiall shape, or figure that is suitable to it, from which also proceeds a wonderfull power of operating, which proper gift it receives from its own *Idea* . . . For *Idea's* are not only essentiall causes of every species, but are also the causes of every vertue, which is in the species' (Cornelius Agrippa, *Three Books of Occult Philosophy*, 1651, I. xi. 26–27). See also 'An Hermetic Philosopher', *Characters*, p. 100.

235. *Dee's Prefaces, etc.* John Dee, the Elizabethan astrologer, published a Preface to Billingsley's translation of Euclid's *Elements*, 1570. His 'preface before the devil' is presumably Dee's account of his dealings with the supernatural powers, contained in the *True and Faithful Relation*. See note to II. iii. 163.

237. *Kelly*: see note to II. iii. 163.

238. *Lescus and th' Emperor*: Albert Laski, Count Palatine of Siradia in Bohemia, was for a time the patron of Dee and Kelly, entertaining them at his castle in Poland in the hope that their experiments might lead to the discovery of the philosopher's stone. Later the two alchemists were received, less warmly, at the court of the Emperor Rudolph II of Austria. See Casaubon, Preface to Dee, *True and Faithful Relation*, D2.

240. *Almanack-well-willer*: a person well-disposed to astrology.

247. *spade*: spayed, gelded.

253. *How many Dukes, etc.* The Butler manuscript includes a passage apparently designed to be introduced here (*Satires*, p. 455).

266. *she is not made of Green Cheese*: proverbial (*ODEP* 431; Tilley, M1116).

268. *a Sea Mediterranean.* An allusion to the recent naming of lunar features after terrestrial mountains and seas by the German astronomer Hevelius. His names first appeared in *Selenographia sive Lunae Descriptio*, Danzig, 1647.

272. *Arms*: creeks, bays.

277. *Planetary Gin, etc.* 'By this Means [i.e. by the influence of the stars] they have found out the Way to make planetary Mousetraps, in which Rats and Mice shall take themselves without the Expence of toasted Cheese and Bacon' ('An Hermetic Philosopher', *Characters*, p. 101).

281. *With Lute-strings, etc.* 'The short endes of lute stringes baked in a juicy pye, will att the opening of it moove in such sort, as they who are ignorant of the feate will thinke there are magots in it' (Sir Kenelm Digby, 'Treatise of Bodies', xxvi. 4, in *Two Treatises*, Paris, 1644, p. 235).

283. *Quote Moles and Spots, etc.* William Lilly claimed to be able to discover moles and marks on a man's body, not by examining his face, but from his horoscope. See Lilly, *History of his Life*, 1715, p. 36.

292. *Cickle*: sickle. Sickles were used as charms in the same way as horseshoes.

293. *Spit fire, etc.* Eunus, a Sicilian slave, gained leadership over his fellow-slaves, in the Servile War of 134 B.C., by claiming the gift of prophecy and breathing fire from his mouth. He did so by concealing a nut inside his mouth, filled with sulphur which he ignited. See Florus, III. xix. 4; Diodorus, xxxiv.

299. *What Med'cine'twas, etc.* 'Let the Sperm of a man by it selfe be putrefied in a gourd glasse, sealed up, with the highest degree of putrefaction in Horse dung, for the space of forty days, or so long untill it begin to bee alive, move, and stir, which may easily be seen. After this time it will bee something like a Man, yet transparent, and without a body. Now after this, if it bee every day warily, and prudently nourished and fed with the *Arcanum* of Mans blood, and bee for the space of forty weeks kept in a constant, equall heat of Horse-dung, it will become a true, living infant, having all the members of an infant, which is born of a woman, but it will bee far lesse' (Paracelsus, *Of the Nature of Things*, trans. J. F., 1650, pp. 8–9).

305. *Whether a Pulse, etc.* The following lines (305–22) satirize recent observations made with the microscope, particularly those carried out by Robert Hooke and described in Hooke's *Micrographia*. Although Hooke's observations were not published until 1665, that is after the publication of the Second Part of *Hudibras*, he had already given many demonstrations with the microscope to the Royal Society in April 1663 and during the months immediately following. See R. T. Gunther, Preface to Hooke's *Micrographia*, in *Early Science in Oxford*, Oxford, 1923–45, xiii. Hooke describes in detail the pulsing of the blood of a louse and mentions the 'many small milk-white vessels, which crost over the breast' of the creature (*Micrographia*, 1667, p. 211).

306. *List*: stripe.

307. *If Systole or Diastole, etc.* 'There seem'd a contrivance [in the louse's body], somewhat resembling a Pump, pair of Bellows, or Heart, for by a very swift *systole* and *diastole* the blood seem'd drawn from the nose, and forced into the body' (Hooke, *Micrographia*, p. 212).

313. *Which Socrates, and Chærephon, etc.* See Aristophanes, *The Clouds*, ll. 143–53.

315. *Whether his Snout, etc.* 'Between these [i.e. the flea's feelers], it has a small *proboscis*, or *probe*, that seems to consist of a tube, and a tongue or sucker, which I have perceiv'd him to slip in and out' (Hooke, *Micrographia*, pp. 210–11).

317. *How many different Specieses, etc.* Hooke gives a detailed description of the mites which live 'on all kinds of substances that are mouldy, or putrifying' (*Micrographia*, p. 214).

322. *That live in Vineger.* Another of Hooke's chapters describes what he calls the 'Eels in Vinegar', visible through the microscope (*Micrographia*, pp. 216–17).

324. *Zany*: an attendant upon a mountebank, who entertained audiences by comically imitating his master.

325. *Whachum.* The 'Key to *Hudibras*' identifies Whachum as '*Tom Jones*, a foolish *Welshman* that could neither Write nor Read' and concerning whom no further information has been found. Other commentators, assuming that Sidrophel is a portrait of William Lilly, have identified Whachum as another astrologer, John Booker, who was for a time associated with Lilly. See note to II. iii. 1093, and Curtiss, 'Butler's Sidrophel', *PMLA* xliv (1929), 1066 ff. The early lines describing Whachum suggest some reference to Booker's career, noted below, but the whole portrait, like the others in *Hudibras*, is general rather than personal.

dash and draw: write speedily and draw up. Lilly records that Booker 'wrote singularly well both Secretary and Roman. In Process of Time he served Sir *Christopher Clothero*, Knight, Alderman of *London*, as his Clerk, being a City Justice of Peace' (*Life and Times*, p. 28).

353. *Holding-forth*: sermon. This Puritan term was derived from the New

Testament expression 'holding forth the word of life' (Phil. ii. 16). 'The Phrase of *Holding-forth* was taken up by *Non conformists* about the Year 1642 or 1643, as I remember . . . in contradistinction to the word *Preaching*' (John Wallis, *Defense of the Christian Sabbath*, 1694, ii. 27).

356. *Conscionable*: equitable.

359. *Rimes appropriate, etc.* The almanacs, prepared by astrologers and sold as chapbooks, generally contained a calendar showing the signs of the zodiac appropriate to each day, and a short verse describing the features of each month. Lilly comments that John Booker wrote 'excellent Verses upon the twelve Months' (*Life*, 1715, p. 28).

361. *When Termes begin, etc.* Most almanacs contained a table showing the dates when the law terms began and ended. They also listed the 'return days', on which the sheriff had to make a return to the courts, declaring how far he had carried out their instructions.

363. *Exchequer*: the Court of Exchequer, one of the four great central courts at Westminster, now merged into the Queen's Bench Division. See Chamberlayne, *Angliae Notitia*, 1677, Pt. ii, p. 106.

370. *for the service of the Great.* Petty offenders were committed to the Bridewell and made to beat hemp, which might subsequently be used in the hangman's rope.

373. *like the Devil's Oracles, etc.* The oracle at Delphi delivered its pronouncements in hexameters. Plutarch comments on the poor quality of oracular verses (*De Pythiae Oraculis*, v).

376. *Bilks*: hoaxes, deceptions.

404. *Fisk.* There is a brief reference to Fisk in *The Devil is an Ass*, 1. ii. 3. Lilly records that he became acquainted with Nicholas Fisk in 1633. He describes him as a 'Licentiate in Physick, who was born in *Suffolk*, near *Framlingham Castle*, of very good Parentage, who educated him at Country Schools, until he was fit for the University; but he went not to the Academy, studying at home both Astrology and Physick, which he afterwards practised in *Colchester*. . . . He came afterwards unto *London*, and exercised his Faculty in several Places thereof. . . . He visited me most Days once after I became acquainted with him, and would communicate the most doubtful Questions unto me. . . . He died about the Seventy-eighth Year of his Age, poor' (*Life*, pp. 29–31).

416. *Bird of Paradise.* 'The Birds of Paradise . . . reside Constantly in the Air, Nature having not bestowed upon them any Legs, and therefore they are never seen upon the Ground, but being Dead. If you ask, how they Multiply? 'Tis Answered, they lay their Eggs on the Backs of one another, upon which they Sit till their Young Ones be Fledg'd' (John Wilkins, *Discovery of a New World*, 1684, 1. xiv. 175).

417. *Heraulds Martlet.* 'The Martlet is always represented in profile, at rest, and with its wings closed. In some early examples the feet are shown: but,

in the Shield of Earl Wm. de Valence in Westminster Abbey, AD 1296, the Martlet appears feetless; and at a later period this mode of representation was generally adopted' (Charles Boutell, *English Heraldry*, 1904, p. 77).

436. *that Cannon-Ball, etc.* Descartes discusses this experiment several times in his letters, published in Paris between 1657 and 1667 (Descartes, *Œuvres*, ed. Adam and Tannery, Paris, 1897–1913, i. 287, 293–4, 341).

442. *Hangs like the Body of Mahomet.* 'They chest him in an yron coffin, (saith *Sabellicus* and *Nauclerus*) they bring him unto the famous Temple of Mecha (in which Citie he was borne) with great solemnitie . . . they convey to the roofe of the Temple mightie Loadstones, they lift up the yron coffin, where the loadstones according to their nature, draw to them the yron, and hold it up, and there hangs *Mahomet* on high' (Henry Smith, *Gods Arrow Against Atheists*, 1609, p. 46). This belief was apparently widely held. See Edward Pocock, *Specimen Historiae Arabum*, Oxford, 1806, p. 186.

454. *Tobacco-Stopper*: an implement for pressing down tobacco in a pipe while smoking. The planet Saturn was represented in books of astrology by a sign, the shape of which resembles a tobacco-stopper.

457. *Dragons Tayl*: 'the descending node of the moon's orbit with the ecliptic' (*OED*).

458. *further leg behind.* See II. i. 104 and note.

Whale: the constellation *Cetus*.

464. *wistfully*: intently.

477. *Sedgwick.* 'William Sedgewick . . . became the chief preacher of the city of Ely, and was commonly called "The Apostle of the Isle of Ely".... Having received revelations, as he pretended, he would forewarn people of their sins in public discourses, and upon pretence of a vision that doomsday was at hand, he retired to the house of Sir Franc. Russel in Cambridgeshire . . . and finding divers gentlemen there at bowles, called upon them to prepare themselves for their dissolution, telling them that he had lately received a revelation that doomsday would be some day the next week. At which the gentlemen being well pleased, they, and others, always after called him Doomsday Sedgwick' (Wood, *Athenae Oxonienses*, 1813–20, iii. 894).

483. *Feat*: event.

494. *accost*: (i) approach; (ii) discover.

498. *dark*: unknown.

530. *Venus you retriv'd, etc.* '*Whachum* having pump'd *Ralph*, and learnt of him the Business they came about, tells it to his Master in *astrological Cant*; *Mars* and *Venus* are the Lover, and his Mistress in Opposition. She is not *Virgo*, therefore a *Widow*' (Grey).

retriv'd: discovered.

536. *One tenth of 's Circle*: i.e. three years. The planet Saturn takes thirty years to revolve round the sun.

569. *Sive and Sheers*. See note to i. ii. 348.

572. *Donzel*: Italian, *donzello*; gentleman.

580. *a wrong Sow by the ear*. Proverbial (*ODEP* 607; Tilley, S685).

599. *Your Ancient Conjurers, etc.* The witches of Thessaly were celebrated for their power to charm the moon down from the sky. Plutarch suggests that the superstition originated during an eclipse (*De Defectu Oraculorum*, xiii. 417). See also Plutarch, *Coniugalia Praecepta*, xlviii. 145 ; Virgil, *Eclogues*, viii. 69.

609. *Your Modern Indian Magician, etc.* 'I remember I there saw a Magician, who perceiving a horrid tempest approaching in a thick black cloud, which would quite destroy their *Seytume*, or olives then in flower, he made a hole in the ground, and with certain words urined in it, which diverted the storm to another part' (Le Blanc, *The World Surveyed*, trans. F. B., 1660, ii. xxiii. 302).

613. *Rosy-crucian*. See note to i. i. 539.

616. *Intelligences*. See note to i. i. 527.

617. *with fumes trapan 'em*. The hermetic philosophers developed in detail the idea, derived from the *Hermetica*, that planetary influences could be invoked and made to act physically upon men by burning fumigations of herbs or incense appropriate to the particular planet whose influence was required. This ritual appears to have been practised by Ficino and by Campanella for Pope Urban VIII. See D. P. Walker, *Spiritual and Demonic Magic*, 1958, pp. 30, 207. It is also described in the second part of the 'Discourse concerning Devils and Spirits', vi. 10, appended to the 1665 edition of Scot's *Discoverie of Witchcraft*.

618. *As Dunstan did the Devil's Grannum*. 'The devil would have tempted him to uncleanness in the likeness of a beautiful Damsel; but he having a pair of hot burning pincers in his hand, caught hold of her with them by the nose, and so spoil'd the devils countenance' (William Winstanley, *England's Worthies*, 1660, p. 18). See also William Stubbs, *Memorials of Saint Dunstan*, Rolls Series LXIII (1874), lxv.

622. *in Planetary nicks*: at critical times of planetary influence.

627. *Bumbastus, kept a Devil's Bird, etc.* See Erastus, *Disputationes de Nova Philippi Paracelsi Medicina*, Basle, 1572–3, ii. 2; Naudaeus, *History of Magick*, trans. J. Davies, 1657, xiv. 185–6.

631. *Kelly did all his Feats, etc.* Edward Kelly, the assistant to the alchemist John Dee (see note to ii. iii. 163) 'carryed with him where ever he went A STONE, which he called his *Angelicall Stone*, as *brought unto him by an Angel*. . . . *It was a stone in which, and out of which, by persons that were qualified for it, and admitted to the sight of it, all Shapes and Figures mentioned in every Action were seen, and voices heard*: The *form* of it was round . . . and it seems to have been of

a pretty bigness: It seems it was most like unto Crystal' (Meric Casaubon, Preface to John Dee, *True and Faithful Relation*, 1659, D2ᵛ, G1ʳ, no pagination).

635. *Agrippa kept a Stygian-Pug, etc.* 'Paulus Jovius . . . charges him with the infamous suspicion of magic, for the reason, which follows: "Agrippa, *says he*, always had a Devil attending him in the shape of a black dog. When death seized him, and he was advised to repent, he took off the dog's neck a collar studded with nails, which formed some necromantic inscriptions, and said to him, *Get away thou wretched beast, which art the cause of my total destruction.* The dog immediately run away to the river Saone, and leap'd in, and was never seen more" ' (*A General Dictionary*, 1734, i. 357). See Paulus Jovius, *Elogia Doctorum Virorum*, Basle, 1556, ci. 237. The 'Author of *Magia Adamica*', to whom Butler alludes in his note, is Thomas Vaughan. Vaughan defended Agrippa in the Preface to *Anima Magica Abscondita*, 1650.

640. *All other Sciences are vain.* An allusion to Agrippa's *De Incertitudine et Vanitate Scientiarum*. See note to i. i. 533.

643. *Behman*: Jacob Boehme. See note to i. i. 536.

654. *Trismegistus.* See note to i. i. 523.

655. *Pythagoras, old Zoroaster, etc.* Zoroaster, Pythagoras, and Apollonius of Tyana were all considered to be 'prisci magi' or precursors of the hermetic philosophy. All three were mystics and were said to have possessed magical powers, including those of divination and healing. See E. M. Butler, *Myth of the Magus*, Cambridge, 1948, pp. 27–28, 49–55, 56–62; D. P. Walker, *Spiritual and Demonic Magic*, 1958, pp. 93, 105.

664. *truth, altho time's daughter.* Proverbial (*ODEP* 674; Tilley, T580).

665. *put her in the Pit.* An allusion to the proverb 'Truth lies at the bottom of a pit (or well)' (*ODEP* 674; Tilley, T582).

667. *he eats his Sons.* An allusion to Ovid's expression *tempus edax rerum*, which became proverbial (*Metamorphoses*, xv. 234; *ODEP* 659; Tilley, T326).

680. *To damn our whole Art for Excentrick.* Butler's source is Melanchthon, *Initia Doctrinae Physicae*, Wittenberg, 1581, pp. 88–89.

689. *Chaldeans*: astrologers. The art of divination by observing the stars was developed by the Babylonians and taken thence to Greece and Rome; hence astrologers became generally known as Chaldeans. See Cicero, *De Divinatione*, i. i. 2.

Genethliacks: astrologers who draw up nativities or horoscopes.

691. *The Median Emp'rour, etc.* See Herodotus, i. 107–8.

697. *When Cæsar in the Senate fell, etc.* See Pliny, *Nat. Hist.* ii. xxx. 30.

701. *Augustus having, b'oversight, etc.* See Pliny, *Nat. Hist.* ii. vii. 5.

708. *Crows and Ravens croak upon trees.* The croaking of crows or ravens was

thought by the Romans to be a bad omen. See Pliny, *Nat. Hist.* x. xii. 14–15.

709. *The Roman Senate, etc.* Pliny notes that the eagle-owl was considered to be a very bad omen. He records two occasions on which the bird appeared in the city of Rome, following both of which ceremonies were held to purify the city (*Nat. Hist.* x. xii. 16 and x. xiii. 17).

711. *Lustrations*: purification by religious rites.

712. *Humiliations*: days of prayer and fasting. From time to time, Parliament set aside special days of humiliation, on which the nation was to acknowledge its errors or seek the assistance of God for the accomplishment of His will. See, for example, Firth and Rait, i. 913.

728. *Found a New World, etc.* A reference to recent discoveries, by means of the telescope, of the features of the moon's surface. There may also be a specific allusion to Bishop Wilkins's *Discovery of a World in the Moone*, 1638, in which it is suggested that the moon may be inhabited.

737. *For Anaxagoras, etc.* See Diogenes Laertius, *Anaxagoras*, ii. 8–12. The page reference in Butler's note suggests that he used the edition of Diogenes Laertius published 'apud Jacobum Nicole' in Paris, 1585, pp. 111, 113.

759. *sweating Lant-horns*: the 'tubs' in which patients were treated for venereal disease by sweating. See note to ii. i. 366.

Screen-Fans: 'a thing made round of crisped paper, and set in an handle to hold before a Ladies face, when she sits neere the fire, in the winter tyme' (Randle Holme, *Academy of Armoury*, Roxburghe Club, 1905, iii. xvi. 83).

782. *the Ganzas.* An allusion to Bishop Godwin's romance *The Man in the Moon, or a Discourse of a Voyage thither by Domingo Gonsales*, 1638. The narrator is carried up to the moon by certain birds called ganzas, which are described as 'a kind of wild swan . . . having one claw like an eagle, and the other like a swan' (*Harleian Miscellany*, 1808–13, viii. 346–61).

786. *Jacobs-staff*: an instrument formerly used for measuring the altitude of the sun.

787. *Wolves raise a Hubbub at her.* Cf. the proverb 'The wolf barks in vain at the moon' (Tilley, D449).

788. *Dogs howle when she shines.* 'The moon does not heed the barking of dogs' (*ODEP* 431).

797. *Art has no mortal enemies, etc.* Proverbial, *ars non habet inimicum nisi ignorantem* (*ODEP* 14; Tilley, A331). 'Owls' and 'geese' are both colloquialisms for 'fools'.

799. *Those Consecrated Geese, etc.* When Rome had been taken by the Gauls in 390 B.C., the Capitol was saved by the cackling of the geese in the temple of Juno. Their noise woke a certain Marcus Manlius, who roused his comrades and successfully warded off the attackers (Livy, v. xlvii. 4).

803. *Athenian Sceptick Owls*: i.e. the Greek sceptics, such as Pyrrho and Sextus Empiricus, who pointed out that sense-impressions were often contradictory, and held that no knowledge was certain. 'Owl' was a colloquialism for a fool, particularly a fool who appeared wise.

819. *Gold-finders*: scavengers.

823. *Witches Simpling, etc.* Portions of the corpses of malefactors were thought to be used by witches in spells and as remedies:

> Hair from the skulls of dying strumpets shorn,
> And felons' bones, from rifled gibbets torn,
> Like those, which some old hag at midnight steals,
> For witchcrafts, amulets, and charms, and spells.

(John Oldham, *Satyres on the Jesuits*, 1681, p. 86.) See also Kittredge, pp. 141 ff.

844. *Berenice's Periwig*: the northern constellation *Coma Berenices*. Berenice was the wife of Ptolemy Euergetes. When he went on an expedition, she vowed her famous hair to Venus if he returned. After his return the hair disappeared from the temple, and was said to have been transformed into a constellation. Callimachus celebrated the event in a poem now lost, but which was translated by Catullus (*Carmina*, lxvi).

849. *Plato deny'd, etc.* Plutarch ascribes to Plato the remark that 'God always plays the geometer' (*Symposiacs*, VIII. ii. i).

864. *Factory*: the act of making; 'business'.

865. *The Ægyptians say, etc.* Butler's source is the first part of Melanchthon's *Initia Doctrinae Physicae* (Wittenberg, 1581, p. 72): 'Herodotus non vult videri ludere, sed ait ab Ægyptiis decem millia annorum, & amplius recenseri, & observatum esse in hoc tanto spacio annorum bis mutata esse loca ortuum & occasuum Solis, ita ut sol ortus sit bis, ubi nunc occidit, & bis descenderit, ubi nunc oritur.'

871. *Some hold, the Heavens, etc.* For the source of Butler's note, see Aristotle, *De Caelo*, ii. 13. 295^a, where the theory of the rapid circular motion of the heavens is attributed to Empedocles (cf. l. 875 below).

877. *Plato believ'd, etc.* For the source of Butler's note, see William Cuningham, *The Cosmographical Glasse*, 1559, i. 11. Cuningham's source is Plato, *Timaeus*, 38 c–d.

881. *The learned Scaliger, etc.* Butler's source is Bodin's *Methodus ad Facilem Historiarum Cognitionem*, viii (Strasbourg, 1599, p. 457). Julius Caesar Scaliger, the Italian philosopher and scientist, made several attacks on the ideas of his contemporary and fellow-countryman, Girolamo Cardan.

887. *Flam*: deception.

890. *Deserv'd to have his Rump well claw'd.* The passage quoted in Butler's note to l. 881 above continues: 'Quod Scaliger cum audisset, flagris dignos putavit qui talia scribunt. Ipse flagris indignus erat, quod earum rerum ignorantia, saepe, & quidem pueriliter, lapsus est.'

895. *Cardan believ'd, etc.* For Butler's source, see Bodin, op. cit. vi. 327. Bodin attributes to the Italian astrologer Cardan the theory that the fate of empires is determined by the influence of the stars, and in particular the tail of the Great Bear, which remained vertical from the foundation of Rome until its conquest (Bodin, vi. 199).

905. *Trigons*: the sets of three signs of the zodiac. The twelve signs were divided into four sets of three, each set corresponding to one of the four elements. Cancer, Scorpio, and Pisces formed the watery trigon; Aries, Leo, and Sagittarius formed the fiery trigon.

913. *th'old Chaldean Conjurers, etc.* See Cicero, *De Divinatione*, II. xlvi. 97, and note to II. iii. 689 above.

917. *Like Idus and Calendæ, etc.* Grey suggests that this is an allusion to Sir Richard Fanshawe's translation of Horace, *Epodes*, ii. 69–70:

> Omnem redegit idibus pecuniam:
> Quaerit kalendis ponere.

Fanshawe renders the lines thus:

> At *Michaelmas* calls all his Moneys in:
> But at *Our Lady* puts them out agen.

(*Selected Parts of Horace . . . Now newly put into English*, 1652, p. 64.)

923. *To swallow Gudgeons*: to be tricked, made a fool of (*ODEP* 633; Tilley, G473).

929. *Some Towns and Cities, etc.* Cicero records that a certain Lucius Tarutius drew up a horoscope for the city of Rome, on the assumption that the moon was in the sign of Libra when the city was founded by Romulus (*De Divinatione*, II. xlvii. 98).

930. *Versal*: universal, whole.

939. *Opposition, Trine, and Quartile*: 'These seven Planets moving in the twelve Signs, do make several Angles and Aspects, with each other; from whose influence the Generation and Corruption of all Sublunaries are caused. . . . A Quartile is three Signs, or ninety Degrees distant; ninety Degrees being the fourth part of three hundred sixty. . . . A Trine is four Signs distant, or 120 degrees. . . . An Opposition is 6 Signs distant, or 180 degrees' (John Gadbury, *The Doctrine of Nativities*, 1658, ii. 32).

956. *Breaks*: goes bankrupt. See II. i. 487.

975. *Like money by the Druids borrow'd, etc.* Butler's source is Franciscus Patricius, *De Institutione Reipublicae*, Strasbourg, 1594, II. vii. 97.

985. *Horary inspection*: i.e. by inspecting a figure of the heavens, erected for the moment at which the question is asked.

990. *Hab-nab*: hit or miss (*ODEP* 270; Tilley, H479).

992. *Discovers how in fight you met, etc.* This and the following lines refer to

402   *Commentary*

episodes in the spurious and anonymous Second Part of *Hudibras*, published in 1663. Butler derived the idea of disclaiming the spurious Second Part from Cervantes, whose hero disclaims the spurious Second Book of *Don Quixote* in the course of the genuine Second Book (*Don Quixote*, II. lix).

993. *At Kingston, etc.*

> Thus they pass through Market-place,
> And to Town-green hye apace,
> Highly fam'd for *Hocktide* Games,
> Yclip'd *Kingston* super *Thames*.
>
> (*Hudibras, The Second Part*, 1663, p. 15.)

with a May-pole Idol, etc. In the spurious Second Part of *Hudibras*, the knight inveighs against the May games, much in the same way as he had attacked the bear-baiting in the First Part, and is again attacked by a mob (ibid., p. 19).

996. *The Dogs beat You at Brentford Fair, etc.*

> Then out they *Snap*, and *Towser* call,
> Two cunning Currs, that would not bawl.
> But slily fly at throat, or tail,
> And in their Course would seldom fail:
> The Butchers hoot, the Dogs fall on,
> The Horses kick, and wince, anon,
> Down comes spruce *Valour* to the ground,
> And both Sir *Knights* laid in a swound.
>
> (ibid., p. 70.)

998. *Fop-doodle*: fool, simpleton.

1007. *the Saltinbanco's part, etc.* In the second canto of the spurious *Hudibras* the knight meets a French mountebank who is attempting to sell quack medicines to a crowd of spectators (op. cit., pp. 37–38).

1009. *stole your Cloke, etc.*

> And sleep they must, then down on Mat
> They threw themselves, left Cloak and Hat;
> But subtle *Quack*, and's crafty Crew,
> Slept not, they'd something else to do . . .
> The Damsel (one that would be thriving)
> In the Squires Pockets fell to diving:
> Their Cloaks were packt up 'mongst the luggage,
> (Thus Men are serv'd when they are sluggish:)
> The Gates but newly open'd were,
> All things were husht, and coast was clear,
> And so unseen they huddle out
> Into the street, then wheel about.
>
> (ibid., p. 64.)

1010. *Chews'd*: tricked.

Caldes'd: deceived; a word coined by Butler, presumably from 'Chaldean', the name given by the Romans to astrologers. See note to II. iii. 689, and cf. 'Elephant in the Moon', l. 494 (*Satires*, p. 15).

1024. *the Vibration of this Pendulum, etc.* The pendulum experiment was performed by Sir Christopher Wren at a meeting of the Royal Society on 22 January 1662, on the basis of which he proposed to set up a universal standard of measurement. See John Wilkins, *Essay Towards a Real Character And a Philosophical Language*, 1668, II. vii. 191.

1034. *Huffer*: boaster. Cf. I. iii. 252.

1093. *Booker*: John Booker (1601–67), astrologer and author of almanacs. It has been suggested that the character of Whachum was based on that of Booker (see note to II. iii. 325).

Lilly: William Lilly (1602–81), probably the best-known astrologer of his time. He published astrological predictions annually from 1644 until his death, and gained notoriety for his forecasts of the outcome of battles in the Civil War. See Lilly, *History of his Life and Times*, 1715, and note to II. iii. 106, above.

Sarah Jimmers: Sarah Jinner, the author of almanacs and predictions in the middle of the seventeenth century, including 'The Woman's Almanack', 1659. Grey and Nash identify her erroneously as Sarah Skelhorn, described by Lilly as a 'speculatrix' (*Life and Times*, p. 101).

1094. *Nimmers*: thieves.

1095. *Napiers bones*: an early aid to multiplication and division, invented by John Napier of Merchistoun, the inventor of logarithms. They consisted of thin strips of bone or ivory, marked out with digits, and are described in Napier's *Rabdologiae, seu numerationis per virgulas libri duo*, Edinburgh, 1617.

1096. *Constellation-stones*: precious stones bearing the influence of particular constellations. Such stones, according to Scot, were engraved by astrologers with the sign of their constellation, and were used as antidotes against poison and for staunching the blood from wounds (*Discoverie of Witchcraft*, XIII. vii. 297–8).

1103. *Cross, nor Pile*: 'head nor tail', i.e. money.

1108. *Rota-men*. The Rota was a club formed by James Harrington for the discussion of political theories. The club was so called after the revolving contrivance used for receiving votes, and because Harrington advocated rotation in the offices of government. Aubrey was a member and, in his life of Harrington, describes its meetings. See also note to I. i. 640.

1110. *fetch*: trick.

1115. *as a Fox, etc.* The story of the fox 'that to save himselfe from the dogges that he heard following him in full crye, did hang by his teeth among dead vermine' on a gallows, is told by Sir Kenelm Digby in his 'Treatise of Bodies', xxxvi. 6 (*Two Treatises*, Paris, 1644, p. 312).

1121. *Not out of Cunning, etc.* Sir Kenelm Digby affirms that the fox's ingenuity is not the effect of reason, but is caused by the action of circumstances on the animal's organs of sense: 'We see how the doubting, the resolving, the

ayming, the inventing, and the like, which we experience in beasts, may . . .
be followed unto their roote, as farre as the division of rarity and density;
without needing to repaire unto any higher principle' (ibid., p. 317).

1134. *Switzers*: Swiss mercenary troops, who were notorious for their
ferocity and brutality.

1148. *dead as Herring*. Proverbial (*ODEP* 131; Tilley, H446).

1153. *give himself one firk*: (i) make any effort; (ii) whip himself.

1158. *High-Places*: seats of idolatry. The high places mentioned in the Old
Testament were the hills on which religious sacrifices were carried out.
Busy, in Jonson's *Bartholomew Fair* (1. vi. 56) calls the fair 'a high place'
(*Works*, vi. 39).

1168. *twelve Free-holders*: the 'twelve free and lawful men, *liberos et legales
homines*' who formed the jury in a court of law. See Blackstone, III. xxiii. 351.

1171. *read his Lesson*: i.e. claim benefit of clergy.

AN HEROICAL EPISTLE OF HUDIBRAS TO SIDROPHEL

HEROICAL EPISTLE: the English equivalent, in general use, for the Latin
Heroides. Turberville, in his translation of Ovid's *Heroides*, 1567, gave them this
title; Drayton published in 1597 the first of his *Englands Heroicall Epistles*; and
the title was also used by Sylvester, Tofte, and Browne. See J. W. Hebel,
Works of Michael Drayton, Oxford, 1931–41, v. 97.

Ecce iterum Crispinus. Crispinus appears in the first satire of Horace (I. i. 120)
as a verbose and tedious writer. Ben Jonson portrays the poet Marston
under this name in *The Poetaster*.

3. *Treppanning*. In surgical operations the skull is cut by means of a small
saw known as a 'trepan'.

10. *of the Tribe of Issachars*. 'Issachar is a strong ass couching down between
two burdens' (Gen. xlix. 14).

13. *William Pryn's, etc.* See note to I. iii. 154.

14. *Retrench'd*: cut off. See II. ii. 23.

22. *Green-Hastings*: green peas, so called because they ripened early.

24. *Drum-heads*: eardrums.

35. *bray'd*: ground. A proverbial expression, derived from Prov. xxvii. 22:
'Though thou shouldest bray a fool in a mortar among wheat with a pestle,
yet will not his foolishness depart from him.'

36. *Nurture*: moral discipline.

39. *Can no Transfusion, etc.* Blood transfusions between animals were carried out several times during the early years of the Royal Society, but the most notorious experiment of this kind was the transfusion of a sheep's blood into a man, a certain Arthur Coga. The operation was performed without mishap, and after it the man showed no unusual reaction. See C. R. Weld, *History of the Royal Society*, 1848, i. 220; Birch, *History of the Royal Society*, 1756, ii. 216.

41. *Nor putting Pigs, etc.* This couplet is repeated in 'The Elephant in the Moon', ll. 217–18 (*Satires*, p. 8).

46. *trying sound from rotten Eggs.* In February 1672 a discourse was read to the Royal Society from Signor Malpighi on the subject of eggs. 'The philosopher had, by very careful and diligent microscopical observations, discovered that, in prolific eggs, before, as well as after, incubation, the first rudiments of the principal parts of the chick are already contained; but that, in addle eggs, instead of such a substance, there is only found a globous, ash-coloured body' (Birch, iii. 16).

48. *curing Wounds, and Scabs in Trees.* In April 1665 Daniel Coxe presented a number of questions to the Royal Society relating to trees and plants. These problems, proposed for research, included 'Wherefore are trees troubled with cancer, hidebound, and some flower so full, that they burst the calix, or case; and how those diseases may be cured' (Birch, ii. 37).

49. *Fluxing them for Claps.* A letter from Martin Lister was read to the Royal Society in February 1671, giving 'several particulars concerning the bleeding of sycamores and walnuts immediately after frosts. This gave occasion of much discourse concerning the motion of sap in trees, and the texture of them' (Birch, ii. 468). The society heard other accounts of the bleeding of trees, including one from Ray on the Bleeding of Sycamores (*Philosophical Transactions*, v. lxviii. 2069; *Abridgement*, i. 558).

51. *Shankers*: chancres, venereal ulcers.

Chrystalines: a name formerly given to the eruptions caused by gonorrhoea.

57. *whimsey'd Chariots.* Cf. 'The Elephant in the Moon', ll. 215–16 (*Satires*, p. 8). The Royal Society frequently discussed plans for the more efficient design of coaches, and models were presented for their inspection (Birch, ii. 22, 27, 30, 41, 45, etc.).

58. *course you without Law*: (i) persecute you without mercy; (ii) race against you without handicap. 'Law' was the term applied to an allowance in time or distance, given to an animal that was to be hunted, in order to give it a fair chance to escape.

60. *making old Dogs young.* In November 1666 a report was read to the Royal Society by Mr. King on the transfusion of blood between two dogs. After hearing his paper, the Society decided to initiate further experiments by

'bleeding a sheep into a mastiff, and a young healthy dog into an old and sick one & *vice versa*' (Birch, ii. 125). In the following year a letter was read from Paris recording that 'the blood of a young dog being transfused into the veins of one that was almost blind from age, and could scarcely stir, the latter was observed two hours after the operation to leap and frisk about' (*Philosophical Transactions, Abridgement*, i. 167).

76. *Naturals*: gifts, powers of mind.

80. *Men find Woodcocks by their Eies.* A distinctive feature of the woodcock is its large eyes.

81. *th' Colledge*: the Royal Society, which held its meetings at Gresham College.

86. *Sir Poll*: Sir Politick Would-be, the foolish Englishman of Jonson's *Volpone*. Grey, Nash, and others have suggested that the allusion is also to Sir Paul Neile, one of the original members of the Royal Society. See Joseph Toy Curtiss, 'Butler's Sidrophel', *PMLA* xliv (1929), 1066 ff.

96. *German Scale.* One German mile is equal to between four and five English miles.

113. *try'd*: shown by experience.

124. *An Artificial Natural*: a fool who pretends to be wise.

THE THIRD PART

CANTO I

16. *by Caligula, the Moon.* 'Et noctibus quidem plenam fulgentemque lunam invitabat assidue in amplexus atque concubitum, interdiu vero cum Capitolino Iove secreto fabulabatur' (Suetonius, *Caligula*, xxii).

53. *such as branded, etc.* An allusion to the proverbial costliness of lawsuits. In medieval times· an accused man whose guilt could not be proved might be forced to undergo trial by ordeal, essentially an appeal to God for a visible sign of the man's guilt or innocence. In one such method of trial the accused man's hand was branded with a red-hot iron and bound up by a priest. His hand was later unbound to see whether the burn had healed and thereby revealed his innocence. See Harold Potter, *Historical Introduction to English Law*, 1948, p. 313. Trial by ordeal was abolished by the Lateran Council in 1215.

55. *read one Verse, etc.*: i.e. claim benefit of clergy.

56. *must sing it*: i.e. at the gallows. Cotton (*Virgile Travestie*, 1670, iv. 145 writes of 'a portion of *Hopkins* metre'

> As people use at Execution
> For the *Decorum* of conclusion.

58. *a shame, the Dev'l might owe him.* An allusion to the proverb 'The Devil owed him a shame and now he has paid it' (Tilley, D261).

61. *Vessel*: body. See note to II. ii. 95.

69. *aggravate*: exaggerate.

85. *fitters*: fragments.

87. *Bowels*: feelings, 'hearts'. See note to I. iii. 912.

104. *Lumber*: odds and ends.

124. *the Riding Dispensation*: i.e. the providential arrival of the Skimmington. Cf. I. iii. 1146 and note.

137. *his inward Ears*: i.e. his conscience. 'Perjury itself is . . . punished with six months' imprisonment, perpetual infamy, and a fine of 20 *l.*, or to have both ears nailed to the pillory' (Blackstone, IV. x. 137).

159. *Longees*: lunges; bows.

160. *Congees*: bows.

206. *Distress*: 'the taking a personal chattel out of the possession of the wrong-doer into the custody of the party injured, to procure a satisfaction for the wrong committed' (Blackstone, III. i. 6).

Forfeiture: 'a punishment annexed by law to some illegal act, or negligence, in the owner of lands . . . whereby he loses all his interest therein, and they go to the party injured' (Blackstone, II. xviii. 267).

225. *all that we determine here, etc.* 'He seems at no loss for an application of a text in Scripture, "Whatsoever ye shall bind on earth, shall be bound in heaven" ' (Nash). See Matt. xvi. 19 and xviii. 18.

244. *upon the Place*: there and then; on the spot.

252. *the Stentrophonick Voice*: the speaking trumpet. It was invented by Sir Samuel Morland, and named after the Greek warrior Stentor, whose voice was 'as strong as the voices of fifty other men' (Homer, *Iliad*, v. 785). See Morland, *Tuba Stentoro-phonica. An instrument of excellent use, as well at sea as at land*, 1671.

262. *Flea*: flay.

264. *Time is, Time was*. The words said to have been spoken by Friar Bacon's brazen head. See note to I. ii. 344.

277. *Raptures of Platonique Lashing*. 'Some old extravagant Fornicators find a Lechery in being whipt' ('A Quaker', *Characters*, p. 149).

278. *Bardashing*: sodomy. 'The Turkes . . . if they have no Beard at all, if they be young, they call them Bardasses that is Sodomitical Boyes' (John Bulwer, *Anthropometamorphosis*, 1650, p. 132).

287. *Call'd thrice upon your Name*. Cf. I. iii. 478; *Don Quixote*, I. i. 3.

289. *transform'd himself t'a Bear, etc.* This account of Sidrophel's transformation into a bear and a goose is a satirical imitation of the transformations of Proteus, as described by Homer and Virgil (*Odyssey*, iv. 454 ff.; *Georgics*, iv. 406 ff.).

290. *tear*: rage.

307. *It Roar'd, Oh Hold, etc.* This episode, of the sorcerer's apprentice transformed into a hedge, satirically follows many such incidents in epic and romance, such as the transformation of Astolfo into a myrtle in Ariosto's *Orlando Furioso*, vi. 33. The passage may refer specifically to the fate of Polydorus, the son of Priam, over whose body a myrtle grew. When Aeneas attempted to tear a bough from the tree, it dropped blood (*Aeneid*, iii. 41 ff.).

310. *Caprich*: whim. See note to II. i. 18.

311. *Who sends me out, etc.* The Butler manuscript contains an alternative version of this passage (*Satires*, p. 456).

319. *Cowitch*. 'There is a certain Down of a Plant, brought from the *East*

Indies, call'd commonly, though very improperly, *Cow-itch*, the reason of which mistake is manifest enough from the description of it, which Mr *Parkinson* sets down in his *Herbal*, Tribe XI. Chap 2. *Phasiolus siliqua hirsuta; The hairy Kidney-bean, called in* Zurratte *where it grows, Couhage . . . the Cods . . . were in clusters, and cover'd all over with a brown short hairiness, so fine, that if any of it be rubb'd, or fall on the back of ones hand . . . it will cause a kind of itching*' (Hooke, *Micrographia*, xxvi. 145).

320. *Guiny-Pepper*: cayenne pepper, imported from Guinea on the west coast of Africa.

321. *Dewtry*. 'The Hearbe called Dutroa, is very common in India, and groweth in every fielde. . . . Out of this blossome groweth a bud, much like the bud of Popie, wherein are certaine small kernels like the kernels of Melons, which being stamped, and put into any meate . . . maketh a man, in such case as if hee were foolish or out of his wittes, so that he doth nothing else but laugh. . . . This Herbe the Indian and Portingall women use much to give their husbandes, and often times when they are disposed to bee merrie with their secrete lovers, they give it to him, and goe in his presence and performe their leacherie together' (Linschoten, *Discours of Voyages*, Hakluyt Society, LXX–LXXI (1885), ii. 68–69).

322. *Advowtry*: adultery.

324. *Manicon*: a kind of deadly nightshade, 'so dangerous, that a very little of the juice thereof is enough to trouble a mans brain, and put him beside his right wits' (Pliny, *Nat. Hist.*, trans. Holland, XXI. xxxi. 112).

326. *Potosi*: the site of the rich silver mines in Bolivia, opened by the Spaniards in the middle of the sixteenth century.

328. *Take Treasure for a Heap of Coals*. A reversal of the proverb *thesaurus carbones erant* (Erasmus, *Adagia*, I. IX. xxx. 346).

329. *Plants with Signatures*. It was commonly believed that a plant revealed its medicinal properties by its 'signature', or resemblance to that part of the human anatomy which it was capable of healing. '[God] hath not onely stamped upon them (as upon every Man) a distinct forme, but also given them particular Signatures, whereby a Man may read, even in legible Characters, the use of them. . . . *Hounds tongue* hath a forme not much different from its name, which will tye the Tongues of Hounds, so that they shall not barke at you' (William Coles, *The Art of Simpling*, 1656, pp. 88–89).

331. *Figures ground on Panes of Glass, etc.* This is probably an allusion to the camera obscura, which was already well known in England when these lines were written. It was popularized by Giovanni Battista della Porta in his *Magia Naturalis*, 1558, translated into English a century later. The Royal Society was interested in the camera obscura. In 1668 Robert Hooke described to them how it might be operated in an undarkened room (*Philosophical Transactions, Abridgement*, i. 269). For another version of this passage, see *Satires*, p. 456.

340. *Hemp on wooden Anvils, etc.* Cf. II. iii. 370 and note.

370. *Chauldrons*: a measure of four quarters; 'tons'.

376. *Grant*: i.e. a right to practise as a sorcerer. A reversion is 'the right of succeeding to the possession of something after another is done with it' (*OED*).

378. *Lady-Monger*: pimp.

381. *Puiney-Imp*: an inferior or junior imp; a nonce-word, formed on the analogy of 'puisne-judge'.

384. *Lancashire.* There was a famous witch trial held in Lancashire in 1612, in which fifteen women and four men were found guilty. Thomas Potts, who acted as clerk of the court, published an account of the trial in his *Wonderfull Discoverie of Witches in the Countie of Lancaster*, 1613. See R. T. Davies, *Four Centuries of Witch Belief*, 1947, pp. 43, 114–15.

388. *Mechanick*: base.

392. *Pharaoh's Wizards.* 'Then Pharaoh also called the wise men and the sorcerers: now the magicians of Egypt, they also did in like manner with their enchantments. For they cast down every man his rod, and they became serpents' (Exod. vii. 11–12).

398. *Cram's*: stuffs with food.

412. *Lapland Hag.* Lapland was notorious for its witches. See notes to II. ii. 344; III. i. 1133.

425. *vapouring and Huffing*: shouting and boasting.

432. *Talismanique Louse*: a model of a louse, made at a propitious astrological moment, for the purpose of warding off lice. See Butler's note to I. i. 524.

437. *Morpion*: crab-louse.

Punese: bed-bug.

439. *perfect Minutes.* See note to III. i. 432.

448. *Carts, or Horses Tail*: i.e. without being carted off to the gallows or whipped.

450. *Pendulums to Watches*: i.e. to be hanged. The pendulum watch is a watch of the modern type, in which a balance wheel replaces the pendulum used in a clock. As Butler remarks in the next lines, the balance will oscillate no matter which way the watch is held. This kind of watch was probably invented by Robert Hooke in about 1660, though a similar type was made on the Continent by Huygens at about the same time. See Richard Waller, *Life of Hooke*, in Hooke, *Posthumous Works*, 1705, vi.

481. *men of Inward light, etc.* It was a recognizable Puritan mannerism to

show the whites of the eyes at excited moments when preaching. The author of the ballad 'The Puritan' describes a preacher

> With Eyes all white, and many a Groan,
> With Neck aside to draw in Tone,
> With Harp in's Nose, or he is none.

(*A Collection of Loyal Songs Written against the Rump Parliament*, 2 vols., 1731, ii. 260.)

500. *Jump punctual*: resemble exactly.

505. *surprize*: seize, take.

521. *Who us'd to judge, etc.* 'Reprieves may also be *ex necessitate legis*: as, where a woman is capitally convicted, and pleads her pregnancy. . . . In case this plea be made in stay of execution, the judge must direct a jury of twelve matrons or discreet women to inquire the fact: and if they bring in their verdict *quick with child* . . . execution shall be staid generally till the next session' (Blackstone, iv. xxxi. 395).

523. *your Love's a Million*. Proverbial (Tilley, L553).

541. *Where all Contracts, etc.* Cf. the proverb 'Marriages are made in heaven' (*ODEP* 409; Tilley, M688).

543. *'tis counted Treason, etc.* 'Imbezzling or vacating *records*, or falsifying certain other proceedings in a court of judicature, is a felonious offence against public justice' (Blackstone, iv. x. 128).

544. *race*: erase.

546. *Nor Marriages clap'd up in Heaven*. 'For when they shall rise from the dead, they neither marry, nor are given in marriage: but are as the angels which are in heaven' (Mark xii. 25).

565. *Like Roman Gaolers, etc.* See Seneca, *Epistolae Morales*, v. 7.

573. *at a venture*: at random.

575. *For what's infer'd, etc.* The expression 'to have and to hold' occurs both in the form of solemnization of matrimony and in legal deeds of conveyance (Blackstone, ii. xx. 298).

588. *at six and seven*: risking one's whole fortune (*ODEP* 594; Tilley, A208).

591. *Beg one another Idiot, etc.* The expression 'to beg for an idiot' originated with the Court of Wards, established by Henry VIII and abolished in 1660. The court had jurisdiction over persons of unsound mind. A guardian might obtain custody of such a person by 'begging' or making a petition to the court. See Holdsworth, *History of English Law*, 2nd edition, i. 262.

597. *For which she's fortify'd, etc.* 'Children born during wedlock may in some circumstances be bastards. As if the husband be out of the kingdom of England, (or, as the law somewhat loosely phrases it, *extra quatuor maria*,) for above nine months, so that no access to his wife can be presumed, her issue during that period shall be bastards' (Blackstone, i. xvi. 456).

601. *pass away*: (i) surrender; (ii) die.

606. *justifie*: make legal.

607. *Nor at her proper cost, etc.* A wife is in no way bound to maintain her husband's bastards. They are supported either by the mother of the child, or, if an order is brought against him, by the father. See Blackstone, I. xvi. 458.

611. *the Eldest hand*: the right to play first in a game of cards.

613. *legal Cuckold*: i.e. a husband who has proved himself a cuckold in a court of law by bringing an action against the adulterer.

614. *truckled*: made to submit.

616. *Johns of Stiles, to Joans of Nokes*: fictitious names formerly used to denote the opposing parties in a legal action.

620. *valuable Consideration*: financial benefit. A term used in the law of contracts. 'This thing, which is the price or motive of the contract, we call the consideration. . . . A contract for any *valuable* consideration [is] for marriage, for money, for work done' (Blackstone, II. xxx. 443).

621. *Writ of Error, nor Reverse, etc.* See I. ii. 163 and note.

627. *Rem in Re*: a phrase coined by Butler from two other legal phrases, *in re* (in the matter of) and *in rem*. 'There is also an information *in rem*, when any goods are supposed to become the property of the crown, and no man appears to claim them. . . . An information was usually filed in the king's exchequer' (Blackstone, III. xvii. 262).

645. *gain th'advantage of the Set*: take the lead in the game.

646. *lurch*: beat, overcome.

653. *an Ague that's reverst, etc.* The ague, a kind of malarial fever, was characterized by a succession of fits, or paroxisms, first cold, then hot, then sweating.

670. *made over*: i.e. transferred their property in trust to another person. This custom appears to have been practised quite frequently. It is referred to again below, l. 1193. Thomas May comments in *The Old Couple*, 1658, Act IV:

> All your widows
> Of aldermen, that marry lords of late,
> Make over their estates, and by that means
> Retain a power to curb their lordly husbands.

See also Jonson, *Epicoene*, II. ii. 141; Congreve, *The Way of the World*, v. iii.

672. *The Foxes weigh the Goose, etc.* 'I will conclude with a famous tale of one of these crafty animals; that having killed a goose on the other side of the river, and being desirous to swimme over with it, to carry it to his denne . . . (least his prey might prove too heavy for him to swimme withall, and so he might loose it) he first weighed the goose with a piece of wood, and then tryed to carry that over the river, whiles he left his goose behind in a safe

place' (Sir Kenelm Digby, 'Treatise of Bodies', *Two Treatises*, Paris, 1644, p. 308).

680. *Cross and Pile*: 'toss-up'. See II. iii. 1103 and note.

688. *Philip and Mary, on a Shilling*. The busts of Philip and Mary face one another on the silver coins of that period. See Edward Hawkins, *Silver Coins of England*, 1876, p. 294.

696. *Prik'd Wine*: wine that has begun to turn sour.

700. *yellow Manto's of the Bride*. Yellow, as well as green, was traditionally a colour signifying jealousy. See Dekker and Webster, *Northward Hoe*, in Dekker, *Works*, 1873, iii. 14. Pliny records that the veils of Roman brides were yellow in colour (*Nat. Hist.* XXI. vii. 22).

702. *Grincam*: syphilis.

707. *Chineses go to Bed, etc.* 'When a woman in Chinese Turkestan is brought to bed, shee forsakes the bed, washeth the child and dresseth it, and then the husband lieth downe and keepes the child with him fortie dayes, not suffering it to depart: is visited meane while of friends and neighbours, to cheare and comfort him. The woman lookes to the house, carries the husband his broths to his bed, and gives sucke to the child by him' (Purchas, *Pilgrimes*, III. i. iv. vi. 92). See also Apollonius, ii. 1013; Diodorus, v. 14; Valerius Flaccus, v. 147; Strabo, III. iv. 17.

711. *Green-men*: gullible, inexperienced men.

736. *made unready*: undressed.

745. *Petard*: 'an Engine (made like a Bell, or Morter) wherewith strong gates are burst open' (Cotgrave, *Dictionarie*, 1611).

754. *inchanting murmurs, etc.* The mandrake was said to utter a cry when pulled out of the ground (Browne, *Pseudodoxia*, II. vi). There were also said to be two varieties of mandrake, 'the white which is supposed the male; and the black, which you must take for the female' (Pliny, *Nat. Hist.*, trans. Holland, II. xxv. xiii. 235).

766. *recruited*: i.e. to which the female had been added.

791. *Our Noblest Senses, etc.* The senses of sight and hearing were traditionally thought to be nobler and higher than the other three. See D. P. Walker, *Spiritual and Demonic Magic*, 1958, pp. 7–9.

793. *Intelligencers*: messengers. These are the three wits, common sense, imagination, and memory, which were thought to receive reports from the five senses and convey them to the soul. The body was thought to receive its impressions direct from the senses, whereas the soul was served by the mind or wits, which in turn were acted upon by the senses. See J. B. Bamborough, *The Little World of Man*, 1952, p. 32.

810. *pawns of Children, etc.* Proverbial (Tilley, W380). Cf. Lucan, vii. 661:

> coniunx
> est mihi, sunt nati: dedimus tot pignora fatis.

821. *Or Stoicks, etc.* Zeno and the Stoics were said to have advocated community and free choice of wives. See Diogenes Laertius, vii. 131.

842. *Banes*: banns of marriage.

858. *Due Benevolence*: the affection due to her. An allusion to Tyndale's translation of 1 Cor. vii. 3: 'Let the man geve unto the wyfe due benevolence.'

862. *Feme-Coverts*: 'The very being or legal existence of the woman is suspended during the marriage, or at least is incorporated and consolidated into that of the husband: under whose wing, protection, and *cover*, she performs every thing; and is therefore called in our law-french a *feme-covert*' (Blackstone, 1. xv. 442).

866. *Lewkners-lane*: a street (now Charles Street, Drury Lane) notorious as the rendezvous of whores. H. B. Wheatley (*London*, ii. 387) notes that in Dryden's *Wild Gallant* the old procuress who is introduced as Lady du Lake tells the heroine that her 'lodgings are in St. Lucknor's Lane'. Mr. Loveby thereupon exclaims 'I am ruin'd. Plague, had you no places in the Town to name but Sodom and Lucknor's Lane for lodgings' (*Wild Gallant*, iv).

868. *Ladies of the Lakes*: i.e. whores. The title was possibly a common colloquialism (see note to l. 866 above). It was coined with an allusion to the Arthurian Lady of the Lake and to the double meaning of the word 'stew', in one sense a pond or lake, in another sense a brothel.

884. *Clergy of her Belly.* As, in certain cases of felony, literate persons could claim benefit of clergy, so a pregnant woman could plead for execution to be deferred until the birth of her child. See Blackstone, iv. xxxi. 394.

892. *Hackney Lady*: whore; a woman available for hire.

905. *little quarrels, etc.* Proverbial. See Erasmus, *Adagia*, III. i. lxxxix. 740; Tilley, F40.

919. *Discords make the sweetest Airs.* Proverbial (Erasmus, loc. cit.).

927. *passes Fines*: makes final agreements. Blackstone (ii. xxi. 348) describes a fine as 'an amicable composition or agreement of a suit, either actual or fictitious, by leave of the king or his justices'. He also notes that such a fine must be 'enrolled of record in the proper office'.

930. *lose*: loose.

941. *at Rovers*: at random.

959. *the Money's on the Book.* An allusion to the instruction, in the Form of Solemnization of Matrimony, that 'the Man shall give unto the Woman a Ring, laying the same upon the book with the accustomed duty to the Priest and Clerk'.

961. *Livery, and Seasin.* Livery of seisin, often mistakenly called 'livery and seisin', was 'the delivery of corporeal possession of a land or tenement' (Blackstone, II. xx. 310). It was carried out by handing over some part of the land or property: in the case of land, a piece of turf or a twig.

964. *flam*: deception. See II. iii. 29.

980. *Trepanners*: tricksters.

986. *Cully*: a person imposed upon, especially by a whore.

987. *Drazels*: sluts.

1000. *Tuition*: guardianship, custody.

1002. *with your Bodies, strive to Worship.* Another allusion to the words of the Solemnization of Matrimony.

1003. *That th'Infants Fortunes, etc.* 'That is, the widow's children by a former husband, that are under age, to whom the lover would be glad to be guardian, as well as have the management of the jointure' (Nash).

1005. *Purposes*: a game of questions and answers, also known as cross-purposes. 'The players sit in a circle, and each is asked in a whisper a question by the one on his left, and receives also in a whisper an answer to a question asked by himself of the person on his right. Each player must remember both the question he was asked and the answer he received, which have at the conclusion of the round to be stated aloud' (A. B. Gomme, *Traditional Games*, 1894, i. 82). Burton includes 'purposes' among 'the ordinary recreations which we have in winter, and in most solitary times busy our minds with' (*Anatomy of Melancholy*, II. ii. 4). See also Pepys, *Diary*, 26 Dec. 1666.

1006. *love your Loves with A's, and B's.* 'I did find the Duke of York and Duchess, with all the great ladies, sitting upon a carpet, on the ground, there being no chairs, playing at "I love my love with an A, because he is so and so: and I hate him with an A, because of this and that:" and some of them, but particularly the Duchess herself, and my Lady Castlemayne, were very witty' (Pepys, *Diary*, 4 Mar. 1669).

1007. *Beast*: a card game, somewhat like the game of nap. For a description of the game, see Charles Cotton, *Compleat Gamester*, xxv.

1012. *sucking of a Vizard Bead.* 'The Visard Mask . . . covers the whole face. . . . This kind of Mask is taken off and put on in a moment of time, being only held in the Teeth by means of a round bead fastned on the in-side over against the mouth' (Randle Holme, *Academy of Armoury*, Chester, 1688, III. i. 13).

1014. *question-and-command New Garters*: new garters, worn by ladies, to be used as forfeits in the game of questions and commands. This game, according to Strutt, 'most probably derived from the basilinda of the Greeks, in which we are told a king, elected by lot, commanded his comrades what they should perform' (*Sports and Pastimes*, ed. Cox, 1903, p. 310).

1017. The Butler manuscript includes a passage apparently designed to be included here (*Satires*, p. 457).

1034. *Executions*: the process of obtaining actual possession of anything acquired by judgement of law; in this case the seizure of the goods or person of the lover by his creditors. See Blackstone, III. xxvi. 414.

1035. *extent*. 'The body, lands and goods, may all be taken at once in execution to compel the payment of the debt. The process hereon is usually called an *extent* or *extendi facias*' (Blackstone, III. xxvi. 420).

1036. *Exigent*. 'Where a defendant absconds, and the plaintiff would proceed to an outlawry against him . . . then a writ of *exigent* or *exigi facias* may be sued out, which requires the sheriff to cause the defendant to be proclaimed, required, or exacted, in five county courts successively to render himself . . . but if he does not appear . . . he shall then be outlawed' (Blackstone, III. xix. 283).

1038. *Scire Facias*: a judicial writ, requiring the sheriff to summon the defendant to court to show cause why execution should not be taken against him. See Blackstone, III. xxvi. 421.

1055. *powder*: force, violence.

1063. *pale as Ashes, or a Clout*. Both proverbial similes (Tilley, A339, C446)

1073. *taking*: troubled state of mind.

1086. *Iron-side*: (i) an allusion to the soldiers of Cromwell's army, who were known as 'Ironsides'; (ii) the name given to Edmund II.

Hardy-knute: King Cnut, who succeeded Edmund II in 1016. He is so called by Butler with an allusion to, and corruption of, 'Harthacnut', the name of Cnut's son.

1119. *pordue*: perdue; 'in an exposed, hazardous position; hidden and on the watch' (*OED*).

1131. *Geomancy*: divination by observation of the earth. This art generally consisted either in throwing a handful of earth on the ground and examining the figure it formed, or in interpreting 'Noise in the Earth, motion, cleaving, swelling of the same' (Agrippa, *Vanity of Arts and Sciences*, 1676, xxxvi. 103). In his essay *Of Geomancy* (trans. Robert Turner, 1783, p. 20), Agrippa notes that in practising this art, the projector would frequently fall into a trance.

1133. *Lapland-Magi*. Lapland was popularly supposed to be inhabited by a great number of witches, and the inhabitants were thought to practise magic on a large scale. See John Sheffer, *History of Lapland*, Oxford, 1674, xi. 54 ff.

1137. *another of the same | Degree, and Party, etc.* This was Sir Erasmus Phillips, the son of Sir Richard Phillips, of Picton Castle in Pembrokeshire. The identification is made by Walter Moyle in a letter of 26 January 1699 (*Works*, 1727, p. 241). Picton Castle was besieged by the Royalists under

Sir Charles Gerard in 1645, and Sir Erasmus and his two sisters were taken prisoner. See A. L. Leach, *Civil War in Pembrokeshire*, 1937, pp. 106, 227–8. Grey was told privately that 'The Officer of the *Cavaliers* sent against the Castle, summon'd Sir *Erasmus* to surrender it; he refused, but offered to *parley* from a Window which was not very high from the Ground: He was a little Man, and the commanding Officer of the *Cavaliers* lusty and tall: The Officer observing this, came just under the Window, and pretending he was deaf, desired Sir *Erasmus* to lean as forward as he could out of the Window; upon his doing so, the Officer who was on Horseback, rais'd himself upon his Stirrups, seiz'd him by the Shoulders, and pulled him out. Upon which the Castle was surrender'd.'

1188. *turn'd her up*: cast her off.

1189. *laid her Dowry out, etc.* The exact meaning of this and the following lines is far from clear, though it is clear enough that the knight's general intention is to separate from his wife, while at the same time retaining control of her property. He would, on marrying the widow, draw up a defective marriage settlement in which her own right to her dowry, which she would bring to the marriage, could later be upset. Her 'jointure', or the benefit she might hope to have from the marriage settlement, would thus be annulled. All that the widow would receive from her own estate, now transferred to the knight, would be the alimony due to her after their separation. Hudibras is particularly anxious to prevent the widow from following the practice, quite common among wealthy or suspicious widows of the time, of handing over their property to a trustee before remarrying. Such a trustee would hold the widow's property for her separate use, and would prevent a second husband from gaining possession of it. See note to III. i. 670, above.

1224. *Saints Bell*: sanctus bell, used with an additional reference to the Puritan 'Saints'. The sanctus bell is rung in churches immediately before the service, and after the pealing of the other bells, to summon the congregation to worship.

1249. *Chouse*: fool, dupe.

1276. *Administrings*: the power to administer political authority. The term does not appear to have been in common use and may have been coined by Butler in imitation of Puritan jargon.

1294. *Prohibited Degrees of Kin.* An allusion to the marriage laws, whereby a person may not marry anyone related to him by 'kindred or affinity'.

1300. *In Nature onl' and not Imputed.* Hudibras draws the theological distinction between natural virtue, inherent in man, and imputed virtue which man shares vicariously with Christ. By comparison with the virtue of Christ, man's inherent virtue is 'impious'.

1308. *Elder*: former.

1314. *he gave his Name, etc.* Partridge (*Dictionary of Slang*) describes Butler's etymology here as 'suspect'.

1322. *Rules all the Sea*: i.e. controls the tides.

1342. *Holy Brother-hood.* The *Santa Hermandad*, or Holy Brotherhood, was set up in Spain in the fifteenth century in order to wipe out robbers and highwaymen. It had powers of summary jurisdiction and was authorized to execute malefactors caught red-handed.

1370. *Rallies*: rails.

1387. *Office of Intelligence*: i.e. the place from which he communicates with us. At the Restoration, newsletters and mercuries were published from the Office of Intelligence. See J. G. Muddiman, *The King's Journalist*, 1923, p. 126.

1388. *His Oracles are ceast.* The power of the pagan oracles was said to have ceased at the incarnation of Christ, in fulfilment of the Old Testament prophecy that the Saviour would 'cause the prophets and the unclean spirit to pass out of the land' (Zech. xiii. 2) and that there would be 'no more soothsayers' (Mic. v. 12). The cessation of the oracles had also been discussed by classical writers, such as Cicero and Plutarch, as an observable fact (*De Divinatione*, ii. lvii. 117; *De Defectu Oraculorum*). See also Browne, *Pseudodoxia*, vii. xii; Milton, *On the Morning of Christ's Nativity*, ll. 173–80.

1394. *Juggles*: practises magic.

1395. *Spirit Po*: the nickname of a certain Richard Duke (1627–1716), of Otterton in Devonshire (*Miscellanea Genealogica et Heraldica*, ed. Bannerman, 4th ser. iii. 31). Roger North describes him as 'a most busy driver in the wheel of faction, which made some call him Spirit Po! as at everyone's service, in short a rigid Presbyterian' (*Lives of the Norths*, 3 vols., 1890, iii. 133).

1398. *Rallying*: joking.

1408. *Condemn'd to Drudg'ry, etc.* The tricks referred to in the following lines were attributed to fairies and mischievous devils, particularly Robin Goodfellow. 'Many mad prankes would they [the fairies] play, as pinching of sluts black and blue, and misplacing things in ill-ordered houses; but lovingly would they use wenches that cleanly were, giving them silver and other pretty toyes, which they would leave for them, sometimes in their shooes, other times in their pockets, sometimes in bright basons and other cleane vessels' (*Robin Goodfellow; his mad prankes and merry Jestes* (1627), reprinted in J. O. Halliwell, *Illustrations of Fairy Mythology*, 1845, p. 122).

1415. *Pug*: imp, small devil.

1416. *Dry Bobbing*: 'a drie bob, jeast, or nip; a stroke that crushes though it cut not' (Cotgrave, *Dictionarie of the French and English Tongues*, 1611).

1417. *intice Fanaticks in the Dirt.* The Will o' the Wisp was sometimes identified with Robin Goodfellow. See *The Ballad of Robin Goodfellow*, vii, in Halliwell, op. cit., p. 164.

1420. *you laugh aloud.* 'Robin Good-fellow would many times walke in the night . . . but when any one did call him, then would he runne away laughing *ho, ho, hoh* !' (*Robin Goodfellow; his mad prankes*, op. cit., pp. 142–3).

1423. *Sophy*: wise man.

1430. *Drubs and Basting*: beating.

1433. *intire*: devoted.

1439. *for a Token*. Cf. i. i. 479 and note.

1440. *Low Countrey Hogen Mogen*: i.e. the devil. See note to ii. ii. 434.

1446. *Ill-affected*: a term applied by the Puritans to their enemies. Cf. 'well-affected', i. i. 738.

1447. *Y' have spous'd the Covenant, etc*. Both Royalists and Independents criticized the Solemn League and Covenant as 'diabolical'. The King forbade it as 'a traiterous and seditious Combination against us and the establish'd Religion and Laws of this Kingdom' (Rushworth, V. iii. ii. 482).

1448. *holding up your Cloven Paws*. 'The manner of taking it was thus: the Covenant was read, and then notice was given, that each Person should immediately by swearing thereunto, worship the great Name of God, and then testify so much outwardly, by lifting up their Hands' (Rushworth, V. iii. ii. 475).

1454. *wooden Peccadilio's*: i.e. stand in the stocks, the punishment for perjury (Blackstone, iv. x. 138). The piccadillo was a stiff collar of linen-covered pasteboard or wire, worn to support a collar or ruff.

1478. *Stools*: Stools of Repentance, formerly placed in Scottish Presbyterian churches, for the use of offenders making public repentance. Clarendon records its use at Stirling in 1650 (xiii. 48).

Poundage: a tax, generally of a shilling per pound sterling, levied on merchandise imported or exported from the country. It provided a subsidy for the monarch, ostensibly for guarding the country by sea. The Long Parliament voted this subsidy to themselves for use against the King (Clarendon, v. 424).

1485. *all the Horridst Actions, etc*. An allusion to the terms used in a legal indictment, of which Blackstone (iv. App. ii) gives the following example: 'Peter Hunt . . . gentleman, not having the fear of God before his eyes, but being moved and seduced by the instigation of the devil . . . did make an assault.'

1512. *Mittimus Anathemas*. An anathema committed a man's soul to the devil, as a legal mittimus entrusted his body to the jailer. A mittimus is a warrant, sent to the keeper of a jail, instructing him to receive a prisoner into custody (Blackstone, iv. xxii. 299). The Presbyterians excluded certain offenders from the sacraments of the Church. An Ordinance of 1645 contained a list of the offences for which a person might be excommunicated (Firth and Rait, i. 789).

1516. *Covenanting Trustees*: the trustees who administered the estates forfeited to Parliament by the Church and by Royalist 'delinquents'. They were required by Parliament to enter into a covenant, swearing on oath to 'discharge the trust committed unto them' (Firth and Rait, ii. 528).

1519. *demise*: transfer (an estate).

1521. *Utlegation*: outlawry; 'a punishment for such as being called into lawe, and lawfully sought, doe contemptuously refuse to appeare' (John Cowell, *The Interpreter*, Cambridge, 1607).

1523. *for a Groat unpaid, etc.* 'There are . . . many obstinate or profligate men, who would despise the *brutum fulmen* of mere ecclesiastical censures, especially when pronounced by a petty surrogate of the country, for railing or contumelious words, for non payment of fees, or costs, or for other trivial causes. . . . And so with us by the common law an excommunicated person is disabled to do any act, that is required to be done by one that is *probus et legalis homo*. He cannot serve upon juries, cannot be witness in any court and, which is the worst of all, cannot bring an action . . . to recover lands or money due to him' (Blackstone, III. vii. 101). 'If, within forty days . . . the offender does not submit and abide by the sentence of the spiritual court . . . there issues out a writ *de excommunicato capiendo*: and the sheriff shall thereupon take the offender, and imprison him in the county gaol, till he is reconciled to the church' (ibid., p. 102).

1539. *Laid out.* A Puritan phrase. Cf. I. ii. 582 and note.

1541. *Nam'd from Blood.* 'Sanctus, from sanguis, blood' (Nash).

1564. *Gresham Carts, etc.* On 4 March 1663, 'Mr. AUBREY presented the [Royal] Society with the scheme of a cart, with legs instead of wheels, devised by Mr. FRANCIS POTTER; which was referred to the consideration of Mr. HOOKE, who was ordered to bring in a report of it to the next meeting' (Birch, *History of the Royal Society*, 1756, i. 206).

1602. *Padders*: footpads, highwaymen.

CANTO II

1. *Breeze*: the gadfly.

2. *Mungrel Prince of Bees.* 'In the utmost edges and sides of the combs, there are seen to breed the bigger kind of bees, which chase and drive the others away: and this vermin is called Oestrus (i.e. the gad-bee or horse flie.)' (Pliny, *Nat. Hist.*, trans. Holland, XI. xvi. 318).

4. *Founders of his House, etc.* 'Of the first Generation of Bees *Aristotle* hath a long discourse. The Philosophers following him have rightly determined in my opinion, that their Generation doth proceed from the corruption of some other body: as of a Bull, Oxe, Cow, Calf' (Thomas Moffet, *Theater of Insects*, 1658, I. iii. 897). See also Varro, *Rerum Rusticarum*, III. xvi. 4; Virgil, *Georgics*, iv. 538–58; Pliny, *Nat. Hist.* XI. xx. 23.

13. *Persian Magi, etc.* The priestly caste of the Magi were reputed among the ancients to beget children upon their own mothers. See Sextus Empiricus, *Hypotyposes*, III. xxiv. 205; Diogenes Laertius, i. 7; Strabo, xv. iii. 20.

19. *Devils Dam, etc.* Sin is described in Milton's *Paradise Lost* (ii, ll. 747–800) as the daughter of Satan and the mother, by Satan, of Death. In turn, Death begets upon Sin a brood of monsters. *Paradise Lost* is the most likely source of Butler's allusion, though it has been pointed out that Milton may himself have found the allegory in St. Basil's *Hexameron*, in Gower's *Mirrour de l'Omme*, and in Phineas Fletcher's *Purple Island*. See J. M. Steadman, 'Grosseteste on the Genealogy of Sin and Death', *NQ* cciv (1959), 367–8; 'Milton and St. Basil', *MLN* lxxiii (1958), 83–84. The scriptural authority for the allegory is Jas. i. 15.

25. *fag'd*: agreed.

35. *no more to purchase, etc.* The following lines allude to the sale and transfer of lands sequestered by Parliament from the Church, the royal family and 'notorious delinquents'. See Firth and Rait, ii. 520, 591, 623, etc.

40. *cross the Cudgels*: yield; 'from the practice of cudgel-players to lay one over the other' (Johnson, *Dictionary*).

43. *Hemp-plot.* Cf. 'A Knave', *Characters*, p. 163: 'He shelters himself under the Covert of the Law, like a Thief in a Hemp-Plot, and makes that secure him, which was intended for his Destruction.' 'Hemp' was a colloquialism for the gallows.

46. *turn'd Plaintiff and Defendant, etc.* The business of purchasing sequestered estates, and subsequently of establishing the ownership of them, was often handed over to solicitors. 'In the course of time, agents came to be regarded as the indispensable links between purchasers and the Sales Trustees' (Joan Thirsk, 'Sales of Royalist Land during the Interregnum', *Economic History Review*, 2nd ser. v. ii (1952), 194).

47. *Laid out.* A Puritan expression. Cf. i. ii. 582 and note.

49. *Gifts.* Cf. i. i. 476 and note.

50. *outlawries*: 'putting a man out of the protection of the law, so that he is incapable to bring an action for redress of injuries; and it is also attended with a forfeiture of all one's goods and chattels to the king' (Blackstone, III. xix. 283).

Scire facias. See note to III. i. 1038.

60. *Was Nam'd in Trust, etc.* The estates seized by Parliament were temporarily vested in certain Trustees, appointed to make arrangements for their sale. Complaints were frequent that the Trustees were in fact embezzling these estates, or retaining them for their own use. See Walker, iv. 48; Henry Elsynge, *List of Members of the House of Commons . . . together with such sums of money, offices and lands as they have given to themselves*, 1648. Some of the Trustees, and other Puritan leaders, in fact formally purchased estates, while others were given land in lieu of wages. See H. E. Chesney, 'Transference of Lands in England 1640–1660', *Trans. Royal Hist. Soc.* 4th ser. xv (1932), 181; Joan Thirsk, 'Sales of Royalist Land during the Interregnum', *Econ. Hist. Review* 2nd ser. v. ii (1952), 188.

66. *outward man*: i.e. the body, as opposed to the 'inward man' or soul. Cf. ii. ii. 77–80.

69. *past*: conveyed, handed down to.

71. *Reprobates*: a Calvinist theological term, signifying those rejected by God and predestined to exclusion from eternal life.

73. *Attaints*. 'When sentence of death . . . is pronounced, the immediate inseparable consequence from the common law is *attainder*. . . . He is then called attaint, *attinctus*, stained or blackened. He is no longer of any credit or reputation; he cannot be a witness in any court; neither is he capable of performing the functions of another man: for, by anticipation of his punishment, he is already dead in law' (Blackstone, IV. xxix. 380).

78. *Utter Barrister of Swanswick*: William Prynne, who was born in 1600 at Swainswick in Somerset. According to Wood he went 'to Linc. inn to obtain knowledge in the common law, where he was made successively barrester, utter barrester, bencher and reader' (Wood, *Athenae Oxonienses*, 4 vols., 1813–20, iii. 845). '*Utter Baristers*, be such as for their longe study and great industry bestowed upon the knowledge of the common lawe, be called out of their contemplation to practise, and in the face of the world to take upon them the protection and defence of clients' (John Cowell, *The Interpreter*, Cambridge, 1607). See also note to I. i. 640.

80. *with Sand-bags*. Cf. 'A Litigious Man' (*Characters*, p. 135): 'He fights with Bags of Money, as they did heretofore with Sand-Bags, and he that has the heaviest has the Advantage, and knocks down the other right or wrong.' A combat with sand-bags, between the armourer and his man, takes place in Shakespeare's *Henry VI* (*2 Henry VI*, II. iii).

88. *Secluded*: kept out. *Chews'd*: tricked.

91. *Reformado Saint*: see note to II. ii. 116.

95. *uses*: practical application of Scripture, as opposed to 'doctrine'. Cf. II. ii. 415.

116. *Sarazen and Christian*: i.e. they were both soldiers and preachers. Cf. also Walker, i. 27: 'As *Mahomet's* Alchoran was the Gallemaufry of Jew and Christian; so they are a composition of Jew, Christian, and Turk.'

119. *lurch*: 'to get the start of (a person) so as to prevent him from obtaining a fair share of food, profit, etc.' (*OED*).

145. *Knaves and Fools being near of Kin*. Knaves and fools were associated in several English proverbs (*ODEP* 341, 342; Tilley, K127, K129, K144).

146. *Boors*: peasants.

Sooter-Kin. 'There goes a report of the Holland women that together with their children they are delivered of a Sooterkin, not unlike to a rat, which some imagine to be the offspring of the stoves' (Cleveland, 'Character of a Diurnal-Maker', in Morley, *Character Writings*, 1891, p. 304). See also Howell, *Familiar Letters*, i. ii. 13, ed. Jacobs, 1892, p. 114.

150. *put by one anothers Bolts*: ward off one another's attacks.

195. *like the Christian Faith, etc.* 'Plures efficimur quotiens metimur a vobis; semen est sanguis Christianorum' (Tertullian, *Apologeticus*, 1). These words became proverbial; see, for example, Aubrey's life of David Jenkins (ed. Clark, ii. 6).

207. *kept the Title, etc.* 'If the claimant be deterred from entering by menaces or bodily fear, he may make *claim*, as near to the estate as he can . . . which claim is in force for only a year and a day. And this claim, if it be repeated once in the space of every year and day, (which is called *continual claim*) has the same effect with, and in all respects amounts to, a legal entry' (Blackstone, III. x. 175).

212. *in Possession*: 'Estates . . . may either be in *possession*, or in *expectancy*' (Blackstone, II. xi. 163).

215. *in a Furious Hurricane, etc.* Clarendon describes the day of Cromwell's death as 'very memorable for the greatest storm of wind that had ever been known, for some hours before and after his death, which overthrew trees, houses, and made great wrecks at sea' (xv. 146). See also Edmund Waller, 'Upon the Great Storm, and of the Death of his Highness Ensuing the Same', *Poems*, ed. Drury, 1893, p. 162.

220. *retriev'd by Sterry.* 'The news of his death being brought to those who were met together to pray for him, Mr Sterry stood up and desired them not to be troubled. "For", said he, "this is good news; because if he was of great use to the people of God when he was amongst us, now he will be much more so, being ascended to heaven to sit at the right hand of Jesus Christ, there to intercede for us, and to be mindful of us on all occasions"' (*Memoirs of Edmund Ludlow*, ed. Firth, 2 vols. Oxford, 1894, ii. 45). See also Robert Baillie, *Letters*, Edinburgh, 1841–2, iii. 425; V. de Sola Pinto, *Peter Sterry*, Cambridge, 1934, pp. 34–38.

224. *False Heaven.* 'Heaven, Hell, and Purgatory, three places within or adjoining Westminster Hall . . . *Heaven* was a tavern, where Pepys occasionally dined' (Wheatley, *London*, ii. 201). See Pepys, *Diary*, 28 Jan. 1660. In 1661 Cromwell's body and those of Ireton and Bradshaw were disinterred, drawn to Tyburn, and hanged. Their heads were placed on poles on the top of Westminster Hall, presumably close to the tavern called Heaven. See Firth, *Cromwell*, 1900, p. 451.

227. *Romulus was seen, etc.* According to Cicero and others, the senator Proculus Julius was walking on the Quirinal Hill, when the spirit of Romulus appeared to him. Romulus announced that he was now a god, renamed Quirinus, and that a temple should be built to him. See Cicero, *De Re Publica*, ii. 20; *De Legibus*, I. i. 3; Livy, I. xvi. 5–8; Plutarch, *Romulus*, xxviii.

233. *laid by the Parliament.* Richard Cromwell 'caused a proclamation to be issued out, by which he did declare the Parliament to be dissolved. And from that minute nobody resorted to him, nor was the name of the Protector afterwards heard of but in derision' (Clarendon, xvi. 11).

237. *now the Saints began their Reign, etc.* The following section describes the divisions and disagreements within Parliament when, after the fall of Richard Cromwell, they attempted to draft a new constitution. They were divided on both religious and political issues, and, 'as a pamphleteer commented, although it might not be true that every member had in his pocket a model of the government he thought best, certainly every bookseller's basket or shop had some new plan for a popular government' (Godfrey Davies, *The Restoration of Charles II*, San Marino, 1955, p. 90).

244. *Hans-Towns*: the towns of the North German Hanse, or Hanseatic League, which were governed by a central council.

245. *Edify*: build; a Puritan term. Cf. Jonson, *Bartholomew Fair*, i. vi. 39 (*Works*, vi. 37).

246. *John of Leiden*: John Beuckelszoon (1509–36), a leader of the German Anabaptists at Münster. He was a fanatic who declared himself King of Zion, and committed polygamy and murder in the name of God. Some of the practices of the Münster Anabaptists, however, resembled those of the later English Puritans. They repudiated infant baptism, destroyed images and musical instruments as being idolatrous, and proposed the common ownership of property. See Ranke, *History of the Reformation in Germany*, ed. Johnson, 1905, pp. 739 ff.

  out-goings. See note to i. ii. 1007.

247. *for a Weather-Cock, etc.* After his capture by the Bishop of Münster, John of Leyden was tortured, executed, and his body hung in a cage from the tower of St. Lambert's Church. See Ranke, op. cit.; Alexander Ross, 'Apocalypsis', p. 29, *View of all Religions*, 1655.

269. *Unless King Jesus*. Millenarianism is chiefly associated with the sect of Fifth Monarchy Men, but it was also common among other independent sects, including the Baptists. When the restored Long Parliament set about the discussion of the form of government to be established, it received many petitions from the Fifth Monarchy Men, one of which proposed 'the proclamation of Christ as head, and the erection of such a government as was contemplated by the godly party in the Little Parliament'. See L. F. Brown, *Baptists and Fifth Monarchy Men*, Washington, 1912, pp. 187 ff.

  tamper'd: worked; plotted.

270. *Fleetwood, Desborough, and Lambard*: the three army leaders who, when the army petitions were rejected in 1659, entered and expelled Parliament. 'There was no Parliament, nor any officer in the army who by his commission was above the degree of colonel, nor had any of them power to command more than his own regiment. Whereupon the officers of the army . . . made choice of Fleetewood to be their general, and of Lambert to be their major general, and of Desborough to be commissary general of the horse' (Clarendon, xvi. 85–86). These officers then nominated a Committee of Public Safety, which included themselves, to govern the country for the time being (ibid. 91).

271. *the Rump*: the remains of the Long Parliament, so called in 1659–60 (Clarendon, xvi. 129).

272. *Agitators*: the name given to the representatives of the common soldiers, elected in 1647, who, together with the council of officers, negotiated with Parliament in matters relating to the army (Clarendon, x. 83). In the course of their protests against the proposed disbandment of the army, and other grievances, they became the principle source of republican feeling among the troops.

the Safety: the Committee of Public Safety. See note to III. ii. 270.

279. *High Places*: temples. See note to II. iii. 1158.

282. *Nimrods*: 'Cush begat Nimrod: he began to be a mighty one in the earth. He was a mighty hunter before the Lord' (Gen. x. 8–9).

284. *Extirpation of th' Excise*. In March 1659 a bill was introduced 'for taking away all laws, statutes, and ordinances, concerning the excise . . . and concerning customs, tonnage and poundage'. The bill, however, never reached a final reading. See Thomas Burton, *Diary*, iv. 296.

286. *Holy-days*. An Ordinance had been passed in 1647 for the abolition of religious festivals (Firth and Rait, i. 954).

Poundage. See notes to III. i. 1478 and III. ii. 284.

287. *Groves*: churches, temples, on the analogy of 2 Kings xxi. 7.

288. *Rectifying Bakers Loaves*. One of the proposals offered to Parliament was that 'all Weights, Sizes, and Measures whatsoever be made equall, of one length, breadth, depth, circumference, weight, and bignesse, within the dominions of the Common-wealth' (Edward Billing, *A Mite of Affection*, 1659, p. 9). See also Davies, p. 94.

291. *Gospel-Ministers, etc.* An allusion to the Presbyterian desire for an educated, ordained, gospel-preaching ministry, as against the sectarian practice of preaching by uneducated laymen. The army was the centre of sectarian activity throughout the Interregnum, and, although preaching by soldiers was prohibited in the New Model Army, there is ample evidence that the more zealous of them ignored the order. See Firth, *Cromwell's Army*, 1905, p. 334. The New Model Army, established under Fairfax in 1645, was entirely dressed in red uniforms (ibid., p. 234).

298. *Camisado*: 'a Spanish word, and doth signifie the investing or putting on of a shirt over the Souldiers apparell or armour; the which is used in the night time, when any suddaine exploit . . . is to be put in practise' (Robert Barret, *Theorike and Practike of Moderne Warres*, 1598, p. 249).

304. *a Ring*. The Puritans generally took exception to the use of the ring in the marriage ceremony, since it was derived from the Catholic belief that marriage was a sacrament, of which the ring was a sacred symbol. See Neal, i. 195.

309. *nothing but her Will.* 'The Thing this Quibble turns upon, is this—The first Response the Bride makes in the Marriage Ceremony is, *I will*' (Grey).

312. *Linsy-Woolsy.* See note to I. iii. 1227.

314. *The Cross, etc.* The making of the sign of the cross in baptism is not mentioned in Scripture, but appears to have been introduced sometime in the fifth century. For this reason the Puritans wished to exclude it from the liturgy. See *A Shorte Treatise, of the crosse in Baptisme,* 'Amsterdam', 1604; Neal, i. 193. In the *Directory for Public Worship* the minister is instructed 'to pour or sprinkle the water on the Face of the childe, without adding any other Ceremony' (Firth and Rait, i. 596). Grey notes an entry in Sir John Birkenhead's mock bookseller's catalogue, *Paul's Churchyard,* 1651: 'An Act for removing the Alphabet *Crosse* from the Children's Primer, and the *Crosse* from off the *Speaker's* Mace' (Cent. II. Class 6. 139).

315. *make all things Recant, etc.* The Puritans applied the title of Saint only to their own brethren of the elect. 'In the Mayoralty of Alderman *Pennington,* the Saints were thrown out of Doors, and the Parishes *unsainted.* For in the Year 1642, the title of *Saint* in the Weekly Bills of Mortality in *London,* was commanded by the Authority then prevailing, to be expunged for the future. . . : This divorcing of the Parishes from their Saints in the said Bills continued until the Year 1660' (Stow, *Survey of London,* ed. Strype, 2 vols., 1720, II. v. 7).

319. *Third Estate of Souls* : i.e. purgatory.

320. *bringing down the Price of Coals.* In 1651, and again in 1654, taxes were imposed upon coal transported from English ports or brought into England from Scotland. The taxes were payable in addition to the existing, and very unpopular, rates of tonnage and poundage. See Firth and Rait, ii. 505–9, 854.

321. *Abolishing Black-Pudding, etc.* In doing so, they would be following God's words to Moses that 'whatsoever man there be of the house of Israel . . . that eateth any manner of blood; I will even set my face against that soul that eateth blood, and will cut him off from among his people' (Lev. xvii. 10). The Levitical law was taken literally by strict Puritans. See *The Triall of a Black-Pudding; or The unlawfulness of Eating Blood proved by Scriptures. By a well-wisher to Ancient Truth,* 1652.

323. *Roots and Branches.* The Root and Branch Petition, presented to Parliament in 1640, on behalf of the citizens of London, demanded the abolition of episcopal Church government 'with all its dependencies, roots and branches' (Gardiner, *Const. Docs.* xxvi. 137).

324. *Eating Haunches, etc.* 'Come and gather yourselves together unto the supper of the great God; That ye may eat the flesh of kings, and the flesh of captains, and the flesh of mighty men' (Rev. xix. 17–18).

327. *Breaking of their Bones, etc.* 'Ask of me, and I shall give thee the heathen for thine inheritance, and the uttermost parts of the earth for thy possession. Thou shalt break them with a rod of iron' (Ps. ii. 8–9).

328. *Secret ones*: a Puritan term for one of their own number, based on the Geneva version of Ps. lxxxiii. 3: '[Thine enemies] have taken craftie counsel against thy people, and have consulted against thy secret ones.'

329. *Thrashing Mountains.* 'Behold, I will make thee a new sharp threshing instrument having teeth: thou shalt thresh the mountains, and beat them small, and shalt make the hills as chaff' (Isa. xli. 15). Reporting on an insurrection by a group of Fifth Monarchy Men in 1657, Thurloe records that 'they encouraged one another with this, that though they were but a worme, that yet they should be made instrumental to *thresh mountains*' (*Thurloe State Papers*, vi. 185).

330. *Hallowing Carriers Packs, and Bells.* 'In that day shall there be upon the bells of the horses, Holiness unto the Lord; and the pots in the Lord's house shall be like the bowls before the altar' (Zech. xiv. 20).

331. *the Legend*: Scripture. The Legend was the service book after Sarum use, containing all the lessons from the Bible and the works of the Fathers required to be read at matins. Its use was prohibited by an act of 3 & 4 Edw. VI c. 10.

351. *a Politician, etc.* The function of the two politicians, whose dialogue occupies most of this canto, is to act as spokesmen for the opposing Presbyterian and Independent parties, and thereby to reveal the hypocrisy common to both. The character of the first politician is, however, derived from that of Anthony Ashley Cooper, first Earl of Shaftesbury (1621–83), though the opinions he expresses could have been held by many independent Members of Parliament. He was probably the shrewdest politician of his time and an adept at political intrigue. In 1643 he raised and commanded troops for the King, but within a year resigned his commission and went over to Parliament, whom he served as a field-marshal. According to Burnet, he was 'one of those who pressed Cromwell most to accept of the kingship', yet in the Parliament of 1656 he joined the opposition to the Protector. After the fall of Richard Cromwell he worked for the restoration of Charles II, and in 1672 was made Lord Chancellor. He later headed the attempts by the Whigs to exclude the Catholic James from the succession and to replace him by Charles's illegitimate son, the Duke of Monmouth. The passing of the Exclusion Bill was prevented by successive dissolutions of Parliament between 1679 and 1681, and Shaftesbury was arrested on a charge of treason, an event which prompted the composition of Dryden's *Absalom and Achitophel.* He was, however, acquitted, amid the acclamation of the London mob, but, attempting to foment further risings, was told that warrants had been issued for his arrest and made his escape to Holland, where he died. See W. D. Christie, *Life of Anthony Ashley Cooper*, 2 vols., 1871. Burnet remarks 'I never knew any man equal to him in the art of governing parties, and of making himself the head of them' (*History of his Own Time*, ed. Airy, 2 vols. Oxford, 1879, i. 172).

357. *trapan*: deceive.

359. *Pragmatick*: busy, interfering.

372. *save his Tide*: seize his opportunity.

380. *Hemp*: the gallows. See note to III. ii. 43.

392. *fast and loose*. See note to I. iii. 1134.

409. *Napiers Bones*. See note to II. iii. 1095.

417. *smoke*: detect.

421. *another*. This politician speaks for the Presbyterians as his colleague speaks for the Independents. Grey, following the 'Key to *Hudibras*', identifies him with John Lilburne, the Leveller, but there is little evidence in the text to associate him with any specific individual.

423. *Haberdasher of small Wares*. Lilburne, whom Grey identifies with this character, was apprenticed to Thomas Hewson, a wholesale cloth merchant, from about the age of sixteen, 'whom', he says, 'I served as faithfully about six years, as ever apprentice served a Master' (*Legall Fundamentall Liberties*, 1649, p. 20).

429. *set his own in Order*. 'Achitophel . . . gat him home to his house, to his city, and put his household in order, and hanged himself, and died' (2 Sam. xvii. 23).

435. *Cavalcade of Ho'burn*. Holborn was the road from Newgate and the Tower to the gallows at Tyburn. See Wheatley, *London*, ii. 220.

440. *his dear delight, to wrangle*. 'The magnanimous judge Jenkins used to say, that if the world was emptied of all but John Lilbourne, Lilbourne would quarrel with John, and John with Lilbourne' (Wood, op. cit. iii. 358).

448. *Pickere*: skirmish; wrangle.

455. *Topiques*: arguments.

471. *Trapes*: slattern, slut.

479. *still the skittisher, etc.* The Butler manuscript includes an alternative version of this passage (*Satires*, p. 458).

496. *Out-goings*. See note to I. ii. 1007.

498. *Jealousies and Fears*. See note to I. i. 3.

510. *run before all others*. An allusion to the terms of the Solemn League and Covenant. See note to I. ii. 626.

520. *Margrets Fast*. On the days appointed for solemn fasting and humiliation all people were required 'diligently to resort to some publique place where the Service and Worship of God is exercised' (Firth and Rait, ii. 425). Members of Parliament usually attended a service at St. Margaret's Westminster (Burton, *Diary*, iii. 11–13). The allusion here is to the debate concerning the fast appointed for 18 May 1659, when opinions in Parliament were divided over the date for the fast, the power of Parliament to make such a declaration, and its wording. The Presbyterian party, who framed the declaration, lamented

that 'these nations are overspread with many blasphemies and damnable heresies against . . . the word of God . . . by denying the authority thereof and crying up the light in the hearts of sinful men as the rule and guide of all their actions'. All ministers were required to read this declaration in public on the Sunday before the fast day. Independents, like Vane, denounced the proposal as a restriction of religious freedom (Burton, *Diary*, iv. 329; Davies, pp. 68–69). Further divisions arose in the Lords during the debate on the declaration. See Ludlow, *Memoirs*, ed. Firth, 2 vols. Oxford, 1894, ii. 60–61.

521. *Providence had been suborn'd.* A certain Thomas Grove moved that an addition be made to the declaration 'to implore a blessing from God upon the proceedings of this present Parliament' (Burton, *Diary*, iv. 332).

539. *weapons with chalk'd Edges.* An entry in Butler's unpublished notebook (numbered folio 18) notes that a confident man's wit 'is like a watchman's bill wth a chalked edge that pretends to sharpnesse only to conceale its dull Bluntnesse from the public view'. The allusions in the following lines are to the early days of the rebellion.

541. *brown Bills*: a kind of halberd, generally carried by watchmen or constables, and bronzed to prevent rust.

542. *Grand Committee*: the committee of both Houses of Parliament, appointed in 1644, which joined with the Scottish Commissioners 'for the better managing the Affairs of both Nations in the common Cause' (Firth and Rait, i. 381). See Gardiner, *Civil War*, i. 305.

543. *Gleaves*: bills, halberds.

553. *Disaffected.* Cf. 'well-affected', i. i. 738.

554. *Malignant.* See note to i. ii. 630.

566. *e're the Blow, become meer Dolts.* 'Ut in Tageticis libris legitur vel Vegoicis fulmine mox tangendos adeo hebetari, ut nec tonitruum nec maiores aliquos possint audire fragores' (Ammianus Marcellinus, XVII. x. 2).

573. *No mean, nor trivial solaces, etc.* 'Est autem hoc ipsum solacii loco, inter multos dolorem suum dividere' (Seneca, *De Consolatione ad Polybium*, xii. 2).

586. *last, and best defence, Despair.* Cf. the proverbial expression 'Despair makes cowards turn couragious' (*ODEP* 137; Tilley, D216).

598. *blinded*: blindfold.

600. *Exauns*: exemptions.

601. *Fine, like Aldermen, etc.* An alderman might 'fine', or pay a sum of money, in order to escape the duties of his office. See Pepys, *Diary*, 1 Dec. 1663.

602. *Efficace*: performance.

605. *like Mahomet.* See note to II. iii. 442.

606. *St. Ignatius, at his Prayer.* St. Ignatius was said, in moments of intense

prayer and devotion, to have undergone levitation. See Maffeius, *Ignatii Loiolae Vita*, I. vii, Cologne, 1589, p. 467.

607. *By Pure Geometry*: a colloquial phrase, meaning 'in a stiff, angular fashion', usually applied to clothes.

610. *obedience is better, etc.* See Ps. li. 16–17.

620. *As Whittington explain'd the Bells.* The tale of Richard Whittington, the scullion who became Lord Mayor of London, became increasingly popular during the seventeenth century. According to one version, Whittington ran away from his master, but

> as he went along
> In a fair summer's morne,
> London bells sweetly rung,
> 'Whittington, back return!'
>
> Evermore sounding so
> 'Turn again, Whittington;
> For thou in time shall grow
> Lord-Maior of London.'

See Richard Johnson, 'A Song of Sir Richard Whittington' in *Crowne Garland of Goulden Roses*, 1612; T. H., *History of Sir Richard Whittington*, ed. Wheatley, Villon Society, 1885.

636. *Calamy*: Edmund Calamy (1600–66), a Presbyterian minister, one of the authors of the Smectymnuus tracts, and a member of the Westminster Assembly of Divines.

Case: Thomas Case (1598–1682), another Presbyterian divine, a frequent preacher to the Long Parliament, 'a great boutifieu and firebrand in the church, a leader and abettor of the pretended reformation' (Wood, *Athenae Oxonienses*, iv. 45). Case was lecturer at St. Mary, Aldermanbury, when Calamy was rector there.

638. *Ny*: Philip Nye (?1596–1672), a leader of the independent faction, a member of the Westminster Assembly and of several ecclesiastical committees during the Commonwealth. He was a regular preacher to the Commons and the author of several theological tracts. Butler wrote a satire 'Upon Philip Nye's Thanksgiving Beard', in which Nye is described as having his beard trimmed before preaching to Parliament on a thanksgiving day (*Satires*, p. 139).

Owen: John Owen (1616–83), an eminent independent divine and theologian, a celebrated preacher to Parliament. He was made Vice-Chancellor of Oxford University by Cromwell.

640. *Adoniram Bifield*: (d. 1660), a Presbyterian divine, one of the two scribes who recorded the proceedings of the Westminster Assembly. He gained some notoriety as an assistant to the commissioners for ejecting scandalous schoolmasters in Wiltshire (1654). See Wood, *Athenae Oxonienses*, iii. 670.

655. *Barnacles turn Soland-Geese, etc.* Soland, or Solan, geese are gannets.
'There are found in the North parts of Scotland and the Islands adjacent,
called Orchades, certaine trees whereon do grow certaine shells of a white
colour tending to russet, wherein are contained little living creatures: which
shells in time of maturity doe open, and out of them grow those little living
things, which falling into the water do become fowles, which we call Barnacles' (John Gerard, *Herball*, 1633, iii. 171, 1588). See also Hakluyt, *Voyages*,
II. i. 63; *Transactions of the Royal Society, Abridgement*, ii. 415; and cf. Cleveland, 'Rebel Scot', ll. 125–6 (*Minor Caroline Poets*, ed. Saintsbury, iii. 60):

> A Scot, when from the gallow-tree got loose,
> Drops into Styx and turns a Solan goose.

657. *Ticket*: licence.

670. *like other Goats.* 'De emptione aliter dico atque fit, quod capras sanas
sanus nemo promittit; numquam enim sine febri sunt' (Varro, *De Re Rustica*,
II. iii. 5).

680. *of Dependences*: i.e., presumably, that men should be reduced to a state
of subjection or dependence on them.

681. *Secret ones.* See note to III. ii. 328.

682. *Raw-heads fierce, and Bloody Bones*: the names of two fictitious monsters,
used to frighten children. See III. ii. 1112; *Satires*, p. 43; Beaumont and Fletcher,
The Prophetess, IV. v, *Works*, ed. Waller, v. 372.

698. *Break one anothers outward Bones.* See note to III. ii. 327.

700. *Kings and Mighty men.* See note to III. ii. 324.

702. *Elves*: demons.

705. *Savage Bears agree with Bears, etc.* Cf. Juvenal, xv. 163:

> Indica tigris agit rabida cum tigride pacem
> perpetuam, saevis inter se convenit ursis.

706. *lug*: bait, tease.

732. *Self-denyals.* An allusion to the Self-Denying Ordinance of 1645. See
note to I. ii. 984.

739. *Ministerial*: subordinate.

753. *Tallies*: 'a stick or rod of wood . . . marked on one side with notches
representing the amount of a debt or payment. The rod being cleft length-
wise across the notches, the debtor and creditor each retained one of the
halves, the tallying of which constituted legal proof of the debt' (*OED*).

755. *burnt our Vessels.* A convicted man, who claimed benefit of clergy,
was burned in the hand before being released from prison. See Blackstone,
iv. 369.

766. *Sprinkle down*: discredit.

768. *Free-grace*: i.e. as opposed to the Calvinist doctrine of predestination, held by the Presbyterians.

772. *Rimmon*: false idol. Rimmon was a Syrian deity worshipped at the temple in Damascus at the time of Elisha. See 2 Kings v. 18.

782. *have Calls to teach it up again*. After the eclipse of the Presbyterians and the rise to power of Cromwell and the Independents, the former began to work for the restoration of the monarchy. Immediately before the Restoration many of them hoped that the new king would support the Presbyterian church. See Clarendon, xvi. 242; Firth, *Last Years of the Protectorate*, i. 31.

802. *past upon account*: given credit in popular estimation.

809. *Picque*: an unnatural appetite for certain foods, generally occurring during pregnancy.

815. *Jobbernoles*: blockheads.

831. *fac'd it down*: browbeat, put down with impudence.

841. *Three Saints*: Prynne, Bastwick, and Burton. See note to i. iii. 154.

846. *Perfect Number of the Beast*. 'Here is wisdom. Let him that hath understanding count the number of the beast: for it is the number of a man; and his number is Six hundred threescore and six' (Rev. xiii. 18). The significance of this passage has been disputed by theologians since the second century. The Puritans often interpreted it as foretelling some political event. See Haller, *Liberty and Reformation*, New York, 1955, pp. 48 ff. Butler's 'Hermetic Philosopher' and his brethren 'have found out who is the true owner of the *Beast* in the *Apocalyps*, which has long passed for a Stray among the Learned; what is the true Product of 666, that has rung like *Whittington*'s Bells in the Ears of Expositors' (*Characters*, p. 103).

869. *Blew Ribands*: the nobility. A broad, dark blue ribbon is worn by Knights of the Garter.

870. *Blew Aprons*: tradesmen.

871. *Calleches*: a kind of light carriage.

872. *Cornets*: embroidered coronets.

883. *Indian Actions*: shares in the East India Company. The company, founded in 1600, originally raised capital for each individual voyage, but were later granted a new charter by Cromwell, establishing them as a permanent joint-stock company. The dividends paid by the company rose and fell steeply during the middle of the century, partly in response to the troubles at home and partly because the traders were dependent on the hospitality of the local Indian rulers, whose power was not always secure. See W. W. Hunter, *History of British India*, 1899–1900, ii. 101 ff.

894. *Fishers Folly Congregation*: i.e. a non-existent constituency. Fisher's Folly was formerly a 'beautiful house, with gardens of pleasure, and bowling-

alleys about it' built by a penurious clerk in Chancery named Jasper Fisher. The house had long since disappeared, but was still remembered in the jingle:

> Kirbie's castle, and Megse's glory
> Spinola's pleasure, and Fisher's folly.

See Fuller, *Worthies*, 3 vols., 1840, ii. 343.

907. *Cut out*: prepare.

908. *Plato's Year*. According to the *Timaeus*, a Great Year was completed when all the heavenly bodies in their orbits returned to the same relative positions. See Plato, *Timaeus*, 39 d; Cicero, *De Natura Deorum*, xx. 51.

909. *Bulls of Lenthall*: the Ordinances issued by Parliament when William Lenthall was Speaker of the House of Commons. He held the office almost continuously from the beginning of the Long Parliament until the Restoration.

910. *Fundamental*. Possibly a play on words. Lenthall was Speaker during the Rump Parliament.

920. *giving aim*: 'to guide one in his aim by informing him of the result of a preceding shot' (*OED*).

935. *from Forty four*: the year when the Self-Denying Ordinance, which was largely to exclude the Presbyterians from Parliament, was proposed. They were then compelled to use their influence by pressure from outside the House. Cromwell finally expelled Parliament in April 1653.

937. *Boutefeus*: firebrands.

946. *pack*: plot.

957. *Help Pamphlets out, etc.* Attempts were made to evade the licensing regulations imposed on the press by obtaining a licence for a harmless book and inserting seditious matter within the published volume. See F. S. Siebert, *Freedom of the Press in England, 1476–1776*, Urbana, 1952, p. 144.

960. *By Letter, etc.* A notorious case of this kind occurred in 1651, when a letter written by one Christopher Love, a Presbyterian minister, to a friend in Scotland, was seized by Cromwell. On the strength of the document Cromwell had Love executed on Tower Hill. See Clarendon, xiii. 117.

963. *Padders*: robber's.

980. *Powdring-Tubs*: normally, tubs used for salting beef. The term was used colloquially for the sweating-tubs used in the treatment of venereal disease, but it appears here to be a euphemism for a prison.

1001. *Piques*: dislike.

1006. *Mundungus*: a slang expression, used to describe ill-smelling tobacco.

1008. *Jobbernoll*: blockhead. Cf. iii. ii. 815.

1017. *Bringing in the King, etc.* See note to i. ii. 513.

1029. *Scorpions Oyl.* 'Take old Oyl as much as you please, put as many Scorpions into it as you can take in *July* . . . add to them white Dittany, leaves of Wormwood, Betony, Vervain, Rosemary, of each j handful, set them a sunning for a long time, then distil them in balneo in a Limbeck. . . . Anointed on the groin, it is prevalent against the bitings of Scorpions, how venomous soever' (Moffet, *Theater of Insects*, 1658, ii. 10. 1053). See also Pliny, *Nat. Hist.* xxix. iv. 29.

1031. *Weapons drest with Salves, etc.* William Foster writes of 'some persons of quality, reputed religious, which use the *Weapon-Salve*' (*Hoplocrismaspongus; or, A Sponge to wipe away the Weapon-Salve*, 1631, 'Epistle Dedicatory'). The ingredients are said to be '*Scull-mosse* or bones . . . Mummy and the Fat of Man' (ibid., p. 40). Foster observes 'this magicall and superstitious unguent every day to spread and come into more hands' (ibid., 'To the Reader'). See Thorndike, *History of Magic and Experimental Science*, 8 vols. New York, 1923–58, vii. 503–5.

1046. *t'a Scantling*: to a certain extent.

1059. *flam'd*: deceived.

1062. *lurch*: beat.

1070. *on the By*: by the way, incidentally.

1074. *like Alegators.* '*Aligators* . . . are frequently hung up in the Shops of *Druggists* and *Apothecaries*' (Grey). The apothecary visited by Romeo had such an alligator (Shakespeare, *Romeo and Juliet*, v. i. 43). See also Garth, *Dispensary*, ii. 127.

1092. *Laid . . . Neck and Heels*: confined; bound up.

1101. *Mahomet (your Chief), etc.*

> For the *Turk*'s Patriarch *Mahomet*
> Was the first great *Reformer*, and the Chief
> Of th'ancient *Christian* Belief,
> That mix'd it with new Light, and Cheat,
> With Revelations, Dreams, and Visions,
> And *apostolic* Superstitions,
> To be held forth, and carry'd on by War;
> And his Successor was a *Presbyter*.

(Butler, 'An Hypocritical Nonconformist', *Satires*, p. 91.)

1108. *Pigs are said to see the Wind.* A popular superstition. It was still a common belief in the Midlands at the end of the nineteenth century, when 'villagers always said that the reason why pigs ran squealing when the wind blew in their faces was because the wind appeared to them as long streaks of fire'. See *NQ*, 7th ser. ix. 14.

1110. *Knights-Bridge.* There was formerly a hospital at Knightsbridge. See Wheatley, *London*, ii. 351.

1111. *Tones*: the characteristic nasal tone of the Puritan preacher. See note to i. i. 228.

1112. *Bloody Bones.* See note to III. ii. 682.

Lunsford: Sir Thomas Lunsford (?1610–?1653), a colonel in the Royalist army and Lieutenant of the Tower. He had an evil reputation and was popularly said to eat up young children.

> From *Fielding* and from *Vavasour*,
>   Both ill affected men;
> From *Lunsford* eke deliver us,
>   That eateth up Children.
>
>   ('The Parliaments Hymnes', *Rump*, i. 65.)

See also Cleveland, 'Rupertismus', ll. 123–4 (*Minor Caroline Poets*, iii. 65).

1117. *Ten-Horn'd Cattle.* The beast in Rev. xvii had ten horns.

1120. *Meroz*: a place mentioned in Judges v. 23: 'Curse ye Meroz (said the Angel of the Lord) curse ye bitterly the inhabitants thereof: because they came not to the help of the Lord, to the help of the Lord against the mighty.' This text was frequently used by Puritan ministers when they preached to raise supporters:

> Then *curse ye Meroz*, in each *Pulpit* did *thunder*,
> To perplex the poor people, and keep them in wonder,
> Till all the Reins of Government were broken quite asunder.
>
>   ('The Rump served in with a Grand Sallet', st. xvi. *Rump*, ii. 122.)

1128. *Marcley-hill.* 'Neere unto the place where *Lug* and *Wy* meet togither, Eastward, a hill which they call *Marcley hill*, in the yeere of our redemption, 1571, (as though it had wakened upon the sodaine out of a deepe sleepe) roused it selfe up, and for the space of three daies togither mooving and shewing it selfe . . . with roring noise in a fearefull sort, and overturning all things that stood in the way, advanced it selfe forward to the wonderous astonishment of the beholders' (Camden, *Britannia*, trans. Holland, 1610, 620 E).

1130. *into Spoons, and Plate.* See notes to I. ii. 557, 569.

1138. *Legion*: the devil. See Mark v. 9; Luke viii. 30.

1149. *Dispensations*: i.e. of Providence; blessings.

Worm'd: deprived.

1162. *snuffled*: spoken through the nose.

1174. *Outgoings.* See note to I. ii. 1007.

1179. *correspondence.* See note to III. ii. 960.

1198. *Root, and Branch.* See note to III. ii. 323.

1199. *Reformado*: resign your commands. A verb coined from the same noun. See note to II. ii. 116.

1200. *T'your Great Croysado General.* 'To' is used in the sense of 'even including'. The Earl of Essex, the commander of the Parliamentary forces, was compelled to resign his commission by the Self-Denying Ordinance of

1645 (Clarendon, ix. 4). Grey, following the 'Key to *Hudibras*', erroneously identifies the General as Fairfax.

1203. *set*: trap.

1209. *sprinkled down*: discredited.

1228. *thorough Reformation*. See note to 1. i. 199.

1237. *The Isle of Wight, etc.* In September 1648 discussions began at Newport, Isle of Wight, between the King and the Parliamentary Commissioners, in an attempt to draw up a treaty. A long theological controversy took place between them concerning the abolition of episcopacy and the establishment of the Presbyterian Church in England (Clarendon, xi. 168).

1239. *Hinderson*: Alexander Henderson, a Scottish divine, had a celebrated disputation with Charles I in 1646 (Clarendon, x. 53). He was not, however, present with the King at Newport, having died in August 1646.

Masses: masters. Possibly an allusion to the expression 'Mas John', a colloquialism for a Scottish Presbyterian minister. See Jeremy Taylor, 'Second Sermon on Titus ii. 7, ? 1661', *Works*, 10 vols., 1862–78, viii. 533.

1242. *Ob-and-Sollers*: disputants; a colloquialism based on an abbreviation of 'objections and solutions'. The abbreviation was not originated by Butler. Cf. 'The Rota', *Rump*, ii. 142:

> Whilst he should give us *Sol's* and *Ob's*
> He brings us in some simple bobs.

1244. *Coursing*: disputing.

1250. *Sir Pride, and Hughson*: Thomas Pride (d. 1658) and John Hewson (d. 1662) were both colonels in the New Model Army and were both knighted by Cromwell.

1257. *Oliver had gotten ground, etc.* 'The treaty went on with a fatal slowness: and by the time it was come to some maturity, Cromwell came up with his army, and overturned all' (Burnet, *History*, i. 77). See also Walker, ii. 18.

1261. *Uxbridge bus'ness, etc.* When Parliament attempted to come to an agreement with the King at Uxbridge (1645), extensive disputations took place between the Commissioners on both sides concerning religion and Church government. See Clarendon, viii. 221.

1263. *a Scoundrel Holder forth*: identified by Grey and Nash as Christopher Love, who preached a sensational sermon in the church at Uxbridge, at the time when negotiations were about to start. He called the King's Commissioners 'men of blood', who 'intended only to amuse the people with the expectation of peace till they were able to do some notable mischieve to them' (Clarendon, viii. 219). The Commissioners, however, could hardly be said to have 'taken Law' from Love or to have been 'forc'd to withdraw' at his command. The allusion is more probably to Henderson, their adviser, who spoke violently of 'the necessity to change the government of the Church for the preservation of the State, which . . . could be preserved no other way' (ibid., 227). Henderson, moreover, was a 'Son o' th'Earth'; his father was a Scottish tenant farmer.

1270. *and Monies.* When the Scots army came to the assistance of Parliament, they asked for £100,000 to be paid to them in advance (Clarendon, vii. 261). The subsequent cost of maintaining the Scottish troops was the cause of popular complaint. See 'A new Ballad, called a Review of the Rebellion', ?1647.

1273. *for better ends*: i.e. the restoration of the monarchy. The Scots again entered England in 1651, under the command of Charles II, when, however, they found little support from the English Presbyterians. See Gardiner, *Commonwealth and Protectorate*, ii. 35.

1287. *Pantomimes*: mimic actors.

1293. *All Countries are a Wise-mans home.* Proverbial: 'Omne solum forti patria est, ut piscibus aequor' (Ovid, *Fasti*, i. 493). See also Lyly, *Euphues, The Anatomy of Wit* (*Works*, ed. Bond, 3 vols. Oxford, 1902, i. 314).

1304. *Nick'd*: defeated by chance, as in the game of hazard, where to 'nick' is to cast a winning throw.

hedg'd in: finds sympathy against himself. To 'hedge in' was a term in gambling, meaning 'to secure oneself against loss (on a bet, etc.) by betting on the other side' (*OED*).

1350. *choust*: tricked.

1376. *venters*: ventures.

1377. *Maggots*: fancies, odd opinions.

1388. *From Conclave down to Conventicle.* 'That is, papists as well as nonconformists' (Nash).

1394. *Dispensations*: the acts of Providence. Cf. i. ii. 1005.

1410. *Like Hawks from bating.* 'Bate . . . is when the Hawk fluttereth with her Wings either from Pearch or Fist, as it were strieving to get away' (Holme, *Academy of Armoury*, Chester, 1688, ii. xi. 7. 238).

1414. *Fift-Monarchy.* See note to iii. ii. 269. The Fifth Monarchy Men hoped for the return of Christ to earth as King, and the establishment of the fifth kingdom foretold by the prophet Daniel, 'which shall never be destroyed: and the kingdom shall not be left to other people, but it shall break in pieces and consume all these kingdoms, and it shall stand for ever' (Dan. ii. 44). The other four kingdoms were identified as the Assyrian, the Persian, the Greek, and the Roman. See L. F. Brown, *Baptists and Fifth Monarchy Men*, Washington, 1912, pp. 12 ff.

1418. *blind-sides*: unguarded sides; weaknesses.

1422. *A Few*: i.e. the elect (Matt. xx. 16).

1443. *Fore-stal'd*: appropriated; purloined.

1448. *great Diana of the Ephesians*. See Acts xix. 28.

1450. *Turn, and wind*: to manage to one's own advantage. Literally, to move this way and that.

1457. *nab*: nibble, bite gently.

1474. *lay . . . Trains*: set snares.

1494. *the Rose*: *sub rosa*.

1505. *That beastly Rabble, etc.* The following lines describe the behaviour of the people of London as Monk and his troops entered the city and put an end to the last of the Rump Parliament:

> In Cheapside there were a great many bonfires, and Bow bells and all the bells in all the churches as we went home were a-ringing. . . . But the common joy that was every where to be seen! The number of bonfires, there being fourteen between St. Dunstan's and Temple Bar, and at Strand Bridge I could at one view tell thirty-one fires . . . and all along burning, and roasting, and drinking for rumps. There being rumps tied upon sticks and carried up and down. The butchers at the May Pole in the Strand rang a peal with their knives when they were going to sacrifice their rump. On Ludgate Hill there was one turning of the spit that had a rump tied upon it, and another basting of it. Indeed it was past imagination, both the greatness and the suddenness of it (Pepys, *Diary*, 11 Feb. 1660).

See also Aubrey, *Brief Lives*, ii. 76; Clarendon, xvi. 131.

1508. *new-chalk'd Bills*. See note to III. ii. 539.

1510. *Baul the Bishops*. See note to I. ii. 530.

1514. *Carbonading*: broiling, grilling.

1525. *Jar*: quarrel.

1526. *Grilly'd*: grilled (Fr. *grillé*).

1534. *Dun*: Edward Dun, the official hangman. He died in 1663, when he was succeeded by the more notorious Jack Ketch. See Horace Bleackley, *Hangmen of England*, 1929, p. 4. A mock-elegy on Dun appeared in 1663, under the title *Groanes from Newgate; or an Elegy upon Edward Dun, Esq., the Cities' Common Hangman, who Dyed Naturally in his Bed the 11th of September 1663, Written by a Person of Quality*. See *NQ*, 2nd ser. xi. 447.

1537. *activ'st Member of the Five*: Sir Arthur Haslerig (?1610–61), whose effigy is appropriately 'mounted on a *Hazel Bavin*'. He was one of the five Members of Parliament accused by Charles I of high treason in 1642 (see note to I. ii. 523). Later he became an active member of the independent faction in the Commons and, after the fall of Richard Cromwell, a member of the Committee of Public Safety and the Council of State. The Parliament in 1659, says Clarendon, 'was governed by Vane and Haslerigge' (xvi. 82). At the Restoration he was imprisoned in the Tower, and died shortly afterwards.

1540. *chosen for a Fift agen, etc.* Haslerig was one of the five Commissioners elected by Parliament to govern the army. The election took place on 11

February 1660, the day on which the mob burned the Rump in effigy. See Ludlow, *Memoirs*, ed. Firth, 2 vols. Oxford, 1894, ii. 223.

1547. *Bavin*: a bundle of brushwood, formerly used in bakers' ovens.

1550. *Cook*: John Cook (d. 1660) was chosen by the High Court of Justice to be one of the counsel against Charles I in the King's trial. In the absence of the Attorney-General Cook found himself chiefly responsible for the prosecution. He was the author, after the trial, of *King Charles his Case, or an appeal to all rational men concerning his trial in the High Court of Justice* (1649). This work received a reply in *The Case of King Charles Truly Stated*, attributed to Butler (*Satires*, p. 366). Later he went to Ireland as Chief Justice of Munster and, at the Restoration, was tried and condemned to death.

Pride: Thomas Pride (d. 1658), a colonel in the New Model Army and a staunch supporter of Cromwell. In 1648, acting on instructions from Fairfax, Pride set a guard round the entrances to the House of Commons, prevented many members from entering, and arrested others, in order to frustrate the intended agreement with the King. This was the celebrated 'Pride's Purge'.

1556. *Like Vermine, etc.* See note to i. i. 524.

1564. *Their Founder, etc.* Saint Ignatius Loyola, the founder of the Jesuit order, started his career as a soldier. It was during convalescence from a wound that he underwent a religious conversion.

1568. *by springing Mines.* An allusion to the Gunpowder Plot.

1574. *Sambenites*: penitential garments worn at the time of the Spanish Inquisition, and so called because they resembled the scapular introduced by Saint Benedict. They were worn by avowed and impenitent heretics at an *auto-da-fé*. 'It . . . is of a black Colour, hath Flames painted on it, and sometimes the condemned Heretick himself, painted to the Life, in the Midst of the Flames. Sometimes also they paint on it Devils thrusting the poor Heretick into Hell' (Limborch, *History of the Inquisition*, trans. Chandler, 1731, II. iv. xli. 295).

1583. *reaches*: contrivances.

1584. *fetches*: tricks.

1585. *Kirkerus*: Athanasius Kircher (1601–80), a Jesuit priest, renowned for his learning, especially in the natural sciences. He lectured at the Roman College on physics, mathematics, and Oriental languages, and wrote a monumental work on Egyptian hieroglyphics, the *Oedipus Aegyptiacus*. See Yates, *Bruno*, pp. 416 ff.

1587. *the Ægyptians us'd by Bees, etc.* 'So many are their virtues worthy our imitation; that the *Ægyptians*, *Greeks* and *Chaldæans* took divers Hieroglyphicks from them; as when they would express subjects obedient to their Prince, they set it forth in figure of a Bee very singular in that virtue; when a King loving to his subjects, they portray it likewise and set it forth by a Swarm of Bees' (Thomas Moffet, *Theater of Insects*, i. iv. 905). See also Pierio Valeriano Bolzani, *Hieroglyphica*, Basle, 1567, xxvi. 185.

1593. *when th' are once impair'd in that, etc.* 'Now these drones be without any sting at all, as one would say unperfect bees.... After the hony is growing once more to maturitie and perfection, then begin they to drive these drones out of dores: nay, ye shall have many bees set upon one poore drone, and kill him out-right' (Pliny, *Nat. Hist.*, trans. Holland, I. xi. xi. 315).

1608. *jump*: agree, tally.

1616. *Luez*: Luz was the Aramaic name for the *os coccyx*, or 'nut' of the spinal column. It was a belief among the Jews that this bone was indestructible and would form the nucleus of the resurrected body.

The learned *Eben Ezra* and *Manesseh Ben Israel* do write, that there is in the Rump of Man a certain Bone, which they call the Bone *Luz*; this, they say, is of so immortal and incomprehensible a Nature, that at the Resurrection out of it all the rest of the Bones and Members shall sprout, just as a Plant does out of a Kernel: and is there any thing that can bear a nearer Resemblance to this Rump Bone than the present *Parliament*, that has been so many Years dead and rotten under Ground? ... And hence it is, I suppose, that Physicians and Anatomists call this Bone *Os Sacrum*, or the holy Bone (Butler, 'A Speech Made at the Rota', *Satires*, p. 325).

See Menasseh Ben-Israel, *De Resurrectione Mortuorum Libri III*, ii. xv, Amsterdam, 1636, p. 202; *Midrash Rabbah*, trans. Freedman and Simon, 10 vols., 1939, viii. 301; Cornelius Agrippa, *Three Books of Occult Philosophy*, trans. J. F., 1651, i. xx. 45.

1624. *Os Sacrum, etc.* This is one of several explanations offered for the name of this bone. The true origin of the name is uncertain.

1627. *several Rude Ejections, etc.* The Rump Parliament, which remained after Pride's 'purge' of the Long Parliament in 1648, was dissolved by Cromwell in 1653. It was recalled again by the army in 1659, shortly before the fall of Richard Cromwell, expelled by Lambert and his troops later in the same year, reassembled in December, and finally dissolved in 1660.

1629. *Reversions*: inheritances. A legal term.

1633. *Kennels*: gutters.

1645. *Before the bluster, etc.* The Butler manuscripts include another version of this passage (*Satires*, p. 462), and of ll. 1649 ff. below (*Satires*, p. 463).

1661. *Entail*: 'bestow as an inalienable possession' (*OED*).

1672. *Bulks*: bellies; bodies.

1690. *Jocky-Rider is all Spurs.* An allusion to the horse races held in the Corso in Rome at carnival time. 'We were taken up the next morning in seing the impertinences of the Carnoval when all the world are as mad at Rome, as at other places, but the most remarkable were the 3 Races of the Barbarie horses, that run in the strada del *Corso* without riders, onely having spurrs so placed on their backs, & hanging downe by their sides, as with their motion to stimulate them' (Evelyn, *Diary*, 28 Feb. 1645; ed. de Beer, 6 vols., Oxford, 1955, ii. 380).

CANTO III

1. *Bug-bears*: hobgoblins; imaginary terrors.

3. *Fern, that Insect-weed, etc.* Ferns were supposed to propagate themselves without seed (Pliny, *Nat. Hist.* xxvii. ix. 55). They are here called an 'Insect-weed' since certain insects, notably bees, were thought to be propagated not by seeds but from the decomposition of matter (see note to iii. ii. 4).

4. *Equivocally*: by equivocal generation, the propagation of plants or animals without seed.

8. *Imps and Teats.* Witches were thought to suckle their imps or familiar spirits from a special teat on their bodies. See note to ii. iii. 146.

15. *Rosi-crusian Virtuoso's, etc.* See note to i. i. 539. 'This is an Art to teach Men to see with their Ears, and hear with their Eyes and Noses, and it has been found true by Experience and Demonstration, if we may believe the History of the *Spaniard*, that could see Words, and swallow Music by holding the Peg of a Fiddle between his Teeth' ('An Hermetic Philosopher', *Characters*, p. 105).

27. *as Resolute appear, etc.* Cf. Ovid, *Fasti*, iii. 644:

Audacem fecerat ipse timor.

30. *run away from death by dying.* Nash compares this line with Martial, *Epigrams*, ii. lxxx:

Hostem cum fugeret, se Fannius ipse peremit.
hic, rogo, non furor est, ne moriare, mori?

34. *Perdue*: in hiding.

36. *Marshal-Legions*: the devil's. See note to iii. ii. 1138.

62. *Believe they lag, etc.* Grey compares these lines with John Taylor, 'An Armado, or Navye' (*Works*, Spenser Soc., 1869, p. 87): 'As Horsemen are none of the best Mariners, so Mariners are commonly the worst Horsemen, as one of them being upon a tyred Hackeney once, (his companions pray'd him to ride faster) *he said he was becalm'd.*'

94. *scruple at*: doubt; question the truth of.

105. *Pug*: devil, demon.

110. *Dun-ship*: a combination of 'dunce' and 'donship'. 'The word don is often used to signify a knight' (Nash).

137. *Rallying*: joking, teasing.

145. *the Reverend writer*: Herbert Croft (1603–91), who in 1675 published

The Naked Truth. Or the True state of the primitive church. By an Humble Moderator (*Somers Tracts*, iii. 329 ff.). Croft submitted that the essentials of religion were common to all Protestant churches and that, for the sake of peace and unity, some compliance by the Established church would be more effectual than persecution and enforced uniformity. 'The appearance of this book', says Wood, 'was like a comet. It drew the eyes of all that could look upon it' (*Athenae Oxonienses*, iv. 312).

158. *Nick*: deceive (with a play upon the name given to the devil).

186. *Leaguer*: siege.

200. *Ridge*: back.

201. *in Querpo*: naked (Spanish, *cuerpo*, body).

210. *Powd'ring Tubs*. See note to III. ii. 980.

211. *two wheel'd Carroches*: a colloquial term for the carts which carried criminals to the gallows. See I. ii. 327 and note.

212. *managing a wooden Horse*. 'The Riding of this Horse, whose back is only two Boards set together like the Ridge of a House, is a kind of Punishment used among Soldiers . . . the sharpness of which ridge doth so gall and cut the Riders Thighs and Breech, that he shall be scarce able to go or stand for a certain time after' (Randle Holme, *Academy of Armoury*, Chester, 1688, III. vii. 7. 310). In 1648 two soldiers were sentenced to 'ride the Wooden Horse at the Royal Exchange, for an Hour at Exchange-time' (Rushworth, IV. ii. 1369).

214. *Eras'd, or Coup'd*: terms of heraldry, used to describe the head or other part of an heraldic beast, when it is represented as being cut off. 'Erased' signifies a jagged cut, 'couped' a clean cut.

220. *Batoons*: blows from a club.

243. *those that fly, etc.* Proverbial (*ODEP* 200; Tilley, D79).

248. *breaking*: going bankrupt.

261. *crown'd their bravest Men, etc.* See note to I. ii. 289.

300. *Bacrack*: a wine produced at Bacharach on the Rhine.

Hocamore: hock (German, *Hochheimer*).

Mum: a kind of beer, originally brewed in Brunswick.

305. *their Sultan-Populaces, etc.* Strangulation appears to have been a common fate of those Turkish Pashas, or military commanders, who proved unsatisfactory to their Sultan. Sir Paul Rycaut records, among similar incidents, the death of Abassa, Pasha of Bosnia, who failed to defeat the Poles in 1634, and was 'strangled by two Kapugees' at the command of the Sultan Amurat IV (*History of the Turkish Empire*, 1680, i. 49).

306. *Bassa's*: Pashas. The name given to Turkish military commanders and provincial governors.

308. *What Fights thou mean'st, etc.* After the Battle of Edgehill, Parliament 'voted that their army had the victory, and appointed a day for a solemn thanksgiving to God for the same' (Clarendon, vi. 101). Again, following Waller's notorious defeat at Roundway Down, 'he was met upon his return to London, after the most total defeat that could almost be imagined . . . with all the trained bands and militia of London, and received as if he had brought the King prisoner with him' (ibid. vii. 172). When the ships of Colonel Popham were severely damaged off the coast of Ireland, 'the House that day . . . passed an Order, *That for this remarkable additional mercy bestowed upon them in the prosperous success given to their Fleet at Sea, upon Thursday next,* 7. June *(the day set apart for publick Thanksgiving) the Ministers should praise God'* (Walker, *Independency,* ii. 196).

350. *the ancient Mice attack'd the Frogs.* An allusion to the *Batrachomyomachia,* or *Battle of the Frogs and Mice,* a Greek mock-epic poem, attributed to Homer.

359. *the Emperour Caligula, etc.* During his expedition to Gaul, Caligula drew up his troops on the sea coast, as though about to cross over into Britain, and commanded them to fill their helmets and cloaks with shells (Suetonius, *Caligula,* xlvi).

381. *won the Amazons, etc.* In some accounts of his life Theseus is said to have fought against the Amazons and subsequently married their queen. See Statius, *Thebaid,* xii. 534; Plutarch, *Theseus,* xxvii.

383. *Rinaldo gain'd his Bride, etc.* Rinaldo, the hero of Tasso's *Gerusalemme Liberata,* is seduced by the enchantress Armida. He later fights against her and her followers in battle, before making her his bride.

402. *breaking Gold.* 'Prior to the exchange of rings, it was accounted sufficient if the contracting parties broke a piece of gold or silver (each keeping a half), and drank a glass of wine' (T. S. Knowlson, *Origins of Popular Superstitions,* 1934, p. 95).

415. *those the Pen had drawn together*: i.e. conscripted or enrolled men.

436. *extend*: seize upon; take possession of.

454. *fingle fangle*: trifle.

458. *like the Swiss, etc.* The Swiss mercenaries were notorious for their courage, brutality, and readiness to fight for money on any side. See More, *Utopia,* II. viii, ed. Lupton, Oxford, 1895, p. 253; Pope, *Dunciad,* ii. 356–8; Oman, *Art of War in the Sixteenth Century,* Ithaca, 1937, pp. 75 ff.

475. *Gallenist, and Paracelsian, etc.* Controversies developed during the seventeenth century between the physicians who followed the traditional methods of Galen, and those who favoured the new methods introduced by Paracelsus as a result of his experiments in chemistry. See Thorndike, *History of Magic and Experimental Science,* 8 vols. New York, 1923–58, vii. 489.

478. *cut . . . out*: prepare.

486. *Piques*: aversions.

496. *Declaration* '[In] the *declaration, narratio*, or *count* . . . the plaintiff sets forth his cause of complaint at length' (Blackstone, III. xx. 293).

510. *sinking*: passing over in silence (a term used in the game of piquet).

521. *Pretence*: claim.

523. *Traverse*: contradict; deny at law.

531. *Chews*: fool, gull.

543. *thrown-up*. To throw up is 'to place one's cards face upwards on the table on withdrawing from the game' (*OED*).

560. *eldest hand*: the first player in a game of cards. See III. i. 611 and note.

577. *Old Dul Sot*. The unreliable 'Key to *Hudibras*' (*Posth. Works*, i) identifies the lawyer as 'One *Prideaux*, a pragmatical Justice of the Peace, noted as much for his extorting Money from Delinquents, as his Disloyalty to his Sovereign'. The portrait is more probably an imaginary one, designed as a general satire on the law.

   told the Clock: counted the hours; passed the time idly.

578. *Bridewel-Dock*: an inlet of the Thames between Whitefriars and Bridewell. On the western bank of Bridewell Dock there was a house of correction, the Bridewell, where petty offenders were sentenced to short terms of imprisonment, and where notorious floggings took place before the Court of Governors. See Wheatley, *London*, i. 242–4.

579. *Hickses-hall*: originally the Sessions House of the county of Middlesex in St. John Street, Clerkenwell, named after Sir Baptist Hicks, at whose cost it was built. In 1619 James I issued a grant to Hicks that the building should become 'a prison or gaol for the county for ever'. Wheatley, *London*, ii. 213.

580. *Hiccius-Dockius*: a formula used by jugglers when performing tricks.

586. *Quarteridge*: payment of a quarterly sum of money.

590. *Puddle-dock*: a wharf at the foot of St. Andrew's Hill, Upper Thames Street, notorious for its dirt and stench. Strype's edition of Stow notes that it was used 'for a Laystall for the Soil of the Streets; and much frequented by Barges and Lighters, for taking the same away' (1720, I. iii. 229). There appears to be no record of a gaol at Puddle Dock. A contributor to *NQ* suggests that 'it was probably only a cage for juvenile delinquents, or one of the sponging-houses belonging to the sheriffs at Puddle-Dock, Blackfriars, a property belonging to the authorities of the city of London' (3rd ser. ii. 352).

599. *Monsters*: the freaks exhibited at fairs by travelling showmen. Trinculo in *The Tempest* (II. ii. 31) thinks of showing Caliban as a 'monster', in the hope that 'not a holiday-fool there but would give a piece of silver'. Among the sights to be seen at Bartholomew Fair were 'large children and tiny men, an occasional tiger or leopard, a mare who had seven feet, a learned pig and a

mermaid' (Rosamond Bayne-Powell, *Eighteenth-Century London Life*, 1937, p. 156).

Puppet-plays. See note to I. i. 559.

602. *Head-burrow*: a constable or parish officer.

605. *Kennel*: gutter.

609. *Impos'd a Tax on Bakers Ears*. 'That is, took a Bribe to save them from the Pillory' (Grey). 'The punishment of bakers breaking the assise [of bread] was antiently to stand in the pillory' (Blackstone, IV. xii. 157).

612. *Arbitrary Ale*: i.e. sold without a licence. Cf. *Characters*, p. 84.

615. *Residentiary Bawds, etc*. 'He uses great Care and Moderation in punishing those, that offend regularly, by their Calling, as residentiary Bawds, and incumbent Pimps, that pay Parish Duties—Shopkeepers, that use constant false Weights and Measures, these he rather prunes, that they may grow the better, than disables' ('A Justice of Peace', *Characters*, p. 83).

620. *Hawker'd*: practised as a hawker (a nonce-word).

621. *To this brave Man, etc*. The Butler manuscripts include an alternative account of the knight's visit to the lawyer (*Satires*, pp. 463–4).

647. *Action of conversion | And Trover*: 'in its original an action . . . against such a person as had *found* another's goods, and refused to deliver them on demand, but *converted* them to his own use' (Blackstone, III. ix. 152).

655. *cross-bill*: a bill filed by the defendant against the plaintiff in the same law-suit. 'A defendant cannot pray any thing in . . . his answer, but to be dismissed the court: if he has any relief to pray against the plaintiff, he must do it by an original bill of his own, which is called a *cross-bill*' (Blackstone, III. xxvii. 448).

685. *Matrimony, and Hanging, etc*. Proverbial. See note to II. i. 839.

688. *Cross I win, and Pile you loose*. Proverbial (*ODEP* 285; Tilley, C834).

690. *Maintenance*: 'a taking in hand, bearing up or upholding of quarrels and sides, to the disturbance or hindrance of common right' (Sir Edward Coke, *Commentary upon Littleton*, III. xiii. 701. 368b).

695. *Common barratry*: 'the offence of frequently exciting and stirring up suits and quarrels between his majesty's subjects. . . . The punishment for this offence . . . if the offender . . . belongs to the profession of the law, [is] . . . to be disabled from practising for the future' (Blackstone, IV. x. 133).

700. *ore the Bar, etc*. An allusion to the expression 'to be cast over the bar', meaning to be deprived of the status of barrister.

715. *From Stile's Pocket, etc*. See note to III. i. 616.

717. *Obnoxious*: guilty; liable to punishment.

718. *Hiccius-Doctius*. See III. iii. 580 and note.

730. *Affidavit-customers*: purchasers of false evidence, sworn on oath.

732. *Tales*. 'If by means of challenges, or other cause, a sufficient number of unexceptionable jurors doth not appear at the trial, either party may pray a *tales*. A *tales* is a supply of *such* men as are summoned upon the first panel, in order to make up the deficiency' (Blackstone, III. xxiii. 364).

742. *Bongey*: a generic term for sorcerers, based on the name of Thomas or Johannes de Bungey, the Franciscan Friar who taught at Oxford in the thirteenth century, and, like his contemporary Roger Bacon, was suspected of practising magic. The two appear in Greene's *Friar Bacon and Friar Bungay*, a play based on popular legends concerning the two friars.

Water-witch. An allusion to the trial of witches by swimming. Cf. II. i. 503 and see note to II. iii. 145.

745. *Trepans*: tricks, snares.

748. *Quirks, and Quillets*: subtleties.

760. *Ply ith' Temples*.

> . . . *Temple-Walks*, and *Smithfield* never fail
> Of plying rogues, that set their souls to sale
> To the first passenger, that bids a price,
> And make their livelihood of Perjuries.

> (John Oldham, 'Thirteenth Satyre of Juvenal, Imitated', *Poems and Translations*, 1683, p. 37.)

Otway writes of your 'Peripatetick Philosophers of the Temple walks, Rogues in Rags, and yet not honest: Villains that under-value Damnation, will forswear themselves for a Dinner, and hang their Fathers For half a Crown' (*Souldiers Fortune*, I. i. 25, *Works*, ed. Ghosh, 2 vols. Oxford, 1932, ii. 96).

761. *Knights oth' Posts*: professional perjurers.

762. *Cross-leg'd Knights*. 'In the round Walk [of the Temple] there remain Monuments of Noblemen there buried, to the number of Eleven. Eight of them are Images of armed Knights; five lying cross-legged, as Men vowed to the Holy Land' (Strype, *Stow's Survey of London*, 1720, I. iii. 271).

768. *According to their Ears, etc.* 'When he is once outed of his Ears, he is past his Labour, and can do the Commonwealth of Practisers no more Service' ('A Knight of the Post', *Characters*, p. 154). It was essential for the perjurer to be well dressed in order to appear an honest citizen. Grey refers to an informer at the trial of Strafford, to whom Pym, his employer, gave money 'to buy him a satin suit and cloak', fearing that 'a person of so vile a quality would not be reasonably thought a competent informer' (Clarendon, vii. 412).

771. *Purveys*: provisions.

AN HEROICAL EPISTLE OF
HUDIBRAS TO HIS LADY

2. *Nebuchadnezar.* See Dan. iv. 31–33.

25. *loss of Ears, etc.* 'Perjury itself is . . . punished with six months' imprisonment, perpetual infamy, and a fine of 20*l*, or to have both ears nailed to the pillory' (Blackstone, IV. x. 138).

26. *Hackney*: hired.

99. *Love, that's the Worlds preservative, etc.* Nash notes that the following lines are a free and satirical adaptation of the address to Venus at the opening of Lucretius' *De Rerum Natura* (i. 1–5, 21–24).

106. *but Heav'n too.* See Matt. xix. 14.

135. *to have Power to forgive, etc.* Cf. Seneca, *De Clementia*, I. xxi: 'Servavit quidem nemo nisi maior eo, quem servabat.' 'Servare proprium est excellentis fortunae' (ibid. I. v). Hudibras again expresses stoical sentiments as he did earlier (I. iii. 1013 ff.).

165. *Breeding Teeth*: cutting teeth, teething.

168. *Cully*: easily deceived.

188. *Philip Ny*: see note to III. ii. 638.

203. *when Necessity's obey'd, etc.* An allusion to the proverb 'Necessity has no law' (*ODEP* 445; Tilley, N76).

234. *fall aboard*: attack, fall upon.

237. *To what a height did Infant Rome, etc.*

By this time *Rome* was grown so strong, that it was able to cope with any of the neighbouring Cities, but for want of Women, its Grandieur was like to continue no longer than a Mans age. . . . *Romulus* ordered Games to be solemnly kept in honour of *Neptunus* Equestris. . . . Whereupon he commanded that the adjacent Countries should have notice given them of a Show that was to be made. . . . Thither also came all the *Sabines*, with their Wives and Children. . . . When the time for the Show was come, and their minds and eyes were all intent upon it, then by consent they made the attack; and giving the signal, the *Roman* youth ran up and down to ravish, or seize their Virgins' (Livy, I. ix, trans. Holland, 1686, p. 8).

See also Plutarch, *Romulus*, xiv; Florus, I. i.

259. *Acting Plays, etc.* See note to l. 237, above.

262. *talk'd of Love, and Flames, etc.* 'The men shew'd a great deal of kindness, whilst they excused themselves, and strove to attone for their fault by love and address, which are the best arguments to pacifie a Womans soul' (Livy, I. ix, trans. Holland).

270. *treaty*: entreaty, persuasion.

293. *Retrench'd*: cut down, reduced.

350. *These*: i.e. 'these words'. Cf. Shakespeare, *Hamlet*, II. ii. 109: 'To the celestial, and my soul's idol, the most beautified Ophelia . . . In her excellent white bosom, these, etc.'; *Twelfth Night*, II. v. 90: 'To the unknown belov'd, this, and my good wishes.'

THE LADIES ANSWER
TO THE KNIGHT

4. *Replevin*: recover; 'the restoration to, or recovery by, a person of goods and chattels taken from him, upon his giving security to have the matter tried in a court of justice and to return the goods if the case is decided against him' (*OED*).

30. *for your Ears*: i.e. as a perjurer. See 'Epistle of Hudibras to his Lady', l. 25 and note.

46. *Propriety*: right of ownership.

49. *Forfeitures*: 'a punishment annexed by law to some illegal act, or negligence, in the owner of lands . . . whereby he loses all his interest therein, and they go to the party injured' (Blackstone, II. xviii. 267).

59. *Saint Martins beads*. The parish of St. Martin-le-Grand was well known for the manufacture of imitation jewellery. 'The rings and chaines bought at S Martines . . . weare faire for a little time, but shortly after will prove alchimy, or rather pure copper' (Geffray Mynshul, *Essayes and Characters of a Prison* (1618), Edinburgh, 1821, p. 48).

61. *like Indian Dames*. 'The *Indians* have their neather Lips in great circlets, beset with pretious stones, which cover all their Chins, deeming it an essential grace to shew their Teeth to the roots' (Bulwer, *Anthropometamorphosis*, 1650, xi. 108).

76. *Jargones*: ciphers.

98. *Ladys of the Post*: i.e. female perjurers. Cf. 'Knights of the Post', I. i. 577.

103. *Deodand*: 'by this is meant whatever personal chattel is the immediate occasion of the death of any reasonable creature: which is forfeited to the king, to be applied to pious uses. . . . Deodands, and forfeitures in general . . . are for the most part granted out to the lords of manors, or other liberties: to the perversion of their original design' (Blackstone, I. viii. 300–2).

134. *Tip't with Gold*.

> eque sagittifera prompsit duo tela pharetra
> diversorum operum: fugat hoc, facit illud amorem;
> quod facit, auratum est et cuspide fulget acuta,
> quod fugat, obtusum est et habet sub harundine plumbum.

(Ovid, *Metamorphoses*, i. 468–71.)

142. *Gossips*: godparents; sponsors at a baptism.

153. *Setters*: confederates of a swindler, employed as a decoy for his victims.

178. *swears his Ears, etc.*: i.e. perjures himself. Cf. l. 30 above.

180. *Perjure booty*: swear falsely for profit.

184. *like Christ*. Cf. 'A Knight of the Post' (*Characters*, p. 154): 'He takes Money to kiss the Gospel, as *Judas* did *Christ*, when he betrayed him.'

192. *Covins*: tricks; treachery.

198. *As they did him*. See 1 Kings xi. 4–9.

   baffle: disgrace.

220. *Too rich a Present, etc.* See Mark x. 38.

261. *Braves*: bravado.

273. *Card*: chart.

277. *Prester John*: the Emperor of Ethiopia, whose customs were described by Elizabethan travellers and ambassadors. The emissaries who visited him in 1520 were not admitted to his presence but had to communicate with him through a third person. When, later, they were received by the Emperor, 'his face was covered with a piece of Blew Taffata, which was to bee moved up and downe, so that sometimes all his face was seene, and sometimes all covered' (Purchas, *Pilgrimes*, II. VII. v. 1079).

283. *Pope Jone*. See note to I. iii. 1249.

285. *Jone the Pucel*: i.e. Joan of Arc, known as *la pucelle*, or 'the maid'.

288. *Grand Constable*: the chief officer of the French royal household.

292. *Long-Robe*: the legal profession.

329. *'less you Fly, etc.* See note to III. i. 597.

370. *vapouring*: boasting.

378. *Salique Law*: the alleged law by which women were debarred from succession to the throne of France. See Shakespeare, *Henry V*, I. ii. 33 ff. Such a law did not, in fact, exist with relation to the monarchy. The *Lex Salica*, a Frankish law-book, was invoked to support the succession of Philip V in 1316, and was again used to challenge the claim of Edward III and his successors to the French throne. This particular meaning of 'Salic Law' appears to have developed as a result of these claims.

APPENDIX A

Butler's Letter to Sir George Oxenden

IN 1933 Ricardo Quintana published extracts from the letter-books of Sir George Oxenden which, as he pointed out, cast new light on the life of Samuel Butler and on several matters relating to the composition of *Hudibras*.[1] Oxenden was employed by the East India Company, which he joined as a boy. He went out to India in 1632, at the age of twelve, and returned home for three visits, the first between 1639 and 1641, the second between 1653 and 1656, and the third between 1659 and 1662. During this last visit he was made President of the Company and was knighted. He died in India in 1669. While he was abroad he kept up a correspondence with his family in England, including his sister Mrs. Elizabeth Dallison and his cousin Lieutenant-Colonel Richard Oxenden. On 6 April 1663 Elizabeth Dallison sent her brother a parcel containing books. One of these was a copy of the First Part of *Hudibras*, as we learn from Richard Oxenden's letter of 30 March:[2]

> S^r amongst some bookes y^t you will receaue from y^r sister Dalyson there is one named Hudibrase wch is ye most admired peece of Drollary y^t ever came forth it was made by o^r Old acquaintance Mr Buttler whome wee did use to meete in Grasenn walkes hee did use to keepe Comp^a wth Ned Kelke & Collonel Mathuse & Dr Morgin & Mr Willm Morgin I onely write this for feare yor multiplicity of Busienesse should cause you to forgett him & y^t you may ye Better understand his Booke hee sends you these Inclosed lines wth ye presentation of his service. . . .

What Richard Oxenden refers to as 'these Inclosed lines' is, in fact, the following letter from Samuel Butler:[3]

> S^r
>
> Yo^r Worthy kinsman & my hon^d Freind Collonell Oxinden hath engaged me to give you this trouble, for he Intending to present you wth a Trifle of mine, a booke lately Printed here, hath beene pleas^d to desire me to give you a short Acco^t of it, It was written not long before ye time, when I had first ye hon^r to be Acquainted wth you, & Hudibras whose name it beares was a West Countrey Kn^t then a Coll: in the Parliament Army & a Com^{te} man, wth whome I became Acquainted Lodging in ye same house wth him in Holbourne

---

[1] Ricardo Quintana, 'The Butler–Oxenden Correspondence', *MLN* xlviii (1933), 1–11.

[2] British Museum Add. MS. 40711, fo. 34.

[3] Ibid., fo. 13^v–14^r.

I found his humor soe pleasant y^t I know not how I fell into ye way of Scribling wch I was never Guilty of before nor since, I did my endeav^r to render his Character as like as I could, wch all y^t know him say is soe right y^t they found him out by it at ye first veiw, For his Esqr Ralpho he was his Clerk & an Independ^t, betweene whome, & ye Kn^t, there fell out Such perpetuall disputes about Religion, as you will find up & downe in ye Booke for as neere as I could I sett downe theire very words, As for ye Story I had it from ye Kn^{ts} owne Mouth, & is so farr from being feign'd, y^t it is upon Record, for there was a Svite of Law upon it betweene ye Kn^t, & ye Fidler, in wch ye Kn^t was overthrowne to his great shame, & discontent, for wch he left ye Countrey & came up to Settle at London; The other Psons as Orsin a Beareward, Talgo[l] a Butcher, Magnano a Tinker, Cerdon a Cobler, Colon a Clowne &c: are such as Commonly make up Bearebaitings though some curious witts heere pretend to discouer ceartaine Psons of Quallity wth whome they say those Characters agree, but since I doe not know who they are I cannot tell you till I see theire Commentaries but am content (since I cannot helpe it) y^t every man should make what applications he pleases of it, either to himselfe or others, Butt I Assure you my cheife designe was onely to give ye world a Just Acco^t of ye Ridiculous folly & Knavery of ye Presbiterian & Independent Factions then in power & whether I have performed it well or noe I cannot tell, Onely I have had ye good fortune to have it Gen^{lly} esteem^d Soe especially by ye King & ye best of his Subjects, it had ye Ill fortune to be printed when I was Absent from this Towne whereby many Mistakes were committed, but I have Corrected this booke wch you will receive my Selfe, wth wch S^r I send you ye best wishes and Reall Affections of

Yo^r Humble & Faithfull
Servt Sam : Butler

London March ye 19th
1662
3

The letter is not written in Butler's own hand, but is presumably a copy of an original which was destroyed.

APPENDIX B

The Original Hudibras

In his letter to Sir George Oxenden, Butler describes how the character of Hudibras was originally inspired by that of a West Country knight with whom he was lodging in Holborn, and how he drew the knight's character so well that 'all y^t know him say [it] is soe right y^t they found him out by it at ye first veiw'. Unfortunately we do not know whom the first readers of *Hudibras* recognized in Butler's description, but within about forty years of the publication of the First Part the idea had developed that Hudibras was Sir Samuel Luke.

Luke was first associated with Hudibras in the poem itself, where the hero declares

> 'Tis sung, There is a valiant *Mamaluke*
> In forrain Land, yclep'd ——
> To whom we have been oft compar'd,
> For Person, Parts, Address, and Beard.[1]

It is generally agreed that Luke is the person here alluded to, though, as Grey pointed out, the allusion is evidence that the hero's character was not modelled on Luke, 'it being an uncommon thing to compare a Person to himself'.[2] He was next mentioned in connexion with Butler by the anonymous biographer whose life of the poet appeared in the 1704 edition of *Hudibras*. The biographer declares that 'our Author liv'd some Time also with Sir *Samuel Luke*, who was of an ancient Family in Bedfordshire', and that, while living with him, Butler 'Compos'd this Loyal Poem'. This statement is, however, not supported by any other known evidence, nor do Butler's earliest biographers, Aubrey and Wood, refer to his residence with Luke. The biographer may well have drawn on popular rumour originating from the allusion to Luke quoted above.

Eleven years later the 'Key to *Hudibras*', published as an appendix to Butler's *Posthumous Works*, not only associated Luke with the poet but described him as 'the chief Hero of his Poem'. 'Hudibras' is, according to the Key, 'a Name which the Author . . . bestows on Sir *Samuel Luke* of *Bedfordshire*; a Self-conceited Commander under *Oliver Cromwel*'. The authenticity of the Key is, however, doubtful, and many of its interpretations are certainly false. According to the essay 'To the

[1] 1. i. 895–8.   [2] Grey, Preface iv.

Reader' which introduces the Key, it was supplied by a Dr. Midgley, on whose authority it is attributed to Sir Roger L'Estrange, but whether L'Estrange was in fact the author and, if so, from what source he obtained the Key, we do not know. It is possible that the author of the Key identified Hudibras with Luke merely on the evidence of the 1704 biography and that the Key itself was issued, without close examination by the bookseller, as a means of increasing the sales of the largely spurious *Posthumous Works*. It must be said, however, that in several ways Luke resembles Hudibras.[1] He was a rigid Presbyterian, the captain of a troop of horse, and scoutmaster-general to the Earl of Essex. He also represented Bedford in the Long Parliament, and was several times appointed to parliamentary committees. His portrait by Cornelius Jansen[2] shows no similarities with Butler's knight, however, and references to him made after the publication of *Hudibras* may have been influenced by his popular association with Butler's hero.

The first person to question this association was Charles Longueville, the son of Butler's friend and benefactor William Longueville, who informed the authors of the *General Dictionary* (1738)[3] that 'Luke was not the person ridiculed under the name of Hudibras'. Zachary Grey, the first editor of *Hudibras*, also had doubts about the identity of the hero, having been informed by a 'reverend and learned person'—probably Warburton—on the authority of a bencher of Gray's Inn, that the original knight was Sir Henry Rosewell of Forde Abbey in Devonshire.[4] The information from Gray's Inn was, however, largely neglected until 1933, when Ricardo Quintana discovered Butler's letter to Sir George Oxenden, which, he believed, supported the claims of Sir Henry Rosewell.[5]

Quintana prefers to accept the testimony of the bencher of Gray's Inn rather than popular tradition, on the grounds that Butler is known to have been associated with Gray's Inn and that the bencher may therefore have learned—indirectly perhaps—of Rosewell's part in *Hudibras* from the poet himself. Butler's description certainly fits the little that is known of Rosewell more closely than what is known of Luke. The original Hudibras was, according to Butler's letter, a West Country knight and a committee-man. There are, moreover, several allusions to the West Country in the poem itself, the action of which takes place 'in Western Clime'.[6] These details are obviously more appropriate

---

[1] For details of Luke's life see *DNB* and Introduction to *Journal of Sir Samuel Luke*, 3 vols., Oxfordshire Record Society, xxix, 1950–3.
[2] Reproduced in *Journal of Sir Samuel Luke*, op. cit.
[3] *A General Dictionary*, 10 vols. 1734–41, vi. 299.
[4] Preface iv.   [5] See Appendix A.
[6] The hero is said to eat 'white-pot' (I. i. 297), traditionally a Devonshire dish, and to have been imprisoned at Exeter (see Butler's note on II. ii. 548).

to a Devonshire man than to a knight from Bedford. Rosewell was, moreover, a committee-man, having been appointed several times by the Long Parliament to committees for the enforcement of General Assessments,[1] and his name appears three times in the lists of Justices of the Peace.[2] He was also repeatedly brought before the Court of High Commission between 1634 and 1640 for refusing to attend services in his parish church, presumably in protest against the Anglican injunctions of Archbishop Laud.[3] Rosewell's claims to be the original Hudibras are therefore stronger than Luke's, though the evidence is not strong enough for a decision to be made in favour of either.

As many of Butler's critics have pointed out, the question is ultimately unimportant. The role of Hudibras in the poem is not to be the object of personal satire, but the embodiment of the pedantry and hypocrisy which it was Butler's purpose to expose. Although an encounter with an actual knight may have prompted him to start the composition of *Hudibras*, Butler ultimately incorporated into his character many vices and absurdities which he recognized in human nature generally. The character of Ralpho appears to have undergone a similar process. He embodies the follies both of the independent sectarians—particularly the Baptists—and of the hermetic philosophers, including Thomas Vaughan, two very different species whom Butler unites rather loosely in the same person. A similar inconsistency has also been noticed in the character of Sidrophel,[4] who is both an experimental scientist and a journeyman astrologer, with resemblances both to the scientist Sir Paul Neile and the astrologer William Lilly. Butler appears to have used Sidrophel in a similar way to the other characters, as a figure to whom to attach both the charlatanism of astrologers and the vain curiosity of scientists. The three leading characters may have been derived in the first place from specific individuals, but, in their final form, they are not consistently related to their originals. The question of the identity of the original Hudibras is not only unsolved, but also irrelevant to the meaning and purpose of the poem.

[1] Firth and Rait, i. 545, 963, 1080 and ii. 32, 295.
[2] Frances B. James, 'Sir Henry Rosewell, a Devon Worthy', *Transactions of the Devonshire Association*, xx (1888), 118.
[3] Ibid.
[4] See Joseph Toy Curtiss, 'Butler's Sidrophel', *PMLA* xliv (1929), 1066–78.

INDEX TO INTRODUCTION
AND COMMENTARY